Touring
Australia

THOMAS COOK

On 5 July 1841 Thomas Cook, a 32-year-old printer from Market Harborough, in Leicestershire, England, led a party of some 500 temperance enthusiasts on a railway outing from Leicester to Loughborough which he had arranged down to the last detail. This proved to be the birth of the modern tourist industry. In the course of expanding his business, Thomas Cook and his son, John, invented many of the features of organised travel which we now take for granted. Over the next 150 years the name Thomas Cook became synonymous with world travel.

Today the Thomas Cook Group employs over 13,000 people across the globe and its Worldwide Network provides services to customers at more than 3000 locations in over 100 countries. Its activities include travel retailing, tour operating and financial services – Thomas Cook is a world leader in traveller's cheques and foreign money services.

Thomas Cook believed in the value of the printed word as an accompaniment to travel. His publication *The Excursionist* was the equivalent of both a holiday brochure and a travel magazine. Today Thomas Cook Publishing continues to issue one of the world's oldest travel books, the *Thomas Cook European Timetable,* which has been in existence since 1873. Updated every month, it remains the only definitive compendium of European railway schedules.

The *Thomas Cook Touring Handbook* series, to which this volume belongs, is a range of comprehensive guides for travellers touring regions of the world by train, car and ship. Other titles include:

Touring by train
On the Rails around France (Published 1995)
On the Rails around Britain and Ireland (Published 1995)
On the Rails around Europe (Second Edition Published 1996)
On the Rails around the Alps (Published 1996)
On the Rails around Eastern Europe (Published 1996)
Touring by car
On the Road around California (Second Edition Published 1996)
On the Road around Florida (Published 1995)
On the Road around Normandy, Brittany and the Loire Valley (Published 1996)
On the Road around the Capital Region USA (Published 1997)
On the Road around the South of France (Published 1997)
On the Road around the Pacific Northwest (Published 1997)
Touring by ship
Greek Island Hopping (Published annually in March)

For more details of these and other Thomas Cook publications, write to Passport Books, at the address on the back of the title page.

TOURING

Australia

Making the most of an

Australian holiday

by car, train, bus and plane

Gareth Powell

PASSPORT BOOKS
NTC/Contemporary Publishing Company

A THOMAS COOK TOURING HANDBOOK

Published by Passport Books, a division of
NTC/Contemporary Publishing Company
4255 West Touhy Avenue,
Lincolnwood (Chicago),
Illinois 60646-1975 USA.

Text: © 1997 The Thomas Cook Group Ltd
Maps and diagrams:
© 1997 The Thomas Cook Group Ltd

ISBN 0-8442-4785-8
Library of Congress Catalog Card
    Number: on file
Published by Passport Books in conjunction
with The Thomas Cook Group Ltd.

Managing Editor: Stephen York
Editorial Assistant: Leyla Davies
Map Editor: Bernard Horton
Colour map: ESR Ltd
City maps: MBD Graphics
Route diagrams: Caroline Horton
Rail and bus information: Peter Bass

Cover illustration by Michael Benallack-Hart
Back cover photograph: Chris Ivin
Copy Editor: Mary Boorman
Picture research: Image Select International
Text design by Darwell Holland
Text typeset in Bembo and Gill Sans using
    QuarkXPress for Windows
Maps and diagrams created using Macromedia
    Freehand and GSP Designworks
Text imagesetting: Goodfellow & Egan Ltd,
    Peterborough
Printed in Great Britain by Fisherprint Ltd,
    Peterborough

*While every care has been taken in compiling this
publication, using the most up-to-date information
available at the time of going to press, all details are
liable to change and cannot be guaranteed. The publishers cannot accept any liability whatsoever arising
from errors or omissions, however caused. The views
and opinions expressed in this book are not necessarily
those of the publishers.*

Written and researched by
Gareth Powell

ABOUT THE AUTHOR

Gareth Powell was born and educated in Wales, and served in the army in the Intelligence Corps in Asia. On his return to civilian life in England he went into book publishing and writing. He was the founder of Mayflower Books. He arrived in Australia some 26 years ago, and founded several magazines including the inflight magazines *Discovery* for Cathay Pacific, *Muhibbah* for Royal Brunei Airlines and *Mabuhay* for Philippine Airlines.

He was associated with the *Sydney Morning Herald* for ten years and at various times was the supplement editor, the travel editor and the computer editor – sometimes all at the same time. He is responsible for a bi-lingual computer magazine which is published in Hong Kong and also edits the travel magazine *Tourism World*. He has written seven books, all non-fiction, all on travel or computers. His writing has appeared in newspapers, magazines and periodicals all over the world.

Gareth travels between Sydney, Hong Kong and England almost as a commuter. He believes that 'Australia is the promised land and travel is the noblest and most delightful of occupations'

PHOTOGRAPHS

All the photographs for this book were supplied by Spectrum Picture Library, with the exception of the following:
Between pp. 32 and 33
Spirit of the Outback train: Leisurail
Kangaroo: Australian Tourist Commission
Sydney Harbour Bridge: Chris Ivin
Between pp. 160 and 161
Cairns skyline and Kynuna pub: Trip
Between pp. 256 and 257
Kalgoorlie hotel: Trip
Between pp. 352 and 353
Sun Pictures: Chris Ivin
Tanunda, Port Arthur coastal view: Trip

ACKNOWLEDGEMENTS

Thomas Cook Publishing would like to thank all those who gave assistance during the preparation of this book, and in particular:
Melissa Brown and her colleagues at Thomas Cook Australia in Sydney; Dave Atherton of Leisurail; John Morley of Rail Australia; Sara Radford, Ruth McIntyre and Ruth Martin of Ansett Australia; Karl Harrison of Thomas Cook Travel Shop, Peterborough.

5

CONTENTS

ROUTES AND CITIES

*In alphabetical order. For indexing purposes, routes are listed in both directions – the reverse direction
to which it appears in the book is shown in italics.
See also the Route Map, p. 8, for a diagrammatic presentation of all the routes in the book.
To look up towns and other places not listed here, see the Index, p. 409.*

7

REFERENCE SECTION

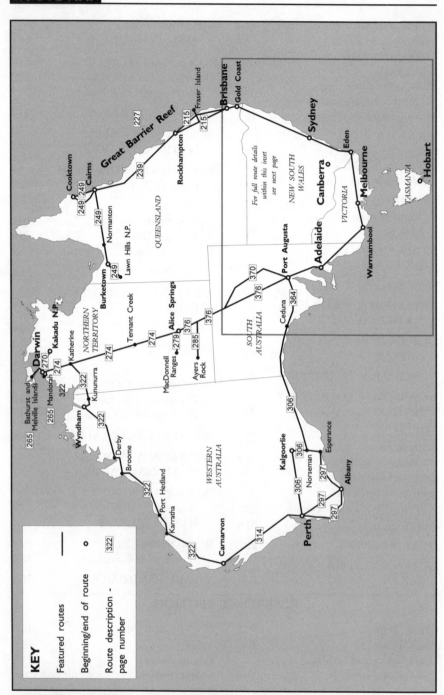

KEY

Featured routes

Beginning/end of route   o

Route description -   322
page number

8

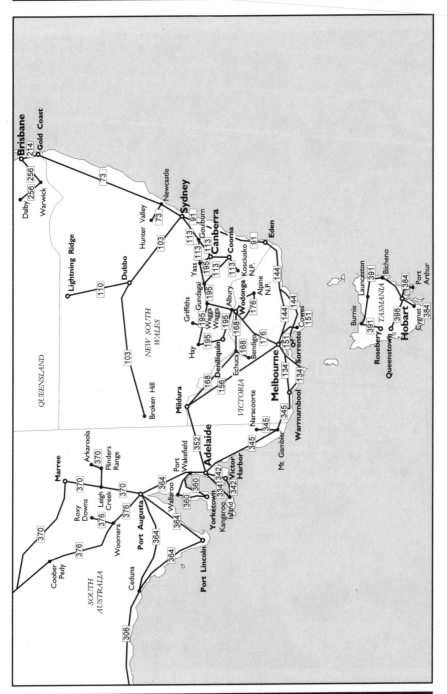

9

Thomas Cook's first Australian office opened in 1880. The Australasian version of *Cook's Travellers Gazette* was published monthly from 1889 to 1939, and one of the earliest covers is shown above.

INTRODUCTION

Writing about Australia is not the same as writing about other countries. It suffers from what has been called the tyranny of distance. Within Australia the distances that need to be travelled from one place to another are immense and present great problems for a travel writer.

Air travel made this book possible. To get to Perth I could have driven from Sydney up through Broken Hill and then down to Port Augusta, across the Nullarbor Plain and down into Perth. It sounds an interesting drive – it is and I have done it more than once – but it is roughly the distance from Oslo to Madrid and in between the centres of civilisation there is kilometre after kilometre of nothing. So empty, so flat that you can see the curvature of the earth.

Although for the last three years I seem to have been perpetually travelling Australia, the fact is that it would take me a lifetime to explore it properly. It would take me ten years of constant travel just to see all of the local museums. But I have been to every town in Australia of any size at least once recently. My judgement of size is based on sacred and profane. If a town does not have a church and a pub it is, in my opinion, not a real town. Thus, though there are 4700-odd – some of them very odd – towns legally listed in Australia, using my test there are just under 1000.

I have written this book for as wide-ranging a bunch of travellers as I could. The typical reader might be someone who has visited relatives or friends before, but now wants to get out and about and see some of the country beyond the city they normally visit. Or you may be a younger traveller with a serious amount of time to devote to a visit and intent on seeing and doing as much as possible, albeit on a tight budget. Or you may just have a normal two weeks' holiday to spend, and want to venture beyond the main tourist sights.

The routes in this book are mixture of fairly short drives from the major population centres, which could be done in a day in some cases, often as circular routes, and epic journeys such as the two connecting routes up the coast of Western Australia. In the south-east of the country, especially, the road system is dense enough to have allowed me to devise routes which interlink with one another, so that you plan a genuine touring itinerary of your choice. But elsewhere there is only one possible road to take, and my recommended route can extend to several thousand kilometres.

Don't be misled. All the routes in this book, except for the very shortest, are meant to be taken in small stages, over a period of days, allowing plenty of time to enjoy the stops, whether they be cities, small towns or national parks. The distances in Australia are too great to do otherwise. Do not regard them as impossible to attempt, or as an endurance challenge. No route has to be driven in full, in any case. If you are coming for a year or even six months, driving most places is an option. But for anything less than that you should plan to fly between major centres and then rent a car for further exploration.

For non-drivers, or for tired drivers, every driving route is accompanied by notes on the alternatives: trains and buses, where they are available between the places described. They are not the fastest method of travel, but they do take the strain off the driver, and off the purse, if you are travelling on a tight budget, especially if you make use of one of the bargain travel passes you cn buy before you arrive.

Final point. I have travelled the world and I cannot think of any other country where I could make the following statement. In researching this book and in my travels around Australia nothing was ever stolen from me; no attempt was made to hustle a tip; no one padded a bill; no one that I can remember was ever unpleasant and everyone treated me as a mate. A truly amazing experience. Try it for yourself. Like me, you will fall in love with the place.

Gareth Powell

How to Use This Book

ROUTES AND CITIES

Touring Australia provides you with an expert selection of over 30 recommended routes between key cities and attractions of Australia's mainland states and Tasmania, each in its own chapter. Smaller cities, towns, attractions and points of interest along each route are described in the order in which you will encounter them. Additional chapters are devoted to the major places of interest which begin and end these routes, descriptions of each state, national park guides, plus some circular routes which explore regions of particular interest. These chapters form the core of the book, from p. 57 to p. 402.

Where applicable, an alternative route which is more direct is also provided at the beginning of each route chapter. This will enable you to drive more quickly between the cities at the beginning and end of the route, if you do not intend to stop at any of the intermediate places. To save space, each route is described in only one direction, but you can follow it in the reverse direction, too.

The arrangement of the text consists of a chapter describing a state and then the state capital, followed by chapters devoted to routes leading from that city to other major destinations. The first state to be covered is New South Wales (pp. 55–56), followed by Sydney (pp. 57–72) and then routes from Sydney: Sydney to The Gold Coast (pp. 73–90), Sydney to Eden (pp. 91–102) and Sydney to Dubbo (pp. 103–109). Dubbo to Lightning Ridge is described in the next chapter, as the route heads into the Outback. Victoria is the subject of the next chapter, followed by routes within that state, and so on.

The order of chapters thus follows the pattern of your journey, beginning in Australia's major cities of Sydney, Melbourne and Canberra. The routes then head north along the coast of Queensland, before exploring the Top End and the Red Centre of the Northern Territory. Western Australian routes start from Perth and then head up the north-western coast. The routes then continue around South Australia heading towards Tasmania, south of the mainland.

To find the page number of any route or city chapter quickly, use either the alphabetical list on the **Contents** pages, pp. 6–7, or the master **Route Map** on pp. 8–9. The routes are designed to be used as a kind of menu from which you can plan an itinerary, combining a number of routes which take you to the places you most want to visit.

WITHIN EACH ROUTE

Each route chapter begins with a short introduction to the route, followed by driving directions from the beginning of the route to the end, and a sketch map of the route and all the places along it which are described in the chapter. This map, intended to be used in conjunction with the driving directions, summarises the route and shows the main intermediate distances and road numbers; for a key to the symbols used, see p. 14.

DIRECT ROUTE

This will be the fastest, most direct, and sometimes, predictably, least interesting drive between the beginning and end of the route, usually along major roads.

SCENIC ROUTE

This is the itinerary which takes in the most places of interest, usually using minor roads and often following coastal routes. Road directions are specific; always be prepared for detours due to road construction, etc. The driving directions are followed by sub-sections describing the main attractions and places of interest along the way. You can stop at them all or miss out the ones which do not appeal to you. Always ask at the local tourist information centre for more information on sights, lodgings and places at which to eat.

TRAINS AND BUSES

In some chapters there are details of rail and bus routes, as an alternative to driving long distances. Information is taken from the *Thomas Cook Overseas Timetable* (see p.38) and table numbers are given.

 ### SIDE TRACK

This heading is occasionally used to indicate departures from the main route, or out-of-town trips from a city, which detour to worthwhile sights, described in full or highlighted in a paragraph or two.

CITY DESCRIPTIONS

Whether a place is given a half-page description within a route chapter or merits an entire chapter to itself, we have concentrated on practical details: local sources of tourist information; getting around in city centres (by car, by public transport or on foot as appropriate); accommodation and dining; communications; entertainment and shopping opportunities and sightseeing. The largest cities have all this detail; in smaller places some categories of information are less relevant and have been omitted or summarised. Where there is a story to tell, we have placed **feature boxes** on subjects as diverse as 'Bushrangers' and 'The Man from Snowy River'.

Although we mention good independently owned lodgings in many places, we always also list the hotel chains which have a property in the area, indicated by code letters after the hotel name. Many travellers prefer to stick to one or two chains with which they are familiar and which give a consistent standard of accommodation. The codes are explained on p. 407, and central booking numbers are also given there.

MAPS

In addition to the sketch map which accompanies each route, we provide maps of major cities (usually the downtown area), smaller towns, regions, scenic trails, national parks, and so on. At the end of the book is a removable full-size **colour road map** of Australia with enlargements of key areas. The **key to symbols** used on all the types of map in this book is shown on p. 14.

THE REST OF THE BOOK

The **Contents** and **Route Map** pages has already been mentioned above. **Travel Essentials** is an alphabetically arranged chapter of general advice for the tourist new to Australia, covering a wide range subjects such as accommodation and safety or how much to tip. **Driving in Australia** concentrates on advice for drivers on the law, rules of the road, and so on. **Background Australia** gives a concise briefing on the history and geography of this fascinating country. **Touring Itineraries** provides ideas and suggestions for putting together an itinerary of your own using the selection of routes in this book. At the back of the book, **Flight Times** is a tabulation of times taken by flights between main cities in Australia, to help in trip planning. The **Conversion Tables** decode Australian sizes and measures. Finally, the **Index** is the quick way to look up any place or general subject. And please help us by completing and returning the **Reader Survey** at the very end of the text; we are grateful for both your views on the book and new information from your travels in Australia.

KEY TO MAP SYMBOLS

Route diagrams

Sydney — Beginning/end of route

Portland — Town mentioned for navigation purposes

51km — Distance in kilometres between two points

Princetown

State Route — (161)

Intermediate town mentioned in a chapter

National Route — (1)

Area Maps

i   Tourist information

▯   Petrol (gas) station

⊼   Picnic site

℄   Public Telephone

City maps

†   Church

♰   Cathedral

✉   Post Office

i   Tourist Information

▲   Camping site

1   National route

(180)   State route

14

KEY TO PRICE DESCRIPTIONS

It is impossible to keep up to date with specific tariffs for lodging and accommodation or restaurants, although we have given some general advice within the Travel Essentials chapter (p.21). Instead, we have rated establishments in broad price categories throughout the book, as follows:

Accommodation (per room per night)
Inexpensive   Under $70
Moderate $70–$150
FairlyExpensive $150–$250
Expensive   Over $250

Meal (two courses)
Inexpensive   Under $20
Medium $20–30
Expensive   Over $30

ABBREVIATIONS USED IN THE BOOK
(For hotel chains, see p. 407)

Ave	Avenue (in addresses)	km	kilometre(s)
Bldg	Building (in addresses)	min(s)	minute(s)
Dr.	Drive (in addresses)	Mon, Tues	Monday, Tuesday, etc.
Espl.	Esplanade (in addresses)	Pde	Parade (in addresses)
hr(s)	hour(s)	Rd	Road (in addresses)
Hwy	Highway, e.g. Princes Hwy	Rte	Route, e.g. Rte 55
Jan, Feb	January, February, etc.	St	Street (in addresses)

TRAVEL ESSENTIALS

ACCOMMODATION

Note first that there is no government standard for rating hotels and motels and many of the stars awarded are fairly irrelevant. Until recently a hotel in Sydney awarded itself seven stars and was only stopped through public ridicule. Each state motoring organisation makes an attempt to classify accommodation, but the standards used are connected with physical aspects, such as telephones in rooms rather than quality of service. In Australia, ever a friendly country, twin beds are the exception, not the rule, and have to be specially requested.

In this book, accommodation costs for hotels in the larger cities are classifed broadly, as 'expensive' ($250 or more), 'fairly expensive' ($250–$150), 'moderate' ($150–$70) or 'inexpensive' ($70 or less). For accommodation listed in smaller places, assume that 'inexpensive' applies unless otherwise noted. Prices are per room, not per person.

Hotels

Hotels, using the word in the international sense, are widely available and most of the chains are represented. Reservation numbers for the major hotel chains are listed on p.407

Although all the standard equipment will be in the room, you will also find an Australian addition – tea and coffee making equipment and ingredients (including fresh milk) in the refrigerator, so that you do not have to call room service for a refreshing cup when you wake up. No Australian would stay twice in a hotel that did not offer this.

Room service is only 24-hour in a few top hotels. In others it tends to stop at midnight and start again for very early breakfasts, although reception will remain open all night.

It is somewhat confusing to learn that the word 'pub' is applied both to a pub in the English sense and to any kind of hotel. Thus the answer to 'What pub are you staying in?' may in fact be 'The Ritz Carlton in Sydney'.

Motels

Australian motels are safe, clean, comfortable and cheap. In many country towns they provide the best accommodation possible. It is possible to set an absolute limit of $70 for two per night and never break it. To save money and avoid noise always choose a motel slightly away from the main highway. All motels, without exception, provide air conditioning, tea and coffee making facilities, a separate bathroom with minuscule tablets of soap to match minuscule towels and a shower, but rarely a bath. Experienced travellers carry their own soap. The décor is uniformly depressing – either multi-coloured brick or colour-washed cement blocks.

All motels will offer breakfast delivered to the room. Almost without exception it will be dreadful – an airline meal on the ground. The best bet is to make a cup of coffee or tea and then drive to a restaurant which is serving breakfast.

Most motels, although individually and privately owned, are members of to a chain – Golden, Homestead, Flag and so on – which allows central booking (see p.407) and also guarantees a certain standard. But I have been travelling Australia for many years staying in motels and have yet to have a bad experience.

Bed & Breakfast, Guest Houses

The equivalent of bed & breakfast in the UK sense is very light on the ground. Places that call themselves bed & breakfast tend to have upmarket aspirations and charge accordingly; closer to the American meaning of the term, they offer genteel weekends away to the well-heeled.

Youth Hostels and Backpacker Hostels

The very cheapest way to see Australia is by bus and hostels, although this is probably only for the young and hardy. Nevertheless, travellers of any age can join **Hostelling International**, represented in Australia by the Youth Hostel

Association, which has hostels throughout Australia, offers an excellent advisory service and supplies a fallback position if all else fails. The initials **HI** in the text of this book indicate Hostelling International hostels. You can join HI through the Youth Hostels organisation in your own country.

At **backpacker hostels** (not HI) you will be asked your nationality before you are given a room. The reason is that most of them, whatever the offical policy, in practice do not accept Australians. The excuse given is that they are too noisy and disturb the rest of the guests.

Camping and Caravans (Trailers)

It is almost as if there were separate tribes in Australia that never mixed. There are those who do all their travelling by air and stay in hotels. Those who drive and stay in motels. And those who drive and stay at camp and caravan sites. Although these three are separated by price they are almost totally classless definitions in that Australia is, as near as can be, a classless society.

There are **campsites** throughout Australia and, almost without exception, in all of the National Parks. In some cases the only way to see a National Park is to hike in, camp and explore from there. Camping, apart from at designated campsites, may be forbidden: when in doubt it is best to check with a ranger as you enter the National Park. Camping gear can be hired from the **Youth Hostel Association** and several camping stores. By camping, while travelling around Australia, you are following a great Australian tradition as exemplified in the song *Once a Jolly Swagman*.

For a long exploration of Australia a **campervan** (or RV) is probably the cheapest and most comfortable way to do it. It is possible to hire fully equipped campervans in all the major cities of Australia and this can be for two-way or one-way trips, sometimes with a surcharge for one-way rental. These do not require a special licence and range from the small but useable to the large and luxurious. Typically they are all booked out over the Christmas holiday period right up to the beginning of February and advance booking during that period is essential.

There are **caravan sites** – trailer parks – everywhere you go in Australia, frequently supplied with power points, shower and toilet facilities and often they are placed at the most scenic points of the coast. At almost all of these sites it is possible to hire a caravan parked on a site by the night – frequently for under $20 a night. This is much cheaper than a motel although, of course, they lack the amenity of a built-in bathroom, and in summer caravan sites can get quite noisy with children playing. But they are inexpensive and the caravan sites normally have the best positions in any given area, simply because they were there first. Parking a campervan by the side of the road for an overnight stay is frowned upon and is not recommended.

AIR TRAVEL

Airports

By and large the airports are well run and the horrendous queues that you find at, say, Hawaii or Hong Kong, rarely ever happen. All international airports – Sydney, Melbourne, Brisbane, Perth and, to a lesser extent, Darwin and Adelaide – have duty-free shopping, although much of it is focused on the Japanese tourist market.

There is no extra airport fee to pay as you leave – the $20 airport tax has normally already been built into the price of the air ticket. Entrance formalities are minimal, with a short immigration and customs form. The laws regarding drugs are very severe. Food and plants of almost any kind are also prohibited. When in doubt declare it at customs.

International Flights

Most of the world's major scheduled airlines, and many charter airlines, fly to Sydney, Melbourne, Perth and other state capitals. Cairns, in Queensland, is also an international terminal. Typical flight times to Sydney are: London 23 hrs; New York 20 hrs; Los Angeles 13½ hrs; Johannesburg 17 hrs; Auckland 2½ hrs; Hong Kong 10 hrs; Singapore 8 hrs. Stopovers in Hong Kong or Singapore are popular with travellers from London and other European airports.

17

There's more to Australia in Ansett's Australia.

It's a vast island that boasts the world's greatest living coral reef (all 1,243 miles of it). An Outback that seems to stretch space itself. Deserts. Tropics. Dreamtime. Rainforests. Snow-capped peaks. Three oceans. Three seas.

And an airline that covers more of it, knows more about it, and can take your passengers to more parts of it than any other.

Welcome to Ansett's Australia. We pioneered air travel Down Under 60 years ago, and today our unbeatable G'Day Airpass covers the most popular destinations (and more).

To discover why there's more to Australia in Ansett's Australia, call 0171 434 7041 or 0345 33 55 05 today for your free map. Seeing is believing.

ANSETT AUSTRALIA

18

Although you can book direct with the airline, which often advertise discounts and special offers, it is often more economical to book a package with a travel agent; these typically offer a choice of other pre-booked elements such as accommodation and car rental, where again the rates are below what you might pay by making your own bookings. The *Thomas Cook Holidays Australia* package, available to UK travellers, is a good example of this type of arrangement.

Internal flights

These are frequent, especially between the main cities. There are two internal airlines – **Qantas** and **Ansett**. This book was written and researched travelling around Australia on Ansett. Compared to international fares, internal flights can be quite expensive. Thus you often find it is cheaper to fly from Sydney to Singapore than Sydney to Perth. Where possible it is best to buy packaged internal air fares outside Australia, as the prices are much lower.

Air Passes

The most economic and convenient way to use the domestic air services is to purchase an air pass through your travel agent before departure. This prepays for a number of domestic flights. For example, Ansett Australia's **G'day Airpass** consists of a number of coupons (minimum purchase 2, maximum 10), entitling you to fly on their services between some 33 Australian airports (and 10 in New Zealand), divided into two main zones (roughly western and central Australia and eastern Australia), plus zones for offshore islands and for New Zealand. Coupons enabling you to travel within a zone are, at time of going to press, £100 each, or between zones £125 each. Unused coupons above the minimum of two can be refunded in full back home if unused; you have to reserve the routes you wish to fly in advance, but these can be re-routed free of charge if necessary when you are in Australia. You can also purchase more coupons at the same equivalent price after arriving, and upgrade from single- to multi-zone after arrival without paying any alteration fees. The only cost involved is the difference, in local currency, between a single- and a multi-zone fare.

Buses

Australia is served by several extensive express long-distance bus services (usually called coaches) that cover the whole country. Buses are comfortable, extremely inexpensive and safe. But the journeys can, on the long routes, seem interminable. If you intend to travel really long distances, remember how large Australia is. It is much quicker to fly from Sydney to London than take a bus from Darwin to Cairns, as many backpackers have found to their cost.

There are several major coach lines, of which the best known are **Greyhound Pioneer, Westerhams, Australian Pacific Tours, AAT Kings, Clipper** and **Gray Line Tours**. Many of them offer passes which run from between 7 to 90 days and are excellent value. As an example, Greyhound Pioneer's Kilometre Pass entitles you to free travel on the company's services for between 2000 and 20,000 km, depending on which pass you buy; prices in early 1997 ranged from Aus$176 to Aus$1344, but a range of discounts apply to YHA members and ISIC member students; furthermore, all passes bought outside Australia attract larger discounts. In the UK, Greyhound Pioneer passes are sold by **Leisurail**, *PO Box 113, Peterborough PE3 8HY; tel: 01733 335599* for brochures.

The routes of major long-distance buses appear on the map on p.37. The *Thomas Cook Overseas Timetable* ('OTT' – see p.38) provides schedules of major bus routes. Where bus travel is available along any of the driving routes in this book, this is noted in the 'Route' section of the chapter and the OTT table number(s) given.

Buses within cities are inexpensive, relatively frequent and quite safe. But they sometimes do not go to precisely the destination you have in mind and at rush hours can be quite packed. In some of the major cities there are tourist explorer buses which provide good value for money.

Children

Children delight in Australia because there is so much to see and do designed especially for them. Take particular care not to expose them to the sun (see 'Health' in this chapter).

19

20

CLIMATE

Australia's climate is normally glorious. Even the winters are very agreeable. There are a few exceptions. Tasmania can get quite cold in the winter – but it is still very pleasant. Melbourne has a variable climate and it sometimes seems that you can experience all of the seasons in one day. But in most of Australia you will never require an overcoat, although you may well require an umbrella.

The Northern Territory is a special case. It has one season which is called The Wet (despite all attempts by the local tourism authorities to persuade people to use a less off-putting name). During these few months the rain can come down in torrential sheets – but only for a short period of time. Then it clears up. This monsoon period tends to see few visitors but for many locals in the Northern Territory this is the best time of the year, with its invigorating mix of sunshine and rain; the visitors who brave it find the area less crowded.

For the whole of Australia you can work on the basis that the seasons are the reverse of the northern hemisphere model. High summer runs from October through to April. Winter is August to October and there is, in many but not all states, a distinct spring and autumn. On the mainland it would be unusual to ever wear an overcoat, although in the high mountains in winter – Australia has three main skiing areas – the weather can be cold and crisp.

The result of this is that Australian fashions tend to concentrate on summer days rather than winter – because there are many more summer days – and the lifestyle is consequently biased towards the outdoors.

Temperatures are always given in degrees Celsius (Centigrade). If you think in degrees Fahrenheit you need to multiply by 9, divide by 5 and then add 32. See the conversion chart on p. 408. Anything between, say, 12° and 26°C – 53° and 79°F – is pretty pleasant, ranging from lightly cool to bearably hot. Anything under 12°C can be looked on as decidedly chilly – certainly to Australians – and when you get down to 5°C (41°F), which is Hobart's minimum temperature, it is cold, no other word for it, and it is time for hot-water bottles and overcoats. At the other end of the scale, anything much over 26°C is very warm, 30°C (87°F) and upwards is decidedly hot and after 35°C you need to consider seriously whether you want to be there at all.

CLOTHING

As a rough rule of thumb, clothing with pretensions to high fashion costs more in Australia than in either Europe or the USA. However, casual dress is more and more accepted even in city offices and therefore the overall cost of dressing is much lower. Australia has some clothing quirks which, although not unique, are the style of the area. On the feet in the summer, thongs – sometimes called flip-flops – are the order of the day. Running shoes or trainers are often worn to offices – they have been worn with dinner suits at formal receptions – and the highly polished shoes one sees in the USA are rarely seen in Australia. There is said to be only one professional shoe-shine stall in the whole of Australia and that is at the Sydney Hilton. It is not patronised by Australians.

During the day polo and T-shirts are accepted at most places.

There are nightclubs that will turn men away for wearing T-shirts, jeans and thongs, but even these are slowly disappearing. The dress code is often stated as 'smart casual' and this seems to be understood as being reasonable in your attire without being stuffy.

In the summer men wear shorts – 'stubbies' – and the further north you go the more common this becomes. In the Northern Territory shorts with long white socks is called Darwin Rig – and this is formal evening wear.

Beach wear is very skimpy, sometimes totally non-existent on certain beaches and topless on most. Australian bikinis typically consist of string strategically placed and operating in defiance of all engineering principles. In recent years having a full tan has become decidedly unfashionable, because of the problems with skin cancer, and cover-up swimsuits are making a major come-back. No fashion magazines in Australia will use models with a definite tan as it is considered an out-dated look.

The one useful tool that comes, as it were, from other civilisations is the fold-up umbrella. It is cheap, convenient to carry and useful when a sudden deluge – there is rarely any other kind of rain – strikes. It is then you will find that Australian cabs are soluble in rain water and an umbrella can help you avoid getting totally soaked.

CONSULATES AND EMBASSIES

Almost every country is represented with a consulate in Canberra or an honorary consulate elsewhere. They are all listed in the chapters on Canberra and the state capitals.

COST OF LIVING

It is very difficult to make valid comparisons because of the differences in lifestyle, salaries, taxation and working practices. But as a general rule it would be fair to say that the overall cost of living is lower than in almost all European countries and much of the USA. It is infinitely lower than that of Hong Kong or Singapore, which is why Australia receives so many migrants.

Most migrants say that the quality of life in Australia is better than that in the country from which they originated, because of the casual, laid-back lifestyle, the relative freedom from serious crime and the comparatively low level of taxation.

Some sample prices in Sydney at time of going to press: unleaded petrol, 72.6 cents per litre; can of Coke from a store, $1.20; medium-sized beer, $2–2.50.

CURRENCY

The only currency accepted in Australia is the Australian dollar ($), divided into 100 cents. In this book, $ means Australian dollar, unless otherwise stated. At the time of going to press, 1 Australian dollar was worth approximately UK£0.46, US$0.77 and Canadian $1.05.

The coins are $2, $1, 50 cents, 20 cents, 10 cents, and the 5 cent coin, which is hardly ever used. The notes are plastic and this new way of printing money is hated by most Australians, who find the notes extremely unpleasing. Notes come in $5, $10, $20, $50 and $100. These are available from automatic teller

21

machines all around Australia and in most cases Visa and MasterCard issued overseas will work in Australian ATMs (there is a small problem with some issued in the USA – check with your bank before you leave).

Almost without exception hotels, motels, restaurants and filling stations accept Visa, MasterCard and, with a few exceptions, American Express and Diners Club. Australia is very much a plastic payment society and in almost every case a credit card will be expected. Indeed, some car rental companies will not let you rent a car for cash.

Note that in Australia, as in other parts of the world, hotels tend to block off part of your credit as soon as you check in. In theory, once you have paid your bill they should unblock your credit, but some of them forget to do so and you can find your card has hit its limit when you have not spent the money. This problem does not apply to American Express or Diners Club.

In theory you can change money at banks. Unless they are specially set up to do, this will take an age and the commission charged will be horrendous. It is better by far to go to a specialised bureau de change such as Thomas Cook (see p. 33). To see how your own currency compares to the Australian Dollar, use the currency converter on the Thomas Cook website – the website address is given on p.39.

CUSTOMS

This is very relaxed both arriving and departing, except in the matter of drugs – sniffer dogs are extensively used – and food, which is banned to stop imported diseases. As you arrive in Australia you will be given several warnings on this subject – most airlines show a video – and the penalties for infringement are very severe.

Your are allowed to bring in duty free 1 litre of spirits, 200 cigarettes and $400 of dutiable goods, plus all the usual personal items. The best way to buy the alcohol and cigarette allowance is at the duty-free shop in the *arrival* hall of your Australian airport. This stops you having to lug a bag of duty-free items with you on your inward flight. There is a considerable saving on duty-free cigarettes – much less on spirits. Wine is not worth bringing in, as the

price differential, even after taking into account the tax, is not in the traveller's favour.

Australia is unique in allowing legal duty-free shops outside airports. You can buy your goods in bond and collect them for your outward flight. This can lead to substantial savings. The duty-free stores are, in effect, bonded customs houses and work in just the same way as at the airport. But typically they have a far wider choice because they are not restricted on space. You have to take your passport and airline ticket with you or you will not be served. Any duty-free goods you buy will be delivered to you at the airport. As you pass through passport control you will be approached by an uniformed officer who will ask whether you have duty-free items to collect. They will then be handed over in a sealed bag. The system works very well and is widely used.

DISABLED TRAVELLERS

In the past, facilities for disabled travellers around Australia have been shameful but now a serious effort has been made to remedy this. Most national parks and wildlife reserves have paid special attention to this problem and many cities have taxis specially equipped for wheelchairs, which charge normal rates. Many restaurant guides now list whether restaurants have wheelchair access or not. Having said that, there is much still to be done, but it is a problem of which everyone is conscious and all new facilities are, almost without exception, equipped so that they can easily be accessed by disabled people.

For advice and information in the UK: RADAR, *12 City Forum, 250 City Road, London EC1V 8AF; tel: (0171) 250 3222* publish a useful annual guide called *Holidays and Travel Abroad (£5 inc. postage)*. In the USA, SATH, *347 5th Ave, Suite 610, New York, NY 10016; tel: (212) 447-7284*.

There are several organisations in Australia that provide information and guides for disabled people. On the Internet there is **Easy Access Australia** – *http://www.vicnet.net.au/~brucean* – which publishes a book of that name, a complete guide to access throughout the country. The book is published from *PO Box 218, Kew 3101, Victoria; tel: (03) 9853 5022. fax: 9853*

9000. The book's author has a complete C5/6 spinal injury and other contributions are by wheelchair users. The price is $19.95 plus $4.90 p &p

Other contact addresses: **ACROD**, *55 Charles St; Ryde, NSW 2112; tel: (02) 9809 4488.* **ACROD**, *33 Thesiger Court, Deakin, ACT.* **Brisbane City Council**, Disability Services Centre, *GPO Box 1434, Brisbane 4001; tel: (07) 3391 2044.* **Disabled Persons Information Bureau**, *Ground Floor, 555 Collins Street, Melbourne 3000; tel: (03) 9616 7704; fax: (03) 9616 8142.* **Darwin City Council**, *Civic Centre, Harry Chan Avenue, Darwin; tel: (08) 8982 2511.* **Disability Information and Resource Centre**, *195 Gillies St, Adelaide; tel: (08) 8223 7522.* **ACROD**, *PO Box 8136, Perth Business Centre; tel: (09) 221 9066.* **Tasmania Paraplegic Quadriplegic Association**; *tel: (002) 381 874.*

ELECTRICITY

Australia uses 240-volt, 50-hertz current and three-pronged plugs and sockets of a pattern unique to the country. Most hotels can supply converters and electrical stores stock suitable equipment (Dick Smith is the best chain for this). Note that this does not apply to laptop computers, which are already set up to take different currents and cycles. If the extension cord to your charger will not fit, and you are staying in a hotel or motel, you will find that the lead for the electric kettle – always supplied in every room – will do as an emergency stop-gap.

EMERGENCIES

Police, **fire** and **ambulance** services throughout Australia are called by dialling **000**. The response in the city will be almost instantaneous. In the country it depends on the distance to the nearest town.

Emergency **clinics** are open 24 hours a day in all the major towns and the standard of service is excellent. One odd anomaly. There is a separate charge made to everyone for using an ambulance. It is not covered by the health service.

The following toll-free phone numbers can be used to report loss or theft of:

Thomas Cook MasterCard Travellers Cheques 1 800 127 495; **MasterCard cards** 1 800 120 113. Emergency assistance in both cases is also available from branches of Thomas Cook in Australia (see pp. 33–34).

FESTIVALS

Further details of the following events will be found in the chapters on the towns where they take place.

January: The Festival of Sydney lasts the whole of January and is a series of major cultural and less serious events.

February: Moomba Festival in Melbourne, with parades through the streets.

In Western Australia it is the Festival of Perth, with artists, performers and writers from all over the world.

March: The Gay and Lesbian Mardi Gras in Sydney brings visitors from all over the world and the parade with its outrageous floats is one of the sights of the city.

In the Australian capital it is the Canberra Festival and in even-numbered years it is the Adelaide Festival, the most important arts festival in Australia. Australian Formula One Grand Prix in Melbourne.

April: In the Barossa Valley in South Australia it is vintage time and there are a series of wine tastings, feasts and performances.

May: In Alice Springs it is time for the Bangtail Muster.

June: In Darwin there is a Beer Can Regatta in which competing boats and rafts are made entirely from beer cans.

August: In Alice Springs it is the Henley-on-Todd Regatta.

September: Melbourne has the Spoleto Arts Festival, with an Italian flavour, and holds the Grand Final of Australian Rules which is, in that city, practically a religion.

November: And again in Melbourne the Melbourne Cup. In Victoria it is an offical holiday but in every other state everything comes to a halt while this classic race is run.

December: The Sydney to Hobart Yacht Race leaves on Boxing Day for what is arguably the greatest ocean yacht race in the world. When it arrives in Hobart it is celebrated by the traditional Little Drink.

FOOD AND DRINK

Some food in Australia is inexpensive beyond belief. At the end of the season fruit can be seen for sale at roadside stalls for $1 a sack of apples or oranges. It used to be that fruit went into and out of season. That no longer applies to any great degree. Home cooking, in the American and British sense, exists, but not to a great extent. The Australian barbecue is, indeed, all-pervasive, although the fondness for immense slabs of steak has diminished in recent years. It is possible, but not probable, that you will get an interesting, well-balanced meal at a barbie. Most Australian families eat out more frequently than their European equivalents. Home-delivered or take-away meals are also extremely popular.

Vegetarian Food

Despite the image of steak-eating, beer-drinking macho Australians, the fact is that the country is slowly becoming more and more vegetarian. Or, to be more precise, is eating less and less meat. Because of the plentiful supply of a wide range of fresh fruit and vegetables, being a vegetarian at any level – from vegan to occasional practitioner – is very easy in Australia. Most restaurants offer vegetarian dishes and most Asian restaurants have several vegetarian specialities. The way things are moving it will not be that long before vegetarian dishes offered on the menu will outweigh meat dishes. This is of great concern to Australia's farmers but is welcomed by the health authorities.

Restaurants

Australian cuisine has taken great strides in the last twenty years. It used to be that the Australian definition of a balanced meal was a meat pie in each hand. No longer. And it used to be that Australian restaurants were either classified as 'Ethnic' – Lebanese, Greek, Chinese, Thai, Vietnamese and so on – or were European imitations. In the past few years this has gone by the board. The ethnic restaurants are becoming modified by the local produce and climate. And in less defined restaurants there is now a true Australian cuisine developing, which has strong Asian influences but still a unique character.

Restaurant prices by and large can be quite expensive and a working basis of an average of $25 a person before wine, with wide variations above and below, is not far off the mark. However, Australians are now also into grazing, with all the popular chains, from McDonalds and Pizza Hut to KFC, represented and these tend to be considerably cheaper.

BYO

Licensing laws in Australia, as in so many other countries, are not based on any observable logic except in one area – licensed premises can serve liquor to anyone over the age of 18. This age rule is strictly enforced.

Many establishments which serve meals have no liquor licence and so Australia has the phenomenon of BYO restaurants. Those letters mean that you are invited to **Bring Your Own** wine with you – glasses will be provided. Most BYO restaurant has a 'bottle shop' (off licence/liquor store) within striking distance and even the smallest bottle shop will have a wide range of wine, with the white kept in the refrigerator (in the tropical north, the red wine as well).

Typically, a BYO restaurant is less expensive than a licensed restaurant, although this does not mean that the food is one whit inferior – indeed, the reverse is often the case.

Pubs

'Pub' in Australia is an all-embracing term applied to both hotels and drinking places. Thus the comment 'it's a decent pub' may well apply to the Sheraton as well as the Nelson, a splendid drinking pub in The Rocks in Sydney. Drinking pubs can be open for almost any twelve hours in 24; most are open until 2300 during the week, midnight on Sat and 2200 on Sundays. Wine bars exist, but are scarce in many of the big cities because of determined efforts by the major hotel chains to prevent them getting a licence.

Beer

The great Australian drink is beer, which is of a light European lager or pilsener style and is served very cold in glasses of three different sizes. These have different names in every state, with the middle size, something under a third of a pint, the normal order. The names you will hear include 'seven', 'pony', 'middy' and 'schooner' among many others. Just ask for a beer and you will normally get roughly half a pint. Beer is always served as cold as possible – it is not unknown for cans to have a few minutes in the deep freeze to give them an extra chill. Australian beer is more alcoholic than the average American beer or British lager – about on a par with most German beers,

Beer is often drunk straight from the can – the 'tinnie' – or a small bottle, and is sometimes supplied in a polyurethane holder to keep it cold. This is especially true in North Queensland and the Northern Territory.

The biggest growth area in beers is **low alcohol**. This has been brought about, in part, by the immensely tough drink-driving laws and random breath testing and, in part, by changing social attitudes towards drinking. The theory is that you can drink four light beers – Toohey's Blue is a well known favourite – without going over the limit. This has been found by test not to be true in all cases, but it tastes like a very good real beer and leaves the drinker relatively sober.

The breweries in Australia have consolidated, which means that beer tends to be much the same with no regional differences. This has led, as in other countries, to the rise of microbreweries producing individual beers with strong flavours. They are still served very chilled.

Wine

Wine is one of the true glories of Australia. It is, overall, of a very high quality and relatively inexpensive although, at the top end, you will see prices to rival those of top European and Californian wines. Work on an average of $12 per bottle for a very drinkable drop and you will not go far wrong, although there are some excellent wines costing much less than that. There are several wine-growing areas of Australia, each with its own style and group of supporters. The most famous is, perhaps, the **Hunter Valley**, which produces a truly remarkable range of red wines. In the **Barossa Valley** the influence of German immigrants has

set an excellent standard for white. In Western Australia it is the **Margaret River Area** and in Victoria the **Yarra.** But there are dozens of other areas and almost all of the wine is extremely drinkable. Note that most wines are classified by the grape. The day when French names like Sauternes and Bordeaux were used are well past. It is arguable that Australia produces wines on a general level that are superior to most of those exported from France. The one exception is champagne – 'sparkling white' in Australia – where the French most definitely still lead the market.

Spirits

The only spirit that is widely drunk – although the full range is available at an average of over $20 a bottle – is rum. This is made in Queensland and that from the town of Bundaberg has a high reputation. A popular drink is Bundie and Coke, especially in Queensland. Spirits are sold on much the same measured system as in, say, Britain but in Australia it is possible to ask for a half measure.

GAMBLING

25

Gambling is endemic in Australia. Australians boast that they will bet on two flies crawling up a wall and there is much truth in this. The traditional Australian gambling game is **'two-up'**, in which two coins are spun in the air from a paddle and you bet whether they will come down heads or tails or one of each. In theory this game is illegal but the police do not enforce the law assiduously. On Anzac Day it is common practice to play two-up in the main streets. The second great Australian gamble comes with the poker machines – 'the pokies' – where the more you play the more certain you are to lose. This does not deter anyone.

Horse racing also attracts an immense amount of betting, either through the totalisator – the TAB – on-course bookies or, illegally, off-course with what are known as SP bookies. Every other sport attracts betting – legal or otherwise – and there are also assorted sweepstakes such as Lotto. It was a sweepstake that financed the building of the Sydney Opera House.

The latest development is the arrival of

casinos – there is now one in every capital city and the competition between them to get the high rollers is immense. It may be that Australians are now over-saturated with opportunities to bet, as the casinos have not proved to be the money-spinners it was anticipated they would be.

HEALTH

Australia has an excellent health service. The public and the doctors complain about it all the time, but the fact is that it is mostly free, it is very efficient and, as a result, Australians are a very healthy race (with the exception of the Aborigines, who have been grossly unfairly treated – in fact mostly untreated – but there are signs that this is now being remedied). There is a government-funded medicine called **Medicare**, similar to the British National Health Service, and there are also medical funds which offer more individual treatment, but there are currently suffering a drop in membership because of the high quality of the Medicare service. However, this excellent free service does not become available to tourists until they have spent six months or more in the country, so that it is vital you have health insurance to cover you during your visit. See also under 'Emergencies'.

Some health warnings are in order. The **sun** in Australia bites like a viper and you must always be aware of the possibilities of both short- and long-term damage. Shirts need to be sun-proof – check the label – and even then you need to avoid prolonged exposure to the sun. Block-out sun creams do work, but not as well as the manufacturers would have you imagine, and their efficiency is easily damaged by sweat and sea water. Most states run perpetual publicity campaigns to warn people about the sun because, sadly, Australia has the highest rate of skin cancer in the world. There is more and more evidence piling up that over-exposure to the Australian sun can be almost as dangerous as smoking.

Whatever you do, try to avoid the noonday sun and keep your swimming and beach games to the morning and the later afternoon when some of the sting has gone out of the day. All this applies especially to young children, whose skin is softer and more susceptible to damage than the skin of adults (adults with the fair complexion of Celtic descent are also particularly susceptible, however). All Australian schoolchildren wear floppy hats as part of their school uniform – frequently with shades hanging down the back like Foreign Legion headgear.

Although Australia has over 200 poisonous insects and animals, the chances of you being bitten are very small. If you are, the current recommended treatment is a compress on the bite itself while you urgently seek medical help. Mosquito bites are a nuisance, rather than a hazard, while bushwalking, so keep sleeves rolled down and wear long trousers. In the north there are occasional outbreaks of **malaria** and Ross River fever but most visitors who become ill do so through over-indulgence in either the sun or alcohol or, frequently, both.

Attacks by **dingoes** are unheard of, notwithstanding the notorious Azaria – 'the dingo took my baby' – case. The danger from **sharks** has been much exaggerated. There have been attacks on swimmers, but if you heed the advice of locals and life-savers in surf areas you are almost certain to come to no harm. The **blue bottle**, a sort of jellyfish, can leave sting marks all over your body; **box jelly fish** (found in northern Queensland) can be lethal: ask a local if it's safe to swim in the ocean and take their advice; remember, there are always swimming pools – over 280,000 in the Sydney area alone.

The only serious danger to tourists from wildlife comes, in the North End, from **crocodile attacks**. If there is a sign warning about them, *do not* go into the water under any circumstances, not even to paddle. Crocodiles can move like greased lightning and will attack in the shallowest of waters.

HIKING

Hiking – bushwalking – is a wonderful way to see the countryside and is perfectly safe providing you follow some basic rules. The biggest danger comes not from getting lost, but from fire. The best way to be safe is to avoid dense scrub and heavy vegetation during periods of high bush-fire danger. Religiously observe all fire bans. Every park has indicators at the

26

entrance and they are also to be seen along most main roads. Warnings are also given in newspapers and on the radio. When the indicator tells you that there is high or extreme fire danger consider some other activity. If you are in a car and you get caught in a bush fire the most sensible thing to do it to wind up all the windows and stay there until the fire passes. Petrol tanks rarely explode.

When walking in the bush dress correctly. You may think that shorts would be cooler, but lightweight, full length trousers will protect you from bites and scratches. You need solid footwear – not thongs and sandals – and you should wear a shirt with long sleeves that can be rolled down when needed.

If you are not an experienced bushwalker stick to the trails and marked paths. The National Parks and Wildlife Service has laid out an immense network of trails covering every national park in Australia and you will never be bored. And, if you stick to the paths, you will never be lost.

HITCH-HIKING

Do not even think of doing it. We have just had a murder trial involving innocent hitch hikers. In all parts of the world this is a most dangerous way of getting around. This is also true in Australia. No matter what your sex and no matter what your belief in your invulnerability, you are putting yourself at serious risk hitch-hiking. Do not do it. The converse holds true. Never pick up hitch-hikers along the road.

INSURANCE

You must have insurance whenever you travel. Your travel insurance, which you should take out before you leave, should cover your baggage, travel cancellation and all medical expenses, including Medivac, so that if you have to be flown in from the outback you will not end up mortgaging your life.

LANGUAGE

Although Australia has become an extraordinary mix of nations, the language of the country is English. There seems to be a three generation rule that applies to new migrants.

The first generation speaks little English; the second is fluent in English and reasonably fluent in their own language; the third generation knows only a smattering of the original language and by the fourth generation it has died out altogether. Thus Australia is very much a monolingual country and the sort of multilingual fluency that you find in some parts of Europe, for example, hardly exists.

The Australian accent is non-regional. You cannot tell whether a person comes from Darwin or Melbourne by their accent. As a general rule the accent becomes more English as you move up the social scale, but even that rule is far from rigid especially as any social scale is hard to define. Australia is effectively a classless society and the language reflects this.

It has been said that the Australian accent comes from speaking with the lips close together so that the flies cannot get in. It is more likely that it is a direct descendant from the Cockney dialect spoken by the first and unwilling migrants. Quite a few words come from rhyming slang and some are Romany in origin.

The most pervasive feature of the Australian language – and to some the most irritating – is the insistence on shortening words and names and then adding 'ie' or 'o' on the end. Thus Fremantle becomes Freeo, Brisbane becomes Brissie, costume becomes cossie, a can of beer is a tinnie (and so is an aluminium boat). Sometimes it becomes ludicrous, as when Christmas present becomes Chrissie pressie – very widely used – or when relatives become rellos or rellies. It can also become quite obscure, as in 'I bought this port in Brissie'. The port could, indeed, be fortified red wine but it could also be a suitcase where port is short for portmanteau – a word sometimes used for suitcase.

This all sounds, to the unaccustomed ear, somewhat juvenile and can lead to misunderstandings. However, Australians generally are the kindest of people and never take offence at a visitor's apparent lack of comprehension.

Note carefully that at almost all times the word 'bastard' is used as a term of affection and not as an insult. 'Mongrel', on the other hand, most definitely is; in the unlikely event that you

How to Speak Australian

Books have been written about the Australian vernacular, and there is not enough space in this one to do it justice. The following, therefore, is a tiny selection of words and phrases which might otherwise leave you puzzled.

Back O' Bourke or **Beyond the Black Stump** – the Outback.

Beauty – mainly pronounced 'bewdy' and an expression of approbation. Sometimes extended to 'bewdy bottler' which is an accolade indeed.

Boomer – large kangaroo but also an expression of approval.

Chuck a sickie – Stay off work to, typically, attend a sporting event. Most Australians are allowed a number of sick days a year and are extremely upset if they become sick on their sick day.

Dunny – outdoor lavatory but also used for toilet in many informal situations.

Esky – a trade name which has become generic and means plastic container for keeping beer, and sometimes food, cold.

Fair go – normally an expostulation asking for tolerance on the part of the other speaker. Also heard as **Fair suck of the sauce bottle.**

Galah. Likewise **dill** and **drongo**. A person of limited intelligence.

Garbo – not a celebrity that wishes to be alone but the rubbish collector.

G'day – Hello.

Good on yer – an expression of approval which is widely used and is normally pronounced as one word.

Hooroo – rough equivalent of farewell.

Kangaroos loose in the top paddock – one of many phrases used to indicate doubts regarding a person's mental state.

Mate – the universal leveller. Everyone will call you mate. Very possibly even the porter who carries your bag to your room. No disrespect is intended. Australia is, indeed, an egalitarian society. Mate is merely the outward sign of this egalitarianism.

No worries – That's okay; don't mention it.

Pom – a person from Britain. It was almost certainly derived from 'pomegranate' which was spoken to rhyme with 'immigrant'.

Septic – someone from the United States. Short for 'septic tank' = Yank.

Shoot through – to depart hurriedly. A Sydney variation is **shoot through like a Bondi tram.**

Tinnies – both beer cans and small aluminium boats.

Tucker – food. This is widely used although it has a quaint bush feel about it. But even in a high class restaurant you may hear of a dish being referred to as 'great tucker, mate'.

Turps – alcohol.

Up and down like a lavatory seat at a mixed party – extremely busy

Ute – short for 'utility', which is a small truck based on a saloon car and is very popular throughout Australia.

Vegemite – a brown paste for spreading on bread, similar to the British Marmite, which is considered by Australians to be part of the true greatness of the country. It is very much an acquired taste.

Wallopers – members of the constabulary.

28

are called a mongrel in a pub, make for the nearest exit. 'Mate' is used between almost all males as a gesture of classless solidarity. 'Guys' – as in 'you guys' – is both uni-sex and classless and is much used. Boarding an internal flight you may be greeted by a hostess who looks at the boarding pass and says, 'Up the back, darls'. Change traveller's cheques in a Queensland bank and the teller says, 'Got your passport and all that bizzo?' Query the decision of a person and you are told: 'Mate, the problem is he's got kangaroos loose in the top paddock'.

The one Australian speech mannerism that confuses many visitors is the habit of placing 'but' at the end of a sentence as if it were a punctuation mark. As in, 'It's a nice day, but'. But what? you may ask. But nothing. It is just a pause in speech. Also confusing is the Australian tradition of understating the case. When answering the universal cry of 'owyergoinmate' – always said as one word – someone may reply, 'Very ordinary, mate, very ordinary'. Which means, in effect, the plague and pestilence have struck.

Australian speech is rich and vigorous and sometimes almost poetic. To describe someone who is perhaps overly well-dressed and therefore not to be trusted the phrase would be, 'As flash as a rat with a gold tooth'. Not Shakespeare. But close.

People from more formal countries might be somewhat taken aback by this informality – I simply cannot ever recall being called 'sir' by anyone in Australia except for a police officer who was charging me for a minor traffic offence – but it is all meant in good part and with the friendliest of feelings. Smile a lot and speak slowly and you will have no problems.

LUGGAGE

Suitcases with designer labels are called 'steal-me bags' in the vernacular. Anonymous well-worn suitcases are more suitable. Only bring what you can easily carry. On internal flights you are allowed one small carry-on bag. The rest must be placed in the hold. You truly do not need large suitcases because the style of dress is informal and suits and formal dresses are simply not essential.

Porters are a dying breed. The story is that they went on strike at Sydney Airport and then cancelled the strike because nobody noticed. Railway porters may, indeed, exist in Australia. It is just that I have never seen one.

MAPS

There is a wide range of maps available. The topographic maps, scale 1:10 000, 1:25 000,

1:50 000, 1:100 000, are sometimes so large-scale as to be confusing unless you want them for a particular reason like bushwalking. The most useful are tourist maps, showing towns, roads, parks, forests and points of interest to the tourist. These can be of Australia, of each State, or of quite small areas (these often have town maps inset). Maps can be bought at newsagents, book shops, and almost always at petrol stations. National Park maps are always available at the National Park itself, or from National Park headquarters in each State.

All tourist information centres have give-away maps of the city centres, as well as a wide range of free brochures which are variable in quality.

MEDIA

Australia is well served by **newspapers**. Each capital city has its own newspaper with the *Sydney Morning Herald* and the *Melbourne Age* being consistently judged among the top twenty newspapers of the world. Commercial **television** is as bad as it is all over the world – this is the nation that brought you *Neighbours* – but cable television means that generally you have 30 channels to choose from and some of them will be worth watching. Commercial **radio**, especially the talk-back programmes, can give you an insight into the Australian way of life, but the jewel in the crown is the Australian Broadcasting Corporation's radio programs, which are superbly produced and very Australian.

NATIONAL PARKS

The glory of Australia lies in its national parks, which are numerous, well maintained and cared for and are inexpensive to enter. There are literally hundreds of National Parks – 300 main ones – throughout the country and to these must be added reserves, state forests and recreation areas. If you saw *Crocodile Dundee* in either version, the bush scenes were all shot in one of Australia's great National Parks, Kakadu (see p.271). In this book a short chapter lists the National Parks of each state. The outstanding ones are described in the route chapters, but any park will repay a visit.

Between them the Australian National Parks

cover an area of more than 24 million hectares and this is being continually expanded. The parks cover everything from relative civilisation near to cities to amazing mountain ranges to deserts and dunes. So popular are the National Parks that the number of visitors – 250,000 to Kakadu alone every year – has put pressure on the environment and it is important to keep to tracks rather than trampling on new vegetation, only to light campfires at designated spots or where a fire has been lit before and to take all your rubbish out with you. It is considered a mark of the civilised person to take away other rubbish even if it had nothing to do with you. Note carefully that many parks do not allow camp fires of any kind, and so spirit stoves are essential equipment.

All native plants and animals are protected within National Parks and picking of flowers and plants is an offence. Pets may not be taken into any National Park.

PASSPORTS AND VISAS

All visitors from overseas must carry full passports valid for 6 months beyond date of stay. Visitors from all countries – including Britain – must have **visas** before they travel. An airline will not let you board without a legal and up-to-date visa. Ignorance of this frequently creates serious problems for passengers leaving Britain on a trip to Australia. New Zealanders are the only nationality exempt from visa requirements. There are four different kinds of visa: Visitor's Visa, valid for six months or less; Working Holiday-makers' Visa, valid for twelve months, which only applies to people under the age of 25 or married couples without children; Temporary Residents' Visa; and Students' Visa.

Visas are obtained from Australia Government offices and this is a painless procedure. You fill in a form, which is usually supplied by your travel agent or airline. Or you can download it from the Internet – *http://www.anzac.com/aust/ visa.htm*, or obtain it from your nearest Australian consulate or High Commission (see box on next page), whom you should contact if you are applying for anything other than a six month Visitor's Visa.

POLICE

Australian police have been going through a fairly traumatic time and have been reformed several times through the use of Royal Commissions. Having said that, the general level of crime in Australia is relatively low. The new, and very tough, gun laws means that firearms are very difficult to buy and keep at home, which keeps the murder rate in the whole of Australia well below that of, say, Los Angeles. The police are not often seen on foot patrols, although this has improved in recent years, but they are very quick in answering an emergency call (dial 000).

POSTAL SERVICES

The Australian Post Office is still a government entity and is relatively reliable – this is open to serious debate – although in most areas there is only one delivery a day. More and more in the cities its business is being taken over by courier services, because the post can be very late indeed at times.

Post offices open Mon–Fri, 0900–1700, and, like the banks, are closed at weekends.

PUBLIC HOLIDAYS

Australia has more public holidays than most countries but not, despite popular belief, as many as, for example, Hong Kong.

The principal **national holidays** are: 1 Jan, New Year's Day; 26 Jan, Australia Day; Good Friday; Easter Monday; 25 Apr, Anzac Day; 8 June, Queen's Birthday (except Western Australia); 25 Dec, Christmas Day; 26 Dec, Boxing Day.

Then there are the **state holiday:**
ACT: 16 Mar, Canberra Day; 3 Aug, Bank Holiday.
New South Wales: 3 Aug, Bank Holiday; 5 Oct, Labour Day.
Northern Territory: 4 May, May Day; 24 July, Darwin Royal Show; 29 Dec, Additional Holiday.
Queensland: 4 May, Labour Day; 16 Aug, Brisbane Exhibition Day.
South Australia: 12 Oct, Labour Day.
Tasmania: 4 Feb, Hobart Cup; 10 Feb, Regatta Day; 2 Mar, 8 Hour Day; Easter Tuesday.

Australian Consulates Abroad

Canada: Australian Consulate, *World Trade Centre Complex*, Suite 602-999 Canada Place, Vancouver, B C V6C 3E1; tel: (604) 684-1177; fax: (604) 684-1856. Australian Consulate-General, Suites 314/316, 175 Bloor Street, East, Toronto M4W 3R8; tel: (416) 323-1155, (416) 323-3909; fax: (416) 323 3910. Australian High Commission, Suite 710, 50 O'Connor Street, Ottawa K1P 6L2; tel: (613) 236-0841; fax: (613) 236-4376

Denmark: Australian Embassy, *Kristianiagade 21, DK 2100 Copenhagen* ; tel: 352 62244, 352 62071; fax: 354 32218

Germany: Australian Embassy, *Godesberger Allee 105-107, 53175 Bonn*; tel: 228-81030; fax: 228-8103130. Australian Consulate-General, 4th Floor, Kempinski Plaza, Uhlandstrasse 181-183, D-10623 Berlin; tel: (030) 88 00 8800; fax: 8800 8899

Hong Kong: Australian Consulate General, *23/F Harbour Centre, 25 Harbour Road, Wancha,;* tel: 28278881; fax: 28276583.

Indonesia: Australian Embassy, *Jalan H.R. Rasuna Said Kav C 15-16, Jakarta Selatan 12940;* tel: 5227111; fax: 5227101.

Malaysia: Australian Embassy, *6, Jalan Yap Kwan Seng, 50450 Kuala Lumpur.*

Netherlands: Australian Embassy, *Carnegielaan 4, 2517 KH. den Haag;* tel: 310 8200; fax: 310 7863

Philippines: Australian Embassy, *1st–5th Floors, Dona Salustiana Ty Tower, 104 Paseo De Roxas, Makati, Metro Manila;* tel: 817 7911; fax: 817 3603.

Republic of Ireland: Australian Embassy, *Fitzwilton House, Wilton Terrace, Dublin 2;* tel: 6761517, 6762441; fax: 6685266.

Singapore: Australian High Commission, *25 Napier Road, Singapore 1025; tel: 737 9311; fax: 733 7134.*

South Africa: Australian High Commission, *292 Orient Street, Arcadia, Pretoria; tel: 342 3740; fax: 342 4222.* Australian High Commission, 14th Floor, BP Centre, Thibault Square, Cape Town 8001; tel: 4195425-9; fax: 4197345.

Sweden: Australian Embassy, *Sergels Torg 12, Stockholm, Box 7003, S-103 86; tel: 613 2900; fax: 247 414*

Taiwan: Australian Commerce and Industry Office (ACIO), *Suite 2608, 26F/International Trade Building, 333 Keelung Road, Section 1, Taipei 110;* tel: (02)720 2833; fax: (02)757 6074

Thailand: Australian Embassy, *37 South Sathorn Road, Bangkok 10120;* tel: 2872680; fax: 2872029.

UK: Australian High Commission, *Australia House, The Strand, London WC2B 4LA;* tel: (0171) 379 4334; fax: (0171) 4658217.

USA: Australian Consulate General, *630 Fifth Avenue, New York, NY 10111;* tel: (212) 245 4000. Australian Consulate General, *1 Bush Street, San Francisco, CA 94104;* tel: (415) 362 6160. Australian Consulate General, *611 N Larchmont Blvd, Los Angeles, CA 90004;* tel: (310) 229 4800. Australian Embassy, *Massachusetts Ave NW, Washington, DC 20036;* tel: (202) 797 3222. Australian Consulate General, *1990 Post Oak Blvd, Suite 800, Houston, TX 77056;* tel: (713) 629 9131. Australian Consulate General, *1000 Bishop Street, Penthouse, Honolulu, HI 96813;* tel: (808) 5245050.

Victoria: 9 Mar, Labour Day; Easter Tuesday; 24 Sept, Melbourne Show Day; first Tues in Nov, Melbourne Cup.

Western Australia: 2 Mar, Labour Day; 1 June, Foundation Day; 5 Oct, Queen's Birthday.

SAFETY

By and large your person and your belongings are safe in most places in Australia. I have lived in Australia for over thirty years and have never been in a fight, never been assaulted and never had cause to call the police. This is not to suggest that Australia is an idyllic, crime-free paradise. It is not. But it is normally pretty safe and pretty law-abiding. All you need to do is take sensible precautions. Statistics tell us that 80 per cent of all cases of violence happen in and around drinking places, normally in the very late evening. The obvious answer is not to drink in dubious bars late at night. And do not get into arguments with strangers in bars about the respective merits of your brand of football versus Australian Rules. To criticise Australian Rules even by merely mouthing faint praise is akin to spitting on the Bible.

In Australia the flaunting of wealth in the form of personal decoration is considered slightly vulgar so it as well to leave serious jewellery at home. Credit card fraud must exist in Australia, although reported cases are few and far between.

SHOPPING

Australia is not a shopper's paradise as far as price is concerned, although it is world class when it comes to variety. Almost all the major shopping companies are represented in Australia. (Marks & Spencers has not yet arrived; nor Harrods. But give it time.) The prices for clothing and luxury and electronic goods are typically higher than they are in Europe or North America.

What can you buy that is worth shipping home? Plainly Australian souvenirs must be high on the list and a broad-brimmed Australian **bush hat** – the brand that everyone knows is Akubra, as worn by Crocodile Dundee, Greg Norman and almost everyone else – bought at the beginning of a trip will help shelter your head from the sun and other inclement weather and will last a lifetime. Do not worry if it becomes battered and bent and somewhat travel-stained. Akubras acquire character in this way and, indeed, there has been a book published on the subject of how headgear soon begins to take on the characteristics of the owner.

Then there is the famous **Drizabone** or its equivalent, a treated canvas raincoat which will indeed keep you dry as a bone in teeming rain.

You may find the full size version, designed for horsemen, somewhat daunting, but shorter jacket versions serve almost as well and are much cooler and lighter to wear.

Moleskins are white working trousers worn by rich farmers and television producers. These trousers are not made literally from the skin of the mole, but from a hard-wearing cotton material which is also extremely soft to the touch. Upsetting traditionalists, some versions are now being made with Lycra woven in, so that they do not get baggy with wear. All of this gear is on sale in different stores all over Australia but the definitive store is **R.M. Williams**, which was started by a famous bushman and stocks the genuine article. It is not just people in the bush who dress in this way; such clothes are essential wear in certain areas of advertising and broadcasting.

SMOKING

Smoking is now banned in all public buildings, airports, taxis, railway trains, buses, at least some sections of restaurants, almost all offices, all aircraft flying within Australia and all aircraft flying from and to Australia.

Cigarette advertising is banned, cigarette sponsorship is being banned, cigarette vending machines are in the process of being totally banned. As a rough rule of thumb you can take it that, unless you are outdoors or in an area where there are signs which specifically permit you to smoke – you can't. There is even a very serious movement to ban smoking in bars and in nightclubs.

Colour section: (i) Touring Australia by car can reveal stunning landscapes and unfamiliar road signs; trains such as the Spirit of the Outback (see p.406) often follow scenic routes which would be impractical by road.
(ii) The unique flora and fauna of Australia are attractions in their own right: red kangaroo; koalas; gum tree flower.
(iii) Sydney (p.57): Darling Harbour; Sydney Harbour Bridge.
(iv) The Big Banana at Coffs Harbour (p.85); community centre, Byron Bay (p.88); Stanwell Park coastline (p.91).

The BIG BANANA COFFS HARBOUR

SWIMMING

Swimming is one of Australia's great outdoor sports and, is perfectly safe if you follow a few basic rules. If the beach is patrolled, and most popular beaches are, especially at holiday times and weekends, the simple rule is to stay between the flags and, if you get into trouble, raise your hand above your head and help will be there immediately. In parts of the north of Australia you will find that some rivers are carefully signposted to show they contain crocodiles. To swim in such rivers is an act of gross folly. Do not do it.

TAXIS

Taxis are reasonably priced, normally airconditioned and the driver will usually take you where you are going with safety and dispatch. Usually. There can be exceptions, as taxi drivers do not get the formal training about destinations that they do in other parts of the world. However, they are very strictly policed and any complaint is acted upon with vigour and alacrity. Merely the threat of a complaint will normally rectify any problem. Every cab has a number at the front. Even making a note of the number will often defuse a situation.

In many cities there is a dearth of cabs between the hours of 1500 and 1530. This is cabbies' change-over time and all attempts to stagger this have been frustrated by the cab drivers, who are conservative in their lifestyle.

Many Australians ride in the front with the driver. This is neither essential nor, in many cases, desirable. Taxi drivers see themselves as the fount of all knowledge – this is a worldwide complaint – but if you sit in the back they tend to leave you alone. Cabs do not usually accept credit cards outside the central business districts of cities.

TELECOMMUNICATIONS

Telecommunications in Australia are world standard and, indeed, in some respects Australia leads the world. There are two dominant carriers – Telstra and Optus – although others are starting up and by the year 2000 there will probably be 50 or so carriers. The mobile telephone network is divided into analogue and GSM digital. The latter is a worldwide

standard, which means that digital mobiles that work in Europe or the Gulf or Asia will work in Australia, provided an agreement is in place between the carriers. The percentage of the Australian population using mobile telephones is approaching a third and coverage is everywhere there is a sufficient population to support the installation of a mobile transmitter. Take it that any town of any size has mobile coverage as have most of the main roads. In the very near future coverage, by way of low-flying satellites, will be total.

More and more telephone kiosks are moving to operation by a stored value telephone card – obtainable at all post offices, many newsagents and petrol stations – although pay phones in shops and restaurants all tend to be coin machines.

The Australian telephone plug is, as in so many countries in the world, unique. Adaptors are readily available and most hotel telephones will accept a standard American RJ11 plug. But not all. Your best bet is to buy the necessary cable or adaptor from the chain of Dick Smith electronic stores which exist almost everywhere.

For overseas calls dial 0011, followed by the country code and then the area code (dropping the first 0 in the case of Britain and other countries whose area codes begin with 0) – then the number. Some country codes:

Canada 1
New Zealand 64
Republic of Ireland 353
South Africa 27
United Kingdom 44
United States 1

Access to the **Internet** is widespread and nearly half a million Australians surf the Net regularly. Penetration rivals that of the USA. There is now a range of cafés which offer patrons Internet access, useful for checking up on e-mail. More useful still is an account with CompuServe, which is easy to access from anywhere in Australia and to which e-mail from the Internet can be automatically transferred.

THOMAS COOK IN AUSTRALIA

There are numerous branches of Thomas Cook in every state of Australia, which provide a full

33

travel service, including domestic and international air tickets, rail tickets, car rental, and travel insurance. There are also foreign exchange bureaux at the gateway airports of Sydney, Melbourne, Adelaide, Perth and Darwin. At all these locations (except for a few of the travel branches) a range of foreign currencies can be changed and Thomas Cook MasterCard Travellers Cheques cashed; they also offer **Moneygram**, a quick international money transfer service which allows you to obtain more cash from home (not available at Thomas Cook airport bureaux de change).

To contact a Thomas Cook travel consultant from anywhere in Australia you can dial 131 771, which is charged at local call rates.

In addition to the above services, all travel locations offer the **Thomas Cook Network Worldwide Customer Promise**. Under this any traveller who has booked his/her travel arrangements through Thomas Cook in another part of the world can obtain, free of charge, air ticket rerouting and revalidation, hotel and car rental reservations, and emergency assistance in the case of lost or stolen Thomas Cook MasterCard Travellers Cheques. **MasterCard** holders can also obtain emergency assistance in the event of loss or theft ot their card.

TIME

There are few public clocks in Australia and those that exist tend to be inaccurate. You can check the time with the Speaking Clock by dialling 1194.

It is important to remember that different states lie in different time zones. The three time zones are **Eastern Standard Time**, which covers New South Wales, Queensland, Victoria and Tasmania; **Central Standard Time** in South Australia and the Northern Territory, which is half an hour behind Eastern Standard Time; and **Western Standard Time**, covering Western Australia, which is 2 hrs behind Eastern Standard Time. And there is the occasional anomaly whereby e.g. Broken Hill, in New South Wales, has opted to be on Central Standard time.

This would be understandable if it were not for **daylight saving**. Some states object to this because it upsets the cows with early milking – honestly, that is the reason given – and so Queensland ignores daylight saving, thus moving 1 hr behind the other Eastern Standard Time states. Western Australia, which has always had ideas of seceding totally from the rest of Australia, also rejects daylight saving and so moves 3 hrs behind Eastern Standard Time.

All of this would still be clear enough, if somewhat complex, but the states cannot agree on which day daylight saving is to be brought in. The map on the facing page summarises the varying time differences and their relation to the rest of the world, but does not attempt to show the dates on which daylight saving applies, which change from year to year and state to state; nor does it take account of relative differences when your home city is in its own daylight saving period. When in doubt check carefully with someone who understands this arcane science, or consult the *current* edition of the OTT (see p.38).

TIPPING

Tipping is not part of the Australian way of life. This may be the only country in the world where cab drivers sometimes give the passenger a lower fare: if the fare on the meter comes to, say, $21 dollars the cab driver will take the note and tell you to forget the small change. In upmarket restaurants ten per cent of the bill would be appropriate but, in every case, tipping levels are much lower than Europe or the United States.

In fact, it is possible to give offence by tipping when it is not appropriate. Australians believe that they live in an egalitarian society, where all people are equal, and some of them find tipping demeaning.

TOILETS

Public toilets do exist – but are few in number and not noted for their scrupulous cleanliness. However, all petrol stations have clean toilets and, although they are supposed to be reserved for customers, there is no problem if you ask politely. All hotels and pubs also have clean toilets which are accessible to the public. In National Parks, those supervised by the National Parks and Wildlife Service tend to be

AUSTRALIAN TIME ZONES

WITHOUT DAYLIGHT SAVING

When it is 12 noon in each of these Australian time zones, it is:

Eastern Standard Time
2 a.m. same day in London and Dublin (GMT); 8 p.m. previous day in New York; 5 p.m. previous day in Los Angeles; 2 p.m. same day in Auckland

Central Standard Time
2.30 a.m. same day in London and Dublin (GMT); 8.30 p.m. previous day in New York; 5.30 p.m. previous day in Los Angeles; 1.30 p.m. same day in Auckland

Western Standard Time
4 a.m. same day in London and Dublin (GMT); 10 p.m. previous day in New York; 7 p.m. previous day in Los Angeles; 4 p.m. same day in Auckland

DAYLIGHT SAVING PERIODS

When it is 12 noon in each of these Australian time zones, it is:

Eastern Standard Time
1 a.m. same day in London and Dublin (GMT); 7 p.m. previous day in New York; 4 p.m. previous day in Los Angeles; 1 p.m. same day in Auckland

Central Standard Time
1.30 a.m. same day in London and Dublin (GMT); 7.30 p.m. previous day in New York; 4.30 p.m. previous day in Los Angeles; 12.30 p.m. same day in Auckland

Queensland time
2 a.m. same day in London and Dublin (GMT); 8 p.m. previous day in New York; 5 pm previous day in Los Angeles; 2 pmsame day in Auckland

Western Standard Time
4 a.m. same day in London and Dublin (GMT); 10 p.m. previous day in New York; 7 p.m. previous day in Los Angeles; 4 p.m. same day in Auckland

NB: All above times may vary by 1 hr if your own city is currently applying its own daylight saving

clean and useable. The slang for a toilet is 'dunny', although this is regarded as common and is gradually disappearing from use.

TOURIST INFORMATION

This can be divided into two areas – official and unofficial. Almost every town has an information centre for tourists. These are manned by locals who are first-rate at sorting out accommodation problems – they will always get you in somehow, somewhere – but may not be totally accurate on local information. Most of the local tourist boards produce brochures which are long on pretty pictures and verbiage,

but short on hard facts. Thus sea is always 'blue' unless it is 'azure'. Sand is always 'golden' unless it is 'white'. Foliage is always 'luxuriant'. Where towns have names of Aboriginal origin, if the correct translation is unflattering it is changed. Thus the translation of the name of the town Trangie, in New South Wales is 'quick intercourse'. You will not see this referred to in tourist brochures.

Note that simply because somewhere has the 'i' sign outside, the international sign for information, it does not mean that this is an official information agency. Many travel agencies and even newsagents in some small country towns have taken to erecting this sign to attract custom. Yes, they will answer your questions, but accuracy is not guaranteed.

TRAINS

The rail service offers a relatively cheap way of travelling around Australia – especially using a rail pass (see below). The network is less dense than in the UK and Europe, but many of the routes recommended in this book are practicable by train, and where this is the case notes on the rail service follow the driving directions. Maps of the main routes can be found on the next page.

Australia possesses a number of long-distance 'named' trains, such as the **Ghan** and the **Indian–Pacific**, some of them among the world's classic rail journeys. See the chapter on Classic Train Journeys, pp 403–405.

Up-to-date **rail schedules** for Australia can be found in the current edition of the *Thomas Cook Overseas Timetable* or OTT (see p.38) and the route information in this book quotes the relevant OTT table numbers (table numbers

sometimes change but all destinations can be traced through the OTT's index).

Train tickets can be booked in Australia at stations or through branches of Thomas Cook, or at the following rail Centres: NSW, *(02) 9929 7614*; Victoria, *(03) 619 5000*; South Australia, *(08) 217 4455*; Western Australia, *(09) 326 2733*; Queensland, *(07) 225 0211*.

The most economical way of using the rail network, however, is to obtain a **rail pass** in your own country before travelling. The **Austrailpass** gives unlimited free travel on Australian trains (including suburban ones) for periods ranging from 14 to 30 consecutive days. The **Austrail Flexipass** entitles you to use trains for a number of non-consecutive days (ranging from 8 to 29 days) within a 6-month period. For details and purchases of these and other passes, contact

UK: *Leisurail, PO Box 113, Peterborough PE3 8HY; tel: 01733 335599.*

USA: *Forsyth Travel Library, 1750 East 131st St, PO Box 480800, Kansas City, MO 64148; tel: 800 367-7984.*

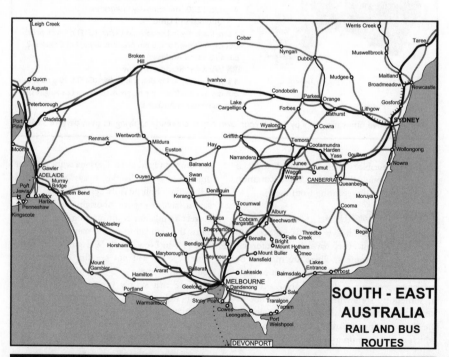

SOUTH - EAST
AUSTRALIA
RAIL AND BUS
ROUTES

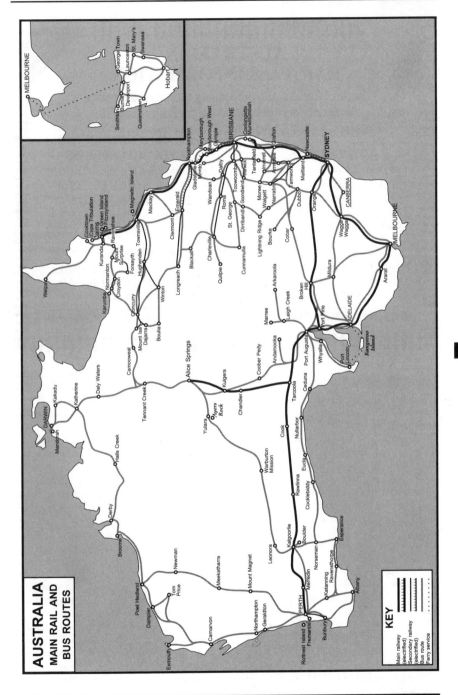

AUSTRALIA
MAIN RAIL AND
BUS ROUTES

KEY

Main railway (electrified)
Secondary railway (electrified)
Bus route
Ferry service

USEFUL READING

Most international guidebook series have a volume on Australia, and often on specific states or cities, useful for extra sightseeing information. The Thomas Cook Travellers range of compact colour guides has a volume on *Sydney and New South Wales* (published by the AA/Thomas Cook Publishing in the UK and Passport Books in the USA – available from any bookstore).

If you intend to use **trains** or **buses** to any extent, you will find it useful, both for pre-planning and for use on holiday, to have the latest edition of the *Thomas Cook Overseas Timetable* (referred to throughout this book as the **OTT**). This gives up-to-date schedules for rail services, and many long-distance bus services, in Australia. Published every two months, it is available at branches of Thomas Cook in the UK, or can be purchased by credit card from **Thomas Cook Publishing**, *PO Box 227, Thorpe Wood, Peterborough PE3 3PU, UK.; tel: 01733 503560; fax: 01733 503596* (from outside the UK the code is 44 1733). Current prices inclusive of postage are £9.80 (UK 2nd class post), £11.90 (Europe airmail) and £13.30 (rest of the world airmail). US readers can order the OTT from Forsyth Travel Library, *1750 East 131st St, PO Box 480800, Kansas City, MO 64148*, for US$27.95 plus $4.50 shipping.

The annual *Penguin Australian Accommodation Guide* is the only comprehensive guide to **accommodation** throughout Australia and has a CD-Rom disk of the details included. In Australia, all the motoring organisations publish accommodation guides to relevant states and these are available at tourist centres. There are no general **restaurant guides** published outside Australia, and very few published within Australia. The two best known are the *Sydney Morning Herald* Good Food Guide and the *Melbourne Age Good Food Guide*. But no similar publication exists for Brisbane or Darwin.

Books to give you a flavour of Australia: *A Town Like Alice*, by Nevil Shute. This is now pretty dated and the forecast that it made for the fictional town in the Gulf country – widely accepted as Normanton (see p.255) – did not

Websites

The Internet is full of sites on Australia. Hundreds, thousands, of them. Many are rubbish, but some are worth accessing and a selection is listed below. For details of the services **Thomas Cook** can provide, including travel, currency and traveller's cheques, visit their website at *http://www.thomascook.com*

Welcome to Australia:
http://www.aussie.net.au/
Official site of the Australian Tourist Commission. Full of information.

Australian Gay & Lesbian Tourism Assoc: *http://aglta.asn.au/about.htm*

Australian Railway Timetable Information: *http://www.com.au/railpage/tt*

Australia – The Final Word
http://www.finalword.com/
Good information on driving.

Cowleys Tourist Destinations
http://www.cowleys.com.au/public/tourist.htm
Lots of gaps but tries to be comprehensive.

Let's Travel Australia
http://www.cybsyd.com.au/lets-travel-australia/
Information on budget travel in Australia.

Australasian Travel and Tourism
http://www.wps.com.au/travel/travhome.htm
Has an excellent links to other pages.

Australia – the Land, the People
http://www.uq.edu.au/~zzgquinn/
Simplistic but useful information plus links.

What follows is a list of destination specific sites. The quality is variable but almost all contain some information.

Sydney:
http://sydney.simplenet.com/index.htm

Sydney Interactive Visitors Guide
http://www.visitorsguide.aust.com/~tourism/

Queensland Tourism And Travel Corporation: *http://www.qttc.com.au/*

Brisbane: *http://sparky.elec.uq.oz.au/brisbane/brisbane.html*

Canberra:
http://www.peg.apc.org/~tomw/ct.html

Melbourne: *http://www.mcmb.com.au/*

North Eastern Victoria
http://www.netc.net.au/Region1/Region.html

Victorian Tourist Operators Assoc:
http://www.world.net/Travel/Australia/vto/

Tasmanian State Dept Of Tourism
http://www.tas.gov.au/tourism/tasman.html

South Australian Tourist Commission
http://www.tourism.sa.gov.au/

Adelaide Regional Guide:
http://www.wombat.com.au/wombat/tour/sa/adelaide/index.html

Western Australian Tourism Commission: *http://www.wa.gov.au/watc/*

Dept Of Conservation And Land Management
http://www.calm.wa.gov.au/tourism/index.html

Perth Convention Bureau
http://www.wa.gov.au/watc/xpcb.html

Northern Territory Tourist Commission
http://www.world.net/Travel/Australia/NT_info/NTTC/

39

come to pass. But it still gives an excellent feel for the outback. *The Lucky Country: Australia in the Sixties,* by Donald Horne. Several times revised, in print for 30 years and still valid. *The Fatal Shore: a history of the transportation of convicts to Australia 1787–1868,* by Robert Hughes.

Wonderful history of Australia as seen through the eyes of the convicts themselves. *A Fortunate Life,* by Albert Facey, published 1981 and still in print. Autobiography of an Australian everyman. He was born 1894, had bush schooling but no formal education and fought at Gallipoli.

DRIVING IN AUSTRALIA

ACCIDENTS

Australia has a very low accident rate compared to other countries and it is continually dropping. If you are in an accident in the city you will observe an odd Australian ritual. The tow trucks will appear first, as if from nowhere, wanting to tow your vehicle away. They will be persistent in asking you to sign a form. Do not sign it. The towies, as they are called, will be followed by the police. All accidents, unless they are minor scrapes, must be reported. Never admit fault and only sign forms for the police. You will find that, as a visitor, you will be treated with great courtesy and kid gloves.

BREAKDOWNS

If you have a breakdown in an urban area, pull off the road, switch on your hazard warning lights and lift the bonnet. If you cannot fix what is wrong with your car, call either the company you hired the car from or the local motorists' association. Explain that you are a visitor and help, for which you may have to pay, will be quickly to hand. Many overseas motoring organisations have reciprocal rights with the Australian motoring organisations – there is a different one for each state – and it is worth making enquiries before you leave. On the few superhighways, telephones can be found every 2 km or so and, again, help will arrive very quickly. If you are in a very rural area, the next car or truck to come along will automatically stop and offer to help or will report your problem through mobile telephone or radio.

CAR RENTAL

All the major rental companies are represented in Australia and they maintain modern, air-conditioned fleets in which the cars, almost without exception, have automatic gear boxes. There is a temptation to hire the lowest priced model, which is fine if you only intend to operate within city areas and use the internal airlines to fly between cities. If, however, you

intend to drive long distances you will find that the extra paid for a higher horsepower, roomier car will be well worth it. It is often difficult, sometimes nigh impossible, for people under the age of 25 to hire a car. The conditions vary, not just between each company, but between each state and each type of car.

DISTANCES

All road distances in Australia and in this book are meaured in kilometres (km), colloquially referred to as 'clicks'. One km is 0.625 miles.

DOCUMENTATION

Your own national driving licence will suffice. International driving licences are not a legal requirement in Australia, although they can be useful if you are involved in an accident.

FOUR-WHEEL DRIVE

Hiring four-wheel-drive vehicles is possible, although much more expensive than ordinary vehicles, and fraught with danger. Many people hiring these vehicles look upon them as a standard saloon with off-road capabilities. In fact, driving a four-wheel-drive vehicle on a surfaced road is an acquired skill. Driving them in the bush requires experience and training. The best way to deal with this is to either go on a four-wheel-drive handling course before you hire one, or only travel in convoy with other, more experienced, drivers. Several tour operators in the country areas offer this facility. The accident rate – not fatalities but mainly over-turns – is very high, and in almost every case is caused by inexperience in the way that a four-wheel-drive vehicle, with its high centre of gravity, handles at any sort of speed. For the record, in researching this book no four-wheel-drive vehicle was needed or used at any point.

FUEL

Petrol (gas) is sold in litres and comes in leaded, unleaded and super unleaded. It is illegal to put leaded petrol into cars fitted with a catalytic converter and that applies to all hire cars, without exception. Very few models – mainly at the sporty end – require super unleaded petrol and it is a waste of money to use it.

Fuel, at about 70 cents a litre, is generally much cheaper than in Europe but more expensive than in the USA. Prices vary, and you will find that in country areas petrol can be as much as 20 cents a litre more expensive than in urban areas. Filling stations abound on the highways. On the back tracks they are a little more difficult to find. The cardinal rule is, when in doubt fill your tank. Keeping your tank topped up at all times will help you on the longer runs. When desperate you can always find someone in a town without a petrol station to sell you petrol – at a price.

OUTBACK DRIVING

If you are driving in the Northern Territory and parts of Queensland you will come across road trains – trucks with three or four trailers. In dry weather they leave a cloud of dust behind them which can reduce your visibility to almost zero. **Overtaking** them is not easy and you need a long clear stretch of road before you should even think of doing so. Better still is to stop, take a rest and then drive on. Driving across the Nullarbor Desert towards Perth you may be dazzled by the lights of an oncoming truck. Get used to it as the road is so straight it sometimes takes 5 to 10 mins to meet and pass.

The most dangerous times for hitting **animals** are dawn and dusk. Keep a special look out for them and reduce your speed. Hitting a full-grown kangaroo at speed is a very serious accident and 'roo bars' are worse than useless.

Make sure you know the **route** and you have discussed it with locals. The police are, as always, a mine of useful information. If you are seriously 'going outback' on unmade roads into the desert, you must carry essential supplies, especially **water** and **fuel**. You simply cannot have too much water; 20 litres a head is a good rule as this could easily last you a week with care. The heat of the day in Australia will mean that you will be running with the air conditioner set on high most of the time. Although this technology has improved tremendously in the past few years, it still means that your fuel

consumption will be relatively high, so when in doubt, fill your tank. If you break down, stay with your vehicle. It provides shade and is a good target for a search party.

All of which sounds somewhat forbidding, although this is not the intention. Australia is a very easy country to drive around and the locals think nothing of covering very long distances in a day – 1000 km being not uncommon.

MOTORCYCLES

These, of course, do exist in Australia and are used for touring, but this is not very common. On long distances between towns a motorcycle is a rare sight. This is in part due to the very long distances between urban centres, the heat and, on the side roads, the dust. Helmets are a legal requirement for both riders and pillion passengers. This is also the case for cyclists.

POLICE

The Highway Patrol has unmarked cars for catching speedsters, as well as roadside radar guns and automatic cameras. Marked police cars have blue lights and if these are flashed at you, pull over on to the verge as soon as it is safe to do so. You must produce your licence.

RECREATIONAL VEHICLES (RVs)

RVs are not as popular in Australia as they are in other countries. They can be hired but most travellers tend to use motels – inexpensive and ubiquitous – with tent camping being reserved for true outback exploration.

ROADS

Australia is not blessed with a great road system and this situation is unlikely to change. It is partly because of the paucity of the population in comparison to the area cover; partly ·it is because the population (in the main) is restricted to narrow strips of land. The result is that although the roads between cities may be grandly named as Pacific Highway or Princes Highway, they are quite often only two lanes wide with passing places every 5 km or so. These passing places are invariably on the upside of a hill which gives cars a chance to soar past caravans and trucks. Warning signs tell you how far it is to the next passing place.

41

There are dual carriageways – the one from Sydney to Newcastle is a good example – but they are very much the exception. You might think that this would all lead to horrendous traffic jams, but they are, in fact, very rare.

All main roads in Australia are numbered following international standards, with tourist routes marked in brown and main routes in green. This is fine if you are following the map or using this guide, but if you ask a local they will be totally confused. Roads are known by their local name and this can change as it passes through various towns. However, the chances of you getting seriously lost are close to zero as there is generally one single route from one town to another, although there may be some sightseeing tours possible.

The major road, which you will come across time and time again, is **Route 1**, which almost completely circles Australia, and for much of its length is known as the Pacific Highway. Again, this is mainly a two-lane (one lane each way) road, with passing places. In some areas of Australia it is a major highway, in others you can drive long distances and see hardly another vehicle. Australians are used to driving far, far greater distances than most Europeans and think little of driving 500 or 600 km to a place to spend a night or so.

Roundabouts (traffic circles, rotaries) are as common in Australian towns as in British ones.

Unsealed Roads

Many of the back roads of Australia are dirt roads, which are scraped at regular intervals to keep them relatively smooth. Driving on them is not difficult and requires no particular skills. Keep the speed moderate so that you can spot pot holes and avoid them. Do not even think of overtaking another vehicle. Australia is dry much of the time so you will probably raise a plume of dust. So will the car in front of you, which will dramatically lower your visibility and may affect your breathing. Lower your speed and drop back until the air is clear. If another vehicle is coming towards you, slow right down and edge to the side of the road. The biggest danger is from flying pebbles, which can be shot from under tyres like bullets and can shatter windscreens. If you reduce your

speed this is very unlikely to happen. Sometimes the road is crossed by a gully. The rule is always to stop and get out and carefully inspect the situation. If the gully is running with water use a stick to probe the depth. Then drive through smoothly in a low gear.

Road Signs

By and large, Australia adheres to international road sign conventions, with some cute and attractive additions which show kangaroos, wombats, crocodiles or whatever. The international formula of mandatory signs being in red and white is adhered to. Yellow and orange are for road works and diversions.

RULES OF THE ROAD

Driving rules and habits will generally be similar to those you are used to. There are some anomalies but they are minor. If you keep in your lane, make your signals early, keep your distance and do not cut in, you will be fine.

The key thing for non-UK visitors to remember is that you **drive on the left**. Unlike British practice, you give priority to traffic joining the road from the right, unless a sign indicates otherwise. At roundabouts and smaller traffic islands you give way to the right.

When two cars going in opposite directions are turning right at an intersection they use the 'diamond turn', i.e. they pass inside each other with left side to left side, instead of driving around each other as they would, for example, in Britain. At **night** you must use dipped headlights, not side lights, when driving, and you cannot park facing the traffic.

Speed Limits

With the sole exception of the Northern Territory (and this will change) there is an absolute speed limit imposed on every road in Australia. In town it is 60 kph (37 mph); in the open country 100 kph (60 mph), and on some motorways 110 kph (just under 70 mph). In other parts of the world there is some laxity allowed in speed restrictions. This is most definitely not the case in Australia and the police patrol all roads. Note that all radar detectors, intended to spot radar scanners before you are caught, are illegal throughout the country.

ROADS • RULES OF THE ROAD

These are relatively easily spotted by the police even when you are mobile.

Drink Driving

This is another area where you simply cannot afford to take the risk. Random breath testing is used in a serious and methodical manner, and on a holiday in Australia you will probably be pulled over for testing once or twice. If there are two of you and you share a bottle of wine for dinner you will be under the limit – but not by a great margin. With beer, two glasses is your limit, unless you drink a low alcohol beer. The absolute limit on low alcohol beers is four cans an hour and even this is pushing it.

This random breath testing has led to a cultural change in Australia, and drinking and driving is very much frowned upon by society at all levels.

Seat Belts

Seat belts must be worn by all passengers at all times in all cars, with the single exception of taxis, and that will probably change in the near future. One prime minister of Australia was fined for being interviewed in a limousine when he was not wearing a seat belt. Infants must be in approved security capsule infant carriers and, in some states taxis are not allowed to carry infants unless they have the necessary safety equipment fitted. Up to the age of four, children are allowed to travel in a properly fitted child car seat and after that they must wear seat-belts. All new buses must be fitted with seat belts and where available they must be worn.

TRAFFIC JAMS AND PARKING

Only two cities in Australia suffer from traffic jams – Sydney and Melbourne. And even these are nothing like the gridlocks seen in other cities around the world. The normal rush hour rules apply and traffic jams disappear in January when schools are on holiday.

The number of ordinary parking meters in Australia is constantly decreasing. They are being replaced by a series of parking bays with one meter which will accept any coins. Parking within the central business district is always possible, but during the day and early evening it is expensive. In some places it can get as high as $25 a day, and a night at the Opera in Sydney, for example, will cost an extra $17 for parking.

Parking illegally will get you a ticket from a 'brown bomber' (the name for parking meter attendants who, to confuse you, are dressed in grey) and this will run from around $50 to something over $100. Even if you have a hire car you will have to pay because the ticket will be forwarded to the hire car company, which will then add it to your credit card bill.

VEHICLE INSURANCE

Car rental agencies offer compulsory insurance plus CDW – collision damage waiver. It is not expensive and it takes away another worry. If you have booked your car abroad you will probably find it is included in the package price.

BUYING A VEHICLE

As in Europe, there is a tradition of young backpackers coming to Australia, buying a second-hand combi-van, touring the country and selling it when they finish the trip. A couple of warnings. Australia is a tough country on cars. The constant high temperatures, the long distances, the sometimes poor road surfaces often result in vehicles bcoming old before their time. So the buyer has to beware.

In Sydney, the lower floors of **King's Cross Car Park**, *Ward St,* opposite the Gazebo Hotel, Kings Cross, are devoted to **The Backpackers Car Market** *(tel: 9358 5000),* where vehicles are sold by their owners. Dealers are not allowed to work here, only individual owners. It costs about $5 a day or $35 a week to have a car on sale here and it must have a 'pink slip' – a certificate of roadworthiness which, in truth, means very little.

Prices are, of course, open to negotiation. The closer to the date of the owner's return air ticket, the more flexible the price. Many have extra camping equipment thrown in. I would not travel around a small park in any of the vehicles I saw on display but, then, I am not a backpacker. Fortunately, insurance can be arranged on the spot. Most insurance companies will *not* provide cover for overseas travellers, owing to the distressing tendency of backpackers to write off vehicles on the very last stages of their travels around Australia.

43

BACKGROUND AUSTRALIA

AUSTRALIA – SHE'S A BIG COUNTRY

When writing about Australia the most difficult point to get across is how large it is. If you look at the continental USA and leave out Alaska and the Great Lakes you have the rough equivalent in size. It is vital that you understand how large the place is, otherwise you will start thinking of day trips to Alice Springs from Sydney or quick jaunts from Darwin to Cairns by bus – I came across examples of both delusions among tourists I met while researching this book.

Put it another way – if you fly by 747 to Hong Kong from Sydney, five hours after take off you will still be over Australia.

So Australia is large. And, as far as people are concerned, it is very nearly empty. Despite the image created by the movie *Crocodile Dundee,* most Australians are city and town dwellers. The majority live in urban surroundings on the coast. If you take quite a narrow strip from Adelaide to Melbourne to Sydney and on to Brisbane, you have covered the most populated area of Australia. The majority of the remainder of the population live in enclaves in Perth – the world's most isolated city – and Darwin.

In theory there are just over 4000 towns and villages in Australia. But if you apply the sacred and profane test – to be a town it must have a church and a pub – and set the lower limits of population at 500, there are not 1000 towns in the whole of Australia. And in some places, like the Northern Territory, towns are so sparse and far apart that anything with a general store and a pub becomes a town, even though the population is in single figures.

GEOLOGY AND GEOGRAPHY

Australia is a very old country. The ranges in the west are made from rocks that were formed more than 300 million years ago, while what is left of the mountain ranges in Central Australia – the Musgraves, the Hamersleys, the Kimberley, Arnhem Land – probably originated 100 million years ago.

One theory is that all of the continents in the south were originally one land mass and broke up well over 200 million years ago. In the east the Snowy Mountains and the Victorian Alps probably came about 65 million years ago and sometime in the last seven million years – yesterday geologically speaking – the inland crust collapsed and settled while the east coast gradually rose. The last volcano probably rumbled in Victoria some 6000 years ago.

Although nature made Australia large and rugged she forgot by and large to supply water. The Aborigines accepted this as part of life. But European settlers stayed close to the rivers, created farms, drained the natural resources of water for irrigation. The result is that now there are very few major rivers in Australia which you could call totally natural. Some have been reduced to a sporadic trickle through the building of dams and weirs and irrigation systems. The Snowy River is no longer a rumbling, tumbling downpour – it is a sedate, meandering river and, at times, can almost disappear altogether. Many waterfalls can only be seen in the rainy season when the dams overflow.

The one exception to this can be found in the high country of Tasmania where the rivers still run wild and free, although plans have been put forward to control, tame and, eventually, destroy them. Now there is a major movement in the other direction, with the federal and state governments realising that water is Australia's most precious commodity and needs to be nurtured, cared for, encouraged. Very soon we should see the Snowy River flowing again in full spate and we may even see the river-boats, which were such a feature of early Australia, once more operating right into the interior.

The one mountain chain worthy of comparison on a worldwide basis is the **Great Dividing Range**, dating back 225 million years from the Palaeozoic time, which runs along the east coast for over 2000 km, starting in tropical rain forest in the far north and ending in sub-alpine moors in Tasmania.

WILDLIFE

Because Australia was isolated as an island continent it developed its own flora and fauna. The over-used word 'unique' is absolutely correct when applied to much of Australia's wildlife.

Animals

The best known of Australia's native animals are the **marsupials**. Marsupials differ from placental mammals in that they give birth much earlier, to complete the offspring's nurture in a special body pouch. There are something like 150 kinds of marsupial in the world and almost all of them is found in Australia. The largest is the **kangaroo**. Even when you have seen hundreds of them they still seem strange, and a herd of kangaroos fleeing in monster hops through the countryside is like a scene from *Jurassic Park*. But although they are very common, visitors rarely see them except in sanctuaries. Or, sadly, dead by the roadside. This is because they are naturally timid creatures and are most active at dusk, dawn and sometimes at night. The one place you can guarantee to see them at any time is Pebbly Beach in New South Wales, where they are almost, but not quite, a pest. A **wallaby** is a kangaroo of small to medium size. A **wallaroo** is smaller yet and about the size of a domestic cat. Western Australia boasts **quokkas** – wallabies small enough to have been mistaken by the Dutch explorers for rats (see p. xxx).

The **koala bear** is not a bear, of course, but another marsupial. Tree-living, and relying mostly on eucalyptus for food and drink, they have become another Australian icon. Current evidence seems to suggest that they suffer severe trauma when cuddled by visitors for photographs and this practice is going out of favour. **Wombats** are also marsupials; bigger than koalas, they live in burrows. They are nocturnal animals and often get run over. Drivers should carefully regard all warning signs.

Australia also has the only two genera of **monotremes** – egg-laying mammals – in the world: the **duck-billed platypus** and the **echidna** or spiny ant-eater. Again, it is extremely unlikely you will see them in the wild but they can be found in dozens of reserves, wildlife parks and sanctuaries.

The wild dog of Australia is the **dingo**, thought to have entered the continent along with the Aboriginal peoples 40–60,000 years ago, and it is fairly widely spread. This is the dog in the famous Azaria trial, 'the dingo took my baby' – and it is now widely accepted that was in fact what happened. Dingoes are difficult to domesticate, although it has been done and many Australian dogs have a strain of dingo somewhere in their family tree. The dingo never became established on Tasmania, which probably accounts for the survival there, until the advent of the Europeans, of the thylacine or Tasmanian tiger (see p. 383).

There are over 700 species of **bird** in Australia, including more than 50 species of colourful parrots such as the **rosella**; other well-known specialities include the **kookaburra** or laughing jackass and the large flightless birds, the **emu** and the **cassowary**. In the reptile kingdom Australia has **crocodiles**, which everyone knows about, and the lesser-known predators, **goannas**, lizards which can grow to over 2m (7 ft) long.

45

Plants

The genus **eucalyptus** or gum tree, perfectly adapted to Australia's many climates, comes in 500 different species. The secret of its success is its ability to conserve water and nutrients in its evergreen leaves. Many other specifically Australian species of plant include colourful and unusual bloomers such as **bottlebrush plants**, **desert peas** and orchids. Deserts can be transformed in a matter of days after one of the infrequent rainstorms by carpets of opportunistic **wildflowers**, and in places such as Western Australia this is a major tourist attraction (see p. xxx). For many visitors, however, Australia's greatest botanica attractions are in the **rain forests** of Queensland and Northern Territory.

PEOPLE AND HISTORY

Aborigines

It is possible that the Aborigines have been in Australia for as long as 150,000 years – certainly for at least 40,000 years. During the last Ice Age it would have been possible for them to have used a land bridge between New Guinea and

Explorers and Expeditions

Reference has been made throughout the text to the many explorers and exploration parties – some daring and successful, some courageous but doomed – who have shaped Australia's history and whose memory often lives on in the names of mountains, deserts and other natural features. This brief checklist does no more than put them in historical context; more details about them are within the remaining chapters of this book.

1606 William Jansz of the Dutch East India Company charted 320 km of Western Australian coastline. The Dutch called the land New Holland.

1616 Dirk Hartog made the first recorded landfall on the Australian Coast.

1642-44 Abel Tasman made two great voyages, in 1642 and 1644. He discovered an island that he called Van Diemen's Land, now known as Tasmania, and the northern coastline of Australia, and was the first European to see both Australia and New Zealand.

1768 Captain James Cook left England on a 3-year expedition to the Pacific in the *Endeavour*. Landing at Botany Bay on the eastern coast, he charted the region, naming it New South Wales.

1787 Captain Arthur Philip sailed with the First Fleet – 11 ships carrying convicts, marines and officers, wives, children, the governor and his staff. This motley crew set up a penal colony on the site of present-day Sydney, New South Wales.

1801 Matthew Flinders was the first to circumnavigate the continent and he charted most of the coastline between 1801 and 1803.

1803 Convict settlement set up at Hobart, Tasmania, then known as Van Diemen's Land.

1806 Captain William Bligh, the ex-captain of the *Bounty*, became governor.

1808 During the Rum Rebellion, Bligh is arrested by officers of the corrupt New South Wales Corps for trying to stop illegal trading in rum.

1810 Merino sheep breeding started, becoming a major economic activity and a viable export.

1813 Gregory Blaxland, Lt Lawson and William Charles Wentworth, and four servants, cross the Blue Mountains (see Sydney–Dubbo p.103–109).

1814 The end of the Napoleonic wars brings a flood of free settlers.

1817 John Oxley, Surveyor-General of New South Wales, set out to discover the course of the Lachlan River.

1824 Another convict settlement began at Moreton Bay, now known as Brisbane, Queensland.

1828 Captain Charles Sturt left Wellington in New South Wales and proceeded past the marshes, which Oxley had considered to be the end of the Macquarie. He followed the dry bed of the Bogan River and, in Feb 1829, reached a river, which he named the Darling.

Australia while sea levels were low. The ending of the Ice Age isolated them for millennia. Their unchanged traditions can therefore be considered to be the oldest continuous human culture. The latest cave paintings discovered would appear to predate the oldest cave paintings in Europe by several centuries (there is some dispute about this). The Aboriginal tribes lived in perfect adaptation to their harsh environment, in nomadic groups, with no hierarchical society of the sort that European settlers recognised. Their religious beliefs were, and are, inseparable from their landscape.

In the early days of colonisation, the Australian continent was, as far as Europeans were concerned, a dumping ground for convicts. And neither the authorities nor the convicts had any regard to the rights of the Aborigines. When James Cook first saw Australia it is estimated that there were about 300,000 Aborigines in Australia. Today there are perhaps 40,000 full-blood Aborigines and 100,000 part Aborigines. The treatment of its Aboriginal people is the shame of Australia's history. Their land was stolen, they were hunted like animals and killed, they were given alcohol, seduced and robbed. Until very recent times – the 1950s – families were split up and

1829 A new colony is formed in Western Australia with its capital at Perth.

1831 Major Thomas (later Lt Col. Sir Thomas) Mitchell, Surveyor-General of New South Wales, discovered the lower courses of the Peel (Namoi), Gwydir, and Dumaresq Rivers and identified the Upper Darling. In 1835 he traced the Darling 300 miles down from Bourke.

1835 John Batman acquired land, now Melbourne, from the Aborigines to pasture sheep.

1836 Adelaide, the capital of South Australia, was founded.

1840 Edward John Eyre led an expedition from Adelaide to try to reach the centre of Australia. The project was abandoned at Mt Hopeless in the Flinders Ranges.

1844 Ludwig Leichhardt, a Prussian scientist, set off from Darling Downs to Port Essington, an early settlement in the far north of the Northern Territory. He crossed the Dividing Range, and discovered the Lynd and Mitchell Rivers. He perished on an overland journey to Perth.

1845 John Mitchell, with Edmund Kennedy as his second in command, discovered the Warrego, Belyando and Barcoo Rivers. His exploration led to the opening up of the rich pastoral areas of Central Queensland.

1850 The shipping of convicts to Australia ceased.

1851 Gold was found by Edward Hargraves at Summer Hill Creek near Bathurst and a succession of gold rushes brought both population and prosperity to Australia.

1854 In Ballarat the miners rebelled. A small band of miners fought, and died, for their beliefs at the Eureka stockade (see Melbourne–Mildura p.156–167).

1860 Robert O'Hara Burke, a police officer, led an expedition from Melbourne, aiming to cross the continent from south to north. W.J. Wills became second in command (see North and West of Cairns pp.249–255). In the same year John McDouall set out from Adelaide and reached the centre of Australia – the first man to do so.

1862 John McDouall, with his third expedition, traversed Australia from south to north, reaching the north coast near Darwin on 24 July. The Overland Telegraph, completed in 1872, follows McDouall's route very closely.

1900 Sydney and Melbourne had become two of the world's largest cities but the country was still a group of states reporting directly to Britain with little internal co-operation.

1901 In Jan, in Centennial Park, the Commonwealth of Australia came into being as a federation of States. A documentary film was made of the event by the Salvation Army.

1914 World War I brought Australians to an understanding of nationhood and an astounding 330,000 volunteers joined up and, again, fought and died at Gallipoli and in France.

1988 Australian Bicentenary.

children taken from their parents so that they could be brought up as White Australians. To this day their life expectancy is about 15 years less than that of average Australians and, in many cases, their living conditions are simply appalling. Most Australians, to some extent or another, feel guilt about the Aborigines and the way they have been, and still are, treated.

Although less than 1% of the population is Aboriginal their plight is a major political problem. The largest numbers are in the Northern Territory and here some of the land has been returned to its traditional owners (a good example is much of Kakadu National Park)

who are organised as land councils and between them in the terrtiory have control over 286,000 sq km. In land rights, despite the furious opposition of most farmers and station owners, the Aborigines are, at long last, starting to get something approaching justice. But the problems still remain. In some states Aborigines can represent 25% or more of the prison population. Unemployment is four times the national average and in remote areas access to health and educational services is either difficult or well nigh impossible.

Is there any reason for hope? Perhaps. The courts do not accept the concept of *terra nulla* (the doctrine that nothing was owned until the Europeans arrived) and several important cases like Mabo and Wik have been settled in favour of the Aborigines. In recent years Aboriginal art has become recognised as a major art form and can be seen in many museums and art galleries. Australia realises that in 2000 the Olympics will turn the spotlight on the nation and if the problem has not been at least partially fixed before then it will be to the eternal shame of Australia.

The question is often asked by visitors: how do you treat Aborigines? And the absolute answer is with respect and dignity. Which is why climbing up Ayers Rock, for instance, shows, at best, a lack of manners. To the local Aboriginal community the rock is sacred and they do not climb over it. Neither should you.

European Arrivals and Colonisation

The Chinese and then the Portuguese may have been the first organised nations to have sighted the Australian continent, in the 15th and 16th centuries. Certainly a Dutch navigator saw the northern tip of Queensland at the beginning of the 17th century. Dutch landings on the west coast (considered barren and inhospitable) followed during that century; Australia's first European name was New Holland.

The European invasion came about, however, through the efforts of a remarkable navigator, **Captain James Cook**. In 1770, he sailed to the eastern coast of Australia in the converted Whitby collier the *Endeavour*, and reported of a land full of promise. The British government of the day saw it as a splendid place to dump convicts and also establish a strategic presence in the South Pacific. In the initial stages the development and exploration of the country was closely tied to the need to find settlements in which to house convicts. It started in Jan 1788 when the first thousand – 750 of them convicts – landed from eleven small ships and started a new nation. **Sydney**, Norfolk Island, Coal River, now the site of the city of Newcastle, and Van Diemen's Land (Tasmania) were all convict outposts. The first major push which was not convict-driven was in 1815 when the Blue Mountains were crossed. What started as exploration motivated by what might be thought of as the 'convict imperative'

became, in the early years of the last century, an expansion into the great unknown land.

In 1825, Van Diemen's Land, which had been one of the harshest and most repressive of the convict settlements, became **Tasmania**. In 1829, the first colony not connected with convicts was established on the Swan River, later to become **Perth**. **Melbourne**, another non-convict city, came as the result of the 'purchase' of 243,000 hectares of land from Aborigines by John Batman in 1835. In South Australia, **Adelaide** – named after the wife of King William IV of Britain – was an 1836 experiment in agricultural settlement. Up at Moreton Bay the convicts took the first steps towards agriculture. By 1839 the convicts were gone and **Brisbane** (named after the governor) became the centre from which free settlers moved into the interior of Queensland.

Darwin came much later in 1869. It was basically a strategic settlement to hold the northern coastline. Originally it was officially called Palmerston until 1911 but the more commonly used name of Port Darwin eventually achieved formal recognition. **Canberra** is the latest comer of them all, set up because of the rivalry between Melbourne and Sydney – still with us to this day – over the siting of the seat of the federal government. In 1911, the clearing of the site for Canberra started and the result is a beautiful city designed by the American architect, Walter Burley Griffin.

Agriculture has always played a major part in the Australian economy. **Camden** near Sydney was an early site and the origins of the wool industry lie there on the farm started by Macarthur whose relatives still live in the area. Then came the big push from New England across the fertile Darling Downs and later the Monaro Plains with Goulburn serving as a centre for that great wool-growing district.

The Gold Rushes and Mass Immigration

The great population leap in Australia and the move into the interior came from gold. The rushes that started in the 1850s tripled the population of Australia to 1.2 million. Among the gold miners were 40,000 Chinese. When the gold ceased to be profitable the new immigrants turned to other ways of making a living. The Chinese turned to market gardening, first to supply the miners and later to supply the new cities. The mix of nationalities became exotic, although the existing residents always complained about the new arrivals. Italians, when they came to the Murrumbidgee Irrigation area, the Greeks who came to Mildura and Renmark along the Murray, the Germans in Adelaide and along the Barossa Valley, all, at first, met with racially inspired hostility and then were slowly assimilated into the community. Now the same problem is being faced by the Vietnamese immigrants, who will no doubt be assimilated too.

Nationhood and the Twentieth Century

On 1 Jan 1901 in Sydney, in the middle of a great heat wave, and after nearly ten years of debate and negotiation, Australia became a nation. The six Australian colonies were, with the passage of the constitution through the British parliament, made into a federation of states, with the capital in Melbourne as a stop-gap measure until Canberra could be built. This was the first step towards Australia becoming an independent nation and, at the same time, the start of the drift away from Britain.

It is difficult for people in other countries to understand how close the ties were to Britain. In both world wars Australia declared war immediately and automatically on the day that Britain did. The Union Jack is, to this day, part of the flag. Until 1996 the majority of migrants came from Britain (the following year the Chinese moved to first place). Until the 1950s Britain was still referred to as 'home' by many citizens and Prime Minister Menzies thought of himself as British to the bone. Millions of Australians still make Britain their number one holiday destination. But the relationship is breaking down and there is a strong possiblity that by 2000, possibly during the Olympic Games, Australia will become a republic and cut all ties for ever.

When World War I started Australians volunteered in their hundreds of thousands. Many were sent to the shambles that was Gallipoli. This is still most seriously remembered in Australia on **Anzac Day** – and the general feeling in Australia is that the nation was let down by the Poms.

In World War II the Australians again surged forward to volunteer – and found themselves fighting in the North African desert when the Japanese declared war and started bombing Australia. It was widely believed that the Japanese would invade. The day was saved by the arrival of the Americans and from that day Australia started to look across the Pacific for a lead. In the Vietnam War Australia was there – 'All the way with LBJ' was the slogan – even though Britian was not involved.

Then came Britain's joining the European Common Market and Australia felt betrayed. The then head of British Tourism told Australian journalists that he could not see one reason why Australians should be treated differently from Hong Kong Chinese and that, yes, a German passport allowed easier access to Britain than an Australian passport. No one in Britain appeared to see how offensive this was and it did more to move the country towards republicanism than any other single factor. The icing on the cake, as it were, was the reports of high jinks of the Royal Family which dominated the Australian press. Few Australians see any future links with Britain being remotely worthwhile. There hangs on a mild sense of tradition – and that is all.

Many Australians see the future in Asia and the Pacific. Although Australia is not part of Asia and never will be, it is an important trading partner with many Asian nations. For example, the Singapore newspaper the *Straits Times* is totally edited, designed and laid out in Sydney and then transmitted to Singapore for printing. The same is true for several Chinese magazines.

Cathay Pacific, the Hong Kong airline, has based all of its booking systems and facilities in Sydney. American Express Asian helpline is based in Australia and the list goes on and on.

Australia is well placed for the next century. It has a reasonably robust economy, a high standard of living, a well educated and a relatively affluent population. Most people who visit Australia seriously think of migrating. Australia has in all senses a place in the sun.

49

TOURING ITINERARIES

Is it possible to see the whole of Australia on a motoring holiday? Yes, if that holiday extended to six months – rushing it – or a year taking it at a medium pace. Australia is a very large country to cover and the only way to see it, if your time is limited, is in instalments. This is the way that this book was created. This is the way that most Australians see Australia. This is the way I recommend for you to get the most out of a visit to that large and wonderful country down-under.

RECOMMENDED ROUTES

In this book I have recommended over 30 driving routes, connecting a selection of the places I think are most worth seeing or staying in. In the rest of this chapter I have given some suggestions for pursuing connected recommended routes in order to make up an itinerary to see a specific part of Australia.

But the routes I have suggested are not necessarily the only way of getting from A to B in all cases, especially in the south-east, where the road network is fuller. In this chapter I have also pointed out some alternative connections between different destinations which I did not have space to cover as a full recommended route.

Likewise the places I have described do not form an exclusive list; you will discover other favourites of your own. In any case, the variety is such that some places you will pass by quickly, others you will immediately fall in love with. I do know of one person who set out to explore Australia and arrived early in the trip at Byron Bay. That was two years ago and she is still there.

The idea with the recommended routes is that you mix and match and add them together create a trip to suit your individual tastes,

subject only to the limitations of time and distance. They do not have to be continuous motoring; in fact, it is very sensible to return your rented car, take a plane (or sometimes a train) to another state capital or major destination, and then rent another car to explore another recommended route from the book. Also, there are no prizes for doing the whole of any route. Some of them are thousands of kilometres, and evne the shortest are probably two-day journeys at minimum.

Alternatively, try to drive in smallish steps from one place of interest to another with any side trips you fancy along the way. The last thing you want to do when on a holiday to Australia is try and break endurance records. If at the end of a segment of the trip you are glad it is over . . . you have not planned it correctly.

Note that I have left out what might be called expedition driving – serious four-wheel-drive exploring in the bush. This can be done, it is enjoyable but it requires expertise and experience and is not easily handled by a visitor on a limited visit.

PRACTICAL HINTS

A few tips that I have found with experience will help to make your trip more pleasant.

1. Try and get as many detailed maps as possible. Australia is totally covered by Ordnance Survey maps but to assemble them all would perhaps be impossible. For example, I have collected all of them for New South Wales and the total is 1876 maps, enough to fill a large filing cabinet. Carrying these would make touring difficult. But it is worth acquiring specific maps for areas of great interest. For example, if you are visiting a National Park – and you must, you really must – the National Parks and Wildlife Office of that state will have maps of the immediate area for sale as well as free sketch maps of specific features. It is worth collecting them all and if you want to cut down on weight you can always mail them home.

2. Do not try to break any records. There are no prizes given for breaking long distance records, unless you count a speeding ticket from the police a prize of some sort. The absolute maximum for a day's drive on good roads in a good car is 300 km. But not all Australia's roads are good and if you are going over back roads you can halve that distance. It is strongly recommended that you stop every hour or so and have a break – a walk around, a cup of coffee, a breather. Many of the accidents in Australia have been caused by driver fatigue and no one would like a visitor to the country to become part of those grim statistics.

3. You do not need to book all of your accommodation ahead unless you are travelling over the Christmas–January school holiday period and, to a lesser extent, at Christmas. But leave yourself enough time to find the sort of place at which you would like to stay. Preferably somewhere off the highway – for peace and quiet; with a pleasant view – for the harmony of your soul; at a reasonable price – for the health of your wallet.

4. If you are flying out of Australia at the end of your holiday, plan to spend the last night at the city from which you will be leaving. Flying can be a nerve-wracking experience and you do not want to add worries about being in time to catch the aircraft to your other problems.

5. Australia can be a harsh and cruel country if you are not prepared. Always listen to local advice. If the road is claimed to be impassable, that will almost certainly be the case. If you are advised not to attempt a particular walk through a National Park, take that advice. If the beach patrol says only swim between the flags, then follow that instruction to the letter. Provided you listen and use your common sense you will not come to any grief.

6. Always keep your petrol tank reasonably full. If it gets below the halfway mark fill up at the very next petrol station. Figures supplied by the breakdown services show that running out of petrol is the main cause of trouble for motorists in Australia.

7. Obey the law and the rules of the road. In other countries a certain amount of leeway is allowed with regard to speed limits and the observance of signs. In Australia this is absolutely not the case and you will be stopped time and time again if you break the speed limit; if you drive without all of the passengers safely buckled in; if you use a mobile telephone in one hand when driving. The police are eager and the fines are ferocious. As a visitor you will probably just be issued with a warning and sent, chastened, on your way but don't rely on it. Far better to observe the laws. Drink driving is, of course, totally banned and random breath testing operates in every state.

8. Leave yourself some slack in your itinerary. This is a holiday and you need time to absorb what you are seeing. There is a complaint called Stendhal's Syndrome, which occurs in tourists who try to see too much, too soon, resulting in fatigue and disorientation. Avoid it by giving yourself some room to manoeuvre. Australia is not going to go away. It will always be here waiting to welcome you on another holiday.

51

NEW SOUTH WALES AND QUEENSLAND

SYDNEY TO THE TOP END

This is very popular with many tourists and gives you a chance to see a lot of the coastline of Australia as well as the Great Barrier Reef and some of the inland towns. It follows, roughly, the Pacific Highway for much of the distance but the trick is to take as many detours as you can so that you can see the countryside and stop and smell the flowers. Sadly, it means that in an average-length vacation you will have to miss Tasmania, South Australia, Western Australia, Darwin and the Northern Territory and Alice Springs with Ayers Rock. But it's a big country and you can't do everything.

The chapters on **Sydney** (pp. 57–72), **Sydney to the Gold Coast** (pp. 73–90), **The Gold Coast** (pp. 211–214) and **Brisbane** (pp. 203–210) combine to give you the following itinerary:

Sydney – Hornsby – Gosford (off the Highway at this point) –The Entrance – Swansea –

Newcastle (back on the Highway) – Raymond Terrace – Bulahdelah (off the Highway after 1 km)–Bungwahl – Forster (back on the Highway) – Taree – Kendall – Kempsey – Nambucca Heads – Coffs Harbour – Grafton – Ballina – Bangalow – off the Highway down to Byron Bay (you would be mad to miss it) – Brunswick Heads – Tweed Heads.

You are now on the Queensland border, on the Gold Coast, and that stretch to my mind is not pretty. It is over-developed, raucous and generally avoidable. (Unless, of course, you want to be noisy and raucous in which case you have found an ideal spot.) This does not apply to Brisbane, however. Coolangatta – Surfers Paradise – Southport – Beenleigh – Brisbane.

Brisbane to Rockhampton (pp. 215–226), **Rockhampton to Cairns** (pp. 239–248), **The Great Barrier Reef** (pp. 227–238) and **North and West of Cairns** (pp. 249–255) will extend your trip along the Queensland coast, including the Great Barrier Reef, and if you wish into the Gulf Country of the north of the state.

Once you are past Brisbane the Pacific Highway becomes the Bruce Highway. Not that a change in name makes a major difference because it is still Route 1. But you will notice a distinct change in the climate because from Sydney you have passed through temperate into a sub-tropical area. The road now winds along the coast heading ever northward.

Brisbane – Caboolture – Nambour (from which you simply must make a detour to Noosa Heads) – Gympie – Maryborough. This is a good place to take a deep breath and visit Fraser Island, which is a National Park, one of the largest sand islands in the world and a small paradise.

You continue to toddle gently along the coast. Maryborough – Bundaberg – Gladstone – Rockhampton – Mackay. You are now running parallel to the Great Barrier Reef, which is one of the wonders of the world and protects Australia from the rolling thunder of the Coral Sea. Then on and on in big swoops with longer and longer distances between the big towns.

Mackay – Proserpine (opposite the Whitsunday group of islands, which are worth a long holiday on their own) – Bowen –

Townsville – Ingham, close to the glory of Hinchinbrook Island National Park – Innisfail – Cairns.

This is about as far as you can get in an ordinary car with complete safety. You can then head on up to Cape York on a four-wheel-drive excursion – there are dozens of them – or, if you have hired your own four-wheel-drive, join a tag-along excursion which means that there is always an experienced driver to pull you out of trouble.

Be warned that once you cross the Daintree River you can, if you are not careful and you hit bad weather, get into trouble.

Heading towards Cape York this time you backtrack inland before you start towards Mt Malloy and then turn north again along what is called the Peninsula Developmental Road that runs through the Quinkin Native Reserve and up the Cape York Peninsula through the Rokery–Croll National Park and right up to the tip of Cape York which is as far north as you can possibly get. The trip from Cairns to Cape York is not for the faint hearted and is not for the inexperienced to travel alone. There is no air conditioning, no beds turned down each night with a chocolate on the pillow. But it is, beyond doubt, one of the great travel experiences of the world.

SYDNEY TO TWEED HEADS INLAND ROUTE

This is an alternative to the coastal route of the Sydney to Gold Coast chapter. It reaches the Queensland border by going inland and over the New England Tableland. Most of this diversion is on the New England Highway that runs from Newcastle to Warwick in Queensland.

Sydney – Newcastle – then turn inland to Maitland – Murrurundi – Quirindi – Werris Creek – Tamworth – Armidale – Glen Innes – Tenterfield.

From there you can go directly over the border to Queensland to Warwick, and so link up with the **Darling Downs** circular route (pp. 256–259) from and to Brisbane.

Or you can follow the Bruxner Highway to the coast, Tenterfield – Casino – Lismore – Bangalow and back onto the Pacific Highway.

NEW SOUTH WALES AND THE A.C.T.

SYDNEY–DUBBO–CANBERRA CIRCUIT

From **Sydney** (pp. 57–72), take the **Sydney to Dubbo** route (pp. 103–109), over the Blue Mountains to Lithgow – Bathurst – Orange – Molong – Wellington – Dubbo. (From Dubbo you could visit the real outback by taking the **Dubbo to Lightning Ridge** route (pp. 110–112). Or you see Broken Hill – but preferably by flying or taking the train from Sydney, Dubbo or Orange.)

At Dubbo turn south-west to Peak Hill – Parkes – Forbes – West Wyalong – Wagga Wagga. Wagga Wagga brings you onto the **Murray and the Riverina** route (pp. 195–200), which returns to Australia's federal capital **Canberra** (pp. 187–194). From Canberra head north back to Sydney on part of the **Southern Highlands Circuit** (pp. 113–120), via Goulburn – Bowral – Mittagong.

SYDNEY TO MELBOURNE COASTAL

Combine **Sydney to Eden** (pp. 91–102) and **Melbourne–Eden** (pp. 144–150) to construct a tour between these two major cities, in either direction, taking in spectacular coastline, resorts such as Shoalhaven, Jervis Bay, Batemans Bay, Eden and Lakes Entrance, and a wealth of first-class National and State Parks, including the Royal National Park outside Sydney, Croajingolong, Gippsland Lakes and Wilson's Promontory.

VICTORIA

MELBOURNE, THE GOLD FIELDS AND THE MURRAY RIVER

As well as the chapter on **Melbourne** (pp. 126–133), this itinerary uses the routes **Melbourne to Mildura** (pp. 156–167) and **Mildura to Wodonga** (pp. 168–175).

Melbourne to the gold fields via Ballarat – Ararat – Horsham –Warracknabeal – Ouyen – Mildura. Mildura – Swan Hill – Echuca, along the banks of the Murray. Take the side-track to Bendigo and from there Rte 149 will take you south-west back to Ballarat and Melbourne.

MELBOURNE TO BRISBANE

This is not one of the recoommended routes described at length in the book, but it is useful if you want to by-pass Sydney and the NSW coast and head straight fro Brisbane and Queensland from Melbourne. The road that makes this possible is the Newell Highway and is the major inland route between Victoria, South Australia and Queensland.

The route runs: Melbourne – Nagambie – Tocumwal – Finley – Jerilderie – Leeton – Griffith – West Wyalong – Cowra – Cabonne – Forbes – Parkes – Peak Hill – Narromine – Dubbo – Wellington – Gilgandra – Coonabarabran – Narrabri – Moree – Goondiwindi – Toowoomba – Gatton – Esk – Warwick – Stanthorpe – Fraser Coast – Brisbane.

MELBOURNE TO ADELAIDE ALONG THE GREAT OCEAN ROAD

Combine the **Melbourne to Warrnambool** (pp. 134–143) and **Adelaide to Warrnambool** (pp. 341–351) routes, and consult the chapters on **Melbourne** (pp. 126–133) and **Adelaide** (pp. 334–341), to put together a truly scenic coastal tour of the south-eastern coast of Australia and stays in its two great cities.

For many the Great Ocean Road from Melbourne is the best drive in the world. Certainly it is stunning in its scenic beauty and its 300 kilometres makes a pleasant two-day drive with plenty of stops. Melbourne – Geelong – Torquay – Anglesea – then up around the mountains and drop down to Lorne, Melbourne's favourite seaside spot – Apollo Bay – Port Campbell National Park with the Twelve Apostles, a most amazing scenic wonder – Warrnambool.

From there Warrnambool – Mt Gambier – Kingston SE – the Coorong National Park, where the mighty Murray River finally reaches the sea – Murray Bridge.

SOUTH AUSTRALIA

ADELAIDE TO MELBOURNE VIA THE BAROSSA VALLEY

After a stay in **Adelaide** (pp. 334–341), from which it is possible to explore the nearby **Fleurieu** (pp. 342–344) and **Yorke** (pp.

53

360–363) **Peninsulas,** you can head east to Melbourne on a journey that takes in the famous wine-making country of the Barossa Valley, the Wyperfield National Park and the Little Desert Wilderness and finally the historic Victoria gold towns before reaching Melbourne. Just follow the **Adelaide to Mildura** route (pp. 352–359) and then **Melbourne to Mildura** (pp. 156–167) in reverse.

SOUTH AUSTRALIA – THE OUTBACK

Combine the Adelaide–Port Augusta section of **Adelaide to the Yorke Peninsula** (pp. 360–363), and the **Port Augusta to Marree** route (p. 370–375), in order to see the serious Outback that South Australia has to offer, including the sights of the Flinders Ranges.

WESTERN AUSTRALIA

PERTH AND THE SWAN VALLEY

Although **Perth** (pp. 290–296) is the most isolated major city on earth, immediately adjacent are the port of Fremantle (described in **Perth to Albany,** pp. 297–305), Rottnest Island, 18 km off the coast and the Swan Valley which is just 30 km from the city centre and this extends into the Avon Valley – about 100 km east of Perth – and runs through the towns of Toodyay, Northam and York. Within driving distance is the Pinnacles Desert, which is in the Nambung National Park, about 250 km north of Perth.

PERTH AND THE SOUTH-WEST

The **Perth to Albany** route, pp. 297–305, can be travelled southwards down the coast and then by the direct route alternative northwards inland via Mt Barker and Kelmscott. Highlights of the coastl run are the Leeuwin-Naturaliste National Park and Margaret River, which is the start of what many people consider the finest wine-growing area in Australia.

From Albany, a small town on the south coast, it is possible to travel west to Esperance, and from there to Kalgoorlie, as noted in the **Perth to Kalgoorlie** chapter, pp. 306–313. The price to be paid for making it a circular tour, however, is some pretty formidable distances.

NORTH OF PERTH

The routes for **Perth to Carnarvon** (pp. 314–321) and **Carnarvon to Wyndham** (pp. 322–329), if combined, give you an itinerary to the top of Western Australia, and directions for connecting to Katherine in the Northern Territory. But for most people the sensible way to see this vast area is to fly to Carnarvon or Broome and use the two driving routes partially, to provide itineraries north and south along the coast from the chosen base city.

NORTHERN TERRITORY

AROUND DARWIN AND THE NORTH

Darwin (pp. 264–269) is a good base for short side-tracks to places such as Mandorah, or a lobger trip into the must-see Kakadu National Park (**Darwin to Kakadu,** pp. 270–273).

ACROSS THE CENTRE OF AUSTRALIA

It is a long hard drive from north coast to south coast, from Darwin to Adelaide, taking in Alice Springs (pp. 279–284) and Ayers Rock (285–286), both of which are easily reached by air, and it is surely only for the masochistic. If you must do it, use routes **Darwin to Alice Springs** (pp. 274–278), **Port Augusta to Alice Springs** (pp. 376–379), and **The Yorke Peninsula** (pp. 360–363).

TASMANIA

Touring Tasmania is a positive delight. Think of the roads as an elongated Y, with Hobart at the bottom of the centre stroke. The roads split at Melton Mowbray and then the left (west) fork becomes the Bass Highway and runs right up to Devonport on the North Coast and then through Ulverstone – Burnie – Somerset – Wynyard – Smithton – Marrawah. The right (east) fork is the Midland Highway that runs through Campbell Town – Launceston – then sharp east to St Helens and down the east coast – St Marys – Bicheno – Triabunna – Sorell and then either down to Port Arthur or back to Hobart. Our routes are more peripheral, making more of a ring around the island. They meet at Queenstown and the great National Parks at the heart of Tasmania, making it very easy to join them into one circular tour.

NEW SOUTH WALES

First, where did the name come from? No one really knows. James Cook called Queensland, together with the present day New South Wales, New Wales in 1770 but he later altered it without explaining why. It has been suggested that the coast looks a little like Glamorgan. He wrote on 22 Aug 1770 'down to this place by the Name of New South Wales'. There have been many attempts to change the name. None have ever succeeded and it is unlikely that it will change now.

GEOGRAPHY

Initially, the state effectively covered half of Australia and, indeed, it has been argued that it extended as far as Fiji. It now takes up about 10% of Australia but is densely populated, with most of the people living on the coastal strip that runs from Victoria right up to the Queensland border in a series of stunning beaches, coves and headlands. The northern stretch, heading towards Queensland, is mountainous, sweeping down to the coastal plain and rain forests cover the slopes running down from the volcanic tablelands. The border with Queensland is only some 500 km south of the Tropic of Capricorn, so it can be quite tropical.

Holding the coastal plain in place, as it were, is the **Great Dividing Range**. This starts dramatically in the north with **Mt Warning**, so named by Captain Cook as a warning to mariners of the dangers of the area, and ends up almost a jumble of foothills in the south of the state. Then as it nears the Victorian border, it reasserts itself with **Mt Kosciusko**, the highest mountain in Australia, rising to 2228m. It is here you find the **Snowy Mountain Scheme**, which provides water and hydro electricity, as well as one of the biggest national parks in Australia (see p.117).

On the other side of the Great Dividing Range in New South Wales the plains start and

55

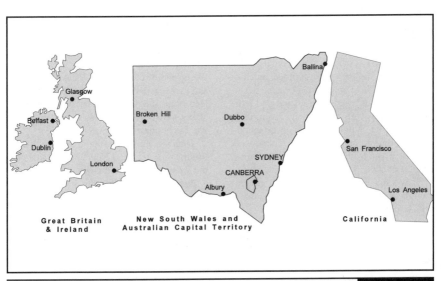

Great Britain & Ireland   New South Wales and Australian Capital Territory   California

this is the agricultural gem of the state, with superfine merino wool and hectares of wheat, which at times can produce one third of the national yield.

And then, beyond the sunlit plains, you come to the outback. D.H. Lawrence in his novel *Kangaroo,* suggested that the bush is a brooding presence that affects the lives of all Australians. There is much poetic licence in this statement but there is also a strong strand of truth. The outback has tempered the Australian character. Even Australians living in the centre of Sydney believe that they have a natural affinity with the bush and the number of townspeople who have a week-ender in the country (a weekend property out of town) is legend. But never in the serious bush country. Never 'back of Bourke' which is, in Australian mythology, the start of the serious outback.

CLIMATE

New South Wales probably has the greatest mix of climates of any of the States of Australia. In Sydney the maximum temperature in the summer is normally around 24°C with a minimum in the winter of about 9°C, which is chilly but not very cold. In Broken Hill the temperature in the summer can get to 32°C and at Sturt National Park, 330 km north of Broken Hill, temperatures of 50°C have been recorded in the summer, which is totally unbearable.

HISTORY

It needs to be remembered at all times that New South Wales started off as a convict settlement, which has irrevocably formed much of its character. The convicts soon became ticket-of-leave men and were able go out and settle the land along with free settlers. From 1813, when **Charles Wentworth** led an expedition over the Blue Mountains, the movement went westwards, and by the 1820s, settlement formed an arc extending 300 km from Sydney.

It was not long before the British government became embarrassed at the charges that it was sending convicts to Australia as slave labour. This monstrous practice stopped for ever in 1852, although convicts were still being sent to Western Australia until as late as 1868.

As settlement spread from Sydney so did specialist agriculture. In late 1805, **John Macarthur**, who had settled in Camden, New South Wales, started breeding merino sheep, claiming – probably falsely – that he was the first person to bring merinos into Australia. He fought with several governments to establish the fine wool trade in New South Wales but died in 1834 before seeing his dreams realised.

It was the discovery of gold in New South Wales that galloped Australia towards full nationhood. Gold brought a flood of seekers of wealth and fortune to the country and the state. The **Reverend W.B. Clarke** found gold in the Lithgow area in 1841 and showed samples to the then Governor Gipps. He is reported to have said, 'Put it away, Mr. Clarke, or we will have our throats cut'.

By 1851 the mood of the times had changed and **Edward Hargraves** found gold at Ophir, near Bathurst. The gold rush was on and it changed Australia irrevocably. In the wake of gold came prosperity and secondary industry. Agriculture was still important but between 1860 and 1900 secondary industry increased by an order of magnitude.

In 1901 the documents for Federation were signed in **Centennial Park**, Sydney.

The two World Wars showed Australia to be a totally loyal part of the British Empire and when Britain declared war Australia followed only minutes later. But in World War II it became apparent that Britain could not defend Australia from the Japanese – only the Americans could do that. After World War II, the people of New South Wales turned more and more towards the USA for inspiration and leadership and the premiers of New South Wales were never slow in stating that the USA was the example to follow.

Britain's entry into the Common Market was the final straw and New South Wales, of all the states in Australia, is closer to an American – perhaps more accurately, a Californian – lifestyle, which has little to do with its British roots.

The Olympic Games in Sydney in 2000 represent the final coming of age for New South Wales.

SYDNEY

The gateway to Australia for most visitors, Sydney is truly one of the great cities of the world. It is immensely fortunate that it is built on a series of fingers of land extending into Sydney Cove, which is protected from the open sea by the heights of Middle Head and South Head. Because of this proximity of high ground and sea, not even the worst attempts of building developers can detract from the singular beauty of the place and the Opera House fits in with the scene to perfection. There is, perhaps, no better place to be than sitting at a waterfront café in Sydney on a summer's day, watching the sea, the sails and the ferries, and sipping a glass of Chardonnay.

TOURIST INFORMATION

NSW Travel Centre, *11-31 York St; tel: 13 2077.* Open 0900–1700 weekdays, 0900–1300 Sat. Accommodation and travel bookings in New South Wales, brochures, information. **Darling Harbour Visitors Centre**, *between Cockle Bay and Tumbalong Park; tel: 9286 0111.* Open 0900–1730 seven days. Maps of Darling Harbour and Sydney. Information on Darling Harbour attractions. Tickets for most Darling Harbour attractions.

Airport Travel Centre, *International Terminal, Arrivals Level, Sydney (Kingsford Smith) Airport; tel: 9667 6050.* Open from first flight arrival to last (approx 0500–2315). Accommodation booking (good standby rates for same day), also tour bookings.

The Rocks Visitors Centre, *(108 George St; tel: 9255 1788; open 0900–1700 daily,* offers $10 guided tours of the Rocks (see p.70) and has a 20 min continuous video show, as well as a small museum about the city of

Sydney. **Sydney Convention and Visitors Bureau**, *80 William St; tel: 9331 4045*; open 0845–1715, is set up to help conventions.

WEATHER

There is a distinct winter, starting about May and finishing in September. High summer runs from late November until the middle of March. Spring and autumn are not so clearly defined but do exist. Sydney never gets really cold, despite what the natives say. It has never snowed there. But it can be nippy enough for a top coat to be welcomed in the coldest weather. In the height of summer it can be very hot but all hotels are air-conditioned, everyone wears loose and minimal clothing and the focus of life moves more to the beach and the surf.

Basically you can expect dry, sunny weather most of the year round. Sometimes there is a local phenomenon called a Southerly Buster, when the wind roars up from the Antarctic and it gets very cold, very quickly. But this never lasts for more than 24 hours, if that. When it rains it normally comes down in torrents and clears up quickly.

ARRIVING AND DEPARTING

Airport

Kingsford Smith is almost certainly the most centrally placed international airport in the world and also one of the most civilised – the formalities for both arrival and departure are quick and relaxed. There are never the dreadful queues, which can be seen at London's Heathrow Airport, for instance. The airport is invariably referred to by the locals as Mascot, after the suburb in which it is found. For **general enquiries**, *tel: 9667 9111;* **flight arrivals and departures** phone the airline concerned (many airlines are represented by Qantas), **international arrivals**, *tel: 13 1223.*

There are two terminals, domestic and international. The distance from the international to the domestic terminal is

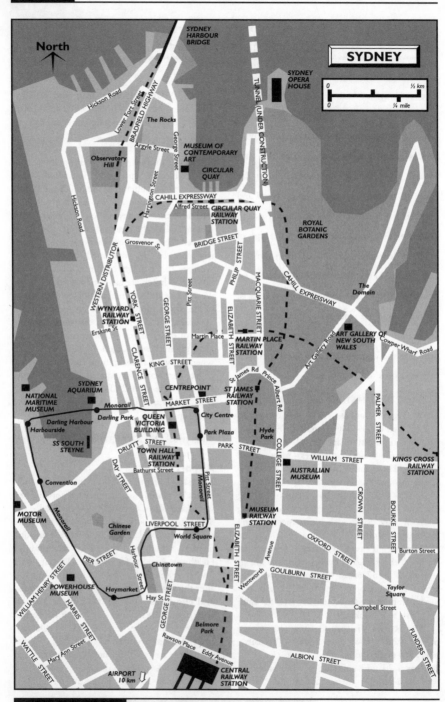

1½ km – there is a shuttle service between them; adult fare $2.50, child $1.50.

The distance from the airport to Central Sydney is 9 km, about 35 mins by **taxi** ($16–$20). An **express shuttle** service operates to and from the airport to the City and Kings Cross, departures from the airport every 10–15 mins every day; *tel: 13 1500.* Adult fare $5, return $8. **Kingsford Smith Bus Service** operates between selected hotels in the City, Kings Cross and Glebe every 10–15 mins from 0600 to last flight, daily; *tel: 9667 3221.* Adult $6, child $4.

There are **car parks** at both terminals – international terminal parking $2.50 per ½ hr – set to actively discourage long term parking.

Facilities in the International terminal include: **Information Service,** *Arrivals Level 1.* **Food** and beverages in the food court plus several bars and restaurants. **Shopping** in the retail court on *Departures Level 2,* duty-free shops beyond the immigration point. **Medical care** at the **Immediate Health Care** centre on *Departures Level 2,* open weekdays 0800–1700, weekends and public holidays 0800–1400. **Currency** exchange at the **Thomas Cook** Bureau de Change outlets on both departure and arrival levels. Cash dispensers are next to them. Australia **Post** on *Departures Level 2,* near the centre of the terminal, including fax. **Lost property: Federal Airports Corporation (FAC),** *Level 3, tel: 9667 9583.*

By Road

There are three main road routes into Sydney and all are comprehensively signposted. It is almost impossible to lose your way.

From the **south** comes the **Princes Highway,** Australia's Route 1, which will keep cropping up in this book, appearing under different names around the country. It comes into Sydney across the Georges River, then sweeps down to the sea at Botany Bay and runs alongside Sydney airport as *General Holmes Dr.* From there it is a freeway called *Southern Cross Dr.,* which runs towards the city – this is the freeway on which you will ride from the airport – and then comes to a confused stop at *South Dowling St.* Here the city fathers are still deciding quite what to do.

There is then a maze of roads, some of which lead to King's Cross and some to the city. It is not, in truth, a grand entrance to one of the grandest of cities.

Coming from the **north,** the **Sydney-Newcastle Freeway** crosses the Hawkesbury River and ends as a freeway at Warrawee. There the road to Sydney is the Pacific Hwy, which wanders through the suburbs of northern Sydney until, at Artarmon, you turn on to the Gore Hill Freeway, which takes you through Naremburn and Cammeray to the Harbour Bridge or the Harbour Tunnel – both cost $2 this way and are free the other. This route gets congested in the rush hours, but that is generally true of all the main roads in Sydney.

From the **west** and the Blue Mountains, the **Western Motorway** joins *Parramatta Rd.* This was the first major road out of Sydney and, in truth, is not a pretty sight and can be somewhat congested. It passes through Leichhardt and Annandale, leaves Sydney University on the right, and enters the city first as *Broadway* and then, as it passes the Central Railway on the right, becomes *George St,* which runs right through the heart of Sydney. From **Liverpool** and **Melbourne,** the **Hume Highway** joins *Parramatta Rd*; turns right and then follows the same route as the road from the Blue Mountains.

The main advice is to avoid the rush hours and, if that is not possible, to drive against the flow. Thus in the evening rush hour it is better to be coming in to the city and in the morning to be leaving. However, the traffic jams, although irritating, are not on the same scale as in cities in other countries. Only two cities in Australia ever experience traffic jams – Sydney and Melbourne – but they are nothing to get over-excited about.

By Train

All of the major train and bus services to and from Sydney are located in and near **Central Station,** *Eddy Ave, Sydney NSW 2000 (between Pitt and Elizabeth Sts); tel: 9379 4054* (Station Master), which is at the top end of *George St,* only slightly outside the city centre. Central Station is the main railway station, serving country and suburban trains.

59

CityRail and State Rail; *tel: 9379 3000* (0600–2200 seven days). **Infoline** for passenger enquiries and timetable information; *tel: 13 1500* (0600–2200 seven days). **CountryLink**, head office *1st Floor, Central Station*; country and interstate rail and coach reservations *tel: 13 2232* (0630–2200 seven days).

By Bus

The Sydney Coach Terminal, *corner Eddy Ave and Pitt St, Central Railway, Sydney NSW 2000; tel: 9281 9366*, open daily 0600–2130, all coach tickets/coach passes available, booking and credit card phone ticketing. At the same address: **Greyhound Pioneer**, *tel: 9212 1500*, open daily 0600–2200. **McCafferty's Express Coaches**, *tel: 13 1499*, open daily 0600–2000. **Backpackers' Bus Booking Centre**, *tel: 9368 0299*, open 0830–1730 Mon–Fri, 1000–1330 Sat.

GETTING AROUND

Orientation

60

To get Sydney into perspective, try and look at it as if from above – a bird's eye view. There is a roughly oblong stretch of water starting at the **Heads**. It has straggly bits going off on each side but if you squint your eyes you can see it is a sort of oblong and it helps to think of it this way when orienting yourself.

Halfway along, at the bottom of the oblong, is the **central business district**. This is connected by the Sydney Harbour bridge and a tunnel to **North Sydney** (which is another central business district in its own right). To the right of central Sydney and accessed through a tunnel running under the somewhat raunchy area of **King's Cross**, running along the bottom edge of the oblong, are the eastern suburbs of **Potts Point**, **Darling Point**, **Vaucluse** and, finally, **Watson's Bay**. These contain most of the seriously expensive real estate in Sydney and are connected by the *New South Head Rd*, which swoops and turns its way along the shore until it ends up at **The Gap** near **South Head** and then swoops back through **Dover Heights** and on to **Bondi Beach**.

Running the other way to the west along the bottom line of the oblong we come first to

The Rocks, the birthplace of Australia, and then past the newly developed **Darling Harbour** to the trendy suburb of **Balmain** and on to **Hunter's Hill**, another most desirable area in which to live.

On the top edge of the oblong, moving to the right, heading east from North Sydney, you pass through a series of suburbs – **Neutral Bay**, **Balmoral**, **Mosman** – and end up at **Middle Head** on the far side of **George's Heights**. The other side of the top edge of the oblong extends west through **McMahons Point**, **Waverton**, **Greenwich**, **Woolwich** and **Longueville**.

Behind all these places lie rows of other suburbs. As a rule of thumb, east is the most expensive area, the northern suburbs come next and moving south and west you quickly come to the less expensive parts of Sydney, with the salutary exceptions of **Paddington** and **Woollahra**.

In many cases these suburbs have a distinct character of their own. Thus Paddington abuts Woollahra but there is a quite distinct difference; Paddington is slightly Bohemian, self-consciously arty and visually, utterly charming, whereas Woollahra has Paddington's charm but also has a feeling of serious wealth.

One theory is that the particular characters of the suburbs derive from the way in which the sea has separated so many of them into distinct areas.

Safety

Sydney is one of the safest cities in the world. It is extremely unlikely that any sensible visitor will be mugged, assaulted or otherwise given a bad time. Plainly, it is intelligent to take sensible precautions and not flaunt your wealth. And, equally obvious, the safebox at your hotel is the place to leave your passport, airline tickets and spare traveller's cheques. But having said that, there is far less street crime in Sydney than any comparable city in Europe or the United States.

The only area where special care should be taken is in King's Cross, especially late at night. This is something of a red-light area and you wander around the bars late at night at your own risk.

Public Transport
The public transport system within Sydney is better than fair but perhaps less than great.

Trains
There is a network of suburban railway lines linking the city to the north and, to a lesser extent the west, but to the east it is severely truncated. All of these lines connect with the Central Railway Station, where maps are provided and tickets can be bought. For all Sydney bus, train and ferry services, timetables and information there is a telephone enquiry line, **Infoline**, *tel: 13 1500*, which is open 0600–2200 seven days a week. Other useful contacts are **CityRail and State Rail**; *tel: 9379 3000* (0600–2200 daily).

Trains in and around the city are, by and large, safe, reliable and dependable. There are sometimes complaints of 'larrikinism' (hooliganism) on the western sections but in normal hours you can take it that this is a crime-free zone.

Buses
Metropolitan buses are clean, frequent, air-conditioned and non-smoking. They are crowded in the rush hours.

Monorail
The Monorail is not loved by the majority of the residents of Sydney. Its construction roused massive opposition and after it was built it was treated with studied indifference. It does not add much to the transportation scene, being used mainly as a tourist shuttle which runs from the city around Darling Harbour and back again. It gives a good view of the city and takes 10 mins to complete a full circuit. Tickets are $2.50 a trip or $6 all day. You can get on or get off near Centre Point, Haymarket near the Entertainment Centre, or at the Convention Centre Harbourside, with some stops in between. There is quite a serious movement to have the whole thing dismantled in time for the Olympics.

At the same time a new light rail system – think of it as an up-dated trolleybus – which will connect The Rocks with Central and up past the Central Railway Station, is being constructed. When open, which will be 'Real Soon Now' or certainly in time for the Olympics, it will make moving around the city even easier.

Ferries
One of the glories of Sydney is its ferry system, which lets you go sightseeing on one of the great harbours of the world at very low prices. All ferries depart from Circular Quay, keep to regular timetables and call at effectively every suburb that has a coastal frontage. For example, if you were going to the zoo (see p.71) you could go by taxi or bus across the Harbour Bridge and then along Military Highway to Mosman and the zoo. But by far the best way is to take the ferry from Circular Quay which drops you directly at the zoo – and throws in a sightseeing trip across the harbour for free.

Passes and Tours
The **SydneyPass** is the most inexpensive way of touring the whole of the city and its harbour. Buy it for 3, 5 or 7 days. With it you can use the entire network of Sydney Transit buses, the Sydney Harbour ferries – a great sightseeing trip – and the CityRail network. Prices for adults are: 3 days, $60; 5 days, $90; 7 days, $80; for children aged 4–16 you pay $10 under each of those prices.

With this pass you can take ferries to all the places that dot the harbour and the coves that adjoin it; take each of the three Sydney ferry cruises, including and especially the **Harbour Lights Cruise**; jump on and off the **Sydney Explorer** and **Bondi and Bay Explorer** buses (see below) and, finally, use your ticket to take you to and from the airport on the **Airport Express.**

The **Sydney Explorer**; *tel:13 1500,* is a bus that operates on a 35 km circuit through the city, stopping at 46 stops and all major attractions; its suburban equivalent is the **Bondi and Bay Explorer**. A ticket for a day of unlimited riding on both services costs $20.

There are over 26 different harbour cruises both by power boat and sailing boat. These can all be booked either at **Circular Quayside Booking Centre**, the **Information Booth at Darling Harbour** or **Shop 208 on Manly**

61

Wharf. All have the same telephone number, *9247 5151*, which is open 24 hours.

A typical cruise with lunch costs between $30 and $43 (somewhat higher at weekends), while a dinner cruise will cost between $40 and $60.

Through the same centre and the same telephone number you can also book seaplane rides across the harbour – 15 mins at $30 a person; helicopter sightseeing trips over Sydney – about 30 mins at $140; or even go parasailing on the harbour from Manly for $39.

Taxis

All taxis operate on a computerised call service. The largest is **Combined Services** *(tel: 9332 8888)*. Two other major companies are **Legion** *(tel: 9289 9000)* and **RSL** *(tel: 9699 0144)*. Cabs can also be flagged down in the street when the light in the centre of the roof is alight to show that they are plying for hire. There is rarely a shortage of cabs except between 1430 and 1530, which is shift change-over time and even then it is hardly a problem. All hotels have a cab rank and it is a perfectly acceptable for anyone to walk up and take the first cab on the rank. The average in town ride is under $10 and out to the suburbs $20. Note that there are no extras for time of day, baggage or number of passengers.

All cabs are air-conditioned. All passengers must wear seat belts. Smoking is prohibited, although sometimes agreement to break the law is reached between the passengers and the driver.

Note that in Australia single passengers tend to sit next to the driver, who will then bore them to death with political views, which are invariably somewhat to the right of the late Genghis Khan. Most of the drivers are totally honest. Their street knowledge does not match that of London cab drivers but most drivers can get you to most places with no problems. Taxis are most strictly policed and complaints from passengers are dealt with immediately and with quite savage penalties.

In Sydney, as in the rest of Australia, taxi drivers do not expect tips although they will always accept one, especially if they have been carrying your suitcases (for which there is no extra charge). Most visitors round the fare up to the nearest dollar. Uniquely, you will sometimes be tipped by the driver. On the clock the fare may come to $18.45 and the driver will tell you to just make it $18.

Driving in Sydney

You can hire a car and drive in Sydney, although it is nowhere near as cost efficient as buying a SydneyPass and using the wide range of public transport. Because Sydney is built on a harbour and inlets run inland at every turn, the roads tend to be narrow and parking is at a premium. Indeed, in some places and at some times it is nigh impossible, and it is always expensive. All of the major car rental companies are represented at the airport, as well as in the city.

Accommodation

Sydney has a wide range of accommodation and it is unlikely you will have a problem getting a room at the price you can afford, except perhaps during public holidays. But it is important to realise that the rates you get from a casual booking are rarely discounted. In almost every case you will get a better rate from a tour operator's package or by booking through a travel agent well beforehand. Discounts as large as 50% off the rack rate can be obtained in this way.

City accommodation can be broken down into areas.

City Centre Accommodation

Expensive ($250 plus): **The Wentworth Hotel**, 61-101 Phillip St; tel: 9230 0700. **Hotel Nikko Darling Harbour**, 161 Sussex St, tel: 9299 1231. **Hotel Inter-Continental Sydney**, 117 Macquarie St; tel: 9230 0200. **Renaissance Sydney Hotel**, 30 Pitt St; tel: 9259 7000. **Hyatt Regency Sydney**, William St; tel: 9356 1234. **The Regent Of Sydney Hotel**, 199 George St; tel: 9238 0000. **The**

Golden Gate Hotel Sydney, 169-179 Thomas St; tel: 9281 6888. **The Ritz–Carlton Sydney**, 93 Macquarie St; tel: 9252 4600. **Sheraton on the Park**, 161 Elizabeth St; tel: 9286 6000. **Sydney Hilton**, 259 Pitt St; tel: 9266 0610.

Fairly expensive ($150–$250): **All Seasons Premier Menzies Hotel Sydney**, 14 Carrington St; tel: 9299 1000. **The Observatory**, 89 Kent St; tel: 9256 2222. **Country Comfort Sydney Central**, corner George and Quay Sts; tel: 9212 2544. **Furama Hotel Sydney**, 68 Harbour St; tel: 9281 0400. **Hyde Park Plaza Hotel**, 38 College St; 9331 6933. **The Waldorf Apartment Hotel** (FL), 57 Liverpool St; tel: 9261 5355. **Sydney Marriott Hotel**, 36 College St; tel: 9361 8400. **Parkroyal at Darling Harbour**, 150 Day St; tel: 9261 1188. **The Waratah Central**, 22-44 Albion St; tel: 9281 0333. **Sydney Boulevard**, 90 William St; tel: 9357 2277. **Hyde Park Inn**, 271 Elizabeth St; tel: 264 6001. **Russell Hotel**, 143A George St; tel: 9241 3543. **The Royal Garden International**, 431 Pitt St; tel: 281 6999. **Grand Hotel**, 30 Hunter St; tel: 232 3755.

Moderate ($70–$150): **The Cambridge** (FL), 9212 Riley St; tel: 9212 1111. **Oxford Koala Hotel** (BW), corner Oxford and Pelican Sts, tel: 269 0645. **Park Regis Hotel Sydney**, 27 Park St; tel: 267 6511. **The Southern Cross Sydney Hotel** (FL), 111 Goulburn St; tel: 9282 0987. **The Castlereagh Inn**, 169 Castlereagh St; tel: 264 2281. **Stellar House**, 4 Wentworth Ave; tel: 264 9754. **Sydney Travellers Rest**, 37 Ultimo Rd, Haymarket; tel: 281 5555. **Hotel Westend**, 412 Pitt St; tel: 9211 4822.

Inexpensive (less than $70): **Metro Motor Inn City**, 306 Crown St; tel: 9360 5480. **YWCA 'Y' on the Park**, 5-11 Wentworth Ave, Sydney 2010; tel: 264 2451. **Sydney Central Private Hotel**, 75 Wentworth Ave; tel: 9212 1005. **Central Railway Motel**, 240 Chalmers St; tel: 9319 7800.

Central Private Hotel, 358 Elizabeth St; tel: 9212 1068. **Criterion Hotel**, Corner Pitt and Park Sts; tel: 9264 3093. **Royal Exhibition Hotel**, 86 Chalmers St; tel: 9698 2607.

63

Accommodation in The Rocks

Expensive ($250 plus): **ANA Hotel Sydney**, *176 Cumberland St, The Rocks, Sydney 2000; tel: (02) 9250 6000*. **Park Hyatt Sydney**, *7 Hickson Rd, The Rocks; tel: 9241 1234*. **Quay West Sydney**, *98 Gloucester St, The Rocks; tel: 9240 6000*. **Old Sydney Parkroyal**, *55 George St, The Rocks; tel: 9252 0524*.

Fairly expensive ($150–$250): **Harbour Rocks Hotel**, *34 Harrington St, The Rocks; tel: 9251 8944*.

Accommodation at the Airport

Fairly expensive ($150–$250): **Sydney Airport Hilton**, *20 Levey St, Arncliffe 2205; tel: 9597 0122*. **Sheraton Sydney Airport Hotel**, *corner O'Riordan and Robey Sts, Mascot 2020; tel: 9317 2200*.

Moderate ($70–$150): **Airport Sydney International Motor Inn**, *35 Levey St, Arncliffe 2205; tel: 9556 1555*. **Sydney Airport Parkroyal**, *corner Bourke and O'Riordan Sts, Mascot 2020; tel: 9330 0600*

Accommodation in Darling Harbour

Fairly expensive ($150–$250): **Novotel Sydney on Darling Harbour**, *100 Murray St, Pyrmont 2009; tel: 9934 0000*. **Ibis Hotel Darling Harbour**, *70 Murray St, Pyrmont 2009; tel: 9563 0888*.

Budget Accommodation

The truly inexpensive places to stay fall into two areas – backpackers and motels. Backpackers are well catered for by several backbacking hostels, of varying quality. They start at about $14 a night and top out at about $30. These all specialise in dealing in catering for overseas tourists, who are often met at the airport. Note that in common with almost all such hostels in Australia, Australians and New Zealanders are not welcome as guests.

AA Tremayne Backpackers, *49 Carabella St, Kirribilli; tel: 9955 4155*. **Apac Backpackers**, *6 Steinton Rd, Manly; tel: 9977 4155*. **Avalon Beach Backpackers Hostel**, *59 Avalon Pde, Avalon; tel: 9918 9709*. **Backpackers Kings Cross**, *162 Victoria St, Potts Point; tel: 9356 3232*. **Glebe Point Village Backpackers**, *256 Glebe Point Rd,*

Glebe; tel: 9660 8133. **Jolly Swagman Backpackers Accommodation**, *King's Cross*. Four hostels; *tel: 9358 6600, 9358 6400, 9357 4733*. **Lamrock Lodge**, *19 Lamrock Ave, Bondi; tel: 9130 5063*. **Surfside Backpackers**, *186 Arden Close, Coogee; tel: 9315 7888*. **Wharf Backpackers**, *48 East Esplanade, Nabky; tel: 9977 2800*.

Motels are where Australians visiting the city tend to stay. There are very few within the city itself but many in the suburbs within easy reach of the city.

The **Youth Hostel Association** *(HI)* exists in Australia but, perhaps, does not have as strong a following as it does in Europe. In the main it is competing with the backpacker hostels – prices are much the same. All information and bookings – *tel: 9261 1111*. The office at *422 Kent St* is a mine of useful information with a wide range of brochures and maps.

There are three youth hostels within the city: **Glebe Point**, *262 Glebe Point Rd, Glebe, NSW 2037; tel: 9692 8418*; **Pittwater**, *Halls Wharf via Church Point, NSW2105; tel: 9999 2196*; **Sydney Central YHA**, *corner Pitt St and Rawson Pl., NSW 2000; tel: 9281 9111*.

Eating and Drinking

The restaurants of Sydney are a constant delight. The definitive guide is the *Sydney Morning Herald*'s **Good Food Guide**, which lists and classifies all serious restaurants. It is available at all newsagents.

The list that follows is of restaurants that I have tested and can recommend. But, in truth, it is rare to have a bad dining experience in Sydney. The competition between restaurants is ferocious and this keeps the standards very high. There are far more restaurants on the south side of the Harbour Bridge than there are on the north side. After North Sydney and *Military Rd* you are in something of a gastronomic wasteland, with few restaurants – a very few – worthy of mention. Most of the people from the north side of the bridge tend to come to the city when dining out.

The prices start at around $20 a person and then go smartly upwards. There are very few restaurants where you would spend more than $100 a person. Low priced is $20 or less per person for two courses, say an entrée and a main. Medium is $20–$30 for the same. Expensive is anything above that.

The one great cost control item is wine. Sydney has far fewer BYO restaurants than, say, Melbourne, but they do exist. In which case you buy your wine – typically $10 a bottle and up – at a local bottle shop and pay $2 corkage. In most restaurants there is a wine list and most wines will run from $18 and then move upwards, sometimes to stratospheric levels. Australians take their wine pretty seriously and the very best commands premium prices. The best way to deal with this is to decide on a price maximum – say $20 – and ask the waiter what you should order. You will have a good wine recommended and be told more about the wine than you want to know.

These restaurants are grouped together roughly in geographic order. All are within an easy taxi ride of the centre of town.

Eating and Drinking in the City Centre

Rockpool, *107 George St, The Rocks; tel: 9252 1888.* Expensive. One of the new and totally serious gastronomic temples of Australia. **Beppi's**, *corner Yurong and Stanley Sts, E. Sydney: tel: 9360 4558.* Expensive. An old-established favourite with the movers and shakers. Booking essential. **Imperial Peking Harbourside**, *15 Circular Quay W., The Rocks; tel: 9247 7073.* Expensive. Chinese food served with great style. Always very busy. Book a table. **Suntory**, *529 Kent St, Sydney; tel: 9267 2900.* Expensive. Superb Japanese in one of the most beautiful settings in Sydney. **The Treasury**, *InterContinental Hotel, 117 Macquarie S.; tel: 9240 1270.* Very expensive. Its many supporters would rate it the best restaurant in Sydney, if not in Australia.

Hard Rock Café, *121 Crown St, Darlinghurst; tel: 9331 1116.* Medium. **Planet Hollywood**, *600 George St, Sydney; tel: 9267 7827.* Medium. Both of these are outposts of the international chains. The food is not great but you do not go there just for the food. **Marigold Yum Cha**, *Levels 4 and 5, 683 George St, Haymarket; tel: 9281 3388.* Inexpensive. Reputed to be the best *yum cha*

(dim sum) restaurant in Sydney. This style of restaurant, where trolleys with selectable and delectable food are wheeled around the tables, are quite popular in Australia. There is probably not a major Australian town that does not have a yum cha, although the quality varies. The name, by the way, is literally Cantonese for 'eat tea'. Always packed with Chinese clientele. **Sydney Tower Restaurant**, *Centrepoint, Sydney; tel: 9233 3722.* Medium. The food is not great but the view is astounding. **Don Quixote**, *1 Albion Place, Sydney; tel: 9264 5903.* Medium. Specialises in suckling pig.

Eating and Drinking in King's Cross and beyond

Bayswater Brasserie, *32 Bayswater Rd, King's Cross; tel: 9357 2749.* Medium. A true brasserie, perhaps the only one in Sydney, which has been consistently successful for many years. **Darley St Thai**, *30 Bayswater Rd, Kings Cross; tel: 9358 6530.* Expensive. The best known and the most expensive Thai restaurant in Australia. **Primadonna**, *33 Bayswater Rd, Kings Cross; tel: 9358 5582.* Medium. Good quality, medium-priced Italian. **A Taste of India**, *370 New South Head Rd, Double Bay; tel: 9327 5712.* Medium. Excellent Indian cuisine. Indian restaurants are comparatively rare in Australia.

Eating and Drinking Just Outside Town

Thai Pothong, *298 King St, Newtown; tel: 9550 4572.* Medium. Highly recommended restaurant in the centre of an area packed with restaurants with wine at bottle-shop prices and traditional Thai, as opposed to Australian Thai, food. **Goodfellas**, *111 King St, Newtown; tel: 9557 1175.* Medium. Stylish brassserie. **Buon Gusto**, *368 Abercrombie St, Chippendale; tel: 9319 4798.* Medium. Italian restaurant that is always crowded and serves far more that you can eat. **Five Doors**, *233 Riley St, Surry Hills; tel: 9211 4454.* Expensive. International style with an excellent wine list and very professional service.

Malaya, *761 George St, Sydney; tel: 9211 0946*, and *86 Walker St, North Sydney; tel: 9956 4306* Inexpensive, Malay/Chinese food.

65

Always room at lunch time but can be crowded in the evenings, when you should book. The *laksa* is considered one of the best of its kind in Sydney. **Bali Indonesian**, *135 King St, Newtown; tel: 9557 3441.* Inexpensive BYO restaurant, which tends to be full in the evenings. Book. **Tetsuya's**, *729 Darling St; tel: 9555 1017.* Japanese cuisine crossed with modern Australia with some amazing, if eclectic, results.

Eating and Drinking in Paddington and Woolahra

Buon Ricordo, *92 Hargrave St, Paddington; tel: 9360 6729.* Expensive. Classic northern Italian cuisine. **Bistro Moncur**, *116 Queen St, Wollahra; tel: 9363 2782.* Expensive. Stylish bistro which has an experimental menu that works most of the time.

Eating and Drinking Further Out of Town

Doyles on the Beach, *11 Marine Pde, Watsons Bay; tel: 9337 2007.* Further out than most listed here but a great Sydney tradition, where you sit in glorious sunshine, sip the wine you have brought and enjoy the freshest seafood. You cannot book a table and on sunny weekends it gets very crowded. Go midweek and enjoy, enjoy. **Centennial Park Café**, *corner Parks Dr. and Grand Dr., in Centennial Park; tel: 9360 3355.* Wonderful place for lunchtime eating in the sun. Mixed clientele with kids enjoying lunch with mum and business people taking a mini-break in the middle of the day. A little way out of town but worth the journey especially on a sunny day.

Pubs

The idea of a pub in the English sense or a bar in the New York sense does not seriously exist in Sydney. There are some pubs worth visiting – and they are almost all in The Rocks area. Other pubs are places for serious drinking and almost all of them are totally devoid of charm or grace.

There are some exceptions, like **The Lord Nelson** and **The Orient** at The Rocks but they are few and far between.

The situation on bars in the city is a strange one. Every time someone has tried to open a bar, the hoteliers have appeared en masse in front of the licensing authorities and demanded that no licence should be given as they cater more than adequately for everyone's needs. That this is a total nonsense is shown by the fact that as this book was being written, a Swiss guest was refused service of a beer in the Sheraton on the Park at 1530 on the grounds that alchohol service in the lounge did not start until 1600. That he was a guest in the hotel made no difference. He and his guests drank water.

There is a small revolt now taking place against this nonsense, especially with the run up to the Olympic Games in 2000, and for the first time in Sydney it is now possible to get a bona fide nightclub licence, where the clientele does not have to buy a full meal in order to get a drink.

Thus the scene is one of rapid change and by the time you get to Sydney there will be more places where you will be able to have a civilised drink although pubs, in the English style, will continue to be few and far between.

Communications

There is no central post office. All branches are open during normal shopping hours but as branches are continually being closed and re-opened within shopping centres they are sometimes difficult to find. Australia Post is not one of the glories of Australia.

The telephone code for Sydney is 02.

Consulates

Canada: *Level 5, 111 Harrington St; tel: 9364 3000.*
New Zealand: *Level 14, 1 Alfred St, Circular Quay; tel: 9247 1999.*
UK: *Level 16, Gateway Building, 1 Macquarie St; tel: 9247 7521.*
USA: *corner Park and Castlereagh Sts; tel: 9261 9200.*

Money

Almost all banks and many hotels will change money but at a ruinous exchange rate. Change your money at a proper bureau de change. On the other hand, almost all banks have automatic teller machines and the majority of these will handle most credit cards. **Thomas Cook** travel agencies all change money and traveller's cheques. **Thomas Cook** change money and traveller's cheques at many locations across Sydney, including at the airport and at: *Shop 509, Hyatt Kingsgate Centre, King's Cross; tel: 9356 2211* and *Shop 22, Lower Ground Flr, Queen Victoria Bldg, George St; tel: 9264 1133*. These two bureaux are open at weekends. In addition, Thomas Cook travel agencies offer the same services, as well as full travel agency facilities, though not always open at weekends. The most central are: *Shop T4, Westpac Plaza, 60 Margaret St; tel: 9251 5411; 175 Pitt St; tel: 9231 2877* (open Sat); *Shop P8 Hunter Connection, 109 Pitt St; tel: 9235 2655*. Travel branches in the Sydney area include: *Westfield Shoppingtown, Macquarie St, Liverpool; tel: 9570 2833; 743 Military Rd, Mosman; tel: 9660 7622; Westfield Shoppingtown, Church St, Parramatta; tel: 9635 6433*.

ENTERTAINMENT

The best guide to shows on in town is published in the Metro supplement of the *Sydney Morning Herald* every Friday, which covers every show, every gig, every happening with complete details.

Sydney's **pop music** scene is very large, with never less than seventy gigs playing at the weekend. Most of these are held in special venues or in clubs – normally RSL, standing for Returned Servicemen's League: they exist in every suburb and are financed by income from slot machines. You do not need to be a returned service person or anything much else to get a temporary membership. The noise level at most of these venues is deafening and the clientele is typically under 30.

There are several major venues for comedy. The best known is the **Harold Park Hotel**, *115 Wiggin St, Glebe; tel: 9682 0564*, which has a show normally Wed–Sat, 2030 ($10). A little way out of the city is the **Comedy Store**, *450 Paramatta Rd, Petersham; tel: 9564 3900*, which has a live show Mon–Sat. **The Double Bay Comedy Club**, *16 Cross St, Double Bay; tel: 9327 6560*, is open Tues–Sun for dinner and show or show only. Australian humour is

robust; much more so than Billy Connolly, for example. If vulgar language offends you these are to be avoided, although the Harold Park Hotel is known for putting on civilised shows.

There is little cabaret as such in Sydney and what there is tends to be in one of the small theatres. The exception to the rule is the **Festival Club**, *corner of Oxford and Pelican Sts, Darlinghurst; tel: 9368 1955*, which attracts a predominantly gay audience but has some superb cabaret artists.

There is no theatre district, as such, in Sydney. Indeed, compared to Melbourne there is a most shameful paucity of theatres. For classical entertainment and serious theatre, the **Sydney Opera House** is plainly the first stop. It is home to the Australian Opera, the Sydney Symphony orchestra, the Sydney Theatre Company, the Sydney Dance Company and Musica Viva and the Sydney Philharmonia. There are always concerts and performances taking place in the various halls. All information and booking, *tel: 9350 7777*. Seats vary in price between $50 and $100.

Sydney is host to those international shows – *Miss Saigon, Crazy for You, Cats* – where you come out humming the tunes. Seats at these shows tyically cost between $80 and $100 and are easily booked through **Ticketek** using a credit card – *tel: 9266 4848*. Note that **Halftix** is in *Martin Pl.* near *Castlereagh St* in the centre of the city and sells same day, half price tickets for cash. You have to turn up personally to make the booking. Telephone bookings are not accepted.

There is also a very active local theatre scene, which is listed every Friday in *Metro*. The standard at these theatres can be variable and you should read the reviews with care before making a booking.

EVENTS

At the beginning of every year Sydney braces itself for two major events. The first is the **Mardi Gras** parade in March, which started as a march in defiance of the laws that made homosexuality illegal, but is now a carnival event where gays strut their stuff with official support from the police, the government, the banks and the airlines. Whatever one's views of

67

Sydney's Past

New South Wales was explored along the coast by Captain James Cook, who in 1770 discovered Botany Bay. He wrote an enthusiastic, if somewhat inaccurate report of the Bay, and this led to it being chosen for a new penal colony.

In fact, the first colony was not established there – Governor Phillip was deterred by the low lying marshy interior, which is now Sydney airport – but a short distance north at Sydney Cove.

Here in Jan 1788, the First Fleet of 1500 souls – 736 convicts, 211 guards and the rest civilian administrators – set up their tents and started the first settlement. That first site on Sydney Cove was the birthplace of modern Australia, the start of European settlement.

Of the original settlers few of either the convicts or their guards had any real skills in farming and were in poor shape when the Second Fleet arrived with more supplies in 1790.

From then on the colony moved forward, with fertile lands westwards towards Parramatta being cultivated. The convicts were used as labourers on the farms, to build roads and to start building rudimentary buildings to house the officers.

As this small colony grew some of the convicts were allowed limited freedom – ticket-of-leave – and became traders and merchants in the growing city or opened up even more land to agriculture.

Quite quickly the convict camp became a colony and was able to supply materials back to the home country. The most important of these was merino wool, which started in Camden with the Macarthur family and rapidly spread inland.

In 1850 gold was discovered within a day's journey, in Bathurst on the western edge of the Great Dividing Range. This brought a surge of instant wealth followed by a period of consolidated expansion.

Now Sydney and the rest of New South Wales had become the leading colonial economy for Britain and the population boomed with immigrants and free settlers coming to the new country.

It was not just gold – there was coal in the Hunter Valley and near present-day Wollongong; red cedar stands right along the coast and farming – especially sheep farming – all added to the general prosperity.

For the present day visitor these waves of expansion can be quite clearly seen in the architecture. The first and major convict wave was responsible for the area around Sydney Cove known, then and now, as **The Rocks**.

The move towards the plains of the west can be seen in the main *Parramatta Rd* running out of Sydney to **Parramatta**, itself a town of colonial buildings. Then the prosperity brought the more solid Victorian buildings in the centre of the city and the need for workers led to the creation of workers' cottages – now very expensive upmarket residences – in **Surry Hills**, **Paddington**, **Glebe** and **Newtown**.

Then, with the final historic flurry, when Australia became a Federation in 1901, the suburbs started to develop the Australian dream – a quarter acre block and a bungalow.

Not many of the present-day inhabitants can claim descent from the convicts of the First Fleet – those that can do so with considerable pride – but the feeling of being 'agin the authorities' is still part of the city's make-up. In Australia this attitude is called 'larrikinism' and there is some considerable grudging admiration in the use of that word.

If you think of Sydney as a larrikin of a city that has grown to become a sprightly adult you will not go far wrong.

flaunting alternative sex, it is colourful, entertaining and, at times, very funny. It brings thousands of tourists from all over the world. In the decade that it has been running it has done more to gain gays acceptance in Sydney society than any other event.

At the same time we have the **Festival of Sydney,** which was for a time a lack-lustre event, not to be compared with the Adelaide festival, but now, under the direction of Leo Schofield, is set to become a major happening.

The Royal Easter Show is when the country comes to the town. The current site is the Sydney Showgrounds but this will move in the next year or so to Homebush, while the Showgrounds will be converted into a film studio and a tourist attraction. The Royal Easter Show is very important to Sydney, as it reminds the inhabitants of the way the city grew, and it attracts large crowds every year, especially if the weather is fine.

In June Sydney has its **film festival** where movies which would not otherwise get a showing appear at the **State Theatre** and other venues.

In August it seems that the whole of Sydney dons its running shoes and takes part in the **Sydney to Surf** race, which is a fun run of 14 km from the city to Bondi. There is horseracing all year around – flat racing only, steeplechasing as such does not exist in Australia – but the major meeting in Sydney is the **AJC Spring Carnival** held at the end of September at Randwick racecourse.

SHOPPING

Sydney has become an international shopping destination possibly because it is easier to shop here than other cities. Certainly the attraction cannot be the prices, which, on the whole, tend to be somewhat higher than elsewhere in the area. It is fascinating to see visitors from Hong Kong – previously thought to be *the* shopping destination of the world – trawling the shops of Sydney.

The lower half of the Central Business District is devoted to shopping and a large percentage of it is a pedestrian precinct. It also contains most of the important shopping malls. Opening hours, which are pretty general for all shops, are 0900–1800 with a late night extension on Thursday to 2100. On Sundays major shops are normally open 1130–1700.

Queen Victoria Building, on *George St* next to the Town Hall and opposite the Hilton, has 200 upmarket shops, cafés and restaurants. **Centrepoint Shopping Centre**, *corner Pitt and Castlereagh Sts,* has 150 speciality shops and stores. **Shop at the Rocks**. This is, of course, one of the most historic and beautiful parts of Sydney but in its restored sandstone buildings it has an amazing range of speciality shops.

Warehouse shopping was late coming to Australia but has now caught on in a big way. The easiest way to do it is to go on a **Shopping Spree Tour**, which takes you around 8–10 warehouses in a minibus. It costs $48 and the tour leaves at 0830 and gets you back, all shopped out, by 1630. Calls at all central district hotels.

To prepare for the rest of your trip around Australia, visit the **Sydney Map Shop**, *Lands Building, 23 Bridge St; tel: 9228 6111.*

SIGHTSEEING

You can spend a lifetime exploring Sydney. By far the best way is to use public transport and, again, the least expensive way is to get a **SydneyPass** (see Getting Around p.61), which will allow you to use a combination of bus, ferry and train to get to and from your destination.

Central
The Sydney Opera House commands the harbour and although very rude things have been said about this building by locals, it is a great architectural achievement – surrounded by controversy in its early days – and is well worth exploring. You can go on a guided tour of the Opera House. These start at 0900 and run pretty continuously until 1600. Cost $9; information *tel: 9250 7111.*

At the moment it is again a centre of controversy because the government gave a developer rights to build alongside the Opera House, which will close off many of the views of the extraordinary building. As this book goes to press this plan is being ferociously resisted. There is no best place from which to view this building. Anywhere you travel on the harbour you will get a new and exciting view.

Also dominating the harbour in a different way is the **Sydney Harbour Bridge**, which is called the 'Giant Coat Hanger', the 'Car Tangled Spanner' and ruder things by the locals. However, it would be dangerous to criticise it, as it is very dear to Sydneysiders' hearts. There is a museum and lookout in the southeast pylon, which has splendid views. The bridge was completed in 1932 and is the second biggest single span bridge in the world, covering 503m. It took 50,000 tonnes of steel to build. The bridge is painted grey – Paul Hogan was one of the riggers responsible for this before he found stardom in *Crocodile Dundee* – although there have been suggestions that it be brightened up for the Olympic Games by painting it a prettier colour. This suggestion is rightly being ignored by the authorities.

Along from the Opera House, and going uphill is *Macquarie St*, one of the great sightseeing roads of Sydney, full of handsome sandstone buildings on both sides of the road reflecting the surge of prosperity in early Victorian times.

The corner of *Bridge St* and *Macquarie St* has the old **Treasury Building**, which has most imaginatively been turned into a hotel; the remarkable entrance hall and lobby are well worth a visit.

On the opposite side of *Macquarie St* stands a statue of King Edward VII on horseback and behind that is the **Conservatorium of Music**. This was originally built as the stables for Government House but is now a training ground for young musicians and the venue for some superb concerts throughout the year.

Nearby are the gates leading to the **Royal Botanic Gardens**, *tel: 9231 8111,* which are truly magnificent throughout the year. It has free guided walks and a trackless scenic train ride runs daily every 15 mins between the Opera House and the Garden's Visitor Centre. Three special places to visit in the Botanic Gardens: the field of wildflowers growing rampant; the tropical glass house; and the walk along the harbour's edge, with some of the finest views of the harbour and, of course, the Opera House.

Next comes the sandstone block, which is the **State Library of New South Wales** with a modern extension which, unusually, enhances rather than detracts from the original architecture. In the foyer the marble floor is a mosaic of an early map of Australia by Abel Tasman, who viewed Tasmania in 1642, some considerable time before Captain Cook came to these shores. The State Library holds regular exhibitions.

In the centre of *Macquarie St* is **State Parliament House**, originally the northern wing of the first colonial hospital. This is the oldest parliament in Australia, having operated in various modes since 1829. Visitors are welcome to watch the politicians from the public gallery, and consider with awe that these people run the most populated state of Australia.

Across the lawns of the **Domain**, behind Parliament House, is the **Art Gallery of New South Wales**, *tel: 9225 1700,* which has a ferociously enthusiastic curator in Edmund Capon, who manages to bring exciting exhibitions to the Gallery on a very regular basis.

Next door to Parliament House is the **hospital**. In front of it stands **Il Porcellino**, a statue of a pig, which is a copy of the original in Florence. It is said that if you make a donation and rub Il Porcellino's nose you will have good luck. The statue has a very shiny nose. Just beyond the hospital is the **Mint Museum**, now a museum of decorative and fine arts, a splendid example of the work of the Colonial architect Francis Greenway.

Continuing up *Macquarie St* we come to **Hyde Park Barracks**, again the work of Greenway, and a masterpiece of Georgian simplicity. This is now an exhibition centre housing a collection of artefacts from the convict era.

Another walk starting from the Opera House swings along the front of Circular Quay with its ferries and comes back up the other side of the harbour to The Rocks. The warehouses and bond stores which still line the waterfront give this a special style (although this is tourist territory, with shops selling the sort of items that you buy and then wonder why when you get home).

The whole area has been restored with great

The 2000 Olympic Games

Sydney is gearing up seriously for the 2000 Olympics and if you have not already booked a hotel room for the event then the bad news is that you are too late. All of the major hotels now have very long waiting lists and all the motels checked said they were booked solid, although in many cases this is by tour companies pre-booking for packaged holidays.

The Australian Tourist Commission has stated that if there isn't room in all the hotels – new ones are being built – then cruise ships will be anchored in the harbour to increase capacity. A large number of visitors to the Olympics will probably be put up in private homes and a scheme is being put in place to take care of this.

Like every other Olympics this one is a planning nightmare with shock, horror stories regularly running in the newspapers suggesting that all is a shambles. But the fact is that much of the construction work is already completed and the infrastructure is in place, so there should be no last minute panics. The design of the logo has been released and, depending on your imagination, it either looks like a cockatoo or an Edna Everage hat. There may be some hiccups at the end with the public transport system – there are budgetary problems – but it would be fair to say that Sydney is much more prepared than Atlanta was at a comparable time.

The slogan of the Olympic Committee is 'Building a Better Sydney', with Circular Quay among the areas listed to be upgraded. But the games themselves will be held in Homebush, which was famous for housing Australia's largest abbatoir and is a somewhat seedy suburb in the west on the Parramatta River. Serious construction work is already under way and there will be a lot of riverside parkland. The facilities would appear to be more than adequate. One way of getting the crowds there and back will be by ferries running on the Paramatta River. There is a 24 hour information line: *tel: 9746 2855.*

Sydney is quite determined to make these the best Olympic Games of all time and Australians are all very supportive and willing to make sacrifices to ensure that this happens.

It is very likely that Australia will, as always, win an inordinate number of medals in relationship to the size of the population. Basically the plan is to beat the Poms – get more medals than Britain. It may well work out that way.

71

style and the place to use as a base for your explorations is **The Rocks Visitors Centre**, *108 George St; tel: 9255 1788* (open 0900–1700 daily), in itself a place worth exploring.

Walk from there up to **Observatory Hill**, which has a group of old sandstone buildings built by convicts in 1857 and is now a museum of astronomy. Open 1400–1700 weekdays, 1000–1700 weekends.

The Rocks is also home to **The Sydney Dance Company** (*tel: 9221 4811*) and the **Sydney Theatre Company** (*tel: 9250 1700*), both of which are on Pier 4 in *Hickson Rd*.

Still using the Opera House as a starting point, you can now explore the other major streets of the city centre. As you walk you will notice that most of the pavements are covered with awnings to keep off the sun and the rain. There was a move in the 1970s to abolish these for not being in the modern style, but luckily they have come back into favour.

The city streets run in parallel up the peninsula with *Macquarie St* as the left boundary and *George St* forming the centre. Much of the centre has been made into a pedestrian precinct which makes it very pleasant for strolling. There are other places worth exploring, which are not directly connected to any one area.

Out of the Centre

Taronga Park Zoo is on a multi-million dollar site at Mosman, with perhaps the greatest views over the sea of any zoo in the world. You can get there by ferry from Circular Quay. It has been extensively modernised in recent times and an adoption system whereby firms and individuals sponsor an animal has been a great success.

It contains Australia's largest collection of native and exotic animals and has a walk-through area where you can see kangaroos and wallabies as in their native habitat. Open 0900–1700; admission $14.50.

Darling Harbour – for information phone either the visitors centre, *tel: 286 0111*, or the Infoline, *tel: 1802 260 568* – is part of the city. You can get there by the **Monorail** (see Getting Around p.61), which loops around Darling Harbour and much of the Central Business District. There are over 200 stores, harbour-side restaurants and cafés.

Here you will find the remarkably good **Sydney Aquarium**, the **PowerHouse Museum**, the **Motor Museum** and the **National Maritime Museum** just next door. It also contains an authentic Chinese garden and the SS *South Steyne*, Australia's oldest steam ferry. These are all open 0930–1700 daily.

For further exploration of Sydney, the National Parks and Wildlife Service runs a **Discovery Programme** of walks, talks and tours *(tel: 985 6333)*.

To follow the history of Sydney you can take a **Ticket Through Time** from the Historic Houses Trust *(tel: 692 8366)*, which allows you to explore seven historic sights including Elizabeth Bay House, the Justice and Police Museum, Vaucluse House and Sussanah Place in the Rocks.

Museums and Art Galleries

Museum of Contemporary Art, *140 George St; tel: 9241 5892*, (24-hr information service). On the water's edge at Circular Quay. Open every day 1100–1800, it has a continually changing program of international and Australian contemporary art. Admission $6. **The Art Gallery of New South Wales**, *tel: 225 1744*, is in a most beautiful Harbour-side setting and has a unique collection of Australian art.

Australian Museum, *6 College St; tel: 9339 8111*. Open daily 0900–1800. This is Australia's oldest and largest natural history

museum. **Australian National Maritime Museum**, *Darling Harbour, tel: 9552 777*. Open daily 1000–1700.

Powerhouse Museum, *500 Harris St Ultimo; tel: 9217 0111*. (Behind Darling Harbour.) Open daily 1000–1700. Australia's largest museum, with over 20 exhibitions covering science, technology, the decorative arts and Australia's social history.

Beaches

What Sydney has in abundance is beaches. In fact, there are so many of them that most Sydneysiders take them for granted. One of the nearest to the city and the most famous outside Australia is **Bondi Beach**. You can get there by the no. 380 or 381 bus from the city or take the train to Bondi Junction and catch the beach bus from the bus terminal just outside the station.

This beach is surrounded by tatty architecture, is not as clean as it could be and has been the scene of some recent regrettable violence – although in fairness that is rare – but it is still Bondi. This is where the beautiful people come to strip down and build up their tans. It is busy from early in the morning – joggers and walkers and early morning swimmers – until late at night. Facing the beach is a row of restaurants and cafés, of varying quality but always crowded.

Manly is a different, more family sort of place. The best way to get there is by ferry from Circular Quay, although in theory it is possible to trek your way around the headlands by bus. As you come off the ferry you are in **Corso**, which is a centre of shops and restaurants. This is a more suburban area than Bondi although, again, it attracts the young and the beautiful in minimal swim gear.

These are but two of the 50 beaches within the Sydney metropolitan area, which extend from **Palm Beach** in the north to the **Royal National Park** in the south. At weekends they can, of course, get crowded but during the week many of the beaches are effectively deserted.

Note that throughout these beaches topless sunbathing is the norm and at some of them nude bathing is legal.

SYDNEY–
THE GOLD COAST

This is one of the most common travel routes used by Sydneysiders going on holiday. You head out of Sydney, turn left and head north – because the further north you go the warmer it gets. This route has the bonus of a possible detour into the Hunter Valley. As in Australia in general, traffic on this route reaches a peak in the school holiday season – especially Christmas and January. Hotels and motels in popular resorts are heavily booked. Unless you have most of your accommodation booked in advance, 20 Dec–30 Jan is not a good time to explore Australia, particularly these coastal resorts.

ROUTE: 873 KM

The Gold Coast

16 Tweed Heads
31
Murwillumbah
51
Ballina 26 Byron Bay
136 1
Grafton
85

Coffs Harbour
47
Nambucca Heads
68

South West Rocks
Kempsey
51
Port Macquarie
Taree 1 84
34
Hunter Valley Wineries
Bulahdelah 82 Forster
15 66 Myall Lakes National Park
Cessnock 49 60 Port Stephens
Newcastle
74
88 1 Gosford
Ku-ring-gai Chase National Park
Sydney

73

ROUTE

Drive north out of Sydney on Hwy 1, the **Pacific Highway**. The Pacific Hwy sounds like a grand super-highway. It is nothing of the sort. Most of the way it is the equivalent of a reasonable suburban road and for much of its length it is only three lanes wide, which makes overtaking hazardous except at specially designated points where the highway, for a short stretch, becomes dual carriageway before reverting to three lanes. At the very start from Sydney you can go along a motorway (one of the few in Australia). You pass superb beaches and, except for holidays and weekends, they are nearly all deserted. These beaches in somewhere like the South of France, would be star attractions. In Australia there are so many of them that they are treated very casually. Almost immediately you are driving along the edge of **Ku-ring-gai Chase National Park**.

At Mooney Mooney, across the inlet of the Hawkesbury River, turn right to **Gosford**. From Gosford the coast road winds past a series of lakes and lagoons to **Newcastle** – the motorway heads inland to the same destination. Along the coast you approach the city with a drive parallel to the Nine Mile Beach. From Newcastle you can side-track to the **Hunter Valley**, one of Australia's premier winegrowing areas, and to Nelson Bay on **Port Stephens**.

At Newcastle the motorway ends and you are back to a three-lane road. Continue along the Pacific Hwy. At **Bulahdelah** turn right along the top of a series of lagoons – Myall and Wallis Lakes – to **Myall Lakes National Park** and **Forster**, which has golden beaches extending on each side. Rejoin the Pacific Hwy just south of **Taree**, then pass more lagoons to **Port Macquarie** and, close by, **Kempsey** and **South West Rocks**. Divert a few kilometres east to visit **Nambucca Heads** and, rejoining the highway again, drive to **Coffs Harbour**.

At this stage the weather is already noticeably different, as you are moving from the temperate – by Australian standards – weather of Sydney into the start of a sub-tropical zone. The highway veers slightly inland towards **Grafton**, separated from the sea by the Yuraygir National Park and Lake Hiawatha. From Grafton follow the highway across the inlet of the Clarence River and past the Banjalung National Park to **Ballina**. From here you can take the coast road, or drive inland along the highway and turn right at the small town of Bangalow, to **Byron Bay**.

Rejoining the highway, continue north to **Murwillumbah**, on the slopes of the long-extinct volcano Mt Warning. A little

further on is **Tweed Heads**, the last town in New South Wales. Once past there you are in Queensland and on the Gold Coast.

TRAINS

Two daily Sydney–Brisbane trains cover this route. Sydney–Kempsey 7 hrs, Kempsey–Coffs Harbour 2½ hrs, Coffs Harbour–Grafton City 1¼ hrs. Only one train stops at Murwillumbah (Grafton City–Murwillumbah 3¾ hrs). The other goes to Casino, where a bus connection takes you on to the Gold Coast. There is also a bus connection from Murwillumbah to Surfers Paradise. OTT table 9017.

BUSES

Four bus companies, including Greyhound Pioneer and McCafferty's, provide between them ten daily services stopping at many of the places on this route. Journey time between Sydney and Murwillumbah is 15 hrs. OTT table 9090.

KU-RING-GAI CHASE NATIONAL PARK

Tourist Information: Visitors Centre, tel: (02) 9457 9322.

The park covers 14,838 hectares of rugged sandstone country surrounding the flood river valley of **Broken Bay**. It is a mixture of open woodland, heaths, eucalypt forest and occasional rain forest pockets. The park is only 24 km north of Sydney. You get there by driving up the Pacific Hwy and turning off towards **Bobbin Head**, or by way of Mona Vale Rd, turning off at **Terrey Hills**. The park is split almost in two by inlets of the **Hawkesbury River**, with **Cowan**, **Coal** and **Candle Creeks** winding their way right into the park on the south side, and **Jerusalem Bay** cutting in on the north side. You can explore the park by water – canoes, cruisers and houseboats to rent at **Akuna Bay** and Bobbin Head.

GOSFORD

Tourist Information: Gosford Tourist Information, Rotary Park, Terrigal Dr., (PO Box 576, Terrigal, NSW 2260); tel: 25 2835. **Central Coast Reservations Hotline**; tel: 1800 806 258 (toll free).

ACCOMMODATION AND FOOD

Gosford Motor Inn *(BW)*, 23 *Pacific Hwy; tel: 23 1333*; **Metro Inn** *(FL)*, *512 Pacific Hwy; tel: 28 4666*; **Galaxy Motel**, *26 Pacific Hwy; tel: 23 1711*; **Rambler Motor Inn**, *73 Pacific Hwy; tel: 24 6577*; **Terranova Park Motel**, *733 Pacific Hwy; tel: 28 1222*; **Holiday Inn Crowne Plaza**, *The Esplanade, Terrigal; tel: 84 9111*; **Clan Lakeside Lodge**, *1 Ocean View Dr.; tel: 84 1566*; **Country Comfort Inn** *(CC)*, *154 Terrigal Dr.; tel: 84 1166*; **Terrigal Pacific Motel**, *224 Terrigal Dr.; tel: 85 1555*; **Terrigal Beach Motel**, *1 Painter Lane; tel: 84 1423*; **Ocean Front Motel**, *102 Ocean Parade, The Entrance; tel: 32 5911*; **El Lago Waters Resort**, *41 The Entrance Rd; tel: 32 3955*; **Tienda Motel**, *309A The Entrance Rd; tel: 32 3933*; **Sapphire Palms Motel**, *180 The Entrance Rd; tel: 32 5799*.

The **Crowne Plaza** in Terrigal (see above) has the upmarket **La Mer** and a more relaxed **Norfolk Brasserie**. The **Willows Restaurant** in the Metro Inn, *512 Pacific Hwy; tel: 28 4666*, has a fixed price menu from $25. **Joel's Restaurant** *on Avoca beach; tel: 82 3666*, has won several awards for its Euro-Australian menu with Asian influences.

SIGHTSEEING

Gosford, 85 km north of Sydney, lies at the head of the major inlet, Brisbane Water, which opens out into the sea slightly south of Broken Bay. Despite being so close to Sydney and still commuter territory, the town is a gateway to an area that offers a series of different travel experiences. It is a dormitory town of Sydney and has a range of resorts running along the coast on both sides. It is every Sydneysider's ambition to own a small seaside cottage or bungalow in the area – a 'weekender' is the local phrase – and this is a part of the coast that focuses mainly on family holidays.

Nearby is **Old Sydney Town**, *tel: 40 1104*, which is a re-creation of that great city prior to 1810. Serious attempts have been made to keep it authentic, although some of the dramatic re-enactments of life in the convict days – the floggings, the duel, colonial justice – have a large component of ham, and are much appreciated by schoolchildren. Open Wed–Sat

and all school holidays 1000–1600. Near Old Sydney Town is **Somersby Falls**, a pleasant spot for a picnic, and close by is the **Wildflower Farm**, open to visitors.

Henry Kendall's cottage, *27 Henry Kendall St*, is where the poet lived for two years from 1874. It was built as an inn in 1838 and has been restored. It has elegant grounds where you can picnic. Open Wed, Sat and Sun, and all holidays 1000–1600; *tel: 25 2270*.

The new **Australian Reptile Park and Wildlife Sanctuary**, *tel: 043 40 1146* (from the F3 take the Gosford Exit to the Pacific Hwy at Somerby; open daily 0900–1700), has one of the world's largest crocodiles in captivity. His name is Eric and he is fed every Sunday. There are twice-daily reptile shows and in the park there are friendly kangaroos, emus, koalas, wombats and dingoes.

Just outside Gosford, 15 mins by road, are the **Glenworth Valley Stables**, *tel: 75 1222*, which offer free range or guided rides, with 200 horses to choose from and nearly a thousand hectares to ride in. Open daily 1000–1700.

From Gosford you can drive down to the coast at **Terrigal** and then follow the coastline north through the seaside resorts of Wamberal, Bateau Bay, Shelly Beach, Toowoon Bay, Long Jetty and finally **The Entrance**, which is one of the pincers that enclose the expanse of Tuggerah and Budgewoi Lake. One of the many attractions of The Entrance is the pelican feeding that takes place at 1530 every day on the shores of Memorial Park.

To the south of Gosford, off the Pacific Hwy, is the **Brisbane Waters National Park** – *tel: 244 911* – which covers 11,372 hectares and borders the Hawkesbury River. It is especially rich in Aboriginal art. There are several walks laid out through open woodlands with occasional pockets of rain forest.

NEWCASTLE

Tourist Information: Newcastle Tourism, *92 Scott St, Newcastle 2300; tel: (049) 29 9299*. Open 0900–1700 Mon–Fri, 1000–1530 weekends; reservations.

ACCOMMODATION AND FOOD

The Esplanade Newcastle Beach Motel,

Shortland Esplanade; tel: 29 5576; **Radisson Hotel**, *corner King and Steel Sts; tel: 26 3777;* **Bimet Lodge Motel**, *121 Union St; tel: 29 6677;* **Novocastrian Motor Inn**, *21 Parnell Pl.; tel: 26 3688;* **Newcastle Star**, *410 King St; tel: 26 1466;* **Newcastle Harbourside**, *107 Scott St; tel: 26 3244;* **Lake Macquarie Flag Motor Inn**, *798 Pacific Hwy, Belmont S. 2280; tel: 45 8622;* **Squid's Ink Motel**, *690 Pacific Hwy; tel: 47 7223;* **Hines Macquarie Motel**, *749 Pacific Hwy; tel: 45 2847;* **Blue Pacific Motel**, *82 Pacific Hwy, Swansea 2281; tel: 71 1055;* **Swansea Motel**, *250 Old Pacific Hwy; tel: 71 1811;* **Lakeside Motor Inn**, *568 The Esplanade, Warners Bay 2282; tel: 48 9666.*

Scratchley's, *Hunter St; tel: 29 1111,* has won best BYO for several years. Right on the waterfront, open 7 days. **Eliza's Café Brasserie**, *The Esplanade; tel: 29 5576,* is informal for light meals. Open daily 0630 till late. **Brewery Brasserie**, *150 Wharf Rd; tel: 29 5792,* is on the ground floor of the Queens Wharf Brewery on the harbour front. **Squid's Ink**, *690 Pacific Hwy, Belmont; tel: 47 7223,* has won several awards for its seafood. Open 7 days from 0700.

SIGHTSEEING

Although Newcastle is technically an industrial city it has some of the finest surfing beaches in Australia – arguably in the world – and a superb harbour. Newcastle is about a 1½ hr drive from Sydney (158 km to the north), is the second largest city in New South Wales, and is Australia's sixth largest city. The whole of the foreshore has been redeveloped and there has been some considerable rebuilding within the city since the famous earthquake of 1990.

The easiest way to see the city is on board the **Newcastle Tram**, which leaves the railway station on the hour 1000–1500, 7 days a week (*tel: 29 1822*). Free Settler Class – which means you can break your journey and catch a later tram – costs $10. Convict Class, without that privilege, is $8. There is an excellent town walk map, free from the information centre, which takes in most of the sights, including the **Newcastle Police Station Museum**, *90 Hunter St.* Open Mon–Fri 0900–1300, Sat–Sun 1100–1600.

By walkway from the Civic Centre is

Queen's Wharf, on the waterfront. This has been redeveloped into a modern, even trendy, area, with shops, restaurants, one of Australia's many mini-breweries and a watch tower.

The city has two landmarks. One of them is **Nobby's Head**, which rises some 30 m above the entrance to the port. On Nobby's Head is **Fort Scratchley**, which was built in the 1880s because of fear of a Russian invasion. The first time the fort saw action was in 1942, when a Japanese submarine surfaced to shell the city and shots were exchanged. The other landmark is the steep slope rising to **King Edward Park** and its obelisk. The city has some attractive terraced architecture and along the foreshore there are lawns and palm trees.

In the suburb of **Shortland** is the **Wetlands Centre** (*tel: 51 6466*), which is home to 100 species of birds and has canoes for hire for further exploration. The Pacific Hwy comes through the city and if you follow it south you come to the great expanse of **Lake Macquarie**, which opens out into the ocean at Swansea. The lake is the largest sea-board lake in Australia and covers 110 sq km with 150 km of foreshore. It contains about four times as much water as Sydney Harbour.

The **Hunter River** flows through the city and Newcastle is the entry town for the wine-famous Hunter Valley, which lies 1½ hrs drive to the north-west. There are several coach tours to the Hunter Valley, including the **Hunter Vineyard Tour** (*tel: 91 1659*), $45 an adult including lunch, with visits to several vineyards and vineries – cellar door tastings included.

SIDE TRACKS FROM NEWCASTLE

THE HUNTER VALLEY

To explore the Hunter Valley, proceed from Newcastle up the New England Hwy, Rte 15, through **Hexham**, **Maitland**, **Branxton**, **Singleton** and on to **Muswellbrook**. To the left of Branxton, around **Cessnock** and down to **Wollombi**, is the main wine country, and to the left of Muswellbrook, down and round to **Denham**, are the Upper Hunter wineries.

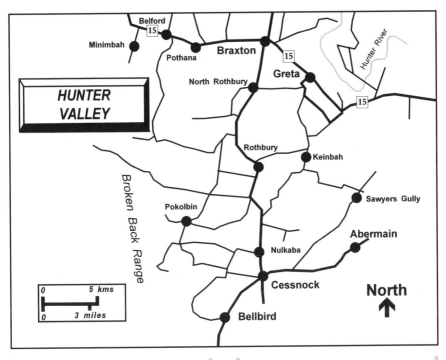

HUNTER
VALLEY

Belford
15
Minimbah
Pothana
Braxton
North Rothbury
15
Greta
15
Hunter River
Rothbury
Keinbah
Broken Back Range
Pokolbin
Sawyers Gully
Nulkaba
Abermain
0   5 kms
0   3 miles
Cessnock
Bellbird
North
↑

The whole area is organised for trips around the wineries with 50 possible winery visits.

Tourist Information for Cessnock and the whole Hunter Valley wine region: **Wine Country Tourist Information**, *Turner Park, Aberdare Rd, or PO Box 152, Cessnock NSW 2325; tel: (049) 90 4477.* Open 7 days 0900–1700; reservations.

ACCOMMODATION AND FOOD

Cumberland Motor Inn *(FL), 57 Cumberland St; tel: 90 6633;* **Cessnock Motel**, *13 Allandale Rd; tel: 90 2699;* **Hunter Valley Motel**, *30 Allandale Rd; tel: 91 2355;* **Neath Hotel**, *Cessnock Rd; tel: 30 4270;* **Country Comfort Inn Hunter Valley** *(CC), Dwyer St, Maitland 2320; tel: 32 5288;* **Endeavour Motel**, *New England Hwy, E. Maitland 2323; tel: 33 5488;* **Molly Morgan Motor Inn**, *New England Hwy, E. Maitland; tel: 33 5422;* **The Hunter Resort**, *Hermitage Rd, Pokolbin 2320; tel: 98 7777;* **Hermitage Lodge**, *corner McDonalds and Gillards Rds; tel: 98 7639;* **Hunter**

Country Lodge, *220 Branxton Rd; tel: 38 1744;* **Tallawanta Motel**, *Broke Rd; tel: 98 7854.*

The restaurants in any wine growing area tend to be superior in quality and this holds true for the Hunter, where several of the better restaurants are, in fact, part of the vinery. **Chez Pok** at Peppers, *Ekerts Rd, Pokolbin; tel: 98 78596,* won the 1994 Hunter Valley Tourism Award. **The Cottage Restaurant**, *Wollombi Rd, Cessnock; tel: 90 3062.* Licensed and BYO. Open Tues–Sat. **The Vines**, *Hunter Country Lodge, Cessnock-Braxton Rd; tel: 38 1744.* BYO. **Arnold's Restaurant**, *Pokolbin Village, Broke Rd, Pokolbin; tel: 98 7619,* features modern Australian cuisine. Open 7 days. **The Cellar Restaurant**, *McGuigan Hunter Village, Broke Rd; tel: 98 7584.* 7 days, BYO.

SIGHTSEEING

The mix of coal mining and wine to be found in the Hunter Valley is quite unusual.

The coal was discovered first. Then came the discovery that the red earth of the Hunter Valley produced some of the great red wines of the world, and so both industries grew up in curious juxtaposition.

Cessnock is an ideal centre for exploring the wine country. It is named after a castle in Ayrshire, Scotland, and has within its area twenty or so villages, all of which were once dedicated to mining. For the first half of this century, coal was the economic mainstay of the area. In 1824, well before coal was commercially mined on a large scale, wine-making was introduced to the area, and now there are some 7000 acres of vineyards in the Hunter. Most, but not all, of the mines in the Hunter Valley no longer operate while the vineyards expand and prosper.

For a suggested drive that will take in most of the major vineyards, leave Cessnock on the *Allandale Rd* – Rte 82. Turn left after the airstrip on to *Broke Rd* and stop at **Lake's Folly** *(tel: 98 7507)*, a vineyard started by a Sydney surgeon, Max Lake. Drive further along and again turn left on to *Palmers Lane*, where you will find four small vineyards. Left off *Palmers Lane* is the **Rothbury Estate** *(tel: 98 7555)*, which was started by a syndicate led by Australia's great wine celebrity, Len Evans.

Allandale Rd continues north and runs through **Rothbury**. On the left is the extension of *Deasys Rd*, which leads to three more vineyards. Soon *Allandale Rd* reaches the New England Hwy. You could, if you wished, make a quick detour to the right to the **Wyndham Estate** winery *(tel: 38 3444)*, which is open every day of the week. The main route continues to the left until you get to *Hermitage Rd* at **Belford**, where there is a tourist information centre. It is also the start of horseback and horse carriage vineyard tours – **Somerset Carriages** *(tel: 98 7591)*.

As you come down *Hermitage Rd* you pass the other end of *Deasys Rd* and the **Hunter Estate Winery** *(tel: 98 7777)*, which has visits every day by appointment. Pass the **Casuarina Restaurant and**

Country Inn, *Hermitage Rd; tel: 98 7888*, and continue until you join *Broke Rd*, which will take you back to Cessnock. Make a detour, turning in the opposite direction along *Broke Rd*, to the **Hungerford Hill Wine Village** *(tel: 98 7666)*, which has gone all out to cater for the tourist, with wine tastings, wine sales, an excellent restaurant and a motel on the premises. Further on in that direction is the **Tyrrell Winery** *(tel: 98 7509)*, a splendid example of a mid-size winery, run by the Tyrrell family.

On the return along *Broke Rd* you pass a dozen vineyards and restaurants, all well-sign posted. One vineyard – **McGuigan's** *(tel: 98 7402)* – has become a resort and leisure centre. *Broke Rd* ends at a crossroads, where there are three information centres. Turn right and drive towards the **Pokolbin Mountain Range**. In this area there are another dozen of some of the greatest vineyards in Australia. Turn back on to *Broke Rd* and you swing past Lake's Folly again, and then back to Cessnock. By my count, on this shortish trip – an easy half day's drive which could take two weeks if you were seriously sampling wines – you come within hailing distance of over forty vineyards, most of which encourage visits and cellar door sales. Bear in mind that wines in the bottle are heavy and a couple of cases in the boot of your car is a weight that you need to consider seriously.

That covers, in outline, the main Hunter Valley wine area. If you drive through Singleton and up to Muswellbrook on Rte 15, you come to the seven vineyards of the upper Hunter Valley.

Remember that if you are driving around the vineyards, after four cellar door wine tastings, your alcohol levels may be too high for safety, and it is, perhaps, better to join one of the many wine tours by coach.

The vintage time is normally around February, when the vignerons will be at their busiest bringing in the crop.

A short drive from the Upper Hunter Valley brings you right to the edge of the 488,060 hectares of the **Wollemi National Park** *(tel: 045 88 5247)*, which is the state's

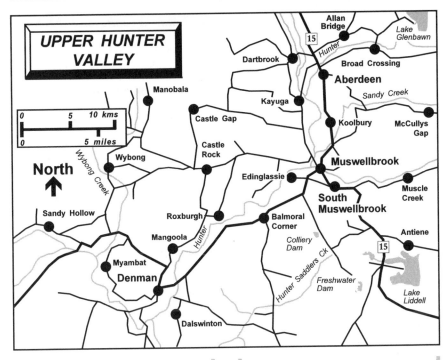

UPPER HUNTER VALLEY

North ↑

79

largest wilderness area, extending as it does from the Hunter River to the **Blue Mountains National Park**.

To the south west of Cessnock, about 32 km, lies the town of **Wollombi**, which is something of a historic treasure and has many sandstone buildings and old cottages that have been restored.

PORT STEPHENS

Port Stephens is about 60km north of Newcastle on the Newcastle F3 Freeway.

Tourist Information: Tourist Organisation of Port Stephens, *Victoria Parade; tel: (049) 81 1579.*

ACCOMMODATION AND FOOD

Central Motel, *corner Government Rd and Church St, Nelson Bay 2315; tel: 81 3393;* **Nelson Lodge Motel**, *Government Rd; tel: 81 1705;* **Marina Resort**, *33 Magnus St; tel: 1800 65 9949;* **Peninsula Motor Inn**, *52 Shoal Bay Rd; tel: 81 3366;* **Port Stephens Motor Lodge**, *corner Magnus and Fingal Sts;*

tel: 81 3366; **Dolphins Motel**, *Dixon Dr.; tel: 81 1176;* **The Anchorage Port Stephens**, *Corlette Point Rd, Corlette 2301; tel: 84 2555.*

Fishermans Wharf Family Restaurant, *Teramby Rd, Nelsons Bay; tel: 81 2977,* is open daily and has a main buffet. **Moffats Oyster Barn**, on the waterfront at *Swan Bay; tel: 97 5433,* is open 7 days and has sea views. **Scales Restaurant**, *106 Magnus St, Nelson Bay,* licensed and BYO, is open 7 nights and offers Hunter beef; *tel: 81 3278.* **Ketch's Restaurant**, *4th Floor Westbury's Marina Resort, 33 Magnus St, Nelson Bay; tel: 81 4400,* has stunning views. **Merretts**, *Corlette Point Rd, Corlette; tel: 84 25555,* is part of the Anchorage Port Stephens.

SIGHTSEEING

Port Stephens has a totally different look and feel. It is as if you are in another country. The white beaches of volcanic sand contrasting with dazzling blue waters make this look like tropical Australia.

The name may mislead you. It applies to the deep water inlet – two and a half times the size of Sydney harbour – coming in between Yacaaba and Tomaree Heads. The main anchorage of Port Stephens is **Nelson Bay**, and it is here that the fishing fleet ties up in the late afternoon.

The Port Stephens area has relatively little industry and is almost completely a holiday region. The white beaches lead into bush land, where there are fine displays of wild flowers in the spring. The waters of the bay are home all year round to bottlenose dolphins. Plainly most of the action in Port Stephens is centred on the water. Nelson Bay is on the south side of the Port Stephens inlet and has dozens of marinas, all offering boats for hire, ranging from power to houseboats. **Pro Dive** at the **D'Albora Marina** *(tel: 81 4331)* – one of the best known marinas in the area – offers 7 day a week scuba and snorkelling lessons in the clear waters. Big game fishing takes place outside of Port Stephens, beyond the heads where the waters of the ocean – as in Sydney Harbour – can be dangerous, especially to an inexperienced sailor. Charter fishing boats are available from, among others, **Kunara Charters**, *tel: 81 4178,* at the Halifax Park Kiosk, Little Beach.

This area is excellent for surfing and there are ocean beaches on each side which, when the wind and tides are right, produce surfing conditions the equal of anywhere in the world.

Oakvale Farm and Fauna World, at Salt Ash, *Nelson Bay Rd; tel: 82 6222,* has animal feeding at 1100 and 1400 each day and tame kangaroos wandering around the grounds. Open every day 1000–1700.

Tomaree National Park – *tel: 87 3108* – stretches along the coast line from Shoal Bay to Anna Bay and covers 896 hectares. There is only one signposted walk, but the park has a series of beaches separated by rocky headlands, behind which are heaths and forests. Sometimes fairy penguins come to the rocky headlands and dolphins are often seen in the waves. 🛦

MYALL LAKES

Tourist Information: Tea Gardens Visitors Centre, *Myall St; tel: (049) 97 0111.*

ACCOMMODATION AND FOOD

Bulahdelah Motor Lodge, *Pacific Hwy, Bulahdelah 2423; tel: 97 4520;* **The Pines Motel**, *Pacific Hwy; tel: 97 4274;* **Myall River Motor Inn**, *3 Yamba St, Hawks Nest 2324; tel: 97 0324;* **Beachfront Motor Inn**, *15 Beach Rd; tel: 97 0324;* **Club Inn Motel**, *Yalinbah St, Tea Gardens 2324; tel: 97 0911.*

Pinetta, *The Pines Motel, Pacific Hwy, Bulahdelah; tel: 97 4274,* open 7 nights a week.

SIGHTSEEING

For many Sydneysiders, Myall Lakes – *myall* is an Aboriginal word for a small, silver-grey wattle – is the preferred summer holiday spot. It is only 2½ hrs drive from Sydney – 220 km – and some of the distance is along the F3 Freeway. The **Myall Lakes National Park**, *tel: 87 3108 (Myall Lakes National Park offices at Raymond Terrace),* covers an area of 21,267 hectares. The water area alone – if you include Myall, Boolambyte and Two Mile Lakes, and Bombah Broadwater, which are all part of the lake system but counted as separate lakes – covers about half of the total area of the park. Indeed, this is the largest fresh water (using that term to include brackish water as well) system in the state. The National Park starts at **Hawks Nest** in the south and stretches all the way up to **Seal Rocks** in the north. Running into it is Myall River, which is in two sections. The Upper Myall starts in the **Craven State Forest** and runs between the **Bulahdelah State Forest** and the **Myall River State Forest**, where it then runs into **Bombah Broadwater**. When it comes out of Broadwater it runs parallel to the coast, with the **Mungo Track** running alongside. As it nears Hawks Nest it broadens at an area with the splendid name of **Pull for Nothing Bay** and then comes in between **Tea Gardens** and Hawks Nest, and opens out into Port Stephens – often mis-spelt Stevens on maps – Bay.

Most activities centre on the water, including sailing, windsurfing and water skiing, while along the 40 km of beach, stretching from

Mungo Beach in the south to Seal Rocks and beyond in the north, there is surfing, scuba diving and beach fishing. **Myall Lakes Houseboats**, *Bulahdelah; tel: 97 4221* and **Luxury Houseboats**, *Myall Marina, Bulahdelah; tel: 94 4495*, offer fully equipped houseboats from 2- to 12-berth for navigating the lakes.

Between the lakes and the beach is a wide area of sand dunes, where, in 1960, there were plans to extract sand. The area was declared a national park to stop any similar attempts. Off shore is **Broughton Island** and **Cabbage Tree Island**, which are both bird sanctuaries and part of the National Park.

Inland a series of footpaths have been developed by the National Parks and Wildlife Service, including the **Mungo Brush Rainforest Walk** and, for the fit, the 21 km walk which links Hawks Nest to Mungo Brush.

Myall Lakes contains a wide range of landforms, wildlife and vegetation. The beach dunes, some of which are over 100m high, are held together with sand grass. In spring the whole park is ablaze with flowers and there are stands of Banksias and paperbarks on the fringes of the lakes themselves. Among the mammals in the park are grey kangaroos, wallabies, possums, koalas and spiny ant eaters, and the whole area is a bird paradise.

Access to the park is by way of the Pacific Hwy at Tea Gardens and Hawks Nest, or turn off at Bulahdelah along *Lakes Rd* to reach Bombah Point. Then turn off along the *Lakes Way*, north of Bulahdelah.

In the south of the park lie the twin towns of Tea Gardens and Hawks Nest, linked together by a bridge, which are well-equipped to cater for visitors, with accommodation, restaurants, boat hire, cruises and many walks and lookouts. There are two main beaches for these towns – **Bennetts**, which is an ocean beach and **Jimmy's**, which is a bay beach.

Although it is now a sleepy town, in the last century Hawks Nest was a relatively important shipbuilding town, but the industry was moved to Nelson Bay as the local stands of useable timber were cleared. Beyond the town, curving around Providence Bay until it nearly gets to Cabbage Tree Island, is **Yaccaba Lookout**, which has splendid views of the whole coastline as well as the off shore islands. Two kilometres down the road from Hawks Nest, where Kore Creek comes out to Port Stephens Bay, is a minute village which rejoices in the name of **Winda Woppa**.

Nearby **Seal Rocks** is something very special. You get there by driving down *Seal Rocks Rd*, which runs off the Lakes Hwy. The road is not sealed all the way, although this is promised in the near future. There is a steep footpath to the **Seal Rocks lighthouse**, which was built in 1875 and gives you wonderful views of the coast and access to **Lighthouse Beach** below. There is a caravan site and petrol is available, but apart from that there is nothing, except a most glorious stretch of coast with Seal Rocks, one of the great scuba diving spots of New South Wales, just off the coast. It is known as one of the most beautiful spots of coastline in the state and is accorded a status that almost amounts to reverence.

Tourist Information: Forster Visitors Centre, *Little St; tel (065) 54 8499.*

ACCOMMODATION AND FOOD

Fiesta Motor Inn, *corner Head and West Sts; tel: 54 6177;* **Forster Motor Inn**, *23-25 Head St; tel: 54 6877;* **Bella Villa Motor Inn**, *19 Lake St; tel: 54 6842;* **Golden Sands Motor Inn**, *6 Head St; tel: 54 6222;* **Great Lakes Motor Inn**, *corner West and Head Sts; tel: 54 6955;* **Jasmine Lodge**, *18 Wallis St; tel: 54 9838;* **Wallis Lake Motel**, *5 Wallis St; tel: 55 5600;* **Lakes and Ocean Hotel**, *10 Little St; tel: 54 6006;* **HI: Dolphin Lodge**, *43 Head St; tel: 55 8155.*

Contasia Family Buffet Restaurant, *Forster Bowling Club, Strand St; tel: 54 5488.* Open 7 days. **Pancake Place**, *Little St; tel: 54 7824.* Overlooking Wallis Lake, open 7 days. **Silhouettes Restaurant**, *12 Beach St, Tuncurry; tel: 54 5751.* Dinner 7 nights. BYO. **The Little Mermaid**, *98 Manning St; tel: 55 5144.* Australian and Scandinavian food. Dinner 7 days, lunch most days, BYO. **Little Snail**, *26 Wallis St; tel: 55 6355.* Seafood specialities. Dinner 7 days. BYO.

SIGHTSEEING

Named after the premier of New South Wales in 1860 and always pronounced 'Foster' by the locals, Forster is, with its twin town, **Cloncurry**, the entrance to the **Wallis Lake Recreation Area**. Running between the two towns is Cape Hawke Harbour, which connects the lake with the sea, and the two towns are connected by a road bridge. The lake runs south from Forster parallel to the sea, with the **Seven Mile Beach** and *Lakes Way* separating the two. Forster's climate is best described as semi-tropical.

You can drive right around Wallis Lake, heading south on the Seven Mile Beach and then turning inland towards **Coomba Park**. If, instead of turning inland, you head south for 2 km, you come to the smaller **Smith's Lake**, which is separated from the sea by Sandbar Beach and offers swimming in calm, warm and protected water.

Back on the road around Wallis Lake from Coomba Park, work your way along back roads to the Pacific Hwy, and then continuing north to **Nabiac** and turning east towards the sea and back to *Lakes Way,* go through **Tuncurry** over the bridge to Forster.

Wallis Lake is large, shallow and salt water. It is fed by the Wallamba, Wang Wauk and, most importantly, the Coolongolook rivers. It supports a fishing and oyster industry and there is a very wide range of water-based recreational activities available, including lake cruises, dolphin viewing, fishing charters, houseboat, boat and water ski facilities. The fish caught are bream, flathead, whiting and mulloway. Scuba diving is very popular on the nearby coral outcrops.

Cruising is widely available with houseboats of different sizes available from **Forster Luxury Houseboats**, *Little St (tel: 54 7733)* and daily cruises offered by **Lake Cruise Forster** *(tel: 55 2225).*

Within easy reach of the town is a series of quite magnificent beaches, which never get seriously crowded, not even in the height of the holiday season. The beaches, called **Nine Mile**, stretching from Tuncurry to **Halliday's Point**, are, of course, not nine miles long. On the northern side of the entrance to Cape Hawke

Harbour is the Bar at Tuncurry, which is fine for surfers and has a rock pool, which is ideal for children. **Forster Main Beach** is patrolled during the season and there are ocean baths at the southern end. **One Mile Beach** is also patrolled during the season while nearby **Burgess Beach** is small, quiet and reached by a steep path, which ensures that it is normally quite deserted.

Horse riding through the Kiwarrak Forest, 20 mins from Forster at Possum Brush, is offered at the **Clarendon Forest Retreat**, *tel: 54 3162.*

The town is of relatively recent date as the area was only seriously surveyed for settlement in 1869. Originally it was to be called Minimbah but was changed to Forster for political reasons.

There was a major timber industry in the region, which fed a shipbuilding industry, but this came to an end after World War II.

Forster has a **Vintage Car Museum**, *tel: 55 4800,* 3 km to the south and 13 km outside the town. Open 7 days 0900–1700. On the shores of Wallis Lake at **Tiona** is the 'green cathedral', created by arching trees. On *Wang Wauk Rd* is the **Grandis**, which is the tallest tree in the state. Of special interest is **Tobwabba Tours and Art**, an Aboriginal-owned enterprise, which organises tours to significant Aboriginal sites and ends with a visit to the Tobwabba Art studios. The tour takes 4 hrs and the studio is open Mon–Fri 0900–1600 *(tel: 55 5411).*

PORT MACQUARIE

Tourist Information: Port Macquarie Tourism, *corner Clarence Hwy*; *tel: (065) 83 1293.*

ACCOMMODATION AND FOOD

Sails Resort, *Park St, Port Macquarie 2444; tel: 83 3999*; **Country Comfort Inn** *(CC), corner Buller and Hollingsworth Sts; tel: 83 2955*; **Beachfront Regency Motor Inn**, *40 William St; tel: 83 2244*; **Sandcastle Motel**, *20 William St; tel: 83 3522*;

Palm Court Motor Inn *(BW), 138 William St; tel: 83 5155*; **Port Aloha Motel**, *3 School St; tel: 83 1455*; **Aquatic Motel**, *Hastings River Dr.; tel: 83 7388*; **Bel Air Motel**

(BU), 179 Gordon St; tel: 83 2177; **HI***, 40 Church St; tel: 83 5512.*
Spinnakers Restaurant at Sails Resort*; tel: 83 3999,* harbour views, open 7 days, licensed. **Riverview Terrace***; tel: 84 4446* overlooks the water, open lunch and dinner Tues–Sun. **Cray's***, at Fisherman's Wharf; tel: 87 1321.* BYO. **Patsy's Place,** *Hay St; tel 84 1143.* Grills and seafood. BYO.

SIGHTSEEING

Port Macquarie, 423 km north of Sydney, can be regarded as three separate destinations, all within 20 mins of each other. To the south lies **Camden Haven** – seaside, the quiet life, holiday accommodation – and to the west and inland is the timber town **Wauchope**, alongside the Hastings River. Port Macquarie itself, founded in 1821 and thus one of the oldest towns in the state, is one of the most important fishing ports on the east coast, as well as being very much a holiday town, based at the mouth of the Hastings River. It has all the attributes of the seaside, with camel rides on the beach – **Coastal Camel Safaris***, tel: 83 7650* – and a 6-acre theme park called **Fantasy Glades** on Parklands Close, which is a great favourite with children. There are cruises up the Hastings River – **Pelican Tours***, tel: 018 652 171* and **Everglades Tours** which you can book at the Tourism centre. **The King Neptune Marine Park**, at the mouth of the river, has seals, dolphins and sharks. Between the town and **Shelly Beach** is the 72-hectare reserve of coastal rain forest called **Sea Acres Rainforest Centres***, tel: 82 3355,* which has a raised boardwalk running through the tree canopies.

Two places to see koalas are **Kingfisher Park***, off the Oxley Hwy; tel: 81 0783* and **Billabong Koala Park***, just past the Pacific Hwy cross-over; tel: 85 1060.* Both open daily.

Port Macquarie has an extensive canal development, which exists so that houses can be sold with water access. This is formed by a series of parallel canals running back from the shore. Next to this canal development is **Settlement City**, which is a shopping area containing everything from the RSL to the up-market **Sails Resort** *(tel: 83 3999)* to McDonalds.

Nearby **Wauchope**, named after Captain Wauch who farmed there from 1841, and pronounced war hope, was, and is, a timber town. It is also now the base for a reconstructed 1880 timber town. This is 3 km to the west of the new town and has steam train rides, demonstrations of working timber machinery, bullock teams and horse-drawn wagons. Wauchope also contains one of those amazing Australian icons which litter and despoil the landscape – a massive model – this time of a bull. It is ugly, not very well made or accurate, and Wauchope is very proud of it. It is, so they tell anyone who is willing to listen, the world's largest fibreglass bull.

Near Wauchope is the **Bellangry State Forest**, with splendid stands of hardwood trees.

Camden Haven, 44 km south of Port Macquarie, is formed by three villages – Laurietown, North Haven and Dunbogan. This is an anglers' paradise. Just outside the town, on **North Brother Mountain**, is a lookout with panoramic views of the area.

KEMPSEY AND SOUTH WEST ROCKS

Tourist Information: Kempsey Tourist Information Centre, *South Kempsey Park; tel: (065) 63 1555.*

ACCOMMODATION AND FOOD

All Nations Hallmark Inn *(FL), 320 Pacific Hwy; tel: 62 1284;* **City Centre Motel***, 95 Smith St; tel: 62 7733;* **Colonial Court Motor Inn** *(BW), 155 Smith St; tel: 62 6711;* **Macleay Valley Motor Inn** *(BW), 465 Pacific Hwy; tel: 62 6988;* **Moon River Motel** *(BU), 157 Pacific Hwy; tel: 62 8077;* **Park Drive Motel***, 161 Pacific Hwy; tel: 62 1361;* **Bay Motel***, Prince of Wales Ave, South West Rocks 2431; tel: 66 6909;* **Costa Rica Motel Resort***, 134 Gregory St; tel: 66 6330;* **South West Rocks Motel***, Gregory St; tel: 66 6330.*

Kempsey Chinese Restaurant*, Smith St, Kempsey; tel: 62 5684.* Open 7 days. **Geppy's Restaurant***, 7 Paragon Ave, South West Rocks; tel: 66 6196.* Wed night live jazz. **The Kiosk***, Trial Bay.* Open 7 days from 0800. Indoor and outdoor eating with views over the bay; *tel: 66 7100.*

SIGHTSEEING

Named after the town of Kempsey in Worcestershire, England by Enoch Rudder, a Sydney merchant, Kempsey is the gateway to the Macleay valley, and to what is called the Holiday Coast. The latter is one of the many efforts of tourist boards around Australia to try and identify their area with a name like Sunshine Coast, Holiday Coast, Paradise Coast, and so on. By and large, the locals totally ignore these appellations.

Kempsey, on the Pacific Hwy, is very well positioned. The **Macleay River** wends its way down to the sea through beautiful forests and rural land to the coast, where it bisects the town. Like almost every other similar town in Australia, it boasts the best year round climate. It is true that it is always pleasant. The Macleay river, as it goes through Kempsey, affords some splendid vistas – the **Riverside Park** is home to a large family of geese.

A central part of Kempsey is the **Aboriginal Heritage and the Djigay Centre**, adjacent to the TAFE college. This has a **Traditional Food Tree Park**, through which you can wander with an Aboriginal guide *(tel: 66 2332)*. There is a strong art scene in Kempsey, both Aboriginal and western, with several galleries. Slim Dusty, one of the icons of Australian folk music, was born here, and every September there is a traditional music festival.

The Kempsey Cultural Centre has been referred to as the 'first Australian building' – a compliment – and houses the tourist centre, a settler's cottage and a museum with a display tracing the story of the Maitland valley. **Boatman's Cottage**, *Ocean Dr., South West Rocks,* open from 1000 daily, has local arts and crafts presented by the South West Rocks Art and Craft Association. Along the coast the beaches are quite remarkable, with the **Arakoon State Recreation Area**, the **Hat Head National Park**, the **Goolawah Reserve** and the **Limeburners Creek Nature Reserve**, all offering clean beaches, clean water, miles of uninterrupted coast and, when the wind is in the right quarter, magnificent surfing. **Crescent Head** provides some of the best surfing in Australia and is the site of the annual **Malibu Classic**.

Skin diving is also well catered for and the base for most diving activity is the small resort of South West Rocks. Because of the close proximity of the Continental Shelf, there are clean, warm semi-tropical waters to dive in for most of the year. **Fish Rock Dive Centre**, *328 Gregory St, South West Rocks; tel: 66 6614,* does a daily dive charter and offers full Scuba courses, as does **South West Rocks Dive Centre**, *100 Gregory St, South West Rocks; tel: 66 6474.*

Deep sea fishing is catered for by **Trial Bay Deep Sea Fishing Charters**; *tel: 015 256 556.*

Trial Bay Gaol, near South West Rocks, 20 km north of Kempsey by way of the Jerseyville Bridge – *tel: (063) 66 6168;* open 0900–1700 daily – is in the Arakoon State Recreation Area. The gaol was built in 1886 but has now been transformed into a museum.

NAMBUCCA HEADS

Tourist information: Nambucca Valley Information Centre, *4 Pacific Hwy; tel. (065) 68-6954.*

ACCOMMODATION AND FOOD

Destiny Motor Inn, *corner Pacific Hwy and Riverside Dr.; tel: 68 8044;* **Miramar Motel**, *Old Pacific Hwy; tel: 68 7899;* **The Nambucca Resort** *(GC), Pacific Hwy; tel: 68 6899;* **Max Motel**, *4 Fraser St; tel: 68 6138;* **Nambucca Motor Inn** *(BU), Pacific Hwy;* tel: *68 6300;* **Blue Dolphin Motel**, *Fraser St; tel: 68 6700.*

Kel's Matilda Restaurant, *Wellington Dr.; tel: 68 6024,* serves what is called 'Fair dinkum cuisine', Mon–Sat. BYO. **Golden Sands Bistro**, *Golden Sands Hotel; tel: 68 6000.* Open 7 days lunch and dinner. **Sawasdee Thai**, *4 Pacific Hwy; tel: 68 9622.* Dinner Mon–Sat. BYO. **Blue Water Brasserie**, *V-Wall Tavern; tel: 68 6394.* Open 7 days.

SIGHTSEEING

Nambucca Heads – at one time spelled Nambucra – is on the coast, facing the Tasman Sea, equi-distant between South West Rocks and Coffs Harbour, and 553 km north of Sydney. It is on the mouth of the **Nambucca River**, which was the reason for the

84

establishment of the settlement. Some of the first European settlers in the area came in 1840 and were ticket-of-leave men – convicts leased on patrol to find and log cedar. The logs were originally taken out overland but were later floated down the Nambucca River and then taken by sailing vessels to Sydney. After the timber fellers came agriculture and by 1867 the site of the town had been established. Soon there was ship building in the area but eventually this disappeared along with the forests and was replaced by dairying, banana plantations and beef. The port was expanded with the addition of a breakwater in 1895.

Nambucca Heads is on the north bank of the river, with the long run of Forster Beach running down to Scotts Head on the other side. On the seaward side of the town is **Beilbys Beach**, which is patrolled in the season and extends south to **Shelly Beach**, which is protected from the sea by Cliffy Point. Just inland from the beach is **Captain Cook Lookout**, which provides excellent views of the area. Even more impressive is the view from the **Yarrahapinni Lookout**, where on a clear day you can see forever.

Crafters Cottage Co-operative, on the Pacific Hwy, 10 km south of Nambucca Heads, exhibits the work of 30 local craftsmen. **The Headland Historical Museum**, *Mainbeach Headland; tel: 68 6380*, is operated by the Nambucca District Historical Society and has displays telling the history of the area. Open 1400–1600 Wed, Sat, Sun.

Close to Nambucca Heads is a major Australian icon. Gordon Parson wrote a song in the 1950s about *A Pub with No Beer*, which was recorded by Slim Dusty and became a hit, not only in Australia, but also overseas. The pub with no beer exists, although the beer supplies have been replenished. To get there go south out of town on the Pacific Hwy and at **Macksville South** turn inland and follow the signs for about 20 km to the **Taylors Arms**; *tel: 64 2101*.

Graffiti has become a pestilence in Australia as it has elsewhere, but Nambucca Heads actually welcomes it on its **Vee Wall Breakwater** on the river, which has become almost a work of art if you don't read the messages. To get

there drive from the town centre through the **Gordon Park rain forest** to the foreshores of the river.

In the middle of the river is Stuart Island, which has the **Nambucca Heads Island Golf Course** *(tel: 69 4111)*, claimed, with considerable justification, to be the only golf course in Australia that is totally surrounded by water.

Escorted four-wheel-drive tours of the area are available from **Nambucca 4WD Tours** *(tel: 68 9963)*. In direct contrast there is a major **Model Train System** on display at *24 Pelican Crescent; tel: 68 7395*. Open Sat 1400–1630 and the same times daily during school holidays or by arrangement.

COFFS HARBOUR

Tourism Information: Coffs Harbour Future, *Marcia St; tel. (066) 52 1522.*

ACCOMMODATION AND FOOD

Aanuka Beach Resort, *Firman Dr., Diggers Beach 2450; tel: 52 7555*; **Pelican Beach Travelodge Resort**, *Pacific Hwy; tel: 53 7000*; **Novotel Opal Cove Resort**, *Pacific Hwy; tel: 51 0510*; **Chelsea Motor Inn**, *106 Grafton St; tel: 52 2977*; **Coffs Harbour Motor Inn**, *22 Elizabeth St; tel: 52 6388*; **Zebra Motel** *(BW)*, *27 Grafton St; tel: 52 1588*; **Town Lodge Motor Inn**, *110 Grafton St; tel: 52 1288*; **Park Beach Resort**, *111 Park Beach Rd; tel: 52 4511*; **Aquajet Motel**, *49 Park Beach Rd; tel: 52 6588*; **HI**, *110 Albany St; tel: 52 6462*.

Deckchairs Bar and Restaurant, *Rydge's Nautilus on the Beach, Pacific Hwy N.; tel: 53 6699*. Open 7 days, licensed. Panoramic views out to sea. **Seafood Mama's**, *between Pelican and Nautilus, Pacific Hwy North; tel: 53 6733*. Lunch Wed–Fri. Dinner 7 nights. Licensed. **Shores**, *Pelican Beach Travelodge, Pacific Hwy N.* Open 7 days, licensed. **Windmill Restaurant**, *1 Pacific Hwy, South Coffs Harbour; tel: 52 2933.* Licensed. Open dinner Mon–Sat. Inside an authentic Dutch windmill.

SIGHTSEEING

The name is misspelled. It was John Korff who found shelter here in about 1847, and who opened a general store. But the surveyors of the day could not get his name right and Coffs

85

Harbour it became. Originally it was two small towns set 3 km apart, but over the years the two grew together.

Unique to Coffs Harbour is the **Big Banana**, which is one of those over-large models which, strangely, are seen by Australian town councils as being a tourist attraction. Yes, it does remind you that bananas are a major crop – in fact, this area is the biggest banana producing region in Australia – but the **Big Banana Leisure Park** *(tel. 52 4355)*, on the Pacific Hwy 3 km north of the town, seems to be somewhat tacky. There is a zoo, 10 mins north of the town, which has a colony of Australian animals, including koalas, flying foxes and dingoes. The **Historical Museum** is in the *High St* to the north of the City Centre Mall *(tel: 52 5794)*, and it tells the story of how the area was developed, first for cedar, then for sugar and finally for bananas and tourists.

There are several excellent picnic spots in and around Coffs Harbour. One favourite is **Sealy Lookout** – drive about 1 km past the Big Banana and then follow the signs through banana plantations to the look-out, which has wonderful views to the north and south over Coffs Harbour and the coast. From Coffs Harbour you can go white water rafting on the Nymboida River with **Wildwater Adventures** *(tel: 53 4469)*, which is thrilling, extremely wet, but with the competent operators in the area, extremely safe. There are also four-wheel-drive tours with **4WD Adventure Safaris** *(tel: 53 6686)* to the rain forest and waterfalls in the hinterland and **Bushland Trail Rides** *(tel: 49 4530)*, which offers rides daily from 0630–1730.

The **Butterfly House** *(tel: 53 4766)* has one of the world's largest displays of live Australian butterflies in a rain forest setting and also has a built-in maze.

The **South Coast Regional Botanical Garden**, off the *High St* on the banks of Coffs Creek and part of the Coffs Creek Walkway, was opened in 1988, and is one of the great attractions of Coffs Harbour. With Coffs Creek on three sides, it has, among other attractions, a mangrove boardwalk and a bird hide in the rain forest setting. At the northern end of the harbour is **Muttonbird Island**, which has a

footpath with superb views of the city, the coast and the hills behind. The equivalent of a National Park at sea, the **Solitary Islands Marine Reserve** is at the very tip of the Great Barrier Reef, and is a place where the confluence of tropical and temperate currents meet to create a perfect breeding place for fish, resulting in a phenomenal, diverse range of marine life. There are twenty good surfing beaches within easy reach of Coffs Harbour.

GRAFTON

Tourist Information: Clarence River Tourist Association, *Pacific Hwy, South Grafton; tel: (066) 42 4677.*

ACCOMMODATION AND FOOD

Fitzroy Motel *(FL), 27 Fitzroy St; tel: 42 4477;* **Key Lodge Motel**, *37 Fitzroy St; tel: 42 1944;* **Civic Motel**, *153 Pound St; tel: 42 4922;* **Roches Family Hotel**, basic, *85 Victoria St; tel: 42 2866.*

Fountain Court Chinese Restaurant, *135 Prince St; tel: 43 1411.* Open 7 nights. Licensed. **Stornelli's**, *Parkview Hotel, Princes St; tel: 42 2402.* Open Tues–Sat. Licensed. Italian cuisine. **Bridge Steakhouse**, *Fitzroy St; tel: 42 1944.* Open Mon–Sat. Licensed. **Copper Grill**, *Royal Tavern, Pound St; tel: 43 2944.* Licensed. Mon–Sat. **Crown Hotel**, *1 Prince St; tel: 43 2944.* Open 7 days. Licenced.

SIGHTSEEING

This town, 660 km north of Sydney and 320 km south of Brisbane, has been called one of the most graceful urban scenes in provincial Australia. It is divided and dominated by the **Clarence River**, which starts in the McPherson Ranges of southern Queenstown and eventually ends up 400 km later at **Yamba** on the coast. There was no bridge across the river until 1932, when the current double deck bridge was built. Grafton is famous for its trees and is often called the Jacaranda city. In 1866, in an early demonstration of conservation policies, the town council decided to consider by-laws for the planting and preservation of trees, with the result there are now well over 7000 trees in Grafton, the most famous of them being the jacaranda. A **Jacaranda Festival** has been held every spring – the last Saturday in October – since 1935.

The Clarence Valley was discovered by Europeans, when an escaped convict, Richard Craig, came across what he called 'the big river'. He received a reward of £100 and a remission of much of his sentence.

Many of the buildings in Grafton are classified by the National Trust, including the **Christ Church Cathedral**, designed by John Horbury Hunt in the Gothic style in 1884 – open seven days 0700–1730 – and the notorious **Grafton Gaol**. Many of the old homesteads have been preserved and the council has bought and restored **Schaeffer House**, *192 Fitzroy St*, which now has an exhibition by the Grafton Historical Society (open Tues–Thurs, 1300–1600 and Sun 1400–1600). The council has also acquired **Prentice House**, *158 Fitzroy St*, which now houses the regional art gallery. Open Wed–Sun 1000–1600.

Next to the main street and the Memorial Park lies the 60 hectare **Susan Island**, named after the boat which brought the first group of wood fellers in 1838. The northern end is covered by a section of rain forest, which houses what is claimed to be the largest bat colony in Australia. There is a footpath and access is by boat or canoe, **Kingfisher Adventures**, *tel: 43 2866*.

There are 24 parks within Grafton, of which the best situated is perhaps **Memorial Park**, overlooking Susan Island and the river. Within an hour's drive of Grafton there are several National Parks, including the 20,032 hectare **Yuraygir** (*tel: 42 0613*), the 17,679 hectare **Bundjalung** (*tel: 28 1177*) on the coast, **Washpool** – which is World Heritage listed – and the **Gibraltar Range** to the west. To the south-west are the **Guy Fawkes River** and, 40 km from Grafton, **Nymboida National Park**, which is difficult to get to.

BALLINA

Tourist Information: Ballina Information Centre, *corner River St and Las Balsa Plaza; tel: (066) 86 3484.*

ACCOMMODATION AND FOOD

All Seasons Motor Inn *(FL), 301 Pacific Hwy;*

tel: 86 2922; **Ballina Beach Resort**, *corner Compton Dr. and Cedar Crescent; tel: 86 8888;* **Ballina Palms Motor Inn**, *corner Bentinck and Owen Sts; tel: 86 4477;* **Richmond Motor Inn**, *227 River St; tel: 86 9100;* **Ballina Centre Point Motel**, *285 River St; tel: 86 6877;* **HI: Ballina Traveller's Lodge**, *36 Tamar St; tel: 86 6737;* **Cubana Motel**, *329 River St; tel: 86 6366;* **Suntori Motel**, *Pacific Hwy; tel: 86 2099.*

Shelley's on the Beach serves breakfast and lunch, Mon–Sun. This is a café above Shelly Beach, with marvellous views out to sea. **Sabis Italiano Ristorante**, *Moon St; tel: 86 7119.* BYO.

SIGHTSEEING

No one is sure where the name Ballina comes from. James Ainsworth settled there in 1847 and he said that the town was called Bullenah, which he thought might have some connection with fish or oysters. As the town is at the mouth of the Richmond River, and has grown through fishing and tourism, this is quite possible. There is also a town in Ireland with the name Ballina, but no connection has ever been established. The town is on the Pacific Hwy and is cut by The Canal and the North Creek, which separates East Ballina from the sea. The climate is sub-tropical and since it is surrounded by water and beaches, Ballina is an ideal tourist resort. Sadly, on the approach to Ballina, there is another of those grotesque, over-large models – this time **The Big Prawn**.

The **Richmond River** was discovered by Europeans in 1828, when Captain Henry Rous sailed there in HMS *Rainbow* and then explored up the river in a ship's boat.

The first European inhabitants were cedar-fellers, who arrived in 1842, and the town was originally called Deptford. In 1889, the government had breakwaters built and the name was changed to Ballina. On display in the town are some amazing vessels. The first is on display in the **Ballina Maritime Museum** *(tel: 81 1002)* and is the raft that was sailed from South America – *La Balsa* – leaving Guayaquil in Ecuador in 1973, carrying a four man crew. It reached the Australian coast after a voyage lasting 178 days and came ashore at Ballina. Also in

87

the town are the pilot vessel *Richmond* and the river boat *Florrie*, which was built in 1880.

You can go cruising in a more modern vessel in the MV **Richmond Princess**, *tel: 018 664 784*, which has 2 hr cruises on Wed, Thur, Sun. The MV **Bennelong** *(tel: 018 664 552)* also has a variety of cruises up the river, including one to Lismore. **Ballina Quays Marina** *(tel: 86 4249)* has houseboats to rent.

In East Ballina is **Shaw's Bay Hotel**, *tel: 86 0234*, (originally called Fenwick House), built of granite with a slate roof, which has a beautiful red cedar dining room and a staircase made from local timber, which was, in fact, carved in Spain. Open daily 1000–2200. Also in Ballina is the **Tropical Fruit Research Station** *(tel: 28 0604)*, which is open to the public.

A short way north of Ballina, along the coast road, is **Lake Ainsworth**, which is a freshwater lake and is safe for children. West of Ballina, on the *Lismore Rd*, is **Alstonville**, which has in its centre **Lumley Park**. This is a remnant of the sub-tropical rain forest which thrived in this area with its basalt volcanic soil. It contains Moreton Bay figs, white booyong, yellowwood and bumby ash. It was in this environment that the red cedar grew and thrived, but was cut down by the early settlers as a cash crop and was, indeed, responsible for much of the European settlement of this area. Alstonville also houses the **National Parks and Wildlife Service** office for the area – *tel: 28 1177*.

BYRON BAY

Tourist Information; Byron Bay Tourist Information Centre, *80 Jonson St, tel: (066) 85 8050.*

ACCOMMODATION AND FOOD

Byron Bay Waves Motel, *35 Lawson St; tel: 85 5966*; **Byron Bay Holiday Inn Motel**, *45 Lawson St; tel: 85 6373*; **Cape Byron Resort**, *16 Lawson St; tel: 85 7663*; **Bay Beach Motel**, *32 Lawson St; tel: 85 6090*; **Byron Motor Lodge**, *corner Lawson and Butler Sts; tel: 856522*; **Byron Sunseeker Motel**, *100 Bangalow Rd; tel: 85 7369*; **Bay Mist Motel**, *12 Bay St; tel: 85 6121*; **Belongil by the Sea Motel**, *4 Childe St; tel: 85 8111*; **HI: Cape Byron Hostel** *corner Byron and Middleton Sts; tel: 85 8788*; **HI: J's Bay Hostel**, *7 Carlyle St; tel: 85 3057*.

This is a wonderland for vegetarians as it is full of vegetarian restaurants but, sadly, they come and go and you must make your own discoveries when you get there. So strong is the feeling of the Byron Bay community against crass commercialism that there is not, as yet, a single example of an international fast food chain in the town.

Beach Café, *overlooking Clarks Beach*, serves a super breakfast, which is only excelled by the view. **Misake Byron**, *Fletcher St; tel: 85 7966*. BYO. 7 days. **Fig Tree**, *Sunrise Lane, off McGettigan's Lane; tel: 84 7273*. Open Thur–Sat. BYO. **Mexican Micks**, *Jonson St*. Dinner Tues–Thur. Cheap. Licensed.

SIGHTSEEING

This is as far east as you can go in Australia without falling off the edge. It is a mecca for many people in Sydney who drive or fly up here as often as they can. It is a magic area with dolphins in the water, whales cruising past at the right seasons of the year and a very special life style. No one in Sydney ever has a bad word to say about Byron Bay. In a sense it is the capital of the alternative Australian world and has always attracted the group that wants to drop out. But it is much more than that and its relaxed life style, superb surfing beaches and numerous walks make it an ideal holiday destination. So ideal that it is impossibly crowded during Christmas and the January school holidays. It is 802 km from Sydney and close to the Queensland Border – 100 km to the Gold Coast – so it has a sub-tropical climate and is mild all year round.

Byron Bay is another town that grew up to service the cedar fellers and a large jetty was built in 1888, four years after the town was named officially. This jetty was never properly protected from the sea and in 1921 the *Wollongbar*, a steamer that carried passengers and goods, was torn from its moorings and sunk. Parts of the wreck can still be seen off Main Beach. After the fishing fleet was seriously damaged in the storm of 1954, it was relocated to **Brunswick Heads** and Byron Bay effectively ceased to be a port.

Byron Bay has yet to come completely to terms with tourism. It would like it – but not too obtrusively. Thus all high rise buildings are banned. **Club Med** had a long and fruitless battle to try to establish a resort here. The local residents, possibly because of the strong influence of the alternative life style, tolerate tourists, are very friendly, but are not out to gouge a tourist dollar. The result is that this seaside town is charming, laid-back and extremely pleasant, even if it lacks five-star hotels.

The name has a connection with the poet Byron. Captain Cook named it after Captain John Byron, the grandfather of the poet, who circumnavigated the globe in HMS *Dolphin* in 1764, and had thus ventured into the Pacific before Captain Cook.

Just 2 km to the south-east of the town is the **Byron Bay Lighthouse**, which has superb views and walks that lead to Watego's Beach (see below), and right out onto the very tip of the headland. This is the perfect spot to watch dolphins playing in the clear water below or spot the whales on their annual migration. There are goats running wild on the headland around the lighthouse. They were originally kept there to feed the lighthouse keepers but now run wild. It is possible to stay in the **Lighthouse Keepers' Cottages**, which have walls so thick that once inside there is absolute silence. (*Bookings; tel: 85 6222.*)

Below the headland is **Watego's Beach**, a surfing mecca in Australia. It is the only beach on the whole of the eastern seaboard that faces north, and, although well sheltered from the wind, it often has the long rolling breakers coming in, which are ideal for surfing.

In the bay, running north towards Brunswick Heads, is the **Julian Rocks Aquatic and Nature Reserve**, which is a major attraction for scuba divers. It is here that the tropical waters from the Coral Sea stream down and collide with the temperate southern waters, and such a convergence always produces a wealth of marine life. As a result it is considered one of the best ten diving sites in Australia. Julian was the name of one of Captain Cook's nephews. **Byron Bay Dive Centre**, *9 Lawson St; tel: 85 7149,* is one of several organisations catering to divers.

Running south from the headland towards Broken Head is **Tallow Beach**, which is 7 km long, golden, windswept and, outside school holidays and summer weekends, frequently deserted. In all, there are 37 km of beaches around Byron Bay, so you need never feel crowded.

The **Byron Environment Centre**, *Cavannah Arcade, Jonson St; tel: 85 70766,* is a good source of information on the area. Hanggliding is a major sport at Byron Bay and **Flight Zone** *(tel: 85 3178)* offers tuition and tandem flights. There are also ultra-light aircraft flights offered by **Skylimit** *(tel: 84 3616),* which cost around $80 for 30 mins.

Back inland from Byron Bay is **Bangalow**, which is right on the edge of the remnant of rain forest known as **The Big Scrub**. Further back into the interior again is the **Booyong Nature Reserve**. In fact, within an easy hour's drive from Byron Bay, there are eight National Parks and 26 Nature Reserves. The Byron Tourist Information Centre has maps and information on all these places.

TWEED HEADS

Tourist Information: Tweed Visitors Centre, *Wharf St; tel: (07) 5536 4244.*

ACCOMMODATION AND FOOD

Las Vegas Motor Inn *(GC), 123 Wharf St, tel: 5536 3144;* **Blue Pelican Motel**, *115 Pacific Hwy; tel: 5536 1777;* **Cooks Endeavour Motor Inn**, *26 Frances St; tel: 553 5399;* **Jack Hi Motel**, *Brett St; tel: 5536 1788;* **Fairlight Motor Inn**, *91 Pacific Hwy; tel: 5536 2633;* **Homestead Tweed Motel**, *58 Boyd St; tel: 5536 1544;* **Murwillumbah Motor Inn**, *17 Byangum Rd, Murwillumbah 2484; tel: (066) 72 2022;* **Poinciana Motel**, *corner Pacific Hwy and Rose St; tel: (066) 72 3666;* **Tweed River Motel**, *55 Pacific Hwy; tel: (066) 72 3933.*

First, a most unusual experience. **Mother Nature's Bush Tucker**, *75 Upper Duroby Creek Rd, North Tumbulgum; tel: 5590 9826,* offers bush food survival kits of 20 local native bush food plants, so that you can grow your own. This is, fortunately, followed by morning tea with home-made scones and cream.

Fishermans Cove, *Coral St; tel: 5536 1646.* Mon–Sat. **Outside Inn**, *21 Wharf St, Tweed Heads; tel: 5536 6558.* Ocean views. Dinner 7 nights. **Thai Star**, *5 Griffith St, Coolangatta; tel: 5536 6202.* Licensed. **Memory Manor**, *106 Riverside, Tumbulgum; tel: 6676 6350.* Open 7 days lunch, dinner Sat. **Oskars on the Beach**, *Greenmount Beach, Coolangatta; tel: 5536 4621.* Open 7 days. Licensed.

SIGHTSEEING

Tweed Heads was named by the explorer John Oxley in 1823 after the Tweed River in Scotland. It is on **Point Danger** and is as far as you can get along the northern coast of New South Wales before entering Queensland. For years this town had a special significance and a substantial source of income, because poker machines were illegal in Queensland but permitted in New South Wales. As a result, the **Twin Towns Services Club** has one of the largest arrays of poker machines in Australia. The law has now been amended but the clubs linger on. These days it is common for Tweeds Heads to promote itself as a double header deal – the twin towns of **Coolangatta** and Tweed Heads – although, in fact, both towns have a distinctive style and this grouping is for promotional purposes only.

The main road to Queensland from New South Wales runs through the centre of the town, which can create traffic problems at the weekends in summer.

At Point Danger, Tweed Heads has a memorial to Captain Cook, with the capstan base made from ballast dumped from the *Endeavour,* and the world's first laser beam lighthouse on top. This was opened in 1970 – the bicentenary of Cook's visit.

The coastline around Tweeds Head is much more pleasant for the tourist than the hustle and bustle of the somewhat tawdry **Surfers Paradise** to the north. In fact, if you are exploring the Gold Coast, with its three theme parks – **Dreamworld, Movie World** and **Sea World**, with the added attraction of the gambling at **Jupiter's Casino** – then Tweed Heads makes an ideal base from which to make forays.

South of Tweed Heads (about 5 km), on *Kirkwood Rd,* is the **Minjungbal Aboriginal**

Culture Museum, which is open seven days, 1000–1600 (*tel: 5524 2109*). It is set in eight hectares of bushland around an old sacred ceremonial bora site, and mangrove and nature walks. The Minjungbal people once inhabited the lower Tweed Valley.

If you want to orientate yourself with general views of the area, the best spot is **Razorback Outlet**, 3 km out of town. Tweed Heads is on two major lagoons that stretch inland. **Terranora Lake** offers fishing and boating, and is famous for its oysters. The other reaches inland to the River Tweed, which goes as far back as Murwillumbah and then enters the 2380 hectare **Mt Warning National Park** *(tel: 27 1177),* which is on the slopes of rain forest clad **Mt Warning**. This is a volcano that has been extinct for some 23 million years.

The park is 12 km south-west of Murwillumbah off *Kyogle Rd.* The entrance to the park is at **Breakfast Creek**. There are two well-signposted tracks. One is a magnificent, if steep, walk leading to the summit, passing through a range of vegetation. There are resting places along the way. The 360° view from the summit is quite remarkable. The other is the **Lyrebird Trail** and only takes 15 mins. It leads to an elevated platform within the rain forest.

To the north-west is the **Border Ranges National Park**; *tel: 28 1177*. It covers 31,508 hectares and is a World Heritage listed park, on the other slope of Mt Warning. It is 38 km west of Murwillumbah off *Summerland Way.*

These are all within easy distance for day trips, with a pleasant drive up the Tweed Valley – quaint villages, sugar cane fields, fruit plantations – to Mt Warning and the parks.

Where the Tweed joins the Rous River, you come to the small village of **Tumbulgum** – the name means meeting of the waters. It was the site of a grog shanty, an unlicensed hotel, as early as 1858. The **Tumbulgum Hotel**, dating from 1887, still exists, and is completely restored and renovated (*tel: 76 6202*). You can explore the two rivers in a hired boat, **Tumbulgum Boat Hire**, *Riverside Dr.; tel: 76 6240.* It is also possible to take a house boat on an exploration cruise – **Tweed River Houseboats**, *161 Pacific Hwy, Murwillumbah; tel: 72 3535.*

SYDNEY–EDEN

The run down to the Victorian border from Sydney – the drive south – has as many charms as the drive north. Between Sydney and Eden there are a number of fascinating towns and, once again, apparently endless stretches of glorious and frequently deserted beaches, interspersed by National Parks and nature reserves.

ROUTE: 483 KM

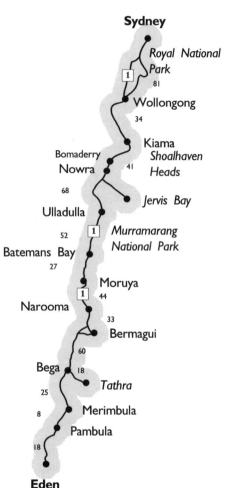

Sydney

Royal National Park
81

Wollongong
34

Kiama
Bomaderry   Shoalhaven
Nowra   41   Heads
68
Jervis Bay
Ulladulla
52   1   Murramarang
Batemans Bay   National Park
27
Moruya   **91**
1   44
Narooma
33
Bermagui
60
Bega   18
25   Tathra
8   Merimbula
Pambula
18
Eden

ROUTE

Start off southwards on the Princes Hwy, Rte 1, as if you were going to Wollongong but turn off after about 20 km from the centre of Sydney, past Sutherland, to the **Royal National Park** and **Audley**. The road meanders through the park – it covers 15,401 hectares, and the countryside is much as it was when the First Fleet arrived – and eventually comes out past Lilyvale at **Stanwell Park**. Here, there is a memorial to the great pioneering aviator, Lawrence Hargraves, whose aircraft design did much to get the Wright brothers airborne. And they were happy to give him the credit. This is also one of the first lookouts on the South Pacific Ocean and you can see all along the coast, beach after beach after beach, all with their own charms, all waiting to be discovered and all, outside the holiday season, pretty much deserted.

You are now going through the outskirts of **Wollongong**, which are something less than

pretty – Fairy Meadow is a particularly misleading name – and into Wollongong itself with, on the horizon, the line of modern sculptures, which is the Port Kembla iron and steel works. Rejoin Hwy 1, driving with **Lake Illawarra** on one side and the ocean on the other, through Minnamurra to **Kiama**. (The Princes Hwy for much of its way is two lanes, which makes overtaking effectively impossible. When it gets to three lanes it is set up specifically for safe overtaking and sometimes, but not often, it even becomes a dual carriageway.)

You head past Gerringong, the Seven Mile Beach National Park and Shoalhaven Heads and then inland to **Bomaderry** and **Nowra**. You can side-track south of Nowra to **Jervis Bay** but the main route on the Princes Hwy keeps fairly close to the coast, with the Budawang Range on the right, until you reach Mollymook and its close neighbour **Ulladulla**.

From Ulladulla you pass Pebbly Beach with its inquisitive kangaroos, Durras with its lake and cross the Clyde River inlet to arrive at **Bateman's Bay**. To your right is Deua National Park (and much farther over is the nation's capital, Canberra) but the route heads on to **Moruya**. Now the Princes Hwy goes through the dairy pasture lands leading to **Narooma**. After 21 km turn left to **Bermagui**, from where it is 19 km back to the Princes Hwy and another 40 km to **Bega**. From here you can side-track to **Tathra** (which can also be reached direct from Bermagui by a coast road and then inland to Bega). The Princes Hwy continues another 59 km through **Merimbula** to the fishing port of **Eden**, just before the Victoria state border.

TRAINS

There are very frequent local services from Sydney as far as Wollongong and Nowra, but none further along this route. OTT table 9014.

BUSES

Melbourne-bound services from central Sydney and the international airport call at many of the towns along this route, but only a couple run (overnight) as far as Eden, journey time approx. 14 hrs. OTT table 9120.

ROYAL NATIONAL PARK

Tourist Information: Visitors Centre; *tel: (02) 9542 0648.*

This is one of 29 National Parks in the Great Metropolitan Sydney area. It is the green lung of Sydney and an easy drive from the centre of the city. Go up *S. Dowling St* as if you were going to the airport. Then join the Princes

Hwy, following the signs for Wollongong. Just past Sutherland at **Audley** there is a clearly signposted road on the left and after ½km you are in the park. The visitors centre is about 3 km further on by the weir at Audley, where you can hire canoes

The Royal National is unusual in that it provides access to small towns. Normally no one is allowed to live in a National Park. Where houses pre-exist they are only allowed to remain for the life of the owner, and then they are demolished. But the Royal is slightly different because there are towns on the edge of the 15,014 hectares, which use the park for access. Therefore you will find the roads through the park busier than you would expect especially during morning and evening rush hours.

But once you get away from the roads it is a peaceful mixture of heathland, scrub forest and, in season, amazing displays of wildflowers. More than 200 species of bird have been identified in the park and there are also wallaby, echidnas, brush-tail possums and even deer, although sitings are not very common.

WOLLONGONG

Tourist Information: Tourism Wollongong, *Crown St; tel: (042) 28 0300.*

ACCOMMODATION AND FOOD

Novotel Northbeach Hotel, expensive, *2 Cliff Rd, tel: 26 3555*; **City Pacific Hotel**, *112 Burelli St; tel: 29 7444*; **Beach Park Motor Inn**, *10 Pleasant Ave, N. Wollongong; tel: 26 1577*; **Boat Harbour Motel**, *7 Wilson St; tel: 28 9166*; **Downtown Motel**, *76 Crown St; tel: 29 8344*; **Normandie Motel**, *30 Bourke St; tel: 29 4833*; **Golden Pacific North Beach Motel**, *16 Pleasant Ave, N. Wollongong 2500; tel: 26 3000*; **Surfside 22 Motel**, *corner Crown and Harbour Sts; tel: 29 7288*; **Blackbutt Motel**, *Shellharbour Rd, Shellharbour 2529; tel: 95 1317.*

Lagoon, *Stuart Park behind North Beach; tel: 26 1766.* Open 7 days, lunch and dinner, licensed. **The Harbour Front Restaurant**, *Endeavour Dr., Belmore Basin; tel: 27 2999.* **Angelo's Trattoria**, *International Centre, 28 Stewart St.* No telephone. BYO.

SIGHTSEEING

Wollongong is so close to Sydney that you would think that the two would overlap. Far from it; they are very distinct entities. Wollongong is totally surrounded by national parks, Lake Illawarra, the steep escarpment behind it and the sea, which prevents any overlapping growth from Sydney. Indeed, there is effectively no more land to develop in Wollongong and although the mix of business may change there in the future, it is unlikely that the population will grow or diminish.

Sir Thomas Mitchell, the surveyor general, covered the area in 1834 and he retained the Aboriginal name, which is said to mean 'sound of the sea'. Wollongong has an odd reputation in Sydney, where it is seen as an industrial town because of the nearby **Port Kembla** steel works although, in fact, it has more beaches and recreation areas than most towns. The best way to view Wollongong's geographical position is to drive from Sydney and stop at the **Bulli Lookout** above Thirroul, which incidentally, is where D.H. Lawrence lived when he was in Australia. You can see that Wollongong is on a coastal strip with a steep forested escarpment rising steeply and the sandstone crests of **Mt Keira** and **Mt Kembla** at the eastern outlets.

Wollongong is moving away from heavy industry to high tech – it has a specialised industrial park associated with the university. The university itself, arguably one of the most go-ahead in Australia, and local tourism are also important to Wollongong.

The Wollongong City Gallery, *corner of Kembla and Burrelli Sts; tel: 28 7500*, is the largest regional gallery in Australia and has a serious collection of Aboriginal art and Colonial works from the Illawarra region. Open Tues–Fri 1000–1700, weekends and public holidays 1200–1600. **The Science Centre and Museum**, on the university's Campus East near the shoreline, has over 120 interactive hands-on exhibits. Open Fri 1900–2100, Sat–Sun 1300–1700 and during school holidays, *tel: 21 5591*.

Wollongong Harbour, originally created for the cedar wood-felling industry, has been superseded for industrial purposes by Port Kembla itself, so it has remained a charming fishing port. There are some superb beaches near the port.

KIAMA

Tourist Information: Kiama Visitors Centre, *Blowhole Headland; tel (042)32 3322.*

ACCOMMODATION AND FOOD

Kiama Terrace Motor Lodge, expensive, *51 Collins St; tel: 32 1966*; **Kiama Ocean View**, *9 Bong Bong St; tel: 32 1966*; **Motel 617**, *132 Manning St; tel: 32 1333*; **The Pines Motel**, *10 Bong Bong St; tel: 32 1000*; **Briggdale Motel**, *18 Hothersal St; tel: 321767*; **Kiama Beachfront Motel**, *87 Manning St; tel: 32 1533*; **Jamberoo Valley Lodge**, *Jamberoo Mountain Rd, Jamberoo 2533, tel: (042) 36 0269.*

Foresters, *Jamberoo Valley Lodge, Jamberoo Mountain Road; tel: 36 0629.* Licensed, 7 days a week. **Harbourside**, *4 Terralong; tel: 32 2799.* Licensed. Not open Sunday night. **Tianas Seafood**, *Collins St; tel: 33 1100.* Dinner Mon–Sat.

SIGHTSEEING

Kiama – the Aboriginal origin of the name is uncertain – is only a 1½ hr drive from Sydney along the Pacific Hwy, and about 2 hrs from Canberra. It lies to the north of **Gerringong** – Werri Beach lies between, followed by the Seven Mile Gerroa Beach – and is at the foot of the Illawarra escarpment, with **Saddleback Mountain** and its superb lookout lying directly behind.

The first European here was the indefatigable George Bass, who in 1797 came ashore and noted the famous blowhole. Then came the timber fellers, followed, as in much of this region, by the dairy farmers.

Kiama is on a heavily indented part of the coast, which means that it is excellent for fishing and has many sheltered beaches. You can also witness the resident pelican population. Its most famous feature was the **Blowhole**, which regularly used to throw up great fountains of spray. The sea has eroded the sides and now this fountain only occurs when there is a strong south-easterly swell. It is important that you follow carefully all the warnings around the Blowhole, as it can be extremely dangerous.

In the town itself the **Post Office**, dating from 1878, is a gem, designed in an Italianate style. In *Collins St*, at the edge of the shopping mall and just north of the roundabout, are the only timber terraced houses – there are plenty of standalone timber houses even in Sydney – that have not been demolished by developers. These were built for quarry workers over a century ago and have now been restored as house craft shops, cafés and galleries. They are classified by the National Trust.

Nearby is the **Pilot's Cottage Museum**, which is open every day except Tues 1100–1500.

A short drive from Kiama is Jamberoo, which has the **Jamberoo Recreation Park**, *Albion Rd, Jamberoo; tel: (042) 36-0114*. Open Sat, Sun and public holidays. Entrance fee $16. It has assorted rides and water slides for children. This was a private village established in the 1840s, and not much has changed since then. The school house, **Minnamurra House** and **Terragong House** have all been classified by the National Trust.

Behind Jamberoo lies the **Minnamurra Rainforest**, which has a walkway to the first falls, where the Minnamurra River falls 50m down from the escarpment in a series of steps.

NOWRA AND SHOALHAVEN

Tourist Information: Shoalhaven Tourist Centre, *254 Princes Hwy, Bomaderry; tel: (044) 21 0788*.

ACCOMMODATION AND FOOD

Avaleen Lodge Motor Inn, *317 Princes Hwy, Bomaderry*, tel: *218244*; **Balan Village Motel** *(BW)*, *175 Cambewarra Rd, Nowra 2541*, tel: *231111*; **Pleasant Way Motor Inn** *(FL)*, *Pleasant Way*, tel: *215544*; **Cross Country Motel** *(BU)*, *corner Kinghorn and McKay Sts*, tel: *217777*; **Marriott Park Motel**, *corner Princes Hwy and Douglas Sts*, tel: *216999*; **Bounty Motor Inn**, *271 Princes Hwy, Bomaderry*, tel: *212233*; **HI: The Coach House**, *30 Junction St, Nowra 2541*, tel: *21 2084*.

Cellar Door Restaurant, *13335 Bolong Rd, Coolangatta; tel: 48 7131*. Part of a winery and thus excellent food. Open 7 days. **Boatshed**, *Wharf Rd; tel: 21 2419*. Licensed.

Open 7 days. Fish specialities. **Captains Table**, *202 Kinghorn St; tel 11 3455*. Open Mon–Sat. Licensed. **Snapper Inn**, *116 Kinghorn St; tel: 21 4692*. Open 7 days. Licensed. **Flappers Restaurant**, *corner Kinghorn and Douglas Sts; tel: 21 5444*.

SIGHTSEEING

Nowra

The name is an Aboriginal word for 'black cockatoo', and was first written as *Noo-Woo-Ro*. It is the centre of **Shoalhaven City**, which is 2 hrs from both Sydney and Canberra. In the Shoalhaven area, which includes Ulladulla and Jervis Bay, there are 109 sea and lake-side beaches and one of the major industries in the area is tourism. The name was given by George Bass, who, sailing down the coast in 1797, discovered the entrance to the river, disliked it intensely and called it Shoals Haven. The first settlers were farmers rapidly followed by timber cutters seeking sleepers for the railway.

From Nowra there are cruises up the Shoalhaven River on the **Shoalhaven Explorer**, daily during the school holidays and Mon, Wed, Fri and Sun at other times. Leaves from Nowra Wharf near the bridge; *tel: 23 1844*. The best known walk is **Bens Walk**, which starts from Hanging Rock at the western end of the Showground – which itself affords excellent views across the Shoalhaven River.

Merogal, *corner West and Worrigeee Sts*, (open Sat 1300–1700, Sun 1000–1700 and most public holidays), was built in 1855 and contains household contents collected by four generations of pioneers. **The Shoalhaven Historical Museum**, *corner Kinghorne and Kalandar Sts*, shows very graphically the way that the area has developed. Open Sat, Sun, public holidays 1300–1600.

Bomaderry

The name Bomaderry can be taken to mean 'fighting ground' or 'running water'. It is 4 km north of Nowra and was created mainly for the railway, which arrived in 1893. The first settler in the area, Herman Meyers, became station master. In fact, the town is still the terminus of the South Coast line. A signposted walk along the Bomaderry Creek starts in *Narang Rd.* You can choose between a 1 hr or a 3 hr walk. Also in *Narang Rd* are the **Shoalhaven Camellia Gardens**, open Sun 1000–1500, Apr–Sept. Other times by appointment; *tel: 22 1200.*

Coolangatta

This small town causes much confusion because it has the same name as a town in Queensland. The reason is that a brigantine of that name was built here in 1843 and wrecked 3 years later on the Queensland Coast, where it gave its name to the other town. This small town houses the **Coolangatta Village Resort**, *1335 Bolong Rd, tel: 48 7131,* a series of buildings dating from before the turn of the century, which have been transformed into hotel rooms – but with all the charm retained. This is probably the best example of a development of this kind in Australia and is strongly recommended.

Kangaroo Valley

This is a very small village and is unusual in that the whole valley has been classified by the National Trust as worth preserving. It contains the **Hampden Suspension Bridge** over the Kangaroo River, which is near a popular swimming and picnic spot, and the **Pioneer Settlement Reserve**, which is next to the bridge and is open daily from 0900–1630 (*tel: 65 1306*). There are, despite the name, no kangaroos to be seen. They are said to have disappeared some time in the 1840s.

 **SIDE TRACK FROM NOWRA**

JERVIS BAY

Turn left off the Princes Hwy 13 km south of Nowra, just after Falls Creek. The road ends at a headland about 20 km further on.

Tourist Information: Shoalhaven Tourist Centre, *254 Princes Hwy, Bomaderry; tel: (044) 21 0788.*

ACCOMMODATION

Anglesea Waterfront Motel Lodges, *2 Admiralty Crescent, tel: 41 5057;* **Bayside Motor Inn**, *corner Hawke and Bowen Sts, tel:*

41 5194; **Huskisson Beach Motel**, *9 Hawke St; tel: 41 6387;* **Jervis Bay Motel**, *Owen St; tel: 41 5781;* **Dolphin Shores Motor Inn**, *53 Beach St; tel: 41 6011.*

SIGHTSEEING

In Australia it is pronounced the way it is spelled, not 'Jarvis', which is the way that Admiral Sir John Jervis, after whom it was named in 1791, would have pronounced it. The naval connection is appropriate as this is very much a naval area. The **Australian Naval Aviation Museum**, *tel: 21 1920,* south-west of Nowra on *Albatross Rd,* has one of the finest collections of military aircraft in Australia. Open daily 1000–1600.

There is no town of Jervis Bay but **Huskisson** and **Vincentia** stand on the bay itself. Jervis Bay is part of the ACT not New South Wales.

Jervis Bay National Park is on a peninsula, with Jervis Bay on one side and St Georges Basin on the other, and contains several naval establishments, which can normally only be visited by appointment. The visitor's centre, on the left as you enter the park, (open 0830–1700 during summer holidays and 0900–1600 at other times), has a complete collection of guides and maps for the area. Within the park itself is **Greenpatch**, which has a sheltered beach and picnic and camping facilities. (National Park information; *tel: 43 0977.*) From Greenpatch, the road leads to **Murrays Beach**, which has several footpaths marked. Along *Stoney Creek Rd* is the ruined **Cap St George Lighthouse**, which was built in the wrong place and became a navigational hazard, encouraging boats to sail too close to the rocky coast line. At the request of the authorities it was shelled by the navy until it was a wreck.

Huskisson, 24 km south-east of Nowra, is named after William Huskisson, who was the Colonial Secretary 1827–1829. There is a population of around 1000.

The sands of Jervis Bay are claimed to be the whitest in the world and every Easter there is a **White Sands Carnival** in Huskisson with floats, stalls, music and

95

fireworks. **Dolphin Watch**, *tel: (044) 41 6311*, has cruises in the bay that leave regularly from the wharf. Nearby the **Jervis Bay Dive Centre**, *Owen St; tel: (044) 41 5598*, offers dives, training and gear hire.

In *Dent St* is the **Lady Denman Heritage Complex**, open daily. There is a mangrove boardwalk and two regional museums – **The Museum of Jervis Bay Science and the Sea** (maritime and surveying) and **The Lady Denham Museum** (history of wooden ship building in Huskisson).Part of the complex is **Laddie Timbery's Aboriginal Art and Craft Centre**, open daily 1000–1700, where all goods sold are made on the site by Aboriginal craftsmen. Activities include boomerang throwing and didgeridoo playing.

Vincentia is across the Moona Moona bridge from Huskisson and was originally known as the Old Township, but was renamed Vincentia – after the battle of St Vincent – in 1952. It has several parks facing on to the beach and there are slipways for launching boats into Jervis Bay at *Holden St* and *Plantation Point*.

On the other side of the peninsula from Jervis Bay is **St Georges Basin**, where on the shore at Sanctuary Point is the **Basin Walk**, which is a scenic stroll following the shoreline from Paradise Beach Reserve to Palm Beach Reserve. It takes under an hour. ▄▌

ULLADULLA

Tourist Information: Milton–Ulladulla District Tourist Association, *Civic Centre, Princes Hwy; tel (044) 55 1269*.

ACCOMMODATION AND FOOD

Albacore Motel *(FL)*, *Boree St; tel: 55 1322*; **Harbour Royal Motel**, *29 Burrill St; tel: 555444*; **Pigeon House Motor Inn**, *156 Princes Hwy; tel: 55 1811*; **Sandpiper Motel**, *78 Princes Hwy; tel: 55 1488*; **Top View Motel**, *72 South St; tel: 55 1514*; **Quiet Garden Motel**, *2 Burrill St N.; tel: 55 1757*; **Mollymook Shores Resort**, expensive, *corner Golf Ave and Shepherd St; tel: 55 5888*;

Mollymook Seaspray Motel, *70 Ocean St; tel: 55 5311*; **Mollymook Seascape Motel**, *22 Princes Hwy; tel: 55 5777*; **Beachpoint Motor Inn**, *17 Shepherd St; tel: 55 3022*; **Mollymook Motel**, *corner Princes Hwy and Golf Ave; tel: 55 1877*; **Paradise Haven Motel**, *39 Ocean St; tel: 55 5514*.

Agee's Restaurant, *Green St*. Lunch weekdays; dinner Mon–Sat. **Harbourside Terrace**, *Wason St. Licenced*.

SIGHTSEEING

Ulladulla – said to be Aboriginal for 'safe harbour' – and the seven lakes district is 227 km south of Sydney, 197 km east of Canberra and 40 km south of Jervis Bay. The district has a wide range of beaches including **Mollymook**, which is patrolled during the season, Bendalong, Ulladulla, Wairo, Merry and Pebbly. Then there are the lakes of Conjola, Burrill, Tabourie, Termeil, Meroo, Bawley Point and Durras.

In the hinterland just behind is **Pigeon House** – it is recognisable as such – which was spotted by Captain Cook in 1770.

Early development was due to stands of cedar. Initially it was known as Wasp Harbour after the name of an early boat, it then became Holey Dollar, which was a corruption of the Aboriginal name of Ulladulla and late in the last century it reverted to its proper name.

On the corner of *Warden* and *Green Sts,* near the swimming pool, is the **Ulladulla Wildflower Reserve**, which covers nearly 12 hectares and has over 100 types of plants, with the canopy overhead consisting of eucalypts and turpentines. **Funland Ulladulla** *(tel: 55 3053)* is one of the largest indoor fun parks in New South Wales – on Princes Hwy and open daily 1000–1700 during the week, to 2200 on Sat and school holidays.

Ulladulla Harbour and Wharf is very much a working fishing port and every Easter Sunday there is a Blessing of the Fleet. On the wharf is the **Ulladulla Dive Shop**, which operates charter vessels and pleasure cruises – Tues, Thur, Sun at 1000, *tel: 55 5303*.

Along the Princes Hwy, 19 km north of Ulladulla, you come to a turn-off. This is the gravelled *Twelve Mile Rd* that leads to **Boyd**

Lookout, which has splendid views of Lake Conjola and the coastline in both directions.

Lake Conjola – drive down *Lake Conjola Rd* from the Princes Hwy – has facilities for most water based activities, and the **Narrawallee Creek Nature Reserve** has a footpath running through forests and mangroves right behind the lake.

A scenic drive from Ulladulla – on gravel roads for the most part – begins at the Civic Centre and then turns left at **Hacketts Restaurant**. From there follow the signs. The drive is about 30 km and takes something under an hour to drive with care, because of the loose surface. There is a car park at **Pigeon House Mountain**, but to reach the lookout you need to climb further up a steep footpath. At one stage you will climb up a series of steel ladders to reach the top of the cliff face. While this is not a skilled climb, a certain level of fitness is required. The view from the top is a 360° panorama. You drive through plantations of native Australian trees – mainly eucalypts – and through heathland, which in the spring and early summer will have a display of wildflowers.

BATEMAN'S BAY

Tourist Information: Eurobadalla Visitors Centre, *corner Beach Rd and Princes Hwy; tel: (044) 72 6900.*

ACCOMMODATION AND FOOD

Esplanade Motel, expensive, *23 Beach Rd; tel: 720200*; **Reef Motor Inn** *(BW)*, expensive, *27 Clyde St; tel: 726000*; **Abel Tasman Motel**, *222 Beach Rd, Batehaven 2536; tel: 726511*; **Argyle Terrace Motor Inn** *(GC), 32 Beach Rd; tel: 725022*; **Country Comfort Inn** *(CC), corner Princes Hwy and Canberra Rd; tel: 726333*; **Bayside Motel**, *60 Beach Rd; tel: 726488*; **Sunseeker Motel** *(FL), Old Princes Hwy; tel: 725888*; **Zorba Motel**, *Orient St; tel: (044) 724804*; **HI**, *Bateman's Bay Tourist Park, Old Princes Hwy; tel: 72 4972.*

Taliva, *236 Beach Rd, Bateman; tel: 72 4278.* French restaurant. Licenced. $25 a head. **Reef**, *Reef Motor Inn, 27 Clyde St; tel: 72 6000.* Licensed. Open 7 days. Seafood specialities. **Bateman's Bay Vietnamese, Thai and Malaysian Restaurant**, *Orient St.* BYO.

SIGHTSEEING

Think of it as Canberra by the sea and you will not be far wrong. It is only 152 km, a few hours drive, from the nation's capital and many of its inhabitants come here for summer weekends and holidays. Bateman's Bay, technically more an inlet, is where the Clyde River runs into the sea and is 8 km across at its widest point. It is crossed by the Princes Hwy – the bridge across a narrow part of the inlet was opened in 1956 – with the town itself being on the southern side. Bateman's Bay was named by Captain Cook after the captain of the *Northumberland*, a ship on which Cook had once sailed.

The town is principally concerned with fishing and oyster leases, although tourism is, of course, an important industry. On the inland side of the bridge and up the river, there is safe sailing, canoeing and swimming. The **MV Merinda** leaves the Boatshed Wharf at 1130 daily for a 3 hr cruise to Nelligen. Deep sea charters are available from **Malua Bay Charters** – *tel: 72 9976.* You can also hire house boats to explore the Clyde River **(Bay River Houseboats**, *tel: 72 5649)*, which will easily accommodate up to eight people and require no special licence.

On the northern side of the bridge, you come to a series of national parks, all of which have their special attractions.

First comes **Murramarang National Park**, which covers 1757 hectares and includes the coastal hills and four offshore islands *(tel: 23 9800)*. This is followed by the small town of **Durras**, reached from the Princes Hwy, which is 500 m from Durras Waters. This inlet was mistaken by George Bass for Bateman's Bay and is a great centre for aquatic sports and camping. The Durras Lakes area has always been regarded as something of a budget holiday spot with prices for caravans and cabins being very affordable.

Next up the coast, again accessible from the Princes Hwy, is **Pebbly Beach**. This is at the south end of the Murramarang National Park and is famous for its tame kangaroos. They are so tame it is often thought that they have been imported just for the tourists. Not so. These are kangaroos from the National Park that have got so used to humans that they lie around waiting

97

to be photographed and fed. A frequent complaint of visitors to Australia is that they never see live kangaroos in the wild. The answer is to go to Pebbly Beach, where several dozen kangaroos are positively guaranteed to be on hand.

The whole of the coastline north from Bateman's Bay as far as **Pretty Beach**, about 30 km, is National Park but it can only be reached at four points from the Princes Hwy. All other vehicular access is cut off and if you wish to explore this area the only answer is to walk.

Four kilometres south of Bateman's Bay lies the suburb of **Batehaven** – most of the buildings are post-1960. There is a **Shell Museum** (open 7 days) and north of the village, behind the dunes that face the sea, is **Birdland** (*55 Beach Rd; tel: 72 5364,* open daily 0930–1600), which is a 2-hectare area of rain forest complete with wombats and koalas.

MORUYA

Tourist Information: Eurobadalla Visitors Centre, *Princes Hwy; tel: (044) 72 6900.*

ACCOMMODATION

Moruya Motel, *201 Princes Hwy; tel: 74 2511;* **Monarch Hotel**, *50 Vulcan St; tel: 74 2433;* **Luhana Motel**, *82 Princes Hwy; tel: 74 2722.*

SIGHTSEEING

Moruya is 6 km up the Moruya River, still in its tidal reaches, where it is crossed by the Princes Hwy. It is on the south side of the inlet, 322 km from Sydney. From the town there is a road running down both sides of the inlet. You cross the bridge from town, and on the northern side, the road runs past Moruya Aerodrome – more an airstrip – and then continues inland from the 6 km **Bengallo Beach** until it reaches **Broulee Head**. There it becomes *Bass Dr.* and passes through the small village of **Broulee** and then winds its way around the coast in a series of tight bends until in reaches Batehaven and, shortly afterwards, Bateman's Bay.

On the town side of the inlet it runs down to **Moruya Heads** and then turns south towards the town of **Congo**. The town started life as a gateway to the Braidwood and Araluen goldfields. In the town is the **Wesleyan Chapel**, which is built from the same local granite used for the pylons of the Sydney Harbour Bridge.

The road out of town to Araluen and Braidwood runs along the north side of the river and after 5 km starts to skirt **Deua National Park** (*tel: 76 2888).* This covers over 80,000 hectares and is a fairly rugged area although there are four camping sites with basic facilities. The park has caves, ridges and small cliffs, all of which have been carved from the limestone rock. The **Deua River** within the park offers excellent canoeing.

NAROOMA AND BERMAGUI

Tourist Information: Visitor Information Centre, *Bruce Hwy, Narooma; tel (044) 76 2881.* **Bermagui Tourist Centre**, *5 Coluga St; tel: (064) 93 4240.*

ACCOMMODATION

Sovereign Motor Inn *(FL), 126 Princes Hwy; tel: 76 2099;* **Whale Motor Inn**, *Wagonga St; tel: 762411;* **Motel Farnboro**, *Princes Hwy; tel: 764611;* **Holiday Lodge Motel**, *Princes Hwy; tel: 762282;* **Amooran Court Motel**, *30 Montague St; tel: 762198;* **Narooma Motel**, *243 Princes Hwy; tel: 764611;* **Beachview Motel**, expensive, *12 Lamont St; tel: (064) 934155;* **Eastview Motor Inn**, *46 Coluga St; tel: (064) 934777;* **Horseshoe Bay Hotel**, *Lamont St; tel: (064) 934206;* **HI: Bluewater Lodge YHA**, *11-13 Riverside Dr.; tel: 76 4440.*

SIGHTSEEING

Narooma

On the south coast and almost opposite Montague Island, Narooma is on the Princes Hwy, where it crosses the Wagonga Inlet, 360 km south of Sydney. The Wagonga Inlet has a narrow entrance to the sea and widens considerably as it goes inland. This means that Narooma, which is on a hilly peninsula, appears to be almost totally surrounded by water. It is encircled by lakes and inlets. Although the town dates from the 1840s, the name – which is Aboriginal for 'sacred stone' – was not made official until 1972.

The information centre is on the beach front and nearby is the small **Lighthouse Museum**. In town, the **United Church**, a wooden building with a timber framed bell tower of considerable charm, is on the State's heritage list. Only 15 km away (go south on the Princes Hwy) is the town of **Tilba Tilba**, which has been virtually unchanged since it was founded in the last century, and is classified by the National Trust as an unusual mountain village.

This area, especially around Montague Island, is famous for big game fishing. South of Narooma, drive 8 km down the Princes Hwy nearly to the Corunna State Forest and then take a left turn down to **Mystery Bay** and **Cape Dromedary**. The mystery comes from a boat disappearing in 1880 and being found at Mystery Bay full of bullet holes, without any passengers. The mystery has never been solved. There are trips to **Montague Island** every Mon, Wed and Fri at 1530, with a park ranger as a guide. You can book through the National Parks office (*tel: 76 2888*) and the cost is $40 a head. You can also cruise up the Wagonga River in the **Wagonga Princess** – bookings taken at the information centre. Every weekday evening **Austwild Tours** (*tel: 76 2845*) runs wildlife spotting tours into the interior of the island. It is possible you might see a platypus in the wild, which would put you ahead of almost every Australian.

To the north of Narooma and before you get to the cheese town of **Bodalla**, there is a gravel road to the right that goes through the **Bodalla State Forest** and ends up at Potato Point on the sea between Lake Tarourga and Lake Brunderee.

Bermagui

This port lies 13 km from the Princes Hwy. The author Zane Grey visited the town in the 1930s and said that it was one of the greatest sports fishing centres on earth. There is a reserve on the headland named in his honour. The name on early maps appears as Pemageua and Bermaguee – it is an approximation of an Aboriginal word meaning 'canoe with paddles'.

Just 8 km to the north is **Wallaga Lake National Park**, which covers 1237 hectares – *tel: (044) 76 2888*. Forested ridges fall steeply to

the shoreline from the foothills of **Mt Dromedary**. The gullies are mainly covered in rain forest. This is the largest lake in southern New South Wales and has families of black swans. More than 220 bird species have been seen in the area, as well as koalas and swamp wallabies. You can only walk in or go in by boat. You can hire boats in Bermagui itself. Wallaga Lake and its surrounds give many opportunities for bushwalking and observing wildlife. On the lake itself, there is swimming, fishing, sailing, boating and water skiing. Boat hire and picnic and toilet facilities are available

BEGA

Tourist Information: Bega Tourist Centre, *Gipps St; tel. (064) 92 2045.*

ACCOMMODATION AND FOOD

Bega Downs Motel *(BW)*, expensive, *corner High and Gipps Sts; tel: 92 2944*; **Bega Village Motor Inn**, *Princes Hwy; tel: 92 2466*; **Bega Southtown Motor Inn**, *Princes Hwy; tel: 922177*; **Northside Motel** *(BU)*, *Old Princes Hwy; tel: 92 1911*; **Princes Motel**, *Princes Hwy, tel: 92 1944*; **Tathra Hotel**, *Bega St; tel: 94 1101*; **HI**, *3 Kirkland Crescent; tel: 92 3130.*

Hideaway Restaurant, *Auckland St; tel: 92 1344.*

SIGHTSEEING

Behind the town of Bega lies a lush green valley, where the cows provide the milk for the famous Bega cheese which has been produced in the area since 1870. The **Bega Cheese Factory** is still operating and open for inspection – 1000–1300 weekdays, 1000–1400 Sun; *tel: 92 1444* – and has a collection of old drays and wagons on display. Open 7 days. One of the famous dairy properties of the area is **Kameruka**, which is classified by the National Trust and is also open to visitors. The town sits in the southern part of the State, and one of its claims to fame is that from Bega it is possible to go skiing in one of the Kosciusko ski resorts and surfing off the beach in the same day. Bega sits at the junction of the Princes Hwy and the Snowy Mountains Hwy and is thus at the junction of the roads that connect Melbourne, Sydney and Canberra. The best way to get

99

Bega into perspective is to drive up to the **Bega Valley Lookout**, where you can see the town, the sea and the Bega River.

George Bass explored as far up as the town, and one of the early cattle runs that followed in 1839 was called Biggah. The town has also appeared on maps as Bika. It became Bega in 1848 and it is thought the word has the Aboriginal meaning of 'beautiful'.

In Bega itself there is a **Heritage Centre and Family Museum** on *Bega St* (open weekdays 1300–1600, Sat 1030–1230), which recounts the history of the area, and 2 km out of town on *Buckajo Rd* is the **Grevillea Estate Winery**, *tel: 92 3006*, open daily 0900–1700. The **Bega Riding School** (*tel: 92 3351*) has trail rides around the countryside.

Candelo is an historic village 39 km southwest of Bega on the banks of the Candelo River (go south on the Princes Hwy and take the turning to the right towards Bombala), which has retained its village atmosphere and many 19th century buildings.

Just outside Bega, on the road to Tathra, is **Jelat Jelat**, which was built for the Gowing family in 1876 and has cedar panelling and a cedar staircase.

SIDE TRACK
FROM BEGA (OR BERMAGUI)

TATHRA

Follow the road east from Bega, about 18 km. There is also a 35 km road south from Bermagui.

Tourist Information: Tathra Beach Store; *tel: (064) 94 1487*.

SIGHTSEEING

Tathra is a small town on the coast, with the **Bournda State Recreation Area** on one side and the 5230 hectare **Mimosa Rocks National Park** (*tel: 76 2888*) on the other side of the *Tathra-Bermagui Rd* . The wharf at Tathra, which was to have been demolished in 1981, has been restored by the National Trust and has a museum housed in an old cargo shed. **Tathra Beach** runs for 3km along the coast and is patrolled during

the season. The beach is well protected from southerly winds and is known for its surf. At the north end of the beach lies **Mogareeka Inlet**, which is the wide, sandy shallow mouth of the Bega River and abounds with bird life. On the inlet, **Bega River Cruises** (*tel: 94 1523*) runs cruises and rents boats.

Historic note: a coastal watch unit in Tathra saw the World War II torpedo attack which sank the USS *William Dawes* off the coast.

MERIMBULA AND PAMBULA

Tourist Information: Merimbula Tourist Office, *Beach St; tel: (064) 95 1129*.

ACCOMMODATION AND FOOD

Merimbula Motor Inn *(FL)*, expensive, *corner Reid St and Princes Hwy; tel: 95 3077*; **Merimbula Seaspray Motel**, *38 Merimbula Dr.; tel: 95 3299*; **Sapphire Waters Motor Inn**, *32 Princes Hwy; tel: 95 1999*; **Kingfisher Motel**, *105 Princes Hwy; tel: 95 1595*; **Merimbula Motor Lodge** *(BU)*, *131 Princes Hwy; tel: 95 1748*; **Ocean View Motor Inn**, *corner Merimbula Dr. and View St; tel: 95 2300*; **Black Dolphin Resort Motel**, *Princes Hwy; tel: 95 1500*; **Colonial Motor Inn**, *corner Princes Hwy and Monaro St; tel: 95 6700*; **Idlewilde Motor Inn**, *Princes Hwy; tel: 95 6844*; **Royal Willows Hotel Motel**, *Princes Hwy; tel: 95 6005*; **Wandarrah Lodge**, *18 Marine Parade; tel: 95 3503*.

The Retreat Restaurant, *Pambula; tel: 95 6674*. Licensed. Dinner Mon–Sat.

SIGHTSEEING

Merimbula
The town is on Merimbula Lake which is not, in fact, a lake but an arm of the sea that offers thoroughly sheltered waters. There is a nature reserve – Bournda – just to the north running on to **Bournda National Park** (2346 hectares of coastal park with lagoons and camping at Hobart Beach, *tel: 96 1434*). Then comes **Kianinny Bay** and the town of Tathra. Just to the north of the town is the **Yellowpinch Wildlife Park**.

Merimbula is a small resort town with surfing, fishing and prawning. It has the **Old School Museum** – a sandstone building in the *High St,* built in 1874, which is the last remaining building of the original town. The museum contains an historical display tracing the growth of the area. Nearby is **Magic Mountain.** Upstream there are oyster leases and oysters are featured on the menu in the town's restaurants.

Merimbula was originally founded as a port in 1855 by the Twofold Bay Pastoral Association, but pretty well all traces of this have disappeared. The wharf was blown up in 1979. In the gold rush of the 1860s, gold prospectors came by boat to Merimbula and then used a track across Big Jack Mountain to get to the diggings in the Snowy Mountains. Now all the boats in the area are either for hire or for recreational use.

Diving is popular in the area and **Merimbula Divers Lodge**, *15 Park St, Merimbula 2548; tel: 95 3611,* runs courses and dives as well as hiring out equipment. Merimbula is also in the path of the whales annual migration, Sept–Nov, with penguins, seals and dolphins often seen in the area. **The Bar** and **Main Beach**, both near the town, offer safe swimming and **Spencer Park**, in the town, also opens onto beaches. The bay is popular for picnics. The golf course has a series of moving hazards well known to Australian golfers – kangaroos.

Pambula

The name comes from an Aboriginal word meaning 'two streams' because two rivers, the Yowaka and the Pambula, enter the bay, with Pambula town just to the north and the Ben Boyd National Park just across the water at Haycock Point. The rivers were once navigable and Pambula was a port, but a great flood in 1860 changed the courses of the rivers, they silted up and the port died, the trade moving to Merimbula.

Pambula was one of the many towns that prospered during the gold rush of the 1850s and there is still some fossicking for gems going on to this day. Syms Covington, who sailed with Charles Darwin on *The Beagle,* settled in Pambula in the late 1840s and later ran the first licensed inn, **The Forest Oak**, which was built in 1856.

Dolphins come up the river to feed and the local kangaroos are a common sight on the beaches and footpaths in the area.

EDEN

Tourist Information: Eden Tourist Information Centre; *Princes Hwy near the roundabout; tel: (064) 96 1953.*

ACCOMMODATION AND FOOD

Twofold Bay Motor Inn, *166 Imlay St; tel: 96 3111*; **Bayview Motor Inn**, *Princes Hwy; tel: 96 1242*; **Coachmans Rest Motor Inn**, *Princes Hwy, PO Box 656; tel: 96 1900*; **Halfway Motel**, *Princes Hwy; tel: 96 1178*; **Centretown Motel**, *167 Imlay St; tel: 96 1475*; **Golf View Motel**, *Princes Hwy; tel: 96 1943.*

Wheelhouse Restaurant, *on the wharf; tel: 96 3392.* Seafood fresh from the trawlers. Licensed. Open Mon–Sat lunch and dinner. **Bianca's Bistro**, *Hotel Australia, Imlay St; tel: 96 1600.* **Great Southern Inn Bistro**, *Imlay St; tel: 96 1515.*

SIGHTSEEING

Eden is the last town of any size on the Princes Hwy before you get to Victoria. It is also the halfway point between Sydney and Melbourne, being 512 km south of Sydney. Eden lies between two halves of a major national park. To the north is Ben Boyd with the **Red Cliffs** – the Pinnacles – which contrast white sandstone with red cliffs. There are marked footpaths throughout the park. Just off the coast is **Leonard's Island** and just before the park starts is **Lake Carallo**. Then to the south the **Ben Boyd National Park** starts again and runs down to Disaster Bay and then becomes the **Nadgee Nature Reserve**, which runs right down to the Victoria border. The town itself is on Twofold Bay and has a long maritime tradition. It is still a major centre for commercial fishing. It is also a centre for whale watching, sea fishing and diving expeditions. The fishing wharves themselves are fascinating, with a resident seal, pelicans overhead and dolphins and penguins often seen in the bay.

Eden was not so named because it was thought to be a paradise by the sea – although that would not have been inappropriate – but because it was the family name of Baron Auckland, who was Secretary of State for the Colonies in 1842, when the town was planned.

Eden was formerly a whaling port, which reached its height in the 1840s, with several boat stations competing ferociously with each other. This history is reflected in the **Eden Killer Whale Museum**, *Imlay St, tel: 96 2094*; open daily 1000–1545, Sat–Sun 1115–1545. Housed here is the skeleton of one of the legendary killer whales – Old Tom. You can also visit what is left of the whaling station.

Across the bay from Eden is a monument to one man's vanity – **Boydtown** and **Boyd's Tower**. The lighthouse was built in 1846 and was to be a feature of Boydtown that would out-shine Eden. The new town never made it and the lighthouse was never lit. But it makes a splendid observation point from which to look back at Eden.

The **whale watching** season is Sept–Nov, when the Humpback, the most common of the species, the Southern Rights, the Minke and the Blue Whale, all pass by on their migration north to the warmer waters of Queensland. When they are sighted off the coast a siren sounds at the Killer Whale Museum. These whales, which were once thought to be seriously endangered, have made a miraculous come-back and each year are sighted in larger numbers. So keen is the interest that regulations have been laid down as to how close boats can approach them. **Cat-Balou Cruises**, *tel: 96 2027*, has half day whale watching cruises Oct–Nov. The boat only leaves the wharf when a whale sighting has been confirmed.

Thirty kilometres south of Eden is **Wonboyn Lake**, which has untouched beaches, dingoes, dolphins and deserted dunes. The best way to explore is by boat, which can be arranged through **Wonboyn Boat Hire** at the caravan office – *tel: 96 9131*.

SYDNEY–DUBBO

If you want to follow in the steps of the Australian pioneers it is fairly easy. You go across the Blue Mountains to where you find 'the vision splendid of the sunlit plains

extended' and then on to the goldfields. If you keep going you hit on the greatest mining find of them all – Broken Hill. It is a fascinating journey but for the original pioneers, a harsh and dangerous one. A holiday exploring up to Dubbo through the goldfields area is a pleasure and a delight. But if you want to go to Broken Hill, unless you really have to drive, take the train or fly.

ROUTE: 413 KM

103

ROUTE

From Sydney take Rte 32, the Great Western Hwy, westwards. As it enters the **Blue Mountains National Park**, after **Penrith**, about 50 km to the west, it ceases to be an expressway. Continue through **Lithgow**, 146 km west of Sydney, and on to **Bathurst**. Here the road begins to head north-west and reaches **Orange** after 56 km. Continue through **Molong**, where Rte 32 turns sharply to the north, to **Wellington**, 100 km further on. From Wellington, **Dubbo** is a further 49 km along Rte 32.

TRAINS

One daily train runs this route from Sydney. Bathurst is 3½ hrs, Orange almost 5 hrs, and Dubbo 6½ hrs, from Sydney. OTT table 9020.

BUSES

Coaches operated by Selwoods Coaches and Greyhound Pioneer run from Sydney to Bathurst (3½–4 hrs) and Orange (4–5 hrs). OTT tables 9104 and 9110.

THE BLUE MOUNTAINS

Tourism Information: Blue Mountains Information Centre, *Echo Point, Katoomba; tel: (047) 82 0756.*

ACCOMMODATION

Lilianfels Hotel, *Lilianfels Ave; tel: 80 1200;*

Alpine Motor Inn *(BW)*, expensive, *corner Great Western Hwy and Orient St; tel: 82 2011;* **Katoomba Town Centre Motel**, *224 Katoomba St; tel: 82 1266;* **Mountain Heritage Country House Retreat**, *Apex and Lovel Sts; tel: 82 2155;* **Clarendon Motor Inn**, *corner Lurline and Waratah Sts; tel: 82 1322;* **3 Sisters Motel**, *348 Katoomba St; tel: 82 2911;* **Skyrider Motor Inn**, *corner Scenic Cliff Dr. and Great Western Hwy; tel: 82 1600;* **Colonial Motor Inn**, *Great Western Hwy; tel: 82 1811;* **Fairmont Resort**, *1 Sublime Point Rd; tel: 82 5222;* **Leura Gardens Ibis Resort**, *Fitzroy St; tel: 841331;* **Where Waters Meet Motel**, *15 Mount Hay Rd; tel: 843022.* **High Mountains Motor Inn**, *193 Great Western Hwy, Blackheath; tel: 87 8216;* **Blackheath Motor Inn**, *Great Western Hwy, Blackheath; tel: 87 8788;* **Redleaf Motel**, *Brightlands Ave; tel: 878108;* **Katoomba HI**, *66 Waratah St; tel: 82 1416;* **North Springwood HI**, *Hawkesbury Lookout; tel: 54 1342.*

EATING AND DRINKING

Pegum's Restaurant, *25 Honour Ave, Lawson;* tel: 59 1844. Closed Tues. BYO. Up-market French cuisine. **Leura House**, *7 Britain St, Leura; tel: 1331.* Open 7 days for dinner. Licensed. Country food. **The Chalet Restaurant**, *46 Portland Rd, Medlow Bath; tel: 88 1122.* Open Thur–Sun. BYO. **Hotel Imperial**, *Station St, Mount Victoria Village; tel: 87 1233.* Licensed. Dinner Fri–Sat. **Rosewood Cottage**, *1 Orient St, Katoomba; tel: 82 2178.* Closed Sun. BYO. **Patrick's La Normandie**, *124 Wentworth St, Blackheath; tel: 87 6144.* Dinner open 7 days. BYO. French cuisine. **Glennella**, *56 Govetts Leap Rd, Blackheath; tel: 87 8352.*

SIGHTSEEING

First try and get it into perspective. There is Sydney. And there, cradling it in enfolding arms, are the Blue Mountains. When you see them, you will wonder why they formed such an impenetrable barrier to the early settlers and stopped them moving out to the 'vision splendid, of the sunlit plains extended', which ran to the north-west. The simple answer is that the earliest explorers approached with logic along

the valleys and as soon as they reached the Blue Mountains they came to impassable cliffs. It was not until someone had the bright idea of following the ridges that the Blue Mountains were conquered. There is much argument as to who was the first across but it is generally accepted that it was Blaxland, Wentworth and Lawson, who came across with horses in 1813. However, there is, however, much evidence to suggest that they were beaten to it by an escaping convict.

Nowadays the crossing of the Blue Mountains is an afternoon jaunt in a car. But on that drive you'll see scenery that will take your breath away. One route out of Sydney takes you up the steep and winding **Bellbird Hill** and then along Bell's Line of Road until eventually you drop down past the Zigzag Railway into **Lithgow**. It does go through some small towns but once you are on the top it is either apple orchards or country all the way.

The second approach takes the motorway that runs off *Parramatta Rd*, by-passes **Penrith**, and then starts a long, slow climb up the mountain going through village after village as it does so. A good way of seeing the Blue Mountains is on a day trip out of Sydney, going up one way and coming back the other. If you start early in the morning you will have time to do some extensive exploring and if you want to go serious bush walking – and this is recommended – you can always come back another day.

If you start off by using *Parramatta Rd* and then the toll way, after 50 km you start the climb up into the mountains through **Lapstone**, **Blaxland** and **Valley Heights**. Along this first half of the journey, your route will be parallel to the railway and then they cross and recross each other several times. The first place of note is **Faulconbridge**. There is a clearly marked sign on the right leading to the house of the artist **Norman Lindsay**. It was here that *Sirens* was made, the movie about his life, featuring one of Australia's most bountiful natural resources, Elle ˙Macpherson, who appeared without the benefit of clothing. You may, like many others, find Lindsay's paintings of the chocolate box Playboy school, but the house and the gardens are splendid and his ship models covetable. Open 1100–1700, closed Tues; *tel: 51 1067.*

From there you go onwards and upwards past Bullabura to Wentworth Falls with **Yester Grange**, *Yester Rd.* This historic house is an art gallery, a museum and is heritage listed. Open seven days a week; *tel: 57 1110.*

Next comes **Leura** – an elegant village built around a central mall – which has **Leuralla Toy and Railways Museum**, *36 Olympian Parade; tel: 84 1169,* and a cliff drive from Leura to **Katoomba**, which offers panoramic views including the Jamieson Valley and the Megalong Valley, and has many lookouts and picnic spots.

At Katoomba, in *Echo Point Rd,* there is a visitor information centre and the road then leads down to a view of the **Three Sisters**, a natural outcrop that is floodlit at night, and also an astounding view over the **Grose Valley** below. You can, if you like, clamber to the bottom, bearing in mind that afterwards you will have to clamber back up again. It is from this viewpoint that you can most clearly see why they are called the Blue Mountains. The blue haze is caused by the minute droplets of eucalyptus oil in the air.

At Katoomba, there is also what is claimed to be the world's steepest incline railway – it used to service a mine – and a skyway that swings above the valley floor. **Katoomba Scenic Railway and Skyway**; *tel: 82 2699.* Both rides are open daily from 0900–1700.

From there continue to **Blackheath** and to **Evan's Lookout**, which has magnificent views across the Grose Valley to **Mt Banks**, and on a clear day, **Mt Tomah** and **Mt Irvine** in the background.

A little further down the main road is a well marked turn off to **Govett's Leap**. Tour guides tell of a lover jumping to his death. Nothing so romantic. Govett was a surveyor and leap is a Scottish word for waterfall. Nevertheless, it is a most beautiful spot, with the **Bridal Veil Falls** drifting down to the valley below. There is a picnic area and a series of well signposted, well graded bus walks. There is also an excellent **National Park Heritage Centre and Shop**; *tel: 87 8877.* If you turn left off the main road you will drop down into the Megalong Valley, passing through a series of giant ferns growing up from the rain forest below. Half way down the steep descent is a parking place and a track running for 600m on a circular route through the rain forest across the creek. Another walk takes you to the **Mermaid's Cave**. You can explore the valley, if you wish, on horseback – **Werriberri Trail Rides**, *Megalong Rd; tel: 87 9171.*

Retracing the route back up the hill from Megalong – this is not a through road – you run alongside the **Shipley Plateau** as you come back into Blackheath.

The next stop is **Mt Victoria**, which has a series of gentle bushwalks to two sightseeing points. Up Mt Piddington Rd is a look-out over the Kanimbla Valley and another is at **Pulpit Rock Reserve**. From Victoria you cut across to the other route to **Bell**. Bell's Line of Road runs down the other side of the valley passing the **Mt Tomah Botanical Gardens**, which are open daily, and then through the fruit orchards of **Bilpin** and **Kurrajong**, where you drop down Bellbird Hill to the plains and on to Sydney. This is a most exhilarating day tour and should not be missed if you can possibly help it.

BATHURST AND THE GOLD TOWNS

Tourism Information: Bathurst Visitors Centre, *William St; tel: (063) 32 2333.*

ACCOMMODATION AND FOOD

James Cook International Motor Inn, expensive, *corner Mid Western and Great Western Hwys; tel: 32 1800;* **Atlas Motel** *(FL), 272 Stewart St; tel: 31 5055;* **Coachmans Inn Motel** *(BW), corner Great Western Hwy and Oberon Rd; tel: 31 4855;* **Country Lodge Motor Inn**, *145 William St; tel: 31 4888;* **Gold Panner Motor Inn**, *Sydney Rd (Great Western Hwy); tel: 31 4444;* **Abercrombie Motor Inn**, *362 Stewart St; tel: 31 1077;* **Bathurst Motor Inn**, *87 Durham St; tel: 31 2222.*

The Terrace on William, *164 William St; tel: 31 1838.* 7 days. BYO. Courtyard dining. **Brooklyn on Mt Panorama**, *Mountain Straight; tel: 31 8075.* **Stagecoach Restaurant**, *corner William and Howick Sts; tel: 31*

105

1264. 7 days, licensed.

SIGHTSEEING

To understand Bathurst clearly, you have to see how it was moulded by the rush for gold. It is one of Australia's oldest inland towns and was founded 2 years after George Evans explored the area in 1813 and called it 'the handsomest country I have ever seen'. Governor Macquarie decided it would be named after the then Secretary of State for the colonies, Earl Bathurst.

The town quickly became the base for explorations inland. The progression was a natural one; over the Blue Mountains and across the plains to Bathurst, and then prepare to head west. But Bathurst's development was pushed along by the discovery of gold nearby in 1851. This first of many Australian gold rushes established Bathurst as a major town with 50 hotels and a population of about 5000. **Bathurst Gold Diggings,** *Conrod Straight, Mt Panorama,* is a reconstruction of a gold mining area. Open Sun–Fri 1000–1600; *tel:* 32 2022.

From the Gold Rush of the 1850s until the turn of the century, many grand public buildings were constructed in the Victorian style, which gives the town so much of its character. They range from the **Old Government House,** which was built in brick for Governor Macquarie's farewell visit to the town, to the 1880 **Court House,** which is the epitome of solid Victorian architecture.

The visitor centre has an excellent booklet describing the different architectural styles, and you can use it as a reference guide on a walking tour of the town. The area's dependence on agriculture is demonstrated daily at **Rossmore Park,** *Limekilns Rd, Kelso, tel:* 37 3634, which has a sheep and cattle stage show.

Near to Bathurst is the **Mt Panorama Motor Circuit** and it is here that Australia's most famous motor race takes place every October. There is a **Motor Racing Hall of Fame** (open daily 0900–1630; *tel:* 32 1872) on one of the corners, which is a public road when racing is not in progress. The track is 6 km long and the speed is 60 kph unless there is a race in progress, when speeds can be well over 250 kph.

There are many ghost towns in the area but the two most famous are **Hill End** and **Sofala.** Hill End is 85 km north of Bathurst and in the 1870s was Australia's largest inland town. Then the gold rush and development stopped and Hill End is now set in a time warp, with almost all the buildings dating back to the 1870s – many of which are well preserved. The town is used frequently by film companies for historical dramas.

Sofala was named after a gold mining town in South Africa and is 45 km north of Bathurst. Most of the town is as it originally was in the 1860s. At that time there were about 40,000 people living in Sofala – now there are less than a tenth of that number.

ORANGE

Tourist Information: Orange Visitors Centre, *Civic Gdns, Byrne St; tel (062) 61 5226.*

ACCOMMODATION

Central Caleula Motor Lodge *(BW),* 60 *Summer St; tel:* 62 7699; **Apple City International Motor Inn** *(FL),* 146 *Bathurst Rd; tel:* 62 6033; **Festival Motor Inn** *(FL), corner Mitchell Hwy and Dalton St; tel:* 62 5755; **Orange Motor Lodge** *(BW),* 110 *Bathurst Rd; tel:* 62 4600; **Oriana Motor Inn** *(BU), Woodward St; tel:* 62 3066; **Down Town Motel,** 243 *Summer St; tel:* 62 2877; **Mid–City Motor Lodge,** 243 *Lords Pl.; tel:* 62 1600.

EATING AND DRINKING

Matilda's Family Restaurant, *Bathurst Rd; tel:* 63 1580. **Metropolitan Hotel Bistro,** *corner Byng and Anson Sts; tel:* 61 1353, dinner Mon–Sat, lunch 7 days. **Orange Ex-Services Club Bistro,** *Anson St; tel:* 62 2666, 7 days. **Blackmans Swamp Restaurant,** 294 *Lords Pl.; tel:* 62 5000, dinner Tues–Sat. **Chloes Restaurant,** *Festival Motor Inn, corner Woodward and Dalton Sts; tel:* 62 5755, Mon–Thur 1800, Fri–Sat 1830. **Jonathans Restaurant,** *Apple City Motel,* 146 *Bathurst Rd; tel:* 62 6033, dinner 7 days from 1830. **Oriana Motor Inn,** *Woodward St; tel:* 62 3066, Mon–Sat 1830. **Patmos Restaurant,** 177 *Lords Pl.; tel:* 625839, lunch Mon–Fri 1200–1400, dinner Mon–Sat. **Temptations Restaurant,** *Central*

Caleula Motel, 60 Summer St; tel: 62 7699, dinner 7 days from 1830. **Welcome Inn**, *87 March St; tel: 624103,* Mon–Sat 1830. **Gumbos Restaurant**, *297 Summer St; tel: 62 3118,* Cajun and international, dinner 7 days from 1800, lunch Mon–Fri 1200–1400. **Golden Bowl Chinese Restaurant**, *Orange City Bowling Club, Warrendine St; tel: 62 0144,* lunch Tues–Sun 1100–1400, dinner 1700–2100 (2200 Fri and Sat). **The Overlander**, *Mid City Motor Lodge, Lords Pl.; tel: 62 1600,* (Indian/Aust), 7 days from 1800. **Phoenix Chinese Restaurant**, *296 Summer St; tel: 62 80117*, days lunch 1130–1430, dinner 1700–2200.

Sightseeing

Orange is one of the stopping points on the way westward. It is a prosperous town in a rich farming area. Half the apple crop of New South Wales is grown on the district's rich volcanic soils. However, it is not called Orange because of some association with fruit. It was named by Thomas Mitchell after William, Prince of Orange (not to be confused with William of Orange) who, like Mitchell, was an aide to the Duke of Wellington.

The volcanic soil comes from the extinct volcano **Mt Canabolas**. The city is situated on the eastern slopes. The area around Orange not only grows fruit, but also produces almost every other kind of agricultural product, and has just started getting into the vineyard business.

The New South Wales government had the idea of a secondary industrial area, which would be called the Bathurst-Orange Growth Centre but, as in so many other cases, only the government thought it was a good scheme and the idea ground to a standstill.

Although there were farmers and stockmen in the area, it was the discovery of gold reefs nearby in **Ophir**, **Lucknow**, Sofala and Hill's End that propelled Orange forward, as well as a hundred other ghost villages in the area. The gold ran out after a few years, leaving Orange a successful, well-established and slightly smug country town serving the immediate area.

Worth seeing is **Bowen Terrace**, which was built in 1876 and is a city terrace in a country town. The main recreation centre of the town is **Cook Park**, *Summer St,* which has a turn of the century bandstand, a begonia conservatory and some trees that were planted over a hundred years ago. The upper slopes of Mt Canabolas have a 2400 hectare flora and fauna reserve. The road up follows the route taken by Mitchell in 1835 – follow the signs – and at the top is the tree filled crater of the volcano.

Side Track from Orange

One weekly train runs on Wed from Orange to Broken Hill, taking approx. 9 hrs; on Mon and Thur it is also possible to catch the **Indian Pacific** (see p.404) at Orange East Fork. From Dubbo there is a bus service by Australian National railways taking 9 hrs. Or you can fly from Dubbo or Sydney. The journey by road is 750 km along Rte 32, now the Barrier Hwy, via **Nyngan**, **Wilcannia** and an awful lot of nothing; the horizon extends so far across the dusty plain that you can see the curvature of the earth.

BROKEN HILL

Tourist Information: Broken Hill Tourists and Travellers Centre, *corner Blende and Bromide Sts; tel (08) 87 6077.*

Remember that Dubbo is on South Australia, not New South Wales, time.

Accommodation and Food

Broken Hill Overlander Motor Inn *(BW), 142 Iodide St; tel: 8088 2566*; **Charles Rasp Motor Inn**, *158 Oxide St; tel: 8088 1988*; **Hilltop Motor Inn** *(FL), 271 Kaolin St; tel: 8088 2999*; **Daydream Motel**, *77 Argent St; tel: 8088 3033*; **Lodge Motel** *(BU), 252 Mica St; tel: 8088 2722*; **Mine Host Motel** *(BW), 120 Argent St; tel: 8088 4044*; **Miners Lamp Motor Inn** *(FL), corner Oxide and Cobalt Sts; tel: 8088 4122;* **HI Tourist Lodge**, *100 Argent St; tel: 88 2086.*

Sightseeing

This is the capital of the far west – 1170 km west of Sydney – and a town created by a single mineral find. In 1883 Charles Rasp, a chemist who was also a boundary rider, pegged out 11 hectares of the broken hill, which he thought might contain tin. It was, in fact, an outcrop of ironstone and the hill itself contained the richest deposit of silver-lead-zinc ever discovered. Two years later Broken Hill Proprietary was floated. The Aboriginal name of the place was *Willyama*, which literally means 'broken hill', and this was used on early maps, but eventually the European name prevailed.

Broken Hill is effectively a one company, one union town. They now live in harmony but it was not always so. A series of brutal strikes led to the formation in 1923 of the **Barrier Industrial Council**, which then proceeded to run Broken Hill as a totally closed shop. This applies to a large extent to this day.

The surrounding countryside is dry and inhospitable. The weather in Broken Hill is always warm and in the summer months of Oct–Mar, extremely hot. Visitors need to pace themselves to cope with the heat.

The town is the only place of any size in the far west of the state and is totally self contained. The centrepiece of the town is a Victorian town hall, which is reminiscent of similar town halls throughout Britain. Twenty five of the buildings in the town are listed. The streets of the town stretch out from the town hall and many are named after chemicals.

One ideal way to get the feel of the town is to go on one of the walking tours (Mon, Wed, Fri, Sat 1000, starting at the **Visitors Centre** – *tel. 87 2782*). You can then go underground at **Daydream Mine**, *tel: 88 5682*. Daily 1 hr tours start at 1000 and finish at 1530. Cost: $10. **Delpars Original BHP Mine**, open Mon–Fri, offer 2 hr tours starting at 1030. Details from the Visitors Information Centre.

Broken Hill is the centre of the **Brushmen from the Bush**, a remarkable collection of artists including Pro Hart and Jack Absolam. There are literally dozens of art galleries in Broken Hill, all showing or selling paintings produced by the Bush

artists. **Pro Hart Gallery**, *108 Wyman St*, open every day 0900–1700 except Sun 1330–1700; **Absolam's Gallery**, *638 Chapple St*, open 1000–1700 daily; and the **Broken Hill City Art Gallery**, *corner of Blende and Chloride Sts*, open Mon–Fri 1000–1700 Sat–Sun 1300–1700, which contains the statue **The Silver Tree**, commissioned by Charles Rasp, are but three examples. The largest commercial gallery is **Ant Hill**, which is opposite the Visitors Centre, open Mon–Sat 0900–1700, Sun 1330–1700.

Silverton is 25 km to the north-west of Broken Hill and access is by way of a surfaced road. This is a ghost mining town and is now widely used as a film set for productions including *Mad Max II*, *A Town Like Alice* and many Australian commercials. The gaol has been converted into a small museum (open daily 0930–1630) and there are half a dozen private art galleries.

White Cliffs is approached by good dirt roads and is 90 km off the Barrier Hwy. It grew up following the discovery of white opals and there are tours through a variety of dugout homes and opal mines. **White Cliffs Dug-Out Motel** – *tel: (080) 916677* – is unique in that it is a motel underground. White Cliffs also houses Australia's first solar power station. 🖾

WELLINGTON

Tourist Information: Wellington Visitor Information Centre, *Cameron Park; tel (068) 45 1733.*

ACCOMMODATION

Garden Court Motor Inn, *Mitchell Hwy; tel: 45 2288*. **Abel Macquarie Motel**, *32 Mitchell Hwy; tel: 45 1011*. **Bridge Motel**, *5 Lee St; tel: 45 2555*. **Wellington Motor Inn**, *37 Maxwell St; tel: 45 1177*.

SIGHTSEEING

At the junction of the Macquarie and Bell rivers, Wellington is 362 km north-west of Sydney on the road from Bathurst to **Dubbo**. One of its better known attractions is the **Wellington Caves** complex (8 km south of

Wellington on a turn-off from the Mitchell Hwy marked **Wellington Gateway Project**. Tours daily every hour on the hour starting at 0900 with the last tour at 1600; *tel: 45 1733)*. These caves have what is claimed to be the world's largest stalagmite and within the **Cathedral**, **Bone**, **Water** and **Garden Caves** are fascinating displays of limestone stalagmites and stalactites. Next to the Wellington Caves is **Hughesville**, where a house made from 9000 wine bottles houses a collection of antiques and local memorabilia. The **Clock Museum** has 170 working clocks on display. **The Wellington Historical Museum**, *corner Warne and Percy Sts, tel: 45 2325,* has an excellent record of the growth of the district with special attention paid to the gold rush. Open daily 1330–1630.

DUBBO

Tourist Information: Dubbo Visitor Centre; *tel: (068) 84 1422.*

ACCOMMODATION AND FOOD

Australian Heritage Motor Inn, *corner Cobra and Brisbane Sts; tel: 84 1188*; **A.A. Cattlemans Country Motor Inn**, *10 Whylandra St; tel: 84 5222*; **Aberdeen Motor Inn** *(BW), 25 Cobra St; tel: 84 1700*; **Atlas Motel**, *140 Bourke St; tel: 82 7244*; **Blue Diamond Motor Inn** *(BW), 113 Wingewarra St; tel: 82 0666*; **Country Comfort Inn Motel** *(CC), Peak Hill Rd; tel: 82 4777*; **Across Country Motor Inn** *(BU), corner Newell Hwy and Baird St; tel: 82 0877*; **Dubbo City Motor Inn**, *57 Cobra St; tel: 82 7033*; **Matilda Motor Inn**, *231 Darling St; tel: 82 3944*; **HI: Kurrajong House**, *87 Brisbane St, tel: 82 0922.*

Jule's Crepes, *213 Macquarie St; tel: 82 9300.* Dinner 7 nights a week. Licensed. **Echidna**, *177 Macquarie St; tel: 84 9393.* **Forest Lodge Restaurant**, *corner Myall St and Wheelers Lane; tel: 82 6500.* Licensed. Australian bush tucker and vegetarian.

SIGHTSEEING

In 1818, 30 years after the arrival of the first fleet explorer, John Oxley documented and reported on the rich grazing land around what is now Dubbo. The first settlers, George Thomas Palmer and John Wylde, arrived 10 years later and in 1828 a property was established called Dubbo, said to be named after the Aboriginal word meaning 'red earth'. A settlement developed nearby and was named after the property.

The greatest attraction in the Dubbo area is the **Western Plains Zoo** *(tel: 82 5888)*, which has one of the largest zoological collections in Australia and is truly an open zoo with the animals wandering nearly wild in something closely approaching their native habitat. There is a 6 km drive around the zoo. Open daily 0900–1700, admission $14.

The Dubbo Museum *(tel: 82 5359)* is on *Macquarie St* and has a blacksmith shop, a village square and a collection of Aboriginal artefacts. On *Obley Rd*, 2 km past Dubbo Zoo, is **Dundullimal**, which is the oldest remaining slab homestead in Australia and is run as a tourist attraction.

Dubbo's Literary History

The *Oxford Literary Guide to Australia* reminds us that the novelist Rolf Boldrewood, who wrote *Robbery Under Arms*, served in Dubbo, under his real name Thomas Alexander Browne, as a police magistrate from 1881. His predecessor, John Oxley Norton, had been murdered by his mistress, Catherine Warren. *Robbery Under Arms* was written in Dubbo during Browne's 3-year stint in the town, as was *Old Melbourne Memories*.

To the north-east of the town is the Talbragar river, about which Henry Lawson, the poet and notorious drunk, wrote a sentimental poem with that title about workers gathering for a funeral and the poem – doggerel? – runs: 'For thirty miles around Trabalagar the boys rolled up in strength, And Denver had a funeral a good long mile in length . . . .'

DUBBO– LIGHTNING RIDGE

Heading towards the 'Back of Bourke' is, to Australians, getting out to the real outback. Dubbo, within striking distance of Sydney, is still civilised country with green fields and ordered vineyards. But start moving further out and there is a change both in the land and the people – these are the people of the bush and they have different attitudes to life.

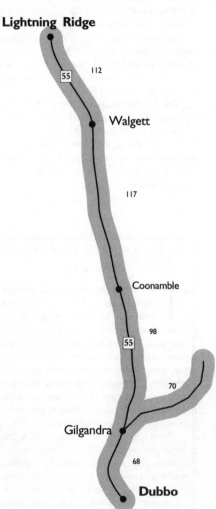

Lightning Ridge

55 112

Walgett

117

110

ROUTE: 395 KM

Coonamble

55 98

Warrumbungle National Park

70

Gilgandra

68

Dubbo

ROUTE

From Dubbo you follow the Castlereagh Hwy, Rte 55, all the way. The first town you come to is **Gilgandra**, a gentle transition to the conditions of the outback because Gilgandra has underground water and an observatory which, together, spell civilisation.

Drive on through **Coonamble** to **Walgett** and you see a major transition. Walgett is the gateway to the back of beyond and it is most certainly pioneer territory. **Lightning Ridge** is the last main stop before you get to Queensland and is a town where the whole economy is based on opals. You are now indeed Back of Bourke, in the serious outback.

BUSES

No trains serve this route, but there is a daily bus (Fraser's coaches) from Dubbo to Walgett (3½ hrs) and Lightning Ridge (4½ hrs). OTT table 9097.

GILGANDRA

Tourist Information: Gilgandra Visitors Centre, *on the Newell Hwy; tel: (068) 47 2045.*

ACCOMMODATION

Castlereagh Motor Inn *(BU), Newell Hwy; tel: 47 2697*; **Cooee Motel**, *corner Newell Hwy and Hargraves Lane; tel: 47 2981*; **Orana Windmill Motel**, *40 Warren Rd; tel: 47 2404*; **Silver Oaks Motel**, *Newell Hwy, PO Box 128; tel: 47 2502*; **Alfa Motel**, *7 Castlereagh St; tel: 47 1188*.

SIGHTSEEING

Gilgandra was known as the windmill town in earlier times as there was no mains water supply. In the 1950s there were some 300 private windmills pumping water to houses. Most of them have now disappeared.

One of the great attractions of Gilgandra – the name is Aboriginal for 'long waterhole' – is the **Gilgandra Observatory**. This takes advantage of the clear night skies, unpolluted by city lights and smog. The observatory is open Thur–Mon with nightly viewing on the 31cm diameter telescope 1900–2200. Closed August.

On the Castlereagh Hwy, 2 km north of town, is the **Australia Collection**, claimed, on dubious authority, to be the biggest collection of Aboriginal art and relics in the state. Open daily.

On Newell Hwy is **Orana Cactus World**, which is a collection built up over 49 years by Lester Myers. Open weekends and at other times by appointment; *tel: 47 2642*. Nearly 15 km north-east of the two (turn off the Oxley Hwy 8 km north of Gilgandra) is the **Native Flora Reserve**, 21 acres of reserved bushland

with rambling pathways. A list of the flora and bird species in the reserve is available at the Gilgandra Visitors Centre.

SIDE TRACK FROM GILGANDRA

WARRUMBUNGLE NATIONAL PARK

Tourist Information: NWPS Warrumbungle; *tel (062) 25 4364.*

This 21,000 hectare park is on the western slopes of the **Great Dividing Range**, 491 km north-west of Sydney. You can reach it from the east via **Coonabarabran**, the west by **Coonamble** and the south through **Gilgandra**. Note that within the park itself pretty well all roads are unsealed and in wet weather can become impassable except to four-wheel-drive vehicles.

On arrival at the park it is a courtesy and a safety measure to check in with the ranger at the **Visitors Centre**, *tel: 254 364.* There is a car fee of $5 and camping overnight on a powered site costs $7.50. There are three sites for campers – **Wambelong, Burbie** and **Blackman**.

Warrumbungle is one of the most dramatic national parks in the state, with peaks and spires climbing their way up to **Mt Exmouth**, which reaches 1206m. Rising from the wooded slopes is the **Breadknife**, a spectacular 90m wall of rock. The rugged landscape is partly due to ancient volcanoes.

The plant and animal life represents both sides of the **Great Dividing Range**. There are many grey kangaroos, swamp wallabies, wallaroos and gliders. There are also koalas but these are shy creatures and are difficult to spot. Among the 180 species of birds are the wedge-tailed eagle and flocks of emus.

A short and gentle walk in the park is to the **White Hum Lookout** on a sloping track, which has a spectacular view of the Warrumbungle range.

In the early morning a great walk for bird-watchers is to **Burbie Canyon**, taking about 1 hr to cover 2 km. For the more energetic there are graded walks, right up to

III

a 16 km hike to the top of Mt Exmouth. Warrumbungles is a tough and sometimes difficult park to get around but the rewards are more than commensurate with the efforts. 🛶

WALGETT

Tourist Information: Information Centre, *Council Chambers, Fax St; tel: (068) 28 1399.*

Almost equidistant between Sydney, Canberra and Brisbane – all about 700 km away – Walgett is in the heart of sheep and opal-mining country.

It was originally known as Walchate, which was the name given to a 'run' – a cattle farm – that covered 32,000 acres but could only graze 300 cattle. It comes from an Aboriginal word that can be translated as 'long waterhole', 'plenty of water' or 'swamp'.

Walgett shire formally came into being in 1906 although there was then no rail connection (that arrived 2 years later) and mail deliveries came by pack horse once a week. The great link through the 1880s were the paddle steamers, which used the **Darling** and **Murray River** systems to carry wool, wood, dried fruit and livestock. Walgett flourished as the centre of a growing pastoral district. And it was a Walgett man, Frederick Wolseley, who invented the powered sheep-shearing machine, which was patented in 1877 and transformed the sheep industry.

Walgett is home to a large number of aborigines, who live either in the town or on the **Namoi** and **Gingie reserves**, and it would be remiss not mention that this often causes tension within the town.

Walgett is a famed fishing spot on the **Barwon** and **Namoi** rivers. In 1902, three bridge workers landed a 250lb cod, which gives visiting anglers something to aspire to. Within easy distance – 75 km – is **Collarenebri**, where the weir on the Barwon River just outside the town, is considered to be one of the best inland fishing locations in Australia.

This is the gateway to the opal fields and within a day's round trip of the town are the **Grawin, Glengarry, Sheepyard, Coocoran** and **Lighting Ridge** fields.

Also within easy driving distance is **Burren** Junction, which has hot, mineralised bore baths, claimed to have remedial properties.

LIGHTNING RIDGE

Tourist Information: Tourist Information Centre; *tel: (068) 29 1462.*

This is one of the most famous opal sites in the world. Opal was first discovered here in 1905. The name is said to come from an incident, when a flock of sheep in the area were struck by lightning. It is on the north-western plains of NSW, 770 km from Sydney.

There are many tours of the opal mines of Lightning Ridge and you will be offered opals galore, at what you will be assured are bargain of the century prices. Sadly, this is rarely the case. Buy because you like the stone, not as an investment. The most rare, and therefore the most expensive stones, are solid with a precious opal face and a jet black base, and can cost well over $3000 a carat. Many of the stones offered are doublets or triplets, where a slice of opal is glued on to a backing of a non-precious opal variety called *potch*. Sometimes, instead of potch, glass or ceramic are used. Such stones can be very attractive when mounted in a setting but they do not compare with the solid stones, which start at $250 a carat for fairly poor quality and then head skywards. Remember the phrase, let the buyer beware.

North of the town, off *Gem St,* is the **Walk-In-Mine**, which demonstrates the ins and outs of opal prospecting. Open daily. Much the same display is at the nearby **Spectrum Mine**.

On *Opal St* is yet another **Bottle House** – more beer than wine – which contains mining and opal memorabilia.

Apart from opal mines and opal shops, Lightning Ridge boasts hot bore baths, where the water is naturally heated to 42°C and is rich in potassium salts. The water comes from the Llanilo Bore, is widely claimed to have therapeutic qualities and has a flow rate of 20 litres a second. The baths are free and always open.

The **Bush Museum** is down a track off *Black Prince Dr.* which is, in turn, off *Pandora St.* You will know you are there when you see a boat in a tree. While this is not the British Museum, it has its own eccentric, and totally politically incorrect, charm.

SOUTHERN HIGHLANDS CIRCUIT

This circular tour heads out through the rich farming districts of Bowral, Moss Vale, Berrima and Mittagong and then south to the Snowy Mountains and Mt Kosciusko, the tallest mountain in Australia. At Cooma you can detour into the heart of Kosciusko National Park and the Snowy Mountains, before picking up the route, again north, right across the park to Tumut, Gundagai, where the 'dog sat on the tuckerbox', and Yass, and then gently back to Sydney. Taking in some of the best scenery in Australia, it can be accomplished easily in a week. It offers the opportunity to stop awhile in Canberra, the nation's capital (see p. 187) or jump onto the Murray and Riverina route (see p.195) at Yass.

113

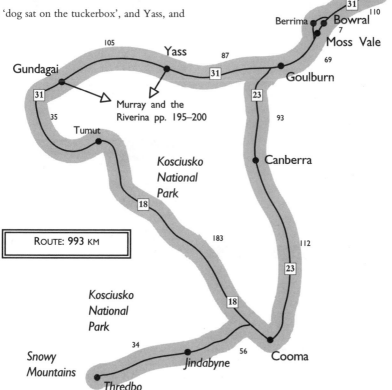

ROUTE: 993 KM

ROUTE

Start from Sydney on the South West Hwy, Rte 31, passing through farming and commuter territory. At **Mittagong**, just over 100 km from Sydney, turn left for **Bowral**, and a little further on, **Moss Vale** (or continue on the Highway to reach Moss Vale via **Berrima**). Nearly 70 km further on along Rte 31 (now the Hume Hwy) lies **Goulburn**. Thirteen kilometres after Goulburn, leave Rte 31 (left) for Rte 23, heading south-west 80 km for **Canberra**. Another 100 km brings you to **Cooma**, gateway to the southern reaches of **Kosciusko National Park**. From here you can side-track into the park for 90 km to **Thredbo**. If you do, retrace the route back to Cooma and head north on Rte 18 for 183 km through the park to **Tumut**. Continue from there up to the junction with Rte 31 and turn right to follow it to **Gundagai** and a further 105 km to **Yass**. Rte 31 continues east to Goulburn, from where you can back-track to Sydney.

TRAINS

There is a frequent commuter service stop from Sydney to Moss Vale (2½ hrs) and Goulburn (3½ hrs). Three daily trains also call at these towns en route to Canberra (4 hrs), as do a further three to Yass Junction (3¾ hrs). OTT tables 9014, 9021, 9026.

BUSES

Greyhound Pioneer coaches run from Sydney to Cooma (6¾ hrs), Jindabyne (just over 7 hrs) and Thredbo (8 hrs); additional services may be laid on in the winter sports season. OTT table 9098.

BOWRAL

Tourist Information: Southern Highlands Visitor Centre, *Hume Hwy, Mittagong; tel: (048) 712888.*

ACCOMMODATION

The Briars Country Lodge, expensive, *Moss Vale Rd; tel: 68 3566.* **Oxley View Motel**, *Moss Vale Rd; tel: 61 4211.* **Bowral Motel**, *Kangaloon Rd; tel: 61 2300.* **Golf View Lodge Motel**, *Boronia St; tel: 61 2777.*

SIGHTSEEING

To all practical intents and purposes, Bowral, Mittagong, Moss Vale and Berrima can be thought of as one very tight, intertwined area.

Bowral is where the richer city folk come to be country people. It has a most wonderful collection of houses and mansions, all in perfectly groomed grounds. As it is 114 km south of Sydney it is just, but only just, outside commuting territory. It is for ever connected with Sir Donald Bradman. He was not born here but this is where he went to school and started his amazing cricket career. There is a **Bradman Museum**, *tel: (048) 62 11247,* which is open but still being developed, and is a long way towards completion. It is in a pavilion on *St Jude St* and overlooks a cricket pitch where the great Don played. Open 1000–1600 daily. Every spring Bowral has a **Tulip Time Festival**, which is held in **Corbett Gardens**.

In theory Bowral and Mittagong are two separate places but in practice they have melded together into one inseparable whole. Mittagong was originally an iron mining town although it seems impossible to believe nowadays. Also in the area is the **Castle Maze**, *corner of Bowral and Bessemer Sts,* open daily 1000–1700, and further along *Bessemer St* is the **Butterfly House**, which is open daily and has literally thousands of live butterflies on display.

BERRIMA AND MOSS VALE

ACCOMMODATION

Berrima Bakehouse Motel, *corner Wingecarribee St and Hume Hwy, Berrima; tel: 77 1381.* **White Horse Inn**, *Market Pl., Berrima; tel: 77 1204.* **Peppers Mount Broughton Hotel**, expensive, *Kater Rd, Sutton Forest 2577; tel: 68 2355.* **Bong Bong Motel**, *238 Argyle St, Moss Vale 2577; tel: 68 1033.* **Golf Ball Motel**, *corner Arthur and Spring Sts, Moss Vale; tel: 68 1511.*

SIGHTSEEING

Berrima has many classic buildings including the court house, which was built in 1838 and now houses the **Berrima Museum.** Open daily; *tel: 77 1505.* At the other end of the street is the **Surveyor General Inn**, which claims, on fairly flimsy grounds, that it is Australia's oldest hotel in continuous operation. Moss Vale is the industrial and agricultural centre of the Southern Highlands, and it forms the third point of a close triangle with Bowral and Mittagong. It has the **Cecil Hoskins Nature Reserve**, **Leighton Gardens** and is generally a pleasant and relaxed country town, which benefits economically from its closeness to Sydney.

Any and all of these towns serve as a gateway to the **Morton National Park** (*tel :87 7270)*, covering 162,000 hectares, with the Shoalhaven River running though it in a gorge and a high plateau in the centre of the park.

GOULBURN

Tourist Information: Goulburn Visitors Centre, *6 Montague St; tel: (048) 21 5343.*

ACCOMMODATION AND FOOD

Goulburn Heritage Motor Lodge *(FL), Hume Hwy; tel: 21 9377;* **Centretown Lagoon Motel** *(BW), 77 Lagoon St; tel: 21 2422;* **Posthouse Motor Lodge** *(FL), 1 Lagoon St; tel: 21 5666;* **Clinton Lodge**, *80 Clinton St; tel: 21 4488;* **Alpine Lodge Motel**, *248 Sloane St; tel: 21 2930;* **Lilac City Motor Inn**, *126 Lagoon St; tel: 21 5000;* **Country Home Motel** *(BU), 1 Cowper St; tel: 21 4877.*

Broadbents Restaurant, *19 Market St; tel: 21 4833.* Licensed. 7 days. **Old Goulburn Brewery**, *Bungonia Rd; tel: 21 6071.* 7 days a week. **Viennaworld Restaurant**, *corner Old Hume Hwy and Lansdowne St; tel 21 6909.* Licensed. Mon–Sat.

SIGHTSEEING

Two hours and 209 km from Sydney and 1 hr from Canberra, Goulburn is a rural city on the Hume Highway, which runs between Sydney and Melbourne. It is the centre of the rich Southern Tablelands farming district, at the junction of the Wollondilly and Mulwarry Rivers. Its early reputation was built on exporting fine merino wool, although when this trade started in the 1830s, coaches took as long as 16 days to reach Sydney.

Within Australia its prison earned it a harsher reputation and it was also a centre for police action against bushrangers (see p.199) in the southern part of the state. When the gold rush came in the 1850s the town was almost deserted as the inhabitants headed for the goldfields north of the town on the Abercrombie River. Goulburn was originally named Strathallan. It was later renamed in honour of the then Secretary of the Colonies. It was the last town in the British Empire to be created a city and a bishopric by Royal Letters Patent.

Many of the buildings in the town date from the last century and there is an excellent walking tour, which takes 1–2 hrs and covers all principal sites. Maps of this tour are available at the **Visitor's Centre** in *Montague St.*

One of the most interesting buildings in the area is **Riversdale** *(tel: 21 4741),* which was built as an inn in the 1830s and has been restored and furnished by the National Trust – open daily except Tuesdays. **St Saviour's Cathedral** was one of the many in Australia designed by Edmund Blackett. It was built of white sandstone in 1874 over an earlier church, which was later demolished and carried out through the front door. Open for tours Mon–Sat 1000–1600, Sun 1300–1600 *(tel: 21 2206).*

St Clair History House is a twenty room mansion built in about 1843, which has been restored by the local historical society. The brewery of 1836 is thought to be the only surviving pre-Federation (1901) brewery in Australia and still serves its own real ale. A landmark of the two is the **Rocky Hill War Memorial**, which was built in 1923. The grounds provide a lookout for views over Goulburn and the country beyond.

Nearby, in a valley one hour's drive to the north-east of Goulburn via Taralga, are the **Wombeyan limestone caves**, which have self-guided tours and a wide variety of accommodation available.

Just outside town is the **Pelican Sheep Station** *(tel: 21 4668),* which is 10 km along the *Braidwood Rd* and has demonstrations of shearing, sheep dog handling and wool preparation. Also just outside town is the **Marsden Weir** on the Wollondilly River, with picnic and barbecue facilities.

115

CANBERRA

See p. 187.

COOMA

Tourism Information: Cooma Visitors Centre; *tel: (064) 50 1742.*

ACCOMMODATION

Alkira Motel, *213 Sharp St; tel: 52 3633*; **Kinross Inn**, *15 Sharp St; tel: 52 3577*; **Cooma Motor Lodge**, *6 Sharp St; tel: 52 1888*; **Marlborough Motor Inn**, *Monaro Hwy; tel: 52 1133*; **White Manor Motel**, *252 Sharp St; tel: 52 1152*; **High Country Motel**, *12 Chapman St; tel: 52 1277.*

SIGHTSEEING

Cooma lies at the crossing of the Monaro and Snowy Mountain Hwys, and could be regarded as the entry point for the Snowy Mountains. Its name comes from an Aboriginal word and has been interpreted as 'lake' or 'swamp'. The water connection is relevant because this was the town of the Snowy Mountain Scheme, the biggest civil engineering work ever carried out in Australia.

While this was being built it was a town of many migrant nationalities, reflected in the **International Avenue of Flags**, which contains the flags of 27 nations, representing all those who worked on the Snowy Mountain Scheme. You can visit the Scheme and see the underground power station at **Cabramurra**, **Talbingo** and **Khancoban**. Check first with the **Snowy Scheme's Information Centre** in Cooma (*tel: 1800 623 776*.)

There is a pleasant stroll around Cooma called the **Lambie Town Walk** that starts at Centennial Park and then ambles around 10km of the town and the surrounding bushland.

Cooma is surrounded by small villages like **Nimmitabel**, once a staging post. The **Royal Arms** (*tel: 54 6422*) was used as a staging post by wheeled carriages as far back as 1850. This inn, featured in the classic film *The Sundowners*, has trout fishing within easy strolling distance. Also nearby is **Llama World**, 19 km out of town on the Snowy Mountains Hwy; *tel: 52 4593*, which is a farm specialising in breeding llamas.

⮑ SIDE TRACK FROM COOMA

Jindabyne is 56 km from Cooma; turn left off Rte 18, 6 km west of the town. Thredbo is another 34 km on. Snow may close the roads between May and Oct, when it is essential to carry chains.

JINDABYNE

Tourism Information: Snowy River Information Centre, *Petamin Plaza; tel: (064) 56 2444.*

ACCOMMODATION AND FOOD

Alpine Gables Motel, *corner Kosciusko Rd and Kalkite St; tel: 56 2555*; **Lakeview Plaza Motel**, *2 Snowy River Ave; tel: 56 2134*; **Aspen Hotel**, *Kosciusko Rd; tel: 56 2372*; **Lake Jindabyne Hotel**, *Kosciusko Rd; tel: 56 2203.*

Azifaz Restaurant, *Central Park, Snowy River Ave; tel: 56 2449.* Licensed. Open 7 nights. Also a night club. **A.J's Balcony Bar and Restaurant**, *Snowy Mountains Plaza; tel: 56 2144.* Open for dinner 7 days. Great views. **Hubert's Restaurant**, *corner Kosciusko Rd and Alpine Way; tel: 56 2052.* Open 7 nights. Licensed.

SIGHTSEEING

This town comes alive during the skiing season, when it offers easy access to the Snowy Mountains. It houses the **NSW Winter Academy of Sport** (*tel: 56 2242*), which is a government establishment but offers both accommodation and training at reasonable prices.

Jindabyne was moved from the banks of the Snowy River bit by bit starting in 1962, to make way for the Snowy Mountains Hydro-electric Scheme. The original town disappeared totally under the water on 22 Apr 1967. It is now on the shores of Lake Jindabyne – the name comes from an Aborigine word meaning either 'feather tailed rat' or 'valley of the waters', depending on which authority you listen to. During the summer it is a perfect base for trout fishing – the lake is very well stocked – and bushwalking, and it boasts staggering

116

views of the Snowy Mountains range. Daily cruises on the lake on MV **Kalinga** throughout the year. **Lake Jindabyne Cruises** – *tel: 56 1195.*

The best place to start a bush walk is probably the **Mt Kosciusko National Parks headquarters** (*tel: 56 2444*), which is about 20 km west of the town, going out on the *Mt Kosciusko Rd.* During the summer it is a 98 km drive to **Charlotte Pass**, where there is a series of walks, some extending up to Mt Kosciusko. Further away, at Thredbo, the ski chair lift operates throughout the year and from there you can get to the steel mesh track (laid by the National Parks and Wildlife Service to stop serious erosion) to the 2228m peak of Mt Kosciusko. During the winter there is skiing at Perisher, Smiggin Holes, Blue Cow and, further down the Alpine Way, Thredbo.

THREDBO AND KOSCIUSKO NATIONAL PARK

Tourist Information: Thredbo Information Centre: *tel: (064) 59 1400.* **Kosciusko NPWS**, *Cooma; tel: (064) 65 2102.*

ACCOMMODATION AND FOOD

Thredbo Alpine Hotel, *Village centre; tel: 59 4200*; **Snowgoose Lodge**, *Banjo Dr.;* *tel: 57 6415*; **Thredbo Alpine Apartments**, *Friday Dr.; tel: 59 4197*; **Alpenhorn Mountain Lodge**, *Village; tel: 57 6223*; **Berntis Mountain Inn**, *Mowamba Pl.; tel: 57 6332;* **HI**, *8 Jack Adams Path, Alpine Village; tel: 57 6376*

Alfresco Pizzeria; *tel: 57 6327.* BYO. **The Credo**; *tel: 57 6844.* Licensed.

SIGHTSEEING

Kosciusko National Park is the largest in New South Wales, covering 690,000 hectares. It contains the highest mountains in Australia and the headwaters of the Snowy, the Murrumbidgee and the Murray Rivers. During the spring, summer and autumn there are walks throughout the park, ranging from mild to extremely strenuous, and in areas of heavy foot traffic walkways have been laid down.

The park has two distinct seasons. In the winter it is a skiers' paradise – both downhill and cross-country. In the summer it is ablaze with wild flowers and plant life and the pleasant temperatures make a welcome relief from the heat of lower lying places. The tree line is at about 1800m, after which you get dwarf snow gums and low lying shrubs. Below the tree line there are fern gullies, forests of mountain ash, candlebark and stringybark and, by contrast, treeless

Skiing

A lthough Australia has more snow-covered mountains than Switzerland, not all of them are suitable for skiing. Consequently downhill skiing has developed in a few well publicised resorts. Thredbo is one of them.

There was, of course, skiing in Australia even in the last century. It is claimed, on little evidence, that the Alpine ski club in Kiandra was the first in the world. Reports of skiing appeared in the pages of the Sydney Morning Herald as early as 1861, and in the 1920s there was a social skiing scene around the slopes of Mt Kosciusko.

But it did not start as a seriously commercial venture until 1956, when an ex-Czech ski-instructor working on the Snowy Mountains project came to Thredbo and realised that the side of the steep valley, on which the resort is now built, would be an ideal ski resort, especially as the Snowy Mountain Authority was building a road, now the Alpine Way, right to the door.

The first lodge for skiers opened in the Thredbo Alpine Village in 1957 and the development of the area as a ski resort has proceeded apace since then.

There are now over 20 restaurants and bars, four ski shops and twenty sets of apartments.

KOSCIUSKO NATIONAL PARK MAP

alpine heaths, most of which have been caused by over-clearing although all farming is now forbidden.

The ski season is relatively short and can sometimes be unpredictable. As a consequence a determined effort has been made to sell Thredbo as a summer resort because the mountains are beautiful, the weather is ideal for walking and the flowers are in bloom to such an extent that they look like a multi-coloured carpet with apparent drifts of snow, which are, in fact, large swathes of white blossom. It is also the closest access to **Mt Kosciusko**. The only problem is the flies, never mentioned in any tourist brochure. You need a good insect repellent.

In Thredbo the ski lift – on the other side of the valley and climbing nearly 600m vertically to the top of **Crackenback** – operates all year round, which means you can go mountain walking with the slope always downhill. 🔼

GUNDAGAI

Tourist Information: Gundagai Visitors Bureau, *Sheridan St; tel: (069) 44 1341.*

ACCOMMODATION AND FOOD

Poets Recall Motel, *corner West and Punch Sts; tel: 44 1777*; **Garden Motor Inn** *(GC), West St; tel: 44 1744*; **Bushmans Retreat Motor Inn** *(BU), corner Mount and Cross Sts; tel: 44 1433*; **Gundagai Motel**, *corner West and Sheridan Sts; tel: 44 1066*; **Sheridan Motel**, *corner Sheridan and Otway Sts; tel: 44 1311*.

The Old Train Stop, *Railway Station; tel: 441 212.* Open 7 days. BYO. **Chan Kong Chinese Restaurant**, *226 Sheridan St; tel: 44 1897.* 7 days. Licensed.

SIGHTSEEING

The famous Australian song says 'the dog sat in the tuckerbox'. This is not precisely correct. One word was altered so that school children could sing it without giving offence. The name comes from the Aboriginal word *gundabandoob-ingee*, which can be translated as 'cut with a tomahawk at the back of the knee'.

The statue of the dog, decorously sitting on the tuckerbox, is to be found at **Five Mile**

The Dog Sat on the Tuckerbox

Australians are a weird mob. There is a statue on Five Mile Creek on the Hume Hwy, 5 miles – 7 and a bit kms – from Gundagai, with a dog sitting on the top of a tucker box – a food container. The original story appeared in 1856 in verse – author unknown – and read, according to every school book in Australia:

'And the dog sat on the tuckerbox, Five miles from Gundagai.'

There is also a recording of Slim Dusty, a major icon of Australian folk song, putting the same words to tune. The explanation given for this strange event was that there was an old time stockdrover, who had trained his dog to sit on the tuckerbox to prevent theives.

All of which is a great nonsense. In the original version, which does not appear in schoolbooks, the dog does not sit on the tuckerbox, he sits in the tuckerbox – but one essential letter has been removed. This is known, understood, and accepted by all students of Australian bush ballads and folk music. But the idea of a dog defecating in a food box is not the image that Australia would like to project to the world.

119

Creek, north of Gundagai just off the Hume Hwy. This is near the remains of the Five Mile pub, which is where camping teamsters gathered before heading off to the next goldfield.

The town is on the banks of the Murrumbidgee River in the foothills of **Mt Parnassus**. The great Australian natural disaster was the great flood of 1852, which swept away the original town and 83 inhabitants. The hero of the flood was Yarri, a koori from the local Wiradjuri tribe, who rescued many people in his bark canoe.

Gold fever came in 1861 and again in 1894 and there are several abandoned buildings and gold mines not far from the centre of town.

An interesting display is the cathedral in

miniature modelled by the late Frank Rusconi over a period of 28 years – it contains 20,948 hand cut pieces of marble. Another masterpiece is his replica of the altar of St Marie's cathedral in Paris – he worked on the original. Both are on display at the tourist information centre during normal working hours and Saturday and Sunday mornings.

The longest wooden bridge ever built in Australia spans the Murrumbidgee at Gundagai. The **Prince Alfred Bridge** was built 1867–1889 and originally formed part of the Hume Hwy. The bridge is classified by the National Trust and is closed to vehicular traffic but you can walk across it. The most imposing building in Gundagai is the **Court House**, built in 1859, and it was here that the trial of the notorious bushranger Captain Moonlight (often spelled Moonlite) was held. It is open for inspection when the court is not sitting.

The tourist centre has a free National Trust walking tour map, which will take you around all the principal sites in Gundagai. The **Gabriel Gallery**, *Sheridan St*, open Mon–Sat, has a collection of photographs taken 1890–1905 by Dr Charles Louis Gabriel, as well as items relating to poets associated with the town – Henry Lawson, Banjo Paterson and others.

Around the town, within easy driving distance, are a series of scenic lookouts including the **Rotary Lookout** at South Gundagai and the lookout on Mt Parnassus. Twelve kilometres out of town on the *Burra Rd,* you come to **Reno**, which also has a great panoramic view of Gundagai and the surrounding countryside.

YASS

Tourist Information: **Coronation Park Tourism Centre**; *tel: (06) 226 2557.*

ACCOMMODATION

Colonial Lodge Motor Inn *(GC), corner McDonald St and Hume Hwy; tel: 226 2211;* **Thunderbird Motel**, *Comur St; tel: 226 1158;* **The Yass Motel**, *Hume Hwy; tel: 226 1055;* **Swaggers Motor Inn**, *Hume Hwy; tel: 226 3188;* **Hamilton Hume Motor Inn** *(BW), 303 Hume Hwy; tel: 226 1722;* **Hi–Way Motor Inn** *(BU), corner Hume Hwy and Grand Junction; tel: 226 1300.*

SIGHTSEEING

This is part of the Canberra region and less than an hour's drive – 62 km – from the capital of Australia. It is about a 3 hr drive south-west of Sydney, 280 km along the Hume Hwy, which now by-passes Yass. There are about 4500 people living in the town and something close to 9000 in the Shire itself.

Yass is famous for its superfine wool and the properties – farms – in the area, the largest of which is owned by publisher Rupert Murdoch. The name is a corruption of an Aboriginal word, appropriately meaning 'running water'. The river Yass runs through the town and after its junction with the Goodradigbee river it forms the Murrumbidgee River, which is dammed 34 km south-west of Yass to form the **Burrinjuck Dam**. This is two and a half times the size of Sydney Harbour, is in the centre of the Burrinjuck State recreation park and offers a wide range of water-sports.

There is basic accommodation – camping, cottages and cabins – in the park *(tel 227 8114)*. Close by the **Lake Burrinjuck Leisure Resort** *(tel 227 7271)* and the **Good Hope Tourist Resort** *(tel: 227 1234)* are the weekend bases for the **ACT Waterski School**. Cruising the lake is the **Lady BJ** *(tel 227 7270)*, which has 3 day camp/cruise safaris and scheduled day cruises along the 100 km of waterways.

There have been vineyards in Yass for over a hundred years. There are now seven major vineries in the area and all are open to the public, offering free wine tastings and cellar door sales.

There are three small museums at Yass. One is the **Railway Station**, *Lead St*, which has been restored and shows the history of the Yass Tramway, one of Australia's many eccentric railway systems. Open Sun 1000–1600. The second museum is the **Hamilton Hume**, which shows the history of Yass and the surrounding agricultural area. Open Sun, Mon, Wed, Fri, Sat.

The third is the **Binalong Motor Museum**, 27 km from Yass, where all the exhibits work, including a 1908 chain drive aero-engined MAB.

NEW SOUTH WALES NATIONAL PARKS

National Parks and Wildlife Service, Sydney; tel: (02) 9585 6444. (Note that most national parks have their own separate offices and these should be contacted directly for more details when you are in the area. The central office will give you the addresses and telephone numbers.)

There are at least 104 national parks in New South Wales – and that is not counting reserves, state forests and other protected areas. This figure is almost certain to be out of date by the time you read it, as the national parks in New South Wales are in a continuing state of evolvement and more parks are added each year. Indeed, it seems that the pace is increasing rather than slowing down.

The most important national parks in New South Wales are described in more detail as part of the various routes in which they occur. The following listing provides an overview of the many and varied parks in all corners of the state.

Unless otherwise stated, all the parks in this listing possess at least one campsite, a picnic area and one or more walking trails. Camping in the bush is possible in those so noted.

In and around Sydney

Greater Sydney is very well provided with national parks, coastal and inland, within a narrow radius of the heart of the city.

Botany Bay *No campsite.*
Bouddi
Brisbane Water. *See p. 75.*
Cattai
Dharug
Garigal *No campsite.*
Georges River *No campsite.*
Heathcote *No campsite but bush camping possible.*

Ku-ring-gai Chase. *See p. 74.*
Lane Cove *No campsite*
Marramarra *No campsite but bush camping possible.*
Royal National Park. *One of Sydney's green lungs. See p. 92.*
Sydney Harbour. *No campsite.*
Wyrrabalong *No campsite.*

On the Coast South of Sydney

For more details of several of these parks, see especially the Sydney to Eden route, pp. 91–102.

Ben Boyd. *See p. 101.*
Bournda. *See p. 100.*
Mimosa Rocks. *No walking trails.*
Murramarang
Seven Mile Beach *No walking trails.*
Wallaga Lake *No campsite, picnic area or walking trails. For more details see p. 99.*

Inland between Sydney and the Victoria Border

Most of these parks are to the west of the recommended Sydney to Eden route.

Budderoo *No campsite.*
Budawang *Bush camping and walking trails but no campsite or picnic area.*
Deua
Macquarie Pass *No campsite.*
Morton
Mt Imlay *No campsite.*
Nalbaugh *Bush camping, but no other facilities.*
Nungatta *Bush camping, but no other facilities.*
Wadbilliga *No walking trails.*

Southern Highlands

See also Victoria National Parks, pp. 184–185, for more national parks in the Australian Alps.

Kosciusko. *Bush camping possible. See p. 117.*

121

National Parks and the NPWS

The National Parks and Wildlife Service (NPWS) has a difficult job in balancing two conflicting claims. The first is the 'green' point of view, which is that the national parks should be as close to nature as possible and therefore any intrusion, except by people on foot – preferably fully accredited 'greenies' – is to be avoided. The second is that the national parks are for everyone to enjoy and therefore vehicular access is essential. This has led to some amazing confrontations, including one where the NPWS banned horse-riding in the Snowy River National Park, which made the legend of the Man from Snowy River (see p. 183) look a bit silly. Reason is beginning to prevail and acceptable solutions are being worked out.

A generally accepted view is that the NPWS is a dedicated group doing a superb job preserving the countryside of Australia, even if sometimes, in their enthusiasm, they go too far.

Note that, without exception, there is a charge for driving into a National Park (and in some there is a charge for any kind of access). The price varies but usually is around $5 per vehicle per visit. If you intend to visit many of these parks the trick is to buy an annual sticker, at $50-$60 if you want it to include Kosciusko, from any NPWS office, which will get you in anywhere.

The observation of some simple rules will help: observe all signs; use bins provided for rubbish or take it away with you; don't bring pets or firearms; observe total fire bans; only light fires in fireplaces provided and bring your own firewood; do not disturb plants, rocks, animals and relics, as they are all protected.

If you are going into the wilder national parks, and there are many, observe the following rules: check with the local NPWS office as to how difficult it will be and how long it will take; check local conditions; bring your own water; make sure you have appropriate clothing; carry a first aid kit with bandages; take a map of the area; wear a hat and sun block cream; carry a plastic bag so that you can take your rubbish away. If you want to be a good citizen take away any other rubbish you see as well.

If you are ever in doubt ask one of the park rangers who are, almost without exception, friendly, approachable, knowledgeable and keen to help you enjoy the park. It is a courtesy and a safety precaution when exploring a national park off the beaten track to register with the rangers as soon as you enter the park. This does not apply if you are just driving in for a picnic but if you are hiking or camping overnight it can be very important.

As well as national parks, states may possess conservation parks, recreation parks, game reserves and regional reserves. The differences between these types of parks were spelled out in the National Parks Act of 1972. A national park is an area with wildlife or natural features of national significance. A conservation park is for the preservation of a state's native flora and fauna. The concept of regional reserves came 14 years later and the idea is to protect areas considered to contain important wildlife and natural features but with the right reserved to mine them later on if need be.

On the Coast between Sydney and the Queensland Border

The Sydney to the Gold Coast route, pp. 73–90, runs past nearly all of these parks.

Booti Booti
Broadwater *No campsite.*
Bundjalung
Crowdy Bay

Hat Head
Myall Lakes *See p. 80.*
Tomaree *Walking trails but no other facilities.*
Yuraygir

Along the NSW–Queensland Border

These parks stretch from the coast, west of Tweed Heads, a good way inland, as far as the line of the New England Highway which leads across the border to Warwick on the Darling Downs route (see pp. 256–259).

Bald Rock
Boonoo Boonoo
Border Ranges *This large park sprawls along the border and at its eastern end runs north into Queensland's Lamington National Park. See p. 90.*
Mt Warning *No campsite.*
Nightcap *No campsite.*

Northern NSW, between the New England Highway and the Coast
Not lying on any of the recommended routes, these parks are nevertheless accessible if you follow the inland journey between Sydney and Brisbane described in Touring Itineraries, p. 51. Alternatively, many can be visited as side trips from coastal resorts on the Sydney to the Gold Coast route, pp. 73–90, as noted below.

Barrington Tops
Cathedral Rock *This park, and Dorrigo and New England, are easy to reach from Nambucca Heads or Coffs Harbour.*
Dorrigo *No campsite*
Gibraltar Range
Guy Fawkes River
Kings Plains *Bush camping allowed, but no other facilities.*
New England
Nymboida *Walking trails but no other facilities.*
Oxley Wild Rivers *Accessible from Port Macquarie or Kempsey*
Washpool
Werrikimbe
Woko

West of Sydney – the Great Dividing Range
The route across the Blue Mountains is described in Sydney to Dubbo, pp. 103–109. Many of these parks lie on or near the Great Dividing Range to the north of the Blue Mountains.

Blue Mountains *Bush camping allowed. See p. 104 for detailed description of this park.*
Goulburn River *No campsite or picnic areas, but allows bush camping and provides walking trails.*

Kanangra-Boyd *No campsite, but bush camping is allowed.*
Nattai *No campsite, but bush camping is allowed.*
Tarlo River *Bush camping and walking trails only.*
Thirlmere Lakes *Picnic site and walking trails only.*
Wollemi
Yengo

West of the Gold Towns
Again the Sydney to Dubbo recommended route, and its continuation Dubbo to Lightning Ridge (pp. 110–112), will steer you towards these parks, some of which are in the true Outback.

Conimbla *No campsite.*
Mt Kaputar
Nangar *Bush camping permitted, but no other facilities available.*
Warrabah *No walking trails.*
Warrumbungle *for more on this park, see p. 111.*
Weddin Mountains

North-west Corner, around Broken Hill
Truly 'Back of Bourke', these parks are likely to be reached by the more enterprising visitors only.

Kinchega
Mootwingee
Sturt

Near Mildura
Several recommended driving routes in this book pass through Mildura, on the northern edge of Victoria. These two parks are accessible by travelling north of Mildura.

Mallee Cliffs
Mungo

North of Griffith
Griffith is the capital of the Murrumbidgee irrigation; see the Murray and the Riverina route, pp. 195–200. Hay is also on that route.

Cocoparra *Just outside Griffith, east along Rte 94.*
Willandra *About 40 km east of the Hay to Ivanhoe road.*

123

VICTORIA

Victoria is the smallest mainland state, covering 227,600 sq km. Yet, despite its size, it has some of Australia's richest farming soil, its wealthiest corporations and its second largest economy. The population of Victoria is 4½ million people, of whom over three-quarters live in Melbourne, making it a very urban, and some would insist urbane, state.

GEOGRAPHY

The borders are marked by the mighty Murray River in the north and the South Australian border – drawn in a straight line with a ruler – in the west. To the south the coast faces Bass Strait, which separates Tasmania from the rest of Australia. Extending from New South Wales in the north-east are the Australian Alps, which bring rugged mountain scenery, skiing in the winter and the source of the Murray, Australia's longest river.

Within its small compass it has deserts, Alps, rain forest and magical seascapes. But unless you get close to the borders it is rare to drive for long without being in some form of civilisation.

Getting around Victoria is much easier than most other states. The road network is normally good – sometimes even excellent – and nothing is desperately far away. The result is that Victoria, unlike many other states, does not have a major internal airline network although Melbourne, of course, has an international airport.

The cities of Victoria are gracious and normally well designed. The broad avenues of Melbourne, wide enough to turn a span of oxen, bear little resemblance to the narrow streets of Sydney. And Victoria has traditionally treasured its past, so the architecture of yesteryear is still well represented.

Victoria divides neatly into five different areas. The **Coastal Region** has typical Australian sandy beaches and equally rugged headlands. The Great Ocean Rd is one of the wonders of Australia. In complete contrast is

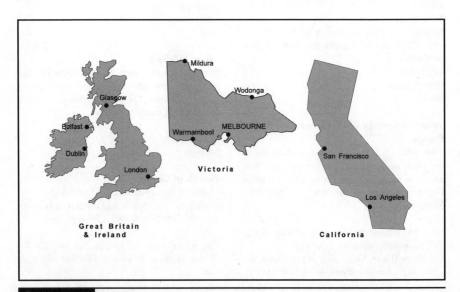

the north-east **alpine region**, which has snow covered mountains, ski resorts and carpets of wildflowers in the spring. The district to the north and west of Melbourne covers the gold-rush towns and the **Grampians**, one of the most beautiful touring areas of this state. Then to the south-east stretches **Gippsland**, with rolling pastures and densely wooded hills preserved for ever in a series of National Parks. And finally the **Murray River**, which has played such an important part in the history of Victoria and created a set of river-boat towns, each with their own distinct character.

CLIMATE

The saying is that if you stand still in Melbourne you can experience four seasons in one day – and this holds more than a grain of truth. Victoria is also rare, if not unique, among Australian states in having four distinct and separate seasons, which mark the passage of the year.

Summer (Dec–Feb) is warm, with an average temperature of 25°C. Spring and autumn are comfortable and only winter is decidedly chilly. There are, of course, exceptions to this. Part of the Alps are under snow for six months of the year and the Big Desert Wilderness in the summer can be as hot as anywhere in Australia. But as a rule these variations hold true.

HISTORY

The attitude of the people of Victoria towards the world is different from the attitude of the citizens of New South Wales. This may have something to with the state's history.

Although an early attempt was made to create a convict settlement in Victoria – in Port Phillip in 1803 – it failed miserably and the convicts were moved on to Tasmania. The people who came to populate Victoria were almost all free, all pioneers, all keen to open up new country. They created, first of all, an agricultural economy, which attracted direct immigration from both Britain and the United States. They pushed hard for, and got, colonial status in 1851, when they ceased to be regarded as an outpost of New South Wales.

Then came gold.

It is impossible at this distance to gauge the

full effect of the gold finds on the people of Australia but cities emptied and new towns were born overnight. From this came the strong surge for political independence by the miners, culminating in the battle of the Eureka Stockade (see p.157), which changed Australia for ever and moved it even further towards being a classless society.

In the 1870s and 1880s fate was kind to Victoria and it expanded in the sun. Then came the great crash of 1893 with banks going to the wall – the sign of ultimate desperation – and it took some twenty years before the state recovered.

For a short time Victoria contained the capital of Australia. In 1901, at the Federation of Australia, the government sat in Melbourne although the deed was signed in Sydney. This created great dissatisfaction among the other states and thus independent Canberra was created in 1927.

Today Victoria produces about a third of the gross national product although that is changing as the economy moves more and more towards service industries. Melbourne is still regarded as being the financial capital of Australia – although that again is changing with electronic communication and the concept of the cyberspace corporation.

125

TRAVELLING IN VICTORIA

In Victoria there are, as a percentage, far more BYO – bring your own wine – restaurants than there are in other states. It is safe to assume that, in the absence of evidence to the contrary, you need to take wine to a restaurant.

The people of Victoria dress more formally than the people of other states. This is especially true of Melbourne. This is not to say that there is the formal stuffiness of, say, London but ties and jackets tend to be worn by businessmen. The way to dress in Victoria is in layers. Then as the weather changes – and it can do it with amazing rapidity – you add or subtract as needed.

The religion of Victoria, no blasphemy intended, is Australian Rules, which is a form of Gaelic football. If you cannot carry on a conversation about one of the teams during the season you may find conversation difficult.

MELBOURNE

It is widely accepted that Melbourne is the queen of Australian cities. It can be argued that its restaurants are superior in range and quality to those of other state capitals. Its architecture, with wide streets and solid establishments, manages to avoid Victorian grimness and blends elegantly into the cityscape. And this while still having an air – totally justified – of financial solidity. Melbourne was, for a while, the capital of Australia. Melbourne was founded by free settlers. If Australia has any class system, then whatever upper class exists . . . it is in Melbourne.

126

TOURIST INFORMATION

The **Victoria Visitor Information Centre** in the Town Hall, *corner Little Collins St and Swanston St; tel: 9790 2121,* can answer any question and can also book you a room. There is a wide range of free brochures available.

ARRIVING AND DEPARTING

By Air

Most people will, of course, fly in to Melbourne. The domestic and international terminals are housed in the same building at **Tullamarine Airport**, which is 22 km northeast of the city centre. There is a freeway into town, which gets fairly congested in the morning rush hour. There is a **SkyBus service** to the city – Franklin St bus terminal and Spencer St train station – which runs every ½ hr, starting at 0600 and stopping at around 2300. Bookings are not neccessary and the fare is $10. A taxi into town will cost just over twice that amount, so if there are two or more of you travelling the taxi is the best bet. There is always a rank of available cabs at the airport.

By Car

Driving into Melbourne you have three major routes. First there is, but of course, Hwy 1, which, from New South Wales, comes from the **east**, along the coast through Orbost, Bairnsdale, Warragul, Dandenong and then into the heart of Melbourne as the Princes Hwy, connecting with the Nepean Hwy at Prahran. However, the main road from Sydney and New South Wales is the Hume Hwy – Rte 31 – which crosses the border into Victoria at Albury–Wodonga and then drops down through Benalla and Seymour until it comes into the heart of Melbourne as *Sydney Rd,* which becomes *Royal Parade*. Don't worry about the names, it is Rte 31 right the way through.

From the **west**, from South Australia, the approach is again along Rte 1, which hugs the coast to Warrnambool and then cuts inland to Queenscliff, the outer suburb of Geelong – stress on the second syllable – and enters as the Princes Freeway by way of the West Gate bridge right to St Kilda and the city centre.

Also entering from South Australia, but further inland, is Rte 8, which comes in through Horsham, Ararat and then through Ballarat and Bacchus Marsh to Melbourne as the Western Hwy (still Rte 8) into the heart of Melbourne.

By Train

All trains to Melbourne come to **Spencer St Station** (The train from Sydney takes 14 hrs, from Brisbane 34 hrs and Perth 58 hrs.

For suburban travel in the Melbourne area trains work very well. **Flinders St Station** is the main suburban station.

Information: V-line – the company that operates public transport in Victoria, *tel: 9619 5000.)*

By Bus

Greyhound Pioneer buses arrive at the **Melbourne Bus Terminal**, *Franklin St*, with others using the **Spencer St Bus Terminal**.

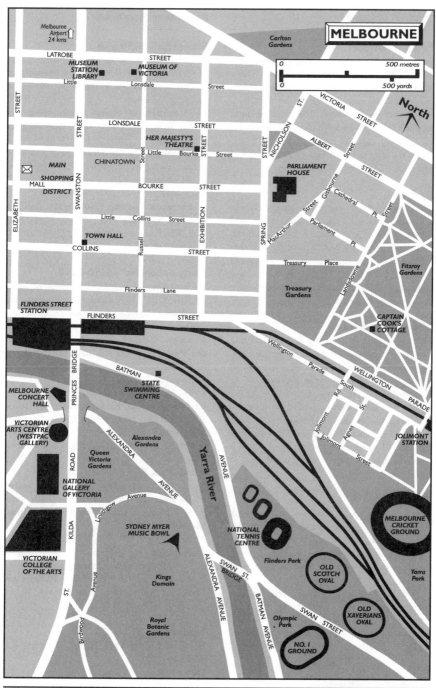

GETTING AROUND

Public Transport

One of the great ways of seeing Melbourne is by tram. **The City Circle Tram** is free. There are ten 'W' class trams, which have been refurbished and are easily recognised by their burgundy and gold colours. The tram operates around the city in two directions and there are 25 specially marked stops along the route. There is a tram every 10 mins or so and the service runs 1000–1800 seven days a week.

By Car

The only area where this guide cannot help you is in turning right at some junctions in the main streets of Melbourne. Signs at traffic lights tell you to get in the left lane to turn right, which is illogical but insisted upon by the authorities 'because of the trams'. To understand the logic and follow it automatically, you need to have been born in Melbourne.

Biking and on Foot

Melbourne is pretty much a flat city and one easy way of getting around is by bicycle. The only problems are the tram lines, as it is easy to get wedged in them. **Bicycle Victoria**, *15-17 O'Connell St, N. Melbourne; tel: 9328 3000*, has an excellent bike riders map of Melbourne.

Walking, because of Melbourne's wide avenues and relatively light traffic, is always a pleasure. Most locals and visitors find that it is usually quicker to walk within the city than to take a taxi.

Taxis

When you do need a taxi, there is a taxi rank on *Swanston St*, outside Flinders St Station, and throughout the city there are ranks aplenty. You can flag down a cab in the street, although this is not as common a practice as it is in Sydney.

The radio controlled cabs are very efficient. **Silver Top** *(tel: 9345 3455)* is the major cab company in metropolitan Melbourne. Others are **Arrow**; *tel: 9417 1111*, **Regal Combined Taxis**; *tel: 9810 0222*, **Astoria**; *tel: 9347 5511*.

STAYING IN MELBOURNE

Expensive – $250 plus

Grand Hyatt Melbourne *(HY), corner Collins & Russell Sts; tel: (03) 9657 1234.* **Melbourne Hilton on the Park** *(HI), 192 Wellington Parade, E. Melbourne 3002; tel: (03) 9419 3311.* **Le Meridien at Rialto Melbourne**, *495 Collins St; tel: (03) 9620 9111.* **The Regent Melbourne**, *25 Collins St; tel: (03) 9653 0000.* **Rockmans Regency Hotel**, *corner Exhibition & Lonsdale Sts; tel: (03) 9662 3900.* **The Sebel of Melbourne**, *321 Flinders Lane; tel: (03) 9629 4088.*

Sheraton Towers Southgate *(SH), 1 Brown St, Southbank 3006; tel: (03) 9696 3100.* **The Windsor**, *corner Spring & Lt Collins Sts; tel: (03) 9653 0653.*

Fairly expensive – $150–$250

Carlton Crest, *65 Queens Rd, Melbourne 3004; tel: (03) 9529 4300.* **Centra Melbourne on the Yarra** *(SP), corner Flinders & Spencer Sts (Postal: PO Box 417, World Trade Centre, Melbourne 3005); tel: (03) 9629 5111.* **Eden on the Park**, *6 Queens Rd, Melbourne 3004; tel: (03) 9820 2222.* **Country Comfort Old Melbourne** *(CC), 5 Flemington Rd, N. Melbourne 3051; tel: (03) 9329 9344.* **Parkroyal on St Kilda Road** *(SP), 562 St Kilda Rd; tel: (03) 9529 8888.* **Novotel Melbourne on Collins**, *270 Collins St; tel: (03) 9650 5800.* **Stamford Plaza Melbourne** *(SP), 111 Lt Collins St, tel: (03)9659 1000.* **Savoy Park Plaza**, *630 Lt Collins St; tel: (03) 9622 8888.* **Holiday Inn Park Suites Melbourne**, *333 Exhibition St; tel: (03) 9663 3333.* **Metro Inn Apartment Hotel Melbourne** *(FL), 133 Jolimont Rd, E. Melbourne 3002; tel: (03) 9654 2844.* **Rydges Melbourne**, *186 Exhibition St; tel: (03) 9662 0511.* **All Seasons Crossley** *(FL), 51 Lt Bourke St; tel: (03) 9639 1639.* **Rydges on Flinders Melbourne**, *corner Spencer St and Flinders Lane; tel: (03) 9629 4111.*

Moderate – $70–$150

Bayview on the Park Hotel, *52 Queens Rd, Melbourne 3004; tel: (03) 9243 9999.* **Downtowner on Lygon** *(FL), 66 Lygon St,*

Carlton 3053; tel: (03) 9663 5555. **St Kilda Rd Travelodge** *(SP), corner St Kilda Rd & Park St, S. Melbourne 3205; tel: (03) 9209 9888.* **All Seasons Hotel Swanston** *(FL), 195 Swanston St; tel: (03) 9663 4711.* **Arden,** *15 Arden St, N. Melbourne 3051; tel: (03) 9329 7211.* **Astoria City Travel Inn** *(BU), 288 Spencer St; tel: (03) 9670 6801.* **City Park Motel** *(FL), 308 Kings Way, S. Melbourne 3205; tel: (03) 9699 9811.* **Elizabeth Tower Motel** *(FL), corner Elizabeth & Grattan Sts; tel: (03) 9347 9211.* **Marco Polo Inn,** *corner Harker St and Flemington Rd, N. Melbourne 3051; tel: (03) 9329 1788.*

Park Squire Motor Inn *(BU), 94 Flemington Rd, Parkville 3052; tel: (03) 9329 6077.* **Ramada Inn** *(FL), 539 Royal Parade (Hume Hwy), Parkville 3012; tel: (03) 9380 8131.* **The Sheraton,** *13 Spring St; tel: 9205 9999.* **The Townhouse,** *701 Swanston St, Carlton 3053; tel: (03) 9347 7811.* **Travel-Inn Hotel** *(FL), corner Grattan & Drummond Sts, Carlton; tel: (03) 9347 7922.* **All Seasons Welcome Hotel** *(FL), 265 Lt Bourke St; tel: (03) 9639 0555.* **Batmans Hill** *(FL), 66 Spencer St; tel: (03) 9614 6344.* **Hotel Enterprize,** *44 Spencer St; tel: (03) 9629 6991.* **Flagstaff City Motor Inn** *(BW), 45 Dudley St, W. Melbourne 3003; tel: (03) 9329 5788.* **Ibis,** *15 Therry St; tel: (03) 9639 2399.* **Kingsway Motel,** *corner Park and Eastern Rds, S. Melbourne 3205; tel: (03) 9699 2533.* **Lygon Lodge,** *220 Lygon St; tel: (03) 9563 6633.* **Magnolia Court Boutique Hotel,** *101 Powlett St, E. Melbourne 3002; tel: (03) 9419 4222.* **New Chateau Hotel,** *131 Lonsdale St; tel: (03) 9663 3161.* **Treasury Motor Lodge** *(BW), 179 Powlett St, E. Melbourne 3002; tel: (03) 9417 5281.* **Ciros Motel,** *204 Lygon St, Carlton 3053; tel: (03) 9639 3322.* **City Limits Motel** *(BU), 20 Lt Bourke St; tel: (03) 9662 2544.* **City Square Motel,** *67 Swanston St; tel: (03) 9654 7011.* **Duke of Wellington,** *corner Flinders and Russell Sts; tel: (03) 9650 4984.*

Cheap – below $70

George Powlett Lodge, *corner George and Powlett Sts, E. Melbourne 3002; tel: (03) 9419 9488.* **Park Avenue Motor Inn,** *461 Royal Parade (Hume Hwy), Parkville 3052; tel: (03) 9380 6761.* **The Victoria Hotel,** *215 Lt*

Collins St (Postal: GPO Box 484G); tel: (03) 9653 0441. **E.M.H. East Melbourne Hotel,** *2 Hotham St; tel (03) 9419 2040.* **Hotel Hollyford,** *650 Elizabeth St; tel: (03) 9347 8558.* **North Motalodge,** *113 Flemington Rd, N. Melbourne 3051; tel: (03) 9329 7433.* **Queens Bridge,** *1 Queensbridge St, S. Melbourne 3205; tel: (03) 9686 3117.* **The Hotel Y,** *489 Elizabeth St; tel: (03) 9329 5188.* **YHA Queensberry Hill,** *78 Howard St, N. Melbourne 3051; tel: (03) 9329 8599.* **YHA Chapman Gardens,** *76 Chapman St, N. Melbourne 3051; tel: 9328 3595.*

Eating and Drinking

Melbourne is a multi-racial city, having one of the largest Greek-speaking populations in the world, more Maltese than Malta, more Asians as a percentage of the population than Sydney, and more ethnic restaurants than the rest of Australia put together. The result of this multi-racial mix is a fascinating range of markets, restaurants and delicatessens, which encourage the people of Melbourne to regard dining out as a most important aspect of life. Melbourne is, indeed, a dining city. If you made a list of the twenty best restaurants in Australia, a dozen would be in Melbourne.

The Age newspaper gives out awards to restaurants every year. At the very top are: **Jacques Reymond Restaurant,** *78 Williams Rd, Windsor; tel: 9525 2178.* Open lunch Tues–Fri, dinner Tues–Sat. Widely considered the best restaurant in Australia. The only restaurant given five chef's hats in *The Age* Guide. Dinner for two $145 plus drinks. **Flower Drum,** *17 Market Lane; tel: 9662 3655.* Open lunch Mon–Sat, dinner seven days. Four chef's hats and widely accepted as Australia's finest Asian restaurant. **Mask of China,** *115 Little Bourke St; tel: 9662 2116.* Open daily. Expensive. Four chef's hats and seen as the contender for the title. **Paul Bocuse Restaurant,** *Daimaru Level 4, Melbourne Central, La Trobe St; tel: 9660 6600.* Four stars. $170 for two plus drinks. Better than his French establishment near Lyon. **Stephanie's,** *405 Tooronga Rd, Hawthorn E.; tel: 9822 8944.* Open Tues–Fri and Sun for lunch, Tues–Sat dinner. Four chef's hats. Run by the great chef, Stephanie

129

Alexander. $130 for two plus drinks. Formal elegant dining at its very best.

Those are the best restaurants in Melbourne and, arguably, the best restaurants in Australia. What follows may not have gained any awards, but they are Melbourne restaurants and therefore a cut above almost anything else.

Ajays, *555 Nicholson St, Carlton North; tel: 9380 5555;* Open lunch Fri, dinner Tues–Sat. BYO. The best of the BYO restaurants. **Chez Bob**, *22 Beatty Ave, Armadale; tel: 9824 8022.* Open Mon–Sat. French bistro style. Licensed. **Kao Thip**, *36 Jackson Court; Doncaster East; tel: 9848 1181.* Open daily for dinner. Licensed. Consistent high quality Thai. **Shanghai Provincial Kitchen**, *113 Little Bourke St; tel: 9663 1811.* Open daily lunch and dinner. Licensed. Northern Chinese food.

Bistro Minootz, *436 Toorak Rd; tel: 9826 9121.* **Caffè Bizzarri**, *470 Toorak Rd; tel: 9827 7179.* **Café Paradiso**, *418 Toorak Rd; tel: 9826 6466.* **Funkies Restaurant**, *445 Toorak Rd; tel: 9827 1822.* **Jac's Bar & Grill**, *445 Toorak Rd; tel: 9827 8244.* **Manhattan Bistro**, *448 Toorak Rd; tel: 9826 9878.* **Topo Gigio**, *432 Toorak Rd; tel: 9827 5555.*

Of course, by the time you try these restaurants, some of them will have closed. That is the price of being trendy. But don't worry – another will have sprung up in its place.

It is highly unusual to be served a bad meal in Melbourne and it is possible to eat lunch for well under $10. You can even have dinner on a tramcar. **The Colonial Tramcar Restaurant**, *tel: 9696 4000,* runs daily, offering lunch and dinner with two sittings for dinner. This is an expensive dinner – starts at $50 a head – but that includes all drinks. You eat and drink as the tram glides its way through Melbourne.

Melbourne also has theatre restaurants – that is, a place where you go to eat and see a show. Typically the food is not marvellous, but that is not the whole point of the exercise. A lot of heckling takes place, but the shows can be surprisingly good. And, after all, this is Australia.

Three worth considering are: **Dirty Dicks Medieval Madness**, *45 Dudley St; tel: 9329 3555.* **Witches In Britches**, *84 Dudley St; tel: 9329 9850.* **A.A.E.The Looney Bin**, *419 Spencer St; tel: 9329 57122.*

Communications

The Post Office is at *90 Collins St, Melbourne 3000; tel: 9299 4321.*

Money

Thomas Cook agencies are located at *Ground Floor, 257 Collins St, tel: 9650 2442; State Bank Galleria, corner Elizabeth and Little Collins St, tel: 9670 8765; Ground Floor, 330 Collins St; tel: 9602 3811.*

ENTERTAINMENT

Sport

Melbourne is a sporting city. Its obsession with Australian Rules – and obsession is the right word – is remarkable beyond belief. It makes the support of a British or American football fan seem a lukewarm, passing affection. Melbourne also loves horse racing, culminating in the Melbourne Cup, when all of Australia comes to a standstill. Its cricket and tennis facilities are among the best in the world.

When it comes to sports, Melbourne is better catered for than any other Australian city. **Flinders Park**, *Batman Ave; tel: 9286 1234,* (open Mon–Fri 0700–2300, weekends 0900–1800) is home of the Australian tennis championships and is also Australia's largest indoor entertainment centre. There are 13 outdoor and five indoor tennis courts in the complex.

Melbourne Cricket Ground, *Yarra Park, Jolimont; tel: 9657 8864.* This sacred shrine is open 1000–1600 with guided tours conducted hourly – $8. Speak only in hushed voices.

In the football season you will hear much discussion about the local teams. You will certainly find the game totally incomprehensible as this variety is only played in Australia and, in the main, Melbourne. It is distantly related to Gaelic football but has acquired a language of its own. It is taken very seriously. The state premier is seen to be a major supporter of a local club – if he were not, he would not survive the next election.

Performing Arts

Melbourne is an artistic city, using the word in its widest sense. It supports far more live theatre than any other city in Australia and as such it

Australian Rules Football

No one can clearly understand the game of Aussie Rules unless they were born in Victoria. I have been to many matches and still have no idea what the devil is going on. But the following may help.

In a senior team there are 21 players, 18 of whom are on the pitch at any one time. They have different positions and tasks – goal kickers, play-makers, and so on. The clubs announce the players in their positions before the game. After a certain deadline the personnel of the team cannot be changed, but alterations can be made to player positions as the coach sees fit. This is part of the game – one coach trying to outfox the other with swift positional moves.

Clubs can interchange players at any time during the match, provided there are only 18 players per team on the field. An interchange steward checks the movements of players in this area.

Each game has four quarters of 20 mins, plus time added on by the field umpires, who can add extra time to make up for lost play. Most quarters run for between 26 and 30 mins. There is a 5-min break at the end of the first quarter and 6 mins at the end of the third quarter. Players stay on the field and are addressed by their respective coaches. At half-time the players leave the field for 20 mins. Each AFL game is controlled by eight umpires – three field umpires, three boundary umpires and two goal umpires. There is also an emergency umpire.

The teams change ends after each quarter and the side with the biggest score at the final siren is the winner. When in Victoria never, ever criticise Aussie rules or compare it to another game. This is akin to spitting on the Bible.

---

has more theatres than all of the other cities in Australia put together. Its art galleries have more hanging space, more important collections. Its operatic performances of the major operas could not, by general consent, be performed in any other city in Australia. And its classical music is consistently world class.

A substantial percentage of the internal tourism of Australia comes from Australians from other cities, including Sydney, coming to Melbourne for a particular show that cannot be held in any other city. The **Sydney Opera House** is architecturally the most important building in Australia but, sadly, it is unsuitable for grand opera.

Sidney Myer Music Bowl, *Kings Domain, near Alexandra Ave; tel: 9281 8000*, or the Bowl, as it is called locally, is an open-air auditorium, with seating for 2000 and room for another 20,000 on the sloping lawn. This is Melbourne's main outdoor concert area.

The State Theatre, *100 St Kilda Rd in Victorian Arts Centre; tel: 9281 8000,* holds 2079 people on three levels. It is decorated in the reds and golds of traditonal grand theatre and can house pretty much any performance. In the same complex is the **Playhouse**, which seats

880 and is used for drama productions, mainly by the Melbourne Theatre Company. The **Melbourne Concert Hall**, also in the Victorian Arts Centre, is a large circular theatre, which also houses the **Performing Arts Museum**. There are literally dozens of other theatres scattered around the suburbs and there is never a night of the year when there are not several productions vying for your patronage.

SHOPPING

Melbourne is also a shopping city. Not just in the central business district – although there you will find as fine an array of shops as in most cities in the world – but in its suburbs. **South Yarra**, **Toorak**, **Carlton**, **Prahan**, **Armadale**, and others. It could be suggested that Melbournians go shopping as a social experience, which might account for the abundance of weekend markets.

Swanston St Walk is a pedestrian boulevard in the city centre, and is an ideal place to wander around a collection of up-market shops – including some of Melbourne's finest – and to eat at one of the outdoor cafés.

The **Sunday Market** at the Victorian Art Centre, *100 St Kilda Rd,* is one of many in

Melbourne, where there is a tradition of shopping for non-essentials, almost as a social activity, on Sunday mornings. **Sailyards market,** open daily 1000–dusk, *corner of Lonsdale and Swanston Sts,* offers clothing, handicrafts and jewellery. **Bourke St Mall** has an array of shops, including two famous Australian department stores – David Jones and Myers. Nearby are the **Royal** and the **Block Arcades.**

Just down from *Bourke St,* in *Little Bourke St,* is **Chinatown,** which is Australia's only surviving area of continuous Chinese settlement since the Gold Rush. It is packed with restaurants shops housed in Victorian age buildings.

SIGHTSEEING

The first residents of the area were probably members of the Wuywurung tribe, who were pushed out when wave after wave of migrating pastoralists came to Victoria in search of land.

One of the most important arrivals was John Batman, who came in May 1835 and started to explore the country to the north and west of Phillip Bay. In doing this he was, strictly speaking, breaking the law. The New South Wales government, which at that time governed all that was to become Victoria, had issued an edict against anyone taking up land outside Sydney. So, by the letter of the law, Melbourne started life as an illegal settlement. Within the year the act was formally recognised by the Colonial Office in London and by 1842 the settlement on the Yarra River was recognised as a municipality. In 1850 Victoria was separated from New South Wales.

Almost immediately after came the gold rush and the population of Melbourne dropped like a stone in a muddy pond as everyone headed out to the diggings and fame and fortune. Few found it. But the money that did come from the goldfields poured into Melbourne and started an era of major civic construction – the Post Office, the Public Library, Parliament House and the Treasury were all erected in the imposing style which gave Melbourne much of its character.

After World War II, there came another major change. The European immigrants who flooded into Melbourne changed its character for ever and for better. Possibly 50% of the city's population have one parent born overseas and something like 20% use another language as well as English. Melbourne has grown up to be a metropolitan, multicultural and urbane city.

Melbourne is a green city, having parks on both sides of the **Yarra River,** which flows down from the **Yarra Ranges** and slowly snakes its way through the city. It has been said that Melbourne has a greater percentage of green space within its city boundaries than any other city in Australia.

It has also been said times without number that it is the most pleasant city in the world in which to work and live. There are many other contenders for that honour but Melbourne certainly has a serious claim to the accolade. If Melbourne has a problem, it is its weather, which can change dramatically within the space of a few hours. But, to Melbournians, that is part of its charm.

One of the special joys of Melbourne is that it is a city of art. The art is not confined to the galleries. It can also be seen in the streets and in the public and commercial buildings. The **National Gallery of Victoria,** *180 St Kilda Rd; tel: 9208 0203,* is glorious on the inside, although there has been debate about the architectural design of the exterior. At the opening which I attended, the then premier of Victoria said, 'People have complained that it looks like a prison on the outside. That is so that we can have more hanging room on the inside.' Quite so. This gallery has the finest collection of art in the southern hemisphere. Open daily, 1000–1700. Admission $6.

Nearby, **Westpac Gallery,** *100 St Kilda Rd in the Victorian Arts Centre; tel: 9281 8000,* has two main exhibition areas and a changing range of exhibitions throughout the year.

The **Aboriginal Desert Art Gallery,** *31 Flinders St; tel: 9654 2516* – open Mon–Sat 1000–1730, Sun 1200–1700 – specialises in Aboriginal paintings and artefacts from the Central Australian desert. On the same theme, the **Aboriginal Gallery of Dreamings** *73 Bourke St; tel: 9650 3277,* (open Mon–Sat 1000–1730, Sun 1200–1700) has a wide range of Aboriginal dot paintings, with some 2500 paintings available. Both of these galleries show a style of art which has only become popular in the last ten years. Before that most Aboriginal art work was sold in shops run by the Missions, and were purchased, in the main, by tourists as souvenirs. Now this distinctive and original art form has become recognised world-wide and is avidly collected.

Other art forms are also widely represented in Melbourne. **Focal Point Gallery**, *300 Lonsdale St; tel: 9663 5445;* open Mon–Sat 1000–1800, Sun 1200–1700, focuses on glass and ceramic art and has works by over 60 of Australia's leading artists. **The Johnston Collection**, *152 Hotham St, E. Melbourne; tel: 9416 2515,* open Mon–Fri 1000–1600 by appointment only, is a decorative arts museum in a historic house. The collection is mainly concerned with interior decoration. In contrast **Makers Mark Gallery**, *101 Collins St; tel: 9654 8488* (open Mon–Fri 0930–1700, Sat 1000–1500) works mainly with contemporary jewellery, sculpture, gold- and silver-smithing.

Physically, Melbourne is just inland from the protected **Port Phillip Bay**, with suburbs like **Brighton** being true seaside resorts. There are many parks within the city as well as National Parks ringing the city. In the You Yangs and Macedon, right around to Kinglake, and from the Dandenongs and the Yarra Ranges down to the Mornington Peninsula (see pp. 151–155), there is a series of magnificent parks and reserves. Although Melbourne is very much an urban setting – the second largest city in Australia – the bush, the country and the sea are only a short drive away.

Within the city the **Royal Botanic Gardens**, *Visitor's Centre and Gate F, Birdwood Ave,* on the south bank of the Yarra; *tel: 9655 2300* (open daily 0730–2030 Nov–Mar, 0730–1730 Apr–Oct), is one of the true glories of Melbourne. The gardens sweep down to the banks of the Yarra and are generally accepted as being the finest gardens in Australia, and very possibly the finest botanic gardens in the world. There are free guided walks, which leave from the visitor centre at 1000 and 1100 Tues–Fri.

On a smaller scale are **King's Domain Gardens**, *off St Kilda Rd,* open Mon and Wed 1000–1600 and weekends 1100–1600. In these gardens is Victoria's first Government House, **La Trobe Cottage**, which was prefabricated

in England and brought out in 1839. The era of great wealth in Melbourne is reflected in **Queen Victoria Statue Gardens**, *off Linlithgow Ave.* The white marble statue by James White was put up in 1907 and has, at its base, representations of Progress, History, Wisdom and Justice, which neatly represent what the Victorian age saw as its virtues.

Pioneer Women's Memorial Gardens, *Alexandra Ave; tel: 9658 8553,* is an extension of the Kings Domain Gardens, built in 1934 as part of Melbourne's Centenary celebrations. This formal, symmetrical garden has a grotto in which stands a small bronze statue of a woman by Charles Webb Gilbert. **Flagstaff Gardens**, *King St; tel: 9685 8553,* cover 7 hectares. The elevated position provides panoramic views of Melbourne. **Fitzroy and Treasury Gardens**, *30 Gisborne St, E. Melbourne; tel: 9658 9800,* open daily 0900–1700, contain **Captain Cook's Cottage** – the one he was born in. It was shipped here from England in 1934 and is furnished in period style. The cottage also has an excellent exhibit on the life and times of the great navigator.

Batman Park, on *Queens Wharf Rd,* is a landscaped park alongside the Yarra River. It is here that John Batman, one of the founders of Melbourne, stepped ashore in 1835. This is one of the many green areas which give Melbourne its feeling of spaciousness. **Alexandra – Queen Victoria Gardens**, *St Kilda Rd, tel: 9658 8553,* is the site of the annual Moomba festival. It was originally a swamp and brickmakers' field but was reclaimed in the 1860s to form this 9.4 hectare park.

Melbourne is a city of churches. **St Pauls Cathedral**, *corner of Swanston and Flinders Sts, tel: 9650 3792,* is Anglican and Gothic. Building started in 1880 and, although it opened for worship the following year, it was not finished completely until 1933. The choir sings a Choral Evensong every day. **St Patrick's Cathedral**, *corner of Cathedral Pl. and Gisborne St, E. Melbourne,* is Roman Catholic and one of the better examples of Gothic Revival architecture. The cathedral was designed by William Wilkinson Wardell, who was also responsible for many of Melbourne's other major buildings.

133

MELBOURNE– WARRNAMBOOL

The Coastal Route along the Great Ocean Rd is one of the great scenic drives of Australia and you could do it easily, if very pressed for time, in one day. But you wouldn't have time to stop and enjoy the views and the charming towns which you drive through. Much better to plan on staying a night here and a night there so that you have time to explore the National Parks that run along the coast and to see the vistas from different viewpoints.

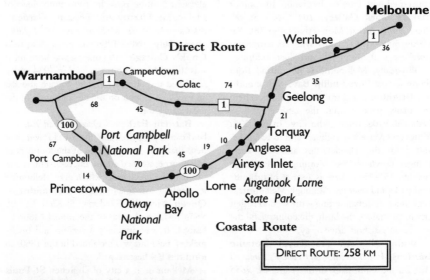

Melbourne

Werribee   1   36

Direct Route

Warrnambool 1   Camperdown

Colac   74   35

Geelong

68   45   1   21

100   16

Port Campbell   **Torquay**

67   **National Park**   19   10   Anglesea

Port Campbell   45   70   Aireys Inlet

14   100

Princetown   Lorne   Angahook Lorne

Apollo   State Park

Otway   Bay

National   **Coastal Route**

Park

DIRECT ROUTE: 258 KM

134

ROUTES

DIRECT ROUTE

Start with the West Gate Freeway from the centre of Melbourne, which takes you across the West Gate Bridge to join up with Rte 83, the Princes Hwy, also called *Geelong Rd*. The Princes Hwy becomes Rte 1 west out of Melbourne. It passes through **Werribee** and **Geelong**, and just after Geelong turns sharply right and heads inland through **Colac** and **Camperdown** to **Warrnambool**.

COASTAL ROUTE

Follow the Direct Route until just after Rte 1 turns inland, a little south of Geelong. At this point turn left onto the very straight road, Rte 100, by way of Mt Duneed south to **Torquay**. Rte 100 officially becomes the *Great Ocean Rd* at Torquay, with a commemorative arch at the eastern view. From Torquay it runs past the famous surfing beaches of Jun Juc and Bells and down to **Anglesea** alongside Point Roadknight. It then drops through a series of small villages – **Aireys Inlet**, Fairhaven and Eastern View on Cinema Point – until it arrives at Victoria's favourite holiday resort, **Lorne**.

The *Ocean Rd* then runs between the **Angahook Lorne State Park** and the sea to the small townships of Wye River, Kennett River around Cape Patton, then Wongarra, Skenes Creek and into **Apollo Bay**. The road then goes inland through the **Otway National Park** (with a turn off to the left down an unsealed road that leads to Cape Otway and its lighthouse). It touches the coast again at the small town of Glenaire then heads back inland to Lavers Hill. Then it is back to the coast at the small town of **Princetown** and through the **Port Campbell National Park**, along the Shipwreck Coast and the amazing sight of the 12 Apostles, to **Port Campbell**.

From there Rte 100 hugs the coast, passing London Bridge, which has fallen into the sea, nearly taking tourists with it, and tight along the coast to Peterborough and then in a large zig-zag north to join Rte 1 and the Direct Route near Allansford. Turn left onto the main route and into Warrnambool, where the Great Ocean Rd ends.

TRAINS AND BUSES

There is a rail line from Melbourne (Spencer St station) to Geelong (1 hr) and Warrnambool (3 hrs). There is a frequent local train service from Melbourne to Geelong but only 3 trains continue on to Warrnambool Mon–Fri and 2 trains on Saturdays. On Sundays just one train runs to Warrnambool but there are 2 bus connections from Geelong. OTT table 9027.

WERRIBEE

ACCOMMODATION AND FOOD

Monte Villa Motor Inn, *78 Old Geelong Rd, Hoppers Crossing 3029; tel: 9748 7700.* **Werribee Motor Lodge** *(BW), 6 Tower Rd; tel: 9741 9944.* **Werribee Park Motor Inn** *(BU), 112 Duncans Rd (Postal: PO Box 437); tel: 9741 7222.*

There is a fully licensed restaurant in **Werribee Park**, *tel: 9741 2444.* Open lunch.

SIGHTSEEING

Although it is only 32 km to the west of Melbourne, this town is very definitely not a suburb even though many of the residents commute to Melbourne. The **Werribee River** and the surrounding farmlands give it an air of bucolic peace, which has nothing to do with the city.

The original settlement had the name of Wyndham but it was changed in 1884 to the Aboriginal name for the town, which means 'backbone' or 'spine'. If you look at the tree-marked course of the river across the plain, that makes sense.

In 1983 the International Union for Conservation of Nature designated **Lake Borrie** (*New Farm Rd; tel: 9742 9209*) and the surrounding area 'wetland of international importance'. The lake was originally a small swamp but it is now part of the Melbourne sewage treatment lagoon series.

The waste has killed off all of the trees but the dead skeletons house the only regularly used breeding colony of Pied Cormorants in Victoria. There are also many other species of wildfowl and waders, and during drought periods Lake Borrie becomes a significant refuge for waterfowl.

Werribee Park Mansion, *K Rd, south of Duncan's Rd; tel: 9741 2444.* Open every day 1000–1545. Admission $8. Set in 10 hectares of formal gardens, this is a magnificent 19th-century Italian mansion, which was built for the Chirnside brothers in 1874–76. The brothers had emigrated from Scotland and had established a farming empire, which at one time included over 1 million sheep. It has been totally restored and is one of Australia's grandest home. The guides are all in period costume.

In the gardens are a lake, a grotto, the Victorian State rose garden and bluestone farm buildings. A substantial part of the grounds is taken over by the **Werribee Research Farm**, which was established in 1912.

Next door to the mansion is **Werribee Zoological Park**, where visitors are taken by safari buses around the exhibits to see zebra, rhino, giraffes and buffalo. Open daily from 1030 with safari buses leaving at regular intervals. Trips last just under 1 hr. Admission $8.

Iramoo Plains Vineyard, *tel: (03) 9741 1290*, has cellar door tastings and sales. Open every Sun 1300–1700 Oct–Apr.

GEELONG

Tourist Information: Geelong Otway Tourism, *National Wool Centre, 26 Moorabool St, Geelong; tel: (03) 5223 2588 or 5222 2900*.

There is a **Thomas Cook Foreign Exchange** branch at *Market Sq., 96 Malop St; tel: 5221 4566*.

ACCOMMODATION

Ambassador Geelong *(FL), corner Gheringhap & Myer Sts; tel: 5221 6844*. **Admiralty Motor Inn** *(BW), 66 McKillop St; tel: 5221 4288*. **Geelong Motor Inn & Serviced Apartments** *(BW), corner Princes Hwy & Kooyong Rd; tel: 5222 4777*. **Hacienda Geelong Motel** *(BW), 15 Mt Pleasant Rd, Belmont 3216; tel: 5243 5844*. **Hamilton Hume Motel** *(FL), 13 The Esplanade; tel: 522 3499*. **Rose Garden Motor Inn**, *14 Settlement Rd (Princes Hwy); tel: 5241 9441*.

Aristocrat Waurnvale *(GC), 90 Princes Hwy, Waurn Ponds 3221; tel: 5241 8211*. **Bay City Motel**, *231 Malop St; tel: 5221 1933*. **Buena Vista Motor Inn** *(FL), 68 High St, Belmont 3216; tel: 5243 6766*. **Colonial Lodge Motel** *(BU), 57 Fyans St; tel: 5223 2266*. **Eastern Sands Motel** *(FL), 1 Bellarine St; tel: 5221 5577*. **Golden Palms Motel** *(HN), 234 Torquay Rd (Surfcoast Hwy), Grovedale 3216; tel: 5243 1077*.

EATING AND DRINKING

Empire Grill, *66 M6 McKillop St; tel: 5223 2132*. Open lunch Mon–Fri. Dinner Mon–Sat. Licensed. Imaginative menu. **Le Parisien**, *16 The Esplanade; tel: 5229 3110*. Open lunch Mon–Fri, dinner Mon–Sat. Licensed. French cooking. **Sawyers Arms Tavern**, *2 Noble St, Newtown; tel: 5223 1244*. Lunch Mon–Fri. Dinner Mon–Sat. Licensed. **The Elephant and Castle Pub Restaurant**, *158 McKillop St; tel: 5221 3707*. Open daily for lunch; dinner Tues–Sat. English pub food.

Savvas Restaurant, *51 Moorabool St; tel: 5229 3703*. Opposite the National Wool Centre. Medium price. Open lunch and dinner

Mon–Sat. **Lamby's Restaurant**, *National Wool Museum, Moorabool St; tel: 5223 2392*. Open 7 days lunch and dinner. In the basement of the 1872 Bluestone Building. Licensed. Medium price. **Portico Restaurant**, *All Seasons Ambassador Hotel, Gheeringhap St; tel: 5221 6844*. Open for dinner seven nights. Licensed. **Fishermen's Pier**, *Yarra St; tel: 5222 4100*. Open daily lunch and dinner. Licensed.

SIGHTSEEING

This is the largest provincial town in Victoria and was named by Governor Bourke in 1837 although it was not incorporated until 12 years later and was only proclaimed a city in 1910. The name comes from the Koori word *Jillong*, which has been variously translated as 'place of the cliff' and 'white seabird'.

Geelong is on **Corio Bay**, where the **Barwon River** enters the sea, and is about an hour's drive down the Princes Hwy from Melbourne. This Highway has something of a confusing start as it wends its way out of Melbourne, but once you see that you are on Rte 1 all is well. The Highway becomes *Latrobe Terrace* as you get nearer the town.

The best way to see the history of Geelong is to take the heritage trail walk, which starts in *Moorabool St* outside the **Wool Museum**. This is in the old bluestone **Dennys Lascelles Woolstore**, which was originally built in 1832. The walk, which is detailed in a brochure available from the tourism centre, takes about an hour to guide you past most of the historic spots in Geelong. The tourist office also has a **Mobility Map** of central Geelong for people with limited mobility.

At the **Geelong Art Gallery** in *Little Malop St (tel: 5229 3645)*, there is a collection of Australian paintings including Eugene von Guerard's *View of Geelong*. The painting is owned by Andrew Lloyd Webber and is on loan to the gallery.

One of the major social events of the year, and a major date in the Australian racing calendar, is **The Geelong Racing Carnival**, *Geelong Racecourse; tel: 5229 4414*, which is held for two days at the end of October, fitting in neatly with the Melbourne Cup.

On the corner of *Myers and Swanston Sts* is the **Old Geelong Gaol** (*tel: 5221 3510*, open weekends 1300–1600), which functioned from 1853 until 1991.

The **Geelong Maritime Museum**, *Swinburne St; tel 5227 0209*, is set in the first Australian Naval College and has a 6m model of the SS *Wandilla*, as well as a wealth of other model ships. Opening hours, 1000–1600 every day except Tues and Thur.

Along the bay is **Eastern Beach**, which has a semi-circular timber promenade, a diving tower and a children's swimming pool. Further along are **Steampacket Gardens**, where an arts and crafts market is held on the first Sun of every month. **The Geelong Botanic Gardens**, *entrance at the east end of Malop, tel: 5226 1267*, are open daily. Established in 1850, they cover 4 hectares with a 15 hectare annexe of botanical woodland, and overlook Corio Bay.

On the western outskirts of Geelong is **Buckley Falls Park**. It straddles each side of the Barwon River, which tumbles over rocks and rapids before it joins with the Moorabool River. The park houses the National Trust listed **Barwon Paper Mill**, which has had its mill race reconstructed and now has water cascading down. Part of the Buckley Falls Park, tucked in a bend of the Barwon River is **Queen's Park**, which was reserved for a botanical garden as early as 1850. Work started in 1860 and the park was redesigned in 1867.

One way of seeing the whole of Geelong and the hinterland very quickly is by way of a scenic flight from **Geelong Airport**, *tel: 5264 1273*, which has a range of ten suggested flight plans.

Nearby is **Barwon Grange** in Newtown, *tel: 5221 3906*; open Sat–Sun 1100–1620 Sept–Apr, closed May–Aug. This well-maintained homestead dates from the last century and is situated on the banks of the Barwon River. All the rooms are furnished in the style of the times.

Also in Newtown, is a pre-fabricated house called **The Heights**, *tel: 5221 3510*; open Wed–Sun 1100–1630. This must have been among the first pre-fabs in the world for it was built in Germany in 1854 and erected in Newtown the following year.

TORQUAY

Tourist Information: Tourist Information Centre, *The Esplanade; tel: 5261 5374*.

ACCOMMODATION

Surf City Motel *(BW), 35 The Esplanade; tel: 5261 3492*. **Torquay Tropicana** *(FL), corner Surfcoast Hwy and Grossmans Rd (Postal: PO Box 409); tel: 5261 4399 or 5261 4495*. **Torquay Hotel**, *36 Bell St; tel: 5261 6046*.

EATING AND DRINKING

When it comes to eating out, the nearby holiday town of Queenscliff is much superior to Torquay and some of its restaurants are also listed below.

Ida's By the Sea, *26 The Esplanade, Torquay (tel: 5261 2253)*. BYO. Seafood specialities. **Pasquini's at Suma Park**, *Marcus Hill; tel: 5258 1724*. Licensed. Historic homestead. Jazz some nights. **Harry's**, *Princes Park, Queenscliff; tel: 5258 3750*. BYO. Beach type kiosk transformed.

Lombardi's Trattoria, *Hesse St, Queenscliff; tel: 5252 3277*. Licensed. Italian style. **Mietta's at Queenscliff Hotel**, *16 Gellibrand St; 5258 1066*. Licensed. Six course gourmet meals on a par with anything in Australia. Extensive wine list.

SIGHTSEEING

For surfers Torquay is the centre of heaven. The surfing beaches run from **Aireys Inlet** to **Point Lonsdale** on the **Bellarine Peninsula**. The most famous beach is **Bells**, which has achieved a mythical, mystical status with surfers. Every spring the **Rip Curl** men's professional titles are held there. Most of the major surfing manufacturers are located here. Quicksilver, Rip Curl, Piping Hot and Billabong all have shops representing them in the *Surfcoast Plaza*.

The town was originally called 'Spring Creek' but was renamed after the Devon seaside town in England. It was at Torquay that the clipper *Joseph Scammell* ran aground in 1891, and its deckhouse was used in the building of **Scammell House** in *Pride St*.

Reflecting one of the major activities of this resort is **Surfworld Museum**, *rear of Surfcoast Plaza, tel: 5261 4606*. Open daily 1000–1700;

137

The Great Ocean Road

A t the turn of the century, most of the villages along the coast, such as Lorne, were cut off by the Otway Ranges and the only way of communicating easily with the outside world was by sea. In 1916, during the middle of World War I, it was suggested that returned servicemen be employed to build roads to hitherto cut-off areas.

From this initiative The Great Ocean Road Trust was founded with two objectives. The first was to provide employment for returned service men, and the second was to create the road as a memorial to those who had served in the war. The suggestion has also been made that the road was also built in conscious emulation of some of the scenic Californian Pacific Coast Highway, especially the section which runs down to Monterey.

The road, which was mainly hacked out of the earth by manual labour, was completed in 1932. It is a long and winding road that starts officially at Torquay and finishes at Warrnambool.

The problem with the road is that although the views are almost constantly breathtaking, the driver of a car sees little of them because this road requires your full concentration. The best way of dealing with this is to pull over at most, if not all, of the viewing stations and parking bays along the way. Otherwise only the passengers will enjoy the views which are, indeed, amazing.

admission $5. It has surfing videos, interactive videos and a wave tank.

Flagstaff Hill Maritime Museum, *tel: 5264 7841*, has recreated a maritime village around the 1872 lighthouse and keepers cottages. In the harbour there are moored ships of the age and underwater movies are screened in the theatre. In the museum the **Loch Ard peacock**, a miraculously unbroken clay figure from Australia's most famous shipwreck, is on display. Open 7 days 0900–1700, $9.50.

The Gippsland Heritage Centre, *tel: 5227 3082* (open 7 days 0900–1700, $7), has 35 separate buildings, several of which are in the National Heritage Estates list. It is a documented history of the town and the lifestyle of the area told through some of the most culturally significant buildings.

Torquay is on the Surf Coast and is a way station to the Great Ocean Rd. But to its east lies the Bellarine Peninsula, which has a series of holiday spots – specifically **Portarlington, Queenscliff, Ocean Grove** and **Barwon Heads**.

The Bellarine Peninsula Railway connects Geelong to Queenscliff. It was built in 1879. The railway is now run by the Geelong Steam Preservation Society, with trips every Sunday and most public holidays, *tel: 5252 2069*.

Tourist Information: Mornington Peninsula Tourism, *Mornington; tel: 5977 0186.*

ACCOMMODATION AND FOOD

Surfcoast Resort, *105 Great Ocean Rd; tel: 5263 3363*. **Anglesea Homestead Motor Lodge** *(BW), 109 Great Ocean Rd; tel: 5263 2600*. **Debonair Motel**, *Great Ocean Rd (Postal: PO Box 134); tel: 5263 1440.*

Saylers Restaurant, *Great Ocean Rd; tel: 5263 1440*. Licensed. **Diana's Café Restaurant**, *113 Great Ocean Rd; tel: 5263 2500*. Dinner and light refreshments. Licensed.

SIGHTSEEING

The Anglesea River – originally called Swampy Creek, as was the town – runs through the centre of this resort, which has safe, patrolled beaches and is surrounded by forested hills. The town originated as a stopover for mail coaches and one of the stations, **McMillans House**, is still standing. Nowadays it is very much an artists' colony and there are many studios and galleries with work for sale.

Googorah is an adventure park in bushland on the west side of the river. (*River Reserve Rd; tel: 5261 4202.*) There is a network of bridges and boardwalks across waterways, connecting bushland islands. The largest island is known as **Sanctuary** and it has the entire range of flora from the Anglesea area. The name *Googorah* is Koori for 'swampy creek', which is precise as the park also serves as a natural firebreak for the town.

Ironbark Basin, *Point Addis and Jarosite Rd; tel: 5261 4202*, is another reserve. Based on what was once a family farm, it incorporates both coastal and forest scenery. The reserve has well maintained and sign-posted tracks and spectacular rugged cliff-top views of the Point Addis coastline. The **Anglesea Golf Course**, *Noble St, tel: 5263 1582*, has many of those moving hazards – kangaroos – which congregate in the early morning and at dusk.

Surf Coast Walk. There is no suggestion that you should complete the whole walk, which is 36 km – although many keen bushwalkers do just that. This marked trail meanders along the coast in six stages, the longest of which should take no more than 3 hrs. It extends from Jan Juc to Moggs Creek and takes in Bells Beach, Point Addis and Distillery Creek Picnic Area. Maps are available from the **Barrabool Shire Office**.

There is another, less strenuous walk – the **Anglesea Heathland Cliff Walk** – that starts at the end of *Purnell St*, goes along to the cliffs and then inland through the forests. The walk takes about 60 mins and pamphlets are available at the tourist office.

For the adventurous, the **Anglesea Hang Gliding School** offers introductory tandem flights at $80.

There is some confusion about the name. It comes from John Airey, a former lieutenant in the navy, who had a station called Eyrie from 1842.

The town was a terminus for the Cobb & Co. coaches from Geelong for many years. The **Split Point lighthouse**, a local landmark, 34m high, was built in 1891. It is not open to the public and can only be viewed from the road. From the lighthouse there is a cliff-top walk with lookouts. Off the main road and well signposted is the **bark hut**, which is a replica of

the 1852 settler's hut that was burned down in the Ash Wednesday bushfires of 1983.

Moggs Creek Picnic Ground is on *Old Coach Rd* – turn right at the bridge – and is in the **Angahook State Forest Park**.

For **accommodation** try **The Light-keepers Inn Motel**, *64 Great Ocean Rd; tel: 5289 6666*.

⬏ SIDE TRACK FROM AIREYS INLET

You can detour to **Angahook Lorne State Park** by way of *Abambra Rd* from Aireys Inlet or from *Old Coast Rd* to the east of Moggs Creek Bridge.

ANGAHOOK LORNE STATE PARK

Tourist Information: Angahook Lorne State Park Office; *tel: 5289 1732*.

The park covers 22,350 hectares and has several major types of vegetation, as well as an extensive bird life. In the park are the **Erskine Falls**, among lush tree ferns and bush. The falls drop 30m. There are many bushwalking tracks laid out ranging from a gentle hour's stroll to serious bushwalking and covering, in all, about 50 km. Also in the park are the **She-Oak Picnic Grounds** and the **Blanket Leaf Picnic Ground**. Both are on *Erskine Falls Rd*.

LORNE

Tourist Information: Surfcoast Tourist Information Centre, *144 Mountjoy Parade; tel: 5289 1152*.

The first thing you need to know about Lorne is that during the Christmas holiday period, extending almost right through until the end of January, it is impossible to get accommodation of any kind unless you have booked previously. And you need to book at any of the popular restaurants if you hope to get a table. Two hours drive away from Melbourne, Lorne is considered the definitive holiday spot and is packed at these times.

ACCOMMODATION

Anchorage Motel, *32 Mountjoy Parade; tel:*

139

5289 891. **Coachman Inn Motel,** *1 Deans Marsh Rd; tel: 5289 244.* **Lorne Hotel Motel,** *Mountjoy Parade; tel: 5289 409.* **Motel Kalimna,** *Mountjoy Parade; tel: 5289 1407.* **Ocean Lodge Motel,** *6 Armytage St; tel: 5289 1330.* **Pacific Motel,** *268 Mountjoy Parade; tel: 5289 1609.* **Sandridge Motel,** *128 Mountjoy Parade; tel: 5289 2180.* **HI: Great Ocean Rd Backpackers,** *10 Erskine Ave; tel: 5289 1809.*

EATING AND DRINKING

Reifs Restaurant and Bar, *84 Mountjoy Parade; tel: 89 2366.* Licensed. Open seven days, lunch and dinner. **Kalimna Restaurant,** *Great Ocean Rd; tel: (052) 89 1407.* Licensed. Seven days. **Kosta's,** *48 Mountjoy Parade; tel: 89 1883.* Open daily 0900-0100. Licensed. Greek influenced cuisine. **The Arab,** *89 Mountjoy Parade; tel: 89 1435.* Open lunch and dinner until late. BYO. **Mark's,** *124 Mountjoy Parade; tel: 89 2787.* Open 7 days lunch and dinner. Licensed.

SIGHTSEEING

Lorne is the first town in Victoria to be declared by the state government as being of special significance and natural beauty. William Lindsay was the first European settler in the area in the 1840s and he came to cut timber. Originally the town was called 'Loutit Bay' after Captain Loutit, who called here in 1841 on the *Apollo,* when carrying wool from Portland to Melbourne. In 1869 the town was surveyed and named Lorne after the town in Argyllshire, Scotland.

For many years the town was effectively isolated by a difficult approach from the interior but the opening of the Great Ocean Rd in 1932 changed that (see p.138).

Rudyard Kipling spent time in Lorne, where he wrote: *Buy my hot wood clematis/Buy a frond of fern/Gathered where the Erskine leaps/Down the road to Lorne.*

The **surf beach** at Lorne is patrolled and very safe, its white sand being protected by two headlands as the Otway ranges sweep down to the sea. **Lorne Surf Shop,** *130 Mountjoy Pde; tel: 5289 1673,* hires out wetsuits and boogie boards. Just after New Year's Day, at the height of the holiday season, the famous **Pier to Pub**

Swim is held, with the field being restricted to 2500 entries.

The Shell Museum, *William St, tel: 5289 1212* (open daily 0900–1630), has an extensive exhibition of shells from around the world.

The Lorne Historical Society, *59 Mountjoy Pde,* has a collection of photographs and memorabilia on the history of the area. Open weekends 1300–1600.

APOLLO BAY

Tourist Information: Great Ocean Road Tourist Information Centre, *115 Great Ocean Rd; tel: 5237 6529.*

ACCOMMODATION

Apollo Bay Motel *(BW), Moore St; tel: 5237 6492.* **Apollo Bay Beachfront Motel** *(GC), 163 Great Ocean Rd; tel: 5237 6437.* **Apollo International Motel** *(FL), 31 Great Ocean Rd; tel: 5237 6100.* **Coastal Motel,** *171 Great Ocean Rd; tel: 5237 6681.* **Motel Marengo,** *Great Ocean Rd; tel: 5237 6808.* **Whitecrest Holiday Resort,** *Great Ocean Rd (Postal: P0 Box 120); tel: 5237 0228.* **Bay Pine Motel & Guest House,** *1 Murray St; tel: 5237 6732.* **Great Ocean View Motel** *(HN), 1 Great Ocean Rd; tel: 5237 6527.* **Skenes Creek Lodge** *(BU), Great Ocean Rd, Skenes Creek via Apollo Bay 3233 (Postal: PO Box 92); tel: 5237 6918.* **The Lighthouse Keeper's Inn,** *175 Great Ocean Rd; tel: 5237 6278.* **Apollo Bay Hotel,** *95 Great Ocean Rd; 5237 6250.* **Koonjeree Motel,** *15 Diana St; tel: 5237 6290.*

EATING AND DRINKING

Beacon Point Restaurant, *Skenes Creek Rd; tel: 5237 6411.* Two kilometres out of town. Highly regarded for its sea food. **Otway Restaurant,** *210 Great Ocean Rd.* BYO. Australian country cooking. **Chris's Beacon Point Restaurant,** *Skenes Creek Rd, Skenes Creek; tel: 5237 6411.* Open daily lunch and dinner. Licensed. Greek style cooking. **Bernie's Restaurant,** *13 km east of Apollo Bay, Great Ocean Rd; tel: 5237 0228.* Open lunch Sun. Dinner daily. Licensed. Fish specialities. **Buffs,** *52 Great Ocean Rd; tel: 5237 6403.* Open daily spring–autumn, Thur–Mon winter. Licensed. Rambling café.

SIGHTSEEING

First came the whalers. Henty's established a whaling station, which operated on and off until 1847. Three years later the timber cutters arrived and the first permanent inhabitants settled where the old whaling station had been sited.

Bass Strait Shell Museum, *12 Noel St; tel: 5237 6395,* has an extremely comprehensive collection of local shells, as well as shells from around the world with some rarities. Open daily 0930–2000. Admission $2.

The Historical Museum, *Great Ocean Rd; tel; 5237 6505.* Open 1400–1700 daily during summer holidays, weekends and school holidays. The museum is in the old Cable Station and it has a photographic history of the area with thousands of pictures on display as well as many artefacts from the early days.

Maits Rest, *Otway National Park, 17 km west along Great Ocean Rd; tel: 5237 6889,* is a rain forest walk with boardwalk and viewing platform.

Eleven kilometres north on the *Barhan River Rd* are **Marriners Falls,** with a 2 km track running through lush forested areas. **Marriners Lookout** is along *Great Ocean Rd,* 3 km to the north. Access is by a steep and narrow road but the effort is worth it because it offers stunning panoramic views of the coast and the Bass Strait.

The *Tuxion Rd* to **Crows Nest Lookout,** 6 km away, has outstanding views but the drive requires the driver's full attention as it is steep and winding in places.

You can go on a fishing trip on the MV **Revolution,** which departs from **Fisherman's Wharf** twice daily 1000 and 1400; *tel: 5237 6529.*

The **Wingsports Flight Academy** *(tel: 5237 6486)* has courses in hang gliding and para sailing and **Torquair Airpark** *(tel: 5261 5100)* offers Tiger Moth flights out along the coast.

Wild Dog Trails *(tel: 5237 6441)* has, despite the name, horse rides into the hinterland.

OTWAY NATIONAL PARK

Tourist Information: Otway National Park, *Cartwright St, Apollo Bay; 5237 6889.*

This park is unusual in that it has very easy access by motor car although its 12,750 hectares have many different ecosystems, ranging from sheltered mountain gullies to exposed dunes to sea shores.

Cape Otway was first discovered by Europeans in 1802, when Matthew Flinders arrived. But it was a treacherous coast, inherently dangerous for sailing ships, and it was not until the lighthouse was built in 1848 that it attracted settlers. The first to move in were, as in most cases, the timber fellers, who worked in the area of what is now Apollo Bay and Lorne. A sawmill opened at **Elliott River** and a tramway, parts of which can still be seen, was built from there to the sea.

After the timber fellers came the settlers, who in 1880 started to clear further timber to open up farm land. Then came the gold boom, with more demand for timber. After World War II there was another timber boom with the demand for houses, and Otway National Park was created to protect the coast above Cape Otway and **Blanket Bay.**

The *Great Ocean Rd* runs right through the National Park with *Lighthouse Rd* – unsurfaced but very well maintained – running down from the centre to the coast. The park is one of the most accessible as you can easily explore it from **Maits Rest** on *Great Ocean Rd,* **Johanna Beach,** or from **Princetown** (see below) to the beach and the river. The lighthouse can be visited (open Tues and Thur 1000–1130, 1400–1530; *tel: 5237 9240.)*

In the park swamp wallabies and ring-tail possums are common and there is a very extensive and varied bird population.

PRINCETOWN

Tourist Information: Mornington Peninsula Tourism, *Mornington; tel: 5977 0186.*

ACCOMMODATION

Apostles View Motel and Country Retreat *(BU), RMB 1435 Booringa Rd; tel: 5598 8277.*

This is one of the stops on the Great Ocean Rd, this time at the mouth of the **Gellibrand River.** It is a centre for scenic drives and bushwalks.

Nearby is the **Glenample Homestead**, *Great Ocean Rd*, 2 km east of the Twelve Apostles (see below). This was constructed from locally quarried sandstone in the 1860s and was the first pastoral settlement to the south of the **Heytesbury Forest**. It was from this homestead that the *Loch Ard* shipwreck rescue operations were directed. The only two survivors of the shipwreck, Eva Carmichael and Tom Pierce, came to this homestead to recover. Open Fri–Mon 1030–1700 mid Sep–mid Jul and every day during school holidays, *tel: 5598 8209*.

The **Otway Ranges Deer and Wildlife Park**, *Great Ocean Rd* near the Twelve Apostles, *tel: 5537 5262*. Open daily 0900–dusk. It has numerous native Australian animals and red and fallow deer, and visitors can feed the animals.

PORT CAMPBELL NATIONAL PARK

Tourist Information: National Park Tourist Information Centre, *Morris St; tel: 5598 6382*.

ACCOMMODATION

Port Campbell Motor Inn *(GC)*, *12 Great Ocean Rd; tel: 5598 6222*. **Southern Ocean Motor Inn** *(BW)*, *Lord St (Great Ocean Rd); tel: 5598 6231*. **Loch Ard Motor Inn** *(HN)*, *Lord St (Great Ocean Rd); tel: 5598 6328*. **Port O'Call Motel**, *Great Ocean Rd; tel: 5598 6206*; **HI: Port Campbell Hostel**, *18 Tregea St; tel: 5598 6305*.

SIGHTSEEING

The town of Port Campbell is very small, with a population of only 200 outside the tourist season. The National Park runs to the east and west of the town in a narrow strip covering 1750 hectares. The park protects the famous limestone formations on the coast. There are footpaths leading to lookouts over the cliffs. There is a small colony of fairy penguin and mutton bird nesting sites. The most important features of the park, all of which you drive past along the Great Ocean Rd, in order are:

The Arch. This is the first of the majestic formations caused by the sea eroding the limestone rocks. **The Grotto** has paths leading down to rock pools.

Loch Ard Gorge is the site of the famous shipwreck in 1878, which claimed the lives of 58 people – only two were rescued. There are steps down the face of the cliff.

Nearby are **The Blowhole, Elephant Rock** and **Mutton Bird Island**.

London Bridge is an amazing double arch formation. Tourists used to be able to walk out over the first arch but on Jan 15 1990, at the height of the tourist season, it collapsed. Luckily at that time no one was on it although two tourists were stranded on the far side of the bridge and had to be rescued by helicopter.

Then come the **Twelve Apostles**. Twenty five million years ago the coast lay under the waves and marine deposits of shell and skeletal debris eventually built to a depth of up to 150m. When the sea receded this became the limestone of the coast, and then the sea started to erode what it had left behind.

The Twelve Apostles are dramatic pillars of limestone standing just off the coast. They are part of the cliff face which has been eroded away and are quite spectacular. They are continuously being hammered by the sea, which has cut archways, blowholes and sheer cliff edges. This is a continuing process and the striations of the limestone layers against the blue of the sea and the white of the crashing waves creates some of the most dramatic scenery in Australia. They range in height from 10 to 50m and are startling in their beauty. There are now only eight apostles to be seen from one of the viewing platforms. This sight alone makes a trip along the Great Ocean Rd worthwhile.

WARRNAMBOOL

Tourist Information: Tourist Information Centre, *600 Raglan Parade; tel: 5564 7837*.

ACCOMMODATION

Central Court Motel *(FL)*, *581 Raglan Pde (Princes Hwy); tel: 5562 8555*. **Mid City Motor Inn** *(FL)*, *525 Raglan Pde (Princes Hwy); tel: 5562 3866*. **Olde Maritime Motor Inn**, *corner Banyan and Merri Sts; tel: 5561 1415*. **Western Coast Motel** *(FL)*, *corner Raglan Pde and Bell St; tel: 5562 2755*. **All Seasons Motor**

Inn and Apartments *(BW), 367 Raglan Pde; tel: 5561 2833.* Centrepoint Motel, *75 Banyan St; tel: 5562 8044.* City Heart Motel, *4 Spence St; tel: 5562 0500.* Colonial Village Motel, *31 Mortlake Rd (Hopkins Hwy); tel: 5562 1455.* Elm Tree Lodge *(BU), 179 Kepler St; tel: 5562 4133.* Log Cabin Motel *(HN), 698 Raglan Pde; tel: 5562 4244.* Mainstream Motel *(GC), 1 Darling St; tel: 5561 4977.* Tudor Motel Warrnambool *(BW), corner Raglan Pde and Banyan St; tel: 5562 8877.* Warrnambool Gateway Motor Inn *(GC), 69 Raglan Pde; tel: 5562 8622.* Motel Downtown Warrnambool, *620 Raglan Pde; tel: 5562 1277.* Flagstaff Hill Motel *(BU), 762 Raglan Pde: tel: 5562 1166.* Mahogany Motel *(BU), 463 Raglan Pde; tel: 5562 5722.* Norfolk Lodge Motel *(BU), 692 Raglan Pde; tel: 5562 6455.* Raglan Motor Inn, *376 Raglan Pde; tel: 5562 8511.* Redwood Manor Motel, *251 Koroit St; tel: 5562 3939.* Riverside Gardens Motor Inn, *corner Simpson and Verdon Sts; tel: 5562 1888.* Motel Warrnambool *(BW), 65 Raglan Pde; tel 5562 1222.* Chateau Lodge Motel *(BW), 8 Spence St; tel: 5562 7144.* Western Motel *(BU), corner Timor and Kepler Sts; tel: 5562 2011.* Turn In Motel, *corner Simpson and Verdon Sts; tel: 5562 3677.*

EATING AND DRINKING

The Mahogany Ship, *Flagstaff Hill Maritime Village; tel: 5561 1833.* Open daily. Licensed. Restaurant Malaysia, *69 Leibig St; tel: 5562 2051.* Breakers, *Banyan St; tel: 5561 3088.* Merihop Café, *78 Leibig St; tel: 5561 3188.* Open dinner Tues–Sat. Licensed. Mediterranean and Asian influenced menu.

SIGHTSEEING

This is the fifth largest provincial city in Victoria. It is right in the centre of the Shipwreck Coast, which runs from Cape Otway through the **Port Campbell National Park** to end up at **Port Fairy**.

Warrnambool was a whaling and sealing port in the early 1830s. It used to be a refuge for sealers and whalers in the past, and was first permanently settled by Europeans in 1839. These were always dangerous waters and between 1836 and 1908 28 ships were wrecked.

When the town was surveyed by Lieutenant Pickering in 1856, he gave it an Aboriginal name taken from a hill by the Hopkins River, which has been variously translated as 'place of plenty', 'place between two waters' and 'running swamps'. Like most of these translations there is no definitive version.

In the town are **The Botanic Gardens**, *corner Queen St and Botanic Rd; tel: 55 64 7800.* They were designed in 1872 by William Guilfoyle, the great designer of the Melbourne Botanic Gardens. There is a bandstand rotunda, a fernery and winding shaded walkways.

On the Breakwater, the **Aquarium** *(tel: 5562 2581; open daily 0900–1700, adults $3.50), has a display of many fish from local waters as well as a large collection of sea shells.*

A popular picnic area is **Cannon Hill**, *tel: 5567 800, off Artillery Crescent,* which has panoramic views of **Lake Pertrobe** and **Lady Bay**. It contains a marble marker, which may just possibly have links with 17th-century Portuguese explorers. The name of the hill comes from the cannon that was installed there to ward off the possibility of a Russian invasion in 1887 during the Crimean War.

The **Middle Island** at Merrii River Mouth can be waded to at low tide and has a fairy penguin colony. There are tracks laid down so that visitors do not disturb the birds.

A small folk museum and history centre operates in **History House**, *Gilles St, tel: 5562 6940.* Open first Sun of each month and every Sun in Jan, 1400–1600. It exhibits old photographs, documents and memorabilia.

Lady Bay, the main beach on *Penrobe Rd,* near the mouth of the Hopkins River, provides safe family swimming and sunning.

Nearby, 12 km west along the Princes Hwy, is the **Tower Hill Game Reserve** – restricted access; *tel: 5565 9202.* This is an ancient volcano crater with an island in the centre. On the island is the **National History Centre** – open 0930–1630 – and there are several self-guided tours of the reserve laid out.

The Blue Hole in *Blue Hole Rd* is a recreational area on the eastern side of the Hopkins River.

MELBOURNE–EDEN

The direct inland run from Melbourne up to the border of New South Wales visits some interesting towns. The scenic detour takes in Wilsons Promontory and other national parks and is worth the diversion.

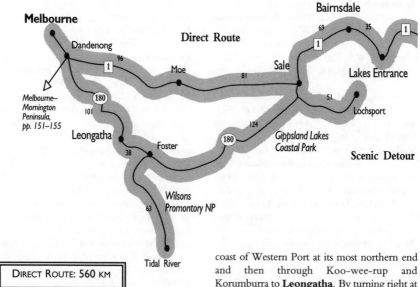

Melbourne
Dandenong
Direct Route
Bairnsdale
Moe
Sale
Lakes Entrance
69 35 1
96
1
81
51
1
Melbourne–
Mornington
Peninsula,
pp. 151–155
180
101
Leongatha
Foster
38
180
124
Lochsport
Gippsland Lakes
Coastal Park
Scenic Detour
Wilsons
Promontory NP
63
Tidal River

144

DIRECT ROUTE: 560 KM

ROUTES

DIRECT ROUTE

From Melbourne travel east along the Princes Hwy (Rte 1) through **Dandenong** (see p.155), **Moe**, **Sale**, **Bairnsdale**, **Orbost**, **Cann River** and on to Eden, a journey of 560 km. To visit **Mallacoota** you will need to turn off right at **Genoa** and travel the 23 km to the coast, retracing your steps along the same road to rejoin the Prince's Hwy.

SCENIC DETOUR

At Dandenong, turn right onto the Gippsland Hwy (Rte 180), touching the coast of Western Port at its most northern end and then through Koo-wee-rup and Korumburra to **Leongatha**. By turning right at **Foster**, 38 km further on, you can take a diversion down to the delights of **Wilsons Promontory**. You then need to retrace your route to Foster and travel east along the Gippsland Hwy past Toora, Welshpool and Alberton on the coast and then inland until you cross the Little Monkey Creek and, passing the Holey Plains National Park, arrive at **Sale** back on the Prince's Hwy and the direct route. At this point you are at the start of the Gippsland Lakes. To the east is the expanse of Lake Wellington and then Lake Victoria.

It is possible to side-track along the coast: just before reaching Sale, take the road on the right and travel between Reeve Lake on the right – followed very quickly by Ninety Mile Beach and the sea – and Lake Wellington on the left, in the **Gippsland Lakes Coastal**

Park. The road peters out after 51 km at **Lochsport**. Back-track to Sale and then follow the direct route to Bairnsdale, Lakes Entrance and Orbost, the coast entrance to the Snowy Mountains (see p.117). Along the coast on the right is Lind National Park and then **Croajingolong National Park**, with Mallacoota and its inlet as an end stop.

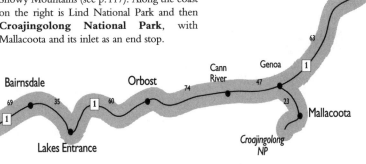

At least 6 trains a day run between Melbourne (Spencer St and Flinders St stations) and **Sale** on weekdays. At weekends 4 trains run on Sat and 3 on Sun (OTT table 9029). Journey time about 2½ hrs.

BUSES

Two bus companies run a service between Melbourne and Eden (and on to Sydney), stopping at all the towns described in this chapter apart from Mallacoota. The journey time to Eden is approx. 15 hrs. Public Transport Corporation have bus connections from Sale to Eden for 5 of their trains. OTT table 9120.

LEONGATHA

ACCOMMODATION

Try **Leongatha Motel**, *18 Turner St; tel: 5662 2375*. **Opal Motel** *(BU), South Gippsland Hwy; tel: 5662 2321*.

SIGHTSEEING

Close to the Strzelecki Ranges, this town in South Gippsland was once the centre of a forest of giant trees. Clearing began in the 1870s, when a labour colony was established to help alleviate unemployment. Soon the area was

cleared and it became cattle raising country, which it remains to this day. The name comes from an Aboriginal word, which has been translated as 'teeth'.

You can experience the delights of this farming life at **Brackenhurst Farm** (*Christoffersons Rd, Nerrena; tel: 5664 9261*), 10 km south-west of Leongatha. Open daily 1530–1700, admission $2. Here you can see the 350-cow herd being milked in rotary milking parlours. There is a collection of antique lamps and firearms at the **Firelight Museum** (*Leongatha Rd; tel: 5668 6272*), 9 km north of Leongatha by way of *Yarragon Rd*. Open weekends and school holidays 1000–1700.

On the Tarwin River and 12 km north of the town off the road to **Mirboo**, is **Moss Vale Park**, 5 hectares of parkland with English and European ornamental trees.

The **Bass Philip Winery**, *Toschs Rd; tel: 5664 3341*, offers three different styles of Pinot Noir and Chardonnay for tasting and has cellar door sales. Open weekends in summer 1100–1800. Another winery is **Tarwin Ridge**, *Wintles Rd; tel: 5664 3211*, which offers Pinot Noir, Sauvignon Blanc and a Cabernet Merlot blend. Open weekends and school holidays.

In the **Mechanics Institute**, *McCartin St; tel: 5662 2031*, is the **Woorayl Shire Historical Society** (open Thur–Fri 1300–1600), which has two spacious rooms housing a collection of historical memorabilia, documents and photographs.

⤴ SIDE TRACK FROM LEONGATHA

WILSONS PROMONTORY NATIONAL PARK

Tourist Information: Wilsons Promontory National Park Visitor Centre, *Tidal River; tel: 5680 9555,* 32 km from the entrance to the park along a sealed road.

ACCOMMODATION

Foster is the best base for accommodation in the area, including **Foster Hotel** *(FL), South Gippsland Hwy, (PO Box 7); tel: 5682 2022;* **Wilsons Promontory Motel**, *26 Station Rd (PO Box 6); tel: 5682 2055.*

SIGHTSEEING

Wilsons Promontory is attached to the mainland by a narrow neck of land – **Yanakie Isthmus** – which you can drive across using the sealed road that runs from Foster to the main park centre of Tidal River. The park has over twenty well signposted safe walks and a total of 80 km of tracks, including one to **Mt Oberon** and another to **Sealers Cove**. As an introduction to the park the **Lilly Pilly Gully Nature Walk** is recommended. It takes about 3 hrs and begins on the main track at Tidal River. You pass through several types of vegetation, including eucalypt forest and rain forest, and granite rock formations.

The park has over 130 km of coastline scenery backed by granite ranges and covers 49,000 hectares. It is a very popular holiday spot and at weekends in the summer the facilities can be crowded although absolute peace and seclusion is nearly always only a short walk away. The name is a slight mystery but it is believed that Governor Hunter named it after Matthew Flinders' friend Thomas Wilson, who lived in London and apparently never visited Australia. The Kooris of the Brataualung clan called this area *Wamoom*. The first Europeans to see this area were George Bass and his whaleboat crew on their 1798 voyage from Port Jackson. They were followed by sealers and whalers, who anchored in Sealers Cove and **Refuge Cove**, where they extracted oil from the blubber.

The coast here is dangerous and, although matters were helped by the construction of the lighthouse in 1859, it continued to claim its tally of ships. Part of the area was reserved by the Victorian government in 1898 and it became a National Park in 1905, since when there have been substantial additions. The park contains grey kangaroos, wallabies, koalas and a wide range of birds, including some almost tame rosellas at Tidal River, which will happily perch on your hand. Australian fur seals can be found on the islands of the park. ⬛

SALE

Tourist Information: Central Gippsland Tourism, *8 Princes Hwy; tel: 5144 1108.*

ACCOMMODATION AND FOOD

The King Avenue Motor Inn *(FL), 20 Princes Hwy (PO Box 1010); tel: 5143 2222.* **Aspen Motor Inn** *(BW), 342 York St (Princes Hwy); tel: 5144 3888.* **Sale Hacienda International Motor Inn** *(BW), corner Princes Hwy and Raymond St; tel: 5144 1422.* **Captains Lodge International Motel**, *46 Princes Hwy; tel: 5144 3766.* **Midtown Motor Inn** *(FL), York St (Princes Hwy); tel: 5144 1444.* **The Princeton Motor Lodge** *(FL), Princes Hwy (PO Box 1010); tel: 5144 6599.* **Swan Motel** *(BU), Princes Hwy (PO Box 80); tel: 5144 3096.* **Sale Motel**, *corner York and Stawell Sts; tel: 5144 2744.* **Wetlands Country Motel**, *Princes Hwy; tel: 5144 3222.*

Timothy's on York, *308 York St; tel: 5144 1933.* Licensed. In weatherboard cottage serving up-market local produce. **The Stockman's Hut**, *Raymond St; tel: 5144 2801.* Licensed. Country style. **Captain's Lodge**, *46 Princes Hwy.; tel: 5144 3766.* Open daily for dinner. Licensed. Australian cooking. **Catchadell House**, *193 Raymond St; tel: 5143 1911.* Open daily for lunch. Dinner Tues–Sat. Licensed. Does not accept credit cards.

The first European to discover Sale, near the junction of the Latrobe and Thomson Rivers, was Angus McMillan in 1841. The first settler was Archibald McIntosh and his property was called, appropriately, Flooding Creek. This name was later to be given to the town but it was formally re-named after Sir Robert Henry 'Fighting Bob' Sale, killed in the Afghan Wars in 1845 and regarded as the best fighting officer in the British army of the day.

Sale grew with the Omeo gold rush of 1851 (see p.182) and was consolidated as a port for the paddle-steamers trading on the **Gippsland Lakes**. The first reasonably useable road to Melbourne was not built until 1865. The railway was completed in 1879. The town became firmly established in modern times as the service and administrative centre for the offshore Bass oil and gas fields of Victoria, which have made Australia 70% self-sufficient in crude oil.

Near Lake Gutheridge on *Foster St*, in the old Sale Borough office building, is the **Historical Museum** (open Sun, public and school holidays, 1330–1600, $2), which has a pictorial and documented history of the town. In the centre of town a **pedestrian mall** has been created at the junction of *Raymond and Cunninghame Sts,* and this has a series of artworks, including bronze bas-relief murals by Annemieke Mein, the **Wall of Fame**.

Sale Regional Arts Gallery (open Mon–Fri 1000–1700, Sun 1000–1400), takes the theme of 'Gippsland and the Environment'. The former **Cobb & Co. Stables**, *Raymond St*, have been transformed into a craft and souvenir market. **Textile Explosion**, *corner Princes Hwy and Raymond St; tel: 5144 4022*, shows the complete process of creating textiles as art works. You can see artists at work, weaving and screen printing. Open Thur–Mon 1000–1600.

Kangaroos and emus wander around the **Fauna Reserve**, *Gutheridge Pde; tel: 5142 3333*. Sale is the centre of the **Gippsland Wetlands**, a collection of lakes and waterways. **The Wetlands Centre of Victoria** (*York St nr Lake Gutheridge*, open Tues–Sat 1000–1600), has information and also runs ecology tours of the area. On the shores of **Lake Wellington**, 25 km from Sale, is **Marley Point**, which is a favoured sailing spot with shallow areas safe for swimming. **The Sale Common State Game Refuge** is on the South Gippsland Hwy *(tel: 5144 3048)* and covers 308 hectares. Nearly three-quarters of this park is freshwater marsh and a boardwalk wends its way through it, allowing visitors to see different habitats.

The historic **Swing Bridge** across the Latrobe River is 5 km to the south of the town and was built in 1883. This is a good fishing and general recreation area.

SIDE TRACK
FROM SALE

GIPPSLAND LAKES COASTAL PARK

Tourist Information: *tel: 5152 0400*.

In the Lakes and Wilderness region of Victoria there are over a million hectares of public land. Indeed, 85% of the land in the whole of **East Gippsland** is dedicated to the public. There are eight Lakes and Wilderness Parks in the area and 400 sq km of estuaries, lakes and rivers to explore. The Gippsland Lakes Coastal Park itself has the **Ninety Mile Beach**, which extends from **Paradise Beach** at one end to the entrance of **Lake Tyers** at the other. Back from the coast there are coastal dunes and then the lakes themselves.

The first European to discover the lakes was probably Angus McMillan in 1840. He came over the mountains to the **Tambo River** and then followed it to where it flows into **Lake King**. He wrote: 'What a glorious sight! Extending to the west further than I could see and to a point that shut it from my view, which I called Tambo Bluff, the noble stream emptied itself into the lake between our camp and it. This magnificent sheet of water was quite alive with pelicans, swans and several kinds of duck.' And it is still much the same – the principal additions being small sailing boats and sailboards.

The best way to explore this park, and its nearby cousin, the **Lakes National Park**, is by boat, with the added benefit that there are no safer waters in which to learn to sail.

147

The park abounds with wildlife, with eastern grey kangaroos, swamp wallabies, emus and possums as well as the pelicans recorded by McMillan. Within the lakes there are many small islands that are bird life havens. **Rotamah Island** has a Royal Ornithologist Society station and bird hides.

Ashore, there are many clearly marked trails around the lakes, which are generally sandy and easy walking. They typically wander through banksia and eucalypt woodland, ending up on or near Ninety Mile Beach. ◩

BAIRNSDALE

Tourist Information: Tourist Information Centre, *240 Main St; tel: 5152 3444* and the **DC&NR office**, *7 Service St; tel: 5152 0400*.

ACCOMMODATION AND FOOD

Bairnsdale Flag Motor Inn *(FL), 598 Main St; tel: 5152 3004*. **Bairnsdale Kansas City Motel** *(FL), 310 Main St; tel: 5152 6266*. **Colonial Motor Inn** *(BW), 335 Main St; tel: 5152 1988*. **Mitchell Motor Inn** *(BW), 295 Main St (PO Box 1041); tel: 5152 5012*. **Main Motel** *(HN), 544 Main St; tel: 5152 5000*. **Riverhill Motor Inn** *(GC), 45 Main St; tel: 5153 1551*.

Tanjil Motor Inn, *384 Main St; tel: 5152 6677*. **Town Central Motel** *(BU), 164 Nicholson St; tel: 5152 3084*. **Bairnsdale Wander Inn** *(BU), 620 Main St; tel: 5152 6477*. **Travelana Motel** *(BU), 49 Main St; tel: 5152 3200*. **Grand Terminus Hotel**, *98 McLeod St (PO Box 126); tel: 5152 4040*.

Riversleigh Country Hotel Dining Room, *1 Nicholson St; tel: 5152 6966*. Licensed. Local fish and wines. Has been called one of Victoria's best provincial restaurants. **Florencio's Steak House**, *306 Main St; tel: 5152 3794*. Open daily. Licensed.

SIGHTSEEING

The town, on the banks of the Mitchell River in the heart of the **Lakes District**, is named after Bernisdale on the Isle of Skye, the birthplace of an early European settler, Angus McLeod, who took up land in 1842. The often repeated story that it was named after the number of babies – 'bairns' – born there to the McLeod family in the early days appears to be a rural myth. The town was gazetted into official existence in 1862. The bridge over the Mitchell River was opened in 1875 and the railway arrived 12 years later. In the 1850s and 1860s Bairnsdale was a port and a centre for the lakes shipping, handling people and goods heading for the Omeo goldfields (see p.182). It is also the centre of an agricultural and vegetable-growing area but it has not always been peaceful. After the visit of the teetotaller and hot gospeller, Tennyson Smith, in 1920, the town split into two factions and rioted.

The Court House in *Bailey St*, next to the Post Office, was built in 1893 and is now classified by the National Trust, although it is still used as a court. It looks like a French château, with gables and conical towers. Open daily.

The **Historical Museum and Resource Centre**, *Macarthur St; tel: 5152 6363*, is open Wed, Thur, Sat, Sun 1230–1800; $3. The building was originally St Andrew's College but now contains much memorabilia regarding the history of Gippsland. In the grounds are early agricultural implements and machinery. **The Krowathunkoolong Keeping Place**, *37 Dalmahoy St*, is an Aboriginal Culture Centre (open weekdays 0900–1700; $3).

Behind the Post Office is the **Port of Bairnsdale**, which is a picnic and swimming area on the Mitchell River with a riverside walking trail.

The ceiling, walls and sanctuary of **St Mary's Catholic Church** – built in 1914 – were painted during the Depression by Francis J. Floreani, who took 4 years to complete this epic work. It is a series of complex and detailed murals, with 400 angels, seraphim and cherubim on the ceiling alone. Open daily. **Macleod Morris State Game Reserve**, *off Paynseville Rd*, covers 520 hectares. There are over 80 varieties of waterbird in this wetlands area and there is a boardwalk and an observation hide. The reserve is open daily, July–Mar.

LAKES ENTRANCE

Tourist Information: Tourist Information Centre, *corner Marine Pde and The Esplanade; tel: (03) 5155 1966*.

ACCOMMODATION AND FOOD

Banjo Paterson Motor Inn *(BW)*, *131 Esplanade (Princes Hwy) (PO Box 591); tel: 5155 2933.* **Bellevue Motor Inn** *(FL)*, *191 Esplanade (PO Box 385); tel: 5155 3055.* **Albatross Motel**, *661 Esplanade (PO Box 449); tel: 5155 1779.* **Coastal Waters Motel**, *635 Esplanade (PO Box 128); tel: 5155 1792.* **Cunningham Shore Motel**, *639 Esplanade; tel: 5155 2960.* **George Bass Motor Inn** *(FL)*, *Princes Hwy; tel: 5155 1611.* **Lakes Waterfront Motel**, *10 Princes Hwy; tel: 5155 2841;* **Riviera Backpackers** *(HI)*, *5 Clarkes Rd; tel: 5155 2444.*

Skippers Wine Bar and Restaurant, *481 The Esplanade; tel: 5155 3551.* Open daily for dinner except Aug. Licensed. Fish specialities.

SIGHTSEEING

The Entrance, as it is known locally, provides access to the Gippsland Lakes and is the home of one of the largest fishing fleets in Australia. The lakes used to be used for commercial shipping but today are only used by yachts, pleasure boats and schools of dolphins, who come into the lakes from spring until the end of summer.

Some 5 km to the north-west, off the road between Metung and Kalimna, is the 178 hectare **Nyermilang Park** – the name is Koori for 'chain of lakes'. Open daily 0900–1600; *tel: 5156 3253.* Built in 1892, it overlooks the lakes. The gardens, which surround the house, are semi-formal and contain local and exotic birds. A display shows the history of the lakes.

Sea Shell Museum, *125 Esplanade; tel: 5155 1538* (open daily) has over 80,000 shells on display and the **Pandora Reef** room has hundreds of deep-water corals showing their underwater colouring. The **Wyanga Park Winery**, *Baades Rd, off Colquhoun Rd; tel: 5155 1508,* is open Mon–Sat 0900–1700, Sun 1000–1700, and offers the usual tastings and cellar door sales. There are boat cruises six days a week from The Entrance to this winery.

ORBOST

Tourist Information: **Slab Hut and Orbost information centre**, *Nicholson St; tel: 5154 2424.* Also the **Rainforest Information Centre**, *Lochiel St; tel: 5161 1375.*

ACCOMMODATION

Orbost Country Roads Motor Inn, *94 Salisbury St; tel: 5154 2500.* **Countryman Motor Inn** *(BW)*, *corner Salisbury and Livingstone Sts (PO Box 462); tel: 5154 1311.* **Orbost Motel Lodge**, *Irvines Rd (PO Box 74); tel: 5154 1122.*

SIGHTSEEING

Yet another town with a name from the Isle of Skye: Orbost is Gaelic for 'winged island' and was the home of the uncle of the squatter Archibald McLeod. During the initial settlement by Europeans there was much tension from European–Aboriginal clashes, with raids and reprisals closing the original station of 1838. This timber town on the Snowy River was finally created in 1878 and a swing bridge was built across the river in 1890. The river, although now only a shadow of its former self, has a tendency to flood and the **Old Pump House**, next to the information centre, has its walls marked with flood heights.

Orbost is the centre for farming on the river flats and is said to be the richest farm land in Australia, possibly the second richest in the world after the Nile Delta. Originally this was swampland and the early settlement was serviced by boats until the arrival of the railway in 1915.

The **Slab Hut** was built by John Moore in 1872 and was a family residence until it was converted into the tourist information centre. **The Historical Museum**, *Nicholson St* (open Mon, Wed, Thur, Fri 1030–1230 and 1400–1600, Sat 1000–1145), covers local history with a series of exhibits and relics.

The Rainforest Centre, *Lochiel St; tel: 5161 1375* (open Mon–Fri 0900–1700, weekends and public holidays 1000–1700), has a 20-min audiovisual presentation on the rain forests of East Gippsland. Outside there are gardens with pathways and elevated boardwalks, which take you through small reproductions of the vegetation, creeks, swamps and waterfalls of the Gippsland area.

Any drive from Orbost tends to be through spectacular scenery. The **Baldwin Spencer Trail** covers 262 km and follows the route taken by Walter Baldwin Spencer when he explored here in 1889. It starts at Orbost, heads south to **Marlo** and in the north through the rain forest of the **Errinundra Plateau** and back to Orbost. Brochures are available at the information centre. **Cabbage Tree Palms Flora Reserve** is 27 km to the east of the town, off the Princes Hwy on Palms Tracks, and contains 20 m high specimens of this relatively rare plant. The seaside resort of **Marlo**, is 15 km to the south on the *Cape Conran Rd*, which meanders along the coast for 18 km.

MALLACOOTA

Tourist Information: Mallacoota Information and Booking Services, *57 Maurice Ave; tel: 5158 0788* and **DC&NR** (the Victorian government department responsible for the park), *corner Buckland and Allen Dr.; tel: 5158 0219.*

ACCOMMODATION AND FOOD

Mallacoota Motel, *Maurice Ave (PO Box 43); tel: 5158 0455*. **Silver Bream Motel**, *32 Maurice Ave; tel: 5158 0305.*

Tide Bistro and Bar; *1 Maurice Ave tel: 5158 0231*. Offers abalone. **Barnacles Seafood Bistro**, *Mallacoota Hotel, Maurice Ave; tel: 5158 0455*. Licensed. **Watts Cooking at the Tide**, *corner Maurice Ave and Allan Dr.; tel 5158 0100*. Open daily lunch, dinner. BYO.

SIGHTSEEING

This inlet is where the Genoa River enters a flooded valley. It started life as a whaling port in the 1830s with Ben Boyd running deep-sea whaling boats from the inlet. Then there was fishing and a brief attempt at gold mining. Now the main product of the area is abalone for the Asian market (although it is occasionally offered in local restaurants). The town is totally surrounded by the Croajingolong National Park (see opposite).

The new viewing platform at **Bastion Point**, *off Betka Rd*, has superb views of the **Howe Range** on the New South Wales border, **Gabo Island** and the whole of The Entrance leading to the complex of lakes.

The Inlet is basically two lakes – Top and Bottom – which are connected by a narrow channel. Bottom Lake is the closest to town.

You can explore both lakes by boat or along the shoreline tracks. One good way of seeing the area is to follow the **Mallacoota Walkabout**, which runs for 7 km from Bastain Point. Part of it is **Shady Gully Walk**, a footpath that runs for about ½ km to **Shady Gully**. Boats can be hired at Mallacoota or Gipsy Point.

⤴ SIDE TRACK FROM MALLACOOTA

CROAJINGOLONG NATIONAL PARK

Tourist Information: CNR Information Centre, *Princes Hwy; tel: 5158 6351.* **CNR Office**, *Allan and Buckland Dr.; Mallacoota; tel: 5158 0219.*

Access to the park is from the Princes Hwy and Mallacoota along gravel roads which are normally passable, but in serious wet weather it is better to check with the CNR office before starting out. The *Old Coast Rd*, west of the Cann River, *Tamboon Rd* and *Wingan Rd* provide access to the **Wingan Inlet** and the western part of the park. The park also has many roads running through it, which are normally passable although they can be closed at times and it is best to check with the tourist office. There are picnic facilities in most of the coastal camping areas and in and around the Mallacoota Inlet.

The park with its musical name – it was once a popular Australian song sung by Slim Dusty – stretches for nearly 100 km from **Sydenham Inlet** to the border of New South Wales. It is considered to be one of Australia's finest national parks, with 87,500 hectares ranging from forested and undisturbed foothills to a wilderness coastline. It has been designated a World Biosphere Reserve by UNESCO. Within the park are two wilderness areas, which were declared in 1992. They are the 15,600-hectare **Sandpatch** and the 7100-hectare **Cape Howe** – both are now protected as areas of high conservation value, which means access is on foot only. ⤴

MELBOURNE– MORNINGTON PENINSULA

The Mornington Peninsula hangs like the toe of Italy to the south of Melbourne and is, for the inhabitants of that city, a favoured weekend retreat. East of the peninsula, in the waters called the Western Port, is Phillip Island, which has its own magical qualities. It can only be approached from the Mornington Peninsula side by boat. By land it means a diversion to the far side of Western Port.

ROUTE: 228 KM

151

Melbourne

20 — Dandenong — 30 — **Emerald**

Mentone — 16 — *Melbourne–Eden, p. 147*

Western Route 20 — 180 — **Eastern Route**

Frankston — 47 — 31 — Koo-wee-rup
13

Mornington
15

Dromana — Hastings
16 — 38 — 51
Portsea 8 — Rosebud
4 — Rye — 12 — Cowes
Sorrento — 181

Phillip — 9
Cape Schanck — Island — **Rhyll**
15

186

Newhaven

ROUTE

From Melbourne head south on the Nepean Hwy hitting the coast of Port Phillip Bay at Mordialloc. You then follow the coastline through a series of almost interlinked small towns – Edithvale, Chelsea, Carrum, Seaford – until you reach **Frankston**. You are still in the greater Melbourne metropolitan area, but you are also at the start of the Mornington Peninsula. After Frankston the road continues parallel to, but a little way from, the sea, until you reach **Mornington**, which is just off the highway at Snapper Point. From there you can either follow the Highway or take the much smaller coast roads to Mt Martha, **Dromana**, at the base of Arthur's Seat, Mt McCrae, **Rosebud**, **Rye**, Blairgowrie, **Sorrento** and, the point of the hook, **Portsea** (where a serving Australian Prime Minister, Harold Hold, was drowned in rough seas).

Back-track through Rye (you can make a side excursion down to **Rye Ocean Beach** in Port Nepean National Park) almost to Rosebud and turn right. After 12 km a further turn to the right takes you 4 km to **Cape Schanck**, with its lighthouse and Angel Cave. Go back to the Rosebud-Flinders Rd and turn right to follow it to Flinders on West Head and on to the seaside town of **Hastings**. From Hastings head north and keep to the right-hand road, following the coast of Westernport Bay, until it meets the Gippsland Bass Hwy. At this junction you can detour to visit **Phillip Island**: turn right, passing **Koo-wee-rup** on Rte 181 around Westernport Bay, turning right onto Rte 186 at Anderson for Phillip Island. Retrace your route to follow Rte 181 north and when it becomes Rte 180 carry on to **Dandenong**. From here you can follow Rte 1 back to central Melbourne, or take the minor road to **Mentone**, where you rejoin the early stretch of this tour.

TRAINS

There is a frequent local train service to Frankston Flinders St Stn (1 hr) continuing to Stony Point, south of Hastings (1¾ hrs). Trains also run to Dandenong (45 mins) but do not continue in the direction of Phillip Island. OTT table 9023.

BUSES

One bus a day (two on Fridays) of the Public Transport Corporation runs to Cowes (3¾ hrs), calling at Dandenong (1 hr). OTT table 9113.

FRANKSTON

Tourist Information: Tourist Information Centre, *51 Playna St; tel: 9789 5529*.

A **Thomas Cook Foreign Exchange** branch is at *8 Station St; tel: 9781 3733*.

Frankston is just within commuting distance of Melbourne (40 km away) and is technically part of the metropolitan area, but it has its own distinctive atmosphere. The name Frankston is something of a mystery. One popular theory is that it is a corruption of Frank Stone's Hotel, one of the early pubs in the area. Another is that

it is named after Frank Liardet, who lived there in 1843. No one knows for certain.

The first brick house constructed in the district is **Ballam Park and Homestead** at *258 Cranbourne Rd (tel: 9789 5529)*. It was built around 1855 by Frederick Liardet, who had French ancestors, and it is somewhat similar in design to a French farmhouse. In the area around the house there is a blacksmith's forge, a display of antique machinery and a museum and resource centre. The park is open daily and the homestead is open Sun and some holidays, 1400–1700. $5.

Petitioning government for better education is nothing new. **The Davey Street School**, *Davey St; tel: 9783 3769*, came into existence when residents made a petition. The government gazetted the present site in 1873 and the school house was built the following year. The current brick building was added on in 1889 and now houses the school museum. Open Mon, Wed 1930–1500.

The railway arrived in 1882 and Frankston became a popular seaside resort for the people of Melbourne. **Frankston Pier** is off Nepean Hwy and was first built in 1857. It was used for taking out fish and firewood and bringing in stores for the townsfolk. **George Pentland Botanical Gardens**, *off Yuille St, tel: 9784 1888*, feature native and fern gardens. Open daily 0800–1800 or later throughout the year. Much less formal is **Sweetwater Creek Reserve**, covering 14 hectares at the foot of Oliver's Hill, near the Nepean Hwy. It has deep gullies and plenty of bird and animal life, including snakes. The Koori called the creek *Narringalling*, which means 'Sweet Water'. There is a splendid view of the bay from Oliver's Hill – it runs out towards Mt Eliza – which you climb to from the reserve. The hill is named after James Oliver, a fisherman who used it as a lookout, although it was originally called Old Man Davey's Hill after William Davey, one of the first to settle in Frankston.

Sage's Cottage is at nearby **Baxter** on *Frankston-Hastings Rd, tel: 5711 337*. Open Wed–Sun and public holidays. It is a vertical timber cottage with a shingle roof, slab walls and herb and vegetable gardens beside the cottage. **Via Mare**, *343 Nepean Hwy; tel: 9770*

0111. Open lunch not Sat. Dinner daily. Licensed. Moderate. Highly recommended.

MORNINGTON

Tourist Information: Mornington Information Centre, *corner Main and Elizabeth Sts; tel: 5975 1644.*

ACCOMMODATION AND FOOD

Brooklands Motor Inn *(FL), 99 Tanti Ave (Postal: PO Box 565); tel: 5975 1166.* **Ranch Motel**, *corner Nepean Hwy and Bentons Rd; tel: 5975 4022.* **Royal Hotel**, *770 Esplanade; tel: 5975 5466.* **Mornington Motel**, *334 Main St; tel: 5975 3711.*

Satay 'n Spice, *Main St; tel: 5975 5154.* Open dinner Wed–Sun. BYO. Malaysian Indian food of a high quality.

SIGHTSEEING

The Mornington Peninsula shire has 190 km of coastline and comprises Mornington, Sorrento and Portsea. It is a major playground for Melbourne, and should be avoided during the school holidays and summer weekends unless advance bookings have been made. It can get very crowded. The peninsula is known for its art and craft galleries, which are almost everywhere you look. On the peninsula there are now very nearly forty vineries, all making cool maritime climate wines and almost all inviting visitors for tastings and cellar door sales.

The McCrae Homestead (*11 Beverley Rd, McCrae, tel: 5987 6244;* open daily 1200–1630) is a National Trust property and one of the oldest houses on the Peninsula. It was built in 1844. **Mulberry Hill**, *Golf Links Rd, Baxter, tel: 5971 4138,* is the former home of Sir Daryl Lindsay and his wife Joan Lindsay, who was an artist and the author of *Picnic at Hanging Rock.* The house is in original condition, complete with its collection of art. Open Sun 1330, 1415, 1500. **Mornington Peninsula Gallery**, *corner Dunns and Tyabb Rds; tel: 5974 4395,* has an extensive collection of drawings, lithographs and posters, and houses travelling exhibitions. Tues–Fri 1000–1630.

The Old Post Office Museum, *corner Esplanade and Main Sts; tel: 5975 3613,* was built in 1863. The museum (open Sun and public holidays 1400–1700, closed mid June–Aug) now houses local historic pieces and old telecommunication equipment. To find out whether you could have made it in television, visit **Studio City**, *1140 Nepean Hwy*, on the road to Mt Eliza, *tel: 5975 9799.* Open daily 1000–1700. It contains a large amount of television memorabilia and a fully equipped studio and control room available to visitors.

DROMANA

Tourist Information: Peninsula Tourist Information Centre, *Point Nepean Rd; tel: 5987 3078.*

This is a popular bay-side beach resort at the foot of Arthur's Seat. One of the great experiences on the peninsula is the ascent from Dromana of **Arthur's Seat**, which rises to 305 m and gives panoramic views over the peninsula. You can drive up the scenic road or take the 20-min ride on the largest chairlift in Victoria, **Arthur's Seat Chairlift**, *Arthur's Seat Rd*, which glides at treetop level to the summit. There is lots of wildlife in the area, including koalas and echidnas. (Open daily 1000–1700 Sept–May; weekends and public holidays the rest of the year; *tel: 5987 2565.* $7.50 adults, $5 children.) At the top is the renovated **Old Viewing Tower**, open dawn to dusk.

Arthurs, *Arthurs Scenic Rd; tel: 5981 4444,* is noted for its superior French cooking. Open Easter to Christmas, Fri–Sun (lunch) Thur–Sat (dinner). Licensed. Expensive.

SORRENTO

Tourist Information: Sorrento Visitor Information Centre, *St Aubins Way.* This is a part-time service and there is no telephone.

ACCOMMODATION AND FOOD

Motel Saltair, *corner Melbourne and Bowen Rds; tel: 5984 1356.* **Sorrento Hotel**, *5 Hotham Rd; tel: 5984 2206.* **Koonya Hotel**, *1 The Esplanade; tel: 5984 2281.* **Oceanic Motel**, *234 Ocean Beach Rd; tel: 5984 1417;* **HI: Bells-Environmental Hostel**, *3 Miranda St; tel: 5984 4323.*

Palms, *154 Ocean Rd; tel: 5984 1057.* Open daily lunch and dinner. BYO. Superior quality, family run restaurant. Expensive.

153

Smokehouse, *182 Ocean Beach Rd; tel: 5984 1246.* Gourmet pizzas. **Sarchi's**, *145 Hotham Rd, tel: 5984 1472.* BYO.

SIGHTSEEING

The original **Sorrento Tramway**, designed in 1889, consisted of a light carriage drawn by two horses. It has been recreated as the **Sorrento Portsea Horse-Drawn Tram Company** *(tel: 5984 1762)*, which runs excursions every Sun and during school holidays. **Collins Settlement Historic Site** (garden open daily 1030–1630) commemorates the landing and settlement here in 1803. There are four graves from that date. An information centre has an educational display. Opening hours vary as to the season. **Marine Aquarium**, *3 St Albans Way*, off Nepean Hwy, *tel: 5984 4478*, has seal shows at 1500. Cruises are available from the aquarium, which allow visitors to swim with dolphins and seals. Open daily 0600 until dark. The **Nepean Historical Society Museum**, *corner Melbourne and Ocean Beach Rds; tel: 5984 4424*, is housed in the **Mechanics Institute**, built from local limestone in 1876. It includes a water cask from the Collins 1803 Settlement and a range of pioneer and shipwreck memorabilia. Open weekends, public and school holidays, 1330–1630. $2.50. In the same grounds is **Watts Cottage**, built in 1869.

PORTSEA

A quiet seaside resort with mainly private houses and just one important hotel, the upmarket **Delgany Country House Hotel**; *tel: 5984 4000* (expensive), whose restaurant, **Two Faces**, *tel: 5984 4166*, is one of Australia's major restaurants – a Michelin two star by French standards. Extensive wine list.

Portsea is where the wealthy of Melbourne have built their discreet mansions. It has some impressive beaches, front and back. The front beach is much the safest. The ocean beach can be dangerous and you should only swim where indicated by the lifesavers.

CAPE SCHANCK

This scenic area overlooks the Bass Strait. In the area is the **Ace Hi Ranch and Fauna Park** (open daily 1000–1700; *tel: 5988 6262)*, an 80 hectare property with ocean views, which has a fauna park, animal nursery and trail ride .

HASTINGS

Accommodation: Hastings Harbour View Motor Inn *(BW)*, *126 Marine Pde; tel: 5979 3333*, is the place to stay.

This is an industrialised area in the Victoria State style – that is, surrounded by farms and orchards – on the western shore of Western Port, a natural deep water harbour. The major attraction is **Hastings Fauna Park**, *249 High St; tel: 5979 1658* ($3), which has wallabies, kangaroos, wombats, deer and a variety of birds.

PHILLIP ISLAND

Tourist Information: Phillip Island Information Centre, *Phillip Island Rd, Newhaven*, just past the bridge from the mainland; *tel: 5956 7447.*

ACCOMMODATION AND FOOD

Cowes

Banfields Motel *(BW)*, *192 Thompson Ave; tel: 5952 2486.* **Coachman Motel**, *51 Chapel St; tel: 5952 1098.* **Tropicana Motor Inn**, *22 Osbourne Ave; tel: 5952 1874.* **The Anchor at Cowes Motel** *(FL)*, *1 The Esplanade; tel: 5952 1351.* **Kaloha Motel**, *corner Chapel and Steele Sts (PO Box 50); tel: 5952 2179.* **Seahorse Motel** *(BU)*, *29 Chapel St (PO Box 54); tel: 5952 2269 or 5952 2003.* **The Continental Phillip Island Motel**, *5 The Esplanade (PO Box 797); tel: 5952 2316.* **Glen Isla Motel**, *234 Church St; tel: 5952 2822.* **New Hollydene Motel**, *114 Thompson Ave; tel: 5952 2311;* **HI: Amaroo Park**, *97 Church St; tel: 5952 2548.*

Black Swan, *10 Thompson Ave, Cowes; tel: 5952 3106.* Italian cuisine. 7 days. Licensed. **Castle Inn**, *9 Steele St, Cowes; tel: 5952 1228.* Licensed. By the sea. Open Mon–Sat. **The Lobster Pot**, *The Esplanade, Cowes; tel: 5952 2316.* Licensed. Lunch and dinner 7 days. **The Jetty Restaurant**, *The Esplanade, Cowes.; tel: 5952 2060.* Open 7 days, both before and after the penguin parade (see p.155). Licensed. **Kellys**, *72 Chapel St, Cowes; tel: 5952 3100.* Daily lunch, dinner. Licensed. French cuisine.

Newhaven

Bridge Motel, *31 Forrest Ave; tel: 5956 7218.*
Sea Breeze Motel, *40 Forrest Ave; tel: 5956 7387.*

Rhyll

Coleshill Lodge Motel, *51 Rhyll-Newhaven Rd; tel: 5956 9304.*

SIGHTSEEING

This 10,000 hectare island lies 120 km south of Melbourne, opposite Mornington Peninsula. The island was originally inhabited by the Bunurong tribe, who called it *Corriong*. It was first discovered by a European in 1798, when George Bass described it as 'a high cape, like a snapper's head'. It was named after Governor Phillip. The commercial centre is **Cowes**, to the north of the island.

One of the highlights of a visit to Phillip Island is the nightly **Penguin Parade**, which lasts for some 50 mins every evening. The time of the parade varies between 1730 in June and July to 2030 in Jan. Typically some thousand penguins come out of the sea to head for their burrows, but the number is smaller in winter and higher in summer. Special measures have been taken to ensure that viewers do not distress the penguins, including the banning of all video and flash lights. If you want to take photographs you must use high speed film. Wear warm clothes because, even in the summer, it can get quite chilly. You must have a ticket to attend the parade and at holiday times booking is essential; *tel: 5956 8691.* There is a charge to see the parade – the money is spent exclusively on running the bird sanctuaries. The best bargain is the **Island Passport**, $29 adult and $13 for children, which gives access to most of the sights and is valid for 12 months.

There are several other places to see bird life on the island, including bird sanctuaries at **Rhyll**, near **Conservation Point**, and at **Swan Lake**. From late spring until autumn, shearwaters – often called mutton birds – can be seen in the rookeries that extend from **Cape Woolamai**. Seals have been always been a feature of the island. Early settlers were seal hunters, who almost annihilated the fur seals although, since they have been protected, a

large colony of them has returned. At **Point Grant** you can see the **Nobbies** rock formations and walk along the cliff-face boardwalks. Just beyond is the home of Australia's largest colony of fur seals – there can be as many as 5000 of them at **Seal Rock** during the breeding season. To get even closer to the seals, **Bay Connections Cruises** in San Remo (*tel: 5978 5642*) runs cruises to Seal Rocks. It also has a sunset cruise around **Cape Woolamai** to see the evening flight of the shearwaters.

The **Koala Conservation Centre**, *Philip Island Tourist Rd, tel: 5956 8300,* has 6 hectares of bush as a haven for koalas, which used to be found all over the island. There is a close viewing area, where a boardwalk takes visitors into the tree-tops. Feeding time is at 1600, when the rangers give an informative talk.

The island has a colony of **pelicans**, which are fed with fish daily at 1100 on the San Remo side of the bridge on the fore-shore opposite the **San Remo Fishing Co-op** (*tel: 5978 5206).* **Phillip Island Wildlife Park**, *Main Tourist Rd, Cowes, tel: 5952 2038,* contains a wealth of Australian wildlife, most of which can be seen at very close quarters. There is a raised boardwalk through the trees to see the koalas. Open daily 0900 with variable closing times.

Phillips Island also has a **Grand Prix Motorcycle Racing Circuit**, where the international Grand Prix events are held every year. And, of course, there is a winery – **Phillip Island Vineyard and Winery** *(Berry Beach Rd, Ventnor; tel: 5956 8465; open daily 1100–1900 Nov–Mar; 1100–1700 Apr–Oct),* which offers cellar door sales and wine tastings.

DANDENONG

Dandenong, known as the market city, is 32 km from Melbourne. It has two major festivals a year – **Oktoberfest** in mid Nov and a **Holland Festival** in Feb.

Heritage Hill, in *Langhorne St,* is a group of historic buildings in a garden setting. The buildings include **Laurel Lodge** and Dandenong's oldest building, **St James Church**, *tel: 5493 4511.* Open Tues, Thur, Sun 1200–1630.

There is a **Thomas Cook Foreign Exchange** branch at *118 Walker St; tel: 9792 0541.*

155

MELBOURNE–MILDURA

This route explores the gold towns – Ballarat, where the rebellion at the Eureka Stockade changed a nation, and Ararat – and visits some stunning national parks, including the Grampians, Little Desert Wilderness (not little and hardly a desert) and the looming vastness of Big Desert Wilderness, before ending in the greenness of the Murray River valley at Mildura, from where further routes lead to Adelaide (p. 352) and Wodonga and Albury (p. 168).

Mildura

79 87

Ouyen

Big Desert Wilderness **Wyperfield National Park** 66

26 **Lascelles**

Hopetoun

61

41 **Warracknabeal**

Little Desert Wilderness National Park **Dimboola**

36

Horsham

65

124 8

74 **Stawell**

111 24 8 31

Halls Gap 124 **Ararat**

Grampians National Park 47 91

112

Ballarat 8

Melbourne

156

MAIN ROUTE: 616 KM

ROUTE

Head west out of Melbourne on Rte 8, the Western Freeway. After 102 km, just before **Ballarat**, the freeway becomes a highway. From Ballarat the road goes through gold country, through Beaufort to **Ararat**, and then inland and north-west to **Stawell**.

From Ararat you can continue on Rte 8 to Stawell or divert west along Rte 124 to **Halls Gap**, which is in the **Grampians National Park** and is a perfect base for exploration. From Halls Gap either take Rte 111 east back to rejoin the main route at Stawell or continue along Rte 124 until it rejoins Rte 8 just before **Horsham**. If you don't make this detour, then proceed to Horsham from Stawell along Rte 8.

Back on the Western Hwy at Horsham, continue to **Dimboola**. Both Horsham and Dimboola are gateways to the **Little Desert Wilderness National Park**.

At Dimboola you leave Rte 8 and strike north-east along Rte 138, the Borung Hwy, to

Warracknabeal. From Warracknabeal head north on Rte 107, the Henty Hwy, to **Hopetoun**, where you are approaching the serious outback. About 50 km to the west is the Wyperfield National Park, with its dried-up lakes, and to the west of that is the **Big Desert Wilderness**, which is harsh and unforgiving and not a place to explore in the summer. From Hopetoun continue on Rte 107 until it joins Rte 121, the Sunraysia Hwy, and turn left to head north for **Ouyen**, joining Rte 79 just south of the town. Ouyen has the Pink Lakes National Park to the west. Follow Rte 79, the Calder Hwy, north to **Mildura**.

TRAINS

One nightly train, the **Overland**, from Melbourne (Spencer St stn) will take you as far as Dimboola (7½ hrs) on this route, stopping (at unsocial hours) at Ararat (5 hrs), Stawell (5½ hrs) and Horsham (6¼ hrs). OTT table 9035.

BUSES

One overnight Public Transport Corporation coach runs from Ballarat to Ouyen (6 hrs) and then to Mildura (7¾ hrs). It is also possible to travel to Mildura with the Public Transport Corporation via Swan Hill during the day, using both train and bus connections. OTT table 9105.

BALLARAT

Tourist Information: Visitor Information Centre, *cnr Sturt and Albert Sts; tel 5332 2694.*

ACCOMMODATION AND FOOD

Bell Tower Inn *(FL), Western Hwy, Alfredton 3350; tel: 5334 1600.* **Sovereign Park Motor Inn**, *223 Main Rd; tel: 5331 3955.* **Bakery Hill Motel** *(BW), corner Humffray and Victoria Sts; tel: 5333 1363.* **Ballarat Mid City Motor Inn** *(FL), 19 Doveton St N.; tel: 5331 1222.* **Ballarat Colony Motor Inn**, *Melbourne Rd (Postal: RSD E674, Ballarat 3352); tel: 5334 7788.* **Central City Motor Inn Ballarat**, *16 Victoria St; tel: 5333 1775;* **HI: Sovereign Hill Lodge**, *Sovereign Hill; tel: 5331 1944 or 5333 3409.*

Emcee's Restaurant, *18 Doveton St, N. Ballarat; tel: 5331 1222.* Open dinner Mon–Sat.

Licensed. **Dyers Steak Stable**, *Little Bridge St; tel: 5331 1222.* **Conders Restaurant**, *12 Sturt St; tel: 5331 7570.* Open Tues–Fri dinner. BYO. Middle Eastern food. **Peals Restaurant**, *1845 Sturt St; tel: 5334 1600.* Licensed. Open Mon–Sat for dinner. **Porters Restaurant**, *corner Mair and Peel Sts; tel: 5331 420.* Licensed. Open Tues–Fri lunch, Tues–Sat dinner. **Priscilla's Cottage**, *109 Eureka St; tel: 5331 5705.* Licensed. Lunch daily. Dinner Sat. An 1860 miner's cottage, now a restaurant, tea rooms and art gallery. **Tokyo Grill House**, *109 Bridge Mall; tel: 5333 3945.* Licensed, dinner 7 days. **Jack's Place**, *10 Camp St; tel: 5332 8545.* Licensed. Open Tues–Sun. Opposite Ballarat court house. **Ansonia**, *32 Lydiard St; tel: 5332 4678.* Open daily lunch, dinner. Licensed. Mediterranean–Asian cooking. **Masons at the Gallery**, *40 Lydiard St N.; tel: 5333 3895.* Open daily lunch. BYO.

SIGHTSEEING

This is the capital of Victoria's gold rush. Starting with the initial strike in 1851, when gold was found at **Poverty Point**, the fields in and near this town produced more than a quarter of all Victoria's gold until the turn of the century. At its peak it was probably the richest alluvial gold field in the world. It was originally called Yuill's Swamp but took the name Ballarat from the Aboriginal word meaning something like 'resting place.'

This is the site of the greatest battle ever fought in Australia, which shaped Australia in a way that can still be most clearly seen to this day. On the gold diggings, all miners in Victoria were made to pay a licence fee and the miners wanted 'no taxation without representation.' On 29 Nov 1854, thousands of miners gathered at **Bakery Hill** and burned their licences. On 3 Dec, the soldiers were called in and the miners, led by Peter Lalor, assembled behind a stockade made from timbers from the **Eureka** claim. In a battle that lasted 15 minutes, 22 miners and six soldiers died.

This epic battle was the start of trade unionism and democracy in Australia. The miners won and Peter Lalor ended up as the first member for Ballarat and, later, Speaker of the House in the Legislative Assembly. The flag used at the

157

Battle of the Eureka Stockade is still flown in Australia to this day. In *Eureka St* there is a memorial park complete with a reconstruction of the stockade.

A sound and light re-enactment of the battle, called **Blood on the Southern Cross**, is held at **Sovereign Hill** (*tel: 5333 5777*) 4 times an evening, Mon–Sat. Each show runs just over an hour. Sovereign Hill, which covers 25 hectares on the Western Hwy going towards Geelong from Ballarat, has rightly won many awards. It is a superb reconstruction of life on the goldfields with shops and mines run by people in period costume. There are guided tours underground using the original tramway. Continuing the theme is the **Gold Museum** on *Bradshaw St*, opposite Sovereign Hill (open daily 0930–1720; *tel: 31 1944*), which has a series of galleries showing the lure of gold.

The **Botanic Gardens** cover 40 hectares on the shores of the man-made **Lake Wendouree** and the **Ballarat Vintage Tramway** (*tel: 5334 1580*), which has vintage trams running at weekends and school holidays along 1.3 km of the original track along the lake shore. In the gardens is the **Adam Lindsay Gordon Craft Cottage**, open 1000–1600 daily Oct–Apr, weekends and public holidays the rest of the year.

Her Majesty's Theatre, *17 Lydiard St; tel: 5333 5800*, is the oldest theatre in Australia and in its time featured stars such as Harry Lauder and Nellie Melba. Those glory days are past although it is still used for live theatres and eisteddfods – singing competitions – which attract huge numbers of entries. A typical eisteddfod will run to more than 6000 on stage performances from some 8000 entries.

Montrose Cottage (open daily 0930–1700) on *Eureka St* has a collection of memorabilia from the Eureka Stockade and is the last miner's bluestone cottage in Ballarat. At the **Great Southern Woolshed**, 100 sheep are still shorn every day to demonstrate the techniques involved. The woolshed is on the Melbourne side of Ballarat on the Western Hwy. Open daily 0930–1700; *tel: 5334 7877*. Five minutes from Sovereign Hill is the **Ballarat Wildlife Park**, *corner Fussel and York Sts, tel: 5333 5933*, which has a wide range of

wildlife, including koalas and Tasmanian devils, with kangaroos, wallabies and emus ranging freely in the 15-hectare park. Open daily 0900–1730 with guided tours at 1100.

Rosella Cottage, on Glenelg Hwy at Smythe's Creek, has kangaroos and wallabies in the extensive grounds. The **Gold Museum** (open daily 0930–1720) gives a presentation showing how gold played such an important part in the development of the area.

ARART

Tourist Information: Tourist Information Centre, *Barkly St, Town Hall Sq; tel: 5352 2096.*

ACCOMMODATION AND FOOD

Ararat Colonial Lodge *(BW)*, *6 Ingor St (PO Box 310); tel: 5352 4644.* **Statesman Motor Inn** *(FL)*, *Western Hwy; tel: 5352 4111.* **Ararat Central Motel**, *249 Barkly St; tel: 5352 4444.* **Golden Gate Motel Ararat** *(HN)*, *Western Hwy; tel: 5352 2474.* **Chalambar Motel** *(BU)*, *Western Hwy; tel: 5352 2430.* **Pendock Motel**, *367 Barkly St; tel: 5352 2521.*

Pyrenees Country Kitchen, *330 Barkly St; tel: 5352 3292.* Open Fri–Sun evenings from 1830. **Café Dominica**, *291 Barkly St; tel: 5352 1002.* Open Tues–Sun in tourist season; dinner only Thur–Sun at other times. Licensed.

SIGHTSEEING

Ararat is named after the nearby mountain, where the first squatter, Horatio S. Wills, rested in 1840 on his journey from New South Wales. After reaching the top of the 600m hill he wrote: 'This is Mt Ararat, for, like the Ark, we rested here.' The first gold in Ararat was found at **Pinky Point**, 6 km out on *Moyston Rd*, but it was not a major strike. The major strike came in May 1857, when a group of seven Chinese miners stumbled across what is now known as the **Canton Lead**. Thus the town might be said to have been founded by Chinese and is the only one in Australia to have that distinction. Ararat celebrates the success of its goldfields with an excess of Victorian architecture. Many of the buildings are listed by the National Trust. None of them have a Chinese flavour.

In town, **Alexandra Gardens** in *Vincent St*

The Victoria Gold Rush

A major force in the development of Victoria was the gold rush of the 1850s. It brought prosperity to the state, riches to very few, death to some and disappointment to most. And, to no small extent, the gold rush formed the character of modern Australia with its emphasis on mateship and its opposition to any authority.

Serious quantities of gold were first found at Clunes in 1851 and the rush was immediate. Within three months there were 8000 miners on the diggings and within a year this had increased to 30,000 adult men. Four years later the figure reached 100,000.

And that was just the miners. It does not count the wives and children and innkeepers and camp-followers (and murderers and thieves) who tagged behind them. It made life very difficult for some. A captain coming into the port of Melbourne stood a very strong chance of seeing his crew head for the hills where the gold was. Sometimes the captain went with them.

The early finds of gold were alluvial and some lucky miners found immense nuggets while others panned it from the rivers. Under the pressure of the mass of miners these sources soon dried up. Gold then had to be dug from the ground, stamped and crushed from the ore, using heavy machinery. The day of the lone miner in the diggings hoping for a fortune was past.

With the companies mining gold the speculators and investors had a heyday and between 1870 and 1890 the towns of Victoria, especially the gold towns, were developed and decorated with fine public buildings, churches, hotels, large houses – all the trappings of prosperity. And most of them are still there – although rarely in the hands of the original owners.

(tel: 5352 2675), has a collection of orchids displayed among large exotic trees. There is also a Japanese Island, an Alpine Landscape, a fernery and an extensive conifer garden. **Ararat Gallery**, *Vincent St, tel: 5352 2836*, has a unique collection of textile art, which is one of the best in Australia. It includes tapestries and costumes from two collections – **The Art of the Japanese** and **Lady Barbara Grimwade**. Open Mon–Fri 1100–1600, Sun and public holidays 1200–1600.

The old bluestone **Ararat Jail** is on *Girdlestone St* and is now open to the public. Open Sun and school holidays 1100–1600; *tel: 5352 3357*. **Langi Morgala Museum** *(corner Barkly and Queen Sts, tel: 5352 4858;* open weekends 1400–1600), covers much of the local area's history with its displays of artefacts – both European and Koori. The name is said to be Koori for 'yesteryear'.

The **Chinese Gold Discovery Memorial** is by a local sculptor, Dorothea Saaghy, as is a life-size statue of a Chinese miner on the actual site of the Canton Lead, just off the Western Hwy to the west of the town. Eventually a Chinese pagoda may be built here.

There are several wineries in the area producing mainly cool climate table wines. **Cathcart Ride Estate Winery** is 5 km away on *Halls Gap Rd;* open daily 1000–1700; *tel: 5352 1997*. **Montara Winery** is on *Chalambar Rd*, 3 km to the south. Open Mon–Sat, 0930–1700, Sun 1300–1700; *tel: 5352 3868*. **Mt Langi Ghiran Vineyard**, *Warrak Rd, Bangor,* off the Western Hwy, *tel: 5354 3207*. Open Mon–Fri 0900–1700, weekends and public holidays 1200–1700. This last makes a wine which is famed throughout Australia.

One of the best views of the Grampians can be found at **Carrolls Cutting**, which is 8 km out on the road from Ararat to Moyston. And **One Tree Lookout**, 6 km out on *Edwards Rd,* has spectacular views of the **Mandurang Valley** to the south and **Bendigo** (see p.172) to the north.

Green Hill Lake, 4 km out of town on the Western Hwy, is ideal for water sports including canoeing and sailboarding, and provides excellent fishing for trout and redfin.

STAWELL

Tourist Information: Stawell and Grampians Information Centre, *54 Western Hwy, Stawell West; tel: 5358 2314*.

ACCOMMODATION AND FOOD

Magdala Motor Lodge *(BW)*, *Western Hwy (PO Box 345); tel: 5358 3877.* **Coorrabin Motor Inn**, *7 Longfield St (Western Hwy); tel: 5358 3933.* **Diamond House Motor Inn**, *24 Seaby St; tel: 5358 3366.* **Goldfields Motor Inn** *(FL)*, *Western Hwy; tel: 5358 2911.* **Hi-Way Eight Motor Inn**, *28 Western Hwy; tel: 5358 2411.* **Central Park Motel** *(BU)*, *3 Seaby St; tel: 5358 2417.* **London Motor Inn**, *10 Horsham Rd; tel: 5358 2200.* **Motel Stawell** *(BU)*, *Western Hwy; tel: 5358 2041.*

Diamond House, *24 Seaby St; tel: 5358 3017.* **Fountain Coffee Shop**, *in the Stawell Mall; tel: 5358 4602.* **The Railway Hotel**, *13 Main St.* Licensed. Bistro meals.

SIGHTSEEING

Originally Stawell was known as The Reefs, as a result of the discovery of gold in 1853 by the shepherd William McLachlan at **Pleasant Creek**. Later quartz was found and mined in the **Big Hill** area and large amounts of gold were produced through reef mining – as opposed to alluvial gold – which contributed to the prosperity of the town. Finally it was named after a chief justice of Victoria, Sir William Foster Stawell. The town is in the **Wimmera** region and is 31 km north-west of Ararat and 233 km north-west of Melbourne. It is the centre of an important agricultural area although, as it happens, mining still takes place in the town in the **Magdala Mine**, which was closed in 1920 but reopened in 1981.

To commemorate the dependence of the town on gold, the town hall has a clock with chimes that play from 0900–1700 with two differs using a gold washing cradle to the tune of *With My Swag on My Shoulder*. Also marking the town's involvement in gold is the **Mt Pleasant Diggings and Alluvial Gold Memorial** at the Shire Buildings, where the Court House has been restored as a museum and is open at weekends. Celebrating God rather than Mammon is **St Matthew's Presbyterian Church**, whose steeple soars over the town.

Stawell is famous for its foot race – **The Stawell Gift** – which has been held every Easter since 1878. Run over 120m, this is one of the richest professional foot races in the world. Since 1986 it has been open to amateurs. The prize money is $100,000. **The Stawell Gift Hall of Fame** (open by appointment, *Main St, opposite Railway Stn; tel: 5358 1326)* has memorabilia associated with the race. Also in town is **Caspers World in Miniature** (open daily 0900–1700; tel: 5358 1877, $7.50), which has dioramas and displays of miniature working models covering 7 Asian countries.

One of the best views of the area is from the **Pioneer Lookout**, which is on the Big Hill on *Scenic Rd*. Nearby – 15 km to the north-west – is **Lake Lonsdale**, which is the second largest lake in the Grampians and is used for boating and is a popular picnic spot. Also close by is **Overdale Sheep Station**, *10 km east of town on Landsborough Rd; tel: 5358 1075.* Open by arrangement. Admission $6. This is a working farm that has a 2 hr tour, which includes shearing demonstrations.

Five kilometres south of the town on the Western Hwy are the **Sisters Rocks**, which are three huge granite tors named after the Levi sisters, who camped there early in the goldfield days and later became residents of Stawell. **Yabby Farm**, *Halls Gap Rd; tel: 5356 4272,* lets visitors fish for trout and yabbies with rods and bait supplied. Open Wed, Thur, weekends and school holidays 1000–1700 Sept–July.

HALLS GAP

Tourist Information: Halls Creek Information Centre, *Great Northern Hwy; tel: 9168 6262.*

ACCOMMODATION AND FOOD

Halls Gap Colonial Motor Inn *(BW)*,

Colour section (i): The Three Sisters in the Blue Mountains (p. 105).
(ii) Outback characters at Silverton (p. 108); paddle steamer on the Murray River (see pp. 168–175, 195–200).
(iii) Melbourne (p. 126): the city skyline and one of its famous trams.
(iv) Cairns (p. 246); the Ettamogah pub at Palmview, Qld (p. 216); pub interior at Kynuna in the Queensland Outback.

Dunkeld Rd (PO Box 13); tel: 5356 4395. **Halls Gap Kookaburra Lodge**, *14 Heath St; tel: 5356 4395.* **Mountain View Motor Inn** *(GC), Ararat Rd (Postal: RMB 2074); tel: 5356 4364.* **Grampians Motel**, *Dunkeld Rd (PO Box 31); tel: 5356 4248.* **Grand Canyon Motel** *(BU), Grampians Rd (PO Box 16); tel: 5356 4248.* **Halls Gap Motel** *(BU), Dunkeld Rd (PO Box 30); tel: 5356 4209.* **Grampians Gardens Motel**, *corner Ararat and Stawell Rds (PO Box 27); tel: 5356 4244;* **HI**, *Grampians Rd; tel: 5356 6221.*

Kookaburra, *Grampians Rd; tel: 5356 4222.* Open daily for dinner. Licensed. Recommended. **Suzy's**, *Lot 5 Dunkeld Rd; tel: 5356 4416.* Open daily for dinner. Licensed.

SIGHTSEEING

This is the tourist centre of the Grampians. The town is named after an early settler, C.B. Hall, who found the gap by following a Koori path across the Grampians.

In the town the **Brambuk Living Culture Centre** *(Dunkeld Rd; tel: 5356 4452; open daily 1000–1700)* shows the Koori culture of the area through displays, live performances and art and craft exhibitions. Nearby is **Lake Belfield**, 5 km along *Dunkeld Rd*, which is too deep and cold for swimming although non-power boating is allowed.

Boroka Vineyard on the *Halls Gap Rd* to Ararat *(tel: 5356 4252)* has not only wine tastings and cellar door sales but panoramic views of the area. **Wallaroo Wildlife Park**, which is next to the vineyard *(tel: 5356 4346)*, has more than 80 species on display. Open every day from 1000 during the holiday periods. Closed Mon–Tues at other times.

GRAMPIANS NATIONAL PARK

Tourist Information: National Park Visitor Centre, *Grampian Rd; tel: 5356 4381.*

The park covers 167,000 hectares and is renowned for its wildflower displays and rugged mountain ranges. The Grampians are in western Victoria, 260 km from Melbourne and 460 km from Adelaide. Approach them from **Ararat** on the Western Hwy or the Henty Hwy or from **Dunkeld** on the Glenelg Hwy.

The **National Park Visitor Centre** is 2½ km along *Dunkeld Rd*, south of **Halls Gap** shopping centre. There are over 900 different plant species in the park but it is the wildflowers coming to glory every spring that attract the most attention. The park has much bird life – over 200 species recorded – and there are also kangaroos, gliders, echidnas and koalas. Most parts of the park are accessible by car.

Halls Gap is in the park and has a circular road going up into the **Wonderland Range** and returning. This road also connects with *Mt Victory Rd* – a side road leads to the **Boroka Lookout** – which goes to **Zumstein** and **Lake Wartook**. Zumstein has kangaroos in abundance. Running south from Halls Gap is the road to Dunkeld, which passes through the **Serra Range** and **Mt Abrupt**.

All of these roads are sealed and can be used in all weathers. The park also has a wealth of secondary roads and they only become a problem after heavy rain, when they may become impassable. When that happens the park rangers are quick to erect warning notices.

Also within the park are more than 160 km of marked footpaths, which range from easy strolls from the visitor's centre to serious bushwalking with overnight stays. Visitors are asked to keep to the tracks because of the problem of soil erosion.

HORSHAM

Tourist Information: Horsham Rural City Visitor Centre, *20 O'Callaghan's Parade; tel: 5382 1832.* **National Parks Information: DC&NR office**, *21 McLachlan St; tel: 5381 1255.*

ACCOMMODATION AND FOOD

Country City Motor Inn *(GC), 11 O'Callaghan Pde; tel: 5382 5644.* **Golden Grain Motor Inn** *(BW), 6 Dimboola Rd; tel: 5382 4741.* **May Park Motor Lodge** *(BW), corner Darlot and Baillie Sts; tel: 5382 4477.* **Horsham Mid City Court** *(GC), 14 Darlot St; tel: 5382 5400.* **Town House Motel** *(FL), 31 Roberts Ave; tel: 5382 4691.* **Commodore Major Mitchell Motor Inn** *(FL), 109 Firebrace St; tel: 5382 0125.* **Darlot Motor Inn** *(HN), 47 Stawell Rd; tel: 5381 1222.* **Glynlea**

161

Motel *(BU)*, 26 Stawell Rd; tel: 5382 1260. **Horsham Motel** *(BU)*, 5 Dimboola Rd; tel: 5382 5555. **Majestic Motel** *(BU)*, 56 Stawell Rd; tel: 5382 0144 or 5382 2888. **Old Horsham Motor Inn**, Western Hwy (PO Box 679); tel: 5381 0033.

Olde Horsham, Old Horsham Village; tel: 5382 2937. Open daily lunch and dinner. Country style cooking. **The Black Forest Restaurant**, 56 Stawell Rd; tel: 5382 0144. Licensed. Traditional country cooking. **Glen Logan**, 37 Doeen Rd, Henty Hwy; tel: 5382 5013. Open dinner Tues–Sat. Licensed. Restored mansion. Australian quality cooking.

SIGHTSEEING

Horsham is the gateway to the Northern Grampians and is within striking distance of the **Little Desert Wilderness** and **Mt Arapiles Tooan State Park**. The city is on the Wimmera River, where it started life as a crossing place. It was named by an early squatter, James Darlot, after the suburb where he was born in Sussex, England. (He named his property Brighton.) The Aboriginal name for the place, *Bongambilor*, meant, elegantly, 'place of flowers'. A post office and a store opened in 1949 and the town came into official existence when it was surveyed in 1854.

An Art Deco building of the 1930s houses the **Horsham Regional Gallery**, which has the **Mack Jost** collection of Australian and European art. (80 Wilson St; tel: 5382 5575; open Tues–Fri 1000–1700, Sun 1300–1630.)

Banksia Hill (tel: 5384 0264 for opening times) in Hutchinsons Rd, Quantong, has more than 5000 banksias and West Australian species.

The Botanical Gardens are in Firebrace St beside the Wimmera River, and were designed, as were so many other botanical gardens, by Will Guilfoyle, who was responsible in the 1870s for the Melbourne Royal Botanical Gardens. It has a magnificent lemon-scented gum and a bunya-bunya pine at the entrance to the gardens. Open every day.

A community enterprise dedicated to working with ultra-fine wool is **The Wool Factory**, Golfcourse Rd, tel: 5382 0333. Open Mon–Fri 0830–1600, holidays and weekends 1000–1500. There are 4 guided tours a day; $5.

Apart from the sheep sheds and the workshops there is a miniature train and a walk-in aviary.

A display of wildflowers from May–Oct draws visitors to **Black Range Farm**, Clarkes Lane, tel: 5383 7506. There are also demonstrations of shearing of cashmere goats and there are panoramic views of the Grampians. The farm offers four wheel drive tours – $60 full day, $30 half day. Visits daily by appointment.

Off the Western Hwy, 11 km from town, is **Dock Lake** (tel: 5382 1832), a recreational reserve where you can go fishing for yabbies.

Olde Horsham Village (tel: 5382 1233, open daily 1000–1730) is a museum, fauna park and also has an art and antique gallery. It is 3 km to the south-east of town and is set in a reserve with many native animals and peacocks.

Laharum is 32 km from Horsham. It contains the **Toscana olive plantation**, off Plantation Rd tel: 5383 8235; open daily 0800–1700 by appointment.

DIMBOOLA

Tourist Information: The tourist office, if you like to call it that, of this small town is the **Muntz Hardware and General Store**.

For **accommodation**, try **Dimboola Motel**, Horsham Rd (PO Box 61); tel: 5389 1177.

Set on the Wimmera River, Dimboola is an agricultural town serving the surrounding area. It is 36 km north-west of Horsham and 335 km north-west of Melbourne. It had its fifteen minutes of fame in 1969 with Jack Hibberd's play of that name, which was later made into a movie.

Dimboola started in about 1859 as a settlement at the junction of tracks from the South Australian border, Horsham, Warracknabeal and Lake Hindmarsh. The name might mislead you. It is not Aboriginal. It was originally called Five Creeks but was changed to the Sri Lankan name, which means 'land of figs', by the surveyor J.G.W. Wilmott in 1863. The area was settled in the 1870s, mainly by German immigrants.

The **Bicentenary Park**, near the Western Hwy, has a steam locomotive parked in the middle as a reminder of the fact that the town once had a railway workshop. The artist

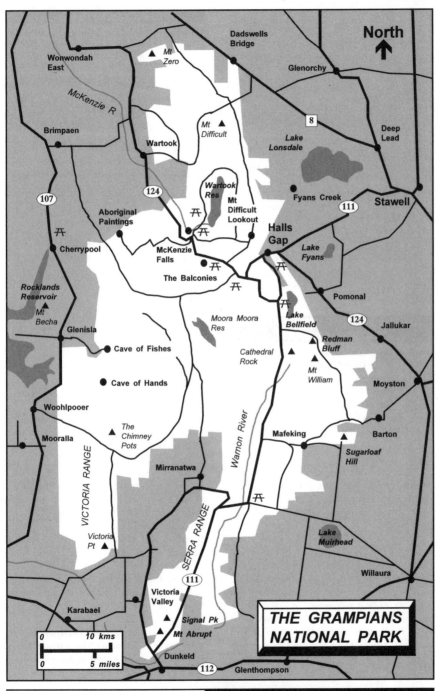

North

Wonwondah East

Mt Zero

Dadswells Bridge

Glenorchy

McKenzie R

Brimpaen

Mt Difficult

8

Deep Lead

Wartook

Lake Lonsdale

107

124

Wartook Res

Mt Difficult Lookout

Fyans Creek

111

Stawell

Aboriginal Paintings

Halls Gap

Cherrypool

McKenzie Falls

Lake Fyans

The Balconies

Pomonal

Rocklands Reservoir

Moora Moora Res

Lake Bellfield

124

Jallukar

Mt Becha

Glenisla

Cathedral Rock

Redman Bluff

Cave of Fishes

Mt William

Moyston

Cave of Hands

Woohlpooer

Warron River

Mafeking

Barton

Mooralla

The Chimney Pots

Sugarloaf Hill

Mirranatwa

SERRA RANGE

VICTORIA RANGE

Lake Muirhead

Victoria Pt

Willaura

111

Victoria Valley

Karabael

Signal Pk

Mt Abrupt

THE GRAMPIANS NATIONAL PARK

Dunkeld

112

Glenthompson

0   10 kms
0   5 miles

163

Sydney Nolan lived in Dimboola during two years of wartime army service. There he painted portraits of the town, which are now on display in the **National Gallery of Victoria**.

On the road to Jeparit at **Antwerp** is the **Ebenezer Mission** (tel: 5382 5033, open daily), founded in 1859 by the Moravian Missionaries to bring Christianity to the local Kooris. The mission, which was closed in 1903, has now been classified by the National Trust. On *Horseshoe Bend Rd* is the **Little Desert Eco-centre** (tel: 5389 1122, open daily), which has demonstrations and slide shows about this nearby – 4 km away – National Park. **Pink Lake** is 9 km to the north-west along the Western Hwy and its amazing pink and mauve colour is caused by salts in the water.

Some 4 km from town is **Picnic Bend**, which is a pleasant recreational area on the Wimmera River with boat launch and picnic facilities.

LITTLE DESERT WILDERNESS NATIONAL PARK

Tourist Information; Park ranger; *tel: 5152 6211* or at the **DC&NR office**, *21 McLachlan St, Horsham; tel: 5381 1255.*

The name is something of a misnomer because with 400mm of rainfall every year it is not a desert, and at 132,000 hectares it is far from little. The soil is sandy but supports mallee and heath plants and in the spring has superb displays of wildflowers.

There are many kangaroos, emus and other animals in the park and 220 different bird species have been counted. There is little water, and if you are hiking you need to carry an adequate supply.

The park runs from the Wimmera River right up to the South Australian border. It was the scene of considerable controversy in its day, when in the late 1960s the government decided to sub-divide and develop the area. There was a serious amount of protest but not until the government lost a seat in a by-election did it come to its senses. Access to the park is by a gravel road from Dimboola, and to the main visitor's area in the north-east section by a sealed road 10 km along from Kiata.

WARRACKNABEAL

Tourist Information: Tourist Information Centre, *Scott St, next to the Post Office; tel: 5398 1632.*

ACCOMMODATION

Warracknabeal Country Roads Motor Inn, *Henty Hwy; tel: 5398 1811.* **Warrack Motel**, *2 Lyle St; tel: 5398 1633.* **Werrigar Motel** *(BU), corner Henty Hwy and Kelsall St; tel: 5398 2144.*

SIGHTSEEING

The name was originally spelled Werracknabeal and is thought to be Aboriginal for 'large gum trees' or, alternatively, 'red gums around a hollow'. The town is 57 km north of Horsham and 339 km north-west of Melbourne.

Warracknabeal serves an agricultural – mainly wheat growing – area in the Mallee region. Edward Eyre was the first European to arrive in the area, when he followed the Wimmera River on an expedition in 1844. A farm – 'a run' – was started by the Scott brothers, Andrew and Robert, in 1845. Then a store opened on the **Yarrambiack Creek** in 1867 and the area was officially opened up for settlement in 1869. The first building in the town came in 1870. The **Log Jail** in *Devereaux St* was built in 1872 and was still in use until the mid 1950s. The town is in an excellent state of preservation – some of the buildings have been listed by the National Trust – and there is a walking tour with black arrows to guide you around 23 points of interest within the town.

The **Agricultural Machinery Museum** is on the Henty Hwy 3 km south of the town (open daily 1000–1700; *tel: 5398 1616*), and has a large collection of early agricultural machinery and implements, most of them in working order and some of them being demonstrated throughout the day. It also contains a replica of the log cottage where Hugh McKay lived when he made the first wheat-stripper-harvester in 1884. Later more than 10,000 of these machines were exported to the United States and Canada. The harvesters are on display at the museum. This is thought to be the first museum of its type in Australia.

The **Historical Centre** (*81 Scott Street, tel:*

5398 1182; open Sun–Fri 1400–1600), has a collection furniture and artefacts from the area covering the last century. Of particular interest is the historic pharmaceutical collection from **Woolcott's Pharmacy**, which operated in the town from 1875 to 1975. **Lions Park** on *Scott St* is reached by way of a footbridge and lies on a bend of the Yarriambiack Creek.

Some 30 km to the north at **Galaquil**, sections of the old **Dog Fence** still remain. This was a vermin-proof barrier built in 1883 from the Murray at Swan Hill along the 36th Parallel to the border. It was the longest wire netting fence in the world and was maintained until 1949.

HOPETOUN

Accommodation in Hopetoun is provided by the **Hopetoun Hotel Motel**, *16 Austin St; tel: 5083 3070.*

This is an agricultural town on the Yarriambic Creek, named after the Earl of Hopetoun, one time Governor of Victoria. *Yarriambic* is Aboriginal for 'creek tribes'. Hopetoun was known as Coorong in its early days, after the lake of the same name. The town is 26 km from Lascelles and 61 km from Warracknabeal along the Henty Hwy. The town can very properly be called the gateway to the **Wyperfield National Park**, one of the most important National Parks in Victoria.

The area was mainly opened up in the 1870s and 1880s by Edward Lascelles – the 'Mallee King' – a close friend of the governor, who came to stay with him several times. The opening of Mallee country to agriculture only became possible with the invention of the stump jump plough, which did not break every time it crashed against a mallee root. The first contest for these ploughs was held in Hopetoun in 1895.

Hopetoun House, the ex-residence of Edward Lascelles, was built in 1891. It is located in *Evelyn St* and listed by the National Trust but it is a private residence and not open to inspection. In the centre of town is **Lake Lascelles**, which is a fine spot for picnics. The **Hopetoun Historical Museum** is in what was the primary school, on *Austin St, off Wyperfield National Park Rd.* Open Sun 1500–1700.

WYPERFIELD NATIONAL PARK

Tourist Information Wyperfield National Park, *RMB 1465, Yaapeet, Vic 3424; tel: 5395 7221.*

This park, which covers 356,800 hectares, is 450 km north-west of Melbourne. You can get to the main camping and picnic grounds in the southern part of the park on surfaced roads by way of **Hopetoun** and **Rainbow**. The ranger's office is 7 km north of the entrance. If you have a four-wheel-drive vehicle it is possible, during dry weather, to enter from the Nhill to Murrayville Rd but check with rangers first. The **Casuarina campsite** is in the north half of the park and access is by way of **Patchewollock**.

Coming in from Rainbow you pass the expanse that is **Lake Albacutha**, which is almost always dry. The lakes in the park are connected by **Outlet Creek**, an extension of Wimmera River and only fill when the river effectively overflows – that last happened in 1976 and 20 years before that in 1956. Even then the water only went as far as **Black Rock**. You then have to go back nearly another 40 years to 1918 to find a full flood, filling all of the lakes.

Wyperfield Park is mallee country. Mallee are shrubby eucalypts with strong root systems. They can be swept by forest fire but the mallee root lives on to send out fresh growth. When the farmers were clearing most of Victoria the mallee was the enemy and it was not until the invention of the jump plough that much of the mallee country was conquered. Altogether there are probably 450 species of native plant in the park and these grow in family groups. River Red Gum and Black Box are found on the flood plains of Outlet Creek and the dried up lakes. The sand plains of the western section are covered with heathland.

The park has emus and grey kangaroos, which can usually be found on the dry lake beds or in the nearby woodlands. There are over 200 species of birds, including the rare Mallee fowl, which builds an earth and leaf litter mound in which to lay its eggs.

There are two major walks within the park. They are both 6 km in length, one running

165

from **Lake Bramruk** and the other at **Black Flat Lake**. There is also a drive tour – the **Eastern Lookout Nature Drive** – which goes through representative areas of the park. Get a leaflet at the ranger's office. If you are hiking and camping you must carry water and it is essential that you register at the ranger's office before setting off.

OUYEN

Tourist Information: Mallee Tourism Association, *Oke St, Community Resource Centre; tel: 5092 1763.*

This town is in the middle of an agricultural area noted for large wheat properties. It started in the early 1900s as a railway station on the line between Melbourne and Mildura and opened up for settlement in 1910. The town is 425 km north-west of Melbourne and 104 km south of Mildura on Calder Hwy. The name is Aboriginal for either 'ghost water hole' or 'wild duck'.

In the town, beside the Calder Hwy, is the **Mallee Stump**, which is claimed to be the largest in Australia, and therefore in the world, and is here as a reminder of the work of the pioneers in clearing the Mallee country. In the town is a **History Resource Centre** (open Fri or by appointment; *tel: 5092 1763*), which has a collection of books, newspapers and documents about the history of the Mallee country. The **Victoria Hotel**, *22 Rowe St; tel: 5092 1397*, is considered to be the finest unrestored example of a country pub in Victoria. West of Ouyen, 30 km away, is **Walpepup Lake**, which has boating and swimming facilities. In the town of **Walpepup** is the **Mallee Research Station**, *tel: 5084 1203*, which covers 1032 hectares, of which 228 hectares is uncleared. Open daily 0830–1630.

SIDE TRACK FROM OUYEN

BIG DESERT WILDERNESS

Tourist Information: Ranger-in-charge, *Big Desert Wilderness, Underbool; tel: 5094 6267.*

The Big Desert is the true Outback, the land of the NeverNever. Even if you make the most tentative exploration you will have really seen the heart of Australia.

This vast park – it covers 113,500 hectares – was Victoria's first declared wilderness (in 1975) and adjoins even larger wilderness conservation areas in South Australia. This is serious wilderness and is therefore hostile to humans who are unprepared. You must carry water and if you are exploring on foot you must have a compass and map-reading skills as well as the appropriate maps. In the summer the temperatures reached mean that walking and exploring during the day are totally out of the question. Even in the other seasons if you are leaving for an overnight walk you must register with the park ranger at Pink Lakes. Note that no facilities or water are provided inside the park.

There are no tracks into the park. There are some old fire trails but these are being revegetated and are not for use. The best approach is from the road that runs from Nhill to Murrayville, which is separated from the park by 5 km of public land. This road can be rough in places. The vegetation is mainly heath and scrub, mallee hanging on for dear life in inhospitable sands. Nearly a hundred different species of bird have been identified in the park and over fifty species of lizards and snakes. ↵

MILDURA

Tourist Information: Tourism Mildura, *101 Deakin Ave; tel: 5021 4424.*

ACCOMMODATION AND FOOD

Boulevard Motor Inn *(BW), 385 Deakin Ave; tel: 5023 5022.* **Central Motel** *(FL), corner Tenth & Madden Aves; tel: 5021 1177.* **Chaffey International Motor Inn** *(FL), 244 Deakin Ave; tel: 5023 5833.* **City Colonial Motor Inn,** *24 Madden Ave; tel: 5021 1800.* **City Gate Motel,** *corner Magnolia & Seventh Sts; tel: 5022 1077.* **Early Australian Motor Inn** *(BW), 453 Deakin Ave; tel: 5021 1011.* **Mildura Motor Inn** *(FL), 376 Deakin Ave; tel: 5023 7377.* **Mildura Plaza Motor Inn Motel** *(GC), 836 Fifteenth St (Calder Hwy); tel: 5021 1155.* **Mildura Inlander Sun Resort**

Motel *(FL)*, *373 Deakin Ave; tel: 5023 3823.* **Sandors Motor Inn** *(BW)*, *179 Deakin Ave; tel: 5023 0047.* **Commodore Motel**, *corner Deakin Ave & Seventh St; tel: 5023 0241.* **HI: Rosemont Guest House**, *154 Madden Ave; tel: 5023 1535.*
Stefano's Restaurant, *Grand Hotel, Langtree Ave; tel: 5023 0511.* Open dinner Mon–Sat. Licensed. Considered one of the best Italian restaurants in Victoria. **Bay Tree Café**, *145 Eighth St; tel: 5021 1244.* Open daily lunch and dinner. Licensed. **The Brolgas**, *373 Deakin Ave; tel: 5023 3823.* Licensed. **Alfred Deakin Restaurant**, *138 Deakin Ave; tel: 5023 0521.* Licensed theatre restaurant that is part of the Northaven Motor Inn. **Pauls**, *corner Tenth and Madden Aves; tel: 5021 1177.* Licensed, open daily. Part of the Central Motel. **Palm Court**, *179 Deakin Ave; tel: 5023 00347.* Licensed, 7 days. Part of Sandors Motor Inn. **The Retreat**, *427 Deakin Ave; tel: 5023 0218.* Licensed. Open Mon–Sat for dinner. **Bellevue**, *corner Deakin Ave and 7th St; tel 5023 0241.* Open dinner Mon–Sat. Licensed. **Chaffey**, *244 Deakin Ave, tel: 5023 5833.* Licensed, up-market. Open dinner Mon–Sat.

SIGHTSEEING

The story is that the name comes from an Aboriginal word meaning 'sore eyes'. If you drive into Mildura from the somewhat arid surrounding countryside, you will perhaps agree that its green and pleasant aspect is, indeed, a sight for sore eyes. It is 544 km north of Melbourne along the Sunraysia Hwy, and grew up as a result of the development of irrigation farming in the area, which was started by the Canadian Chaffey brothers in 1887 but really only got into its stride in this century. The city layout is based on the Californian cities of Ontario and Upland, where the Chaffeys had started other irrigation schemes. It is the Australian birthplace of large-scale irrigation farming. In a sense, it is also a gateway to the great Australian outback because **Wentworth**, where the great rivers, the Murray and the Darling, meet, and where the **NeverNever** starts, is only 29 km to the west.

The best way to view the city is to take the **Chaffey Trail**, which starts off from the Tourist Information Centre. It takes in **Old Mildura Homestead**, *Cureton Ave*, which is a reconstruction of the first homestead established in 1847 (open 7 days 1000–1600). **Rio Vista** was built in 1889 as the home of W.B. Chaffey, one of the founders of Mildura. Open Mon–Fri 0900–1700, weekends 1300–1700.

From there the trail runs along *Deakin Ave*, which was originally designed so that trams could run along the centre plantation. **Psyche Bend Pumping Station** shows the engineering that was required to make the irrigation work. Open Tues 1300–1630, Thur 1300–1630, Sun 0915–1230. On the cliffs over the river is the **Mildura Blass Winery**, *tel: 5025 2303*. Guided tours Mon–Fri 1100 and 1430. Tastings and cellar door sales 7 days a week. Then to the Mildura wharf, which was built in 1892 to handle the paddle-boat traffic.

There are several paddle-steamers working out of Mildura up and down the Murray, including the **Melbourne**, which operates twice daily from Mildura Wharf and the **Rothbury**, which has a series of day cruises. For both *tel: 5023 2200*. Longer cruises are offered aboard the **Coonawarra** *(tel: 1 800 03 4424)* and a dinner cruise is available on the **Avoca** *(tel: 5021 1166)*. The Murray is an ideal river to explore by houseboat: **Matahari Houseboats** *(tel: 5023 4620)* and **Sunraysia Houseboats** *(tel: 5027 3621)*, among several.

The **Golden River Zoo**, which is privately owned and is only 4 km from Mildura along *Flora Ave* *(tel: 5023 5540)* has, besides many Australian animals, lions, monkeys, bears and pumas. Finally, one easy way of surveying the area is by hot air balloon flight with **Cameron Balloon Flights** *(daily; tel: 5021 2867)*.

Mildura is surrounded by National Parks. Only 75 km away is the 48,000 hectare **Hattah-Kulkyne** *(tel: 5029 3253)*, which was listed in 1982 by UNESCO as a World Biosphere Reserve. A 2 hr drive away – 130 km – is the **Murray-Sunset National Parks Pink Lakes** area, although exploration to the centre of the park requires four-wheel-drive. To the north-east of Mildura – 110 km – is the **Mungo National Park** *(tel: 5023 1278)*, which is part of the **Willandra Lakes World Heritage** area.

167

MILDURA-WODONGA

It rises high in the Alps at Mt Pilot and as it comes down from the Alps it grows and extends; coming through Victoria it defines one of the state boundaries, waters the land and provides entertainment, recreation and pleasure to many people. The Murray River is the mightiest river in Australia, and Mildura is a good place to start an exploration of it.

This route follows its course most of the way, introducing you to riverboat towns such as Robinvale, Swan Hill and Echuca, and the major wine-growing centre of Rutherglen. Finally on to Wodonga, forever chained to its twin sister Albury, and close to Lake Hume and its aquatic delights.

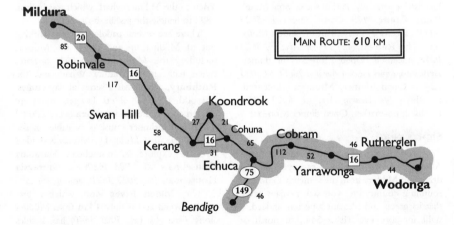

MAIN ROUTE: 610 KM

168

From Mildura head north a little way along Rte 79 just into New South Wales and then turn right onto Rte 20, the Sturt Hwy, south-east for 79 km as far as Euston. There turn right onto Rte 16; **Robinvale** is 6 km further on, just across the border back into Victoria. From Robinvale the road follows the Murray River valley to **Swan Hill** and **Kerang**.

At Kerang you can take a 27 km detour to visit **Koondrook** and another 25 km to rejoin the main route at **Cohuna**, or drive straight down Rte 16 to Cohuna. From Cohuna follow Rte 16 to **Echuca** (from where you can make a side track to **Bendigo**).

From Echuca the road heads east, north and east again to **Cobram**, where it catches up again with the Murray Valley and follows it through **Yarrawonga** and **Rutherglen** to **Wodonga**, on the Murray and Riverina route (see p. 198).

BUSES

Several coaches of the Public Transport Corporation run from Mildura to Swan Hill

(2¾ hrs) and on to Bendigo (5 hrs), some stopping at Kerang (3 hrs). Others take in Swan Hill (3 hrs), Kerang (3¾ hrs), Echuca (5½ hrs) and Wodonga (10 hrs). OTT tables 9105, 9109 and 9126.

ROBINVALE

Tourist Information: Robinvale-Euston Tourist Information Centre, *Bromley Rd; tel: 5026 1388.*

ACCOMMODATION

Motel Robinvale, *112 Bromley Rd; tel: 5026 3090.* Homestyle Motel *(BU), 36 Ronald St; tel: 5026 3513.* Robinvale Hotel, *70 Perrin St; tel: 5026 3030.*

SIGHTSEEING

In the middle of the grape, citrus fruit and vegetable growing area around the Murray River, the town is almost encircled by a loop in the river. This attractive and elegantly laid-out town is the largest township between Swan Hill and Mildura. It was a planned town almost from the start. Herbert Cuttle bought land here in 1912. In 1924 he had it sub-divided and a township surveyed and planned, and a bridge was built across the Murray River. Herbert Cuttle named the town after his son, Captain George Robin Cuttle, VC, who was killed in World War I, near Villers Bretonneux in France. The two towns were twinned in 1984.

Robinwood on *River Dr.* is the Cuttle home, built in the 1920s. Nearby is a massive windmill for bringing up artesian water, which is believed to be the biggest windmill in the southern hemisphere.

McWilliams Wines, *22 Moore St,* off the Murray Valley Hwy, *tel: 5026 4004,* is one of the biggest wine companies in Australia and this is possibly its largest winery. Open for cellar door tastings weekdays 0900–1200 and 1300–1630. The tasting room, an original log cabin, is almost a historical museum of the Robinvale area. Robinvale Wines and Vineyards, 5 km from the centre of town on *Sea Lake Rd, tel: 5026 3955,* produces organic and non-alcoholic wines in a totally chemical free winery. It is run by the Caracatsanoudis family. Open Mon–Sat 0900–1800, Sun 1300–1800.

An unusual farm, which produces almonds as a primary crop, is Kyndalyn Park, *tel: 5026 9216.* (Open Mon–Fri 0900–1700). The property has over 800 hectares of almond trees.

The Euston Weir is 2 km south of the town on *Swan Hill Rd* and has a fish ladder to help fish climb from one level to another. Much further out, 65 km to the south-east on *Murray Valley Rd,* is Wilga Park Flora and Fauna Sanctuary, which specialises in plants from the more arid parts of Australia.

SWAN HILL

Tourist Information: Swan Hill Information and Development Centre, *306 Campbell St; tel: 5032 3033.* Open Mon–Sat.

ACCOMMODATION AND FOOD

Burke & Wills Motor Inn Swan Hill *(BW), 370 Campbell St; tel: 5032 9788.* Lady Augusta Motor Inn *(FL), 375 Campbell St; tel: 5032 9677.* Swan Hills Resort Motor Inn *(FL), 405 Campbell St; tel: 5032 2726.* Australian Settlers Motor Inn *(BW), 354 Campbell St; tel: 5032 9277.* Lazy River Motor Inn *(BU), Murray Valley Hwy; tel: 5032 2123 or 5032 2124.* Murray Downs Motor Inn, *Murray Downs Dr.; tel: 5033 1966.* Oasis Hotel/Motel *(GC), 287 Campbell St; tel: 5032 2877.*

Silver Slipper Restaurant, *405 Campbell St; tel: 5032 2726.* Licensed. Open for dinner Mon–Sat. Oasis Bistro and Monkey Bar, *287 Campbell St; tel 5032 2877.* Monkey Bar open for dinner seven nights. Licensed. Oasis open for lunch and dinner. Not licensed. Peppercorn Tree Restaurant, *396 Campbell St; tel: 5032 4427.* Dinner Tues–Sat. Licensed. Part of the Campbell Motor Inn.

SIGHTSEEING

The origin of the name is romantic. The explorer Major Mitchell stayed here in 1836, on the banks of the Murray River. His night's rest was disturbed by the noisy swans that inhabited the marsh around the hill, hence the name. There are still swans, although the town has grown up to become a regional centre and a major holiday centre. The big boast of the town is that, although it is set in north-west

169

Victoria, it still manages more sunny days a year than the Gold Coast.

Swan Hill is 350 km north of Melbourne, 825 km west of Sydney and 515 km east of Adelaide. The Murray was a major factor in the growth of the town, as the arrival of the paddle-steamers in 1853 allowed Swan Hill to become a centre for agriculture – the crops were wheat, barley, stone fruit and vegetables. The paddle-steamers ran for 80 years and were crucial to the development of the area. Perhaps the easiest way to see Swan Hill is to take the 1½ km **Swan Hill walk**, which takes you right around the town – maps at the Information Centre.

This is yet another town with a big symbol – this time a **Murray Cod**, which is 11m in length and 6m in height. It was originally made for a movie called *Eight Ball*. It is in *Curlewis St*, opposite the railway station – one train a day to Melbourne – and is as ugly as you feared. However, it does signify that Swan Hill is the gateway to a major inland fishing area. There is excellent fishing on the **Murray**, the **Little Murray**, **Murrumbidgee**, **Wakool** and **Edward Rivers**, mainly accessed from **Tooleybuc**, 30 mins to the north; and actually in New South Wales – **Merrin Creek** and **Boga**, **Charm**, **Pooma**, **Tooim** and **Kangaroo Lakes**.

The **Pioneer Settlement** (*tel: 5032 1093*), the first of its kind, is right on the banks of the Murray. It includes several original buildings and the staff wear period costumes. There is a Cobb and Co. coach and a wide range of agricultural machinery, much of it in use. A sound and light show re-enacts the pioneer days every night. Open every day of the year.

In *Curlewis St*, between *McCallum and Pritchard Sts*, is the **Burke and Wills Tree**, which was planted over 100 years ago to commemorate the visit to Swan Hill of the famed, and doomed, explorers (see p.254). It is believed to be the largest Morton Bay Fig tree in Australia and is 30m high, 44m wide and has a trunk with a diameter of 4m.

The Murray River is central to the life of Swan Hill and the **Pyap**, an original paddle-steamer, allows you to cruise the river as they did in the old days. Cruises leave every day at 1030 and 1430 from the wharf at the Pioneer Settlement; *tel: 5032 1093*. There are houseboats for hire at **Kookaburra Houseboats** (*tel: 5032 0003*), which allow you to cruise the Murray and stay out on the river.

Hilltop Fauna Park (*tel: 5033 1515*), which is only a few minutes drive north of Swan Hill on the Murray Valley Hwy, has kangaroos, deer, emus, donkeys, and is open daily.

Tyntynder Homestead is a National Trust building 16 km north of Swan Hill on Murray Valley Hwy, 3.2 km north of **Beverford**. It was built in 1846, is set in old world gardens and is the first example of brick veneer building seen in Australia. A brick facing was added to the original log construction in 1850. It has a collection of over 800 antique dolls.

Swan Hill Pheasant Farm and Aviaries, *tel: 5030 2648,* is a 20 min drive away on *Chillingollah Rd*, and is the largest commercial free range pheasant farm in Australia. It also has peacocks and other birds in a country setting. Open daily, except Tues, 0900–1700.

There are wineries in the area. The first to make wine commercially was **Best's St Andrew's Winery** (*tel: 5037 2154*), which is 6km off the Murray Valley Hwy at Lake Boga, and has tours through the winery and distillery at 1100 and 1500 each weekday.

Another vinery is **RL Buller**, *tel: 5037 6305,* 15 km north on the Murray Valley Hwy. Open Mon–Sat 0900–1700 for tastings and cellar door sales.

Across the **Lift Bridge** – built in 1896 – and 1½ km away, lies the new development of Murray Downs, which contains the **Murray Downs Homestead**, *tel: 5032 1225,* open daily. This was originally the station house for the largest river frontage property on the Murray River and is a gracious Victorian living time capsule.

Lake Boga – named by explorer Major Mitchell after the Bogan Aboriginals – is 14 km south of Swan Hill on the Murray River Hwy. It houses a restored Catalina flying boat – this was a repair depot for Catalinas in World War II. There is extensive wildlife with turtles and pelicans. This is a major water sports area, and you can hire most of the gear at **Lake Boga Jet Ski Hire** (*tel: 5056 0672*).

KERANG

Tourist Information: Lester Smith Lookout Tower, *Wellington St, Murray Valley Hwy; tel: 5453 3100.*

ACCOMMODATION

Downtown Motor Inn, *77 Wellington St; tel: 5452 1911.* Motel Kerang, *76 Bendigo Rd; tel: 5452 1311.* Motel Loddon River *(BU), Murray Valley Hwy; tel: 5452 2511.* Commercial Hotel, *corner Victoria & Wellington Sts; tel: 5452 1031.*

SIGHTSEEING

Kerang is noted as the home of thousands of birds, particularly ibis, who migrate each spring to the rookeries. The first settler was an Irishman, Woodford Patchell – a graduate from Trinity College, Dublin, and therefore a wholly decent man – who created the town in the late 1850s, when he started farming using irrigation methods (he was arguably Victoria's first irrigator), and built a bridge across the Loddon River. Later the railway came and the town developed, although it still has a population of just 4000. The history of the town, including Patchell's notes on irrigation, can be seen in the Kerang Historical Museum, off Murray Valley Hwy. Open weekends 1330–sunset.

The Lester Smith Lookout Tower (20m high) started its career as a water tower. It now provides excellent views of the area, as well as housing the tourist information board. Open daily 1030–1600.

The ibis rookery on Middle Lake, 2 km from town, which you reach by way of the Murray Valley Hwy, has what is said to be the largest ibis rookery in the world. It is estimated that, in total, 200,000 ibis make Kerang and the surrounding area their nesting place. There is a bird hide from which you can observe the ibis.

KOONDROOK

Koondrook lies on the Murray River in the centre of a pastoral and citrus fruit growing area. It has an historic lift span bridge across the river linking it to Barham in New South Wales. It is the gateway to the Gunbower State Forest, which is, in fact, an island, covering 26,400 hectares, and running from

Koondrook down to Torrumbarry, with the Murray on one side and Gunbower Creek on the other. It was declared a state forest as long ago as 1874, but as this is a state, as opposed to a national park, the timber has been harvested in a major way over the years. It still has widespread forest and an amazing range of animal and bird life.

On Gunbower Island is the Shannkrist Zoological Reserve, *tel: 5453 2544,* open daily; $5. This has a water buffalo herd, emu flock and a variety of farm animals in an alternative farming enterprise. There is also an evening tour of nocturnal animals and an escorted evening forest drive – $10.

In town, The Tram Gallery (*corner Forest and Station St; tel: 5453 2281*) is an art gallery and gift shop, which is housed in three trams.

ECHUCA

Tourist Information: Echuca–Moama and District Tourism Association, *2 Leslie St, Customs House; tel: 5480 7555.*

ACCOMMODATION AND FOOD

Port of Echuca Motor Inn *(FL), 463 High St; tel: 5482 5666.* All Rivers Motor Inn *(FL), 115 Northern Hwy; tel: 5482 5677.* Caledonian Hotel Motel Echuca, *110 Hare St; tel: 5482 2100.* Echuca Philadelphia Motel *(BW), 340 Ogilvie Ave; tel: 5482 5700.* Nirebo Motel *(FL), 251 Hare St; tel: 5482 2033.* Paddle Wheel Motel *(HN), 385 High St; tel: 5482 3822.* Riverboat Lodge Motor Inn *(GC), 476 High St; tel: 5482 5777.* Echuca Motel, *268 Ogilvie Ave; tel: 5482 2899.* Fountain Motel & Rivergum Restaurant *(BU), Northern Hwy; tel: 5482 3200.* Hopwood Motor Inn, *Northern Hwy; tel: 5482 2244;* HI: Echuca Gardens Hostel, *103 Mitchell St; tel: 5480 6522.*

Bridge Hotel, *Hopwood St; tel; 5482 2247.* Open daily for lunch and dinner. Licensed. Steam Packet Hotel, *610 High St; tel: 5482 3411.* BYO. Open daily lunch and dinner. Riverside Restaurant, *Murray Esplanade; tel: 5482 5133.* Open daily lunch and dinner. The only licensed restaurant on the banks of the Murray River. Echuca Cellar Door, *2–10 Radcliffe St; tel: 5480 6720.* Licensed. Cock 'n

Bull, *17 Warren St; tel: 5480 6988*. Australian modern cuisine. Licensed. **Ogilvie's**, *340 Ogilvie Ave; tel 5482 5700*. Dinner Tues–Sat. Licensed. Recommended.

SIGHTSEEING

Located at the junction of the Murray, Goulburn and Campaspe rivers, this is one of the oldest river towns in Victoria, dating from 1853. The town was founded by an ex-convict, Henry Hopewood, and during the riverboat era, it boomed as a port on the Murray River and a railroad terminus. By the 1880s it was Victoria's second largest port, only surpassed by Melbourne itself. Then the railways extended to the other towns and Echuca's glory days were over. In 1969 the National Trust declared the port an historic area.

The **Coach House Carriage Collection**, *57 Murray Esplanade; tel: 5482 5244,* is housed in a corrugated iron carriage factory that dates back to 1905. It has 35 coaches on display, all of which have been fully restored. There is, of course, a Cobb & Co. coach as well as a London Hansom cab. Open daily 0930–1500. Admission $4.

The **Port of Echuca Wharf Museum**, *45 Murray Esplanade, tel: 5482 4248,* is extensive, comprising of the restored Echuca wharf, where the riverboats used to come in, the riverboats themselves – *Pevensey, Adelaide, Alexander Arbuthnot* – and finally the historic buildings surrounding the wharf. Originally the wharf was 1.2 km long, but it has now been reduced to one fifth of that size. The wharf itself was built on three levels to take account of fluctuations in the height of the river. Open daily 0900–1700; $6.

The **Historical Society Museum**, *1 Dickson St; tel: 5482 4225,* is housed in the old police station. It has original river charts, riverboat photographs and a wardrobe of colonial clothes. Open Mon, Wed, public and school holidays 1300–1700.

Gumnutland and Garden Railway, *565 High St; tel: 5482 5490,* appeals to younger children. There are over thirty buildings in this model village, all built from local timbers, plants and, of course, gumnuts. Open Mon–Fri 0900–1600; weekends, holidays 0900–1700.

There are cruises on the **Emmylou** paddle-steamer between Echuca and the **Moana Wharf**, some 2 km away. There are also longer two night cruises – the paddle steamer will comfortably hold 18 passengers; *tel: 5482 3801.*

The **Pride of the Murray** *(tel: 5482 5244)* also has river cruises, which depart daily at 0945, 1100, 1205, 1315, 1430. The cruises last 1 hr and have a detailed commentary. $8. The **Canberra** *(tel: 5482 2711)* is a vintage paddle-steamer driven by a steam engine and was originally used for wool bales. Departs daily at 1100, 1130, 1245, 1400, 1500 for 1 hr cruises, again with commentary. $8.

There are more than 40 restored vehicles in the **National Holden Motor Museum**, *7 Warren St; tel: 5480 2033,* showing the motoring history of Australia from the turn of the century. It has historic film footage and some Holden prototypes. Open daily 0900–1700. $5. **Raverty's Museum**, *Murray Valley Hwy; tel: 5482 2730,* (open most days 0930–1700; $30), also has a collection of restored vintage motor vehicles.

Sharps Magic Movie House and Penny Arcade, *Bond Store, Murray Esplanade; tel: 5482 2361,* has Australia's largest collection of working Penny Arcade machines. There is also an old movie house showing flickering, silent classics of yesteryear. Open daily 0900–1700. $8.

Red Gum Works, *Murray Esplanade; tel: 5482 5711,* is Victoria's oldest family owned sawmill and has demonstrations of woodturning and timber cutting. Open daily 0900–1700. **World in Wax Museum**, *630 High St; tel: 5482 3630.* Open daily 0900–1700; $6. A sort of lesser, Antipodean, Madame Tussauds. Has some sixty life-sized wax portraits of everybody from Paul Hogan to Dame Nellie Melba.

SIDE TRACK
FROM ECHUCA

Take Rte 75 46 km south to Bendigo.

BENDIGO

Tourist Information: Tourist Information Centre, *26 High St, Kangaroo Flat; tel: 5447 1383.*

ACCOMMODATION AND FOOD

All Seasons International Motor Inn *(FL), 171 McIvor Hwy; tel: 5443 8166.* Julie-Anna Inn *(FL), 286 Napier St (Midland Hwy) (PO Box 249); tel: 5442 5855.* Bendigo Haymarket Motor Inn, *5 McIvor Hwy; tel: 5441 5654.* Cathedral Motor Inn *(BW), 96 High St (Calder Hwy); tel: 5442 5333.* Heritage Motor Inn *(BW), 259 High St; tel: 5442 2788.* Lakeview Motor Inn *(BW), 286 Napier St (Midland Hwy); tel: 5442 3099.*

Bazzani, *Howard Pl.; tel: 5441 3777.* Open for dinner daily; Sun–Fri lunch. Licensed. Sophisticated. Greystanes, *57 Queen St; tel: 5442 2466.* Open Lunch Tues–Fri, dinner Tues–Sat. Licensed. Recommended. Metropolitan Restaurant, *224 Hargreaves St; tel: 5443 4916.* Licensed. Open daily lunch and dinner. Maxines, *15 Bath Lane; tel: 5442 2466.* Open Tues–Sat, dinner; Tues–Fri lunch. Italian style.

SIGHTSEEING

Set in the fertile valleys of the Campaspe and Loddon rivers, Bendigo is a prosperous town that was founded by the gold rush and then kept growing. The name comes from that of a British bare-knuckle fighter, real name William Thompson, who was famous at the time of the naming of the town in 1851. Plainly the authorities thought this name not quite the article so renamed it Sandhurst after the English military school. The locals, however, took no notice and went on calling it Bendigo, and this became official in 1891.

In the centre of town, in *Pall Mall*, is the Alexandra Fountain, which was a gift to the town from successful miner George Lansell. It used more than 200 tonnes of Harcourt granite in its construction. The Bendigo Creek Linear Park *(tel: 5443 1677)* runs for 5 km from the Botanic Gardens along the banks of Bendigo Creek. Tying in to this is the Bendigo Bushland Trail, *tel: 5444 6666*, which links other footpaths and bicycle tracks to the Linear Park. Follow this up to One

Tree Hill and Diamond Hill for excellent views of Bendigo.

Bendigo was originally built on gold and the Central Deborah Gold Mine, *(76 Violet St; tel: 5443 8070; open daily 0900–1700, $12)*, is an original quartz reef gold mine that was re-opened in 1972. The mine is 422m deep and has 17 levels. Tours are conducted on the second level and visitors are able to see the working conditions, as well as how the quartz was processed on the surface.

Although the Chinese brought much to Victoria, the only remaining truly Chinese building is in Bendigo – the Bendigo Joss House, *Finn St, Emu Point; tel: 5442 1685.* Open daily 1000–1600. It is constructed of timber and local bricks and is painted in the Chinese style.

Following on from that, the Golden Dragon Museum at *5 Bridge St, tel: 5441 5044*, has the world's longest – more than 100m – Imperial dragon, as well as the oldest. There is a rich collection of Chinese procession regalia going back to the 1880s. Open daily 0930–1700; $5.

George Lansell lived at Fortuna House, *Chum St; tel: 5442 0222.* This baroque mansion was, in its time, the largest private residence in Australia. It is now occupied by the Army Survey Regiment, but there are guided tours on most Sundays at 1300. ◢

COBRAM

Tourist Information: Log Cabin and Tourist Information Centre, *corner Punt Rd and Station St; tel: 5872 2132.*

ACCOMMODATION AND FOOD

The Charles Sturt Motor Inn *(FL), 31 Mookarii St; tel: 5872 2777.* Cobram Colonial Motor Inn, *corner Murray Valley Hwy and William St; tel: 5872 1866.* Regency Court Motel *(GC), 1 Main St; tel: 5872 2488.* Cobram Classic Motel, *corner Murray Valley Hwy and Station St; tel: 5872 1633.*

Old Currency, *corner Station and Main St; tel: 5872 2990.* Open Tues–Sat nights. BYO. Situated in a former State Savings Bank building.

SIGHTSEEING

This small agricultural town, specialising in dairy products and famous for its peach orchards, is 20 km to the south of **Tocumwal** in New South Wales, 35 km west of **Yarrawonga** and 251 km north of Melbourne. The name is a local Aboriginal word meaning 'head'. The twin town of **Barooga** is connected by a bridge over the Murray.

Opposite the Log Cabin information centre – which holds tastings of local cheeses – is a reconstructed **pioneer's cottage**, set in parkland.

On the banks of the Murray, at *Horseshoe Rd,* is the **Horseshoe Lagoon**, which has fishing and bushwalking. **Thompsons Beach**, off Murray Valley Hwy, before the bridge, is a natural sand beach with swimming and water skiing, said to be the best in the area.

Near Cobram, on the Murray Valley Hwy, is **Heritage Farm Wines**, the only vineyard in Australia that is still worked with draught horses. The usual cellar door tastings and sales are offered, but there is also a display of old bottles, winery and agricultural equipment. (Open daily 0900–1700; *tel: 5872 2376.*) Also out of town, on the road from **Benalla** to Tocumwal – get there by way of the Murray Valley Hwy – is **Matata Deer Farm**, where visitors can see and feed the red and fallow deer. Open Sat–Thur and public holidays 1000–1600; *tel: 5873 2302.*

YARRAWONGA

Tourist Information: Yarrawonga Mulwala Tourist Association, *Irvine Parade; 5744 1989.*

ACCOMMODATION AND FOOD

Belmore Motor Inn, *14 Belmore St; tel: 5744 3685.* **Central Yarrawonga Motor Inn,** *111 Belmore St; tel: 5744 3817.* **Lakeview Motel,** *1 Hunt St; tel: 5744 1555.* **Quality Motel** *(BU), 51 Telford St (Murray Valley Hwy); tel: 5744 1956.*

Woodlands Lakeside Motor Inn, *Murray Valley Hwy; tel: 5744 2355.* **Burkes Royal Mail Hotel** *(BU), 96 Belmore St; tel: 5744 3033.* **Ski-Land Motel,** *Murray Valley Hwy (Postal: RMB 1070); tel: 5744 3937.*

Shag's Nest Restaurant, *Belmore St; tel: 5744 1450.* Open nightly. Licensed. **Left Bank,** *Belmore St; tel: 5744 1756.* Open daily 0930–1630, dinner Fri–Sat. BYO. **Lussinos,** *132 Belmore St.*

SIGHTSEEING

Yarrawonga is on the shores of **Lake Mulwala**, an artificial lake that covers 6000 hectares. The lake is the result of a 1930s agreement between NSW, Victoria and South Australia to harness the waters of the Murray River. Part of this project was the **Yarrawonga Weir**, completed in 1939, which in turn formed Lake Mulwala. Despite its utilitarian origins, Lake Mulwala has also become a major water sports destination. The name is variously translated as 'the place where wong pigeon nested' and 'water running over rocks', so it is clearly anyone's guess. What is certain is that this is another town whose name was immortalised in a popular country song – *I'm going back again to Yarrawonga.* Possibly because the name rhymes so elegantly with 'linga longa'.

Yarrawonga proudly boasts that it gets more sunshine than Brisbane, and is only equalled by Darwin. Reflecting the river history of the town, the information centre has the paddlewheels of the paddle steamer *Pilot* on display. These were recovered when the lake was drained in 1985.

From the Yarrawonga foreshore, there are cruises along the Murray River in the **Lady Murray**, *tel: 5744 2005.* (Daily 1200 and 1400). On Lake Mulwala you can cruise on the **Paradise Queen, Lake Resort and Mulwala Water Ski Club,** *Yarrawonga Foreshore; tel: 5744 1843.* Twice daily cruises.

The Old Yarra Mine Shaft, *tel: 5744 1899,* on *Irvine Parade* is open daily 0900–1700, $2. It has a collection of gems, minerals and fossils, and a blue grotto with glow worms. Also in the town is the **Tudor Clock Museum,** *21 Lynch St; tel: 5744 1249.* Open daily 1000–1630; $3.

Byramine Homestead is the former house of Elizabeth Hume, and is 15 km west of the town on the Murray Valley Hwy. Recently bought by the council, it has been closed for renovations, so check with the tourist office.

RUTHERGLEN

Tourist Information: **Rutherglen Information Centre**, *corner Main and Drummond Sts; tel: (060) 32 9166.*

ACCOMMODATION AND FOOD

Wine Village Motor Inn, *217 Main St (Murray Valley Hwy); tel: 32 9900.* **Motel Woongarra** *(BU), corner Drummond and Main Sts; tel: 32 9588.* **Rutherglen Motor Inn** *(GC), 10 Moodemere St (Murray Valley Hwy); tel: 32 9775.* **Walkabout Motel**, *15 Moodemere St; tel: 32 9572 or 32 9174.* **Star Hotel Motel Rutherglen**, *Main St; tel: 32 9625.*

The Shamrock, *Main St; tel: 32 9439.* Lunch, dinner Mon–Sat. Great food. BYO. Booking essential. **The House at Mount Prior**, *Mount Prior Winery, Howlong Rd; tel 26 5256.* Open daily for dinner. Lunch at the associated **Terrace Restaurant**. Licensed. **Tuileries**, *Drummond St; tel: 32 9033.* Lunch Thur–Sat. Dinner Tues–Sat. Licensed. Formal, traditional quality.

SIGHTSEEING

This is the wine capital of Victoria and lies 274 km north-east of Melbourne. It is surrounded by vineyards in the oldest vine growing area of Australia.

The name comes from the home town in Scotland of John Wallace, hotel owner and member of the Legislative Council in the 1850s. This was when the gold boom came to Rutherglen and, indeed, a gold mine was still operating until 1965. But wine started at almost the same time. Lindsey Brown, reputed to be the first vigneron in the area, is reported as saying, 'There was more gold to be got from the first six inches than lower down'.

The first vines were planted in 1851 and **Seppelt's Clydeside Winery** was established in the same year. The Murray District Winegrowers' Association was formed in 1883. The government then stepped in by passing a Planting Bonus Bill in 1889, which led to vast quantities of inferior wines that ruined the industry.

To make up for this, a viticultural college was established in 1896, and was important in researching the answer to phylloxera,

which, in 1897, ravaged the vineyards of Australia, reducing them to just 2000 hectares. Many were given over to sheep and other crops.

The **Rutherglen Historical Museum**, *Murray St*, is in the old school building. Open Sun 1330–1630. The first **Rutherglen Wine Festival**, held in 1967, was, perhaps, the first sign of the Australian wine industry coming of age.

The following wineries – this is nowhere near an all-inclusive list, more a small sampling – welcome visitors for tastings and cellar door sales. All of them are off the Murray Valley Hwy, unless otherwise stated.

Campbells, *tel: 32 8111.* Open Mon–Sat, 0900–1700, Sun 1000–1700. This is one of the oldest, as the family has been producing wine since 1870.

Fairfield, *tel: 32 9381.* Open Mon–Sat, 1000–1600. At one time, this winery, founded by George Morris in 1859, was the biggest vineyard in the southern hemisphere. The vineyard was effectively destroyed by phylloxera and passed into other hands. In 1973 George Morris' grand-daughter bought the property, replanted 3 hectares of vines and restored the house. The cellars once held three million litres of wine at a time. Tours of **Fairfield House** – school and public holidays 1100, 1300, 1500 (not Sundays).

G. Sutherland Smith, *tel: 26 2070.* Open weekends and public holidays, 1000–1700. Very high quality wines with a serious reputation. **Jones Winery** *tel: 32 8496.* Open Mon–Sat, 0900–1700, Sun 1000–1700.

Mt Prior Vineyard and Cellars, *Howlong Rd*, 11 km to the north-east. (Open daily 1000–1700; *tel: 26 5591.*) Established in 1860, a 40 hectare property with homestead and gardens.

In line with the Australian love of big symbols, the **water-tower**, which was built in 1899, has been re-modelled as a wine bottle. In the same style, the town, which is famed for its fortified wines, has a sign as you enter reading: 'Sydney may have a nice harbour, but we have a great port'.

In town is the **Wine and Gold Museum**, open Mon–Fri 0900–1700, Sat 0900–1200.

MELBOURNE–WODONGA

The Victorian Alps run to the east and north-east of Melbourne. This route contains some side tracks into this beautiful area and, if you opt for the 355-km Scenic Detour, heads into the heart of the region and to skiing country, before arriving at Wodonga and the Murray River, from where you can join routes to Mildura (pp. 168–175) and via Wodonga's twin town Albury to the Murray and the Riverian route (pp. 195–200).

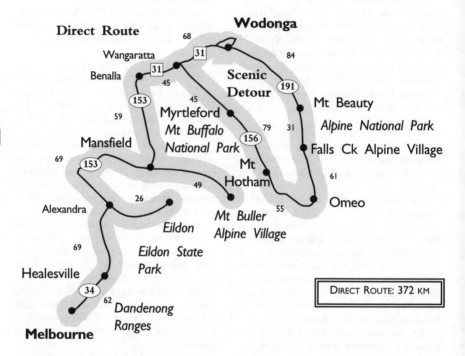

176

DIRECT ROUTE: 372 KM

DIRECT ROUTE

➡️ Take Rte 34, the Maroondah Hwy, east out of Melbourne. While still in the greater Melbourne area you can turn off right towards Olinda to visit the **Dandenong Ranges National Park**. The first stop along the main route is· **Healesville**, some 62 km outside the city. Another 64 km takes you to

Alexandra, from where you can side-track to **Eildon** and its State Park on the edge of the Alps.

A little way north-west of Alexandra the highway becomes Rte 153, and at Merton turns sharply east to **Mansfield**. This is a jumping off point for a side track to **Mt Buller**. (You can by-pass Mansfield by remaining on Rte 153, or rejoin the main highway from Mansfield by taking Alt Rte 153 north.)

The highway continues north to **Benalla**, just before which you should turn right onto Rte 31, the Hume Hwy, to **Wangaratta**. From there you can complete the direct route to **Wodonga** by continuing on Rte 31 for another 68 km.

SCENIC DETOUR

To see the best of the Alps, turn right off Rte 31 shortly after Wangaratta, onto Rte 156. First stop is **Myrtlesford**, near **Mt Buffalo National Park**. Another 79 km brings you further into the Alps and to **Mt Hotham**.

Follow Rte 156 to **Omeo**, from where you begin the return stretch north up Rte 195. About 11 km after Anglers Rest, turn left into the **Alpine National Park** on Rte 191, taking you to **Falls Creek** and **Mt Beauty**. From Mt Beauty Rte 191 takes another 84 km to reach Wodonga.

All the roads in the Alpine area are pretty well maintained but the firm rule is that if you are going into the mountains and there is snow around you must carry chains, even if you never need to use them.

BUSES

Several coaches make weekend runs from Melbourne to Mansfield, taking about 3 hrs. OTT table 9101b. For more details of buses to the ski resorts, see later on in this chapter and OTT tables 9101d and 9101f.

DANDENONG RANGES NATIONAL PARK

Tourist Information: Park Information Office, *Lower Picnic Ground, Upper Ferntree Gully; tel: 9758 1342.*

This park could be considered one of the

green lungs of Melbourne. It is right on the doorstep and easily accessible. Two main roads lead into the park: *Mt Dandenong Tourist Rd* (Rte 22), which runs from the Burwood Hwy at Upper Ferntree Gully to *Canterbury Rd* at Montrose, and *Monbulk Rd*, which starts at the same place and runs to the Maroondah Hwy at Lilydale. There is an excellent network of roads within the park.

The ranges were once covered in forests and the park combines three of the largest remaining sections – Sherbrooke, Doongalla and Fern Tree Gully. There are over 350 species of indigenous plants in the park. In the spring there are amazing wildflower displays, with wattles and pea-flowers coming into bloom. The Sherbrooke Forest section has lyrebirds, as well as many other species. There are few mammals other than those of nocturnal habit.

HEALESVILLE

Tourist Information: Yarra Valley Regional Tourism Association, *127 Maroondah Hwy; tel: (03) 5962 2600.*

ACCOMMODATION AND FOOD

Healesville Motor Inn, *45 Maroondah Hwy; tel: 5962 5188* or *5962 5251.* **Terminus Motel**, *23 Harker St; tel: 5962 4011.* **Sanctuary House Motel**, *Badger Creek Rd; tel: 5962 5148.*

Mt Rael Lodge, *140 Yarra Glen Rd, Healesville; tel: 5962 4017.* Licensed. Open lunch Fri–Sun, dinner Thur–Sat. Superb but pricey food.

SIGHTSEEING

Healesville is a town in the Yarra Valley, and in the heart of the premium wine country of Victoria. The town was named after Sir Richard Heales, who was a coachbuilder and also the Premier of Victoria from 1860 to 1861. Healesville is 87 km north-east of Melbourne along the Maroondah Hwy.

Agriculture started in the district in the 1830s and timber felling became important in the 1860s. The town was surveyed in 1864 and the first inn and saw mill were built the following year.

One of the main reasons for visiting

Healesville is the **Healesville Sanctuary**, *Badger Creek Rd*, off Maroondah Hwy; *tel: 5962 4022*, which covers 32 hectares. This quite remarkable place has been a sanctuary for sick or injured wildlife since 1934, when it opened as the Colin Mackenzie Sanctuary. The first platypus bred in captivity was born here in 1943 and there is now a Platypus Research Station. Open daily 0900–1700.

The sanctuary is packed with a large collection of Australian wildlife, including over 200 species of bird. It also has the most comprehensive platypus exhibition in the world.

Badger Weir Park, *Badger Weir Rd, off Don Rd; tel: 5962 3719*, is landscaped parkland, with walks through fern gullies. Open daily from 0800–2000 during the summer and 1700 in the winter.

Victoria's tallest tree, a mountain ash, is in **Black Spur**, on the Maroondah Hwy on the road to **Narbethong**. Regarded by many as Victoria's most beautiful forest area, the 10 km drive passes many footpaths through the forests, with parking areas. If you drive north to Marysville, you come to the **Maroondah Reservoir**, which is surrounded by superb, lush countryside.

You can travel by motorised trolley between Healesville and **Tarrawarra**, coming back by way of the Yarra Valley. The **Yarra Valley Tourist Railway** *(tel: 5962 2600)* operates daily on the hour 1100–1600.

Healesville has a literary connection, as the poet **C.J. Dennis** spent his last thirty years at Arden in Toolangi – 19 km north – on the edge of the **Toolangi State Forest**. He died there in 1938. Dennis wrote *The Sentimental Bloke*. His last book was *The Singing Garden,* a tribute to the garden at Arden, which covers two hectares and features massive rhododendrons and the John Masefield tree, commemorating that poet's visit to Arden.

The 5000 km National Trail for walkers and horse riders runs from Healesville all the way north to **Cooktown** in Queensland.

Gruyere is 8 km to the south, and this is home to the **Yarra Yering**, **Prigorje** and **Warramate** wineries, in one of the great red wine areas of Australia.

I personally believe that Dr Bailey Carrodus

at **Yarra Yering** *(Briarty Rd; tel: 5964 9267;* open Sat 1000–1800) produces the best red wine in the country, bar none. And the vineyard has stunning views across the Valley.

SIDE TRACK
FROM ALEXANDRA

Rte 168, a spur of the Maroondah Hwy, leads 26 km east from the main route at Alexandra to Eildon, its lake and National Park.

EILDON

Tourist Information: Visitor Information Centre, *Main St; tel: 5774 2909*.

ACCOMMODATION

Eildon Holiday Resort Motel, *corner Snobs Creek Rd and Goulburn Valley Hwy (PO Box 35); tel: 5774 2415*. **Eildon Parkview Motor Inn**, *Hillside Ave; tel: 5774 2165*. **Golden Trout Motel**, *Riverside Dr.; tel: 5774 2508*. **Eildon Lake Motel**, *Girdwood Parade; tel: 5774 2800*.

EATING AND DRINKING

At Eildon Boat Harbour is **Smiffy's Licensed Restaurant and Bar**, *tel: 5774 2237*, open Fri, Sat, Sun for dinner and lunch. **Hillside Restaurant**; *tel: 5774 2031*. BYO.

SIGHTSEEING

This is a very new town. It was created in the 1950s to accommodate workers who had come to construct the dam. The original name was Sugarloaf Dam. The current name comes from Eildon Hills in Scotland, where King Arthur, a much-buried man, is reputed to have a grave.

The road running between the town and the nearby **Fraser National Park** is steep and winding, but does not require a four-wheel-drive vehicle, and offers views over **Lake Eildon**, the **Goulburn** and **Acheron Valleys**, and south, to the **Cathedral Ranges**.

Lake Eildon is Victoria's largest lake,

covering some 138 sq km with 525 km of shoreline. As a result Eildon has become a water sports centre – the lake dock area is 2 km from the town – with all sorts of craft for hire.

Lake Eildon Holiday Boats (*tel: 5778 7335*) has houseboats for hire and **Eildon Boat Harbour and Ski Boat Hire** (*tel: 5774 2107*) has sailboards, power boats and jet skis.

The lake is set in a valley surrounded by tree-covered mountains and is part of the **Goulburn Irrigation System**. The original dam was built between 1915 and 1927, but this was extended between 1952–1955 to raise the capacity to the current 3.38 million megalitres.

At the end of the dam, away from the town, there is a viewing platform as well as slipways for launching boats. At weekends a ferry boat sightseeing trip operates from the boat harbour.

At **Snob's Creek**, off the Goulburn Valley Hwy about 6 km from town, is **Snobs Creek Fish Hatchery**, *tel: 5774 2207*. Admission $5. Run by the state department responsible for parks, it produces trout, salmon, cod and perch. The visitors centre at the fishery has more than thirty species of Victorian fish on display in tanks set up to resemble their native habitat.

EILDON STATE PARK

Tourist Information: Park office; *tel: 5772 1293*.

This steep and rugged park covers 24,000 hectares on the southern and eastern shores of Lake Eildon running up into the **Enterprise Range**.

Access is from the *Jerusalem Creek Rd* from Eildon or from the road that runs from Eildon to **Jamieson**.

Some of the features of the park are the magnificent stands of Blue Gum trees and the fern gullies along **Jerusalem Creek** and its tributaries.

It is linked to **Fraser National Park** and together they cover 27,000 hectares. This was once a heavily forested area but during the gold rush, most of the trees were felled for timber, and the trees are now eucalypts which have grown since then.

MANSFIELD

Tourist Information: Mansfield Tourist Information, *Old Railway Station; tel: 5775 1464*.

ACCOMMODATION

Mansfield Valley Motor Inn, *Maroondah Hwy; tel: 5775 1300*. **Alzburg Inn**, *39 Malcolm St; tel: 5775 2367*. **Mansfield Motel** *(BU), 3 Highett St (Midland Hwy); tel: 5775 2377*. **Highton Manor** *(Motel Section), Highton Lane; tel: 5775 2700*.

SIGHTSEEING

Lying 183 km north-east of Melbourne, Mansfield is a timber town in the centre of a large grazing district at the foot of the Great Dividing range. From the town there is easy access to the **Mt Buller Alpine resort** (see below). The town is an all-year round resort.

During the winter, **The Ski Centre** at *32 High St* is open *(tel: 5775 2095)*.

Delatite Vineyard and Winery, which is 8 km along *Mt Buller Rd (tel: 5775 2922)* is open daily 1000–1700.

A picturesque area of land on the Goulburn River is the **Upper Goulburn Historic Reserve**, which is off *Gould St,* and here the river is suitable for canoeing, fishing and fossicking – panning for gold.

Within the area there are numerous defunct gold mines and ruined houses dating back to the 1850s.

SIDE TRACK FROM MANSFIELD

Rte 164 goes east some 49 km to Mt Buller and its Alpine Village.

MT BULLER

ACCOMMODATION

Mt Buller Chalet Hotel, *Summit Rd; tel: 5777 6566*. **Abom Hotel**, *Summit Rd (PO Box 42); tel: 5777 6091*. **Arlberg Hotel**, *189 Summit Rd (PO Box 312, Mansfield*

3724); tel: 5777 6260. **Kooroora Hotel** (open snow season only), *1 The Avenue (PO Box 83); tel: 5777 6050.* **HI**, *The Ave, Mt Buller Alpine Village; tel: 5777 6181.*

SKIING

Mt Buller has the largest integrated lift system of the three resorts, with 13 chairlifts, 13 T-bars and Pomas, and an extensive snow making capability. It is unique in that on runs serviced by eight major lifts it offers a money back Ski Guarantee – if you cannot ski because of a lack of snow you get your money refunded.

All of these resorts are serviced by coaches from Melbourne. It is possible to start early in the morning – 0400 – be skiing on Mt Buller by 0900, ski all day, leave Mt Buller at 1700 and be back in Melbourne at 2300.

This particular service is operated by **Alzburg Inn Resort** (*tel: 1 800 033 023*), but a service to Mt Buller is also offered by **Australian Pacific Tours** (*tel: 13 1304*).

Similar services for **Mt Hotham** are run by **Trekset** (*tel: 1 800 80 32 05*) and for **Falls Creek** by **Pyles Alpine Coach Services.** ⬛

MYRTLEFORD

ACCOMMODATION

Golden Leaf Motor Inn, *Ovens Hwy; tel: 5752 1566.* **Standish St Hotel Motel**, *101 Standish St; tel: 5752 1583.* **Myrtleford Country Motel** *(BU), 258 Myrtle St (Ovens Hwy); tel: 5752 1438.*

SIGHTSEEING

At the junction of the Ovens and Buffalo Rivers, Myrtleford is in a major tobacco and hop growing area. It has an excellent view of the Alps from various points around the town and is surrounded by wooded slopes.

The town started life as a camping area for miners, when gold was found nearby in the gold rush of the 1850s.

The Old School Museum (*corner Elgin and Albert Sts, tel: 5727 1417,* open Sat 1400–1700) is in a building dating from 1870.

It includes a series of display areas which reflect the gold and agricultural background of the town.

Nearby, in the *Happy Valley Rd,* are **Rosewhite Vineyards**, with cool climate wines, cellar door tasting and sales. Open daily except Tues and Thur, 1000–1700; *tel: 5752 1077.*

MT BUFFALO NATIONAL PARK

Tourist Information: Mt Buffalo National Park; *tel: (03) 5755 1466.*

ACCOMMODATION

Mt Buffalo Chalet, *Mt Buffalo Rd, Mt Buffalo National Park (PO Box 76); tel: 5755 1500.* **Tatra Inn**, *Mt Buffalo National Park, Cresta; tel: 5755 1988.*

SIGHTSEEING

This park has imposing granite tors (outcrops), waterfalls, snow gums and, in season, spectacular displays of wildflowers, as well as views of the Alps. The park was gazetted in 1898, making it one of the earliest national parks in Australia. It was extended in 1898 and now covers 31,000 hectares.

The reason it is called Mt Buffalo is that the explorers Hamilton Hume and William Hovell, who were in the area in 1824, thought that the granite mass looked like a buffalo. It was an almost impassable buffalo at that, and it wasn't until 1854 that it was climbed by Europeans.

Access to the park is by way of a surfaced road – good surface but very winding and extra care should be taken – from **Porepunkah** near Bright. There are good surfaced roads throughout the park, but in snow conditions chains must be carried.

The park, at it highest point, rises to 1723 m at **The Horn** on the granite range that runs for 11 km at an average height of 1000 m. During the winter this area is very popular with cross country skiers.

The plants and animals in the park are diverse and are able to cope with the cold winters, cool summers and high rainfall, which are typical of the area.

The sub-alpine vegetation includes snow

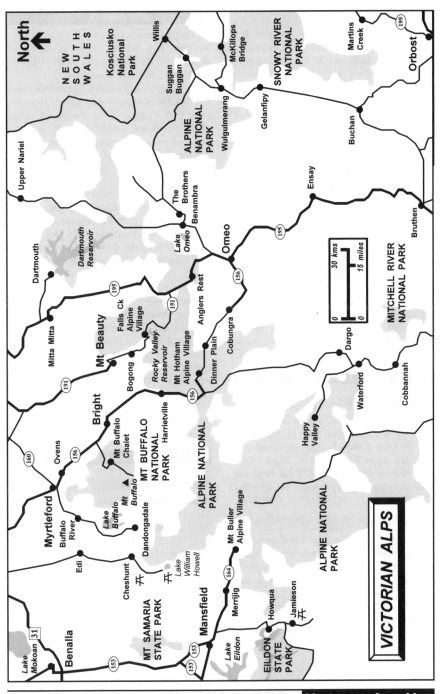

gums, alpine ash and Buffalo sallee, which is a small willow-like tree unique to this area. The ground cover beneath the trees is mainly Buffalo sallow wattle and the heaths, often covered by snow for a quarter of the year, are a mixture of low grasses, mosses and other native plants.

The range of animal life includes echidnas and platypuses in the lowlands, although the latter are very elusive, and if you ever see one in the wild (as opposed to the zoo), you join a small and privileged group. There are also possums in the woods and a fair collection of wombats. There is even the occasional swamp wallaby.

Nearly a hundred reptiles have been spotted within the park, including the tiger, brown, copperhead and white-lipped snakes. And there are over 130 bird species, including the lyre bird, which is to be found in the dense forested gullies around The Chalet.

Within the park there are 90 km of well-signposted and marked walks. Perhaps the easiest and most pleasurable is the **Gorge Nature Walk**, which starts at Crystal Brook and extends 2 km through spectacular scenery.

MT HOTHAM

ACCOMMODATION

Snowbird Inn Hotel (open snow season only), *Alpine Rd (PO Box 108); tel: 9525 5777 or 5759 3503*. **Zirkys Lodge** (open snow season only), *Alpine Rd (PO Box 46, Bright 3471); 5759 3518 or 9816 3762*. **SCV Mt Hotham** (open snow season only), *Alpine Rd (PO Box 359, Toorak 3142); 9826 0428 or 5759 3543*.

SKIING

This resort is somewhat smaller and, perhaps, a little more intimate. It is at a height of 1850 m and has a skiing area of 375 hectares. The resort is serviced by two Pomas, 1 T-Bar and 7 chair lifts.

The skiing is divided into beginner 18%, intermediate 53% and advanced 30%, which makes it more suitable for the average skier than Falls Creek.

OMEO

Although Omeo is known as the capital of the Victorian Alps it is an all-year round tourist destination. The name is said to come from a Koori word meaning 'mountains'.

The gold rush of the 1850s pushed the town forward, but because of the relatively large distance from Melbourne, this was known as one of the wilder and rougher goldfields and was regarded for many years as the last frontier. After gold came agriculture with large sheep and cattle runs making the town, which served the area, prosperous.

Dating back to the wild and woolly days of the goldfields is the town's **log jail**, built in 1858, and found in **A. M. Pearson Memorial Park**. Open weekends; *tel: 5759 1366*.

Follow *Benambra Rd* 8 km out of town and you come to **McMillans Lookout**, which, at 933 m, has spectacular views over the Omeo Valley and beyond to the Upper Snowy Valley and, on a clear day, as far as Mt Kosciusko.

The **Oriental Claims Historic Area** – even the name has a historic ring about it – is 2 km out of town on *Alpine Rd; tel: 5759 4344*. There is a footpath to an amphitheatre surrounded by small gravel cliffs, which were all man-made. They were dug away by the Chinese prospectors searching for gold.

Some 25 km out of town on the *Alpine Rd* are **Victoria Falls**, with good views from the access road.

FALLS CREEK

ACCOMMODATION

Astra Lodge (no facilities for children under 12), *23 Sitzmark St (PO Box 74); tel: 5758 3496*. **Attunga Alpine Lodge**, *49 Arlberg St; tel: 5758 3255*. **Karelia Alpine Lodge**, *70 Parallel St; tel: 5758 3278*.

Falls Creek Motel (closed Oct 11–Dec 26), *85 Falls Creek Rd; tel: 5758 3282 or 9844 2762*. **Trackers Mountain Lodge**, *88 Schuss St; tel: 5758 3346*. **Cedarwood Alpine Lodge**, *96 Schuss St (PO Box 124); tel: 9525 5777 or 5758 3393*. **Cooroona Lodge**, *8 Slalom St; tel: 5758 3244*.

The Man from Snowy River

Banjo Paterson made a major mark as a poet on Australia. He wrote the words to *Once a Jolly Swagman* (also known as *Waltzing Matilda*), although it may have been set to an English folk tune from Northumberland.

And he also wrote *The Man From Snowy River*, which is an epic about a bushman who rode across the Snowy Mountains chasing a runaway horse.

Every Australian knows the opening lines – 'There was movement at the station, for the word had passed around, that the cold from old Regret had got away.' Indeed, many Australians know every single word and will, when taken with an excess of alcohol, insist on reciting it to you.

There are a large number of claimants to having been the rider on whom this truly stirring poetry is based, among them 'Hellfire' Jack Clarke, Lachlan Cochran and Owen Cummins. In his definitive book, *Australian Folklore*, Fearn-Wannan lists the five main claimants. In fact, it was none of them, because it has been pretty well established that Paterson created the great rider from his imagination.

In an article 'Looking Backward', Banjo Paterson wrote:

'They have turned up from all the mountain districts – men who did exactly the same ride, and could give you the chapter and verse for every hill they descended and every creek they crossed. It was not small satisfaction to me to find that there really had been a Man from Snowy River – more than one of them.'

SKIING

Splits into 17% beginner, 43% intermediate and 40% advanced – biased towards the more experienced skier. It runs 9 Pomas, 6 T-bars and 6 chair lifts but, as always, this is simply the current position, as the ski fields are always being upgraded and extended. As it stands, it can move 25,000 skiers an hour and there are 90 different runs.

The resort is at a height of 18,427m and, to improve upon nature, there is snow-making equipment covering 96 hectares, although the total area is 451 hectares.

MT BEAUTY

Tourist Information: Australian High Country Visitors Centre, *Kiewa Valley Hwy; 5754 3172*.

ACCOMMODATION

Snowgum Motel, *Kiewa Valley Hwy, Tawonga S. 3698 (PO Box 266, Mt Beauty 3699); tel:* *5754 4508*. **Allamar Ranch Motor Inn**, *Kiewa Valley Hwy, Tawonga S. (PO Box 231); tel: 5754 4365*.

Bogong Moth Hotel, *Kiewa Valley Hwy, Tawonga S. (PO Box 155, Mt Beauty 3699); tel: 5754 4644*. **Meriki Motel**, *Tawonga Crescent; 5754 4155*.

SIGHTSEEING

Victoria's largest hydro-electric scheme is **Kiewa** on the Kiewa Valley Hwy (**Visitors centre:** *tel: 5754 3172*). There are guided tours of the **McKay Creek Power Station** (Tues, Thur and weekends between 1200 and 1530 except in winter when there are only weekday tours).

The water from the scheme comes from the rocky valley reservoir, which is at a height of 1615m on the **Bogong High Plains**, and is covered in snow for three months of the year.

WODONGA

See Murray and the Riverina, p. 198.

VICTORIA NATIONAL PARKS

Department of Conservation and Natural Resources, *240 Victoria Parade, E. Melbourne; tel 9412 4011.* (Note that most national parks have their own separate offices and these should be contacted directly for more detail when you are in the area. The central office will give you the addresses and telephone numbers.)

Even though Victoria is the smallest state in Australia it has a wealth of parks – 34 national parks and 41 state parks at the last count. Some of the parks are big and basically deserts, some are small and verdant, but all are interesting. The state parks in Victoria come under a lighter hand than the national parks in that they are more open for recreational use and, indeed, in some of the parks, logging is allowed, although this is very restricted.

The following section lists the most note-worthy national and state parks in Victoria, many of which are describe din more detail in the recommended routes for Victoria on the preceding pages. Unless otherwise stated, each park will have at least one campsite, picnic area and walking trail.

In and around Melbourne

Melbourne is ringed with state and national parks. Churchill and Dandenong Ranges are actually within Greater Melbourne.

Arthurs Seat State Park
Brisbane Ranges
Bunyip State Park
Churchill *No campsite.*
Dandenong Ranges *No campsite. See p. 177.*
French Island State Park *See the Melbourne to Mornington Peninsula route, pp. 151–155, for this and Point Nepean.*
Kinglake

Lerderderg State Park
Organ Pipes *No campsite.*
Point Nepean *No campsite.*

The Great Ocean Road

These parks all fall on the Melbourne to Warrnambool route, pp. 134–143.

Angahook Lorne State Park *See p. 139.*
Otway *See p. 141.*
Port Campbell *No picnic area.*

South-west Victoria

These parks and those under the next heading are best explored by taking the Melbourne to Mildura route, pp. 156–167.

Mt Richmond and Discovery Bay *No campsite.*
Grampians Bush camping possible. *See pp. 161, 163.*
Little Desert Wilderness. *See p. 164.*
Lower Glenelg *Bush camping possible.*
Mt Eccles

Sunset Country and The Big Desert

Big Desert Wilderness *See p. 166.*
Hattah-Kulkyne *Bush camping possible.*
Wyperfield *See p. 165.*
Yanga-Nyawi (Murray-Sunset) *Bush camping possible.*

The Victorian Alps

The Alpine and Snowy River National Parks are continuous with Kosciusko National Park in New South Wales, forming one large alpine area with winter sports and summer resorts.

Alpine *Bush camping possible. See p. 177, and box opposite.*
Baw Baw *Bush camping possible. For serious hikers, the Alpine Trail starts here and follows the mountains all the way to Mt Kosciusko, in New South Wales.*

The Bogong Area, Alpine National Park

Alpine National Park falls into three very distinct parts. The smaller middle and eastern portions are joined to the larger western part by a comparatively narrow strip of park formed by the Barry Mountains. The western part has Mt Buller Alpine Village on its western fringes (see p. 179). The middle portion, described in the scenic detour to the Melbourne to Wodonga route (pp. 168–175), includes the Bogong Area.

Bogong is Aboriginal for 'big person'. For thousands of years Aborigines went to the high plains at the first thawing of the snow to have a Bogong moth feast; the insect was considered a major delicacy. The Bogong Area contains the most extensive and botanically rich area of alpine vegetation in the Victorian Alps: more than 300 species of plant have been recorded. The wildflower meadows in summer are spectacular.

The 646,000 hectares of this park contain some of the best skiing and ski-resorts in Australia. It also includes the highest peaks in Victoria and some remarkable mountain scenery. It lies 365 km north east of Melbourne and 90 km south east of Albury-Wodonga. From the south you can take the Omeo–Mt Hotham–Harrietville Rd, which is mainly gravel but usually open throughout the year. The High Plains Rd from Omeo Hwy to Falls Creek is mainly gravel and is often closed during the winter season. Access from the north-west is by way of the Kiewa and Ovens Valley Hwys. It is important to realise that it is a legal requirement to carry chains for your car during the winter when you visit this park, whether you intend to go into snow-covered areas or not.

Although, in general, horse riding in National Parks is frowned upon it is permitted in some sections of the park for the months of Dec–Apr.

Tourist Information: Alpine National Park, *Kiewa Valley Hwy, Mt Beauty; tel: 5757 2693.*

185

Burrowa-Pine Mountain *Bush camping possible.*
Cathedral State Park
Eildon State Park. *See p. 179.*
Errinundra
Mitchell River *Bush camping possible.*
Mt Buffalo *No picnic areas. See p. 180.*
Snowy River

SE Victoria –The Tasman Sea Coast

The majority of these parks are on or close to

the Melbourne to Eden route, pp. 144–150.

Alfred *No campsite, picnic area or walking trail*
Cooprancambra *No campsite or walking trail, bush camping possible*
Croajingolong *Bush camping possible. See p. 150.*
Gippsland Lakes Coastal Park *See p. 147.*
The Lakes *See p. 148.*
Lind *No campsite or walking trail.*
Wilsons Promontory *No picnic area. See p. 146.*

AUSTRALIAN CAPITAL TERRITORY

The Australian Capital Territory is home to the nation's capital, Canberra, and is an odd sort of a place with its own laws, style and government. The map on p. 55 shows its position and size, surrounded by the much greater expanse of New South Wales.

Australian Capital Territory has been a site of continuous habitation for many years. The earliest evidence of Aboriginal occupation of the area dates from 21,000 years ago. When the Europeans came to Australia the main tribe in the area was the Wiradjuri. They came every year in the late spring to eat themselves silly on what were considered a great delicacy, bogong moths.

COMMONWEALTH OF AUSTRALIA

The first European explorer in the area was Charles Throsby who came in 1821. He named the area Limestone Plains; farming started there within three years and within ten all of the land in the area was settled.

Then came Federation and the Australian Capital Territory was formed as a theoretical entity. On a scorching hot day, 1 Jan 1901, the Commonwealth of Australia was created by federating the six Australian states.

They did not all come willingly to the party – Western Australia still talks about seceding and going it alone – and many concessions had to be made. The most important was that the national capital would be established within the state of New South Wales, would 'not be less than one hundred miles from Sydney' and

would be totally independent. This was proposed by the splendidly named politician King O'Malley, who managed to get enough votes to support the motion. It was also decided that it had to have a sea outlet, which complicated matters more than somewhat. Thus from 1901 to 1908 sites were inspected and rejected for all sorts of possible reasons.

Eventually a compromise was struck and the Australian Capital Territory was set to be in both the Yass-Canberra District with an enclave in Jervis Bay, which is used by the Royal Australian Navy for its Naval Training College.

THE NEW CAPITAL

The territory came into existence in Jan 1911 and covered what was then called 910 sq miles – 1356 sq km. The then Minister for Home Affairs, appropriately King O'Malley, said, 'this city must be the finest capital city in the world.' Australian politicians often speak like that.

An international architectural competition to design Canberra was announced and drew an amazing 137 entries. Again there was much debate but the entry of a Chicago-based architect, 37-year-old **Walter Burley Griffin**, won first prize. He had earlier worked in the studio of Frank Lloyd Wright. To gauge the level of the competition you should know that the second prize went to Saarinen, the famous Finnish architect.

It is said that it was the magnificent drawings that accompanied Griffin's proposal that swung the jury. These had been created by his wife, Marion Mahoney Griffin, who was also an architect.

The ACT has now ceased to be a rural centre – 95% of its income comes from work connected with the federal government. And Jervis Bay provides the essential outlet to the sea.

CANBERRA

Canberra pretty much started as a nothing place in a nowhere land. Only inter-state jealousy created the, arguably, great national capital that exists today. The Australian Capital Territory now covers 2366 sq km and has a population of over 300,000. Canberra is in many ways still a country town, dignified with the name 'city' because it is the nation's capital. However its capital status endows it with enough important buildings and memorials to make a visit almost obligatory.

TOURIST INFORMATION
Visitor Information Centre, *Northbourne Ave, Dickson, tel: (06) 204 0044 or Freecall, 1800 026 166.*

ARRIVING AND DEPARTING

Airport
Canberra, although the nation's capital, does not have an international airport. The domestic airport is 7 km from the city. To get into the centre of the city you can take an **ACT Mini Bus**, which runs regularly in time with arriving and departing flights and costs around $7. Or take a taxi, which costs around twice that price.

By Train
You can also get there by train and the main station is on *Wentworth Ave* in Kingston. Most interstate buses arrive in the middle of the city at the **Jolimont Centre**, *67 Northbourne Ave.*

By Road
Getting to Canberra from Sydney is easy. You head out on *Parramatta Rd* and then turn left on to the Hume Hwy just past **Goulburn**. The drive, mainly on reasonable motorway, is 305 km and takes 3½ hours of steady driving. This road is notorious as being the most heavily patrolled in Australia and if you exceed the posted speed limits you will, without a doubt, be pulled up by the police.

GETTING AROUND
The easiest way of exploring the city is Murray's **Canberra Explorer Bus**, run hourly 1015–1615, starting at the Jolimont Centre. It covers all the main sights with an informed commentary from the driver. A 1-day ticket is $18 and a complete tour costs just under $9.

Public Transport
The city is well catered for by buses run by **Action (timetable information** *tel: 6207 7611).* Most buses start their journeys at the **City Bus Interchange**, *11 East Row.* A day ticket costs around $6 and a weekly ticket is about $3. Most politicians leave Canberra at the weekends, as do the civil servants, so it can be very difficult to find a bus then, and you will find it easier to walk or take a taxi.

The **Canberra City Tram** is called the **Downtowner** and is really a bus made to look like a tram. It is free and runs around the shopping streets of the city centre; one passes every 10 mins 0900–1630, but not at weekends.

Taxis are available at stands. For radio cabs try **Aerial Taxis**; *tel: 6285 9222;* **Diamond Radio Taxis**, *Queanbeyan; tel: 6297 3000.*

Driving in Canberra
Canberra has the best laid out and best maintained road system in Australia – politicians look after their own – and driving around the city is a positive delight. The city has never seen traffic jams as experienced in Sydney and Melbourne. You may encounter a problem when crossing **Lake Burley Griffin**, where the layout of the bridges has even the locals confused. There are, in theory, three bridges crossing the lake although most visitors only find one. But as Canberra is contained in such a small compass this is the least of problems.

STAYING IN CANBERRA

Central Canberra:
Rydges Canberra, *London Circuit; tel: 247 6244.* **Rydges Capital Hill**, *corner Canberra Ave and National Circuit; tel: 295 3144.* **Capital Parkroyal** *(SPH), Binara St; tel: 247 8999.* **Country Comfort Inn Canberra** *(CC), 102 Northbourne Ave; tel: 249 1411.*

Diplomat Boutique Hotel *(FL), corner Canberra Ave and Hely St; tel: 295 2277.* **Downtown Spero's Motel**, *82 Northbourne Ave; tel: 249 1388.* **Acacia Motor Lodge**, *65 Ainslie Ave; tel: 249 6955.*

Southern Suburbs:
Barton: **The Brassey Hotel**, *Belmore Gardens; tel: 273 3766.* **Macquarie Private Hotel**, *18 National Circuit; tel: 273 2325.* Deakin: **Embassy Motel** *(BW), corner Adelaide Ave and Hope Circuit; tel: 281 1322.* **New Deakin Inn Motel**, *70 Kent St; tel: 281 1011.*

Forrest: **Forrest Motor Inn** *(FL), 30 National Circuit; tel: 295 3433.* **Telopea Park Motel**, *16 NSW Crescent; tel: 295 3722.* Kingston: **Monaro Motel**, *27 Dawes St; tel: 295 2111.* Yarralumla: **Hyatt Hotel Canberra**, *Commonwealth Ave; tel: 270 1234.*

Northern Suburbs:
Braddon: **Olims Canberra Hotel**, *corner Ainslie and Limestone Aves; tel: 248 5511.* **Kythera Motel**, *100 Northbourne Ave; tel: 248 7611.*

Lyneham: **Canberra City Gate Motel** *(BW), corner Northbourne Ave and Mouat St; tel: 247 2777.* **Canberra Lyneham Motor Inn** *(BW), 39 Mouat St; tel: 249 6855.* **Edmund Barton Motor Inn**, *193 Mouat St; tel: 248 5111.* Dickson: **Canberra International Hotel**, *242 Northbourne Ave; tel: 247 6966.* O'Connor: **HI**, *Dryandra St; tel: 248 9155.*

Eating and Drinking
Kalinka Russian Restaurant, *55 Woolley St, Dickson; tel: 249 8082.* Licensed. **Canberra Yacht Club**, *Mariner Pl., Lotus Bay, Yarralumla; tel: 273 1784.* On the waterfront. Open daily for lunch, Mon–Sun for dinner. Licensed.

Communications
The central post office is in *Alinga St; tel: 6209 1370.* Open Mon–Fri 0900–1700.

Consulates and Embassies
Austria: *12 Talbot St, Forrest ACT 2603; tel: 6295 1533.*
Belgium: *19 Arkana St, Yarralumla ACT 2600; tel: 6273 2501.*
Canada: *Commonwealth Ave, Yarralumla, ACT 2600; tel: 6273 3844.*
China: *15 Coronation Dr., Yarralumla ACT 2600; tel: 6273 4471.*
Finland: *10 Darwin Ave, Yarralumla ACT 2600; tel: 6273 3800.*
Germany: *119 Empire Circuit, Yarralumla ACT 2600; tel: 6270 1911.*
Greece: *9 Turrana St, Yarralumla ACT 2600; tel: 6273 3011.*
Netherlands: *120 Empire Circuit, Yarralumla ACT 2600; tel: 6273 3111.*
New Zealand: *High Commission, Commonwealth Ave, Yarralumla ACT 2600; tel: 6270 4211.*
Norway: *17 Hunter St, Yarralumla ACT 2600; tel: 6273 3444.*
Republic of Ireland: *20 Arkana St, Yarralumla ACT 2600; tel: 6273 3022.*
South Africa: *High Commission, Rhodes Pl., State Circle, Yarralumla, ACT 2600; tel:6273 2444.*
Singapore: *High Commission, 12 Forster Cres., Yarralumla, ACT 2600; tel: 6273 3944.*
Spain: *15 Arkana St, Yarralumla ACT 2600; tel: 6273 3555.*
Sweden: *Turrana St, Yarralumla; tel: 6273 3033.*
Switzerland: *7 Melbourne Ave, Forrest ACT 2603; tel: 6273 3977.*
UK: *British High Commission, Commonwealth Ave, Yarralumla, ACT 2600; tel: 6270 6666.*
USA: *21 Moonah Pl., Yarralumla ACT 2600; tel: 6270 5000.*

Money
There is a **Thomas Cook Foreign Exchange** branch located at *Shop DG18/19 Ground Floor, Canberra Centre, Bunda St; tel: 257 2222.*

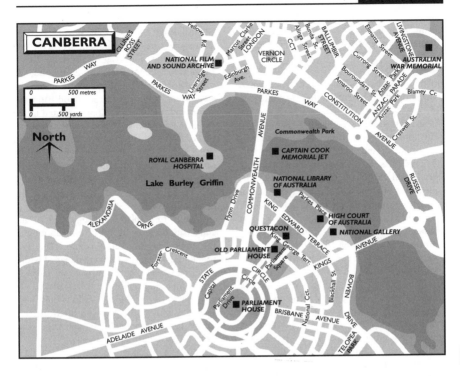

ENTERTAINMENT

The local newspaper, the *Canberra Times*, is not, by any stretch of the imagination, an international newspaper. But it does list, every Thur, every concert, gig and happening in the area. There is also the quarterly *Canberra What's On*, which is fine except that times, prices and sometimes venues have changed.

As throughout Australia, rock bands mainly play the pubs – the **Moosehead's Pub**, *London Circuit*, the **Rose and Crown Tavern** and **Matilda's Tavern** both at *Weston*, probably lead the charge. Classical music performances are held at the **Canberra Theatre Centre** in *Civic Sq. (tel: 6257 1077)* and the **Canberra School of Music**, *Llewellyn Hall (tel: 6249 5700)*. Plays and other performances are also held at the Canberra Theatre Centre.

Canberra has very liberal licensing laws and is, incidentally, pornography headquarters for Australia. Videos banned in every other state except the Northern Territory are freely available and are, indeed, a major industry.

EVENTS

Canberrra is a city that greatly enjoys its festivals even if it does not actually let its hair down. It starts over the last weekend in Feb with the **Royal Canberra Show**, which is a farming exhibition and is considered by country folk as a lead-in to the Royal Easter Show in Sydney. Then comes the **Canberra Festival** at the beginning of Mar, celebrating the foundation of this very new city. This has street parades – not to be compared with the Mardi Gras in Sydney – concerts, drama and discreet fireworks. **Floriade**, possibly the best of them all, is a spring festival of flowers. It runs mid Sept–mid Oct with truly wonderful gardens blazing with colour, and concerts and exhibitions.

SHOPPING

Canberra is not a shopping destination but the usual stores can be found at average Australian prices. Shops are open on Fridays until 2100. Sunday shopping is the exception apart from some supermarkets in the satellite towns. A main shopping area is the new **Canberra Centre**, between *City Walk* and *Bunda St.*

SIGHTSEEING

In the early days nothing much happened. A new property, **Duntroon**, was established in 1825, which was later bought by the government and turned into a military college in 1910. The homestead was a large and wonderful edifice with verandahs. Today it houses the Officers' Mess and the Commandant's Office of the **Royal Military College**. Despite the splendours of Duntroon, Canberra was still not a big town. In 1826, the population was only 116. There was a small Anglican church and a school, both finished in 1845, and **Yarralumla House**, which was built 1891. This was later to become the residence of the governor-general. But it was basically a one-horse town.

Federation in 1901 changed that, when it became obvious that Australia had to have a capital. The obvious choice was either Melbourne or Sydney but the rivalry between these two cities should never be underestimated — the choice of one would have led to serious political repercussions in the other. The Act of Federation signed on 1 Jan 1901, stated that: 'The Seat of Government of the Commonwealth shall be determined by the Parliament and shall be within territory granted to, or acquired by the Commonwealth. It shall be within the State of New South Wales and be distant not less than one hundred miles from Sydney. Such territory shall contain an area of not less than one hundred square miles granted to the Commonwealth without any payment.' The Australian Capital Territory was created in 1908 as a 2368 sq km enclave in New South Wales with access to the sea at **Jervis Bay**. In 1911 land for a capital city was acquired by the commonwealth government and nearby **Mt Stromlo** was selected as the site for an observatory, which was built in 1926.

In order to build Canberra as a capital city, to all intents and purposes from scratch, an international contest was held. This was won in 1912 by the American landscape architect Walter Burley Griffin, whose plan was for a city with a population of 25,000, which was expected to grow in time to 75,000. Of his

original design he wrote: 'The site may be considered an irregular amphitheatre with **Mt Anslie** at the north-east, flanked by **Black Mountain** and **Mt Pleasant**, all forming the top galleries; with the slopes to the water, the auditorium — the waterway and flood-basin, the arena; with the southern slopes reflected in the basin, the terraced stage and setting of monumental Government structures sharply defined rising tier on tier to the culminating highest internal hill, **Capital Hill**; and with **Mugga Mugga**, **Red Hill** and the blue distant mountain ranges forming the back scene of the theatrical whole.'

Central to his plan was a large artificial lake and a parliamentary triangle to contain most of the important national buildings. The surrounding residential areas were designed with a geometric street pattern, circular and radial in shape. And, despite the fact that work did not proceed as fast as Burley Griffin would have wished — two World Wars and the depression of the 1930s intervened — by and large what exists today is what he envisaged.

Much of the current quality of Canberra is the result of the National Capital Development Commission, which was established after the last war to complete the establishment of Canberra as seat of government; to develop it fully as the administrative centre; to create the buildings, avenues, lakes, parks and other features appropriate to Australia's national capital and to design living areas with a high standard of amenities and attractive surroundings.

In the 1960s the last of the public service departments, which had been languishing in Victoria, was transferred to Canberra and the city went through a boom period with new towns added to the circumference of the city.

Canberra arouses strange emotions in people. It is well designed, well ordered, full of beautiful parks and elegant buildings. Yet, it drives the Scottish comedian Billy Connolly, for example, into a frenetic rage. In his book on his tour of Australia he wrote: 'Incredibly, the government held an international competition to design the capital city. The winner was an American — Walter Burley Griffin — who can be held single-handedly responsible for the city plan. If there's any justice at all, I'm sure he's

The Origins of Canberra

The area was first explored by a European, Charles Throsby Smith, in 1820–21 and became known as the Limestone Plains. He wrote: ' - happy to report that the country is perfectly sound, well-watered with extensive meadows of rich land on either side of the rivers, contains very fine limestone, slate, sandstone and granite fit for building, with sufficient timber for every useful purpose.' Later the explorer and botanist, Allan Cunningham, again reported that the area had agricultural potential and the first 'run' – the first farm – was taken up by Joshua Moore on the banks of the Molongolo River in 1824. He gave it an adaptation of a local Aboriginal name – Canberry. The initial property consisted of slab huts built at roughly the current position of the **Royal Canberra Hospital**. In the hospital grounds there is a fountain, which is inscribed: 'On this site Lieutenant J.J. Moore, the first settler in this district, built his residence about AD 1826. Some stones from it now form this fountain AD 1954.'

From Canberry came the later name of Canberra. The official story is that it comes from an Aboriginal word meaning 'meeting place', either of rivers or of tribes joining together to feast on Bogong Moths. Another theory is the name comes from a term meaning 'tomahawk chop on the back of the knee'. That name is a considerable improvement on some that were suggested when the project was initiated, the daftest of which was *Sydmeladperbrisho,* the combined names of all the state capitals.

roasting in hell. This is probably the most inert, sterile town on earth.' There are, however, many who would seriously disagree. Canberra is, by any standards, a beautiful city. It is most unusual among Australian inland cities in that it is blessed with a solid rainfall, averaging 625mm a year, keeping the city and its extensive parklands green throughout the year.

Many of the historic buildings that were part of early Canberra have been well maintained. **Lanyon**, built in 1835, is a fine example of the superb homes built by original settlers. The Laynon Homestead was almost totally self-sufficient as can be seen by the dairy, workers' barracks, storerooms and kitchen, surrounding the main house. The turret of the ivy-covered kitchen holds a bell, which was rung to call the shepherds and labourers to their work. The house was extended in 1859 and again in 1905. The interior has been painstakingly restored. Open Tues–Sun 1000–1600.

In 1845, **St John's Church of England** was completed. It is built from bluestone from nearby Mt Pleasant and sandstone from Black Mountain. The east window above the altar is one of the first stained-glass windows to be made in Australia. Near the church is Canberra's first school, which remained the only school in the area from the early 1840s until

1880. The schoolhouse has been restored and is open Wed 1000–1200, Sat, Sun 1400–1600. **Blundell's Farmhouse** was built in 1858 by the Campbells of Duntroon as a home for their head ploughman, who lived there for a decade before moving on, to be replaced by the Blundells. They lived in this tiny cottage for more than fifty years, raising three daughters and five sons. It has been totally restored to the original style by the Canberra Historical Society. You can view the parlour, the main bedroom, the original kitchen, the girls' bedroom, the new kitchen, the garden and the shed. Open daily 1400–1600, Wed 1000–1200.

Those are the old attractions of the city – now let us look at what has been achieved since it became a capital.

In Canberra the first rule of sightseeing is the **Parliamentary Triangle**, containing most of Australia's important national monuments. You can easily take a full day to explore them all and all are within easy walking distance, laid out on both shores of Lake Burley Griffin, which separates yet unifies the city.

The most important new addition to the city is **Parliament House**, which seems to meet with universal approval. Its design was again decided by international competition and it was opened in May 1988. It is situated on

Capital Hill and its circular form blends into the original hill. The apex of the triangle is the 81 m flag post on Parliament House, which is visible from most approaches to the city. The flag is 12.8 by 6.4m, flies 24 hours a day, being floodlit at night, and has to be replaced every two weeks for repairs and maintenance. The building itself is an impressive construction, set on a 32 hectare site, although much of it is underground. Its curved central roof is covered in lawn, making it appear a natural outgrowth of the landscape. It has two ring roads systems surrounding it with **Capital Circle** being the inner and **State Circle** the outer. Parliament House is not on the site envisaged by Walter Burley Griffin. He planned Capital Hill to be the site for a **Peoples' Hall** while Parliament itself would be on a lesser elevation, **Camp Hill**, mid-way between the two houses of parliament, which has now effectively disappeared. But as is normal in these matters, the politicians took priority over the people. The argument has been put forward that the new Parliament does, indeed, belong to the people and is therefore in a true sense a Peoples' Hall, although this does not convince everyone. Free guided tours are every ½ hr or you can make your own exploration of much of the building using a self-guiding brochure. Open daily 0900–1700.

Book in advance for a seat at Question Time, when you will hear insults hurled with gay abandon; *tel: 277 5399*. Question Time in the Australian parliament does not inspire a deep belief in the democratic process.

The new house had to compete in size with the **Old Parliament House**, which was constructed when Parliament moved to Canberra in 1927. Even though at the time of its building it was clearly seen as a stop-gap solution – 'something more than temporary but less than permanent' was how a contemporary comment put it – it was used until the new building opened some sixty years later. Again, there are guided tours of the building. There is also a sound and light show, precisely titled **Order, Order**, which offers a slightly sanitised version of parliament in action. The title reflects the fact that the Australian parliament was always a robust forum for discussion, and some of the performances when the house is sitting have

been, and still are, more reminiscent of a bar brawl than a political discussion. (*King George Terrace; tel: 270 822*. Open daily 0900–1600.)

Also in Old Parliament House is the **National Portrait Gallery**, where you can see the famous and infamous who created modern Australia. Do not confuse this with the nearby **National Gallery**, *Parkes Place; tel 240 6411*, which has arguably Australia's greatest collection of Australian art and regularly houses major travelling exhibitions. The upper four galleries are all devoted to Australian art. The other galleries try to show a representative collection of other art but, as the gallery has not yet been collecting for a century, this is somewhat limited. The range of Australian art is the gallery's glory – from Aboriginal art to the Heidelberg School to the post-modernists. There is a quick once-over-lightly tour run by volunteer guides, which takes 30 mins, when you can spot those areas you wish to return to for more serious consideration – sometimes with a surcharge for major exhibitions, making it one of the few public buildings in Canberra to charge for entry. Open 1000–1700. Admission $3. There is a sculpture garden in the grounds of the gallery, open at all times and free of charge.

Blasting out of the lake to a height of 140m on calm days, which is most of the time, is the **Captain Cook Memorial Jet**. The water comes out of the nozzle at speeds in excess of 260 kph and at any given moment 6 tonnes of water is suspended in the air. It automatically switches itself off when the wind rises so that spectators and cars are not soaked.

At **Questacon**, the **National Science and Technology Centre** has over 180 exhibits – 200 are intended as the final figure – which are continually being updated. You can freeze your shadow to a wall, play a harp with no strings or experience virtual reality. There is a spiralling ramp, which takes you past the six major galleries. An enormous Foucault pendulum hangs down in the centre, proving that the earth does, indeed, rotate, and a Japanese theatre shows some of Japan's achievements. It is perfectly possible to spend a day in this splendid place and nothing less than a 2 hr visit will do it justice. It is staffed with enthusiastic and knowledgeable volunteers. Highly recommended.

(*King Edward Terrace; tel: 270 2800.* Open daily 1000–1700.)

The High Court of Australia is within easy strolling distance of the National Gallery. The architecture is stunning, with a long, 24m high, glass façade, dominating the approach from *King Edward Terrace*. It is normally open to the public daily 0945–1630 and has a series of murals by Australian artist, **Jan Senbergs**, showing the development of the country under its Constitution, which is the driving force of the High Court. There are three courtrooms, each with a visitors' gallery, where you can see the slow and ponderous march of justice when the courts are in sessions. The ushers of the High Court are renowned for the depth of their knowledge and their keenness to tell visitors how the courts work. They are approachable, friendly and well informed.

The National Library of Australia, opened in 1968, houses the country's premier collection of the records and journals of the nation. Among its many treasures is the journal of **Captain James Cook** on his epic journey of discovery on the *Endeavour*. There are around 100,000 works housed in the library but it also has a policy of continuous exhibitions, which are run on three levels at the front of the building. Viewed from outside, the building has echoes of the Parthenon in Greece and is widely regarded as one of the more attractively designed and presented tourist attractions of Australia. Guided tours last about ½hr but you may find you end up staying half a day. (*Parkes Pl.; tel: 262 1279.* Open daily 0900–1600.)

The Australian War Memorial, approached by *Anzac Parade*, is the central core of Walter Burley Griffin's concept. It does not glamorise war but tries, instead, to show the heroic efforts of those involved. Multimedia is used to put across the story of Australia at war. This is a sacred spot for almost all Australians and should be approached in the appropriate mood. There are guided tours by volunteers during the day although you may find the experience too emotional to cope with in a single visit. Open daily 0900–1645 with closing marked by the playing of the Last Post.

Outside the Parliamentary triangle, Canberra has many other delights for the visitor,

apart from the ever-present gardens and green spaces which so lighten the city.

The **National Capital Exhibition**, *Regatta Point, Commonwealth Park; tel: 257 1068*, on the north shore of the lake, shows how and why Canberra evolved through a series of multimedia displays. Open daily 0900–1700. Visiting it raises the thought that it is wrong for politicians to be sited in such an elegant, well organised place. It gives them a rose-tinted view of the country. It would be far better if they were housed in an under-privileged Aboriginal community so that they can see the wrongs that are wrought in their name.

A good place for viewing Canberra is from **Mt Ainslie** to the north. The road to Mt Ainslie is pleasant and meandering and passes clumps of volcanic rock. Although the summit is an impressive 842m above sea level it is only 260m above the level of Lake Burley Griffin, although it still affords spectacular views. To the south is **Red Hill Lookout**. To the west, the best viewing position is **Government House Lookout**, which offers a view of Yarralumla, the residence of the governor general. The house has open days.

The **Royal Military College at Duntroon** is at the east end of the lake and is based on the early homestead. The chapel there is recreated from the **Changi** prisoner of war camp in Singapore. A self-guided tour takes you around the establishment. It is also possible to attend ceremonial events such as Trooping the Colour and Beating the Retreat.

On weekdays the **Royal Australian Mint** offers the unique experience of operating a coin press to make your own Australian dollar, which is, indeed, legal tender. There is a self-guided tour along galleries which overlook the factory floor, with informative panels explaining exactly which process is being carried out. This is the only true factory within the city boundary of Canberra. (*Denison St, Deakin; tel: 202 6999.* Open Mon–Fri 0900–1600, Sat–Sun 1000–1500.) **The National Museum of Australia Visitor Centre** has 3 main themes – Aboriginal and Torres Strait Islander culture; Australian society and history; the environment. A Discovery Trail has a self-guided walk. Next to **Scrivener Dam**, 13 km west of

193

the city – used to control the Molonglo River to keep Lake Burley Griffin at the right height – is the **National Aquarium and Australian Wildlife Sanctuary**, *Lady Denman Dr.*; *tel: 287 1211.* It has 26 display tanks, a tunnel through the 1½ million litre **Riverland** so that fish swim around and above you, and, in the sanctuary, a wide collection of Australia's unique wildlife. Open 0900–1730 daily.

On the top of Black Mountain is the 195 m high, telecommunications edifice, **Telstra Tower** – there are arguments as to whether it enhances or damages the landscape. It has viewing galleries and a revolving restaurant, giving stunning views. (*Black Mountain Dr., Acton; tel: Freecall 1800 806 718.* Open 0900–2000 daily. $3.) On the slopes of Black Mountain below the Telstra Tower, is the **Australian National Botanic Gardens**, *Clunies Ross St, Black Mountain; tel: 250 9540.* This has one of Australia's finest collections of plants, laid out in themed groups over an area of 42 hectares. You can explore a rain forest gully, a sample of mallee shrublands or an open eucalypt forest, by following a series of marked trails. This is almost certainly the most comprehensive collection of Australian botanical species in the world. Guided tours on weekends at 1000 and 1400, starting at the **Information Centre** next to the car park. Open daily 0900–1700.

Cockington Green is an English landscape in miniature and it fascinates children, who see it as a massively extended dolls house. It is, in fact, a series of very precise models built throughout to a scale of 1:12. The periods and venues are, perhaps, a little mixed, with a Scottish castle followed by a Kentish oasthouse followed by Stonehenge, but the workmanship is excellent and the general effect fascinating. Unlike most displays of this kind it has model people to scale, which makes the buildings come to life. It is now being extended to add important Australian buildings and townscapes. There is also a miniature steam train offering free rides. To get there drive along *Barton Hwy* and then on to *Gold Creek Rd* – it is well signposted. (*Gold Creek Road, Gungahlin; tel: 230 2273.* Open daily 0930–1630.)

The **National Dinosaur Museum**, *corner Gold Creek Rd and Barton Hwy, Gungahlin; tel:* 230 2655, has several reconstructions of Australian dinosaurs as well as other relics. This is Australia's largest dinosaur display, with a multimedia exhibit showing their past place in the world. Open daily 1000–1700 and 0900–1700 during school holidays.

The **National Film and Sound Archive**, *McCoy Circuit, Acton; tel: 209 3111,* is totally fascinating even though only a very small part of its collection can be exhibited at any one time. The Archive is housed in the Art Deco splendour of what was once the Institute of Anatomy, and is very cramped. It is not widely known that Australia was a major pioneering country as far as films were concerned and there are fragments of documentaries going back as far as 1887, and a wonderfully preserved documentary of the signing of the document of Federation in 1901. The Salvation Army, which actually made what could be thought of as the world's first feature film in *The Soldiers of the Cross,* was mainly responsible for this pioneering work. The exhibition is divided up into a number of small theatres and within the space available a most wonderful exhibition has been created. Open daily 0900–1700.

Out of Town

Bywong Town Gold Mining Village is 28 km north of Canberra at *Millyn Rd, Geary's Gap; tel 236 9183.* By following the signs off the Federal Hwy, it is easy to find. This has a goldmine with working machinery. Guided tours, including panning for gold, are at 1030, 1230 and 1400. Incidentally, this is the genuine article, not a specially created tourist display.

The Space Centre, *Paddy's River Rd, Tidbinilla; tel: 201 7838,* is in the grounds of the **Tracking Station**. Open late in summer, admission free. It has on display, interplanetary spacecraft, a piece of the moon and the sort of food they eat in space. That is not what they serve in the adjacent **Moon Rock Café**.

Looking at space from a different direction is the **Mt Stromlo Observatory**, *off Cotter Rd, Weston Creek; tel: 249 0276,* some 20 mins drive from Canberra. This observatory was first opened in 1924 and has an exploratory exhibition, which shows the work done there. Open daily 0930–1600. Admission $5.

MURRAY AND THE RIVERINA

This is a circular tour beginning and ending in the Australian Capital Territory and taking in the south-west interior of New South Wales. On the way you will visit Mad Dan Morgan country and Albury, on the Murray River, which, with its twin town, Wodonga, is the inland entry point to the state of Victoria. From there you travel the Riverina Highway to Deniliquin and Hay. On the return stretch, you pass the Murrumbidgee irrigation area and can visit Griffith, its main town.

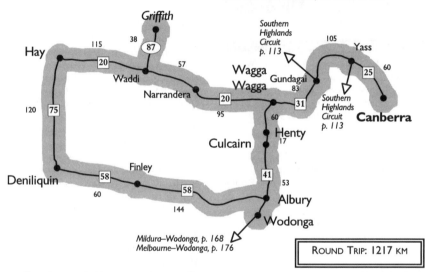

ROUND TRIP: 1217 KM

Mildura–Wodonga, p. 168
Melbourne–Wodonga, p. 176

195

ROUTE

From **Canberra** take Rte 25, the Barton Hwy, to Yass, where you link up with the Southern Highlands Circuit (see p. 113). You join the Hume Hwy, Rte 31, just before reaching the town; follow this road west to Coolac, where it becomes a freeway and takes on the name the Sturt Hwy, to **Gundagai**. Turn right 38 km after Gundagai onto Rte 20 and carry on to **Wagga Wagga**. Just after Wagga Wagga, turn left onto Rte 41, the Olympic Hwy, and proceed to **Henty** and **Culcairn**. From Culcairn it is 53 km to **Albury** and its twin town

Wodonga (from where you can join the Mildura–Wodonga route, p. 168).

From Albury head west along Rte 58, the Riverina Hwy, through **Finley** to **Deniliquin**. Here you join Rte 75, the Cobb Hwy, turning north to **Hay**. At Hay you turn right to rejoin Rte 20 and 115 km later, at **Waddi**, you can take the 38 km detour north to **Griffith** along Rte 87. Retrace your route to Rte 20 and continue east through **Narrandera** until you reach Wagga Wagga again. From there head back to Canberra along the first part of the route, but in the reverse direction.

TRAINS

No trains connect Canberra to the rest of this route, but you can pick up Sydney–Melbourne services (two daily) at Yass Junction. From there Wagga Wagga is 2¼ hrs and Albury is 3½ hrs. Also from Yass Junction, a Sat only train runs to Griffith (5 hrs). OTT table 9026.

BUSES

Public Transport Corporation coaches connect Canberra with Albury (4¾ hrs) by way of Gundagai (2½ hrs). Greyhound Pioneer buses run from Canberra to Yass (45 mins), Gundagai, Wagga Wagga and Albury. OTT table 9109.

GUNDAGAI

See Southern Highlands Circuit p. 119.

WAGGA WAGGA

Tourist Information: Tourism Wagga Wagga, *Tarcutta St; tel: (069) 23 5499.*

A **Thomas Cook Foreign Exchange** branch is located at *Shop 28, Wagga Wagga Market Place, Baylis St; tel: (069) 31 7922.*

ACCOMMODATION

Barters of Wagga Wagga *(FL), 143 Maurice St; tel: 21 1922;* **Old Wagga Inn** *(BW), corner Morgan and Tarcutta Sts; tel: 21 6444;* **Boulevarde Motor Inn,** *305 Edward St; tel: 25 5388;* **Centralpoint Motel,** *164 Tarcutta St; tel: 21 7272;* **Club Motel** *(BU), 73 Morgan St; tel: 21 6966;* **Park Motel,** *1 Tarcutta St; tel: 21 4301.*

SIGHTSEEING

The name was made famous in England in the 1950s by the Australian comedian Dick Bentley, who allegedly came from this town; it comes from an Aboriginal phrase meaning 'place of the crows'. It was first settled by the largest Aboriginal tribe in New South Wales, the Wiradjuri. Locals call it Wagga. This is the largest inland city in Australia and is renowned as the 'Garden Town of the South'. The 8.9 hectare **Botanic Gardens** take pride of place. Wagga, just off Hume Hwy, is almost equidistant from Sydney and Melbourne (450 km or so both ways), and is mid-way between

Sydney and Adelaide. It is the most important town in the Riverina agricultural area. The Murrumbidgee runs through Wagga to form a beach, which boasts Australia's only inland lifesaving club patrol.

The economy of the region is almost wholly agricultural, first wheat and now cattle and sheep. There are many National Trust walks starting from the visitors centre. The **Wollundry Loop** runs for 10 km and circumnavigates the lagoon, but the ultimate challenge is the 32 km **Wiradjuri walking track**. There is also a self-drive **Red Arrow** 28 km motor tour that takes in 31 of Wagga's main attractions.

The 129-hectare **Lake Albert**, formed at the turn of the century by diverting water from Crooked and Stringybark Creeks, offers sailing, fishing, canoeing and water skiing.

Nearby is the **Charles Sturt University**, which overlooks the Murrumbidgee and has a viticulture course with its own winery in *Boorooma St*, N. Wagga. It is named after the explorer Charles Sturt, who travelled up the Murrumbidgee in a whaleboat in 1829. The other winery in the town is the **Wagga Wagga Winery,** *tel: 22 1211,* 10 km upstream on the river; open for tastings 1100–1700.

South of the Sturt Hwy and west of Wagga, is the **Aurora Clydesdale Stud and Pioneer Farm,** *tel: 28 2215,* where you can see these magnificent creatures working. Open daily except Thur. Also nearby is **Junee,** the headquarters of the state's diminishing rail system. The railway line runs though the town. The Renaissance-style railway station was built in 1883, five years after the arrival of the railway. Worth seeing is the **Monte Cristo Homestead** *(off Olympic Way),* which is a two-storey Georgian mansion on a hill overlooking Junee. Open daily 1000–1600. It has iron lacework verandahs, a collection of carriages, an operational smithy, and it is claimed, on very little evidence, a ghost. From Junee there is a scenic road to **Mt Ulandra**.

CULCAIRN

Tourist Information: Tourism Albury-Wodonga, *553 Kiewa St, Albury; tel: 6023 8173.*

Accommodation options in Culcairn

include **Morgan Country Motel**, *corner Olympic Way and Melrose St; tel: 29 8233*, and **Cuclairn Hotel**; *tel: (060) 29 8501*. The glory days are gone. The Sydney–Melbourne train used to stop here overnight, and, for a long time, the **Culcairn Hotel**, built in 1891, was the largest hotel between the two cities. The town's other major claim to fame is that it has Australia's largest sub-artesian domestic water supply. In 1926, a 39m deep shaft was constructed, giving the town un-limited drinking water. As a result, the few streets are tree-lined, and at one time it was known as the 'Oasis of the Riverina'. Half the buildings in Culcairn are Heritage classified by the National Trust. Across from the railway sta-tion is the old stationmaster's house, now restored as a museum with remnants of the old railway days. It also has references to the bushranger Mad Dan Morgan, referred to by some as 'blood thirsty', and by others as the 'traveller's friend'. He was shot dead in 1865. Such was his fame that this area is still referred to as **Mad Dan Morgan country** (see p.199).

HENTY

Places to stay in Henty include **Central Hotel**; *tel (069) 29 3149* and **Doodle Cooma Arms**; *tel: (069) 29 3013*.

SIGHTSEEING

Henty is 12 km north of Culcairn and is well within Mad Dan Morgan's territory. It was here that he shot and killed Sergeant Smyth, the leader of a troop of mounted police. A memo-rial to the sergeant is on the road to the west of the town. Henty was originally known as Doodle Cooma, but wiser heads prevailed and it was renamed after a squatter in the area. This is where Hadlie Taylor, a local farmer, unveiled his invention, the header-harvester, at the town's agricultural show in 1914. It revolu-tionised farming, and there is a memorial in the centre of the town, with the original machine on display in **Henty Park**.

ALBURY

Tourist Information for Albury and Wodonga: Gateway Information and Tourist Complex; *tel. (060) 41 3875*.

ACCOMMODATION AND FOOD

A wide range of accommodation is available in Albury; what follows is a brief selection.

Albury Manor House Motel, *593 Young St; tel: 41 1777*. **Albury Georgian Motor Inn**, *599 Young St; tel: 21 8744*. **Meramie Motor Inn**, *595 Kiewa St; tel: 21 8100*. **The Albury Regent Motel**, *Dean St; tel: 21 8355*. **Allawa Motor Inn**, *corner Hume Hwy and Olive St; tel: 21 6133*. **Commodore Motel** (GC), *515 Kiewa St; tel: 21 3344*.

EATING AND DRINKING

Albury Kebab Place, *462 Dean St; tel: 6041 6220*. **Ambassador Restaurant**, *467 Dean St; tel: 6021 5535*. **Beefeater's Bistro**, *324 Wodonga Pl. (Hume Hwy); tel: 6021 6216*. **Bahn Thai Restaurant**, *592 Kiewa St; tel: 6041 5555*. **Cafe Victor**, *corner Dean and Elizabeth Sts; tel: 6021 8447*. **Cultura Cafe & Restaurant**, *515 Kiewa St; tel: 6041 3884*.

SIGHTSEEING

You cannot write about Albury – named after an English village – without mentioning its sis-ter town of **Wodonga**. The two form the **Albury-Wodonga region**, which is the only planned growth area in Australia. The romantic way of describing Albury is 'where the moun-tains meet the Murray', and this is, indeed, accurate. The Murray River at Albury forms the boundary between New South Wales and Victoria and played an important role in the development of Australia. It was here, in 1824, that the explorers Hume and Hovell crossed the Murray. The town was surveyed in 1842. Originally it was simply called The Crossing Place.

Albury was at the vanguard of the 'green' movement, as in 1870 it was decided to pre-serve existing trees and plant more to line the streets. The first bridge across the Murray was opened in 1861. Up until that date, the only way across was by punt. The paddle steamers started coming up the river from Adelaide in 1855, loaded with settlers and supplies. In 1858 the first paddle steamers were built in Albury.

In 1936, the **Hume Weir** was built, creat-ing one of the largest artificial lakes in Australia – **Lake Hume**. This lake is central to much of the holiday activity in Albury, with all forms of aquatic recreation. You can even go trout fishing at the **Hume Weir Trout Farm**. Worth seeing is the **Ettamogah Pub**, *Burma Rd, tel: 26 2366*. This was the cartoon creation of Ken Maynard – an outback pub where trouble was always brewing. Ettamogah is said, facetiously, to be Aboriginal for 'let's have a drink'. In 1987, a pub based on the cartoon was created, and although the customers are not quite as colourful as in the drawings, it is still an amazing place to have a beer.

The Regional Museum is a converted old pub in *Wodonga Pl., Noreuil Park*. It tells the history of the area and the long rivalry between the towns on each side of the river. Open daily 1030–1630. There are many protected buildings dating from the 1860s, including the **Courthouse**, where the magistrate Thomas Browne once reigned – better known under his pen name Rolf Boldrewood, as the author of *Robbery Under Arms*. The **railway station** is a masterpiece of Victorian Italianate excess and is classified by the National Trust.

On the Murray, the **Gateway Tourist Complex** is at the site of the original Crossing Place. Between Sept–Mar, when there is enough water, the paddle steamer, *Cumberoona*, still pulls into the original wharf at Echuca (see p. 171), which was built in the 1860s.

WODONGA

Tourist Information: Tourism Albury-Wodonga, *553 Kiewa St, Albury; tel: 6023 8173*.

ACCOMMODATION AND FOOD

The Blazing Stump Motel *(FL), Tallangatta Rd (Murray Valley Hwy); tel: 56 3433*. **Belvoir Village Motel**, *corner Melbourne Rd and Moorefield Park Rd; tel: 24 5344*. **Stagecoach Motel** *(BW), 188 Melbourne Rd; tel: 24 3044*. **Motel Wellington Wodonga**, *46 High St; tel: 24 2400*. **Murray Valley Motel** *(BU), 196 Melbourne Rd; tel: 24 1422*. **Warrina Motor Inn**, *31 High St; tel: 24 2211*. **Sanctuary Park Motel** *(BU), 11 High St; tel: 24 1122*.

The Steak Pit, *Elgin St; tel: 24 1262*. Licensed. **Blazing Stump Motel Restaurant**, *Talangatta Rd; tel 56 3433*. Licensed.

SIGHTSEEING

This city on the Murray River is always mentioned together with Albury. It is 306 km north-east of Melbourne. Wodonga, an Aboriginal word meaning 'edible nut', 'edible plant growing in a lagoon' or 'bulrushes' – interpretations differ – was the original name. When the town was surveyed in 1852, it was changed to Belvoir, after Lord Belvoir of Leicestershire, an English Member of Parliament of the time. But, in 1869, the name reverted to Wodonga as the townspeople refused to call it Belvoir, on the grounds that they didn't know how to pronounce it. The town's founders are generally regarded as being Charles and Paul Huon, who established 'runs' (farms) there in the 1830s. The expansion of the town kept pace with the increased use of the Murray for trade.

This is the home of the **Flying Fruit Fly Circus**, which has achieved a measure of international fame. It can also claim that the **Murray Grey** cattle, one of Australia's distinctive breeds, was developed in the area.

The Royal Australian Artillery Ordnance Corps Museum, *31 Supply Battalion, Gaza Ridge Barracks, Bandiana; tel: 55 2525*, is 4 km out of town, and has a major display of army memorabilia. It was once the largest army storage depot in the Southern hemisphere. Open Mon, Tues, Fri 1000–1500, weekends 1000–1600; $3. **Stonleigh Cottage**, *50 High St; tel: 55 9200*, is the oldest remaining building in Wodonga, dating from 1857. It is now a florist's shop, but inspection can be arranged. Eric Sumsion spent a considerable amount of time in the 1950s renovating and re-establishing the **Sumsion Gardens** *(end of Huon St; tel: 55 9200)* which overlook **Lake Huon** and are named in his honour.

DENILIQUIN

Tourist Information: Tourism/Visitor Services, *George St; tel: (03) 5881 4150*.

ACCOMMODATION AND FOOD

Deniliquin Country Club Motor Inn, *68 Crispe St; tel: 5881 5299*. **Settlement Motor Inn**, *327–331 Victoria St; tel: 5881 3999*. **Centre Point Motel**, *399 Cressy St; tel: 5881*

Bushrangers

C onsidering Australia's convict history, it is perhaps natural that the major heroes of the country should be criminals – bushrangers. The bushrangers were effectively Australian highwaymen and the greatest of them all was **Ned Kelly**. He is such an integral part of Australian folklore that the phrase 'as game as Ned Kelly' is still used to this day. Ned was probably born in 1855 and was most articulate, sending letters to the general public and making speeches. In these he stated his bushranger philosophy, a mixture of Irish nationalism and Australian republicanism. His family had, undoubtedly, been badly treated by the police, and he truly believed that Australia should be a republic. His ideas are still alive today. The Ned Kelly gang terrorised the police and some of the population for over 2 years. Most of the gang eventually died in a shoot-out at **Glerowan Inn**, but Ned wore armour and was captured by being shot in the legs. He was hanged despite public petitions for his reprieve.

Not many mourned **Mad Dan Morgan**. He was of Welsh descent and probably suffered from schizophrenia, for he frequently went into mad rages. He was referred to as 'a blood-smeared monster, festooned with the bones of countless victims'. He worked in Victoria and New South Wales, and was a committed socialist who did much to improve the working conditions of station hands. But he also murdered and robbed. He was eventually gunned down at Peechelba Station in northern Victoria in 1865. After his death a bush-ballad appeared telling of the 'tragic deed of Morgan's death.'

The darling of them all was **Bold Ben Hall**, who was, by all accounts, handsome and dashing. He worked in the Lachlan River district of New South Wales in the 1820s, and was regarded by many (including policemen) as a man of decency and kindness. He was betrayed to the troopers and shot dead by the Aboriginal tracker Billy Sdargin.

3544. **Deniliquin Golf Leisure Resort**, *Memorial Park; tel: 5881 3835.* **Deniliquin Motel**, *286 Wick St; tel: 5881 1820.* **Peppin Motor Inn**, *Crispe St; tel: 5881 2722.*

Bus Stop Café, *344 Whitelock St; tel: 5881 4446.* **China Plate Restaurant**, *378 Victoria St; tel: 5881 5605.* **Deniliquin Bowling Club Restaurant Bistro**, *Wick St; tel: 5881 3011.* **Ho's Chinese Restaurant**, *142 End St; tel: 5881 2089.* **Tee Jays Restaurant**, *399 Cressy St; tel: 5881 7220*

SIGHTSEEING

The largest irrigation area in Australia surrounds Deniliquin, which also boasts the largest rice mill in the southern hemisphere. This is also an area renowned for premium merino sheep. Denilquin is 737 km from Sydney, say 8 hrs driving, 543 km from Canberra (6 hrs) and 280 km from Melbourne (3 hrs).

In the centre of town, opposite the Deniliquin town hall in *Cressy St,* is the **Island Sanctuary**, a wildlife reserve with kangaroos, emus and 80 different bird species. It is also the beginning of a riverside walk running along the Edward River to **McLean Beach**, an inland beach with swimming and picnic facilities.

Deniliquin is the centre of the Wetlands area and, at the **Office of State Forests** in *Victoria St,* there is information on all the wetlands in the Murray area and how to get there. South of Deniliquin is the **Moira Lake Wetland System**, which extends over 1200 hectares of lakes and swamps and has a large ibis rookery.

The first major hotel in the area was the **Imperial Hotel** on *Hay Rd,* which was opened in 1872. It was destroyed by fire but has been authentically recreated and is now the reception area for the **Pioneer Tourist Park** (open 7 days, *tel: 81 5066*). Within the park is a display of pioneer antique steam and pumping equipment, most of it in working order, collected from the early camps on the Snowy River.

The town has a series of connecting lagoons and parks, with **Waring Gardens** featuring an aviary. Nearby is **Steven's Weir**, which was built on the Edward River to divert water into 360 farms in the surrounding area. This has become a picnic area and fishing spot.

The old **Deniliquin police inspector's residence** has been fully restored by the local historical society. Open Tues 1000–1200.

At the edge of the **Tuppal Forest**, *8 km along Lawson Syphon Rd*, is a popular picnic and camping spot. For overnight stays there are air-conditioned family units to rent *(tel: 81 5518)*.

HAY

Tourist Information: Tourist and Amenities Centre, *407 Moppett St; tel (069) 93 1003*.

ACCOMMODATION AND FOOD

Bishops Lodge Motel (FL), *35 Sturt Hwy; tel: 93 3003*. **Bidgee Motor Inn**, *74 Lachlan St; tel: (069) 93 2260*. **Cobb Highway Inlander Motel** (BU), *83 Lachlan St; tel: 93 1901*.

Hay Services Club Restaurant, *371 Murray St; tel: 93 1623*.

SIGHTSEEING

Situated on the Sturt and Mid-Western Hwys and the Murrumbidgee River, Hay is the commercial centre for the surrounding farming area. This was a stopping point for the famous Cobb & Co. coaches which, for a few short years, held outback Australia together. In the **coach house**, *corner of Cobb Hwy*, in the centre of the town, is *Sunbeam*, the original coach that travelled between Deniliquin and Wilcannia. The town has many restored buildings dating from the last century, including the **Court House**, the now defunct **Railway Station** and the **Conservation and Lands Department**. All of the buildings are floodlit at night.

GRIFFITH

Tourist Information: Griffith's Visitor Centre, *Jondaryan and Banna Aves; tel: (069) 62 4145*.

ACCOMMODATION AND FOOD

The **Gemini Hotel** *(FL), 201 Banna Ave, PO Box 478; tel: 62 3833*; **Yambil Inn Motel**, *155 Yambil St; tel: 64 1233*; **Bagtown Inn Motel**, *2 Blumer Ave; tel: 62 7166*; **Acacia Motel**, *923 Irrigation Way; tel: 62 4422*; **Citrus**

Motel, *Jondaryan Ave; tel: 62 6233*. **Griffith Motor Inn**, *96 Banna Ave; tel: 62 1800*.

Golden Chopsticks, *14 Probert Ave; tel: 62 6629*. Open Tues–Sun, dinner. **Pizzeria Villagio**, *4 Yenda Pl.; tel: 65 1588*. BYO.

SIGHTSEEING

Like Canberra, this is a relatively new city designed by the American architect, Walter Burley Griffin. Right in the middle of the Riverina and the Murrumbidgee Irrigation Area, it services a large, agricultural area. To get an overview of the area, either take a quick trip in a light aircraft; **Griffith Aero Club** at the aerodrome, *tel: 64 1666*; or a hot air balloon trip at dawn; **Balloon Aloft**, *tel: 64 2322*.

The wine produced in Griffith is known as irrigation wine, and connoisseurs swear it has a faint taste of salt, although mere ordinary consumers have never been able to detect it. **Winemakers of the Riverina**, *tel: 64 1625*, have put together a case of a dozen local wines, which will give any visitor a clear idea of the quality of the wine offered. The biggest winery in the area is **McWilliams Wines** in Hanwood, *tel: 63 0001*, which is 8 km south of Griffith and, perhaps sadly, has both the **Big Barrel** and the **Big Bottle**. **De Bortoli Wines** at Bilbul, 10 km from Griffith, *off Yoogali Rd, tel: 64 9444*, is renowned for its sweet Botrytis (Noble Rot) wine. They are generically known in Australia as stickies and are drunk at the end of dinner. There are six other vineyards in the area; all welcome visitors.

The **Pioneer Park Museum**, *Scenic Hill; tel: 62 4196*, has forty historic buildings, including an early store and farm equipment from the turn of the century. The museum is in **Pioneer Park**, which is 18 hectares of native bushland, and has a series of lookouts, each with a view of Griffith. **The Griffith Regional Art Gallery** (open Wed–Sat, 1030–1630; *tel: 62 5991*) is in a 1930s art deco building and has two galleries. One has a permanent collection of Australian designed jewellery and the other is home to an ever-changing range of travelling exhibitions.

The Griffith Wine and Food Festival is held at Easter and attracts participants from all over Australia, as well as international interest. The Visitors Bureau has details.

QUEENSLAND

More than 20 per cent of Australia is occupied by Queensland, which extends from the arid wastes of the Simpson Desert through the lush greenery of rain forest out to the wonders of the Great Barrier Reef.

Every state in Australia makes the claim that it is the holiday state, but this probably holds more true for Queensland than anywhere else. It has pretty much something for everyone. In the southern part of the state it is the somewhat brash, honky-tonk appeal of Surfers Paradise and the Gold Coast. In the north it is the relatively isolated splendour of the Cape York peninsula. The state capital, Brisbane, is a sophisticated city with much to offer the visitor although it is now being challenged by Cairns as an entry point to the state.

GEOGRAPHY

The easiest way to think of the layout of Queensland is as three roughly parallel strips. A hundred kilometres out at sea the Great Barrier Reef, then the coastal strip with its endless beaches and inland, still running roughly parallel, the Great Dividing Range, running up the centre and only living up to its name at the extreme ends. But it does define the state and separates the coastal plains from the inland.

One distinguishing feature of the countryside of Queensland is the massive area of sugar

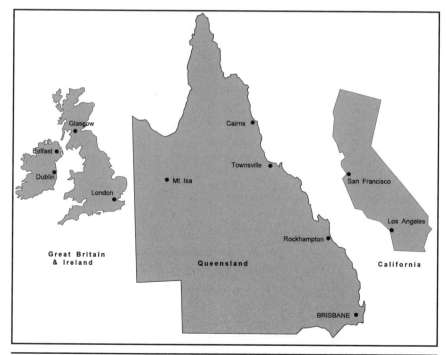

Glasgow

Belfast

Dublin

London

Great Britain & Ireland

Cairns

Townsville

Mt Isa

Rockhampton

Queensland

BRISBANE

San Francisco

Los Angeles

California

cane fields, which covers the river flats and defines the countryside for 1400 km from Nambour to Mossman.

Queensland is not over-populated. Although it is the second largest state in Australia its 3 million inhabitants are not spread evenly over the 1,727,530 sq km of the state. Instead, they tend to be clustered in the south-east corner, leaving the rest of the state as a vast area dotted with small farming settlements and towns with the occasional small 'metropolis' like **Mt Isa** to give it presence.

THE COAST

The south-east corner with the **Gold Coast** and the **Sunshine Coast** is still defining itself as far as tourists are concerned and the area is undoubtedly going through some growing pains as it tries to decide whether to be a tropical Blackpool or Coney Island or a desirable destination for overseas visitors. At the moment vulgarity is winning the battle. The exception to this is **Brisbane**, which, since Expo 88, a significant happening in the life of the city, has become a pleasant and truly international place, avoiding the excesses of Surfers Paradise and the Gold Coast, and has a distinctly urbane, if tropical, appeal. This crowded part of Queensland is also popular with Australians as a place to retire and for the past few years it has led the country in net population growth.

Urban development in Queensland away from the south-east corner is basically around coastal towns – Bundaberg, Rockhampton, Mackay, Townsville and Cairns – all of which are going through a period of major growth.

Off shore there are 700 named islands which face the 5400 km coastline. The islands are enclosed by the **Great Barrier Reef**, one of the wonders of the natural world, which runs for 2400 km from Bundaberg in the south to the tip of the Cape York Peninsula in the north. Although the reef does eventually come to brush the shore, normally there is a 100 km wide channel between the reef and the mainland and the result is some of the safest sailing waters anywhere in the world, and paradoxically some of the most dangerous. Because while yachts can sail the Whitsunday Passage with impunity provided ordinary care is taken,

larger ships have had a distressing tendency to run on to coral reefs in the darkness and the area has, literally, hundreds of commercial wrecks. But holiday yachting has been pretty much exempt from these disasters.

OUTBACK QUEENSLAND

Once you travel north or west of the crowded corner you come to a vast and pretty empty country. There are over 300 National Parks in Queensland and together they cover an area of 27,000 sq km, more land than is contained in many countries. Most of the roads across the area are good if narrow, the only major exception being at the very northern tip of Cape York Peninsula where most, if not all, of the roads are unsealed and in the far north impassable except by four wheel drive.

On the other side of the Great Dividing Range is the outback of Queensland, that vast scorched land with properties – farms – as big as English counties. In that wide plain there is one mountainous anomaly, the Selwyn Range, which has one of the world's richest deposits of silver, copper, lead and zinc and is the source of wealth and employment for Mt Isa. In the rest of this arid outback you find towns like **Longreach**, which is where Qantas started, and **Birdsville**, the start of the notorious Birdsville Track (see p.375). To the north, heading toward the Gulf of Carpentaria, is the **Gulf country**, which is good for cattle-raising but in the wet season becomes a morass of unpassable roads, some of the smaller towns and homesteads being cut off for weeks.

And then, almost as an exclamation mark atop Queensland, there is **Cape York Peninsula**, which extends out into the Torres Strait with much of its 700 km spike occupied by Aboriginal reserves or National Parks. It is a rugged land and yet, like most of Queensland, a very welcoming one.

CLIMATE

More than half of the state lies above the Tropic of Capricorn and the weather is normally pleasant with only two distinguishable seasons – a short winter, when it never gets cold, and a long, pleasant summer, which is normally an endless succession of sun-drenched days.

BRISBANE

Brisbane is inland on the Brisbane River. At Moreton Bay, where the river comes out to the sea, there is said to be an island for every day of the year. Some of these are large islands that shelter the coast from any storms coming in from the sea – South Stradbrooke, North Stradbrooke, Moreton and Bribie Island, which is opposite the Gold Coast.

The northern outer suburbs of Brisbane, which run along the Redcliffe Peninsula and the bay – Scarborough, Redcliffe, Margate, Woody Point, Brighton and Sandgate – are now true Australian suburbia, with not much to attract the visitor. Even the beaches are less than attractive when compared to those of the islands further north.

On the other hand, two of the suburbs to the south of the mouth of the Brisbane River – Wynum and Manly – have their own attractions, mainly connected with boating. There are marinas, boating areas and harbours right along the waterfront.

TOURIST INFORMATION

Queensland Tourist and Travel, *123 Eagle St; tel: 3833 5400* or **Queensland Government Travel Centre**, *Edward and Adelaide Sts; tel: 3833 5412* or **Brisbane City Council Information Booth**, *Queen St Mall; tel: 3229 5918*.

ARRIVING AND DEPARTING

If you are flying in to Brisbane the airport is about 10 km from the centre. There is a SkyTrans bus ($6 a person), which is timed to meet incoming flights and runs between 0500 and 2030. The price of a taxi to town will be between $15 and $20.

If you come by train or bus you arrive at the **Transit Centre** in *Roma St*. Taxis have a rank outside and local buses also leave from there.

GETTING AROUND

As Brisbane is a small city, it is entirely reasonable to explore the city on foot. However, Brisbane also has an excellent public transport system, although this ceases at midnight.

Taxis can be hailed in the street and are always at the rank in *Roma St*. To book a taxi try **B&W Cabs**; *tel: 3238 1000*, **Yellow Cabs**; *tel: 3391 0191*.

Cyclists are well catered for, with maps at the tourist office showing bike routes around the city. There are several places near *Roma St* where you can rent bicycles.

If you are using the buses, trains and ferries, the best buy is the **Roverlink**, which gives you unlimited travel for one day at $8. For information on all types of travel; *tel: 13 1230*. The suburban buses are called **Cityxpress**, with **Citybus** covering the centre of the city.

Citysights open-top tram – a bus in disguise – runs daily, except Tues, 0900–1600 and a pass costs $10. The tram takes you around all the sights of the city and it is an excellent way to get oriented.

The electric Citytrain network runs out to the suburbs and leave Central Station in *Ann St*.

Brisbane is bisected by the river and ferries run across it from several places. Prices start at $1.20. Two main departure points in the city are in *Eagle St*; Waterfront Place and the Riverside Centre.

STAYING IN BRISBANE

Accommodation

There is a wide choice of lodging, listed here in arough order of price, most expensive first.

203

Conrad International Treasury Casino, *William & George Sts; tel: 3306 8888.* **The Heritage – A Beaufort Hotel,** *corner Margaret and Edward Sts; tel: 3221 1999.* **Sheraton Brisbane Hotel & Towers,** *249 Turbot St; tel: 3835 3535.* **Brisbane Hilton Hotel,** *190 Elizabeth St; tel: 3231 3131.* **Carlton Crest Hotel,** *corner Ann and Roma Sts; tel: 3229 9111.* **Country Comfort Lennons Hotel** *(CC), 66 Queen St; tel: 3222 3222.* **All Seasons Abbey Hotel,** *160 Roma St; tel: 3136 1444.* **Albert Park Hotel,** *551 Wickham Terrace, Spring Hill 4000; tel: 3831 3111.*

Brisbane Parkroyal, *corner Alice & Albert Sts; tel: 3221 3411.* **Hotel Grand Chancellor,** *corner Leichhardt St & Wickham Terrace, Spring Hill 4000; tel: 3831 4055.* **Radisson North Quay Hotel,** *293 North Quay; tel: 3236 1440.* **Ridge Hotel,** *corner Leichhardt and Henry Sts; tel: 3831 5000.* **Novotel Brisbane,** *200 Creek St; tel: 3309 3309.* **Brisbane City Travelodge** *(SP), Roma St (PO Box 5, Roma St, Brisbane 4003); tel: 3238 2222.* **Camelot Inn** *(FL), 40 Astor Terrace; tel: 3832 5115.* **Gazebo Hotel,** *345 Wickham Terrace; tel: 3831 6177.* **Mercure Hotel Brisbane,** *85 North Quay; tel: 3236 3300.* **Metro Inn Tower Mill Hotel,** *239 Wickham Terrace; tel: 3832 1421.* **Wickham Terrace Motel** *(BW), 491 Wickham Terrace, Spring Hill 4000; tel: 3839 9611.*

Metropolitan Motor Inn *(FL), 106 Leichhardt St, corner Lt Edward St; tel: 3831 6000.* **Astor Motel,** *193 Wickham Terrace; tel: 3831 9522.* **Bellevue Hotel Brisbane,** *103 George St; tel: 3221 6044.* **Gregory Terrace Motor Inn,** *397 Gregory Terrace, Spring Hill 4000; tel: 3832 1769.* **Spring Hill Terraces Motel,** *260 Water St, Spring Hill 4000; tel: 3854 1048.* **Soho Motel,** *333 Wickham Terrace; tel: 3831 7722.* **Embassy Hotel** (no parking), *corner Edward and Elizabeth Sts; tel: 3221 7616.* **Majestic Hotel,** *382 George St; tel: 3229 0772. Fax 07–3229 0772.* **Marrs Town House Motel,** *391 Wickham Terrace, corner Twine St; tel: 3831 5388.* **Explorers Inn,** *63 Turbot St; tel: 3211 3488.* **HI: Brisbane City,** *392 Upper Roma St, Queensland 4000; tel: 3236 1004.* **HI: Brisbane Gardens,** *15 Mitchell St, Kedron 4031; tel: 3857 1245.*

Eating and Drinking

Daniel's Steakhouse, *145 Eagle St; tel: 3832 3444.* Lunch and dinner Mon–Fri. Licensed. **Friday's,** *123 Eagle St; tel: 3832 2122.* Open seven days. Licensed. There are three restaurants in the complex. **Il Centro,** *1 Eagle Street Pier; tel: 3221 6090.* Lunch Sun–Fri. Dinner daily. Licensed. Italian cuisine. **Jo-Jo's,** *Queen and Albert Sts; tel: 3221 2113.* Open daily. Licensed. **Michael's Riverside,** *Waterfront Pl., 123 Eagle St; tel: 3832 5522.* Licensed. High quality, perhaps the best in Brisbane. **Oshin,** *256 Adelaide St; tel: 3229 0410.* Lunch Mon–Fri. Dinner Mon–Sat. Licensed. Japanese food. **Siggi's at the Port Office,** *Edward St; tel: 3221 4555.* Open daily. Licensed. **Tortilla,** *26 Elizabeth Arcade, off Charlotte St; tel: 3221 4416.* Open daily for dinner, weekdays lunch. Licensed. Spanish cuisine.

Communications

The post office is at *261 Queen St; tel: 3405 1202 or 3405 1448.*

Consulates and Embassies

New Zealand: *288 Edward St; tel: 3221 9933.*
UK: *BP House, 193 North Quay; tel: 3236 2575.*
USA: *383 Wickham Terrace; tel: 3831 3340.*

Money

Queensland banking hours are, like most of Australia, Mon–Fri 0930–1600. Major branches can be found in the centre around *Queen* and *Edward Sts.*

There are two **Thomas Cook Foreign Exchange** branches at *195 Adelaide St; tel: 3236 4966* and *Shop 135 Level Q, Myer Centre, Elizabeth & Albert Sts; tel: 3221 9749.*

SHOPPING

Shopping is a major scene in Brisbane, mainly because of the international tourists, who use Brisbane as a gateway to the Queensland coast. Central for all shopping activities is **Queen Street Mall,** which runs from *Edward St* to *George St,* and has hundreds of shops. A pedestrian precinct only, it is a warm and relaxed place for shopping, browsing or just watching the crowds go by.

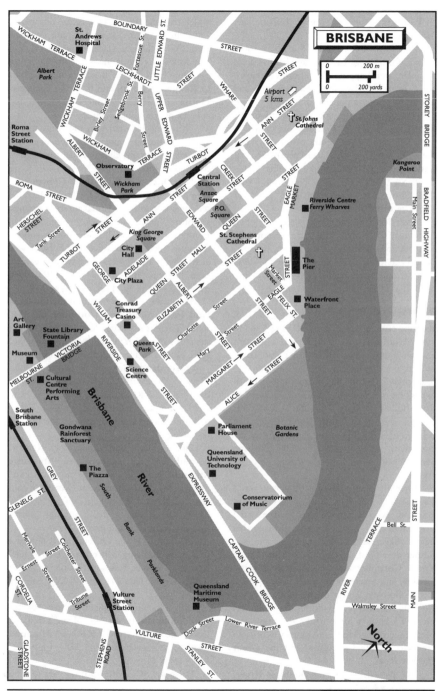

BRISBANE

| 0 | 200 m |
| 0 | 200 yards |

Airport 5 kms

Paddy's Markets (*corner Florence and Macquarie Sts, New Farm; tel: 3252 7211;* open Mon–Fri 0900–1600, Sat and Sun 0830–1600) is across from Kangaroo Point and has five acres of undercover shopping. Fresh fruit, vegetables, meat, stores, hardware, toys, jewellery, new and second hand clothing, books and fabric.

There is a maze of speciality shops in the picturesque suburb of **Paddington**, which is only 3 mins from the centre of the city. The shops are mainly in *Given and Latrobe Terrace* at **Paddington Circle**. Open Mon–Fri 0900–1700, Sat 0900–1600. **The National Trust Gift Shop** is in **The Mansions** (*tel: 3221 4965),* next to Parliament House.

Riverside Centre Markets are only open on Sunday 0700–1600, and there are normally over 300 stalls featuring glass blowers, weavers, potters and leather-workers; there are children's activities and, quite often, a five piece calypso band. It is at the *Riverside Centre, 123 Eagle St.*

Brisbane came of age when it held the Expo in 1988. Until that time it had been a pleasant enough country town rather than a city, which moved along gracefully with no excitement, little pzzazz. **Expo 88**, a true international exposition of world class standards, changed all that. Buildings were refurbished, restaurants opened, the whole **South Bank**, which had been an ugly warehouse and industrial area the city centre, was brought to life. Brisbane became one of the most exciting cities in Australia.

When the Expo closed, although it was a traumatic experience for many of the citizens of Brisbane, who felt somewhat deflated, the magic remained. Since that date Brisbane has never looked back. The river banks have been further developed, specifically with the **Eagle Street Complex** and the **Gateway Marine Centre**, and several new hotels have opened. Today Brisbane is one of the most attractive cities in Australia and is becoming more and more of a gateway for tourists – the airport has been much upgraded and extended – who come to explore Queensland and the **Great Barrier Reef**.

The city is defined by the **Brisbane River**, which meanders through the centre of the city, and, with its bank-side gardens and developments, gives the city shape and character. It is also a means of transportation, with the ferries operating from next to the **Botanic Gardens** to **Kangaroo Point**, and from the **Customs House** to the same destination. The ferries stop at half a dozen points along the river.

There is a wide range of museums and art galleries in Brisbane, giving lie to the suggestion that love of a warm climate is the sure sign of the artistic philistine.

The **Queensland Cultural Centre** contains the **Queensland Art Gallery**, which has serious collections of Australian art, paintings, sculpture, prints, ceramics, major French, European, Asian and English works, antique furniture, silver, glassware and pottery, as well as frequently being home to travelling exhibitions. It is at South Bank; *tel: 3414 7303.* Open daily 1000–1700. Wed late closing at 2000.

Also at the Cultural Centre is the **Queensland Performing Arts Complex**; *tel: 3840 7400.* There is no charge for admission to visit the premises, which include a concert hall, theatres, plaza, art gallery, museum and library.

Queensland Museum is in the *Cultural Centre, S. Brisbane; tel: 3840 7635,* and is open daily 0900–1700, with a late opening Wed to 2000. It houses a vast range of exhibits relating to anthropology, geology, zoology, history and technology.

The old South Brisbane dry dock is incorporated into the **Queensland Maritime Museum**, which is next to the old site of Expo 88, near the Cultural Centre at *Dock St, S. Brisbane; tel: 3844 5361.* Open daily 1000–1700. $4. It has on display the steam tug *Forceful,* models, documents and historic pictures.

The history of the Queensland Railways is told at the **Railway Museum**, which is adjacent to Redbank Railway Station; *tel: 3288 4747.* Open Tues–Fri 0900–1630, Sat–Sun 0900–1700.

Early agricultural implements, coaches, the fully restored rail motor No. 74 and a doll collection are all on display at **Redland Museum**, *Smith St, Cleveland; tel: 3286 3494.* Open Sun 1100–1600. $1.

Museum of Contemporary Art (*8 Petrie*

Terrace, Brisbane; tel: 3392 0033; open Mon–Sat 1200–1700) has among its many exhibitions, a young artist's gallery and, on the street, a micro gallery for the passing parade.

The oldest art society in Queensland has been operating since 1887. It has local works on display at the **Royal Queensland Art Society Gallery**, 419 Upper Edward St; tel: 3831 3455. Open Tues–Fri 1000–1600, Sat 1400–1600.

Victoria Barracks Museum is at Petrie Terrace, Brisbane; tel: 3233 4326. Open Sun 1300–1600, but will open on weekdays if requested. Displays uniforms, photographs, weapons and other memorabilia of Queensland military units dating from pre-Federation days.

Of all the cities in Australia, Melbourne is the only one still running an active and extremely effective tram service, although at one time they were common to all state capitals. The **Brisbane Tramway Museum** (20 Tramway St, Ferny Grove; tel: 3351 1776; open Sun 1330–1600, $4) shows the history of the Brisbane City Council Transport System and, importantly, includes rides on the trams.

Brisbane is very much a city of green spaces and gardens. One of the glories of the city, the **Botanic Gardens** in Alice St, is open from sunrise to sunset with guided tours 1100 and 1300 Tues–Fri. Tel: 870 8136. They were designed in 1855 by Walter Hill. **Southbank Parklands** (tel: 867 2020) consists of sixteen hectares of landscaped parklands on the south bank of the river, with restaurants, 'The Piazza', a beach area, boat rides and entertainment.

Queensland Aboriginal Creations is a curio section within the Department of Community Services. It has a comprehensive selection of authentic Aboriginal artefacts and handicrafts. Open Mon–Fri 0830–1630, 135–147 George St, Brisbane; tel: 3224 5730.

The Brisbane Antique and Art Centre (791 Sandgate Road, Clayfield; tel: 3262 1444; open Mon–Sat 0900–1700, Sun 1000–1700) and the **Cordelia St Antique and Art Centre** (Old Church, corner Cordelia St and Glenelg St; tel: 07 844 8514; open Wed–Sun 1000–1700) are but two of the many antique centres in Australia, which bring groups of dealers together under one roof. The word antique is used in a looser sense than perhaps in Europe,

and collectables would be a more accurate term.

Cleveland Bayside Markets, Bloomfield St, Cleveland; tel: 3821 1666, are on the bay and dedicated to local arts and crafts. Open Sun 0900–1500.

One of the two remaining convict-built buildings in Brisbane is now the **Commissariat Stores** (115 William St, Brisbane; tel: 3221 4198; open Tues–Fri 1100–1400, Sun 1100–1600, $1). Inside are three floors of displays, including Aboriginal and convict relics, artefacts, costumes, furniture and paintings. It was built in 1829 on what was the town's original wharf. It also houses the offices of the **Royal Historical Society of Queensland**.

There are over 200 exhibiting potters housed in a magnificent century old church hall at the **Potters Gallery**, corner Malt and Brunswick Sts, Fortitude Valley; tel: 3358 5121. Open Wed–Fri 1000–1600, Sat 1100–1700, Sun 1400–1700.

Brisbane's Municipal Administration is in **City Hall** in King George Sq, which contains an art gallery, museum, concert hall and public library. It was built over a period of ten years starting in 1920, and its centrepiece is the clock tower, which was, for many years, the highest structure in the city. The doors open at 0700 every morning. **Parliament House** next to the **Botanic Gardens**, is a fine example of French Renaissance architecture and was opened in 1868. It is in a parkland setting opposite the Botanic Gardens – corner of George and Alice Sts; tel: 3226 7562. The Public Gallery is open for visitors when Parliament is sitting: Tues and Thur 1030–1300, 1430–1800, 1930 until House rises, Wed 1430–1800, 1930 until House rises. There are guided tours Mon–Fri, 1000 and 1400.

The **Treasury Building** is between George and William Sts, and is a solid 1890s structure, which now houses the **Conrad Treasury Casino**. Set in a reserve of natural forest, and including Queensland heritage buildings, a pub, a general store, a slab hut, a shipwright's cottage and **Earlystreet Historical Village** is the site of the home of three former Queensland Premiers. It is in the suburbs at 75 McIlwraith

Ave, Norman Park; tel: 07 398 6866 and is open daily, 1000–1630. $6.

In the **Parklands** area, which is next to the Cultural Centre, there are several attractions as well as a beach on the Brisbane River. In the area, the **Gondwana Rainforest Sanctuary** is a great rain forest experience, complete with a pool containing crocodiles. One hundred native animals live in the sanctuary, including koalas, green tree frogs, lizards and Tasmanian devils. (*South Bank, S. Brisbane; tel: 3846 4155;* open daily 1000–2200, $9.50.) Another attraction in Parklands is the world's largest collection of Australian butterfly species in their own flowering forest environment at the **South Bank Butterfly House**, *South Bank, S. Brisbane; tel: 3844 1112/1137.* Open daily 1000–1800. $6.

The **Southern Cross** is the aircraft in which Sir Charles Kingsford Smith – a native of Brisbane – made the first air crossing of the Pacific Ocean. It is on display at **Brisbane Airport** and can be viewed at any time.

Our World Environment is a pavilion that enables visitors to experience both desert and Antarctic environments. It is at *South Bank, S. Brisbane; tel: 3844 6555.* $8.

Old Windmill, at *Wickham Terrace*, was built originally by convicts in 1828 under Captain Patrick Logan, an infamous prison warden, who was later murdered. The design was faulty so a treadmill had to be used to drive the grindstones. Since then it has been used as a fire lookout, a meteorological station and as the transmission station in the 1930s for some of the world's first television transmissions. Although the grounds are open every day, there is no entry to the actual windmill.

Out of Town

Within easy driving distance of the city are many attractions. Situated 11 km from the city, on the banks of the Brisbane River at Fig Tree Pocket, Lone Pine Koala Sanctuary is a fauna sanctuary – the largest of its kind in Australia – with native animals and birds and although, yes, it does contain koalas, it also has lots of kangaroos. (*Jesmond Rd, Fig Tree Pocket; tel: 3222 7278;* open daily 0845–1700. $10.)

The **Cosmic Skydome** in the **Thomas**

Brisbane Planetarium, 6 km to the west of the city, is the largest planetarium in Australia and uses an elaborate projection system to throw an image of the night sky on the inside of the overhead dome in the star theatre. It is at *Mt Coot-Tha Botanic Gardens, Mt Coot-Tha Rd, Toowong; tel: 3377 8896.* Open Wed–Fri 1530 and 1930, Sat 1330, 1530 and 1930, Sun 1330 and 1430. Children under the age of six are not allowed in.

The Bunya Park Wildlife Sanctuary, *Bunya Park Dr., Eatons Hill, Brisbane; tel: 264 1200,* has 8½ hectares of natural Australian bush, with one of the world's largest breeding kangaroo colonies as well as a wide range of other Australian wildlife. The sanctuary has picnic and barbecue facilities available. Open daily 0930–1700, $9.50.

Native Australian animals, horse and buggy rides, train rides and picnics are the main attractions at the **Forest Of Fame**, *Jamieson Rd, Atkinson Dam, Eowood; tel: 075–86 4474.* Open daily 0900–1700. $4.

A fort, which has now become a historical fort, is **Fort Lytton National Park**, *South St, off Lytton Rd, Lytton; tel: 3393 4647.* Open daily except Sat 1000–1600. $2.

A town of the past has been recreated at **Caboolture Historical Village** *Beerburrum Rd, Caboolture; tel: 071–95 4581.* Open daily 0930–1530. $3. **Claremont**, *1A Milford St, Ipswich; tel: 3202 2005,* is a National Trust historical homestead. Open Sun 1000–1600, $2.

A nursery surrounded by pine forest, **King Country** (*58 Dinwoodie Rd, Thornlands; tel: 3206 4051;* open 0800–1700) has rain forest and native orchid display gardens with stags, elks, crows nests, native orchids and ferns.

Queensland domestic architecture is very distinctive, with its emphasis on verandahs and general airiness. **Mayes Cottage Gallery** is in an early Queensland cottage, built in 1871 and restored. (*36 Mawarra St, Kingston; tel: 3209 3966;* open Tues–Sun 1000–1500).

Built in 1886, **Miegunyah** has been restored and stands as a memorial to the pioneer women of Queensland. (*31–35 Jordan Terrace, Bowen Hills; tel: 3252 2979;* open Tues–Wed 1030–1500, Sat–Sun 1030–1600). A magnificent three-storey stone residence, built by

Andre Stombuco in the 1880s, **Palma Rosa**, *9 Queens Rd, Hamilton; tel: 3262 3769*, is open on Sun 1400–1630. $1.50.

Brisbane's oldest surviving home is **Newstead House**, *Newstead Park, Breakfast Creek Rd, Newstead; tel: 3252 7373*. It was built in 1846 for Patrick Leslie with convict labour and has been restored and appropriately furnished. Open Mon–Fri 1100–1500, Sun 1400–1700. $3. **Ormiston House** is on the site where sugar cane was grown commercially for the first time in Australia. The original section was constructed in 1853. It is at *Wellington St, Ormiston; tel: 3286 1425* and is open Sun 1330–1630. $2.50.

In Ferny Hills, which is close to the centre of town, there is the **Australian Woolshed** (*tel: 3351 5366*) which has shows at 1000, 1100 and 1400, with working sheepdogs and a shearing demonstration and, believe it or not, a parade of trained sheep.

For the kids and the young at heart there are many attractions, including scary rides in a bobsled or grass skiing at **Samford Alpine Adventureland**, *Eatons Crossing Rd, Samford 4520; tel: 3289 1581*. Open Sat–Sun and school holidays 1000–1700.

A games centre with Grand Prix racing cars, waterslides,18 hole putt putt, bumper boats, slot car racing and video games are at **Mirage Grand Prix**, *2098 Ipswich Rd, Oxley; tel: 3379 9444*. Open Mon–Tues 1000–1700, Wed–Sun 1000–2200.

One of the world's largest scale (1:48) model railways is on display at **The Train Place**. Over 10,000 man hours went in to making the true-to-scale buildings and bridges. Open daily 0930–1700, *Tamborine Rd, Wolffdene Via Beenleigh; tel: 075–46 4221*. $4.

Visitors to the **Popcorn Factory and Confectionery Warehouse** can see the full popcorn manufacturing process and buy confectionery at wholesale prices. The warehouse is at *Building 4, 358 Nudgee Rd, Hendra; tel: 3268 4877* and is open Mon–Fri 1000–1630.

Licoriceland, *21 Jijaws St, Sumner Park; tel: 3376 6945*, is the only licorice factory in Queensland and you can see the sticky black stuff being made. Open Mon–Fri 0930–1530, except Jan.

SIDE TRACKS FROM BRISBANE

NORTH STRADBROKE ISLAND

Tourist Information: Stradbroke Island Visitors Centre, *near the ferry terminal, Dunwich; tel: (07) 3409 9555.*

Captain Henry John Rous was commander of the HMS *Rainbow*, which carried Governor Darling to the area in June 1827. The father of Rous was Viscount Dunwich, Earl of Stradbroke. Hence the name. Nearby is **Rainbow Beach**, which is where the ship was anchored, and Rous' father is remembered again at **Dunwich Point**. The island, which is 40 km long, is the largest in the bay, and originally was much larger. Until 1896 the two Stradbroke islands were connected, but a storm cut the sand spit at **Jumpinpin**. **South Stradbroke** island is effectively deserted while North Stradbroke boasts sealed roads connecting the minor towns of **Dunwich, Amity** and **Point Lookout**. The island's main occupation is rutile mining and most of the residents are employees of Consolidated Rutile. To get there go by ferry from **Toondah Harbour** at **Cleveland**. **Stradbroke Water Taxis** (*tel: 3286 2666*) has a regular car ferry service to the island at $63 per car return.

The interior of the island is rugged motoring and hardly suited to even four-wheel-driving. Some of the roads are for mining vehicles only and it is important to look out for signs as the drivers of these believe, rightly in this case, that the road is theirs. The road to the east out of Dunwich goes through the centre of the island to **Main Beach**. On the way it passes **Blue Lake**, which is a National Park and a freshwater haven for the island's wildlife. After that comes the **Eighteen Mile Swamp**, leading to Main Beach, after which you run out of surfaced road.

If you are thinking of camping – there are camping areas there – be warned that the area is notorious for its mosquitoes which appear, from empirical experience, to be immune to insect repellent.

Surf Lifesaving

Surf lifesaving began early this century when the first official surf lifesaving club in the world was founded at Bondi on 6 Feb 1906. Up until 1902 it was illegal to swim in the surf during daylight hours. This was more a case of morality rather than safety. Men and women were allowed to 'bathe' in the early morning and late evening only, and at separate times.

In 1902, William Gocher announced to all, including the police, that he would defy the ban and enter the water at **Manly Beach** (near Sydney) at noon. He was apprehended but no charges were laid, and soon the sport of surf bathing became very popular. Groups of experienced surfers began to form surf clubs to help protect less proficient swimmers from the dangers of the ocean.

The Surf Bathing Association of New South Wales was founded on 18 Oct 1907. This was later changed to the Surf Life Saving Association of Australia.

In the 1994–95 season, surf lifesavers performed 11,455 rescues. Inflatable Rescue Boats were the most commonly used rescue device, used in 4304 of these rescues. The second most used piece of equipment was the rescue board, with 3214 rescues. Surf lifesavers in Australia have now performed a total of 393,438 recorded rescues.

The north road goes to Amity and Point Lookout. Amity is a minor stopping point and most visitors head on to Point Lookout. This is very much a seaside town straggling out along the point.

Stradbroke Riding and Canoe (*tel: 3409 8279*) offers half day canoe trips and 1 and 2 hr horse rides into the interior. The beaches are all splendid, although **Home** and **Cylinder**, which are patrolled, can get quite crowded at holidays weekends. Unpatrolled, and therefore less crowded, are **Deadman's Beach** and **Frenchman's Bay**.

ProDive North Stradbroke (*tel: 3409 8074*) offers dives and equipment to **Flat** and **Shag Rocks**, which are known for grey nurse sharks – not dangerous – and moray eels – nearly blind and only dangerous if provoked.

MORETON ISLAND

The spelling is incorrect. It was named after James Douglas, the Earl of Morton, but was misspelled in the account of Cook's voyages by John Hawkesworth, which was published in 1773.

The island is 40 km from Brisbane. It can claim that **Mt Tempest**, which soars to 280 m on the island, is probably the highest

dune in the world. And the island itself is the second largest sand mass in the world – beaten to the title by **Fraser Island**. Most of its 19,260 hectares is National Park, and the island only has small villages such as **Bulwer, Kooringal, Cowan Cowan** and **Tangalooma Resort**, which was a whaling station until 1962. The 1857 red and white painted sandstone lighthouse on the northern tip of the island is still in use.

Note that there are no sealed roads and this island is very much four-wheel-drive territory. There is daily access (except Mon) from *Holt Street Wharf, Pinkenba*, Brisbane, on the **Tangalooma Flyer**; bookings are essential. The **Moreton Venture** car ferry runs from **Whyte Island** to Kooringal and Tangalooma. And the **Combie Trader Vehicle and Passenger Ferry** runs daily from **Scarborough Point** (on the Redcliffe Peninsula north of Brisbane). You need a vehicle permit, which costs $15 and is available from the ferry operators.

There are several tours of the island available from Brisbane. An example is **Moreton Island Service** (*tel: 07 3203 6399*) which runs tours every Mon, Fri, Sat at $55 a person. This includes the ferry trip, an island tour and a barbecue lunch. ⏏

THE GOLD COAST

The Gold Coast has an image problem. It is seen as being loud, vulgar and not quite the article. There is, sadly, much in this. It combines some of the attractions – and demerits – of Blackpool, Disneyland and a three ring circus on a strip of land, liberally covered with skyscrapers, running along the coast. It is where Australia comes to celebrate coming of age – the loss of innocence. And it is where Australia comes to retire.

TOURIST INFORMATION

Surfers Paradise, *The Mall, Cavill Ave; tel: 075 38 4419.* **Coolangatta**, *Beach House Plaza, Marine Parade; tel: 075 36 7765.*

ARRIVING AND DEPARTING

Driving in from New South Wales, you come into Queensland and the Gold Coast at Coolangatta, which is down the road from Tweed Heads, the last stop in New South Wales. You can also get to the Gold Coast – either Surfers Paradise or Coolangatta – by bus from the Transit Centre in Brisbane for $12. The trip takes an hour or so.

You can fly in to the domestic airport of Coolangatta, the Gold Coast Airport. Transit buses run to Coolangatta and Surfers Paradise; **timetables and information**; *tel: 5536 6841.*

GETTING AROUND

The whole of the Gold Coast, with its main highway running parallel to the coast, has a 24-hour local bus service called **Surfside Buses**, which runs between Coolangatta and Southport. A one-way ticket is $4 but there are day rover passes available.

In Coolangatta, the bus station is on the corner of *Warner and Griffith Sts.* For radio taxis the number to call is *5536 1144.*

STAYING ON THE GOLD COAST

Broadbeach

Conrad Jupiters Hotel, *Broadbeach Island; tel: 5592 1133.* **The Pan Pacific Hotel Gold Coast**, *81 Surf Parade; tel: 5592 2250.* **Happy Holiday Inn Motel**, *2 Albert Ave; tel: 5570 1311.* **Broadbeach Motor Inn**, *2651 Gold Coast Hwy; tel: 5570 1899.* **Hi Ho Motel Apartments**, *Queensland Ave, corner Old Burleigh Rd; tel: 55382777.* **Golden Rainbow Motel**, *2689 Gold Coast Hwy; tel: 55703400.* **Golden Nugget Motor Lodge**, *2733 Gold Coast Hwy; tel: 5539 9495.* **Montego Motel**, *2671 Gold Coast Hwy; tel: 5539 9956.*

Burleigh Heads

Fifth Avenue Motel *(BW), 1953 Gold Coast Hwy; tel: 5535 3588.* **Outrigger Resort Gold Coast** *(FL), 2007 Gold Coast Hwy; tel: 5535 1111.* **Burleigh International Motor Inn**, *1896 Gold Coast; tel: 5535 0033.* **Casino Motel**, *1761 Gold Coast Hwy; tel: 5535 7133.* **Gregory Motel**, *Gold Coast Hwy, corner Ikkina Rd; tel: 5535 3282.* **Elite Motel**, *1935 Gold Coast Hwy; tel: 5535 2920.*

Coolangatta

Beachcomber International Resort, *122 Griffith St; tel: 5536 5566.* **Beach House Seaside Resort**, *52–58 Marine Parade; tel: 5536 5566.* **Bombora On The Park Motel**, *Goodwin Park; tel: 5536 1888.* **Chateau Royale Hotel**, *1 Garrick St; tel: 5536 7111.* **Coolangatta Airport Motel**, *95 Golden Four Dr.; tel: 5536 6244.* **Greenmount Beach Resort**, *Hill St; tel: 5536 1222.* **Ocean View Motel**, *corner Clark St and Marine Parade; tel: 5536 3175.* **Coolangatta YHA**, *230 Coolangatta Rd; tel: 5536 7644.*

Southport

Earls Court Motor Inn, *131 Nerang St; tel: 5591 4144.* **Park Regis Hotel**, *2 Barney St,*

211

corner *Brighton Parade (PO Box 344, Surfers Paradise 4217); tel: 5532 7922.* **San Martino Marine Parade Motel,** *134 Marine Parade; tel: 5591 6666.*

Surfers Paradise

ANA Hotel Gold Coast Hotel, *22 View Ave; tel: 5579 1000.* **Gold Coast International Hotel,** *corner Gold Coast Hwy and Staghorn Ave; tel: 5592 1200.* **Paradise Island Resort Hotel,** *1 Paringa Dr., Paradise Island 4217; tel: 5531 5600.* **Ramada Hotel,** *corner Gold Coast Hwy & Hanlan St, Paradise Centre; tel: 5579 3499.* **Surfers Paradise Travelodge Hotel,** *2807 Gold Coast Hwy; tel: 5592 9900.* **Cavill Inn Motel,** *25 Cavill Ave; tel: 5531 5559.* **Chevron Hotel,** *Ferny Ave; tel: 5539 0444.* **Ocean Blue Resort Surfers Paradise Motel,** *122 Ferny Ave; tel: 5579 4444.* **Pink Poodle Motel** *(BW), 2903 Gold Coast Hwy; tel: 5539 9211.* **Trickett Gardens Holiday Inn Motel,** *24 Trickett St; tel: 5539 0988.* **Iluka Beach Resort Hotel,** *corner The Esplanade and Hanlan St (PO Box 736); tel: 5539 9155.* **Islander Resort Hotel,** *6 Beach Rd; tel: 5538 8000.* **Mercure Hotel Beachcomber Gold Coast** *(AC), 18 Hanlan St (PO Box 1028); tel: 5570 1000.* **Chateau of Surfers Paradise Hotel,** *corner The Esplanade and Elkhorn Ave (PO Box 922, Surfers Paradise, 4217); tel: 5538 1022.* **D'Arcy Arms Motel,** *2923 Gold Coast Hwy; tel: 5592 0892 or 5592 0882.* **Paradise Inn Motel,** *2826 Gold Coast Hwy; tel: 5592 0585.* **Silver Sands Motel,** *2985 Gold Coast Hwy, corner Morkwell Ave; tel: 5538 6041.* **Delilah Motel,** *72 Ferny Ave and corner Cypress St; tel: 5538 1722.* **Surfers City Motel,** *3314 Gold Coast Hwy; tel: 5539 8988.* **Marriott Surfers Paradise Resort Hotel,** *158 Ferny Ave; tel: 5592 9800.*

Money

There is a **Thomas Cook Foreign Exchange** branch in Broadbeach at *Shop G79, Oasis Shopping Resort; tel: (0755) 922 888.*

SIGHTSEEING

Starting at the Queensland-New South Wales border, the Gold Coast runs for 35 km as a series of beaches from Tweed Head to Main Beach. It is 85 km from Brisbane and is surrounded by seven national parks. In theory, there are towns along the whole of the shore, but, in fact, it is, to all intents and purposes, a continuous ribbon of development, where many Australians – over two million visitors last year – go for their holiday.

In the centre is **Surfers Paradise**, which is the Blackpool or Atlantic City of Australia, with lesser resorts (less glitz and noise) on either side. **Tweed Heads, Coolangatta** (which contains the airport that services the area), **Burleigh Heads** and **Broadbeach** to the south, with **North** and **South Stradbroke Islands** running to the north. The Pacific Hwy runs along the coast from Tweed Heads to Coolangatta, and then the Gold Coast Hwy takes over. It parallels the shore, diverging from the Pacific Hwy at **Tugun,** then through Surfers and **Southport** – a side road to **The Spit** – and finally slightly inland to **Oxenford,** and then on to join the Pacific Hwy.

Surfers Paradise, as a name, is correct, for there is good surfing on the beaches, two dozen of which are patrolled. The surf can be deceptive and care should be taken on unpatrolled beaches. You can learn to surf at the **School of Surfing,** *Surfers Paradise Beach; tel: 07 5535 6978,* for $12 a lesson. It boasts that if you can swim, it can teach you to stand on a surf board in only two lessons.

There are dozens of theme parks and animal parks in the area. Entertainment is continuous, even if it can be more than a little expensive.

Grundy's Entertainment Centre is a family-style entertainment centre, with games, rides, children's amusements and daily stage shows. (*Paradise Centre, Cavill Ave, Surfers Paradise; tel: 075 38 9011.* Open daily 1100– 2100.) Nearby, in the Surfers Paradise Beer Garden, is the **Surf Museum.**

In the heart of Surfers, **Ripley's Believe It Or Not,** *Raptis Plaza, Cavill Mall; tel: 07592 0040,* is based on the famous newspaper strip and has a collection of outlandish gadgets, unbelievable inventions and illusions, displayed using audio-visual techniques. Open daily 0930–2300. $9.50.

Jupiters Casino, *Gold Coast Hwy, Broadbeach; tel: 076 92 1133,* was one of the first in

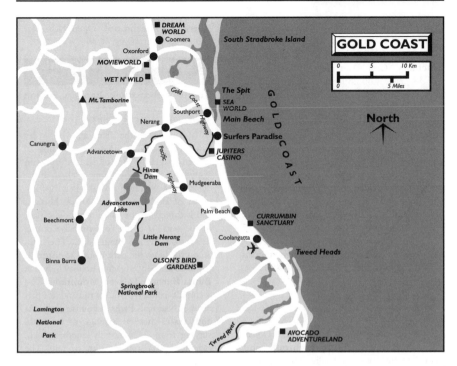

DREAM WORLD
Coomera
South Stradbroke Island

Oxonford
MOVIEWORLD
WET N' WILD

Gold
The Spit
SEA WORLD
Main Beach
Surfers Paradise
Coast Highway
Southport
Nerang

Mt. Tamborine

Canungra
Advancetown
Pacific
JUPITERS CASINO

Hinze Dam
Highway
Mudgeeraba

Advancetown Lake
Palm Beach
CURRUMBIN SANCTUARY
Beechmont

Little Nerang Dam
Coolangatta
Binna Burra
OLSON'S BIRD GARDENS
Tweed Heads

Springbrook National Park

Lamington
National
Park
Tweed River
AVOCADO ADVENTURELAND

GOLD COAST

0   5   10 Km
0   5 Miles

North

G O L D C O A S T

213

Australia, but is now under heavy competition, with several casinos opened, and opening, in the past few years, and turnover and profits dropping. Open daily 24 hours. It has free 'Learn to Play lessons' for blackjack, roulette and craps at 1015 Tues–Sat.

Sea World has 25 hectares of attractions, including aquariums, dolphin and sea-lion shows, rides and a monorail. (*The Spit, Main Beach; tel: 075 88 2222.* Open daily 1000–1700. $29.) Other theme parks are only a short drive away. They have all had a fairly lean time, with several of them closing down. The ones that have survived have the most to offer.

Dreamworld Parkway, *Coomera; tel: 075-73 1133,* is a 24 hectare family theme park. Open daily 1000–1700, $29. There are rides, shows and attractions, and an Imax theatre, which shows special movies on a monster-size screen, really giving the impression of audience involvement. Not suitable for sufferers of vertigo.

Near **Oxenford**, 23 km north of Surfer's Paradise, is **Warner Bros Movie World**,

Pacific Hwy, Oxenford; tel: 075 73 3999. One of its problems is that visitors keep comparing it to similar attractions in California. It is not as large, not as spectacular (because of understandable financial constraints), but it is still a more than worthwhile place to visit and can take up a whole day. It contains the usual movie-related shows, a demonstration of special effects and a studio tour. Open daily 1000–1700. $29.

The nearby **Wet 'n' Wild Water Park**, *Pacific Hwy, Oxenford; tel: 075 73 2277,* has speed slides, an adventure play pool, a wave pool, a dive-in movies stunt show and un- limited free rides after admission. Open Mon–Sun 1000–1630 Sep–Oct; Mon–Sat 1000–2200, Sun 1000–1700 Nov–Feb; Mon– Sun 1000–1630 Mar–Apr. $14.50.

The mad sport of diving into space with rubber bands tied to your feet is very popular in this area. A typical service is **Bungee Down- under**, *Seaworld Dr., The Spit, Gold Coast; tel: 075-311103.* Open 1000–dusk. $69. After your few seconds leap into space you can buy photos and a video of your daring 15 seconds of fame.

One of the most common publicity pictures of the Gold Coast is of a young tourist positively covered in lorikeets. **Currumbin Sanctuary**, *Gold Coast Hwy, Currumbin; tel: 075 34 1266,* is on 28 hectares of parkland full of Australian wildlife. There is a miniature trail that travels 25 km around the tracks. The lorikeets, members of the parrot family, come in to be fed – a syrup mixture on a tin plate – twice a day and have absolutely no fear of humans. Open daily 0800–1700. $12.

Queensland is a major centre for avocado growing. **Avocado Adventureland** is an avocado plantation that has become a tourist attraction. It is in *Duranbah Rd,* off the Pacific Hwy, 1 km south of Coolangatta; *tel: 066 77 7222.* The plantation is set among rain forest and there are attractions such as native animals to feed and boat rides. Open daily 1000–1700.

⇄ SIDE TRACK FROM THE GOLD COAST

Exploring the country behind the Gold Coast – **Binna Burra**, **Springbrook** and **Mt Tamborine** – is a delight. The country is only a half-hour drive from the coast. Among the attractions are **Olson's Bird Gardens**, *Currumbin Creek Rd, Currumbin Valley; tel: 075 33 0208,* which has gardens and rainforest with pheasants, parrots and finches in large landscaped aviaries. Open daily 0900–1700. $7.50.

Mt Tamborine is 34 km to the north west – go via Nerang and Oxenford – and much of it is in the **Tamborine National Park**. This is very much an area of arts and crafts shops and little tea rooms. One attraction is **Mt Tamborine Country Market**, *Showgrounds Main Western Rd, Mt Tamborine; tel: 075 45 1736.* It is a monthly market, where stall holders sell only 'homemade', 'home baked' or 'home grown' products. Open second Sun of every month 0830–1500.

Out past Nerang, near **Advancetown**, is the **Advancetown Lake and Hinze Dam**, *tel: 075 33 2158,* which is a swimming spot and a picnic area surrounded by mountains including **Springbrook**, **Binna**

Burra and **Beechmont**. Open Nov–Mar 0830–1800, rest of year 0730–1700.

LAMINGTON NATIONAL PARK

Tourist Information: Rangers Station *Binna Burra; tel: (07) 5533 3584* and *Green Mountains; tel: (07) 554 0634.*

Named after the late, and not very lamented, Lord Lamington, governor of Queensland at the turn of the century, who visited the park once and celebrated the occasion by shooting a koala. It is 100 km north of Brisbane, covers 20,500 hectares and is thought to be the most popular park in the state. It is full of waterfalls coming down from the mountain ridges. The main access road into the park from **Canungra** – paved all the way – reaches holiday lodges at **Binna Burra** and **Green Mountains**. The accommodation is privately run and not part of the National Parks administration. At both places there is a range of footpaths varying from 2–24 km in length, which, together, cover some 160 km of trails. The most important trail is the one that covers the 22 km from Binna Burra to Green Mountains.

This park is sub-tropical and densely forested. The trees are mainly booyong, marara and carabeen, while below the tree canopy are ferns, orchids, mosses and vines. The park is renowned for its bird life.

The weather in the park is changeable – it tends to be much cooler than the surrounding countryside – and if you are going on one of the longer hikes, be prepared for extreme weather conditions. ◢

⟷ Connection to Brisbane

From Surfers Paradise it is 20 km along the Gold Coast Hwy to the junction with Rte 1, the Pacific Hwy. From there it is 47 km north to the outer suburbs of Brisbane. Continue along Rte 1 as it becomes the South East Freeway 20 km into the centre of the city; for the airport, fork right near Underwood onto the Gateway Arterial, which takes you some 20 km to the airport.

BRISBANE–ROCKHAMPTON

Driving anticlockwise around the coast of Australia, the great navigator's dictum keeps springing to mind – keep Australia on your left. And, indeed, the road from Brisbane to Rockhampton – Route 1, which is here called the Bruce Highway – does precisely that. It is marked National 1 throughout and although you may have to turn off it towards the sea for short distances to visit the coastal towns of this route, you simply cannot get lost. If you deviate to the right you come very quickly to the South Pacific Ocean. If you deviate to the left you will see, looming in front of you, the Great Dividing Range.

215

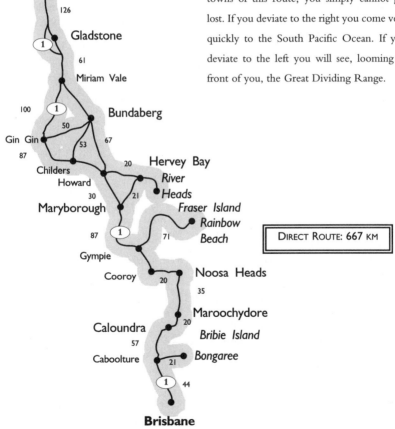

Rockhampton

126

Gladstone

1

61

Miriam Vale

100   **1**

50

Gin Gin

53   67

87

Childers   20   Hervey Bay

Howard   *River*

30   21   *Heads*

Maryborough   *Fraser Island*

87   **1**   71   *Rainbow*
Beach

Gympie

Cooroy   20   Noosa Heads

35

Maroochydore

Caloundra   20

57   *Bribie Island*

Caboolture   21   *Bongaree*

1   44

Brisbane

Bundaberg

DIRECT ROUTE: 667 KM

ROUTE

From Brisbane you take Rte 1, the Bruce Hwy, north. The road passes through an almost totally built-up area – this is where most of Australia wants to come to retire and a large percentage wants to come to spend their holidays. On your right as you leave Brisbane is the Redcliffe Peninsula – nearly all suburbs – acting as the northern arm of Moreton Bay. You then pass through Burpengary to **Caboolture**. At that point the highways diverge, with the Daguilar Hwy heading inland to Kingaroy – peanut country – and the Bruce Hwy forging straight ahead. You can turn off right, to visit **Bribie Island**, but the main highway heads to **Caloundra**, a short turn to the right off Rte 1. From there proceed up the coastal road to **Maroochydore**, and still sticking to coast roads, to **Noosa Heads**.

From Noosa Heads take the inland road a short distance to rejoin Rte 1 at **Cooroy**. About 30 km further on is **Gympie** and your first chance to detour to **Fraser Island**. From Gympie the road runs directly to **Maryborough** but, again, you can take a detour towards the coast and **Tin Can Bay** (halfway to Rainbow Beach and the Fraser Island ferry) and rejoin the highway at Maryborough.

On your right is Fraser Island, running parallel with the coast. From Maryborough 21 km of coastal road takes you to **Hervey Bay** and another opportunity to cross to Fraser Island. From Hervey Bay take the road west to **Howard** to rejoin Rte 1, which heads towards Childers and **Gin Gin**, still keeping roughly parallel to, but inland from, the coast. Turns to the right from either place will take you to **Bundaberg**; alternatively you can head north from Howard without rejoining Rte 1.

From Bundaberg either drive coastally through **Avondale**, or rejoin the highway at Gin Gin and head north. Either way will bring you to **Miriam Vale** and then to **Gladstone**, a minor detour from the highway to the right. From Gladstone head north to rejoin Rte 1 and carry on to **Rockhampton**.

TRAINS

There is no shortage of trains along this route, including many of the famous services such as

the Queenslander (see p. 405). OTT table 9013 lists them. Most leave from Brisbane Roma St Stn. Gympie is 3 hrs, Maryborough 4½ hrs, Bundaberg 5½ hrs, Gladstone 8 hrs and Rockhampton 9½ hrs.

BUSES

Greyhound Pioneer, McCafferty's and other operators offer a good choice of services along this route. Journey times are longer than those of the trains, however, Rockhampton, for instance, is nearly 13 hrs by coach from Brisbane. OTT table 9082.

BRISBANE TO CALOUNDRA

Inland along the *Glass Mountains Rd,* 20 km away, is **Landsborough,** but before you get to Landsborough you pass through **Palmview,** which is at the Caloundra turn off on the highway.

There you will find a series of edifices celebrating a cartoon series drawn by Ken Maynard in the *Australasian Post,* a weekly of very light reading. First comes the **Ettamogah Orchestral Fountains,** *Lot 1 Frizzo Rd, Palmview; tel: 074 94 5455.* Open daily 0900–1700. $4.50. This consists of 800 water fountains choreographed to 15-min music soundtracks backed by 22 banks of coloured lights. No one is suggesting that it is art but it is quite fascinating.

Right alongside is the **Ettamogah Pub,** *tel: 074-94 5444,* which does look like the pub in Maynard's cartoon, sloping walls and all. Open Mon–Sat 0900–2200. It is very much a purpose-built tourist attraction, but nevertheless it has a certain character. There is another one in Albury, NSW (see Murray and the Riverina, p. 198).

In Landsborough itself is **The Big Kart Track,** *Glass House Mountains Rd, Landsborough; tel: 074-94 1613.* To roar around the 1200m of track in a kart costs $30 an hour. Open Sun–Thur 0900–1700, Fri–Sat 1000–2200.

More sedate is **Landsborough Historical Museum,** *Landsborough-Maleny Rd; tel: 074-941755,* which traces the history of the Landsborough shire dating back to 1924. Open Sun, Mon, Tues, Thur 1000–1600.

SIDE TRACK
FROM CABOOLTURE

Turn right from the highway near Caboolture to Bongaree at the southern tip of the island, a distance of 21 km.

BRIBIE ISLAND

Tourist Information: Bribie Island Tourist Information Centre, *Benabraw Ave; tel: 07 3408 9026.*

ACCOMMODATION

Blue Pacific Hotel Motel, *Ocean Beach, Woorim; tel: 3408 1004.* **Bribie Island Hotel-Motel**, *25 Sylvan Beach Esplanade, Bellara; tel: 3408 7477.* **Bribie Waterways Resort Motel**, *155 Welsby Parade, Bongaree; tel: 3408 3000*

SIGHTSEEING

Bribie Island is 31 km long and separated from the mainland by the narrow **Pumicestone Channel**. It was named after an escaped convict who lived there. There is a bridge across the Channel to **Bellara**, one of the three towns at the south end of the island. The north-west coast is a **National Park** and is only safely explored by four-wheel-drive vehicles.

CALOUNDRA

Tourist Information: Tourist Information centre, *Caloundra Rd; tel: 074 91 0202.*

ACCOMMODATION

Alton's Palm Breeze Motel *(BU)*, *105–111 Bulcock St; tel: 5491 5566.* **Anchorage Motor Inn & Islander Restaurant**, *18 Bowman St; tel: 5491 1499.* **Caloundra Motel**, *30 Bowman St; tel: 5491 1411.*
Caloundra Ocean Views Motor Inn, *115 Bulcock St; tel: 5491 1788.* **Caloundra Safari Motel**, *corner Minchinton St and Orsova Terrace; tel: 5491 1011.* **Caloundra Suncourt Motel**, *135 Bulcock St; tel: 5491 1011.* **Dolphins Motel**, *6–8 Cooma Terrace; tel: 5491 2511.* **Kronks Motel**, *corner Minchinton and Ormuz Aves; tel: 5491 2088.*
Oasis On Golden Beach Resort, *corner North St and Landsborough Parade; tel: 5491*
0333. **Oasis Resort & Conference Centres**, *corner Landsborough Parade and North St; tel: 5491*
0333. **Rolling Surf Motel**, *10 Levuka Ave, Kings Beach; tel: 5491 1300.*

SIGHTSEEING

The name could have derived from *callanda*, an Aboriginal word meaning beautiful, but there is no confirmation of this. Caloundra is very much a tourist town in the traditional Australian sense. It is a separation point between miles and miles of beaches to the north and Bribie Island to the south, with its national park and suburbs.

The nearest beach to the town is **Bulcock Beach**, but **Golden Beach** is perhaps preferable. The beaches are ideal for swimming and windsurfing. Inland there are foreshore parks with bunya trees.

Corbould Park Racecourse, *Pierce Ave Caloundra; tel: 074 92 6788,* is one of the best horse racetracks in Queensland and has other activities suited to the family almost every day throughout the school holidays. Racing every Saturday.

Also in Caloundra, at *Landsborough Parade,* is a replica of Captain Cook's ship the **Endeavour**, which was originally a Whitby collier until taken into service with the Royal Navy. This is built to two-thirds to scale, so the real ship was considerably larger although, by today's standards, still very small. The working gear and the rigging are authentic reproductions. Open daily 0900–1630, $5; *tel: 0749 1278.*

There are over 3000 teddy bears and related items set up in fantasy scenes at the **Teddy Bear World and Museum**, *26 Bowman Rd, Caloundra; tel: 074-92 5050.* Open daily 1000–1600. $3.

At the Caloundra Aerodrome, on *Pathfinder Dr.,* is the **Queensland Air Museum**, *tel: 074 91 0202.* It has many aircraft on display, including an Armstrong Whitworth Meteor. Open Wed, Sat, Sun 1000–1600; $3.

This part of Queensland seems to attract potters. The **Green Frog Pottery** in *Sydal Street, tel: 074 91 9727,* has no charge for watching the potter at work. Workshop open Mon–Fri 0800–1630.

217

MAROOCHYDORE

Tourist Information: Maroochy Tourist Information Centre, *corner Aerodrome Rd and Sixth Ave; tel: (074) 79 1566.*

ACCOMMODATION

Avenue Motor Inn, *106 Sixth Ave; tel: 5443 3600.* **Beach Motor Inn**, *Sixth Ave; tel: 5443 7044.* **Blue Waters Motel**, *64 Sixth Ave; tel: 5443 6700.* **Coachman's Courte Motor Inn**, *Sixth Ave; tel: 5443 4099.* **Heritage Motor Inn**, *69 Sixth Ave; tel: 5443 7355.* **Maroochy River Motel**, *361 Bradman Ave; tel: 5443 3142.* **Maroochy River Resort – The Coach House**, *2/46 David Low Way; tel: 5448 5566.* **Maroochydore Motel**, *Duporth Ave; tel: 5443 1999.* **Pacific Paradise Motel**, *612 David Lowe Way; tel: 5448 7181.* **The Waterfront Hotel**, *2/46 David Low Way; tel: 5448 4488.* **Wun Palm Motel**, *137 Duporth Ave; tel: 5443 4677.* **Maroochydore YHA**, *24 Schirmann Dr.; tel: 5443 3151.*

SIGHTSEEING

The town is on the coast, where the **Maroochy River** comes out to the sea, and is a major tourist centre. Maroochydore extends into the Maroochy estuary with **Pincushion Island** as a pimple off the point. On the right hand side of the peninsula runs **Maroochydore Beach** facing out to the South Pacific. This runs south until it becomes part of **Alexandra Headland** and, almost immediately, **Mooloolaba**, where the **Mooloolaba River** comes to the coast at **Point Cartwright**. Mooloolaba – you will frequently see it spelled with a 'h' on the end – is, in effect, a suburb of Maroochydore, although it perhaps has more charm.

Two kilometres south of the airport, on the north side of the river, is **Nostalgia Town**, *David Low Hwy, Pacific Paradise; tel: 48 7155,* which has as its theme 'a laugh at the past', with displays taking themes of nostalgia – the war years and the Roaring Twenties, for example. There is an Enchanted Railway ($4) and Albert's Incredible Time Trip ($4).

You can cruise the river with **Maroochy River Cruises**, *Maroochydore; tel: (018) 71 3275,* which has different cruises throughout

the day. There are also several cruises from Mooloolaba – **Gemini Reef Cruises**, *The Wharf, Mooloolaba; tel: 44 6077* and **Sunshine Coast Ferry**, *The Wharf, Mooloolaba; tel: 78 0088.*

Bli Bli is 10 km north-west of the town, again along the river, and there you will find yet another theme park, **Bli Bli Castle** (*David Low Hwy, Bli Bli; tel: 074 48 5373*). In fact it does not look or feel very much like an authentic castle, having been built of concrete block, but it has a drawbridge over the moat and it tries, by way of demonstrations and dioramas, to show the medieval way of life. Open daily 0900–1700. $6. In the same area is **Ski & Skurf**, which is a cable water ski park. That is, you are towed at a rate of knots by a continuous cable rather than a speed boat. (*David Low Way, Bli Bli; tel: 074-48 7555;* open Mon–Fri 0900–1800, Sat–Sun 0700–1800; 2 hrs $25.)

The Wharf Mooloolaba, *Parkyn Parade, Mooloolaba Spit; tel: 44 8088,* is more a themed shopping and entertainment centre than a genuine working wharf. It was created in the style of a 19th century fishing village, and has a marina, speciality shops, tavern, amusement centre and restaurants. Open daily 0800 to late. At the same place is **Underwater World**, *Parkyn Parade, Mooloolaba Spit; tel: 074-44 8488.* Open daily 0900–1800. $13.50. This includes an oceanarium, an ocean discovery centre, the theatre of the sea, performing seals and a transparent tunnel through the base of the aquarium so that you have fish surrounding you. It also has shoals of barramundi, Australia's favourite dining fish.

Driving from Surfer's Paradise you reach **Buderim** just before you get to Maroochydore. This has a **Pioneer Cottage**, *5 Ballinger Crescent; tel: 074 45 3739,* which is an original settler's home dating from 1876. It has been restored and furnished in the style of the times. Open daily 1100–1600.

NOOSA HEADS

Tourist Information: Tourist Information Centre, *Hastings St; tel: (074) 47 4988.*

ACCOMMODATION AND FOOD

Sheraton Noosa Resort, *Hastings St; tel:*

5449 4888. **Netanya Noosa Resort**, *75 Hastings St; tel: 5447 4722.* **The Caribbean Noosa Motel**, *15 Noosa Parade; tel: 5447 2247.* **Noosa Haven Motor Inn**, *119 Noosa Parade; tel: 5449 8905.* **Noosa Parade Holiday Inn Motel**, *corner Noosa Parade and Key Court; tel: 5447 4177.* **Noosa Village Motel**, *10 Hastings St; tel: 5447 5800.* **Beach Breakers Resort**, *75 David Low Way; tel: 5447 2829.* **Chez Noosa Resort**, *263 David Low Way; tel: 5447 2027.* **Club Noosa Resort**, *Noosa Dr.; tel: 5447 5377.* **Koala Beach Resort**, *44 Noosa Dr.; tel: 5447 3355.* **The Nautilus Noosa Resort**, *124 Noosa Parade; tel: 5449 9188.* **Noosa Harbour Resort**, *Quamby Pl.; tel: 5447 4500.* **Noosa Quays Resort**, *4 Quamby Pl.; tel: 5449 2699.* **Noosa Shores Resort**, *86 Noosa Parade; tel: 5447 5766.* **Reef Hotel Motel**, *Noosa Dr.; tel: 5447 4477.* **Seahaven Beachfront Resort**; *tel: 5447 3422.* **Tingirana Motel**, *Hastings St; tel: 5447 3274.* **HI: Halse Lodge Guest House**, *2 Halse Lane; tel: 5447 3377.*

The restaurants in Noosa seem to cater either for the up-market resort crowd or surfers, with not a lot of choice in between. **Laguna Bay Beach Club**, *Hastings St; tel: 49 4793.* Open seven days. Licensed. Ocean views. Greek-Italian cuisine. **Café le Monde**, *Hastings St; tel: 49 2366.* Open seven days, breakfast, lunch, dinners. Licensed. Live music. Pricey. **Eduardo's on the Beach**, *25 Hastings St; tel: 47 5875.* Open for breakfast, lunch and dinner every day. BYO. International cuisine. Medium price. **Saltwater**, *8 Hastings St; tel: 47 2234.* Open seven days lunch and dinner. Seafood. Licensed. **Rosers**, *1 Hastings St; tel: 47 3880.* Licensed. Open seven days lunch, dinner. Seafood.

SIGHTSEEING

This vies with Byron Bay for the title of the most popular resort in Australia. The real estate prices for properties near the beach rival those of the best suburbs in Sydney. Noosa Heads was originally named after an escaped convict, James Bracewell, when it was known as Cape Bracewell. He lived here among the Aborigines. Eventually, Bracefield was pardoned but the name of the town was changed

to Noosa, an Aboriginal name, possibly meaning 'shade' or 'shadow'. The area was first explored by Europeans in 1842, and in the 1960s became a favourite place for surfers because of its north-facing beach and perfect surfing waves. After the surfers came, inevitably, the developers and Noosa became a favoured resort.

You can get to Noosa Heads by road north out of Caloundra along the coast or from inland through Eumundi on the Bruce Hwy. The town, which is protected by a headland and defined by a river, overlooks Laguna Bay. It is a totally up-market tourist resort with *Hastings St*, the main drag, lined with shops, restaurants and bars, all reflecting a civilised approach to tropical living.

The town planning rule is that no building should be higher than the trees, which helps preserve Noosa Heads' distinctive flavour. Behind, also preserving the area, is the **Noosa National Park**, which covers some 432 hectares with rain forest and open eucalypt woodland, and has rocky headlands running right to the sea with two beaches – Granite and Alexandria Bay. The best view of Noosa Heads is up *Viewland Dr.* to **Laguna Lookout** in the National Park. Just to the north is the much larger **Cooloola National Park**.

Every evening at sunset it is almost traditional to walk along *Gympie St* and see the sun setting on the other bank of the river among the mangroves.

Nearby at **Tewantin** – 6km from Noosa Heads – is the tourist complex of **Noosa River Harbour Town**, *1 The Esplanade, Tewantin; tel: 074 49 0844.* Open 1000–1700 for shops, nightclubs and restaurants stay open until late. You can also take a cruise from here with the **Everglades Water Bus**; *tel: 074 47 1838.*

Tourist Information: Maryborough and District Tourist Information Centre, *30 Ferry St, Maryborough; tel: (071) 23 2682.*

ACCOMMODATION

McNevins Parkway Motel, *188 John St; tel: 22 2888.* **Maryborough Motor Inn Motel**, *corner Queen and Ferry Sts; tel: 22 2777.* **Arkana**

Inn *(BU)*, *46 Ferry St; tel: 21 2261.* **Cara Motel**, *196 Walker St; tel: 22 4288.* **Royal Hotel**, *340 Kent St; tel: 21 2241.* **Lamington Hotel-Motel**, *corner Ferry and Queens Sts; tel: 21 3295.* **Maryborough City Motel**, *138–140 Ferry St; tel: 21 2568.* **Maryborough Motor Inn Motel**, *corner Queen and Ferry Sts; tel: 22 2777.* **Mineral Sands Motel** *(FL)*, *corner Ferry and Albert Sts; tel: 21 2366.* **Spanish Motor Inn**, *499 Alice St; tel: 21 2858.* **Tinana Hotel Motel**, *Gympie Rd; tel: 21 5082.*

SIGHTSEEING

The Mary River is named after the wife of the then governor of New South Wales, Sir Charles Fitzroy. It was named in 1847. The town's name comes from the river. The town is 255 km north of Brisbane and is one of Queensland's oldest cities, first settled in 1843. Maryborough has a range of well preserved public buildings mainly around *Wharf St* – it was an important wool shipping port, although that activity has now ceased – which has earned it the title of the Heritage City. The town was proclaimed a port in 1859 and a municipality in 1861.

The **Railway Museum** is understandably at the *Main Platform, Railway Station, Lennox Street (tel: 071 23 9261)* and is open by appointment. Note this is the old railway station. It has a display of equipment used by Queensland Railways in the 19th and 20th centuries, including some fully restored locomotives.

The late William Olds was one of Australia's foremost model engineers. **Olds Engine House and Works**, *78 North St, tel: 071-21 3649*, displays some of his famous models. Open Thur 0930–1600, or by arrangement. $2.

Brennan and Geraghty's Store, *64 Lennox St, Maryborough; tel: 21 2250*, with adjoining residence and cottage, was acquired by the National Trust. The same family ran it for more than a century and much of the original style, stock and records have been retained and restored. Open daily 1000–1500. $3.

In *Alice St* is the **Original Maryborough Site** of the first settlement of Maryborough. The settlers moved to the present site in 1852 after hostilities with the local Aborigines. The site offers a series of walking routes near the

river's edge so that you can imagine the way of life of early settlers.

Built in 1883 and restored to its former glory in the mid 1950s, **Baddow House**, *364 Queen St, Maryborough; tel: 071-23 1883*, now houses memorabilia and collectors items. Open daily 1000–1600. $3.

HERVEY BAY

Tourist Information: Hervey Bay Central Booking Office, *363 The Esplanade; tel: (071) 24 1300.*

ACCOMMODATION AND FOOD

Hervey Bay Resort Motel, *249 The Esplanade, Pialba 4655; tel: 28 1555.* **Playa Concha Motor Inn** *(FL)*, *475 The Esplanade, Torquay 4655; corner Ann St; tel: 251544.* **Shelly Beach Motel**, *509 The Esplanade, Urangan 4655; tel: 28 9888.* **Fairway Motel**, *29 Boat Harbour Dr., Pialba 4655; tel: 28 1008.* **Fraser Gateway Motor Inn** *(BW)*, *68 Main St, Pialba; tel: 28 3666.* **Golden Sands Motor Inn**, *44 Main St, Pialba; tel: 28 3977.* **Kondari Resort Hotel Motel**, *49 Elizabeth St, Urangan; tel: 28 9702.* **Tower Court Motel**, *459 The Esplanade, Torquay; tel: 25 1322.* **Hervey Bay Motel**, *518 The Esplanade, Urangan 4655; tel: 28 9255.* **Reef Motel** *(BU)*, *410 The Esplanade, Torquay 4655; tel: 25 2744.*

Seven Seas Motel, *573 The Esplanade, Urangan 4655; tel: 28 9699.* **Sunseeker Motel**, *354 The Esplanade, Scarness 4655; tel: 28 1888.* **Bay View Motel**, *399 The Esplanade, Torquay 4655; tel: 28 1134.* **Point Vernon Motel**, *189 The Esplanade, Point Vernon 4655; tel: 28 1418.*

Torquay, one of the five towns of Hervey Bay, is the centre of all activity. **Gringo's**, *449 The Esplanade; tel: 24 5466.* Open lunch and dinner. Mexican food. **Sails Brasserie**, *433 The Esplanade; tel: 25 5170.* Open daily lunch and dinner. The definitive restaurant in the area. Licensed. Seafood. Pricey. **Dolly's**, *410 The Esplanade; tel: 25 5633.* Open daily; dinner. Live music and smorgasbord. Licensed.

SIGHTSEEING

In Australia it is normally pronounced as it's spelt, not 'Harvey'. The area – in fact, five suburbs in search of a centre – is named after the surgeon on Cook's *Endeavour*, who later became the Earl of Bristol. It is 34 km north of Maryborough and is the access point for Fraser Island. It has a good, though surfless, beach, extending for 13 km and possibly the best whale watching in Australia. There are a couple of dozen cruise boats that will take you whale watching, although there are restrictions on how close they can approach the mammals. One operator is **Polymetric Products**, *63 Old Maryborough Rd, Pialba; tel: 28 2603*, and you can easily book through one of the several information centres or, indeed, anywhere that you are staying. During the season of migration, which runs from late Aug–Oct, as many as three dozen whales can come into the bay at the same time.

The Big G'day Australian Wildlife and Theme Park, *Maryborough-Urangan Rd, Hervey Bay; tel: 24 1733*, is open daily 0900–1700. $7. The park covers 15 hectares of bushland and is stocked with a large variety of wildlife, including crocodiles.

⬛ SIDE TRACK FROM HERVEY BAY OR GYMPIE

To get to Fraser Island you take a ferry – in Queensland known as barges – from one of two places. A 71 km drive from **Gympie** leads through Tin Can to **Rainbow Beach**. Nearby **Inskip Point** offers a 10-min crossing by the *Rainbow Venture (tel: 074 86 3154)* to **Hook Point** at the southern end of the island. $45 return for vehicle and passengers.

Alternatively, it is a short drive from Hervey Bay to **River Heads**. From there the *Fraser Venture (tel: 071 25 4444)* makes the journey to **Wanggoolba Creek** – $55. In both cases it is advisable to book. Permits are required to take a vehicle on to the island and these cost $15 and can be obtained from any Queensland National Park and Wildlife Service office or from the Hervey Bay City Council in Torquay *(tel: 071 25 0222)*.

FRASER ISLAND

Tourist Information: Fraser Island

Tourist Information Centre, *8 Rainbow Beach Rd, Rainbow Beach; tel: (074) 86 3227* or, on the island itself, **Fraser Tourist Information Centre**, *Eurong; tel: (071) 25 0222*.

Fraser Island is the largest sand island in the world, extending over 184,000 hectares. One version claims it is named after Captain James Fraser, who was killed by Aborigines when he came ashore from his wrecked ship *Stirling Castle*, or after his wife Mrs Eliza Fraser from the same shipwreck, who was – according to several conflicting accounts that she gave – captured by the Aborigines.

As a sand island it is truly a massive place, 20 km long and 15 km wide, with dunes rising to 200m. The island is so large that Captain Cook mistook it for part of the mainland. Fraser Island was declared a native reserve in 1860, when it had an Aboriginal population of between 2000 and 3000. By 1904 they had all been dispersed to the mainland as timber cutters moved in.

The trees ran out in 1925 and nothing much happened until 1949 when rutile sand mining leases were applied for and issued. Massive demonstrations from the early conservationists, led by John Sinclair, caused the government to set up an inquiry. In 1976 sand mining had effectively ceased and in the following year half of the island was declared a National Park. The island was added to the World Heritage List in 1993.

The **Great Sandy National Park** covers 52,000 hectares on the northern third of the island and is almost totally sand. Some of the sand dunes can reach heights of 235m. The sand, amazingly, supports tall forests, for over the centuries a mat of vegetation has grown up to give them support and sustenance. There are stands of rain forests inland, often surrounded by forests of blackbutts. Nearer the shore, the coastal dunes have salt resistant shrubs and trees. There are freshwater lagoons and extensive swamps. The easiest way to get around the park is by four-wheel-drive vehicle, but parts are being banned to vehicles because of erosion.

In the centre of the island is rain forest – growing in sand – and a series of freshwater

221

lakes. Of these the best known is perhaps **Lake Mackenzie**, the water of which is normally totally clear.

This is one of the few places in Australia where the only way to get around is to walk, use a trail bike or a four-wheel-drive vehicle. There are no sealed roads and driving conditions can be tricky, especially after heavy rain.

When driving on the island you must keep to the tracks to protect the vegetation as well as your vehicle. Much of the island is ecologically fragile because of the depredations of tourists and there is a strong movement to either ban or limit the number of vehicles visiting the island. There are already some vehicle-free areas, which you should carefully observe. When driving you should have four-wheel-drive constantly engaged to avoid spinning your wheels in the sand. Lowering your tyre pressures to 102–125 Kpa (15–18 psi) will help you maintain traction. The speed limit on the inland tracks is 35 kph and on the beaches 60 kph.

The first stop is **Central Station**; it has many dingoes, reputed to be Australia's purest strain, which should under no circumstances be fed. **Dili Village** is the former sand mining centre and beyond that you get to **Happy Valley**. There are two signposted tracks from there leading inland. One goes to **Lake Garawongera** and the other to **Yidney Scrub** and then past a series of lakes, until after 45 km it returns to the beach. On the east coast is **Seventy Five Mile Beach**, which at times can seem like a city road during the rush hour. Drive carefully and enjoy the scenery. 🏖

BUNDABERG

Tourist Information: Bundaberg District Tourism and Development Board, *corner Mulgrave and Bourbong Sts; tel: (071) 52 2333.*

ACCOMMODATION AND FOOD

Alexandra Park Motor Inn, *66 Quay St; tel: 52 7255.* **Bougainvillea International Motor Inn**, *73 Takalvan St; tel: 51 2365.* **Reef Gateway Motor Inn** *(FL),* 11 *Takalvan St; tel: 532255.* **Sugar Country Motor Inn**, *220*

Bourbong St; tel: 071-531166. **Bert Hinkler Motor Inn** *(FL), corner Takalvan and Warrell Sts; tel: 52 6400.*

Spinnaker Stonegrill and Bar, on the river front at *Quay St; tel: 52 8033.* Open daily lunch and dinner. Licensed. Jazz at weekends.

SIGHTSEEING

The first part of the name Bundaberg comes from an Aboriginal tribe – the Bunda. The name was chosen by District Surveyor Thompson in 1869. The town is 15 km inland on the **Burnett River** and about 50 km from the Bruce Hwy. This is sugar cane country and during the crushing season driving in the area has two hazards – both picturesque – cane trains and fires. The cane trains cross the roads and the cane fires, deliberately set to clear away insects and debris, can light up the sky for miles. This is also where the famous **Bundaberg Rum** comes from. In Australia you will rarely find another brand and a Bundie and Coke is a universally popular drink.

Sugar growing was established in the area in the 1870s using the Pacific Islands indentured labourers – *kanakas* – who were frequently brought against their will in one of the less glorious chapters of Australian history.

Bundaberg is the home town of two of Australia's heroes – the singer **Gladys Moncrieff** – 'Our Glad' – and the pioneer aviator **Bert Hinkler**, who made the first solo flights between England and Australia.

To understand how central sugar is to the area's economy, visit the **Isis Central Mill**, (south on Isis Hwy, on your right a few kilometres before the Gin Gin turn-off). Tours every week day at 1400 from mid Jul–Nov, the crushing season. This mill crushes just under a million tonnes of cane a year and generates $30 million of income for the district.

You can also visit the **Bundaberg Mill**, *Whittered St;* $3, but only in the distilling section. There are five tours a day during the week and four a day at weekends. The tour lasts 1 hr and afterwards you are invited to sample the product. There is a rum museum, which is a transported colonial Queensland building, **Spring Hill House**. Tours start at 1000.

The English home of the local hero Bert

Bert Hinkler

In 1921 Bert Hinkler flew the 1270 km from Sydney to Bundaberg and thus set a world record for continuous flight in his Baby Avro, a light aircraft. Then, in 1928, he flew from London to Darwin in just over 15 days. It should be understood that the previous record for the flight was 28 days and he was the first person to make the trip solo. As a result his visit to Canberra on March 14 1928 was a great civil celebration. In England the magazine *Punch* came up with:
'Hinkle, Hinkle, little star,
Sixteen days and here you are!'

He was one of a group, all ex-World I aviators, who decided to stay in aviation: the most famous of them was Sir Charles Kingsford Smith, who said 'My intentions are to take up flying in Australia after the war. It is an honourable and interesting career, and at home there will be possibilities for our services.'

Those possibilities and efforts by men like Hinkler and Kingsford Smith resulted in the formation of Qantas – Queensland and Northern Territory Aerial Service – in 1922, as well as the use of aviation to connect the remote country towns of Australia.

Hinkler is well remembered in the town and there is a replica of his Baby Arvo built from wires and canvas in the tourist office on *Bourbong St.*

Hinkler was at *29 Lydgate Rd, Thornhill, Southampton.* Hinkler lived there from 1926 until his death in 1933. It was in this house that he planned his world-conquering flights, including the flight to Australia. In 1982 it was in danger of demolition and the people of Bundaberg bought it and brought it back to the town of his birth, where it is now the **Hinkler Museum**, *corner Mt Perry Rd and Young St; tel: 52 0222*, in the centre of the **Botanic Gardens**, 4 km from the centre of town on the road to Gin Gin. Open daily 1000–1600.

There is also a **Hinkler Glider Museum**, *corner Mulgrave and Bourbong Sts; tel: 52 2333*. Open daily 0900–1700. It has Bert Hinkler's first aircraft on display; a lightweight glider which he flew on **Mon Repos Beach** in 1912. The beach is also famous for its **turtle rookery** (open daily Nov–Feb), where loggerhead female turtles clamber over the beaches in the dark to lay their eggs. Information leaflets are available from the Tourist Information Centre or at Mon Repos Beach.

An overall view of the history of the region is given by the **Bundaberg and District Historical and Museum Society**, *Young St.* Open Mon–Sat 1000–1600. $1.50. On display are memorabilia of early life in Bundaberg and a full size aeroplane, with Bert Hinkler connections, hangs from the ceiling.

Paradise Park, Paradise Lane; tel: 55 1085, is a private enterprise animal hospital and nursery for the region. There are 100 volunteers who help run the hospital. There are over a hundred varieties of animals and birds and the park has many kangaroos, wallabies and koalas. Open daily 0900–1700. $5.

223

Tourist Information: **Gladstone Regional Information Office**, *56 Goondoon St; tel: 07972 4000.*

ACCOMMODATION

Country Plaza International *(FL), 100 Goondoon St; tel: 72 4499.* **Country Club Motor Inn** *(GC), corner Far St and Dawson Hwy; tel: 72 4322.* **Camelot Motel** *(BW), 19 Agnes St, corner Elizabeth St; tel: 79 1222.* **Amber Lodge Motel**, *129 Toolooa St; tel: 72 4144.* **Gladstone Motel**, *88 Toolooa St; tel: 72 2144.*

Gladstone Village Motor Inn, *corner Dawson Hwy and Chapman Dr.; tel: 782077.* **Gladstone Reef Hotel** *(FL), corner Coondon and Yarroon Sts; tel: 721000.* **Mawarra Motel**, *6 Scenery St; tel: 72 1411.* **Mid City Motor Inn**, *26 Goondoon St; tel: 72 3000.* **Siesta Villa Motor Inn**, *104 Glenlyon St; tel: 72 4922.* **Why-Not Motor Inn**, *23 Coon St; tel: 72 4222.* **A1 Motel** *(BU), Toolooa St; tel: 72 1655.* **Park View Gladstone Motel**, *42*

Roseberry St; tel: 72 3344. **Rusty Anchor Motor Inn**, *167 Goondoon St; tel: 72 2099.* **Sun Court Motor Inn**, *Far St; tel: 72 2377.* **Rocky Glen Hotel Motel**, *Dawson Hwy; tel: 72 2977.* **Queens Hotel Motel**, *corner Goondoon and William Sts; 72 6615.*

SIGHTSEEING

Gladstone is named after William Ewart Gladstone, the British prime minister, who in his time as Colonial Secretary advocated settlement of northern Australia as a new colony with the capital of what was then called **Port Curtis**. The entrance to Port Curtis was explored by Owen Stanley in HMS *Rattlesnake* in 1848 and then a settlement was established with 200 convicts. They were harassed in turn by mosquitoes and local Aborigines. Three months later Port Curtis was abandoned when Gladstone ceased to be Colonial Secretary and his replacement abandoned the idea of settling northern Australia.

In 1854 the region was opened to settlers and the town of Gladstone grew on the site of Port Curtis. There was a strong movement before the turn of the century to make Gladstone the capital of Queensland but this, like Port Curtis, failed.

The town has exploded in size since the 1960s, when the bauxite refinery at **Parson's Point** came on line, handling ore from Weipa on the Cape York Peninsula, and eventually becoming the world's largest single-stream bauxite plant, covering 80 hectares. It supplies about a quarter of all Australia's aluminium. The refinery and dock area, with its array of wharves totally dominate the Gladstone landscape.

But despite the industry, Gladstone is a pleasant town and is a good starting point for the Great Barrier Reef. It has a splendid new marina, where you can catch boats to many of the islands on the reef.

One way of seeing the town is to take the driving circuit, which starts at the Visitors Information Centre, covers the central area, the waterfront and the south-east and west sides of the town. The centre has a free map of the 30 km tour.

Worth seeing in town is the **Regional Art Gallery and Museum**, *Goondoon St; tel: 72 2022*, which is housed in an elegant Georgian style-building. It has three basic areas and the one used for visiting exhibitions normally has an interesting collection on display. Open Mon–Fri 1000–1700, Sat 1000–1600.

Out of Gladstone and on to the Bruce Hwy, ou come to **Port Curtis Historic Village**, *tel: 78 1486*, which is a re-creation of an historical village – not the original Port Curtis, which never got to this size – with railway station, church, homes and regular market days. Open daily 0800–1600; $1.

In the town are the **Toondoon Botanical Gardens**, *Glenlyon Road; tel: 72 2022*, which has a display of gardens complete with a lake, surrounded by 34 hectares of natural bush with a marked 3 km bush walk that takes in two lookouts. Open daily 0900–1730.

In *Flinders Parade* is the **Rotary Waterfall** – Rotary as in donating club rather than movement. It is lit-up from dusk until 2130, later at the weekend, and is situated at the foot of *Auckland Hill*. Behind the waterfall there are 111 steps that take the energetic to the **Auckland Point** lookout, with its views of the harbour and the island.

 **SIDE TRACK FROM GLADSTONE**

CARNARVON NATIONAL PARK

Tourist Information: Rangers Office; *tel: (079)84 4505.*

Although the best known part of the park is the gorge, the area covered extends to 251,000 hectares on the **Great Dividing Range** and the **Consuelo Tableland**. But the magnet is the gorge which winds for 30 km through white sandstone walls, which at times are as high as 200m. The creek that cut the gorge runs all year round, with the result that there is luxuriant vegetation at all times. Wallabies, possums and kangaroos often come to drink in the creek.

The access to Carnarvon Gorge is along the Carnarvon Developmental Road via Consuelo, 20 km south of **Rolleston**. This is along partially sealed roads. After heavy rains the unsealed portion of the roads tends to be impassable and you should check first with the park rangers.

At the gorge itself there is a track running for 9.3 km from the Visitor's Centre along the creek – it crosses it 18 times on the way – to **Cathedral Cave** with Aboriginal paintings inside. There are steps and ladders to help you make an easy ascent to **Boolimba Bluff**, which has staggering views of the whole area. This is a strenuous walk and climb but the results are well worth it. ⛰

ROCKHAMPTON

Tourist Information: Capricorn Information Centre, *Highway 1, Gladstone Road; tel: (079) 27 2055* or the **Riverside Information Centre,** *Quay St; tel: 22 5339.*

ACCOMMODATION

Cattle City Motor Inn *(BW), 139 Gladstone Rd; tel: 27 7811.* **Centrepoint Motor Inn** *(FL), 131 George St; tel: 27 8844.* **Country Comfort Inn Rockhampton** *(CC), 86 Victoria Parade; tel: 27 9933.* **Albert Court Motel** *(BW), corner Albert and Alma Sts; tel: 27 7433.* **Archer Park Motel,** *39 Albert St; tel: 27 9266.* **Regency on Albert Street Motel,** *28–34 Albert St; tel: 22 6222.*

Travellers Motor Inn *(FL), 110–116 George St; tel: 27 7900.* **Castle Court Motor Inn,** *75 Gladstone Rd; tel: 27 5377.* **Central Park Motel** *(GC), 224 Murray St; tel: 27 2333.* **Country Lodge Motor Inn** *(FL), 112 Gladstone Rd; tel: 27 8866.* **Duthies Leichhardt Hotel,** *corner Denham and Bolsover Sts; tel: 27 6733.* **Fitzroy Motor Inn,** *corner Fitzroy and Campbell Sts; tel: 27 9255.* **Golden Fountain Motel,** *166 Gladstone Rd; tel: 27 1055.* **Motel 98,** *98 Victoria Parade; tel: 27 5322.*

A1 Motel Rockhampton South *(BU), Gladstone Rd, (Burke Hwy); tel: 27 4944.* **Ambassador on the Park Motel,** *161–165 George St; tel: 27 5855.* **The Motel Lodge,** *100 Gladstone Rd; tel: 27 3130.* **Porky's Motel,** *141 George St; tel: 27 8100.* **Post Office Hotel-Motel,** *corner Musgrave and* Burnett Sts; tel: 27 3899. **Simpsons Motel,** *156 George St; tel: 27 7800.* **Tropical Gateway Motor Inn,** *122 Gladstone Rd; tel: 27 8822.* **HI:** *60 Macfarlane St; tel: 27 5288.*

SIGHTSEEING

The town, familiarly known to every Australian as Rocky, was named in 1856 by Henry Wiseman, the Commissioner of Crown Lands. He created the name from a word for town – Hampton – with a prefix to indicate that it was near the rocks in the **Fitzroy River,** above the old bridge.

In its wilder early days Rockhampton was known as 'the town of the three S's – sin, sweat and sorrow.'

The town started very quietly in 1857 as a store and an inn, although it was grandly called a port. It was the centre for the remarkable Archer family, who came there to raise beef. Rockhampton's fortunes rocketed as a result of exaggerated reports of gold at nearby **Canoona** – 60 km to the south-west – and Rockhampton instantly expanded into a shanty town.

In the 1860s the discovery of copper in **Peaks Down** and **Mt Morgan** led to a consolidation of the town, which had become a centre of one of the premier beef regions in Australia. It still is today.

Rockhampton is 40 km from the coast, right on the Tropic of Capricorn and an hour's drive from **Gladstone.** It could be thought of as the capital of Capricornia and is, indeed, the start of the Capricorn Hwy, which goes out to **Winton** and then heads into the NeverNever. There is a marker at the southern end of the town, next to the tourist information centre, indicating your position. The river neatly divides the town, which is connected by the Fitzroy Bridge.

The town's prosperity in the last century is reflected by the fact that more than fifty buildings have been classified by the National Trust. The *Quay St* historical precinct has several of these buildings, including the city's **Custom House,** built of sandstone, with a copper dome.

The city is further beautified in the spring and early summer by amazing displays of bauhinia and bougainvillea flowers.

225

The **Botanical Gardens**, *tel: 31 1254*, are extensive and said to be some of the best in tropical Australia. The gardens incorporate a mini zoo and aviary. Open dawn to dusk.

Within easy driving distance are limestone caves, which are thought to have originally been part of the Great Barrier Reef. The **Cammoo Caves**, *Bruce Hwy*, 21 km north of Rockhampton; *tel: 34 2774*, are inhabited by bats. Open daily 0800. Tours every hour from 0930–1600. $7.

The Dreamtime Cultural Centre is reputed to be Australia's largest Aboriginal Cultural Centre and is also on the Bruce Hwy, north of Rockhampton opposite the turn-off for Yeppoon. Open daily 1000–1730; *tel: 36 1655*. It is set in some 12 hectares of natural bushland and there are two tours a day at 1100 and 1400. $8.

Further along off the Bruce Hwy, 22 km north of Rockhampton, is **Gangalook Museum**, *tel: 34 2827,* which has a slab cottage, antique machinery and vintage cars. Open seven days a week 0900–1600; $5.

Aboriginal Dreamtime

I t is generally held that the Australian Aborigines were probably migrants from the Asian mainland in prehistoric times. But the Aborigines themselves know that they came from the Dreamtime. This is a consistent feature of their beliefs, no matter which of the several hundred Aboriginal languages they speak. Although there are some words that run through most of these language versions, and the grammar is much the same, most of the languages differ as much as the languages of Europe.

The central core of the belief of Australian Aborigines is centred around the traditions of their clans, rites and customs. They strongly believe in the spiritual significance of the land. Over-simplifying it, one could say that most Australian Aborigines believe that their clan members are all descended from a common ancestral being.

Complex rituals, art and traditions link the clan to the land, and Aborigines believe that their spirits will return there when they die. They believe that to destroy or damage a sacred site is a threat to both the living and the spirits. This is not a belief that is generally shared by other Australians which results, at times, in friction.

Linking the Aborigines to their ancestral being are totems. Each person has a totem, which is also sometimes called 'Dreaming'. The clan honours them and the Dreamtime creators. These totems can take different forms – normally animal – and these are closely reflected in all Aboriginal art.

Aboriginal art is quite remarkable and much sought after and can attract very high prices. The distinguishing features are abstract geometrical patterns and representational designs, and a bold use of colour. Some paintings are on bark and some, perhaps the grandest, are to be found in caves and on rocks.

Although some Aborigines still live as nomads in the Northern Territory, parts of Western Australia and Queensland, large numbers live among white Australians. Their plight is, indeed, sad, and their life expectancy is the lowest in Australia.

At the time of the first settlement by Europeans, it is estimated the aboriginal population of Australia was between 150,000 and 300,000. By the 1970s the population had declined to about 160,000 because of lack of resistance to the diseases introduced by Europeans, disruption of the Aboriginal way of life, and, in the early period, government indifference. Now the figures have risen again and are today thought to be in excess of 250,000.

226

THE GREAT
BARRIER REEF

Until you go there it is totally impossible to grasp the immensity and variety of the Great Barrier Reef. Captain James Cook called it 'a wall of coral rock rising almost perpendicular out of the unfathomable ocean'. And, yes, in places along this 2000 km Queensland coastline, it is. But it is also a series of islands, most uninhabited, ranging from 'continental' islands – large pieces of the mainland, which are the tops of drowned mountains – to coral cays, formed when wreckage and floating plants catch on to a piece of coral just coming out of the sea and hang on there long enough for a minute island to form (see p.230).

The islands of the reef range from National Parks – the whole of the reef is in fact a gazetted area – to resort islands. In a very few cases, the resorts have intruded on the natural beauty; Hamilton Island is a particularly bad example. In others, the development has been kept in tune with the nature of the area, of which a most excellent example is Lizard Island. The islands range from large and affordable to small and exclusive, which is another way of spelling expensive. Resorts like Lizard, Orpheus and Bedarra have an international reputation, charge international prices and do not allow children.

ARRIVING AND DEPARTING

Getting to the reef depends very much on where you want to get to. You can, of course, fly in and land on the Great Barrier Reef itself from any major airport in Australia – there is a full scale jet airport on Hamilton. You can helicopter in from almost any Queensland resort town. Or you can go in by ferry. But, remember the Reef is 2000 km long and where you are going directly affects which part of the mainland you leave from. Does the reef ever meet the mainland? Yes, it does. Just across the Daintree River on the far northern side of Cairns the reef actually comes in to the shore – which is rain forest – before veering out again.

TOURIST INFORMATION

Queensland Government Travel Centre, *corner Adelaide and Edward Sts, Brisbane; tel: (07) 3221 6111.*

227

LADY ELLIOT ISLAND

Tourist Information: Lady Elliot Island Resort, *tel: 071 53 2485.*

Lady Elliot is 90 km east of Bundaberg and is the southern extremity of both the **Reef Marine Park** and the Great Barrier Reef. The island is a danger to navigation and the lighthouse, still properly maintained, was built in 1873, replacing the original of 1866, which was blown down in a storm. It has been converted to automatic operation but, as a lighthouse, it would be fair to say that it has been something less than a resounding success.

The name of the island comes from a sloop called *The Lady Elliot*, which ran aground on the **Hinchinbrook Reef** in 1816, starting a persistent maritime fashion. There have probably been more wrecks on the reef of Lady Elliot than any other piece of coastline in Australia.

The island was one of the starting places of the Australian beche-de-mer industry in

Australia, supplying these gastronomic delicacies to the Asian market. Lady Elliot – actually a coral cay, which is part of the reef – has suffered the depredations of guano mining in the last century and over-grazing by goats, although vegetation is slowly returning. The 42 sq km island was formed over a 3000-year period and you can learn about its life cycle on a guided reef walk. A complete circuit of the island takes less than 1 hr. Lady Elliot is a real skin diver's paradise, with amazing 40m visibility on a clear day and a wealth of marine life as well as several wrecks in the immediate area. It is also unusual in that you can dive straight from the beach.

There are 10 major dive sites, including **Coral Gardens**, **Lighthouse Bommie**, **Moiri** and **Shark Pool**. Visibility is almost always excellent and can extend to 50m in the right conditions. The coral is in good condition and snorkelling and glass bottom boats make viewing attractively easy. However, as an anchorage holding it can be very dangerous.

This is a most attractive destination for bird-watchers, as the island boasts more than 57 varieties. More that 200,000 individuals nest here in the summer, as do sea turtles.

To get to the island you have to travel on one of the daily 30-min twin-engined flight – book with **Sunstate**, *tel: 13 1313* or *(071) 52 2322*. This is the only coral cay on the reef with its own airstrip, which was built in 1969.

The accommodation is perfectly acceptable, if not at the luxury end of the market. It has permanently erected safari style tents and motel type rooms called **Reef Units**.

HERON ISLAND

Tourist Information: Queensland National Parks & Wildlife Service, Heron Island Information Centre; *tel: (079) 72 5690* or **Heron Island P&O Resort**; *tel: (079) 78 1488*.

Heron Island is a very small coral cay 70 km north-east of Gladstone on the mainland, 100 km from Rockhampton and 500 km north of Brisbane. It lies right on the Tropic of Capricorn and barely rises 2.5m above the reef. It extends to 17 hectares – a complete tour of the place hardly occupies a full hour. But, despite its size, it is part of a most extensive reef.

Heron is in a lagoon that covers 40 sq km and most of the coral flats can be walked over at low tide. Two thirds of the cay is National Park. On the other third, the north-eastern end, there is a resort and a marine research station. The research station is Queensland's first and studies the different forms of marine and reef life. Heron Island is a turtle rookery with the greenback, hawksbill and loggerhead migrating to lay their eggs on the beaches. The island is a sanctuary for 30 species of birds, including 100,000 black noddy terns and reef herons. During the migration season, humpback whales regularly pass the island.

Heron has been very lucky to escape the blight of feral goats although there was at one time a turtle canning factory operating on the island (open 1925–30). But in the main it has survived unscathed. And the island lives up to its name – herons can be seen around the coral, which is exposed at low tide.

Heron is spectacular in that the beach runs straight into the coral. This, sadly, is far from being the best coral on the Reef but the aquatic life is nothing short of astounding. Indeed, it is reckoned, by some authorities, to be among the best in the world. This near and easy access gives brilliant snorkelling conditions and there is a small drop-off wall to hover around on the eastern side of the island. Skin diving is also catered for through the resort. Although the dive sites are very near, all diving is off a boat – there is no diving straight off the beach.

The vegetation on the island is mainly casuarina and pandanus with occasional pockets of dense bush and the island is renowned for the variety of its bird life. In the season they can be very noisy and being struck by an aerial dropping is a hazard.

There is a small harbour with a jetty, which was created by dredging, and this has resulted in the death of some coral, although the full environmental effects have not yet been fully tabulated.

The resort is owned by P&O (*tel: 079 78 1488*) and is mid-level rather than top of the market, although the cost of staying there is increased by the ferry fare for the 2 hr catamaran trip, $120; or the 30 min helicopter trip, $355 (both return prices). Both helicopter flights and the catamaran service operate daily from Gladstone. The catamaran ride across open water in rough weather can be a serious test of stamina and sea sickness pills are strongly recommended.

The resort accommodation consists of lodges with shared facilities or motel-like suites. Prices are inclusive of all meals. No camping is allowed on the island. Most of the guests who come to Heron Island are primarily interested in skin diving and most of the facilities are geared to their needs.

There is a strange anomaly. Heron Island time is 1 hr behind Australian Eastern Standard Time. No one is able to give a satisfactory explanation as to why this should be so.

GREAT KEPPEL ISLAND

Tourist Information: Great Keppel Island Resort; *tel: (079) 39 5044.*

Keppel is a 14 sq km continental island, as opposed to a coral cay. It is only 13 km from the coast at Rockhampton, just north of the Tropic of Capricorn in the group called the **Keppel Islands**. The name comes from Captain Cook, who chose it in 1770 to honour Rear Admiral Augustus Keppel, who later became the First Lord of the Admiralty.

Great Keppel is blessed with brilliant white sand beaches – 28 km of them – and has plenty of coral to explore, although it is a fair distance from the reef. The beaches are some of the best on the islands and finding a deserted one is just a matter of strolling far enough. A fringing reef protects the 17 beaches of the island. The island is thickly forested although there are several tracks that lead to the 175m summit of **Mt Wyndham**.

The island attracts day trippers from the mainland and both the diving and snorkelling are good. Surrounding Great Keppel are the 17 islands of the Keppel group, all effectively undeveloped because of a lack of water and because most of them are now national parks.

Great Keppel is one of the few islands which caters for backpackers and budget travellers. It has a hostel with two 16-bed dorms, while a lodge has motel-style units. The resort specialises in package holidays and has nearly 200 units. The island is a place for an active holiday

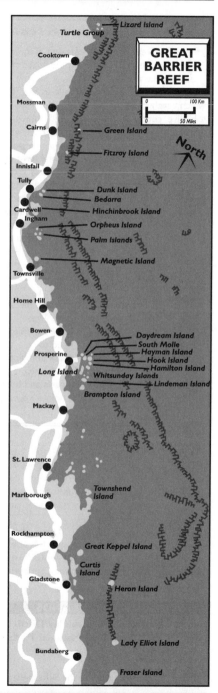

229

The Great Barrier Reef

The Great Barrier Reef is one of the wonders of Australia, and of the world. It stretches for over 1200 km from the coast of Papua New Guinea to Bundaberg in Queensland. In the north it is relatively narrow – between 15 and 25 km wide. But in the south, beyond Cairns, it extends far out to sea. The 700-plus islands in the Reef range from atolls which barely clear the water to major landmarks. The Reef is not a dead accretion of rocks – it is alive, continually extending and renewing itself. It is a huge system built by tiny creatures, which are only a few millimetres in size. These living coral polyps excrete a limy skeleton, which remains as coral when they die and new polyps grow on the dead skeletons.

So far 340 different types of coral have been identified but it is likely that the number will increase over the years. Coral will only grow and thrive in clean, salt water so the preservation of the outer edge of the Australian continental shelf is vital for the future of the reef. Coral cannot live above water but sometimes dead coral will accumulate, floating jetsam will stick and slowly the reef will rise above the water level. This is how a cay is formed, which, eventually, becomes colonised by grass, which in turn brings the sea birds and then, centuries later, trees grow and another part of the reef has become an island.

Despite its size the reef is a delicate creature, easily disturbed by the Crown of Thorns starfish, resort development and the impact of tourists. In 1979 almost all of it was proclaimed a **marine park** and now it is managed to balance the needs of all users with the health of the reef itself always the primary concern.

The reef, apart from its coral, also has an amazing range of aquatic life in a mind-boggling range of colours, sizes and types. These colours and decorations are a form of protection against predators and the result for the visitor is a wonderland of flashing colours. To enjoy the fish and the sea life you don't need to be a scuba diver. Most of the activity takes place in very shallow waters and a snorkel, mask and flippers will do very well.

The beauty is not just below the sea. The reef is home to 240 different species of birds. There are probably 2900 coral reefs and hundreds of continental islands and coral cays, most of which have an abundance of unique vegetation.

230

and squash, tennis, golf, archery, volleyball and skydiving are all catered for – it is very popular with the younger crowd. The night-life on Great Keppel is famous, possibly notorious, and 'getting wrecked on Keppel' was once an advertising theme for the resort.

There are two flights daily from Rockhampton by **Air Sunstate**, which is now a subsidiary of Qantas. Ferries and cruises leave from **Rosslyn Bay Harbour** on the Capricorn Coast, south of Yeppoon.

WHITSUNDAY ISLANDS

Tourist Information: Whitsunday District Office of the Queensland National Parks & Wildlife Service, *Airlie Beach; tel: (079) 46 7022.*

There are over 70 islands in the Whitsunday group and they form the best known and the most visited part of the Barrier Reef islands. The name came from Captain Cook, who sailed through on July 3 1770 – Whitsunday. Because of the protection provided by the reef these are some of the safest sailing waters in the world and bareboat chartering – yacht supplied with no crew – is a major tourist industry. Captain Cook had it right when he said 'the whole passage is one continuous safe harbour.'

All bar five of the islands in this group are National Parks and much of the mainland facing the Whitsundays is also a series of National Parks. Almost 95% of the total area has been classified. All of the waters are zoned and, by and large, the rule is you can look but not take, although in some Zone A areas limited fishing is allowed. All of the islands are continental islands with full vegetation. Many also have fringing reef systems to make up for it.

The main centre for access to the Whitsundays is **Airlie Beach**, which is where most of the cruise, tour and bare boat charter operators are based.

BRAMPTON ISLAND

Tourist Information: Brampton Island Resort, *Brampton Island; tel: (079) 51 4499*.

This island National Park, established in 1932, covers 464 hectares and is a hilly, continental island. Strictly speaking, it is part of the **Cumberland Group**, which is sometimes referred to as the **Southern Whitsundays**, but the line dividing the two groups is totally arbitrary and can be ignored. The **Brampton Holiday Resort** is one of the oldest on an island, having opened in 1933 as a holiday farm. The only earlier resort in the reef area is **Lindeman**.

Some of the slopes of the island have been denuded by domestic animals but most are still heavily forested. From the turn of the century, Brampton was used by the Queensland government as a nursery for palm trees and the island still has splendid stands of them. There are 11 km of walking tracks to the various coves and beaches and wonderful views can be seen from the 213 m high **Brampton Peak**. The walk to the summit starts near the golf course belonging to the resort and is a 2 hr round trip, allowing for time at both lookouts. The island has much wildlife including cockatoos and grey kangaroos. Nearby is **Carlisle**, which is an undeveloped National Park covering 520 hectares – a little larger than Brampton – and is densely covered with vegetation and uninhabited.

At low tide it is possible to walk across the reef to Carlisle and the reefs at **Oyster** and **Dinghy Bays** are perfect for snorkelling. You can also walk across to the much smaller **Pelican Island** at low tide. Note that the waters are part of the **Marine National Park** and no shell or coral collecting is allowed.

There is a beach resort, *tel: (079) 51 449*, owned and managed by Qantas, which is middle-range and low key and has a rattle-trap of a train, built in 1962, to take guests from the jetty to the resort. The resort itself is at **Sandy**

Point, which is the north-central corner of the island looking across to Carlisle. Generally this is more of a family resort with none of the 'get wrecked' atmosphere of Great Keppel.

Good snorkelling is to be found in the channel between Brampton and Carlisle. There is serious skin diving on **Credlin reef** and the nearby **Catacombs**.

Brampton is accessible by plane and launches from **Mackay**. **Roylen Cruises**, which once owned the resort on the island, has a cruise to Brampton, leaving Mackay every day at 0830, *tel: (079) 555 1303*.

LINDEMAN ISLAND

Tourist Information: Club Med, *Lindeman Island; tel: (079) 46 9598*.

Lindeman is the most southerly island of the Whitsunday Group, 32 km from the coast, and covers 8 sq km. The whole island is a National Park and it boasts a small mountain, **Mt Oldfield**, which is 210 m high and has panoramic views. There are paths leading to the summit and also to most of the beaches on the island.

Lindeman got its name in 1868, not from the winemaker, but from a Royal Navy sublieutenant, George Sydney Lindeman, who charted safe passages through the Whitsundays.

Much of the island is covered in eucalypts although the vegetation has suffered badly from attacks by feral goats. These have now been eradicated and the native plants are making something of a comeback. The island has 20 km of marked walking tracks with lookouts affording wonderful views across the **Pentecost**, **Hamilton** and **Whitsunday Islands**. The island also has seven splendid beaches. It is well known for its butterflies, the best known being the Blue Tiger, which can be seen Oct–May. All walks basically start from the airstrip, including the 4 km walk to the top of Mt Oldfield. This walk goes right around the peak and there are amazing views across the Whitsundays.

Lindeman is blessed or cursed, views greatly differ, with a **Club Med** *(tel: 1 800 80 1823)*, opened in 1992. This was Australia's first Club Med and provides all of the usual facilities, which means that you can be active every minute of the waking day. The resort has, on occasion, been savagely attacked in the media

231

but it also has a large group of supporters. Lindeman it is not the best island for scuba although you can dive and there is a dive school on the island, which gives introductory lessons.

Departures daily by air or launch from **Shute Harbour, Mackay** and **Hamilton Island**. Or you can fly to Hamilton Island and take a launch from there.

HAMILTON ISLAND

Tourist Information: Hamilton Island Resort, *Hamilton Island Post Office; tel: (079) 46 9999.*

Hamilton Island covers 6 sq km, has daily direct jet connections to Cairns, Brisbane, Sydney and Melbourne and is separated from Whitsunday Island, which lies to the north, by the Fitzalan Passage. The island is some 16 km south-east of Shute Harbour in the heart of the Whitsunday Islands, about 900 km north of Brisbane. This island is somewhat controversial as the resort is perhaps more suited to the high-rise central business district of a city rather than a tropical island. It has been described with elegant accuracy as the Gold Coast revisited. In fact it is a town rather than a resort, specialising in packaged tours.

Uniquely it has a modern jet airport and can be reached by scheduled flight from almost anywhere in Australia. There is one major resort and two minor ones and the whole island is packaged for tourists, with almost every activity available. There is a 20-hectare fauna park with kangaroos, koalas and a dolphin pool as well as eight swimming pools and nine restaurants. As a general rule all the facilities on the island are expensive, sometimes alarmingly so.

The **Hamilton Island Resort,** *tel: (079) 469 100,* was originally built for the international jet set by entrepreneur Keith Williams, who managed to get a deer farming lease changed to one for tourism. The resort was built with major backing from, among others, Ansett Airlines. It was opened just in time to be hit by a long strike by the airline pilots and was eventually placed in receivership. All the buildings, the jet airstrip and the massive infrastructure flew totally against all conservation policy – and there was hardly a murmur of protest. There is no way in the world that it

could be built in these days, but in the 1980s things in Queensland were different.

Today the resort is sold to a wider market although the prices are still very high, especially if you want to use any of the facilities or restaurants on the island. At any one time Hamilton can accommodate up to 2000 tourists.

However, the east side of the island is relatively undeveloped and there is a walk around the coastline at **Catseye Beach**, which then starts to climb until you reach the summit of **Passage Peak** with views north to the Whitsunday Islands. Hamilton Island has fringing coral reef, with the best snorkelling at Catseye Beach. You can also visit the Outer Reef by high speed catamaran or helicopter.

You can fly direct to Hamilton Island from Brisbane, the Gold Coast, Cairns, Townsville, Melbourne or Sydney. The island's catamaran departs twice daily from Shute Harbour.

SOUTH MOLLE ISLAND

Tourist Information: South Molle Island Resort, *South Molle; tel: (079) 46 9433.*

South Molle is the central island in the Whitsunday Passage, 8 km north-east of Shute Harbour, and is the largest of the **Molle** group. The island is effectively joined to **Mid Molle** and **North Molle** islands and you can walk to Mid Molle at any time. The name Molle comes from Colonel George Molle, Lieutenant Governor of New South Wales in 1815.

South Molle is a hilly island with grasslands and patches of rain forest on its slopes, which is still slowly recovering from the effects of overgrazing in earlier years. The island is only 4 km long and 2 km wide at its broadest point – the total area is 4 sq km – but it has 12 km of sand and coral shorelines, although it is not blessed with great beaches.

Tracks lead up to the 198m peak of **Mt Jeffreys**. Most of the island is national park and there are some fine short walks, all of which are well signposted. There is a 3 km walk to the top of **Spion Kop** – the name comes from the Boer War – which gives a fine view of the surrounding sea and islands.

South Molle Island Resort is a low-key. mid-level, laid-back and very Australian establishment in the north of the island and its site is

232

also the terminus for the ferry from the mainland. The resort offers a wide range of activities including most sports and, unusual in these resorts, almost all activities are free.

From South Molle there are cruises to the outer reef and the waters around the island are excellent for snorkelling and diving. The resort also offers trips to the underwater observatory on **Hook Island**. The island offers golf, day and night tennis, squash and a full range of water sports.

You can get to South Molle by high speed catamaran from Shute Harbour, which takes about 30 mins. Alternatively, fly to Hamilton Island and take the launch from there.

DAYDREAM ISLAND

Tourist Information: Daydream Resort; *tel: (079) 48 84888.*

Originally known as **West Molle**, this Whitsunday island is very near Shute Harbour – 5 km – which makes it the closest of the group to the mainland. It lies neatly between South Molle and Shute Harbour and in all covers less than 2 sq km – 17 hectares to be precise – which makes it one of the smallest islands in the Whitsundays. Most of the volcanic rock and coral island is covered with dense bush, with a beach running the whole length of the east side. Daydream is not a bright marketing name invented by an advertising agency. It was the name of a gaff rigged ketch, owned by Paddy Murray, who bought the island in 1934 and renamed it.

Daydream Resort (*tel: 079 48 84888*) totally dominates the island. It was opened in 1990 and is managed by the Travelodge chain. While the island is one of the smallest in the Whitsundays this resort is one of the biggest. In its favour it does offer excellent facilities. Snorkelling among the fringing coral and most aquatic sports including sailboarding, jet-skiing, parasailing, coral viewing in glass bottomed boats and reef fishing are available. Most of its normal activities and non-powered water sports are free. The resort has a small marina and a beach club at the opposite end, the south end, of the island for the use of guests.

There are two beaches on the island – **Sunlover's** is small and behind the resort, and

the other beach runs in front of the **Beach Club** at the other end of the island. You can walk from the resort to the Beach Club but it can be quite a climb in the heat of the day.

The island can easily be reached by launch from Shute Harbour – eight services a day – or Hamilton Island, and the resort does not try to stop day-trippers.

HOOK ISLAND

Tourist Information: Whitsunday Connections Travel Centre, *43 Shute Harbour Rd, Airlie Beach; tel: (079) 46 6900.*

Hook is the second largest island in the group to the north of Whitsunday. The island, part of which is National Park, has two fjord type inlets cutting into the southern end – **Nara** and **Macona**. These 5 km long inlets provide safe and scenic anchorages for yachts. Hook is a true wilderness island and **Hook Peak**, which rises to 459m, is the highest mountain in the islands. There are few walking tracks on this rugged island but there are a number of excellent beaches and superb diving.

The snorkelling opposite the island's resort at the north end of the island is some of the best in the area, which means some of the best in the world. The coral is in fair condition, the water normally very clear and the aquatic life is spectacular. Near the resort is an underwater observatory, where you can observe the fish and the coral from 10m down without getting your feet wet. Open 1000–1400, $8.50.

There is a low-key, basic resort at the southern end, which also has camp sites and is very popular with backpackers. There are also camp sites at **Curlew Beach** and **Stonehaven Beach** (*tel: 079 45 2165*) but these are only accessible if you have your own boat. The passage between Hook Island and Whitsunday Island is narrow and sometimes creates strong currents, which can be dangerous to swimmers and divers moving too far offshore.

For access, ferries run daily from Shute Harbour at 0830 and 1400, returning at 0930 and 1500. $12 return.

HAYMAN ISLAND

Tourist Information: Hayman Island Resort, *Hayman Island; tel: (079) 46 9100.*

233

Hayman is the most northerly of the Whitsunday Group; 28 km north-east of Shute Harbour and about 900 km north of Brisbane. The island is 4 sq km and is generally quite mountainous with eucalypt and Hoop Pine covered hills. Most of the island is national park and there are some fine short walks and several marked trails. The island is close to the outer reef with launches available to take you there for snorkelling, coral viewing and diving.

Hayman Island is one of the most luxurious and expensive resorts on the reef – it was set up as a five-star international hotel resort and is not interested in catering for the great unwashed. There has been a resort on the island since 1950. This was taken over and totally rebuilt over a period of two years and $260 million. It re-opened in 1987 with a flourish of trumpets as being the definitive resort for the rich and tasteful. By and large they stayed away and the early years were marked by desperate efforts to widen the target audience so that the empty rooms could be filled. This has happened and now the resort regularly features in the top ten resorts of the world.

It is still expensive, still very up-market. Thus Hayman sometimes acts in an odd way. There is a superb restaurant called **La Fontaine**. In this restaurant on this tropical island gentlemen are expected to wear ties.

Rooms at the resort are not cheap, starting at $350 a night and going up – that is room only, although in fairness all activities are free.

The easiest way to get to Hayman is to fly to Hamilton and then make the 1 hr trip on a launch. This is no ordinary launch. It is a luxury cruiser and you check in during the trip and sip champagne while you do so.

LONG ISLAND

Tourist Information: Club Crocodile; *tel: (079) 46 9400* or **Palm Beach Resort**; *tel: (079) 46 9233.*

As its name implies this is a long narrow island – 11 km long and never more than 1½ km wide. In all it covers 12 sq km. It is only ½ km from the mainland. Long Island was given its prosaic name by the explorer Matthew Flinders, although for a time it was called Port Molle. It is covered in rain forests with tracks

leading to lookout points. There are some 20 km of bushwalking tracks on what has been claimed to be the prettiest island in the Whitsunday Islands. There is good snorkelling and it is close to good scuba diving sites since it is nearer the outer reef than most other Whitsunday islands.

There are two resorts on Long Island but they are small, low key and unobtrusive and have had chequered careers with name and management changes galore. **Club Crocodile** is at the north end of the island while **Palm Beach** is about a third of the way down.

The island has wallabies, fruit bats, goannas and a wide variety of birds.

You can travel to the island by launch from Shute Harbour or Hamilton.

MAGNETIC ISLAND

Tourist Information: Tourist Information office, *Pier, Picnic Bay; tel: (077) 78 5155* or **The Ranger**, *22 Hurst St, Picnic Bay, Magnetic Island; tel: (077) 78 5378.*

Magnetic Island is only 8 km and 20 mins off the coast near Townsville, and is a granite based island of 5184 hectares, which boasts a dramatic coastline with 23 beaches. This is a favourite getaway island for the population of Townsville. And, indeed, it has permanent residents – about 2500 – who commute to the city. This island is also a favourite destination for backpackers because it has such a wide range of affordable accommodation.

The name Magnetic was given because the compass of the *Endeavour* swung wildly as it sailed past. No one has ever been able to repeat that anomaly. There are four settlements on the island and there is vehicular traffic but nearly two-thirds of the island is a National Park, which fortunately restricts further development. Bicycles, motor cycles and mini vehicles are available for hire on the island. There is an excellent leaflet produced by the National Parks, available at the tourist office, with details of all of the many walks on the island.

The easiest way to get Magnetic Island into focus is to think of it as a rough triangle with the main settlement of **Picnic Bay** at its southern point. The right side of the triangle, the east side, is where most of the development has taken place and you can drive through **Nelly Bay** to **Arcadia** and then right through to **Horseshoe Bay**, which is at the top of the triangle in the north. The National Park covers some 2790 hectares and fills much of the centre of the triangle, only taking in the coast in the north and for a third of the east coast.

Picnic Bay is where the ferries arrive and this town has all the facilities. Then travelling up the east coast you come first to **Rocky Bay**, which has an excellent beach, and then the small settlement of Nelly Bay, which boasts among its attractions **Shark World**, where you can see the sharks being fed at 1130 and 1430. Just beyond Nelly Bay is a ruin, which is what is left of the **Magnetic Quay** development, a project to build a marina and hotel that went bankrupt. On from there is **Geoffrey Bay**, which has a walk on the fringing coral and after that Arcadia, which has a pleasant beach and, back from the road, the **Alma Bay Lookout**. The road then splits with the left fork taking you to Horseshoe Bay and the right to **Radical Bay Lookout**.

The hillsides of the island are strewn with boulders and mostly covered with open eucalypt woodland of bloodwoods, stringybark and grey ironbarks. There are also small pockets of rain forest in the gullies. The island also has a fringe reef, which has excellent snorkelling.

The waters surrounding Magnetic Island are part of the Great Barrier Reef Marine Park, which means that some activities may be restricted in some zones some of the time. More details can be obtained from the Great Barrier Reef Marine Park Authority or the Department of Environment and Heritage in Townsville.

High-speed catamarans from Townsville take 20 mins to reach the island and cost around $15 return. It is possible to ferry a vehicle across but as this costs $85 for a short stay it is better to hire on the island.

ORPHEUS ISLAND

Tourist Information: Department of Environment and Heritage, Queensland National Parks and Wildlife Service, *Ingham 4850; tel: (077) 76 1700* or **Orpheus Island Resort**; *tel: (077) 77 7533.*

Orpheus is a volcanic island, which is almost totally national park – 1300 hectares were declared as such in 1979 – and is set in the midst of coral reef. The island, surrounded by a maze of reefs and small islands and fringed by beach after beach, is just under 100 km north of Townsville and about 20 km off the coast of **Ingham**. It is long and narrow, extending 11 km but never wider than 1 km. It is the second largest of the **Palm Group islands**. The name come from the HMS *Orpheus,* which was the largest warship in Australia until it was wrecked in 1863.

The island is largely composed of granite with some volcanic rocks in the north. It has a series of wooded hills with sheltered bays and seven spectacular beaches surrounded by spectacular fringing reefs. These reefs are considered some of the finest on the Reef islands.

At **Pioneer Bay** there is a marine research station. The area reputedly boasts over 1100 different species of fish, 340 species of coral, dolphins swimming offshore and, during the migration season, humpback whales on their way to their breeding grounds.

There are also 50 different species of birds and giant turtles regularly come ashore to lay their eggs.

The best snorkelling is found off the northeast tip, where a great variety of marine life may be seen in shallow water.

Orpheus has one major five star resort, which has been open since 1930 and is thus one of the original reef resorts. The atmosphere is laid-back but luxurious, with studio units and two bungalows. It occupies leased land overlooking Hazard Bay.

Camping is permitted near **Yank's Jetty**, **South Beach** and at **Little Pioneer Bay** but permission must be first obtained from the **Queensland National Parks and Wildlife Service** office at Ingham. No fresh water is available and all supplies must be brought from the mainland.

Most people coming to Orpheus fly in by seaplane from either Townsville or Cairns. Coming by sea you either need your own boat or take a water taxi from **Dungeness**, near Lucinda on the mainland. The cost is much the same as flying.

235

HINCHINBROOK ISLAND

Tourist Information: Hinchinbrook Island Resort; *tel: (070) 66 8585.*

Hinchinbrook is claimed to be the world's largest island National Park, being 35 km long and 25 km wide – all of it National Park – and is the largest island off the Queensland coast. Hinchinbrook is 120 km north of Townsville and 9 km north of Ingham on the Bruce Hwy. The highest point of the island is **Mt Bowen** at 1142 m, which consists of a series of steep granite crags, ending as cliffs, which protect the beaches on the south side.

The valleys of the island are almost continuously running with water and, as a result, many of the gullies have luxuriant pockets of rain forest with milky pine, palm figs and vines. More than 66 species of birds, 22 species of butterflies and 29 species of mangroves have been counted on the island. The island has many wallabies, most of which are quite used to humans and hang around the resort mornings and evenings. There are also huge goannas and the island is home to many turtles.

The island is a wilderness area, which has been relatively untouched by the European incursions into Australia. There is a mangrove swamp clogging the bay between the island and the mainland, which runs for 30 km. Indeed, when Cook first sailed by, he thought the island was part of the mainland and called it Mt Hinchinbrook. This swampland is cut by channels and inlets from nine rivers, which come from the mainland. There are over 20 different types of mangroves in the swamp. There is a boardwalk through the mangrove swamp from **Missionary Bay** but, as always whenever mangroves are concerned, you need to be sure you have an adequate supply of strong insect repellent. Indeed, the whole of the island suffers from mosquitoes and sand flies at certain periods of the year and insect repellent is a must.

At the far end of the beach at **Shepherds Bay**, there is a 2 km track leading to **Macushla Bay**, which has a camping area. For the fit and energetic there is an **East Coast** trail, which is a 2–4 day walk through rain forest with creek crossings and some rough tracks. The track is signposted throughout.

The resort on Hinchinbrook is on leased land at the tip of **Cape Richards**, which is as far from the mainland as is possible on this island. It was first established in 1975 and it provides seclusion and a quiet holiday in a natural environment. The resort can only take a maximum of 50 guests so it never feels crowded.

By launch it is 41 mins from **Cardwell** on the mainland. There are also sea plane services from Townsville and Cairns. There are two daily boats from Cardwell – about $50 return. Sailors should note that there are no safe anchorages on the eastern side of the island.

BEDARRA ISLAND

Tourist Information: Bedarra Bay Resort; *tel: (070) 68 8233.*

Bedarra only covers 1 sq km and is a rarity among the reef islands in that it is privately owned. It is 35 km to the north-east of Cardwell, 6 km south of **Dunk** and 5 km from the mainland. The island has been in private hands since 1913, when it was bought for £20. Now it is mainly owned by Qantas, which runs two exclusive resorts, **Bedarra Bay** and **Hideaway Resort**, which take perhaps 50 people as a maximum. These resorts are expensive, starting at $500 a day, but that includes everything, even free drinks. The design of both is very much in sympathy with the nature of the island and they are totally unobtrusive. The hotels have gone through hard times and Hideaway Resort has a tendency to open and close with the seasons.

There are several excellent beaches on the island, all easily reached from the resorts, and many others which can only be reached by dinghy. Exploring the island basically means taking the 1.5 km walk between the two resorts through dense rain forest, which can take as long as 45 mins. The resorts themselves call this walk 'strenuous'.

Access to Bedarra is via a 45-min flight to Dunk Island and then by motor launch or water taxi to Bedarra. Day visitors are not welcome.

DUNK ISLAND

Tourist Information: Dunk Island Resort; *tel: (070)68 8199.*

Dunk, at 10 sq km, is the largest island in the

Family Group and is about 160 km north of Townsville and 120 km south of Cairns. It is a very popular resort island with Australians. The majority of the island – 7.3 sq km – is National Park with extensive footpaths through rain forest lush with vegetation, caused by the island's high rainfall. The backbone of the island is a forest-covered ridge, which is separate to the national park and covers 730 hectares on the low-lying ground in the western part. This is also where the resort complex owned by Qantas is to be found.

Rain forest on the island grows right down to the sea and some of the beaches on the island are only accessible by boat. There are 13 km of marked footpaths throughout the island including one reaching up to **Mt Kootaloo** at 271 m.

Dunk is famous for its butterflies – the most famous of these is the bright blue Ulysses butterfly, which is used as an emblem for the island and a logo for the resort. It also has a wide variety of bird life – 150 species have been spotted.

Dunk Island Resort can handle 400 guests at a time but it is not Great Keppel. It is very much a low-key resort, where the guests choose their own activities. The architecture of the resort reflects the horrors of the time it was built, in the late 1960s and early 1970s. Luckily the structure has been disguised by plant growth, which has softened the rough edges and camouflaged the more offensive architectural follies.

Dunk Island was the home of **E.J. Banfield**, who lived there from 1897 to 1932. He was a journalist and while there wrote *Confessions of a Beachcomber,* which has been continuously in print since it was first published. It is highly recommended reading for anyone who is going to Dunk because it is both a guide to the island and a most literate and interesting read.

Access is by plane from Cairns or Townsville. A daily flight from either lasts just under an hour and costs about $100. Or by launch or water taxi from **Mission Beach** at $18.

Along with Heron Island this is the only true coral cay which is also a resort. The island covers 13 hectares in a heart shape but at its highest is barely 3 m above sea level. It is 660 m long and 260 m wide at its broadest point. When the tide is out some 300 hectares of reef are exposed and the ranger conducts reef walks. Both the reef and the island are National Parks.

Although the island is green, this is not how it got its name. Green was the name of the chief astronomer on the *Endeavour.*

Green Island is a true coral cay at the late stage of development and has vegetation, which somewhat resembles rain forest on the mainland, but without the variety. The island has more than 50 bird species, which are welcome visitors. Less welcome is the fact that this island had the first reported sighting of the Crown of Thorns – a starfish which destroys coral – and 27,000 were removed from one reef alone. The island has some great beaches, which can get quite crowded at holiday weekends. In all the island has over 200,000 visitors a year.

To get away from the bustle of the interior there are footpaths through the rain forest type vegetation and, as always, after a few metres you are away from any other people. Around the cay is a 500-hectare marine park reef and there is an observatory – nowadays considered somewhat old-fashioned – which extends 6 m below the sea and allows comfortable viewing. The reef is easy to explore on foot at low tide. Also on the island is the long established **Marineland Melanesia**, which is a combined museum, gallery and aquarium with large captive crocodiles on display; admission $7.

This is one of the most accessible of the coral cays as it is only 27 km north-east of Cairns, making it an easy day trip by powered catamaran. There is a smallish but five star resort – maximum 90 people – that has been developed at great expense by a Japanese corporation. Rates start at $350.

Getting there from Cairns is easy as there are launches and catamarans galore. A return trip will cost about $45.

237

GREEN ISLAND
Tourist Information: Green Island Resort; *tel: (070) 51 4644.*

FITZROY ISLAND
Tourist Information: Fitzroy Island Resort; *tel: (070) 51 9588.*

Fitzroy is a large – 4 sq km – continental island, less than 30 km south-east of Cairns, and is the third most northerly island in the Great Barrier Reef.

The island is covered with eucalypt and tropical rain forests with she-oak, Indian beech, native nutmeg, tamarinds and turpentine.

The beaches are covered in coral, which makes them less than ideal for sunbathing, but the coral fringe of the island is ideal for snorkelling.

The low key, budget priced resort at **Welcome Bay** offers bunk houses and cabins as well as camping. The maximum number of visitors is 144 at the resort and 50 campers. There is also a backpackers hostel with bunkrooms. The island is rarely crowded although it attracts many day trippers from Cairns at holiday weekends. All of the, limited, development there is, is on the north side of the island with walks running from Welcome Bay to the **Lighthouse**, which was built in 1943 and has been rebuilt twice since, and then back by another route. The lighthouse is not in the traditional style and is an ugly piece of government architecture.

Starting from the same spot at Welcome Bay, there is also the **Secret Gardens walk**, which runs up a rain forest valley that is almost perpetually damp.

Fitzroy is very much a water sports area and most of the equipment is for hire from the resort. There are fifteen excellent dive sites around the island, which has a dive shop.

There are several cruises to Fitzroy operating out of Cairns, of which the most active is **Great Adventures**; *tel: (070) 51 0455.*

LIZARD ISLAND

Tourist Information: Lizard Island Resort; *tel: (070) 60 3999.*

Lizard Island, 93 km north-east of Cooktown and 270 km from Cairns, is a high granite – coarsely crystalline and pinkish grey – island. It was here that Captain Cook, in 1770, managed to spot a gap through the reefs, which would allow him to sail the *Endeavour* into open sea. The sighting of the passage was possible because the reef is only 20 km away. The island was then, as now, inhabited by many large lizards and is a continental island surrounded by a fringe of coral.

The National Park covers most of the island, extending to 1010 hectares of mainly grassland. The walk to **Cook's Look**, where Captain Cook spotted the gap, is relatively easy but it is as well to take water in the summer. Indeed, Lizard Island can be very hot and it is advisable to wear a hat, use powerful sun protection and carry water.

Throughout the island there are patches of open forest. There are also coral cays and rocky outcrops to the south of Lizard Island, which are also part of the National Park. These off-shore cays are the **Turtle Group**, 91 hectares; **Nymph Island**, 65 hectares; and **Two Islands**, 15 hectares. There is also the unimaginatively named **Three Islands**, which covers 41 hectares and has a dense cover of grasses and low shrubs while **Rocky Islets**, 32 hectares, has substantial vegetation.

In the area around Lizard the water is clear with visibility frequently down to 50m and it is generally considered one of the best destinations in the world for snorkelling and diving. It invariably appears in lists of the ten best diving spots in the world.

Close to the shore are the **Clam Gardens** in **Watson's Bay**, but all around the island there are superb snorkelling spots. There are daily trips to **The Cod Hole** on the outer reef, which is widely regarded as one of the world's most spectacular diving sites. The reefs and waters surrounding the island are managed within the Great Barrier Reef Marine Park and some activities are rightly prohibited, including commercial fishing, spear-fishing and the collection of corals or shells, dead or alive.

The island has over 40 species of birds and 11 species of lizards, the best known being the large sand goanna, after which the island was named. There is a camping area located just back from the beach at the eastern end of **Watson's Bay**.

Lizard Island Resort is expensive which, when the cost of the flights are added, makes it a holiday only suited to the wealthy. There are regular flights – a spectacular scenic trip over the coastline and reef – to the island from Cairns.

ROCKHAMPTON–CAIRNS

1 Km = .7 mi

ROUTE: 1029 KM

One of the most popular routes for visitors from overseas, it nevertheless involves a lot of driving on what is not always the most interesting of roads. However, it provides access along its length to parts of the Great Barrier Reef. Rail tours up and down this coast (generally starting in Brisbane) are also very well patronised.

Cairns

1

88

Innisfail

150

Ingham

112

Magnetic Island

Great Barrier Reef

Townsville

37

Ayr

182

239

Proserpine

1

126

Great Barrier Reef

Mackay

36

Sarina

90

Clairview

208

1

32 *Yeppoon*

Rockhampton

37

ROUTE

The first 340 km of this run leaves you almost no chance of any detours. You start on the Bruce Hwy – Rte 1 – heading north. You could, if you wish, make a short detour to your right through **Emu Park** to **Yeppoon**, opposite **Great Keppel Island**, and then back again to rejoin the highway but you would only have advanced 3 km. The road then has no outlets to the right because it is mainly a military training area and so you pass through **Yaamba**, **Glen Geddes**, **Marlborough** to **Clairview**, on the sea near **Broad Sound**, without a single deviation. A pretty boring 200 km or so, the only consolation being that this is very easy driving. From **Clairview** the road hugs the coast until it passes the **West Hill National Park**, where it bears inland to **Sarina**, which has a short detour to the right to **Sarina Beach**.

Mackay is only 37 km from Sarina and from there the Bruce Hwy continues up to **Proserpine**, 126 km away, which is part of the complex of **Airlie Beach** and **Shute Harbour**, and could rightly be considered the entrance to the **Whitsunday Islands** of the **Great Barrier Reef** (see p. 230).

From Proserpine the Bruce Hwy – still Rte 1 – heads along the coast for 182 km to **Ayr**, with no detours possible, and from Ayr it turns inland for 37 km to **Townsville**. Townsville to **Cairns** is a distance of 350 km. Other than the towns of **Ingham** (112 km from Townsville) and **Innisfail** (150 km from Ingham), there is not one single detour to the right worth talking about, except that just past **Ingham** there is a very minor trackway down to **Halifax** and **Lucinda** facing the south end of **Hinchinbrook**, and at **Miriwinni**, 24 km past **Innisfail**, there is a road that runs down to **Bramston Beach** with the **Eurbemangee Swamp** on the right. And that is it. Otherwise the road runs straight on, never changing its all-Australian name of Bruce and always remaining Rte 1, the round-Australia highway.

TRAINS

This is the best-served route in the book as far as rail is concerned. Many of Australia's best-known trains, including the *Queenslander*, the *Sunlander*, the *Spirit of the Outback*, cover all or part of this route. See pp. 403–405 for more details. There is a lot to be said for avoiding the long stretches of driving by letting the train take the strain. With some variations depending on which service you take, timings from Rockhampton include Mackay 6 hrs, Townsville 12½ hrs, Ingham 15 hrs, Innisfail 18 hrs and Cairns 20½ hrs. OTT table 9013.

BUSES

If your budget doesn't run to a rail tour up this coast, there's no shortage of buses either, and the journey, although less comfortable, is often faster. Daily services are provided by Greyhound Pioneer, McCafferty's and others, calling at many places, including Mackay (4¾ hrs), Townsville (10 hrs), Ingham (11½ hrs), Innisfail (14½ hrs) and Cairns (16 hrs). OTT table 9082.

MACKAY

Tourist Information: Tourism Mackay, *The Mill, 320 Nebo Rd; tel: (079) 52 2677.*

ACCOMMODATION AND FOOD

Dolphin Resort *(FL), Beach Rd; tel: 54 9666.* **Ocean International Hotel** *(FL), 1 Bridge Rd, Illawong Beach; tel: 57 2044.* **Alara Motor Inn,** *52–56 Nebo Rd; tel: 51 2699.* **Central Hospitality Motel,** *2 Macalister St; tel: 51 1666.* **Four Dice Motel** *(FL), 166 Nebo Rd; tel: 51 1555.* **The Lantern Motor Inn,** *151 Nebo Rd; tel: 51 2188.* **Mackay Motor Inn,** *208–212 Nebo Rd; tel: 52 2822.* **Marco Polo Motel** *(FL), 46–50 Nebo Rd; tel: 51 2700.* **Miners Lodge Motor Inn** *(BW), 60–62 Nebo Rd; tel: 51 1944.* **Shakespeare International Motel** *(BW), 309 Shakespeare St; tel: 53 1111.* **White Lace Motor Inn,** *73 Nebo Rd; tel: 51 4466.* **Coral Sands Motel & Valencia Restaurant,** *44 Macalister St; tel: 51 1244.* **Country Plaza Motel Mackay,** *40 Nebo Rd; tel: 57 6526.* **Culbara Motel,** *corner Bruce Hwy and Campbell Ridge Rd; tel: 59 5251.*

Metro Motor Inn, *34–38 Nebo Rd; tel: 51 1811.* **Paradise Lodge Motel** *(BU), 17–19 Peel St; tel: 51 3644.* **Pioneer Villa Motel,** *30 Nebo Rd; tel: 51 1288.* **Sugar City Motel** *(GC), 66 Nebo Rd; tel: 51 2877.* **Bel Air Motel,** *10 Nebo Rd; tel: 57 3658.* **Bona Vista Motel,** *corner Malcomson St and Norris Rd; tel: 42 2211.* **Boomerang Hotel–Motel,** *Nebo Rd; tel: 52 1755.* **Cool Palms Motel,** *4 Nebo Rd; tel: 53 1477.* **El Toro Motel,** *Nebo Rd; tel: 51 2722.* **Golden Reef Motel,** *164 Nebo Rd; tel: 57 6572.* **Gorries Motel Mackay,** *186 Nebo Rd; tel: 52 2033.* **International Lodge Motel,** *Macalister St; tel: 51 1022.* **Kooyong Motor Hotel,** *corner Harbour Rd and Evans Ave; tel: 51 4844.* **The Mackay Town House,** *73 Victoria St; tel: 57 6985.* **Metropolitan Hotel–Motel,** *corner Gordon and Carlyle Sts; tel: 57 2802.* **HI: Larrikin Lodge,** *32 Peel St; tel: 51 3728.*

Toong Tong Thai, *10 Sydney St; tel: 57 8051*. Open 7 days. BYO. **Hog's Breath**, *corner Wood and Victoria Sts*. Open 7 days. Tex-Mex. Licensed. **Waterfront Restaurant**, *8 River St; tel: 57 8131*. Open daily from 1000. Licensed. The fashionable eating spot in Mackay.

SIGHTSEEING

The name is always pronounced in Australia Mac-Eye. The town was named after Captain John Mackay, who in 1860 led a party overland from **Armidale** in search of pastoral land. He returned with cattle two years later and founded the town. The early pioneering days were not all beer and skittles. One early record cited it as a place of 'brute force, savage debauchery and disgusting language.'

Mackay has always been an important sugar town – it is sometimes referred to as the sugar capital of Australia – and an artificial deep water port was built in 1939 to service the eight sugar mills in the area. Inland coal mines were developed from 1969 and at **Hay Point** to the south of the town, a coal terminal, the world's largest, was built to handle the output.

Mackay is fortunate in that it has some elegant architecture — the result of sugar and coal wealth – broad, well laid out streets and, within the town boundaries, three beaches. These are **Harbour Beach** which is patrolled, **Town Beach**, and to the south, **Illawong Beach** with its fauna reserve. **The Illawong Fauna Sanctuary**, *tel: 57 7591*, has local fauna and there are lots of other entertainments for children. Open 0900–1830; $2. There are also crocodiles, which are fed every day at 1000.

Between Mackay and **Sarina**, 37 km to the south, are some of Australia's most beautiful beaches including **Sarina Beach** at the midway mark, which runs back to sand dunes. All beaches in the area are in potential stinger waters and swimming in the summer months can be dangerous. You must check carefully before you go swimming. There are several cruises out to the Reef available from Mackay. Two operators from Mackay Harbour are **Roylens Cruises** with catamarans to the Reef and the **Whitsundays**; *tel: 55 3066*, and **Elizabeth E II**; *tel: 57 4281*.

In the town there is a large recreational area surrounding the **Botanical Gardens**, *Queen's Park, Goldsmith St; tel: 57 2741*. Open 0600–1800. Inside the gardens is an orchid house with a display of both local and overseas varieties. In the centre of town there is more greenery in the **City Heart Mall**, and on the banks of the Pioneer River there is **Caneland Park**, which runs down from *Mangrove Rd*.

Greenmount Homestead, *tel: 59 2250*, is run by the Mackay Historical Society. Open Mon–Sat 0930–1230, Sun 1000–1530; $3. It has been renovated, restored and refurnished in the style of the last century and has many items of memorabilia pertaining to Mackay.

One way of seeing the area is to take a seaplane – a rare form of transport in Australia – to **Redbill Reef** and **Bushy Island. Fredricksons** *(tel: 42 3161)* has a flight departing daily at low tide. $140. Another way of getting an overview of the area is with **HeliJet Helicopters**, which fly from the airport *(tel: 3574)* and offer scenic flights over the northern beaches, **Eungella National Park** and **Cape Hillsborough**. To the north-east, 45 km on sealed roads, is the **Cape Hillsborough National Park**. This is a coastal national park with vegetation ranging from rain forests to hoop pine. There are several lookouts on the ridges overlooking the coast and a wealth of beaches, which attract kangaroos and wallabies.

Some 80 km from Mackay is the **Eungella National Park** (QNP&WS, *corner Wood and River Sts; tel: 52 2677*), which is 50,800 hectares of largely inaccessible wilderness rising to a peak of 1280m at **Mt Dalyrmple**. There are no roads through the park and access is by way of **Eungella** and then **Broken River**, which is a camping area within the park. From there the only way to explore is on foot and there is a relatively easy 2.2 sign-posted circuit from Broken River and a relaxed 8.4 km walk to **Crediton Creek** from the same starting place.

SHUTE HARBOUR

Tourist Information: Whitsunday District Information Centre, *corner Mandalay and Shute Harbour Rds, Airlie Beach; tel: (079) 46 6673*.

ACCOMMODATION

Motel Shute Harbour, *Shute Harbour Rd; tel: (079) 46 9131.*

Proserpine

A & A Motel, *Main St; tel: (079) 45 1888.* **The Lodge at Laguna Quays Resort**, *Private Mail Bag, Proserpine Post Office; tel: 47 7777.* **Motel Astro**, *Bruce Hwy; tel: 45 1288.* **Proserpine Motor Lodge**, *Bruce Hwy; tel: 45 1588.* **Whitsunday Anchor Motel & Guest House**, *32–36 Herbert St; tel: 45 1200.* **Whitsunday Palms Motel**, *Bruce Hwy; tel: 45 1868.*

Airlie Beach

Colonial Palms Motor Inn *(BW)*, *Shute Harbour Rd; tel: 46 7166.* **Whitsunday On The Beach Resort**, *267–269 Shute Harbour Rd; tel: 46 6359.* **Airlie Beach Hotel-Motel**, *16 The Esplanade; tel: (079) 46 6233.* **Airlie Beach Motor Lodge**, *6 Lamond St; tel: 46 6418.* **Beaches Resort**, *356–362 Shute Harbour Rd; tel: 46 6244.* **The Islands Inn Motel**, *Shute Harbour Rd; tel: 46 6755.* **Whitsunday Terraces Resort**, *Golden Orchid Dr.; tel: 46 6788.* **HI: Club Habitat**, *394 Shute Harbour Rd; tel: 46 6312.*

SIGHTSEEING

Proserpine is a sugar town on the Bruce Hwy and is the turn off to **Airlie Beach** – 25 km away – and **Shute Harbour**, which are both on a peninsula extending into **Repulse Bay**. This peninsula is being developed for tourism because of its proximity to the **Whitsunday Passage** islands, and the towns almost merge.

There are literally dozens of cruises, self-sail yachts and power boats available out of Shute Harbour. Indeed, as a passenger terminal, it is now only second to Sydney. Shute Harbour is the ideal spot to start a cruise of the 74 tropical islands of the Whitsunday group. Most are deserted but some, such as **Hamilton** and **Daydream**, are developed as tourist resorts (see Great Barrier Reef chapter pp.227–238). A selected listing of cruises and boat charters in Shute Harbour: **Apollo III**; *tel: (008) 075 042*; **Iluka**; *tel: 46 6897*; **Coral Trekker**; *tel: 46 7197*; **Whitsunday Connections**; *tel: (008)*

075 127; **Queensland Yacht Charters**; *tel: 46 7400*; **Whitsunday Rent A Yacht**; *tel: 46 9232*; **Gretel**; *tel: 46 7529*; **South Molle Cruises**; *tel: 46 9433.*

There are conducted rides into the rain forest at the foothills of the **Conway Range**, available from **Brandy Creek Trail Rides**, *Shute Harbour Rd, Proserpine; tel: (079) 46 1121.* Two rides a day 0900–1200, 1500–1800. $35.

In nearby **Cannonvale** is the **Whitsunday Wildlife Park**, *Shute Harbour Rd, Cannonvale; tel: 46 1354*, which is about 8 km from Airlie Beach. This has a comprehensive collection of Australian fauna, with kangaroos and wallabies roaming around the grounds. Open daily 0830–1730; $12. The **Whitsunday Aquarium**, *Jubilee Pocket Rd, Airlie Beach; tel: 46 6142*, has a display of reef fish and turtles as well as a collection of 3000 shells. Open daily 1030–1630; $5.

This is a major skin diving area and there are several companies in Airlie Beach that teach everything from a resort ticket to a full open-water course. Three companies are **Pro–Dive**; *tel: 46 6508*; **Oceania Dive**; *tel: 46 6032*; **Reef Enterprise Dive**; *tel: 46 7228.*

From Proserpine, 30 km to the south east of the town on the *Shute Harbour Rd*, is **Conway National Park**, which extends off-shore to include many of the Whitsunday islands and in all covers 23,800 hectares.

TOWNSVILLE

Tourist Information: Highway Information Centre, *Bruce Hwy on the southern approach to Townsville; tel: 78 3555.* **Townsville Information Centre**, *Flinders Mall; tel: 21 3660.*

Townsville airport is 5 km to the north and there is a shuttle bus that is scheduled to meet most flights, which takes you into town for $8. Buses stop at the **Transit Centre** on the south side of Ross Creek in *Palmer St*, while the train station is across the other side of the creek on *Flinders St*.

The taxi stand at the mall takes telephone bookings; *tel: 7072 1555.*

ACCOMMODATION AND FOOD

Aquarius on the Beach Hotel, *75 The*

Strand; tel: 72 4255. **Sheraton Breakwater Casino,** *Sir Leslie Thiess Dr. (PO Box 1223); tel: 22 2333.* **Townsville Reef International** *(BW), 63 The Strand; tel: 21 1777.* **Townsville Travelodge,** *Flinders Mall; tel: 72 2477.* **Cluden Park Motor Inn,** *corner Flinders and Bruce Hwys, Wulguru 4811; tel: 78 4555.* **South Bank Motor Inn** *(FL), 23 Palmer St, S. Townsville 4810; tel: 21 1474.* **Colonial Gardens Resort,** *The Lakes, Woolcock St; tel: 25 2222.* **Colonial Rose,** *23 Bowen Rd; tel: 25 1422.* **Monte Carlo Motor Inn,** *45 Bowen Rd, Mundingburra; tel: 25 2555.* **Robert Towns – A Greentree Inn,** *261 Stanley St; tel: 71 6908.* **Seagulls Resort,** *74 The Esplanade, Belgian Gardens 4810; tel: 21 3111.* **Town Lodge Motor Inn** *(GC), 15 Victoria St (PO Box 939); tel: 71 2164.* **Hi Roller Motel,** *36 Bowen Rd; tel: 79 2179.* **Raintree Motel,** *corner Bowen Rd and Carmody St; tel: 75 3066.* **HI: Adventurers Resort,** *79 Palmer St; tel: 21 1522.*

Cactus Jack's, *Palmer St; tel: 21 1478.* Licensed. Tex-Mex. Licensed. **Covers,** *209 Flinders St East; tel: 21 4630.* Open Tues–Sun for dinner. Licensed. Up-market. **Victoria Bridge and Fisherman's Wharf,** *Flinders St; tel: 21 1838.* Open daily lunch and dinner. Licensed. On the riverside. Calls itself Australia's longest waterfront restaurant but is, in fact, a range of restaurants of different styles. **Larrikins,** *95 Denham St; tel: 72 5900.* Open daily. Australian food – emu, crocodile, barramundi. Licensed. **Yongala,** *11 Fryer St; tel: 72 4633.* Dinner Mon–Sat. Licensed. Greek-style food in historic surroundings. **Spinnakers on the Breakwater,** *Sir Leslie Thiess Dr.; tel: 21 2567.* Open lunch and dinner. Licensed. Sea surroundings. Seafood specialities. Up-market.

SIGHTSEEING

Australia's largest tropical city and the business and cultural centre of North Queensland, Townsville is also the centre for higher education and research. It lies wholly in the tropics and three-quarters of its rainfall comes between Oct–Mar. The name of the city sounds like a duplication of the word, but is logical in that it is named after Captain Robert Towns, who was the major financial backer of John Melton Black, the founder of the settlement starting in 1864. Towns only visited the place once, in 1866.

Although Townsville spreads itself, the centre is compact. The best place to see Townsville and the surrounding area is from **Castle Hill** at **Mt Cutheringa.** There is a footpath on the slope nearest the city, which starts at the top of *Blackwood St* – or you can go by way of *Gregory St* to *Stanton Terrace* – and if you get to the highest lookout at 300m you have 360° views extending out to **Magnetic Island.** It is possible to drive up to the lookouts. The rock face is floodlit at night.

Just off shore from Townsville – about 16 km – is **Magnetic Island,** of which the majority, 2790 hectares, has been declared a National Park. Cruise operators go from Townsville to Magnetic Island, and also Orpheus, Hinchinbrook and Dunk Islands (see Great Barrier Reef pp. 227–238): **Pure Pleasure Cruises;** *tel: 7721 3555.* **Magnetic Marine;** *tel: 7772 7122.* **Coral Princess Cruises,** *Breakwater Marina; tel: 7721 1673.* There are also amphibious air services to Orpheus, Dunk and Hinchinbrook.

Regarded as Townsville's premier attraction, **Great Barrier Reef Wonderland,** *Flinders Street East; tel: 72 4249,* has what is claimed to be the world's largest living coral reef aquarium. It has a walk-through tunnel and all the fish, plants and corals come from parts of the Great Barrier Reef. Open daily 0900–1700; $12. There is also an **Omni-Imax Theatre** – $10 – which was the first in the southern hemisphere and shows virtual reality films, which are not for people suffering from vertigo. Screening is every hour starting at 0930.

Townsville is in the cyclone belt and the devastating result of one of these freak acts of nature can be seen at the **Maritime Museum,** *Palmer St; tel: 21 5251.* Open Mon–Fri 1000–1600, Sat–Sun 1300–1600; $3. On display are the relics from the *Yangala,* which went down with all hands in a cyclone in 1911. There also relics from several other wrecks and the museum covers all of North Queensland Maritime history.

The Australian Institute of Marine Science, *Cape Ferguson; tel: 78 9264,* makes

Captain Cook

If you go to Lizard Island, to the north of Queensland, you will find that it is a continental island with a steep hill in the centre. If you climb it you will find that, although not technically difficult, it is very tiring, and you need to take a lot of water and frequent rests.

Captain Cook, in his uniform of a captain of the Royal Navy, climbed that peak in the noonday sun to find a passage for the *Endeavour* out of the dangers of the Barrier Reef, where it had been entrapped for a 1000 km. When Cook got to the top, the day was too misty for him to see clearly. So he returned to the base, slept on the ground and climbed again in the dawn's breaking light. From the peak he saw the channel which is now known as Providence Channel.

In all, Captain Cook had three great voyages of exploration in the South Pacific Ocean and the North American coastal waters.

In 1768, as lieutenant-in-command of the *Endeavour*, he undertook his first great voyage to the South Pacific, on which he safely carried a group of British astronomers to the recently discovered island of Tahiti to observe the transit of the planet Venus across the sun in June 1769. From there he went to New Zealand and charted the coastline for the first time – all 3860 km of it. In 1770, he discovered the eastern coast of Australia, which he charted and claimed for Great Britain under the name of New South Wales.

In 1772, in command of the *Resolution*, and accompanied by another ship, the *Adventure*, he set out on his second great expedition, a search for the fabled southern continent, Terra Australis. In July 1776, Cook sailed again to determine whether a Northwest Passage between the Atlantic and Pacific oceans existed north of the North American continent. After searching in vain for a Northwest Passage as far north as the Bering Strait he turned back. He returned to the Sandwich Islands, where he was killed by the locals.

Cook is, indeed, the Columbus of Australia.

244

Townsville the centre for marine research in North Queensland. Visitors are very welcome to walk around the facilities of the research station and watch a slide show, which shows what the Institute does. Open daily. Tours Fri 1000–1200, Mar–Nov.

Townsville Museum, *81–99 Sturt St,* is in what was the Magistrates Court, built in 1877. The museum concentrates on the history of the area although it often has displays from other states and overseas. Open Mon–Fri 1000–1500, Sat–Sun 1000–1300; $2.

Worth seeing is the **Sheraton Breakwater Casino-Hotel**, *Sir Leslie Thiess Dr., tel: 22 2333,* which is yet another casino designed to make untold fortunes from Asian gamblers – especially the high rollers. It has yet to fully live up to its promise and is open continuously.

Castling Street Heritage Centre, *5 Castling St; tel: 72 5195,* is a collection of heritage houses furnished in the style of the period and operated by the National Trust. Open Wed 1000–1400, Sat–Sun 1300–1600.

Just out of town **Town Common**, *Pallarenda Rd; tel: 74 1382,* is a short drive – 5 mins – from the city centre, on the coast at Pallandera. Open daily sunrise–sunset. It is alive with animal life, especially in the wet season. This 3240 hectare sanctuary is on wetlands fed by the **Bohle River**, which originates in the **Many Peaks Range**, and there is a wide diversity of bird, animal and plant life. There are hides near the **Pink Lily** freshwater lagoon and the **Long Swamp** and footpaths throughout the reserve. There is also a 7 km road you can use to drive through the area.

Anderson Park is 6 km from the centre of town and covers 37 hectares. (*Hugh St, Mundingburra; tel: 22 0347;* open daily sunrise–sunset.) The garden also houses the **Kokoda Pool**, which is a memorial to the infamous Kokoda trail.

Billabong Sanctuary, *Bruce Hwy, 17 km south of town; tel: 78 8344.* This is a zoo for Australian animals, specifically those from the tropical north and has a two hectare billabong with saltwater crocodiles, cassowary and water-fowl. In the grounds are koalas, wombats, dingoes and parrots and there are feeding shows throughout the day. Open daily 0800–1700, $13.

INGHAM

Tourist Information: **Ingham Tourist Information Centre**, *Lannercost St; tel: (077) 76 5211.*

ACCOMMODATION

Herbert Valley Motel, *Bruce Hwy; tel: 76 1777*. **Ingham Motel**, *62 Townsville Rd; tel: 76 2355*. **Lees Hotel**, *58 Lannercost St; tel: 76 1577*.

SIGHTSEEING

The Bruce Hwy runs north west from Townsville and after 113 km reaches Ingham. The town is just over 10 km in from the sea and is backed by the **Mt Fox National Park** with the **Gorge Range** and the **Lumholtz National Park** to the north west. The name comes from William Bairstow Ingham, who settled in the district in 1873 and established the first ·sugar cane farm. The town, originally called Lower Herbert, was named after him 9 years later. From the 1890s onwards it grew as the centre for the large number of sugar cane plantations in the area. It was very much a focus for Italian immigration between the wars.

The claim is made that this is the original town of the pub 'with no beer' – **Lee's** – which was drunk dry by American servicemen in 1942, celebrating winning the Battle of the Coral Sea. Dan Sheahan, a local of the town, wrote a poem of that name which was published in 1944 and this inspired Gordon Parsons to write the song, which was recorded by Slim Dusty on April Fool's Day, 1957.

The town's main road is wide and planted with trees and many alamanda – the yellow bloom is the emblem of the district.

Most of Ingham's attractions are outside the town. To get to the **Broadwater State Forest**, *tel: (077) 76 27770,* you take the Bruce Hwy north out of Ingham and after 3 km turn off at *Hawkins Creek Rd*. Broadwater is about 40 km further on. There is a footpath which runs

for 2 km from the picnic ground through dense rain forest, passing a fig tree whose buttressed trunk has a circumference of more than 40m.

About 24 km south of Ingham, 6 km off the Bruce Hwy and just past Waterview Creek, is **Jourama Falls National Park**, *tel: 77 3112.* This has a series of cascades over salmon coloured granite rock formations set in the middle of dense bush with clear pools suitable for swimming. There is a mildly strenuous 2½ km footpath along the creek through palm and casuarina groves to two lookouts.

Wallaman Falls is reached by way of Trebonne but the road is unsurfaced for 30 km of the 48 km journey and in the wet season it is wise to check with the ranger (*tel: 77 5125*) before starting off. These are the second highest falls in Australia dropping some 300m from Stoney Creek into the Herbert River. Wallaman is also claimed to be the longest sheer drop waterfall in Australia. The access road winds through scenic rain forest and takes you to a lookout over the falls.

INNISFAIL

Tourist Information; **Cassowary Coast Information Centre**, *Bruce Hwy; tel: (070) 61 6448.*

ACCOMMODATION

Barrier Reef Motel, *2 River Ave; tel: 61 4988.* **Black Marlin Motel** *(BU), 26 Glady St; tel: 61 2533.* **Carefree Motel**, *14 Owen St; tel: 61 2266 or 612186.* **Moondarra Motel**, *21 Ernest St; tel: 61 1989.* **Robert Johnstone Motel**, *corner Fitzgerald Esplanade and Grace St; tel: 61 2444.* **Walkabout Motel**, *20 McGowan Dr.; ·tel: 61 2311.* **Riverlodge Motel**, *84 River Ave; tel: 61 3888.*

SIGHTSEEING

The town was originally called **Geraldton** but this created confusion with the town of the same name in Western Australia and its name was changed to Innisfail in 1910. It lies on the Bruce Hwy to the north of Ingham, near a number of National Parks with the Johnstone River running through the town. Between Innisfail and the sea is **Ella Bay National Park** and next to it the **Eubenangee Swamp**

National Park. Then, following the Bruce Hwy north towards Cairns, on your left you come to the **Bellenden Ker National Park**, with the Bellenden Ker range of mountains your constant companion for the rest of the 80 km journey. Taking the Palmerston Hwy west you pass through the **Palmerston National Park** before reaching the **Atherton Tableland** and the town of **Millaa Millaa**.

The town itself is a working town, not given over to tourists, and it has the genuine feel of a Queensland country town serving the needs of the surrounding countryside – mainly the sugar plantations – and the small fishing fleet.

In the town is the **Historical Society Museum**, *11 Edith St*. Open Mon 1300–1500, Tues–Fri 1000–1200 and 1300–1500. $1. It is housed in the old School of Arts building and is run by volunteers.

On *Fitzgerald Esplanade* at the end of *Grace St*, there is a **fish depot**, where you can buy fresh seafood off the boats.

For the visitor most of the attractions of Innisfail are just outside the town.

The last remaining wetlands between Townsville and Cairns are preserved in the **Eubenangee Swamp National Park** (*tel: 51 9811*) which covers 7830 hectares. Car access is off the Bruce Hwy from Miriwinni. There is a long boardwalk providing access to the interior of the park – don't forget your insect repellent – which is full of bird life and also has its fair share of crocodiles. Off the boardwalk vines make the going difficult.

The Palmerston Hwy out of Innisfail up to the Atherton Tablelands cuts through the **Palmerston National Park** (*tel: 64 5115*) which covers 14,200 hectares. It has some wonderful rain forest scenery along with gorges, waterfalls and extremely clear, freshwater swimming holes. There are forestry tracks covering the park, which can be bumpy going but in the dry season are normally accessible. Running through the park is the **North Johnstone River**, which during and after the wet season provides excellent white water rafting. At the **Tchupala Falls** there is a self-guiding trail through the rain forest.

The peaks of the **Bellenden Ker National**

Park (*tel: 76 6304*), which range up to 1622m, are almost always swathed in mist and the climb to **Bartle Frere**, Queensland's highest mountain, is only for experienced bushwalkers. The 31,000 hectare park is mainly undeveloped although there are picnic sites with low waterfalls and swimming sites near the turn offs from the Bruce Hwy at **Babinda**, **Pawngilly** and 5 km south of **Gordonvale**.

CAIRNS

Tourist Information: Far North Queensland Promotion Bureau, *corner Grafton and Hartley Sts; tel: (070) 51 3588.*

ARRIVING AND DEPARTING

Cairns airport is about 4 km north of the city and is newly built and elegantly designed. A taxi into town along the Cook Hwy costs around $8 and there is a shuttle bus – $5 – which connects to the major flights and goes directly into the city. The airport also has the usual car hire agencies and this might be a better bet because daily rates can be extremely low, and at $50 starts to compete easily with a taxi both ways and transport around the town.

At the moment buses pull in at the end of the Esplanade at Trinity Wharf coach station and trains stop about half a kilometre away in *McLeod St* but there are plans for a transit centre combining them both in *Bunda St*. For radio taxis *tel: 7051 5333*.

ACCOMMODATION AND FOOD

Cairns International Hotel, *17 Abbot St; tel: 31 1300*. **Radisson Plaza Hotel**, *Pierpoint Rd; tel: 31 1411*. **Matson Plaza Hotel**, *The Esplanade; tel: 31 2211*. **Cairns Hilton Hotel**, *Wharf St; tel: 52 1599*. **Country Comfort Inn Cairns** *(CC), corner Lake and Florence Sts; tel: 51 5733*. **Holiday Inn Cairns**, *corner Esplanade and Florence Sts; tel: 31 3757*. **Pacific International Hotel** *(FL), corner Spence and Esplanade Sts; tel: 51 7888*. **Acacia Court Hotel** *(BW), 223 The Esplanade (PO Box 431); tel: 51 5011*. **Fairways Motor Inn** *(FL), 702 Bruce Hwy; tel: 54 4444*.

Mercure Hotel Harbourside, *209 The Esplanade; tel: 51 8999*. **Outrigger Country Comfort Inn Motel** *(CC), corner Abbot and*

Florence Sts; tel: 51 6188. **Tuna Towers Motel**, *145 Esplanade St (PO Box 1100); tel: 51 4688.* **All Seasons Cairns Village Resort Motel** *(FL), corner Bruce Hwy and Anderson Rd; tel: 54 7700.* **Balaclava Motel Hotel**, *423 Mulgrave Rd; tel: 54 3588.* **Cairns Angler Motel**, *287 Lake St; tel: 31 1666.* **Cairns Holiday Lodge Motel** *(BW), 259 Sheridan St, corner Thomas St; tel: 51 4611.* **Cairns Tropical Gardens Motel**, *312 Mulgrave Rd; tel: 31 1777.* **Compass Motel** *(BW), 232 Mulgrave Rd; 51 5466.* **HI:** *20–24 McLeod St; tel: 51 0772.* **HI:** *93 The Esplanade; tel: 31 1919.*

Donnini's, *Pier Marketplace; tel: 347 3128.* Open daily lunch and dinner. Licensed. Italian cuisine. **Tawny's**, *corner of the Hilton hotel; tel 51 1722.* Open dinner nightly, lunch Fri. Licensed. Seafood. Up-market. **Sawasdee**, *89 Grafton St; tel: 31 7993.* Open daily lunch and dinner. BYO. Thai cuisine. **Gypsy Dee's**, *41 Shields St; tel: 51 5530.* Open daily for dinner. **Pronto**, *74 Grafton St; tel: 51 2407.* Open lunch and dinner. Italian cuisine. **La Fettucine**, *43 Shields St; tel: 31 5959.* Open daily for dinner. BYO. Italian cuisine. **Damari's**, *171 Lake St; tel: 31 2155.* Lunch, Mon–Fri. Dinner nightly. Licensed. Up-market. **Dundee's**, *corner Aplin and Sheridan Sts; tel: 51 0399.* Open dinner seven nights. Licensed. Australian food – crocodile, emu and fresh seafood. **Taste of China**, *36 Abbott St; tel: 31 3688.* Lunch and dinner 7 days. Licensed.

Communications

The post office is at *13 Grafton St; tel: 7051 4200.*

SIGHTSEEING

The most northerly city in Queensland was originally known as Thornton but in 1876 the city was named after the then governor of Queensland, Sir William Cairns. (Local pronunciation drops the 'r' so that it sounds like the town on the French Riverina.)

Like so many Australian cities its growth was directly related to the gold fields. There was rivalry between **Port Douglas** and Cairns over the **Hodgkinson River** gold fields. Both

believed the gold, transported by dray, should be taken to their port.

Cairns received official approval and later also catered for the **Palmer River** gold field and the tin mines at **Herberton**, which opened in 1880. Despite this, Port Douglas started to overtake Cairns in importance and by 1882 was well ahead – buildings in Cairns started to be moved elsewhere.

But as gold declined and timber, grazing and sugar became more important so Cairns' fortunes revived. It became a city in 1923, a year before the railway link was made to Brisbane. The railway never made it to Port Douglas, which started to decline.

Cairns is a most visually attractive city, having broad thoroughfares and much colonial architecture with some imposing public buildings. Some of this character is being eroded by tourist development and many of the traditional Queensland houses have already disappeared but the essential charm is still there. One good way of seeing the town is to take the **Esplanade Walking Trail**, which runs for 3 km from the centre, north along the foreshore.

The oldest area of the city is around the wharves, which still exist, on **Trinity Inlet**. The hotels and business houses combine to form the **Barbary Coast**, an area which, despite substantial development, is still quite full of character. Cairns is the centre for the marlin fishing industry and also is a major point of access for the northern islands of the Barrier Reef.

Marlin Jetty is where the marlin sports fishing boats are based as well as most of the boats that make the run to the islands. Some of the operators are: **Big Cat Green Island Cruises**; *tel: 51 0444;* **Great Adventures**; *tel: 51 5644;* **Hostel Reef Trips**; *tel: 51 2866;* **Ocean Free**; *tel: 51 4400;* **Ocean Spirit Cruises**; *tel: 31 2920;* **Reef Jet Cruises**; *tel: 31 5559;* **Sunlover Cruises**; *tel: 35 2444.*

One of the more popular short local trips is on board the paddle-wheeler SS *Louisa*, which runs a 2½ hr tour up Trinity Inlet through the Everglades. (*Marlin Jetty; tel: 31 3065.* Operates daily, $15.)

In the city there is much of interest. In *Anderson St* is the **Environmental Park** with a boardwalk over a remnant of lowland tea tree swamp. During the wet this walk shows you the original vegetation of Cairns.

The Botanical Gardens, *94 Collins Ave and Greenslopes St, Edge Hill; tel: 50 2454,* were created in the 1880s, cover 400 hectares and rise to **Mt Whitfield** – 370m – in a range of coastal wetlands and rain forest. (Open daily 0730–1730.*)* They are linked to **Flecker Botanic Gardens** by boardwalk. On the road to the airport are signs showing the way to a series of mangrove walks, which have boardwalks and hides so that you can see the life of the mangrove swamps. These swamps also have a very active insect life so you will most definitely need a repellent.

Housed in the **School of Art** that was built in 1907, **Cairns Museum and Art Gallery**, *corner Lake and Shields Sts; tel: 51 5582,* has a display showing the construction of the rail link between Cairns and **Kuranda** and the contents of a joss house, which stood, until recently, in *Grafton St.* It also has displays covering the Aboriginal history of the area – the Tjapukai and Bama Aborigines – and the way in which Cairns, a late developer of a town, was formed by the gold fields and maritime trade. Open daily 1000–1500.

Cairns is richly endowed with beaches, all within a short drive. Starting 10 km to the north is **Palm Cove**, both a beach and a resort. Then come **Trinity** and **Yorkeys Knob**.

The bungy jump craze has come to Cairns and jumps cost from $60. **A.J. Hackett Bungy Jump**, *The Pier Marketplace; tel: (070) 31 1119.* Open daily 0900–1700. You are driven out to the bungy jump at *McGregor Rd,* Smithfield which is north of Cairns. Better or worse, depending on your point of view is **Rapjumping** (*tel: (018) 450 120; open daily),* which is abseiling head first in what is termed 'a perfectly safe manner.' Again you are picked up, taken to the jumping sites and returned.

There are over 100 freshwater and saltwater crocodiles at **Wildworld Australia**, *Captain Cook Hwy, tel: 55 3669.* Open daily 0900–1700. Shows are held throughout the day.

The House of 10,000 Shells, *32 Abbott St; tel: 51 3638,* lives up to its name with an extensive shell collection and museum with a display

of Australiana, souvenirs, semi-precious and coral jewellery. Open Mon–Sat 0900–2200, Sun 1100–2200. **Gallery Primitive**, *26 Abbot St,* is a few doors along and has a comprehensive range of Pacific native art even though, again, it is basically a shop.

Out of Town

Out of town is **Kuranda** – a most magic place. Kuranda can be reached by road, by the **Kuranda Scenic Railway** – highly recommended; 30 km long with 15 tunnels and 100 curves and a restored Victorian station at the Kuranda end – or by the **Skyrail Rainforest Cableway** running 7½ km from the **Smithfield Shopping Centre**, north west of Cairns to Kuranda.

It is a most charming town, which feels as if it is locked in a 1960s time warp and Sergeant Pepper's Lonely Heart Club Band may appear at any minute. And, indeed, there is a group of locals who dress as members of that band on market days and – unusual, this – ask visitors to please *not* photograph them.

One of its prize assets, which is renowned throughout Australia, is **The Tjapukai Dance Theatre**, *21 Coondoo St; tel: (070) 93 7544.* Shows daily 1100 and 1330. This is certainly the best Aboriginal dance talent in Australia, which is presented using all the skills and techniques of the modern theatre. It is totally stunning and under no circumstances should be missed. It has won almost every award available in Australia. Quite right too.

Also in Kuranda is the **Australian Butterfly Sanctuary**, *Rob Vievers Dr; tel: (070) 93 7575.* Open daily 1000–1500. There are guided tours starting almost every 15 mins and they last about an hour. According to the *Guinness Book of Records,* this is Australia's largest butterfly farm. It breeds and flies up to 35 indigenous and protected species of butterflies in a rain forest enclosed by a massive walk-through flight aviary. Nearby is **The Kuranda Wildlife Noctarium**, *8 Coondoo St; tel: 93 7334.* Open daily 1000–1600. This has a display of nocturnal fauna set in simulated rain forest at night. It has been described as 'the world's best live display of Australian nocturnal animals in a natural rainforest setting.'

NORTH AND WEST OF CAIRNS

Cairns is the capital of tropical North Queensland and, in a sense, it is the jumping-off point into the real tropics. Cairns itself is a tropical town but as soon as you leave the outskirts, travelling north or west, you soon realise that this green and tropical area is very different to other parts of Australia.

Driving the Cape York Peninsula is like embarking on an expedition. The change is quite remarkable. Sealed roads intermittently become just graded dirt. Bulldust, the ultra fine powder, is everywhere, choking engine filters, which have to be cleaned every day. In the Wet, many of the roads to the north, sealed or not, are impassable. In the dry they can be a challenge.

In the dry, a conventional vehicle could easily make the run as far as Cooktown, if you head first for Lakeland and then turn inland for the last 54 km of the trip. In theory, you could also drive along Peninsula Developmental Rd as far as Weipa although your car will not be pristine upon arrival. This is real frontier country and a four-wheel-drive is the best option, especially if you intend to explore off the main road. You must carry enough supplies, especially water and petrol, to get you from place to place with a safe reserve.

ROUTES

NORTHERN ROUTE

At Cairns, Rte 1 changes its name from the Bruce Hwy to the Captain Cook Hwy, and makes an 87 km run north to **Mossman**, with **Port Douglas** a minor detour on the right. After Mossman you continue north in a series of zigzags, turning left to visit **Daintree** (36 km) and then onwards, on a road suitable only for four-wheel-drive, to **Cooktown**. An alternative is to head inland to **Mt Molloy** and then north on the Peninsula Developmental Rd to Lakeland and then east on the Cooktown Developmental Rd.

WESTERN ROUTE

Getting into the Gulf Country from Cairns, you can take either the Gulf Development Rd, which starts on the **Atherton Tablelands** or the Burke Development Rd out of **Cloncurry**, which is the last section of the route known as the Matilda Hwy. This chapter's recommended route takes the first option.

Head south out of Cairns along Rte 1 and turn right at Gordonvale for **Atherton**. From there head south to **Ravenshoe**, and there turn right along the Kennedy Hwy to **Mt Garnet** and, after passing through part of **Undara National Park**, to **Mt Surprise**. By now you are on the Gulf Developmental Rd. Some 90 km after Mt Surprise you reach **Georgetown**. Continue west 150 km to **Croydon**, and another 153 km to **Normanton**, just off the coast of the Gulf of Carpentaria. From Normanton the road takes you another 230 km in an arc to **Burketown**, from where you can reach **Lawn Hills National Park**.

These are mainly sealed roads – with an unsealed and often corrugated 70 km stretch between Croydon and Normanton – and, in the dry season, suitable for any normal vehicle

249

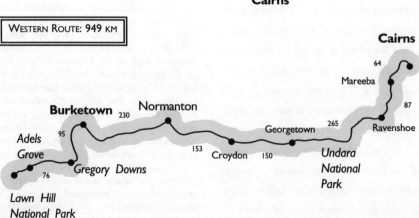

if driven slowly and carefully over the unsealed sections. Other roads, notoriously the Normanton to Chillagoe run, should only be attempted with a very fully equipped four-wheel-drive and a very experienced driver, and even then only in the dry season. If you are visiting the Gulf you need to be pretty self-sufficient, as there are few banks, the petrol stations are often hundreds of kilometres apart and the accommodation tends to be very basic.

TRAINS

No trains cover either of these routes in any depth, but there are one or two relatively short rail trips within the area around Cairns and the Gulf Country, which are well worth taking, including the Savannahlander, the Gulflander, the Inlander and the Kuranda Scenic Railway. More details are given on p. 405. See OTT tables 9007–9010 for timings.

BUSES

Coral Coaches provide services out of Cairns to Port Douglas (1½ hrs) and Cooktown (8 hrs). Whitecar Coaches run to Atherton (1¾ hrs) and Ravenshoe (2¾ hrs). Cairns-Karumba Coachlines run a thrice-weekly service from Cairns all the way along the Western Route, including Undara (4½ hrs), Georgetown (6¼ hrs), Croydon (8½ hrs) and Normanton (10½ hrs). OTT tables 9070 and 9089.

PORT DOUGLAS

Tourist Information: Port Douglas Information Centre, *23 Macrossan St; tel: (070) 99 5599.*

ACCOMMODATION AND FOOD

Sheraton Mirage Port Douglas, *Davidson St; tel: 99 5888.* **Radisson Royal Palms Resort**, *Port Douglas Rd; tel: 99 5577.* **Reef Terraces Resort**, *Port Douglas Rd; tel: 99 3333.* **Club Tropical Resort Hotel**, *corner Wharf and Macrossan Sts; tel: 99 5885.* **Lazy Lizard Motor Inn** *(BW), 121 Davidson St; tel: 99 5900.* **Rusty Pelican Motor Inn** *(FL), 123 Davidson St; tel: 99 5266.* **Whispering Palms**, *20-30 Langley Rd; tel: 98 5128.* **Central Hotel Motel**, *Macrossan St; tel: (070) 99 5271.* **Port Douglas Motel**, *9 Davidson St;*

tel: 99 5248. **Coconut Grove Motel**, *58 Macrossan St; 99 5124.* **Sassi Islandpoint Motel**, *Island Point Rd; tel: 99 5313.* **HI: Port O'Call Lodge**, *Port St; tel: 99 5422.*

Going Bananas, *87 Davidson St; tel: 99 53400.* Open dinner Mon–Sat. Licensed. Strange tropical castaway type up-market restaurant. **Nautilus**, *17 Murphy St; tel: 99 5330.* Open nightly for dinner. Licensed. Open air setting. Up-market. **Catalina**, *Wharf St; tel: 99 5287.* Lunch, dinner Tues–Sun. Licensed. Seafood specialities. **Rusty's Bar and Bistro**, *123 Davidson St; tel: 99 5266.* Open daily. Licensed.

SIGHTSEEING

Port Douglas at one time – in the 1880s – looked as if it would be the port of North Queensland. Then Cairns surged ahead when the railway line opened. In 1911 there was a devastating cyclone and business moved from Port Douglas to nearby **Mossman**.

Port Douglas became a backwater – down at one time to a population of 250 – until the advent of the disgraced entrepreneur Christopher Skase. He conceived and built what is now the **Sheraton Mirage Resort**, which has since been followed by four other major resort hotels including the **Radisson Royal Palms Resort**, and the whole area has become an explosion of tourist facilities.

· Incidentally, **Quintex**, the company founded and run by Skase, went belly up owing $1.6 billion. Skase is currently in Majorca and has successfully resisted all attempts at extradition. In Port Douglas he is generally regarded as a saint who has been cruelly abused by the authorities.

The town stands on a long low spit of land 6 km from the main Captain Cook Hwy and its roads are lined with palm trees – a Skase innovation. Although this is basically an up-market resort – and the prices in the top hotels reflect this – it is still a Queensland small town with much of the charm intact.

Although much is made of scuba diving around the Barrier Reef, the truth is that generally the water is so shallow that if you just snorkel you will see most of the sites with none of the expense and minimal risk.

If you want to learn how to scuba you can get a resort certificate, which will allow you to dive in the company of a qualified diver. One place offering this facility is **Port Douglas Dive Centre** (*Anzac Park, tel: 99 5327;* open daily 0845–1730), with training courses and escorted trips out to the reef.

There is a paddle steamer that cruises **Dickson Inlet**, where you can see wild birds and possibly crocodiles. **Lady Douglas Paddle Wheeler** (*tel: 99 5189*) departs daily 0930, 1025, 1315 and 1425. $20.

Rainforest Habitat, *Port Douglas Rd; tel: 99 3235*, is a spread of planned rain forest within an immense canopy. It is as near as you can get to the rain forest with all its variations encompassed in a small space. There are professional guides on hand or you can explore on your own. Open daily 0800–1630. Admission $14.

The canopied rain forest is surrounded by a further area, which has wallabies, koalas, crocodiles and emus.

Ben Cropp is a well known Australian skin diver and photographer and his **Shipwreck Treasure Trove Museum**, *Ben Cropp's Wharf; tel: 99 5858*, contains a display of a treasure trove salvaged from the sea. There is a continuous showing of movies portraying Ben Cropp's adventures around Australia exploring old ship wrecks. On display are relics recovered from the *Pandora*, which was lost in 1791 while carrying the captured mutineers of the Bounty back to England for trial. Open daily 0900–1700; $4.

The Ballyhooley Steam Cane Train departs from Marina Station to St Crispins Station. Hourly 0900–1700. Return $6.

From the Marina there are a wide range of cruises out to the Reef. The best known and most popular is **Quicksilver** (*tel: 99 5500*), whose 300 passenger catamarans depart every day at 1100 and go out to **Agincourt Reef**. The $118 price includes use of snorkel gear, a ride in a semi submersible and lunch.

Mossman, 14 km from Port Douglas, was named after Hugh Mosman, but was misspelled deliberately to avoid confusion with Mosman in Sydney, which was named after Archibald Mosman, Hugh's father.

DAINTREE

Tourist Information: Daintree National Park, *Daintree; tel: (070) 51 9811* or *92 8188.*

ACCOMMODATION

Daintree Wilderness Lodge, *83 Cape Tribulation Rd, Alexandra Bay (PO Box 352, Mossman); tel: (070) 98 9105.* **Daintree Cape Tribulation Heritage Lodge**, *Turpentine Rd, Cooper Creek, via Mossman; tel: 98 9138.* **Daintree Eco-Tourist Lodge**, *Daintree Rd; tel: 98 6100.* **Silky Oaks Lodge Resort**, *Mossman River Gorge; tel: 98 1666.* **Demi View Mossman Motel**, *41 Front St; tel: (070) 98 1277.*

SIGHTSEEING

Daintree is only a small town, situated 80 km north of Cairns and 5 km west of Mossman, and would not be worthy of further note except that it is the entrance to the **Daintree National Park** and it could be thought of as the gateway to the **Cape York Peninsula**. Below the Daintree River crossing you will find nothing but sealed roads, resort hotels and civilisation. Above the Daintree River you are entering into the true top end.

There have been many bitter battles fought by conservationists to keep this area of rain forest unsullied and the struggle still rages on. However, because eco-tourism has brought such prosperity to north Queensland the support is now very much on the side of the greens, although developers are still trying to build throughout the Cape York peninsula and are ardent advocates of upgrading and surfacing the road to encourage even more tourism.

The park itself covers 56,450 hectares and is a World Heritage area of the wet tropics. It has rugged ranges covered with forests and woods, and the many tributaries of the Daintree River come tumbling down the slopes in series of waterfalls. Right through the park is the deep gorge of the **Mossman River** with footpaths leading into the ever luxuriant rain forest. Animals in the park include tree kangaroos, ringtail possums, the golden bower bird and tree frogs. This is the only place in Australia where the rain forest actually grows down to the coast, where it makes contact with the

Barrier Reef. The forest near the road, which runs up the spine of Cape York, often demonstrates a curious phenomenon. It can be pouring with rain on the road but in the rain forest there is but a gentle mist. The canopy of the rain forest is so dense that it acts as an effective umbrella.

There is a 3-km footpath from the car park at the Mossman picnic area but most of the park is only suitable for experienced bushwalkers.

The Daintree river at Daintree is wide with a ferry crossing. The ferry runs 0600–2400, pedestrians $1, vehicles $5, and goes on to the 35 km of the Cape Tribulation Rd, which is partly sealed but in the Wet can be formidable barrier except for a properly equipped four-wheel-drive.

Ranged between the ferry and the town itself there are a series of tour operators offering cruises of the Daintree River. Most of the tours take an hour or so and cost around $10–15. You will see prolific bird life along the the river and from Apr to Sept it is very likely that you will see crocodiles sunning themselves on the banks, especially at low tide.

Among the better known operators are: **Daintree Rainforest River Train Tours**, tel: 90 7676; **Daintree River and Reef Cruise Centre**, tel: 98 6115; **Crocodile Express**, tel: 98 6120; **Daintree Lady**, tel: 98 6146; **Daintree River Cruises**, tel: 98 2065 or 018 77 1850; **Daintree Wildlife Safari**, tel: 98 6125.

In the village itself is the **Timber Museum, Gallery and Shop**, which has a timber workshop with craftsmen turning out turned bowls and other items. On display in the museum is a large collection of old wood working tools.

COOKTOWN

Tourist Information: Cape York Pennisula Tourism Association; tel: (070) 69 5569 or **Port Douglas and Cooktown Tourist Information Centre**, 23 Macrossan St, Port Douglas; tel: (070) 99 5599.

ACCOMMODATION AND FOOD

The **Sovereign Resort Hotel**, Charlotte St (PO Box 100); tel: 69 5400. **Sea View Motel**,

Charlotte St; tel: 69 5377. **Cooktowns River of Gold Motel**, corner Hope and Walker Sts; tel: 69 5222. **Cooktown Motor Inn**, 12 Charlotte St; tel: 69 5357.

Endeavour Inn, Charlotte and Furneaux St; tel: 69 5384. Dinner nightly. Licensed. Australian cuisine. **Sovereign Hotel**, Charlotte and Green Sts; tel: 69 5400. Open daily lunch and dinner. Licensed.

SIGHTSEEING

Cooktown is 240 km north-west of Cairns and is named after Captain Cook. In June 1770, he had holed the *Endeavour* on the Barrier Reef, some 70 km to the south-east. A sail was patched over the hole, still with a large chunk of coral stuck in, and the ship was slowly brought to the Inlet, which Cook named the Endeavour River. The ship was lightened, beached, repaired and refloated. C.S. Forester was later to give a splendid fictional account of this, transposed to South America with Horatio Hornblower in charge.

It is claimed that the workbenches and rough shelters that were set up for work on the *Endeavour* – Australia's first white settlement – formed the basis for Cookstown. The site of his landing is now **Endeavour Park**. All of this is recorded in the **James Cook Historical Museum and Joseph Bank Gardens**, Helen St; tel: 69 5386. Open daily 0930–1600, $5. The museum was built in 1889 as St Mary's Convent and was a senior school for girls. It was used by the military in World War II and then abandoned in 1945. A developer was all set to demolish it, when the Queensland National Trust and the Catholic Church stepped in and restored it as a museum. The museum has, among many other exhibits, Cook's cannon and anchor, which were jettisoned in the efforts to get the *Endeavour* off the reef.

Cooktown originally grew as a result of the **Palmer River** gold rush of 1873 – at one point it had nearly a hundred pubs; now it has three hotels – but today its economy almost totally depends on tourism as a departure point for the Cape York peninsula.

Worth seeing is the **cemetery**, which has the grave of the remarkable Mrs Mary Watson, who died in tragic circumstances fleeing an attack by Aborigines in the early pioneer days, and a **Chinese shrine** dedicated to the 18,000 Chinese who came to the region during the gold rush.

The best view of the town is from **Grassy Hill Lookout**, which has an old lighthouse and a memorial to Captain Cook, who used this vantage point to plot a course through the Reef. Cooktown is also the start of the **Bicentennial National Trail**, which runs 5000 km from Cooktown to **Healesville** in Victoria and is much used by hikers and horse riders.

In theory you can drive to Cooktown during the dry season along the **Bloomfield Track** in a conventional car but a four-wheel-drive is a much better bet. During the wet season it is the only way to drive that route, which at times is even closed to four wheel traffic. The same applies out of Cooktown to **Laura** – fine for conventional vehicles – and then through the **Lakefield National Park**. In the dry season you could probably make it on the road that runs through this ½ million hectare wilderness – but a four-wheel-drive vehicle is a much safer proposition.

The inland route from Cairns to Cooktown is fine for conventional vehicles even though a lot of the road is unsealed and you get rattled around a lot on the corrugations. The road can be closed in the wet season and you should check with the **RACQ** (*tel: 51 4788*) before setting off.

GULF COUNTRY

This is the land of **Gulf Savannah**, which was so superbly described by Neville Shute in his book *A Town Like Alice*. It extends from the border of the Northern Territory across the top end of Queensland coming to a stop at the Great Dividing Range. To the north of it is the Gulf of Carpentaria and the Cape York Peninsula. Most of its coastline consists of mangrove swamps and it was these that prevented the ill-fated Burke and Wills expedition from actually reaching the sea, although they knew they were close.

This is a large, flat and essentially empty landscape which is hot, tough and home to

---

Burke and Wills

The Burke and Wills expedition was a tragedy. Robert O'Hara Burke and the scientist W.J. Wills led an expedition from Melbourne to the Gulf of Carpentaria – a trans-Australian crossing. The expedition was financed by the Victorian public and they set off in 1860. They nearly made it to the Gulf, getting within 50 km. They returned to Coopers Creek, where one of the party, Grey, died of dysentery. Not long afterwards Burke and Wills also perished. There is a statue to commemorate their deaths in *Spring St,* Melbourne. In July 1862 the first successful south to north crossing was carried out by John McDouall Stuart, who travelled from Adelaide to Darwin. The telegraph line was later constructed along the trail that he had blazed.

---

thousands of crocodiles. The area is dominated by weather. During the Wet, which lasts from Dec–Mar, all of the dirt roads are effectively closed and even sealed roads can become impassable with floods. The time for visitors to explore the Gulf Country is Apr–Oct.

The two main towns, in an area which is not over-populated, are **Normanton** and **Burketown**, but these are not serious tourist destinations. The two major tourist attractions are the difficult of access **Lawn Hill National Park** and the **Undara Lava Tubes**. Getting to the Undara Lava Tubes is not a problem – only half a day's drive from Cairns – but Lawn Hill is a serious expedition.

UNDARA

Lava tubes, massive tunnels created by lava flow that run for distances of up to 35 km from the side of a dead volcano, are found on the **Yarramulla Station**, which is reached via 15 km of unsealed road off the Gulf Development Rd, 130 km from **Ravenshoe**. Or you can fly in on one of the regular chartered flights from Cairns. The site has been very well developed for tourists and offers a wide range of amenities. The only way to see the lava tubes, which can be up to 19m high and 20m long, is by conducted tour ($52 for half a day).

NORMANTON

Tourist Information: Normanton Carpentaria Shire Council, *Landsborough St; tel: (077) 45 1268*

It is important to get the size of this town into perspective lest you be misled. The population is listed at the moment as 1190. That is not the population of a major town. It has seen more boisterous times, as in 1890 when it was the port town (it is 80 km inland on the **Norman River**) for the gold rush to the **Croydon** gold fields, to which it was connected by rail. Now its glory days are well past and it is basically a collection of stores and buildings waiting for another gold rush.

Worth seeing is the very first **Burns Philp Store**; *tel: (077) 45 1235*, in the main street, *Landsborough St.* Open normal working hours.

The last camp of the Burke and Wills expedition can be found on the left hand side of the road to Burketown on the eastern bank of the Little Bynoe River. There is a signpost marking the track that will get you to the site.

Dorunda Barramundi Lodge, *Dorunda Station, via Normanton; tel: (070) 53 4500*, is a Gulf wilderness fishing lodge 200 km north east of Normanton. Camping is available at the 25 km long private lake, and hire boats and rods are available.

The **Normanton Penitentiary**, *Haig St,* is one of the attractions of the town and was the main penal establishment for the Gulf Savannah during the heyday of the Croydon gold rush. Contact the police station for admission.

The famous **Gulflander** train (see p. 405), the line to nowhere, leaves from **Normanton Railway Station**, *Matilda Street; tel: (077) 45 1391*, on Wed on its journey to Croydon and returns Thur. It carries both passengers and cars.

BURKETOWN

Tourist Information: Burke Shire Council, *Musgrave St; tel: (077) 45 5100.*

Burketown has about 250 residents. At one time the place had promise and tried to become important. Captain Stokes sailed up the Albert River in 1841 to choose the town site and wrote that he would call them 'The Plains of Promise' and that he could foresee the horizon 'would be broken by a succession of tapering spires rising from Christian hamlets'. He was wrong. The **Burketown to Normanton telegraph line** was in competition with the Adelaide to Darwin line, and Burketown was to be the terminus for the trans-oceanic cable connecting Australia to Asia and Europe. This did not happen and Burketown missed its moment of glory.

The **Morning Glory** is a peculiar cloud formation that usually occurs from Sept–Nov. Tubular clouds roll out of the Gulf in the early morning, extend from horizon to horizon and are accompanied by violent winds. Then there is the **Artesian Bore**, which was so graphically described in *A Town Like Alice*. Boiling mineralised water pumps out of the bore and creates a billabong.

SIDE TRACK
FROM BURKETOWN

LAWN HILL NATIONAL PARK

255

This is right at the other side of the Gulf Savannah area, nearly on the edge of the Northern Territory. It can be reached by going south from Normanton along the Burke Development Rd 194 km south to the **Burke and Wills Road House** and then turning right, covering another 145 km to **Gregory Downs**; the same point can be reached more quickly from Burketown by driving south for about 100 km. The route continues from there by unsealed trail 76 km westwards to **Adel's Grove**, where there is a kiosk, *tel: (077) 48 5502*. Neither drive is for the inexperienced or the fainthearted and a four-wheel-drive is strongly recommended, although in the dry season you could make it in a conventional vehicle. The Park is a gorge of luxuriant growth, in striking contrast to the surrounding countryside. Camping is allowed and can be booked with the Park Rangers on *(077) 48 5572.*

DARLING DOWNS

This almost-circular tour from Brisbane takes in some of the finest agricultural land in Australia. Nearly all of the interesting scenery for the traveller occurs in and around the Great Dividing Range. Further inland the roads are flat and the landscape uninspiring.

Darling Downs was the first area in Queensland to be settled after the Moreton Bay penal colony. It is neatly defined on its southern border by the New South Wales border and could be thought of as lying between two highways – the Warrego Hwy to the north and the Cunningham Hwy to the south.

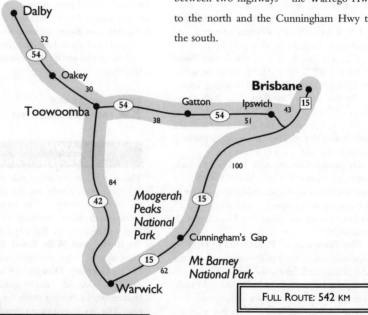

FULL ROUTE: 542 KM

ROUTE

Take Rte 1 south out of Brisbane until it turns onto the South East Freeway, at which point continue on what is then Rte 15, *Ipswich Rd.* After a few more km this road merges with Rte 20 to become the Ipswich Motorway, heading west and still numbered Rte 15. Remain on Rte 15, by-passing Ipswich, until about 100 km outside Brisbane you reach **Cunningham's Gap**. Continue another 62 km to **Warwick**. From Warwick head north on Rte 42 to **Toowoomba**.

Colour section (i): The Great Barrier Reef (p. 227): aerial view of Green Island; diving in the Reef.

(ii) Twin Falls, Kakadu National Park (p. 272); saltwater crocodile, Kakadu; Katherine Gorge (p. 276)

(iii) Ayers Rock (p. 285).

(iv) The Exchange Hotel, Kalgoorlie(p. 311); Hay St, Perth (p. 290).

From Toowoomba you can return to Brisbane by heading east along Rte 54, the Warrego Hwy, via **Gatton** and **Ipswich**. This cuts about 164 km off the tour. To take the full route, however, follow Rte 54 in the opposite direction out of Toowoomba, north-west, via **Oakey** to **Dalby**.

After visiting Dalby the simplest and quickest way to return is by going back to Toowoomba and then on to Brisbane as described above. The network of roads to the east of Dalby does, however, give connections to Rte 1 north of Brisbane at Caboolture, Gympie and many other places on the Brisbane–Rockhampton route (see p. 215).

TRAINS

On Tues and Thur evenings the Westlander runs to Charleville from Brisbane, stopping at Toowoomba (1¾ hrs) and Dalby (5 hrs). OTT table 9012.

BUSES

A good bus service to the Darling Downs is provided by a variety of companies, including Greyhound Pioneer and McCafferty's. One route connects Brisbane to Toowoomba (2½ hrs) and Dalby (3½ hrs). Another links Brisbane and Toowoomba with Warwick (3 hrs direct, 3½ hrs via Toowoomba). OTT tables 9073, 9074 and 9076.

CUNNINGHAM'S GAP

Tourist Information: Queensland National Parks; tel: (074) 631 579.

Just beside the 676 hectares of **Moogerah Peaks National Park** is the gap in the Great Dividing Range where Allan Cunningham discovered the Darling Downs. The park gives spectacular views over Cunningham's Gap to the **Fassifern Valley** and is reached just off the Cunningham Hwy (Rte 15). Just to the south is **Mt Barney National Park**, the eastern edge of the Great Dividing Range, covering 11,900 hectares. **Mt Barney** itself reaches 1360m.

WARWICK

Tourist Information: Warwick Tourist Information Centre, 49 Albion St; tel: (076) 61 3122.

Discovery and Settlement

The first known European visitor to the area was the botanist Allan Cunningham, who led an expedition from Sydney in 1827 to explore the area inland from the Great Dividing Range. After only six weeks he came upon the valley and was immensely impressed by its potential. He reported that he saw 'a beautiful and well watered valley', which he named after Ralph Darling, the then governor of New South Wales. He then discovered two routes to the Queensland coast from the Darling Downs. The first of these was Spicer's Gap and the second was Cunningham's Gap, which is now used by the main road from Brisbane to the Darling Downs. By 1840 sheep farming had started in the area, and such was its success that it brought in a surge of other farmers, many of whom acquired their land by dubious means.

ACCOMMODATION AND FOOD

Alexander Motel, Cunningham Hwy and Wentworth St; tel: 61 3888. **Buckaroo Motor Inn** (BU), 86 Wood St; tel: 61 3755. **Centre Point Mid City Motor Inn**, 32 Albion St; tel: 61 3488. **City View Motel** (GC), corner Cunningham Hwy and Yangan Rd; tel: 61 5000. **Horse & Jockey Hotel/Motel**, corner Palmerin and Victoria Sts; tel: 61 2722. **The Jackie Howe Motel**, corner Palmerin and Victoria Sts; tel: 61 2111. **McNevins Gunyah Motel**, New England Hwy; tel: 61 5588. **Village Motor Inn**, 57 Victoria St; tel: 61 1699. **The Warwick Homestead**, 17–19 Albion St; tel: 61 1533.

Criterion Hotel, 85 Palmerin St. Licensed. Pub food.

SIGHTSEEING

The town, which is 162 km inland and south-west of Brisbane, started in 1840 on the banks of the Condamine River with the **Canning Downs Run**, and was important as the birthplace of pastoral farming in south-east Queensland. It was illegally settled until government permission was given in 1842. Then it became a pioneer in the cross-breeding of sheep and back in 1850 tried breeding Peruvian llamas for mohair, with no success.

The town grew with the arrival of the Cobb & Co. coach service in 1865 and the railway in 1873. The city, which achieved that status in 1936, likes to refer to itself as the **Rose and Rodeo City** because rosebushes are a feature of the town – there are superb displays in **Queen Elizabeth Jubilee Rose Gardens** in **Leslie Park** – and it houses the office of the **Australian Rough Riders Association**. There is a major rodeo in Warwick in the last week of Oct and this has been held almost every year since 1929.

Many of the buildings in Warwick are sandstone, built before the municipality was officially recognised, demonstrating the wealth of the area.

One of the town's major attractions is the **Pringle Cottage and Museum**, *Dragon St*, which was built in 1863 and has a collection of Victorian mechanical antiques. Open daily except Tues, 1000–1200 and 1400–1600, admission $3.50.

The **Jackie Howe Rest Area** on the corner of the *Cunningham Hwy* and *Glengallan Rd* has a massive pair of shears as a monument to **Jackie Howe**, whose record of shearing 321 sheep by hand in one day in 1892 has never been surpassed. Jackie Howe used to rip the sleeves off his shirt to give himself room to move and the sleeveless blue singlets widely used by Australian workers are to this day called 'Jackie Howes'. Howe is always referred to as a 'gun shearer' and the word 'gun' has come to mean the best in any area of endeavour.

The region is rich in minerals and fossicking for gems and minerals is popular, especially in the **Dalrymple Creek** area. On the outskirts of Warwick near the entrance to Rosenthal Station stands **Leichardt's Tree**, which is said to be the place where Ludwig Leichhardt started the 1848 expedition from which he never returned. In the area is **Warwick Dam**, which is popular for water-sports and especially for fishing.

Historical Footnote

Warwick can claim a minor place in Australian history. In 1917, the prime minister, Billy Hughes, spoke there on the subject of conscription, which was totally rejected in Australia and never became law. An egg was thrown and hit Billy Hughes on his hat but the local police constable refused to prosecute. This incident led to the formation of the Australian Commonwealth police force.

TOOWOOMBA

Tourist Information: Toowoomba **Tourist Centre**, *City Hall, 541 Ruthven St; tel: (076) 32 1988.*

ACCOMMODATION AND FOOD

Park Motor Inn *(FL), 88 Margaret St; tel: 32 1011.* **Raceview Motor Inn**, *52 Hursley Rd; tel: 34 6777.* **Tudor Lodge Motel** *(FL), Cohoe St; tel: 38 1822.* **Blue Violet Motor Inn** *(BW), 31 Margaret St; tel: 38 1488.* **Garden City Motor Inn** *(GC), 718 Ruthven St; tel: 35 5377.* **Allan Cunningham Motel & Pioneer Steak House** *(BW), 808 Ruthven St; tel: 35 5466.* **Bridge Street Motor Inn**, *291 Bridge St; tel: 34 3299.* **Burke & Wills Toowoomba Hotel**, *554 Ruthven St; tel: 32 2433.*

Clewleys Motel, *683 Ruthven St; tel: 38 3466.* **Coachman Motel**, *4 Burnage St; tel: 39 3707.* **Colonial Motel** *(BW), 730 Ruthven St, New England Hwy; tel: 35 3233.* **Downs Motel**, *669 Ruthven St; tel: 39 3811.* **Flying Spur Motel** *(BU), 277 Taylor St; tel: 34 3237.* **Gateway Motel**, *41 Margaret St; tel: 32 2088.* **Glenfield Motor Lodge** *(FL), corner Ruthven and Stenner Sts; tel: 35 4466.* **Jacaranda Place Motor Inn**, *794 Ruthven St; tel: 35 3111.* **James St Motor Inn**, *corner James and Kitchener Sts; tel: 38 3066.* **Jefferys Motel & Caravan Park**, *864 Ruthven; tel: 35 5999.* **Leichhardt Motor Inn**, *682 Ruthven St: tel: 38 4644.* **Ruthven St Motor Inn** *(BU), 786 Ruthven St; tel: 36 1366.* **Cosy Motel**, *195A West St; tel: 38 3900.*

258

Apart from the above, dining possibilities include **Herries Town House**, *210 Herries St.*, licensed, Italian cuisine, and **Spotted Cow**, *Ruthven and Campbell Sts*, licensed, English pub-style meals.

SIGHTSEEING

Toowoomba is 127 km west of Brisbane, lying 600 m high on the edge of the Great Dividing Range, and is known as a garden city. The town started off life as a staging post called The Swamp. No one is certain of the origin of its current name. In 1840 there was a station there called Toolburra. This was changed by Thomas Alford, an early settler, to Drayton, after a town in Somerset, but his house was called Too-woomba. Drayton is now a suburb of the town. It is suggested that the name may be an Aboriginal word for 'swamp' or 'underground water'. Nowadays Toowoomba is the commercial centre for the Darling Downs.

One of the main attractions of Toowoomba is the **Cobb & Co. Museum**, *27 Lindsay St*, which displays several of the coaches that linked outback settlements. Open Mon–Fri 1000–1600, weekends 1300–1600, admission $3. **The Regional Art Gallery**, *Ruthven St*, has the Lindsay collection of colonial art. Open Tues–Sat 1000–1600, Sun 1300–1600.

There are many gardens throughout the city, including the **Botanic Gardens** on *Lindsay St*, which are part of **Queens Park**, while the **Japanese Garden – Ju Raku En –** is in *West St* at the University of Southern Queensland.

In the area, 40 km south of Toowoomba, is **Rudd's Pub**, which holds an important place in Australian literary history. Here, Steele Rudd wrote a number of Dad and Dave stories and the pub has a storyteller, who gives recitations of parts of *On Our Selection*, a major landmark in Australian writing.

Seeing the environs of Toowoomba is made easier by taking one of the self-guided driving tours available from the tourist centre. For example, there is a 48-km circuit taking in **Spring Bluff**, where the old railway station has wonderful gardens worth visiting. Then there is a 100-km circuit to **Heifer Creek**, which is known as the **Valley of the Sun.**

DALBY

Tourist Information: Tourist Office, *Thomas Jack Park, Drayton and Condamine Sts; tel: (076) 62 1966.*

ACCOMMODATION

Dalby Manor Motor Inn *(FL)*, *18 Drayton St; tel: 62 1011.* **Pathfinder Motor Inn** *(BW)*, *62 Condamine St; tel: 62 4433.* **Dalby Parkview Motel**, *31 Drayton St; tel: 62 3222.* **Motel Myall**, *corner Drayton and Myall Sts; tel: 62 3399.* **The Gallery Motor Inn**, *128 Drayton St; tel: 62 2300.*

SIGHTSEEING

Dalby is at the crossroads of three highways – the Warrego, Bunya and Moonie – and is 84 km north-west of Toowoomba. It was named in 1854 after a town in the Isle of Man and is the centre of one of the richest grain-growing areas in Australia.

The **Pioneer Park Museum**, off the *Warrego Hwy* 2 km west of the town centre, has a collection of old farm machinery and buildings. The town also has a memorial to an insect – the cactoblastis caterpillar. Cactus escaped from a garden at the end of the last century and quickly spread across the farming land of Queensland. By the 1920s a large part of the agricultural land in Queensland was covered with this blight. Then in 1925 the government imported the cactoblastis, which quickly ate its way through the cactus. (The same idea – eradicating one pest by introducing another – was tried in recent years with the cane toad, which was intended to destroy a beetle threatening the sugar crop. It didn't succeed but bred in ever-increasing numbers. Now the cane toad is a serious menace.)

There is a self-drive tour of the town and you can get information at the tourist office.

Nearby, 29 km to the south-west, is **Lake Broadwater Conservation Park**, which has boating and other water sports. **Jimbour House**, which is Heritage listed, is 27 km to the north and the grounds are open daily. This is where Ludwig Leichardt's expedition through the Northern Territory started. The **Bunya Mountains National Park** is 60 km to the north-east.

259

QUEENSLAND NATIONAL PARKS

TOURIST INFORMATION

Queensland Conservation and Land Management, *tel: (07) 9334 0333.*

OVERVIEW

The national parks of Queensland are possibly more varied, and numerous, than in any other state of Australia. Near Brisbane they are fragmented and numerous, small areas spread across the landscape.

This means, for instance, that **Tamborine Mountain**, one of the most important areas, is split up into seven small parks with development and farming between. Tamborine, which lies 45 km north-west of the Gold Coast acquired a national park by default when a forestry official in 1908 declared 130 hectares at **Witches Falls** as 'unfit for any other purpose'and it became Queensland's first national park. Since then eight others have been added in piecemeal fashion, covering parts of the northern slopes of Mount Tamborine. The parks are **Panorama Point, Macrozamia Grove** and **MacDonald Park** which each cover less than 20 hectares. Then comes **Joalah**, 40 hectares; **The Knoll**, 85 hectares; **Palm Grove**, 118 hectares; **Witches Falls** 130 hectares; **Cedar Creek**, 230 hectares. Access to the parks is by way of Oxenford on the Pacific Highway between **Beenleigh** and **Nerang** (see p. 214).

Near Rockhampton there is **Fraser Island** with its **Great Sandy National Park**. And inland along the **Dawson Highway Carnarvon** with its amazing gorge. In this area there are well over 30 national parks.

Near Townsville both **Magnetic Island** and **Hinchinbrook Island** are national parks and altogether there are twenty in the region. The **Great Barrier Reef** in its entirety is managed as a marine park – all 350,000 sq km. There are some minor pieces outside the park but these represent less than two per cent of the total, so that the Great Barrier Reef is totally secure from any direct assault.

Within reach of **Cairns** and, further north, **Cooktown** at the entrance to the Cape York Peninsula, there are 41 national parks. It is perfectly possible to visit half a dozen of them in a day's easy driving.

REGION BY REGION

In the following listing, parks have, unless otherwise noted, at least one campsite, picnic area and walking trail. Where bush camping, i.e. in the wild rather than at an organised site, is permitted, this is stated.

The Great Barrier Reef and Coast

See the chapters on the Great barrier Reef itself (pp. 227–238) and the coastal routes which give access to it: Brisbane to Rockhampton (pp. 215–226) and Rockhampton to Cairns (pp. 239–248).

Bowling Green Bay *Bush camping possible.*
Byfield *Bush camping possible, no other facilities.*
Cape Hillsborough
Cape Palmerston *Bush camping possible, picnic and barbecue area, no other facilities.*
Cape Upstart *Bush camping possible, no other facilities.*
Conway
Cumberland Islands *Picnic area, no other facilities.*
Eungella
Great Barrier Reef Marine Park
Hinchinbrook Island
Keppel Islands Group
Magnetic Island *No campsite.*
Mt Aberdeen *Bush camping possible, no other facilities.*
Whitsunday Islands *Bush camping possible.*

Coral Sea and South Pacific Coast
See Brisbane to Rockhampton route, pp. 215–226, for more details of these parks.

Bunker Group
Burrum River *No facilities.*
Capricorn/Bunker Group *No campsite but bush camping possible.*
Cooloola *Bush camping possible.*
Eurimbula *No picnic area or walking trails.*
Great Sandy *Bush camping possible.*
Litabella *No facilities.*
Mt Colosseum *Bush camping possible, no other facilities.*

In and around Brisbane
See the Gold Coast chapter, pp. 211–214, Brisbane, pp. 203–210, and the Darling Downs route, pp. 256–259, for more details of some of these parks.

Blue Lake *No campsite, picnic area or walking trail.*
Brisbane Forest Park
Bunya Mountains
Crows Nest Falls
Girraween *Bush camping possible.*
Lamington *Bush camping possible.*
Main Range *Bush camping possible.*
Moreton Island *Bush camping possible, no picnic area.*
Mt Barney *Bush camping possible, no picnic area.*
Mt Mistake *No facilities.*
Natural Arch *No campsite.*
Sundown *Bush camping possible, no picnic area.*
Tamborine group (see previous page).

The Outback
Barcoo *No facilities.*
Bladensburgh *No facilities.*
Diamantina Gate *No facilities.*
Epping Forest *No facilities.*

Idalia *No facilities.*
Mariala *No facilities.*
Simpson Desert *Bush camping possible.*

Cape York and Gulf Country
See the chapter on North and West of Cairns, pp. 249–255.

Archer Bend *No facilities.*
Bellenden Ker *Bush camping possible. No campsites or picnic areas.*
Bulleringa *No facilities.*
Camooweal Caves *No walking trails.*
Cape Tribulation *No walking trails.*
Cedar Bay *Bush camping possible. No campsites or picnic areas.*
Dagmar Range *No facilities.*
Daintree *No campsite.*
Edmund Kennedy
Endeavour River *No facilities.*
Herbert River Falls *Walking trails but no other facilities.*
Jardine River *No picnic area or walking trail.*
Lakefield *No picnic area but bush camping possible.*
Lawn Hill *Accessible from Burketown or Normanton. See p. 255.*
Mitchell and Alice Rivers *No facilities.*
Rokeby *No facilities but bush camping possible.*
Staaten River *No facilities.*
Starcke *No facilities.*
Undara

261

Central and Southwest Queensland
Carnarvon *Bush camping possible. Accessible from Gladstone; see p. 224.*
Currawinya *No facilities but bush camping possible.*
Chesterton Range *No facilities.*
Great Basalt Wall *No picnic area or walking trail.*
Porcupine Gorge
Thrushton *No facilities.*
White Mountains *No facilities.*

THE NORTHERN TERRITORY

The Northern Territory – most locals call it the Territory – is perhaps the Australia of visitor's dreams. It is harsh, magnificent and extends for ever. About a quarter of the Territory is not fit for man nor beast – sand dune and claypan desert, where survival is the issue. Yet it is irresistible. Visitors come for a quick look – and stay a lifetime.

GEOGRAPHY

The Territory extends for 1,346,200 sq km (519,771 sq miles) and represents about a sixth of the Australian continent although it has less than 1% of the Australian population – around 168,000 people. It is 1610 km from north to south and 934 km from east to west, with most

of it within the Tropic of Capricorn. It is bigger than most of Europe and several of the properties, the farms, are bigger than European countries.

The Northern Territory is divided into two broad climatic regions, the **Top End**, which is subject to the north-west monsoons – the Wet – and the **Red Centre**. These are very broad groupings and within them there is a multiplicity of variables – climate, soils, drainage – which have resulted in a mind-boggling range of flora and fauna. There is, of course, no such thing as a final count but in the Northern Territory there are more than 2800 species of plants, in excess of 350 types of birds, 100 native mammals, including 40 marsupials, and more than 50 species of fish. There are more than 100 different species of butterfly. The Top End has **Darwin** and **Kakadu** – one of the world's greatest National Parks – and other delights.

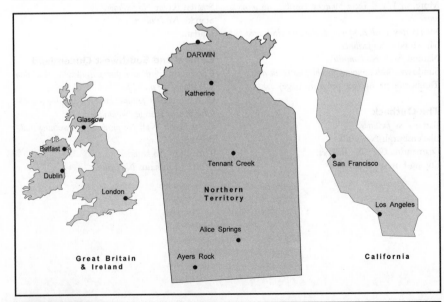

The Red Centre has **Ayers Rock**, or Uluru, the **Olgas** and **Alice Springs** – 'Alice' to everyone who lives in Australia. **Tennant Creek**, on the Stuart Highway between Darwin and Alice can be seen as the separation point between the Top End and the Red Centre, for it is here you break away from the light woodland coverage and start to pass through vast pastoral properties on your way to Alice Springs.

DRIVING IN THE TERRITORY

Although the Northern Territory can be one of the most rugged places on earth it has a good road system. The three main highways are the **Stuart** which runs from Adelaide to Darwin, the **Barkly** from Townsville through Mt Isa, and from Perth the **Victoria** which you join at **Kununurra**. These are sealed roads although, once again, it should be remembered that the distances involved can be immense. While four-wheel-drive has its definite attractions, 85 % of the Territory's normal tourist attractions are serviced by all-weather roads and it is possible to see almost everything you want to see using a normal two-wheel-drive vehicle. Where four-wheel-drive vehicles are essential you can take a local tour and let someone else worry about the driving.

You will find that the gaps between fuel and food stops on these roads are never more that 200-plus km, with 300 km being the outside limit. Nevertheless, a good rule is to fill up whenever you can so that if you should have a wander off the beaten track you won't run out of fuel.

The biggest danger in the view of many drivers in the Territory is the dreaded **road train**. This consists of a prime mover with three trailers hooked on behind. They often reach 50 m in length and have so much mass and momentum that they cannot brake easily or swerve out of danger. If you are overtaking a roadtrain you need one whole kilometre clear for the manoeuvre. Do not even think of trying to overtake on a curve or when you do not have a totally clear view ahead.

In the Wet you may find some problems with floods and you should never try to blast through unless you are fairly certain of your depth and the state of the road. Having said that it is a courtesy and a custom of the Territory to help a motorist in distress and if you get stuck someone will always tow you out.

ABORIGINAL LANDS

The Territory, which took control of its own destiny in 1978 is managed from Darwin – capital of the Territory and the Top End. Nearly a quarter of the residents of the Territory are Aboriginal – a far, far higher percentage than anywhere else in Australia. About a third of the Territory is Aboriginal land – under the direct or nominal control of the Aboriginal community – following a series of fiercely fought court battles. Until the early 1970s the generally held view of the government was that Australia was effectively empty when the European settlers arrived and therefore the Aborigines had no claim whatsoever. This *terra nulla* belief was overturned starting with the Land Rights Act of 1976 and since then much of the traditional land has been returned to its original owners. The transition has taken place much more smoothly than anyone forecast.

If you will be travelling through Aboriginal Land you must have a permit. All organised tours obtain these permits for you; otherwise you must apply in writing to the relevant Land Council.

In the Top End – **Arnhem Land**, **Borroloola** or **Nhulunbuy** the relevant authority is: **Northern Land Council**, *9 Rowling St, P O Box 42921, Casuarina NT 0811; tel: (08) 8920 5100; fax: 8945 2633.*

For the **Melville** or **Bathurst Islands**: **Tiwi Land Council**, *Nguiu, Bathurst Island, Via Darwin NT 0822. Tel: (08) 8947 1838; fax: 8947 1840._*

For Central Australia: **Central Land Council**, *33 Stuart Hwy, P O Box 3321, Alice Springs NT 0871; tel: (08) 8951 6211; fax: 8953 4343.*

The councils have the absolute right to refuse admission. Within the Territory there are a number of places or objects that hold special significance for Aboriginal people. Some are open to the public. Treat these sites as reverently as you would your own country's most sacred monuments..

DARWIN

For Australia and Australians this city – a flattering description for a place with a population of less than 70,000 – is, indeed, the last frontier. This is the way that Australians like to think of Australia. It is a rough, tough, knockabout sort of place. Think of it as the Paul Hogan of Australian cities and you will not be far wrong.

TOURIST INFORMATION

Darwin Regional Tourist Association, *31 Smith St Mall; tel: (08) 8981 9733.*

ARRIVING AND DEPARTING

It could be argued that the only way to get to Darwin is by air or by cruise liner. For almost every visitor the answer is to fly from any Australian state capital or Cairns and land at Darwin. There are also direct international flights to Darwin from **Singapore, Bali, Brunei** and **Tokyo**. For many Territorians, as people of the Territory tend to call themselves, it is quicker and easier to fly overseas than internally within Australia. All flights arrive at **Darwin Airport**, 12 km north-east of the city centre. There is a shuttle bus which meets all international flights and all of the important domestic flights, which costs $6 and goes to the central Transit Centre, *69 Mitchell St.* Taxis are plentiful and cost something just under $15.

Almost all the national coachlines offer tours to and from and within the Territory in air-conditioned coaches. But it should always be remembered that distances covered are quite extensive – the bus journey from Cairns takes very nearly two days of hard travel.

GETTING AROUND

One way of seeing Darwin to get it into perspective is to use the splendidly named **Tour Tub**, an open sided but sun-shaded bus which travels around ten destinations all day *(tel: 8985 4779).* Main bus stop is in *Knuckey St*, opposite Woolworths at the end of the Mall.

Public Transport

The city – no larger than an English town – is easy to stroll around although it can get quite hot unless you are in the shade. There is an excellent and inexpensive bus service with a maximum fare of $1.70. The Bus Terminus *(tel: 8999 6540)* is on *Harry Chan Ave*, at the bottom of *Cavenagh St.* Buses go as far as Humpty Doo, which is about 50 km from town on the road to Kakadu.

Car rental in the area is very inexpensive if you avoid the main companies out at the airport. In the centre of town, on the corner of *Smith and McLachlan Sts*, there are several agencies which rent cars for as little as $25 a day.

Taxis can be hailed or booked; *tel: 8981 8777.*

STAYING IN DARWIN

Accommodation

Accommodation in Darwin is almost always fairly full and prices tend to be 20–30% above those for the equivalent accommodation in the Eastern states. More accommodation is being built but it is essential that you book and confirm accommodation before travel.

Beaufort Darwin Hotel, *The Esplanade; tel: 8982 9911.* **Diamond Beach Hotel Casino**, *Gilruth Ave, Mindil Beach; tel: 8946 2666.* **Darwin Travelodge** *(SPH), 122 The Esplanade; tel: 8981 5388.* **Novotel Atrium Darwin (Accor)**, *corner Peel St and The Esplanade; tel: 8941 0755.* **Frontier Darwin Hotel**, *3 Buffalo Court; tel: 8981 5333.* **Hotel Darwin**, *corner Herbert St and The Esplanade; tel: 8981 9211.* **Poinciana Inn Motel** *(FL), Mitchell St; tel: 8981 8111.* **Mirambeena Tourist Resort**, *64 Cavenagh St; tel: 8946 0111.* **Top End Hotel** *(BW), corner Mitchell and Daly Sts; tel: 8981 6511.* **Plaza Darwin –**

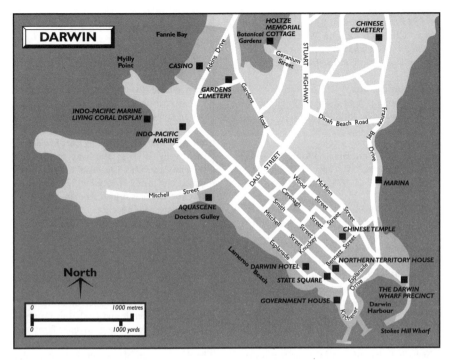

A Rydges Hotel, *32 Mitchell St; tel: 8982 0000.* **Cherry Blossom Hotel**, *108 Esplanade; tel: 8981 6734.* **Asti Motel** *(BU), corner Smith and Packard Pl.; tel: 8981 8200.* **Air Raid City Lodge**, *35 Cavenagh St; tel: 8981 9214.* **Darwin Motor Inn**, *97 Mitchell St; tel: 8981 1122.* **Don Hotel**, *12 Cavenagh St; tel: 8981 5311.* **Metro Inn Motel** *(FL), 38 Gardens Rd; tel: 8981 1544.* **Palms Motel**, *100 McMinn St; tel: 8981 4188.* **Tiwi Lodge Motel**, *53 Cavenagh St; tel: 8981 6471.* **HI: Darwin YHA**, *69 Mitchell St; tel: 8981 3995.*

Eating and Drinking

Almost all restaurants in Darwin are closed on a Sunday, when the town seems to take a deep breath before the week to come.

Swiss Restaurant, *60 Smith St, Harry Chan Arcade; tel 8981 5079.* Open lunch Mon–Fri, dinner Tues–Sat. BYO. Authentic Swiss cuisine. No credit cards. **Texas Junction**, *64 Smith St, tel: 8941 0990.* Open for dinner Wed–Sat 1930 until late. Dining and dancing and occasional cabaret.

Hanuman, *28 Mitchell St; tel: 8941 3500.* Open lunch Mon–Fri, dinner every night. An Indonesian name but serving Thai and Nonya – a Singapore mixture of Malay and Chinese food. **Peppis**, *84 Mitchell St; tel: 8981 3732.* Open lunch Mon–Fri. Dinner every night. Licensed, international cuisine. **Vorassi Tavern**, *Frontier Arcade, 21 Cavenagh St; tel: 8981 7033.* Open lunch Mon–Fri, dinner Mon–Sat. Italian cuisine. Licensed. **Thai Garden**, *109 Smith St; tel: 8981 8168.* Open for dinner Tues–Sun. Family Thai restaurant. BYO. **Charlie's Restaurant**, *29 Knuckey St; tel: 8981 3298.* Open lunch and dinner, 7 days a week. Licensed. Italian food. **Café Capri**, *37 Knuckey St; tel: 8981 0010.* Open seven nights, licensed. Italian cuisine.

Mama Luisa, *2 Pavonia Pl.; tel: 8985 3903.* Dry season lunch daily. Dinner Mon–Sat. Italian and Spanish cuisine. Licensed. **La Chaumiere**, *13 Shepherd St; tel: 8981 2879.* Open lunch Mon–Fri, dinner Mon–Sat. French cuisine. Licensed. **Boardroom Restaurant**, *MGM Grand Darwin, Gilruth Ave;*

tel: 8943 8888. Licensed. Part of the gambling casino. **Christo's On the Wharf**, *Stokes Hill Wharf; tel: 8981 8658.* Open lunch Tues–Fri. Dinner Tues–Sun. Local seafood specialities.

Communications

The post office is at *48 Cavenagh St*, on the corner of *Edmunds St; tel: 8980 8227.*

Money

There is a **Thomas Cook Foreign Exchange** branch at *Shop 1A Star Village, Smith Street Mall; tel: 8981 4088.*

EVENTS

In the dry season there is a wide range of festivals. In the middle of June is the **Bougainvillea Festival**, which has bands, plays and parades. Then at the end of July they hold the **Beer Can Regatta** in Fannie Bay, when boats made from beer cans race against each other. Most of the spectators are putting the same brand of cans to their original intended use. Only a week or so later comes the barefoot **Mud Crab Tying Competition**, which can be hazardous for the competitors and hilarious for the spectators.

SIGHTSEEING

Shaded by dense, green tropical vegetation, Darwin is Australia's most northern state capital. This city at the Top End of the Northern Territory has long welcomed visitors to its shores. Macassans from **Indonesia** traded with coastal Aborigines for hundreds of years. The first European to have an impact on what was to become Darwin was Lt Stokes of the HMS *Beagle*, who named the coastal inlet after **Charles Darwin**. The coast inlet which provides the harbour is about twice as large as that of Sydney. Geographically it is mid-way along the complex and convoluted northern coast of Australia. In 1824 there was an expedition in 1824 to establish a convict settlement which failed. In 1867 a new site was chosen and officially called Palmerston although that, too, did not long last. In the 1870s, the discovery of gold drew substantial numbers of Chinese settlers, who at one time made up the majority of local residents.

Amy Johnson

Amy Johnson was, for a long time, Australia's sweetheart. Although she was not Australian – she was born in Sheffield – the fact that she was the first woman to fly solo to Australia made her an immediate honorary Australian.

She flew solo to Australia in 1930, and although she missed beating Bert Hinkler's record by 3 days, she was feted and became Australia's 'Queen of the Air.' She gained her pilot's licence in 1928, and she was also the first British woman granted a ground engineer's licence.

Her objective was to fly solo to Australia and to beat the record of 16 days (see p. 223). She was sponsored by Lord Wakefield of the oil company who, with Amy's father, put up the £600 to buy a used DH Gypsy Moth – G-AAAH.

On 5 May 1930, she set off in the single-engined aircraft and landed in Darwin on 24 May, completing an epic flight of 11,000 miles. She was the first woman to fly alone to Australia but she did not break Hinkler's record.

She never stopped flying. The following year she set a record for her flight across Siberia to Tokyo, and in 1932 she broke the record for a solo flight to Cape Town. She joined the Air Transport Auxiliary which delivered aircraft to the RAF in 1939. Two years later she disappeared somewhere over the Thames estuary.

In 1911 Darwin passed to Commonwealth control – until that time it had been seen as part of South Australia. In 1919, Ross and Smith landed at Darwin on their historic flight from England to be followed in 1930 by Amy Johnson, the first woman to fly from Europe to Australia.

During World War II Darwin was seen as the first line of defence against Japanese invasion. Women and children were evacuated and the Japanese air force bombed Darwin 63 times, killing nearly a thousand people in total.

On Christmas Day 1974, **Cyclone Tracy**

brought Darwin to its knees. The majority of the buildings were destroyed and 66 people were recorded dead or missing. The population dropped to 12,000 but has since risen again and now stands at around 80,000.

Darwin is built from the end of a truncated peninsula, from which it extends north for about 8 km. The tallest building in Darwin at the moment – this will very soon be challenged – is the **Northern Territory House** on the corner of *Mitchell and Bennett Sts*. From the front of the building you look towards **State Square**, containing the **Northern Territory Parliament House** and the **Supreme Court**.

Less than 50m from Northern Territory House along *Bennett St* is the **Smith Street Mall**, which is the heart of what you might care to think of as the central business district. Thirty metres in the other direction is the **Darwin Hotel** – one of the few buildings to survive the cyclone – and then the parkland of the **Esplanade** on the edge of the harbour.

The **Darwin Wharf Precinct** at *Stokes Hill Wharf, tel: 8981 4268,* is a new development of restaurants, shops and bars with some tourist attractions – there is even a bungy jumping tower at times in the season – and is a good starting point for seeing some of the other sights of the city.

The focal point of the city centre is the *Smith St Mall,* which is shady, vehicle free, has a wealth of sidewalk cafés and eating centres and is a pleasant place on a summer's day. The city has more than 300 speciality shops altogether, all with a fairly relaxed Territorian approach to life. The Mall also includes the **Hotel Victoria** – the Vic – which was once a frontier bar in the true sense of the word but has now been gentrified, although the punkah fans are still there.

One tour using the **Tour Tub** (see p.264) is to the **Oil Storage Tunnels**, which were constructed in World War II. These existed because Darwin was the only Australian city to be bombed during the war. (Sydney was shelled by Japanese submarines but that was more of a gesture than a serious attack.)

There are several different ways of touring this facility. You can walk there after visiting Government House or you can take The Tour Tub from the *Smith St Mall,* which will drop you off at the tunnels and then pick you up an hour later, letting you have a quick tour of Darwin at the same time.

The tour of the tunnels are semi-guided – you are given an introductory talk and then allowed to find your own way around. Open 1000–1400, Tues–Sat; *tel: 8989 5982*. $4.

Museum of Arts and Sciences, *Conacher St, Fannie Bay; tel: 8989 8211*. Open Mon–Fri 0900–1700, Sat–Sun 1200–1700. This brilliant collection of Aboriginal art is well laid out with lots of helpful information. It is perhaps the best of its kind in Australia. The art from the off-shore islands is nothing less than superb. If you are thinking of buying any of this marvellous art form have a look around here first and you will soon be able to tell the difference between the great, the average and the meretricious. There is also an exhibition showing the effects of Cyclone Tracy. Well presented, air-conditioned, helpful staff.

Indo-Pacific Marine, *Stokes Hill Wharf; tel: 089 81 1294,* is an exhibition of living coral reefs from the Darwin area. Twice winner of the National Tourism Award. One of the better displays of its kind, it is packed with information about the wonders of the living coral reef and how it grows and propagates. Open daily 0900–1600 also Mon, Wed, Fri, Sun 1900–2130.

Australian Pearling Exhibition, *Stokes Hill Wharf, Darwin; tel: 8941 2177*. Open daily 1000–1700, Sat–Sun 1000–1800. Small but totally fascinating museum with mementos and displays telling the fearful history of pearl diving on whose fortunes Darwin was built. Features audio and visual presentations, part of a pearling lugger and a live display of the pearling ecosystem.

One excellent way of seeing the harbour is to take a harbour cruise. **The Spirit of Darwin** departs twice daily, 1345 and 1745 Apr–Sep, and 1745 Mon–Sat Oct–Mar from the Cullen Bay Resort Marina for a 2 hr cruise of the harbour *(tel: 8981 3711)*.

The **Aviation Heritage Centre**, *557 Stuart Hwy, Winnelie; tel: 8947 2145,* tells the history of aviation in the territory with special focus on the bombing of Darwin by the

267

Japanese. Its major exhibit is a massive B52 bomber on permanent loan from the USA. There is also the wreckage of a Zero fighter shot down in the first air raid on Darwin in 1942. Open daily 0830–1700.

Every day at high tide hundreds of fish come in to be fed at **Aquascene** at *Doctors Gully,* which is at the end of the Esplanade. Among the fish are milkfish, mullet, catfish and batfish Feeding times, of course, depend on the tide; *tel: 8981 7837.* Admission $4.

East Point Military Museum, *tel: 8981 9702,* 7 mins from the city centre at the **East Point Reserve,** has an extensive photographic display as well as a collection of firearms, artillery and armoured vehicles. It also has a 15 min movie with footage of the 1942 bombing of Darwin. The reserve itself has sweeping views of the harbour and is very popular at sunset when the colours are spectacular and wallabies come out of the rain forest to feed. Open daily 1000–1700 Oct–Apr, 0900–1700 May–Oct.

There are more than 700 hectares of parks in this green city, the main one being the **Botanic Gardens,** about 4 km from the centre at *Gardens Rd, off Gilruth Ave; tel: 8989 5535.* They always appear, blessedly, to be several degrees cooler than the city. The site is more than a century old and has the largest range of tropical palms – about 400 species – in the Southern hemisphere, with some of them being more than a century old. Open 0700–1900 daily.

Fannie Bay Gaol Museum, *East Point Rd, Fannie Bay; tel: 8989 8290.* Open daily 1000–1700. Darwin was always a tough town and the gaol reflects this. The gallows, last used in 1952, are still there. You can buy souvenirs made by prisoners in other prisons in the territory in the shop **Rogues Gallery,** which is open weekdays.

Crocodylus Park, *McMillan's Rd, Berrimah; tel: 8947 2510,* is 5 mins from the airport with a museum and a lot of live crocodiles. There are external viewing platforms and holding pens for large crocodiles, which are being managed for longer term research by world crocodile expert Dr Graham Webb. Open daily 0900–1700. Feeding and tour 1100 and 1400.

SIDE TRACKS FROM DARWIN

THE BATHURST AND MELVILLE ISLANDS

These islands are only 80 km north of Darwin but they are, indeed, another world. Together Bathurst and Melville Islands cover approximately 8000 sq km. Melville is the largest island off the Australian coast after Tasmania.

The islands are the home of the Tiwi people, who have lived for thousands of years with minimal contact with mainland Aboriginal people. Thus their culture and very specifically, their art, is unique.

Although the islands are only a short flight from Darwin the only way that you can get there is by an organised tour, which, typically, allows you half a day on the island, although longer tours can be arranged.

The first serious European contact was in 1911 when the Catholic Church established a mission on Bathurst Island. **Nguiu** is the main township with a population of about 1200 people. **Milikapiti** and **Pularumpi** are the two principal towns on Melville Island, both of which have a population of about 300.

Fort Dundas was the first European settlement in north Australia and was established in 1824, near where Pularumpi stands today. The settlement only lasted for a few months and was then abandoned. In 1942 World War II brought Bathurst Island two small claims to fame. It was the first Australian soil to be strafed by enemy aircraft. And a Tiwi, Matthias Ulungura, captured the first Japanese prisoner of war, a pilot who crashed on Melville Island.

Visiting the islands as a member of an organised group you will undoubtedly be taken to **Bima Wear,** which is a local workshop producing fashions that incorporate Tiwi artistic styles.

Also on the agenda will be a visit to the **Patakijiyali Museum,** which has display galleries depicting Tiwi culture and heritage. At the **Tiwi Pima Art Centre** you will see Pukamani burial poles, animals and human figures. This is a unique art, which despite having some similarities to other schools of art in Australia, is very much an art form in its own right.

GOVE PENINSULA AND NHULUNBUY

Nhulunbuy is 650 km east of Darwin, on the edge of the Gove Peninsula and surrounded by the Arafura Sea. It is considered by many to provide the best fishing in the Top End. Nhulunbuy now has a population approaching 4000 and is a major base for fishing expeditions into the Arafura Sea to catch reef or game fish. The easiest way to get there is to fly in on a 45 min flight by domestic airline, although four-wheel-drive access is possible during the dry winter provided permits have been acquired to pass through Arnhem Land via the Central Arnhem Hwy. ⬛

MANDORAH

A good day trip – a long day trip – from Darwin ends up a little beyond the Territory Wild Life Park on the *Cox Peninsula Rd,* which eventually winds its way down to Mandorah. This small seaside town is opposite **Port Darwin** at the end of one of the encircling arms that protect the large and sheltered harbour. Mandorah is 140 km from Darwin by road but there is a six times daily ferry run by **Darwin Harbour Ferries**, *tel: 8978 5094.* $15 return. To go to Mandorah itself the ferry trip is much the preferred method. On the other hand, the road towards Mandorah, which almost circles back on itself, passes many delightful attractions.

To go by road you leave Darwin on the Stuart Hwy, which is sign-posted clearly from the centre of the city, and turn off at **Howard Springs**, which is just over 25 km south-east of Darwin and effectively a suburb. The **Howard Springs National Park** is an oasis of rain forest and parklands with a spring-fed swimming pool with fish and turtles. The fauna includes goannas, birds and wallabies. Open daily 0800–2000.

Some 5 km further along the Stuart Hwy, 40 km from Darwin, after the turn off from Arnhem Hwy but before you get to the very small town of **Noonamah**, you can find a less friendly form of fauna at the **Darwin Crocodile Farm**, *Stuart Hwy; tel: 8988 1450,* which demonstrates crocodile breeding. There are typically 7000 of them in captivity at any one time. Open 7 days a week, feeding at 1400. The café offers crocodile burgers for the discriminating.

Then, almost immediately after Noonamah, and 12 km after the junction with the Arnhem Hwy, you turn right on to *Cox Peninsula Rd,* which takes you first to **Berry Springs Nature Park**, which has a pleasant spring-fed pool where you can swim surrounded by wet monsoon forest. Next to it is the **Lakes Tourist Resort,** *off Cox Peninsula Road, Berry Springs; tel: 8988 6277,* where you can swim, fish or canoe on **Lake Deane**. Within striking distance is **Majestic Orchids** but it is not very easy to find. It is not signposted, so phone *(tel: 8988 6088)* to book and get directions. This is the largest tropical orchid cut flower farm in Australia with 2 hectares of shade-house and some 320,000 orchids. You can also go horseback riding on trails around the farm. Bookings are essential.

Next door is the **Territory Wild Life Park**, which has been voted the best tourist attraction in the Northern Territory. There are few who would argue. (Open 0830–1800 daily; *tel: 8988 6000).* Free shuttle trains take you around 6 km of track running through 400 hectares of natural bush and you can see everything from buffalo to a 3½m long saltwater crocodile. There are also demonstrations of flying birds of prey with eagles and falcons swooping out and back to their handlers, who all seem to be female.

You can continue along the *Cox Peninsula Rd,* which climbs to **Observation Hill**. At this point you run out of sealed road but, except in the Wet, the ungraded road wends its way through the **Delissa Wagait Larrakia Land Trust** down to Mandorah. ⬛

DARWIN–KAKADU

The drive from Darwin to Kakadu National Park can be an adventure in its own right. Along the way you will pass many attractive places to stop and visit. In theory it is possible to visit Kakadu on a day trip from Darwin but that is rather like doing Rome on a Tuesday. Kakadu and its surroundings deserve more time. For many visitors, Kakadu is the prime reason for venturing into the Top End of Australia, and few are disappointed.

During the Wet about 1300 mm of rain cascades on to Kakadu. It is a marvellous time because the rain comes in shattering storms with sunny periods between.

The dry seasons, known as *Wurrgeng* and *Gurrung* to the Aborigines, are when most visitors arrive (May–Sept). It can get very hot in Kakadu – about 35°C would be the maximum – and, of course, very humid. But there is always plenty of shade in the National Park.

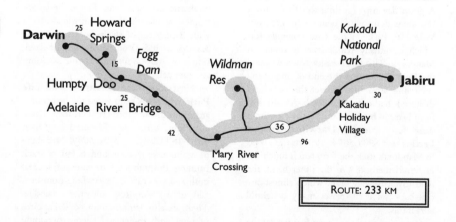

ROUTE: 233 KM

ROUTE

You head out of Darwin on the Stuart Hwy, Rte 1, and 10 km after **Howard Springs** you turn to the left and head east along Rte 36, the Arnhem Hwy. The Highway passes **Humpty Doo**, **Adelaide River Bridge**, **Mary River Crossing** and enters the **Kakadu National Park** about 40 km after the **Bark Hut Inn**.

Continue for nearly 140 km to the Park Headquarters near **Jabiru**.

BUSES

One daily Greyhound Pioneer bus runs from Darwin in the early morning to Cooinda in the National Park, taking about 5½ hrs. OTT table 9084.

DARWIN TO KAKADU

The Arnhem Hwy from Darwin to Kakadu is virtually a causeway running through, almost atop, the **Mary River wetlands**. These wetlands are alive with wildlife and driving through you will see more species of birds than you will anywhere else in Australia outside a zoo.

In the Wet this road can be flooded – sometimes for many kilometres at a time. But it is sealed all the way to Kakadu and is hardly ever impassable. Even when it is flooded, if you motor at a steady speed you are unlikely to get into trouble.

Most tourists stay away from the Top End during the Wet, which many Territorians consider to be an error of judgement. In the Wet the countryside is green and alive and the rain, when it comes, is more a sudden torrential tropical downpour than a sullen drizzle, and soon clears away.

One of the problems with the Wet – Nov–Mar – is that some, but never all, of the attractions of Kakadu may be closed, but this seems to many to be a small trade-off for the extra wildlife that can be seen at that time.

About 11 km after you have turned on to the Arnhem Hwy you will come to **Humpty Doo**, scene of one of the greatest agricultural investment disasters seen in Australia. Humpty Doo was to be the centre of one of the world's largest rice-growing areas and many millions of dollars were invested before the whole scheme was aborted.

At Humpty Doo you will find **Grahame Gow's Reptile World**, *tel: 8988 1661,* which has on display a wide range of venomous reptiles. Open daily 0830–1730.

Next comes **Fogg Dam**, which is just off the Arnhem Hwy some 60 km out from Darwin. This was established in the 1950s as a water source for one of the doomed rice-growing projects and the 2.3 sq km of wetlands around the dam is now home to spectacular numbers of water birds – pied geese, brolgas, ducks, herons, egrets, ibis, corellas, cockatoos and many, many more.

Best time to view the birds is at dawn and dusk but at any time it is spectacular. You can view them from purpose-built vantage points complete with informative signs along the low dam wall.

There is also a signposted 3.6 km walk through the pockets of monsoon rain forest, for which you will need your insect repellent.

At the **Adelaide River Bridge**, 64 km from Darwin along the Arnhem Hwy, you will come across a wonderful sight. When you explain it later you will not be believed unless you have photographs to support your claim – and not even then. Cruises on the **Adelaide River Queen** ($30 and up for a 90 min cruise) leave here along the Adelaide River in search of – honestly – leaping crocodiles.

There are normally half a dozen cruises a day but check for times as these vary with the state of the river; *tel: 8988 8144.* The crew members put out meat bait and the crocodiles leap vertically out of the water as high as 2m to take it. And sometimes sea eagles swoop in to try and snatch it from their jaws.

Next is the **Leaning Tree Lagoon**, which is 90 km from Darwin and a picnic spot as well as a site for bird-watching. You come off the bitumen and in the Wet it is possible for a normal two-wheel drive vehicle to get bogged down, so take care.

Off the Arnhem Hwy and 170 km from Darwin are the **Wildman** and **Shady Camp Reserves**, which incorporate a large part of the Mary River flood plain.

Boat cruises on the Mary River can be booked from the **Point Stuart Wilderness Lodge** *(tel: 8978 8912)* and cost about $25. You will definitely need industrial-strength insect repellent in this area to drive off the mosquitoes.

Also within the reserves is the **Rockhole Billabong and Shady Camp**, renowned for being the definitive spot to catch the Top End's barramundi. Information can be obtained at the **Ranger Information Station** at the corner of Point Stuart and the *Rockhole Rds; tel: 8978 8986.*

A further 120 km along the main route you arrive at **Kakadu National Park**.

KAKADU NATIONAL PARK

Tourist Information: Kakadu National

271

Park Bowali Visitor Centre, *Kakadu Hwy, Kakadu National Park; tel: (08) 8979 9101*, open 0800–1700. This is full of all the information you could possibly need, as well as being the best place from which to begin exploration.

Make sure you get a copy of the *Visitor Guide to Kakadu National Park*, which neatly spells out all the options. Also get a copy of the schedule of ranger-guided walks and talks.

Time spent in the Park with a tour guide or ranger means that while exploring art sites you learn about Aboriginal Dreamtime and culture. When you are taken on a bushwalk your enjoyment is enhanced by the expert commentary and observations of the guides.

There is a fee of $15 a person to enter the park. Most attractions within the park are accessible by sealed, all-weather roads. The exceptions are **Jim Jim**, **Twin Falls** and **Maguk**, which are accessible only by four-wheel-drive. One way to deal with this is to use two-wheel drive conventional vehicle to get to the park and then take a guided tour to specific spots. This will give you the advantage of an informed commentary and a safe and enjoyable excursion.

There are very few marked long-distance bushwalks within the park – this is being remedied – and if you are venturing on a serious expedition you must register with the park rangers before you leave.

This is justifiably the most famous national park in Australia because within its huge area of just under 20,000 sq km it offers a wide variety of different environments. It has everything ranging from the rivers and billabongs of the wetlands to woodlands, forests, coastal mud flats and stone escarpment country.

The name Kakadu comes from the local Gagudju aborigines, who now manage the park through the Gagudju Association with the active assistance of the Australian National Parks and Wildlife Service. The Gagudju Association is funded mainly by royalties coming from the mining of uranium along the eastern border with **Arnhemland**.

Basically the park is the catchment area of the **South Alligator River**. Trying to describe just the biology of the area would take a whole book. There are over 900 species of plant life, some of them unique to the area, some 300 varieties of birds, 75 reptiles, 50 native mammals, 30 amphibians, countless thousands of insect species and a quarter of all Australian freshwater fish.

As well as all this it shows evidence of continuous occupation for over 20,000 years and has galleries of intricate rock work dating back to almost prehistoric times.

The Gagudju have a strong and ancient tradition of painting on protected rock surfaces. Two of Kakadu's formations feature extensive galleries of paintings. **Ubirr** has some of the world's oldest surviving paintings and, as an added bonus, the views from the top of the rock are stunning. **Nourlangie Rock** has paintings around its base with **Narmarrgon, the Lightning Man**, probably being the best known figure. To understand and appreciate the paintings it is almost essential to have the services of a guide or ranger.

Another way of viewing Kakadu is by water. Near the entrance to the park is the **Gagudju Cooinda Lodge** and here you can hire flat-bottomed boats to glide along **Yellow Water**, which is a land-locked billabong fringed by pandanus, bamboo, paperbark and monsoon rain forest. As you ease silently through these glassy, still waters you will see pelicans, brolgas and cormorants diving for fish – an almost endless panorama.

Near where you set off is the **Warradjan Cultural Centre**, *Cooinda Rd, Yellow Water*, which is built in the shape of a warradjan (pig-nosed turtle), and has a display where the Aboriginal people of Kakadu tell visitors about their culture.

In the Wet, the torrential rain which comes between Dec–Mar can make access to some – but never all – of the sites difficult. The most favoured times are Jun–Aug, when there is still plenty of water although the weather is typically dry.

As the Dry comes to an end the waters contract until November, when the season starts again with the Build-up – oppressive weather and electrical storms, which are dissipated with the torrential downpours of the Wet.

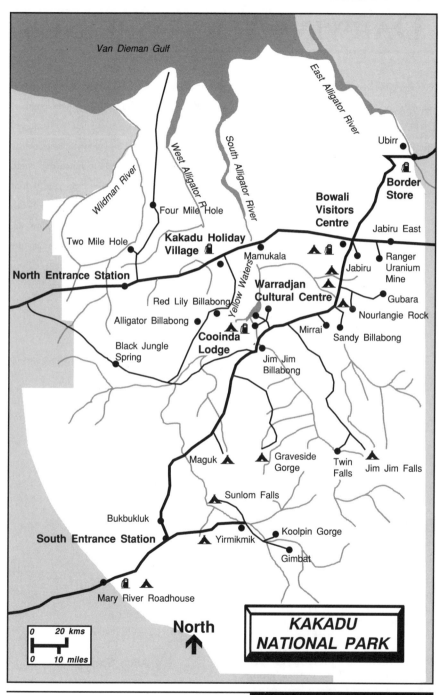

Van Dieman Gulf

East Alligator River

West Alligator River

South Alligator River

Wildman River

Ubirr

Border Store

Four Mile Hole

Bowali Visitors Centre

Jabiru East

Two Mile Hole

Kakadu Holiday Village

Mamukala

Jabiru

Ranger Uranium Mine

North Entrance Station

Yellow Waters

Warradjan Cultural Centre

Red Lily Billabong

Gubara

Alligator Billabong

Nourlangie Rock

Cooinda Lodge

Mirrai

Sandy Billabong

Black Jungle Spring

Jim Jim Billabong

273

Maguk

Graveside Gorge

Twin Falls

Jim Jim Falls

Sunlom Falls

Bukbukluk

Koolpin Gorge

South Entrance Station

Yirmikmik

Gimbat

Mary River Roadhouse

North

0 20 kms
0 10 miles

KAKADU NATIONAL PARK

DARWIN–ALICE SPRINGS

The route between Darwin and Alice Springs requires no navigation skills. You leave Darwin on the Stuart Hwy and follow it all the way through to Alice. This is a well maintained sealed highway with petrol and food stops along the way. The sheer length of the journey can be tiring but with an air-conditioned vehicle and plenty of stops on the way, it can take you pretty much the length of the Northern Territory from the Timor Sea down to within 300 km of the South Australian border. If you were to follow the road on from there you would eventually get to Adelaide, and you would have driven across Australia from north to south.

274

ROUTE: 1484 KM

ROUTE

Head south from Darwin on Rte 1, the Stuart Hwy. The first stop of any note is **Pine Creek**, which is 230 km from Darwin. The Stuart Hwy carries on from Pine Creek another 90 km to **Katherine**. From Katherine the road runs south through **Mataranka, Daly Waters, Newcastle Waters** and **Renner Springs** towards **Tennant Creek**, 627 km from Katherine. Another 249 km brings you to **Barrow Creek**, from where you continue for 283 km through **Ti-Tree** to **Alice Springs**.

BUSES

Greyhound Pioneer and McCafferty's buses run the length of this route daily. Katherine is 5 hrs from Darwin; Daly Waters is 9 hrs, Tennant Creek 14¼ hrs and Alice Springs 19¾ hrs. OTT table 9125.

DARWIN TO KATHERINE

There are still a few sites of interest in **Pine Creek**, including the **Miners Park**, which has on display the original crude mining machinery. Pine Creek was the site in 1871 of the first gold rush in the Northern Territory. The gold was found when they were digging holes for the poles to hold the Overland Telegraph – a double benefit. The decision was made to import indentured Chinese labourers – practically slave labour – and eventually this led to a racial backlash, when the Chinese outnumbered the European Australians in the area by five to one. In 1888 the Chinese were banned from the Northern Territory.

About halfway between Pine Creek and Katherine, turn left and travel about 20 km east of the Highway to visit the impressive **Edith Falls**, within the **Nitmiluk National Park** (see next page). The Falls are formed on the edge of the Arnhem Land escarpment and throughout the year plunge into a large pool fringed with pandanus, in bush surroundings.

KATHERINE

Tourist Information: Katherine Region Tourist Association, *corner Stuart Hwy and Lindsay St; tel (08) 8972 1886* or **Katherine Gorge National Park**, *Katherine 5780; tel: (08) 8972 1799*.

ACCOMMODATION AND FOOD

Frontier Katherine Motel, *Stuart Hwy; tel: 8972 1744*. **Pine Tree Motel**, *3 Third St; tel: 8972 2533*. **Knotts Crossing Resort**, *corner Giles and Cameron Sts; tel: 8972 2511*. **Katherine Hotel/Motel**, *Katherine Terrace; tel: 8972 1622*. **Paraway Motel**, *corner O'Shea Terrace and First St; tel: 8972 2644*. **Crossways Hotel**, *corner Katherine Terrace and Warburton St; tel: 8972 1022*. **Kuringgai Motel**, *Giles St; tel: 8971 0266*. **Palm Court Motel**, *corner Third and Giles Sts; tel: 8972 2722*. **Riverview**

Motel & Caravan Park, *440 Victoria Hwy; tel: 8972 1011*. **Springvale Homestead Tourist Park**, *Shadforth Rd; tel: 8972 1355*. **HI: Palm Court**, *corner Third and Giles Sts; tel: 8972 2722*.

Buchanan's, *corner O'Shea and First Sts; tel 8972 2644*. Part of **Paraway Motel**. Licensed. Possibly the best restaurant in town. **Matilda's**, *Stuart Hwy, 3 km south of town; tel: 8972 1744*. Part of the **Frontier Motor Inn**. Licensed. The other best restaurant in town. Note that the bars of Katherine are typical of the Territory and are not recommended for those who are timid in spirit.

Although Katherine could hardly be called a shopping mecca it does have two shopping complexes with large supermarkets open daily.

SIGHTSEEING

Katherine is within easy striking distance of Darwin – 330 km down the Stuart Hwy which runs through the town where, for a short while, it is renamed *Katherine Terrace*. It is both a fully formed township with a decidedly urban feel and the Northern Territory outpost on the very edge of some of Australia's most spectacular wilderness regions. Katherine – the locals pronounce it so that the last syllable rhymes with 'wine' – was named in 1862 by the explorer Stuart after the daughter of one his benefactors. It regards itself as a perfect launch place for a tour of the Northern Territory.

The town has a population of 9400, partly as the result of the nearby air force base of **Tindal** – the largest in Australia and off limits to visitors. Katherine is the central town for an area about the size of Victoria. Only 30 km from the town centre is **Katherine Gorge** (see next page), one of Australia's unique attractions. And the town itself has much to offer the visitor.

An important attraction of Katherine is that it helps you slip into the Territory pace of life. Darwin is informal and laid back. Katherine takes that natural approach one step further. As an introduction to the true spirit of the Northern Territory it has no equal.

The history of the area is presented in the **Katherine Museum**, *Gorge Rd; tel: 8972 3945*; open Mon–Fri 1000–1600, Sat 1000–1400, Sun 1400–1700. The **Katherine**

Railway Museum and Gallery, *Railway Terrace,* is the old railway station, built in 1926, but now the local headquarters for the National Trust. There is a considerable display of railway memorabilia as well as information on the history of Katherine. Open Mon–Fri 1300–1500.

The **Katherine School of the Air**, *Giles St; tel: 8972 1833,* claims, almost certainly correctly, to be the largest classroom in the world. It broadcasts daily to children over a distance of 800,000 sq km. During term time you can see it in operation and how this early form of remote learning has, in some small part, conquered the tyranny of distance. Open daily 0900–1200.

Out of Town

Near to town are some delightful hot springs. Go along the Victoria Hwy for 3 km, turn off at **Riverview Caravan Park** and you come to **Katherine Hot Springs**. While no medicinal benefits are claimed, these hot springs on the banks of the Katherine River make for pleasant swimming. A short stroll away is the **Lower Level Nature Park**, itself a pleasant spot.

Springvale Homestead *(tel: 8972 1122)* is 8 km from Katherine via *Zimmin Dr.* or Victoria Hwy, then *Shadforth Rd.* It is the oldest homestead still standing in the Territory and was once run by Ted Ronan, a Territory figure who wrote *Vision Splendid* and other novels about the Outback. It offers tourist version corroboree and crocodile spotting tours. There is a swimming pool, motel and camping. Free short walking tours daily 1000 and 1430 Apr–Oct.

A little further out are the **Cutta Cutta** and **Tindal Caves**, *tel: 8972 1940,* which are 27 km south of Katherine by way of the Stuart Hwy. These are limestone rock formations that lie about 15 m below the surface. There are well marked and signposted walking tracks. Cave tours are conducted daily – hourly 0900–1500. (Open all year except in the height of the Wet when they can be inundated.) Admission $11 for both caves.

The main natural attraction near Katherine is the **Nitmiluk National Park**, which includes the Katherine Gorge and Edith Falls – both of which are essential Top End experiences.

The singular version of the name **Katherine Gorge** is a little misleading, as it is more a system of 13 gorges. Each is separated from the other by rapids, covering 10 km in all. These gorges have been carved over the centuries from sandstone in shades of deep brown-red and ochre with striations ranging at times from almost a pink to a red so dark to be almost black. As at Ayer's Rock (Uluru), the colours of the cliffs on each side of the gorges change during the day, the most intense colours being seen at dawn and dusk. Note that in the summer Dry the gorges are serene and peaceful but during the Wet the water can be whipped into waves up to 2 m high, so care needs to be taken with the timing of your visit.

Experiencing the gorge can be done in several ways. Drive by sealed road to the **Park Visitors Centre** *(tel: 8972 1886)* which is 31 km east of Katherine. There are boat tours from the jetty, which is about 1 km away, and these reach as far as the fifth gorge in a series of cruises and then there are walks past the rapids for the longer trips. These tours range in length from 2 hrs to a full day.

If you are fit and adventurous you can hire a canoe (**Kookaburra Canoe Hire**; *tel: 88 72 3604)* from $25 a day, take your time and explore all the gorges. To get an admittedly expensive overview before you even start, you can survey the gorges in either a small fixed winged aircraft or, even more spectacularly, by helicopter – **Brolga Airways**; *tel: 8971 7000.*

The Nitmiluk National Park covers 180,000 hectares and has over 100 km of marked walking trails, which range up to serious bushwalking expeditions in the area in and around the Katherine River as it winds its way through the gorge and then out into the open to become a gentle, meandering, tree-lined river. It is essential that you register with the park ranger before setting out on any of these major walks.

← → **Connection to Kununurra**

The Victoria Hwy runs some 450 km west from Katherine to Kununurra and from there to Wyndham and the Carnarvon–Wyndham route (see p. 322).

Life in the Outback

Life in the serious outback is hard, frequently uncomfortable and sometimes downright dangerous. Three institutions have worked in harmony for many years to bring some form of relief. They are the **Flying Doctor Service**, the **School of the Air** and the **Bush Radio**, which keeps everyone in touch. This used to be pedal driven and in *A Town Like Alice* there is a superb description of how it was used and how desperately important it becomes in an emergency.

The Royal Flying Doctor Service was formed by the Reverend John Flynn – Flynn of the Outback – in 1928. He had started a hospital in Oodnadatta in 1912 and found that people were dying of relatively simple problems like appendicitis, which turned into peritonitis simply because no medical help was available within easy travelling distance. Although he could not fly an aircraft and all of his long-distance communication technology was based around prayer he forged ahead. The man who made it work was Alf Traeger, who in 1928 invented the treadle radio where pedalling supplies the power.

Now the service provides total medical coverage for the people beyond the Black Stump. Each station (farm) has a radio and can call for help, knowing it will arrive within a couple of hours rather than a week or a fortnight when it would be too late. The radio also runs a chat room, rather like the Internet, every evening, when neighbours, who may be many hundreds of kilometres apart, can gossip. These are called 'galah sessions' after a particularly noisy bird.

The radio is also used for the School of the Air, which started in 1951 and means that families in the outback no longer need to be split up while the kids go off to boarding school. There are now 14 schools of the air scattered around the outback. With satellite communication it is now possible to use imaging as well as voice with video conferencing just around the corner.

To try and get an idea of the size and scope of these schools, the one in Alice has over a dozen teachers to support some 150 odd students in an area covering 1.3 million sq km and the furthest student is 1000 km from base.

277

KATHERINE TO TENNANT CREEK

As you drive this section of the route it will be brought home to you that during World War II this was the front line for Australia. You will see airfields and hangars and large storage sites. **Larrimah**, which is 180 km south of Katherine and halfway between Darwin and Tennant Creek, was a major staging post during the war and at one time more than 3000 service personnel were housed there.

Later on you come to **Daly Waters**, which you might consider Australia's first international airfield, as in the 1930s it was a refuelling stop for Qantas. It also contains the **Daly Waters pub**, which claims to be the oldest in the Territory – its liquor licence has been held continuously since 1938. The pub was opened to cater for the airline passengers arriving on the new Qantas airlines. Just off the Stuart Hwy is the old aerodrome and its 1929 hangar has a photographic and text display on the history of aviation in the region, particularly Qantas. Open daily 0800–0900, 1500–1600.

The scenery changes constantly with the landscape losing its lush greenery and starting to become more arid. Some authorities insist that **Newcastle Waters** marks the change-over point between The Top End and Central Australia, although many arguments are advanced for other places. Newcastle Waters has another claim to fame. It is on the junction of three major stock routes including the famous 220 km **Murranji** stock route, which ran west from Newcastle Waters to **Top Springs** and played a major role in Australia's droving history.

Newcastle Waters was chosen as the starting point for Australia's Bicentennial **Last Great Cattle Drive**. The **Drover's Memorial Park** features a bronze statue of **The Drover**. But at the time of writing, there were no facilities for visitors in Newcastle Waters.

After Newcastle Waters you come almost immediately to **Elliott** – population 600 – named after Captain Elliott, who was in charge of the interim camp for northbound troops during World War II. And then, still on the Stuart Hwy, it is under 600 km to the **Three Ways Roadhouse**, which is where the Barkly Hwy comes in from the east from Queensland. Three Ways also has the **Flynn Memorial**, dedicated to the achievements of Flynn of the Outback – John Flynn, founder of the **Royal Flying Doctor Service**.

TENNANT CREEK

Tourist Information: Visitor's Information Centre, *Paterson St; tel: (08) 89 62 3388.*

ACCOMMODATION

Desert Sands, *Paterson St; tel: 8962 1346.* **Tennant Creek Hotel**, *146 Paterson St; tel: 8962 2006.* **Eldorado Motor Lodge**, *Paterson St; tel: 8962 2402;* **The Tavern**, *53 Paterson St; tel: 8962 1033.* **Safari Lodge Motel**, *12 Davidson St; tel: 8962 2207.* **Bluestone Motor Inn**, *1 Paterson St; tel: 8962 2617.* **Goldfields Hotel Motel**, *603 Paterson St; tel: 8962 2030.*

SIGHTSEEING

The town of Tennant Creek is located 504 km from Alice Springs, 26 km south of Three Ways and 11 km south of the original creek. This was discovered in 1860 by John McDouall Stuart and named after John Tennant of **Port Lincoln** in South Australia. In 1872 it became the site for the Overland Telegraph Station. In the 1930s gold was discovered and it was the centre of Australia's Last Great Goldrush. The gold mainly petered out although finds are still being made, but the town remained and now contains about 3100 people.

The history of Tennant Creek can be seen in the **Tennant Creek Museum**, *Leichhardt St.* Open daily 1530–1730; $2. Nearby is the **Aboriginal Mural** in *Paterson St*, which is a community project emphasising Aboriginal mythology in relation to contemporary life.

Battery Hill is on *Peko Rd*, 1½ km to the east of town, and is the site of the **Tennant**

Creek Gold Stamp Battery. This is an operating gold crushing battery and mining museum. Open Mon–Fri 0900–1600. From there you can tour the goldfields and visit different types of mines such as **The Burnt Shirt Mine** or the **Golden Forty**. And you are encouraged to go gold fossicking with all equipment supplied. Some of the mines are still operating and at one of them, **Dot Mine**, a Tennant Creek miner will give you a first hand account of the mine and a miner's life. Note that this is rugged country and you should take care when exploring. Further along on *Peko Rd*, just past the Battery, is **Bill Allen Lookout**, which is a good place to view Tennant Creek and the surrounding area. There are plaques at the lookout, which show where the mines were dug and other local points of interest.

Yet further along the same road, 12 km east of town, you come to **Noble's Nob Open Cut Mine**, which was once the richest gold mine in Australia.

Off Stuart Hwy, 2 km north of Tennant Creek is the **Mary Ann Dam**, which has created an artificial lake suitable for small boats and canoes and swimming. **The Overland Telegraph Station**, which was built in 1872, is 12 km north along Stuart Hwy. **The Conservation Commission** (*tel: 8962 3388*) has now made this into a living museum with self-conducted tours.

Out of Town

One of the major attractions within easy driving distance of the town are the **Devil's Marbles**, 104 km south of Tennant Creek along the Stuart Hwy. They are a collection of precariously balanced gigantic granite boulders. According to Aboriginal mythology they are the 'Eggs of the Rainbow Serpent.'

There is a sort of miniature and much less impressive version of the Devils Marbles closer to town called the **Devil's Pebbles**, and the two should not be confused. The latter is an extensive area of granite boulders 17 km north along the Stuart Hwy, which look as if some giant has scattered them across the desert. Best time for viewing is at sunset, when they glow in the dying rays of the sun.

ALICE SPRINGS

At the heart of the Red centre, surrounded by the crags and cliffs of the MacDonnell Ranges, Alice Springs seems set in a harsh and waterless environment. This is far from the truth. There a wealth of lush – by Red Centre standards – natural water sources including the magnificent Standley Chasm, Ellery Creek Big Hole, Redbank, Glen Helen and Ormiston Gorges.

TOURIST INFORMATION

Central Australian Tourism Industry Association, *Gregory Terrace and Hartley St; tel: (08) 8952 5800.*

ARRIVING AND DEPARTING

Alice Springs airport is 14 km south of the town and has connections to every major Australian city. There is an airport shuttle bus *(tel: 8953 0310)* that meets incoming flights and costs $9. There are always plenty of taxis which cost about $20 or so.

The train station is on the west side of the Stuart Hwy, just off *Larapinta Dr.* The Ghan (see p.404) arrives there from Adelaide, and sets off on its return journey, every Fri.

STAYING IN ALICE SPRINGS

Accommodation
Plaza Hotel Alice Springs, *Barrett Dr.; tel: 8952 8000.* **Alice Springs Pacific Resort** *(FL), Stott Terrace; tel: 8952 6699.* **Lasseters Casino Hotel**, *93 Barrett Dr.; tel: 8952 5066.* **Vista Hotel Alice Springs**, *Stephens Rd; tel: 8952 6100.* **Alice Motor Inn** *(FL), 27 Undoolya Rd; tel: 8952 2322.* **Red Centre Resort**, *North Stuart Hwy; tel: 8952 8955.* **Desert Rose Inn**, *115 Railway Terrace; tel: 8952 1411.* **Frontier Oasis Resort**, *10 Gap Rd; tel: 8952 1444.* **Desert Palms Resort**,

Barrett Dr.; tel: 8952 5977. **Desert Oaks Motel**, *corner Stuart and Lasseter Hwys; tel: 8956 0984.* **Alice Springs Gapview Resort Hotel**, *Gap Rd; tel: 8952 6611.* **Territory Motor Inn**, *Leichardt Terrace; tel: 8952 2066.* **Swagmans Rest Motel** *(BU), 67–69 Gap Rd; tel: 8953 1333.* **White Gum Holiday Inn Motel**, *17 Gap Rd; tel: 8952 5144.* **Elkira Motel** *(BW), 65 Bath St; tel: 8952 1222.* **Outback Motor Lodge** *(BW), South Terrace; tel: 8952 3888.* **Midland Motel**, *4 Traeger Ave; tel: 8952 1588.* **Jim's Place Motel**, *Stuarts Well, South Stuart Hwy; 8956 0808.* **Mount Nancy Motel** *(BU), 6447 North Stuart Hwy; tel: 8952 9488.* **Wauchope Hotel Motel**, *Stuart Hwy, Wauchope Well; tel: 8964 1963.* **Heavitree Gap Motel**, *Emily Gap Rd; tel: 8952 4866.* **Diplomat Motor Inn**, *corner Hartley St and Gregory Terrace; tel: 8952 8977.* **Stuart Lodge Motel**, *Stuart Terrace; tel: 8952 1894.* **Todd Tavern Motel**, *corner Wills Terrace and Todd Mall; tel: 8953 1333.* **Melanka Lodge Hotel**, *Todd St; tel: 8952 2233.* **HI: Pioneer Hostel**, *corner of Parsons St and Leichhardt Terrace; tel: 8952 8855.*

Eating and Drinking
This is definitely not gourmet territory but you get good portions and very fair value for money.

Melanka Steak House, *94 Todd St; tel: 8952 2233.* Open seven nights for dinner. Licensed. Pub food. **Camels Crossing**, *Fan Arcade, Todd St; tel: 8952 5522.* Nightly. Mexican food. **Terrace**, *134 Bath St; tel: 8952 1222.* Open seven nights for dinner. Licensed. Part of the **Elkira Motel**. **Golden Inn**, *9 Undoolya Rd; tel: 8952 6910.* Lunch Mon–Sat, dinner seven days. Licensed. Asian food. **La Casalinga**, *105 Gregory Terrace; tel: 8952 4508.* Dinner seven nights. Italian cuisine.

SIGHTSEEING

It was the presence of water that provided the initial reason for the existence of Alice Springs as a European pioneer settlement. The water led to a station for the electric telegraph, which led to a town.

The first installation of the telegraph in Australia was in 1853 between Melbourne and Williamstown in Victoria. South Australia – its boundaries extended to the north as far as Darwin – wanted to keep up. The Colonial Office in London was asked to appoint a Superintendent of Telegraphs and sent Charles Todd and his wife Alice, who arrived in Adelaide in November 1855.

Todd had shipped out the equipment needed to set up the first telegraph line in South Australia between Adelaide and Port Adelaide. Then, in 1857, a line from Adelaide to Melbourne was started and was operating by the following year.

The next step was a line that would connect Australia with the rest of the world.

John McDouall Stuart took three attempts at the trek between Adelaide and Darwin to prove it could be done. In April 1860 the party passed through the Red Centre on their way north to the coast. Construction of the line started ten years later.

As it was being surveyed, a waterhole was found in the Todd River, which was named Alice Springs, after Alice Todd, the wife of Charles Todd after whom the river had been named. This waterhole was permanent and was therefore chosen to become first a base station and then a telegraph repeater station.

The telegraph line started operating in 1872. The line had come through the **Heavitree Gap**, the gateway to Alice Springs, the year before, and gradually a town grew up nearby. Originally it was called Stuart – this was officially the case until 1933 – but local usage changed it to its current name.

Now it is a town of 24,500 people nestling at the foot of the **MacDonnell Ranges** and is the urban heart and gateway to Australia's **Red Centre**. This is not the wild and woolly west. Rather it is a town which is rapidly growing to meet the commercial demands of tourism and readers of *A Town Like Alice* may be a tad disappointed.

The history of the town has not been forgotten. The Telegraph Station was closed in

1932, and converted into a hostel for Aboriginal children. Restoration of the Telegraph Station started in 1963 and is still there as a memento of pioneer times (see below).

It is not generally remembered that Alice Springs was the administrative headquarters for Central Australia, which was an administrative area from 1927–1931. Therefore Alice Springs could, quite correctly, be seen as the capital of the Red Centre.

But Alice Springs is really a country centre and the best way to see it as such is to go to its most visited landmark, **Anzac Hill**. This is off *Wills Terrace* and gives you an instant overview of the town.

The centre of the town is marked by the Todd River, which is almost always dry, and is where the amazing **Henley-on-Todd Regatta** is held every October: bottomless boats are run rather than rowed.

Todd Mall in the centre of the town was once the main street but has now been made into a pleasant pedestrian precinct.

Historic Buildings
The restored **Alice Springs Telegraph Station**, *tel: 89523 993,* is 3 km north of Alice Springs just off the Stuart Hwy. The reserve features the original buildings and equipment, an illustrated history of the telegraph station and the surrounding grounds are a pleasant place for a picnic. Open daily 0800–2100 Oct–Apr, 0800–1900 May–Sep; $2.50.

You can relive the work of **Flynn of the Outback** – the Rev. John Flynn, who was stationed here over a long period and founded the Royal Flying Doctor Service (see Darwin–Alice Springs p.277).

He died in 1951 at **Adelaide House**, *48 Todd Mall; tel: 8952 1856.* It was the first hospital of the district, with the first nurse arriving in 1916. It has on display an early pedal operated Treager radio and a Morse typewriter. In theory, open Mar–Nov Mon–Fri 1000–1600, Sat 1000–1200, but check first. Admission $2.

Stuart Town Gaol, *Parsons St; tel: 8952 4511,* is constructed from locally quarried stone from the range near Heavitree Gap. Open Tues and Thur 1000–1230 and Sat 0930–1200.

280

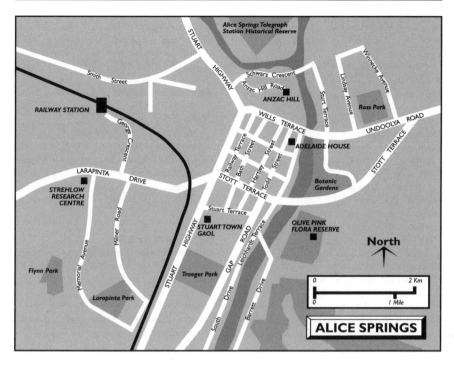

Tours

Camel riding is nothing like riding a horse – it is typically more comfortable and if you are in a camel train all you need to do is sit still and enjoy the scenery. No experience needed. **Alice Springs Camel Outback Safaris**, *Stuart Hwy, Stuart's Well; tel: 08956 0925,* has all sorts of camel rides available, starting with 1 hr jaunts all the way up to safaris that can last 3 weeks. Open daily 0730–1700.

Another place that offers camel riding is the **Frontier Camel Farm**, *Ross Hwy; tel: 8953 0444.* Open daily 0900–1700. It has a camel museum and kangaroos wandering around the grounds. It also offers a camel tour along the dry bed of the Todd River and then to the first and only winery in Central Australia.

The Winery is on *Petrick Rd,* off South Stuart Hwy, 10 km from town; *tel: 8955 5133.* The wines are an interesting and unique experience and there is also a restaurant. It is fair to say that this is the only winery in the world where you are positively encouraged to arrive by camel. Open daily 0900–1600.

Museums and Galleries

The **Araluen Centre**, set in 5 hectares of gardens, has two art galleries which exhibit local art and craft. It is an excellent place to look around before buying any Aboriginal art. It is also the performing arts and entertainment centre and you should check locally for programme details. (*Larapinta Dr., tel: 8952 5022;* open Mon–Sat 1000–1700 Feb–Nov.)

Aboriginal Dreamtime Caves Diarama Village, *Larapinta Dr.; tel: 8952 1884,* has a display depicting the myths and legends of the Australian Aborigines and has a wide range of Aboriginal arts and crafts for sale. Open 1000–1700 Mon–Fri, Feb–Nov.

Some 24 km north of Alice Springs on the Stuart Hwy is the **Historic Bond Springs Homestead**, *tel: 8952 9888,* which is a heritage working cattle station, offering everything from a smoko to lunch. Complete with school room, blacksmith shop and overnight stay cottages.

The Museum of Technology, Transport and Communications, *Memorial Dr.;*

tel: 8953 4475, has an aviation museum as well as displays of technology, transport and communications.

Panorama Guth, *65 Hartley St, Alice Springs; tel: 8952 2013,* is a 360° painted landscape of Central Australia, which you view from a platform as if from a lookout. Henk Guth is not universally accepted as being one of the world's great artists but there is also an art gallery – works by Albert Namatjira – and an Aboriginal museum. Open daily Mon–Sat 0900–1700, Sun 1400–1700. $3.

Strehlow Research Centre, *corner Larapinta Dr. and Memorial Ave; tel: 8951 8000,* is fascinating but flawed in that almost all of the original material of the collection cannot be displayed because of Aboriginal attitudes towards non-Aborigines and, in many cases, women, viewing them. Some of the items willed to this centre would appear to have ended up in private hands and considerable controversy surrounded the establishment of this collection. The result is visually stunning although there are very few genuine Aboriginal artefacts on display. Open daily 1000–1700.

The Ghan Railway

The Ghan, named after the presumed Afghan nationality of the camel train leaders, was, and still is, Australia's most famous train. It was, in its old days, slow, unreliable and much given to breaking down – on one occasion it arrived 3 months late – but it was the only true link with the Outback, arriving in Alice Springs originally in 1929. It is now being sold into private hands and it may well be that its glory days will return (see also Classic Trains p.404).

There is an exhibition run by the **Ghan Preservation Society,** *Norris Bell Ave, off S. Stuart Hwy; tel: 89555 047,* with an old local shed, a working steam engine and train rides. Open daily Mar–Dec.

Gold Mining

Lasseter is an Australian legend – a man who found and lost a major reef of gold. Unkind cynics merely see him as an eccentric with a few kangaroos loose in his top paddock. Others believe implicitly that he found such a reef and that whoever rediscovers it will make a fortune

beyond the dreams of avarice. Perhaps. What is fairly certain is that no one is likely to make such a fortune at **Lasseter's Hotel and Casino,** *93 Barrett Dr.; tel: 8952 5066,* which has all of the basic gambling games. It also has a minor claim to fame as it was featured in the film *Priscilla, Queen of the Desert.* Open daily 1000 until very late.

On display at the **Minerals House,** *58 Hartley St, Alice Springs; tel: 8951 5658,* is a series of displays on the geology of Central Australia. And if you want to dig for a fortune, information on fossicking regulations and requirements is available. Open Mon–Fri 0800–1630.

Parks and Gardens

The Mecca Date Garden is claimed to be the first date farm in Australia, *Palm Circuit; tel: 8952 2425.* Open Mon–Sat 1000–1700, Sun 1000–1600 except Nov–Mar.

The oddly named **Olive Pink Flora Reserve** – Olive Pink was an early activist for Aboriginal rights – is an arid zone botanic garden with examples of native shrubs and trees from a 300 km radius of Alice Springs. (*Tuncks Rd, Golf Course Causeway; tel: 8952 21547.*) The plants are well sign-posted and described and there is also an Information Centre. Open daily 1000–1600.

School of the Air

Distance learning is thought of as a modern concept that started with the Internet. In fact, in Outback Australia, is has been around since 1951. At the **School of the Air,** *80 Head St; tel: 8952 1800,* you can listen to a live broadcast of day to day classes and see the children's work and hobbies. Open Mon–Fri 0800–1200 Feb–Nov, except for school holidays. Admission $2.

Flying Doctor Service

The Royal Flying Doctor Service is an amazing service, which has made the outback habitable – or at least a little less inhospitable. The service headquarters (*Stuart Terrace; tel: 8952 1129*), let you see the communications radio in operation and browse around the museum, which tells the history of this remarkable service. Open daily Mon–Sat 0900–1600, Sun 1300–1600; $1.50.

Out of Town

Five kilometres out of town is a serious attempt to reproduce the life of the pioneers at the **Old Timers Folk Museum**, *S. Stuart Hwy; tel: 8952 2844.*

Further along in that direction **The Pitchi Richi Aboriginal Cultural Experience**, *Palm Circuit; tel: 8952 1931,* has an outdoor museum, an Aboriginal guided tour and visitors can try their luck at playing a didgeridoo, spear and boomerang throwing and whip cracking. Also on display are the quite remarkable sculptures of the late William Rickets, an artist who is still little known even in Australia, although this will change. Open daily 0900–1600.

SIDE TRACKS
FROM ALICE SPRINGS

WEST MACDONNELL RANGES

The West MacDonnell region is well situated for day trips from Alice Springs. The region is known as **Albert Namatjira country** after the famous Aboriginal watercolourist.

Take the *Namatjira Dr.* out from Alice Springs. On your right will be the vast expanse of the **West MacDonnell National Park**. The **Ellery Creek Big Hole** is 96 km along the Drive. It is a large waterhole with a high red cliff and a sandy creek, which is fringed by river red gums. The pool is cool and deep and there are camping and picnic facilities.

Further along *Namatjira Dr.* – about 40 km – is **Glen Helen Gorge**, in which the Finke River is constrained between high sandstone banks as it starts its journey out to the **Simpson Desert**. There is a lodge on the edge of the Gorge with accommodation, a restaurant and a **Conservation Commission information shelter**.

Serpentine Gorge is 107 km west of Alice Springs and is a narrow, winding gorge with semi-permanent waterholes and

gorge scenery, which can be green and verdant. There are well marked walking trails and an abundance of wildlife.

The Ochre Pits are also on *Namatjira Dr.*, about 118 km west of Alice Springs. This ochre quarry was once mined by Aborigines, who used it for traditional ceremonial body decoration and other paintings.

Further along the road, about another 25 km, is the **Ormiston Gorge and Pound**, which is one of the most spectacular features of the West MacDonnell Ranges. There is a deep waterhole and a footpath as well as camping facilities.

Ormiston Gorge is right at the eastern extremity of the West MacDonnell National Park and the nearby small town of **Glen Helen** marks the end of the sealed road although outside the wet season *Namatjira Dr.* continues to be perfectly drivable with a normal two-wheel-drive vehicle.

Redbank Gorge is on the unsealed portion of *Namatjira Dr.*, some 170 km west of Alice Springs. This is a deep and narrow chasm in the range and the waters that flow through are amazingly cool, indeed, positively icy and not encouraging to swimmers. The creek has ghost gums growing along its banks, which contrast with the spinifex and scrubland in the dry area around the gorge.

HERMANNSBURG AND PALM VALLEY

A second tour out of Alice Springs follows *Namatjira Dr.* 12 km to **Iwupataka** and then along *Larapinta Dr.* to **Hermannsburg**.

Hermannsburg was, until recently, a **Lutheran Mission** and is claimed to be the oldest Aboriginal community in the Red Centre, dating from the 1870s. That is about as far as you can sensibly tour with a conventional two wheel drive vehicle. To explore **Palm Valley** you need a four-wheel-drive vehicle set up for running on loose surfaces and even then it is not a drive for the inexperienced. The best way to tour Palm Valley is by way of one of the many four wheel drive tours out of Alice Springs.

283

Then you need not worry about the driving.

To get to Palm Valley, which is 21 km south of Hermannsburg, you drive down the Finke River bed which is, for most of the year, loose sand, making it relatively easy to get stuck. The valley is an oasis in an area of dry and barren country but the trip is worth the effort because of the valleys population of the rare Red Cabbage Palm – *Livistona mariae*. These exist nowhere else in the world and there are over 3000 of them in Palm Valley. They have existed in this area for something in excess of 10,000 years.

Also off *Larapinta Dr.*, 18 km to the west of Alice Springs is **Simpsons Gap**, which has steep-sided ridges, huge ghost gums and timbered creek flats. The best way to see it is to follow one of the several footpaths in the area, which range from moderate to strenuous. **Standley Chasm** is further down off *Larapinta Dr.*, about 54 km west of Alice Springs. The chasm is a break in the MacDonnell Ranges and there is a 1½ km walk along the creek bed between the strong red walls of the chasm, past a series of spring-fed pools which sustain a wide range of plants.

The **Tnorala Conservation Reserve – Gosses Bluff** – can be accessed either by way of *Namatjira Dr.* or *Larapinta Dr.* In both cases you are on unsealed roads for part of the 200 km journey west of Alice Springs. The reserve contains a spectacular crater caused by a comet crash 130 million years ago. It is jointly managed by the Conservation Commission and the Aboriginal custodians and owners. The easiest way to explore this area is by taking a four wheel drive tour out of Alice Springs.

EASTERN MACDONNELL RANGES

Head out of Alice through the Heavitree Gap and along the Ross Hwy, until, after 10 km you reach **Emily Gap**. From here on in you are in the Eastern Macdonnell Ranges.

The Eastern MacDonnell Ranges is an ideal region for day trips from Alice Springs and the countryside, with its gaps and gorges, draped in mauve and misty blue colours is quite distinct from the country in the West MacDonnell Ranges.

Amongst the sights worth seeing in the area are **Emily and Jessie Gaps Nature Parks**, which are both off the Ross Hwy. The first is 23 km off the Ross Hwy and the second is 10 km further along. These gaps in the ranges have been created by streams cutting their way through the rock. They are both popular spots for a picnic and there is a range of wildlife in the area.

Further along is the **Arltunga Historical Reserve**, which is also off the Ross Hwy, 108 km east of Alice Springs. This was a gold town, which made its first strike in 1887. It is all pretty much in ruins now but you can still see the workings and the gravestones and there is a mine to explore. The police station and gaol have both been restored and there is a Visitor Centre, which has a lot of information on the area.

The Ross River Homestead, at the end of the Ross Hwy, 88 kms east of Alice Springs, is a historic homestead, which has concentrated on becoming a touring attraction with plenty to do, including horse- and camel-riding, boomerang-throwing and whip-cracking.

AYERS ROCK AND
THE OLGAS

TOURIST INFORMATION

Ayers Rock Resort Visitors and Information Centre, *Ayers Rock Resort; tel: (08) 8956 2240.*

ARRIVING AND DEPARTING

You can drive to Ayers Rock from Alice Springs, first on the Stuart Hwy and then, 210 km later at Erldunda, on to the Lasseter Hwy for another 247 km to the Ayers Rock Resort. Or there are frequent coaches for most of the major tour companies, which offer round trip day tours for around $150. Far easier is to fly in direct to Connelan airport with Ansett. There are direct flights from Sydney, Alice Springs,

Cairns and Perth. There are shuttle coaches between the airport and the Yulara village, which costs about $10 and taxis cost the same. However, hire cars are quite expensive, as there is a 'remote surcharge', so a saloon will cost something around $70–$90 a day. As is true in most locations in Australia you can hire a four-wheel-drive vehicle but there is an excess charge of $5000. If you are not an experienced four wheel vehicle driver hiring one is not a good idea as they are easy to turn over.

STAYING IN YULARA

Outback Pioneer Hotel, *Yulara Dr.; tel: 8956 2737.* **Sails In The Desert Hotel**, *Yulara Dr.;*

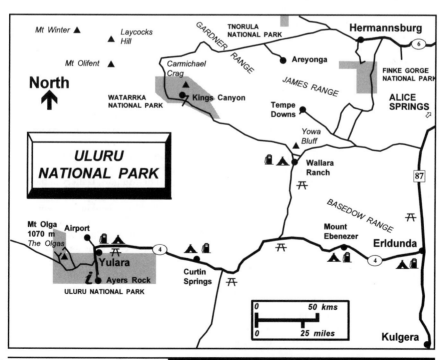

tel: 8956 2200. **Spinifex Lodge Hotel,** *Yulara Dr.; tel: 8956 2131.* **HI: Outback Pioneer Lodge,** *(PO Box 10) Yulara; tel: 8956 2170.*

SIGHTSEEING

Let us start with some basics. Ayers Rock, or using its correct Aboriginal name, **Uluru**, is one of those natural manifestations which are almost beyond comprehension. It is the largest rock in the world and rises 348m above the flat plane. The circumference around the base is more than 5 km. The rock moves through an incredible range of colours as you watch, especially at sunrise and sunset, as if it were some sort of supernatural light show. Perhaps it is.

While in Northern Territory terms Uluru is just down the road from Alice Springs, it is actually over 400 km away and in a reasonable car the journey will take 4 hrs, or 20 mins by air to the special airport of **Yulara**. Often visitors arrive in Sydney with Ayers Rock pencilled into their itinerary as a day trip. Unless you are chartering a private jet plane that is simply not possible. The **Yulara resort** offers accommodation to visitors to the area, available at every level from backpackers to a five star hotel. Normally such a venture would be intrusive and vulgar but Yulara blends in with the countryside, creating no visual offence.

Uluru and the **Olgas – Kata Tjuta** – are part of the **Uluru National Park.** Uluru is 20 km from Yulara and the Olgas are a further 30 km from Uluru. Viewing areas have been set up for visitors to take advantage of the sunset and sunrise colours, which can vary from a bright orange/red to the deep brown of the main body of rock to a solid and moody purple. A spectacular sight comes after rain on the rock, when it takes on a silver sheen.

Visitors are often tempted to climb Ayers Rock (it is forbidden to clamber around the Olgas). Most experienced people within the park recommend that you don't. It is an ascent of 1.6 km and very steep in parts, and it is sadly common for elderly visitors to find that it is slightly more than their heart can take, resulting in park rangers having to lower them down with stretchers – no easy task. Luckily the mortality rate is almost zero but the risk is definitely there. The second point is that the local

Aboriginal people feel uneasy when they see people clambering around an area in which there are many sacred and significant sites. They are much too polite to have a confrontation but there is no doubt that the Aboriginies would prefer visitors to enjoy the delights of Uluru without clambering all over it.

You will almost certainly find that a walking tour around its base with a guide is less physically taxing and also more spiritually rewarding.

Kata Tjuta – the Olgas – are 50 km away from Yulara by excellent paved road and seem overshadowed by Uluru. This is an illusion. The tallest peak on Kata Tjuta, **Mt Olga**, is more than 200m higher than Uluru. The distinctive domes and striated, weathered surfaces of Kata Tjuta match Uluru in colour and some visitors prefer its subtleties and hidden pleasures. Whatever view you take, both are remarkable, well worth the journey and humbling experiences. The entry fee into Uluru–Kata Tjuta National Park is $10 per person.

The climate in the area is typical Central Australian weather. The summer has warm to hot days with mild nights. The winter, warm days with cool to cold nights. There is an insignificant annual rainfall. What must be mentioned is the flies. In the summer they are a serious nuisance and you see people wearing veils to avoid them. An industrial strength insect repellent is an absolute essential during the summer.

The Indiginy Amphitheatre, *tel: (08) 8956 2240,* at the **Ayers Rock Resort** has didgeridoo playing and Northern Territory music for an hour under the star-filled skies. Mon–Sat 2030 during summer months, 1930 in the winter. **The Mulgara Gallery** in the **Sails in the Desert Hotel,** *Ayers Rock Resort; tel: (08) 8956 2200,* has working resident artists and an impressive collection of Australian arts, crafts and gifts. Open daily 0800–2000. More basic but perhaps better value for money is the **Maruku Arts and Crafts**, near the **Ranger Information Centre,** *Uluru–Kata Tjuta National Park; tel: (08) 8956 2153,* which is an Aboriginal-owned outdoor gallery selling the works of more than 800 artists and crafts people of the region. Open daily 0830–1200, 1500–1700 Dec–Apr, 0830–1700 May–Nov.

NORTHERN TERRITORY NATIONAL PARKS

TOURIST AND GENERAL INFORMATION

Park and Wild Life Commission, *tel: (08) 8924 4143.*

The Northern Territory is blessed with some of the most famous national parks in Australia, and indeed in the world. Although the number of parks is not great, the wide variety of terrains and attractions is remarkable, from stark desert to tropical rain forest.

REGION BY REGION

Top End – accessible from Darwin

Kakadu *Bush camping possible. Kakadu National Park is only 2 hours drive from Darwin and yet its 20,000 sq km is a World Heritage region containing a vast expanse of parkland with a wide range of vegetation and geography and including such stunning sites as Ubirr and Nourlangie Rock, Yellow Waters, Jim Jim and Twin Falls. See pp. 270–273.*
Litchfield *Accessible from the town of Adelaide River, between Darwin and Pine Creek on the road to Katherine.*

South-west of Katherine

These parks lie along the Victoria Highway, connecting the Territory to Kununurra at the top end of Western Australia; see p. 329.

Gregory *Bush camping possible. A park of two halves, separated by the Stokes range, which is Aboriginal land.*
Keep River

Near Katherine

The major attractions on the otherwise pretty empty Darwin to Alice Springs route, pp. 274–278.

Elsey
Nitmiluk (Katherine Gorge) *Bush camping possible. This park is a must if you are driving south from Darwin. See p. 275.*

Around Alice

The centre of Australia contains the best-known natural monument in the country, but also many other parks which are easy to visit using Alice Springs as a base.

Arltunga Historic Reserve. *In the East Macdonnell Ranges, forming a visitable group with N'dhala Gorge and Trephina Gorge. See p. 284.*
Finke Gorge *This, the West Macdonnell Ranges and Hermannsburg are close to Alice Springs and together make a worthwhile side-trip from there. See pp. 279–284.*
N'dhala Gorge
Trephina Gorge
Uluru *As well as the sacred monolith of Uluru or Ayers Rock, the park contains Kata Tjuta, otherwise known as the Olgas, an impressive cluster of rock domes. The resort of Yulara and the airport may this world-famous site very easy of access from all parts of Australia. See pp. 285–286.*
Watarrka *Bush camping possible.*
West Macdonnell *Bush camping possible. See pp. 279–284.*

287

WESTERN AUSTRALIA

Western Australians frequently do not see their state as being part of Australia. They think it too large, too remote, too different. Many of them believe it should be a country in its own right. It is, after all, Australia's largest state and is isolated by desert from the other population centres in the east. The state has a wide range of contrasts, from the cities and settlements clinging to its coast and enjoying one of the world's ideal climates, to the sun-dried outback, which lies sere and wizened after centuries of sunning.

GEOGRAPHY

Western Australia covers 2,525,500 sq km. In a sense it is almost as much part of Asia as it is Australia. Perth is closer to Jakarta and Singapore than it is to Sydney. The northern coastline only has the narrow straits of the Timor Sea separating it from the islands of Indonesia. The distance from north to south is the same as the distance between Oslo in Norway and Madrid in Spain. It is bigger than Texas, Japan, New Zealand and the British Isles, all added together.

Once you get away from the coast most of that immense land area is outback, with the **Nullarbor Plain** in the south, the **Great Sandy Desert** in the north and the **Gibson and Great Victoria Deserts** in between. And the rugged wilds of **The Kimberley** are in the extreme north of the state. Although the population of Western Australia is about 1.8 million, almost 1.4 million live in the Perth area, which means that in most parts this is Australia's emptiest state.

The state can be split into a series of geographical groupings. The Kimberley is centred around **Broome**. Also in the Kimberley is

Derby, 2300 km from Perth by road, which is the nearest town to the impressive **Windjana Gorge**. Further south is the **Pilbara**, a major iron ore area and also the **Kirninji National Park**, with spectacular mountains and plains of the Hamersley Range. **Exmouth** is the centre of what is called the Coral Coast, including the **Ningaloo Marine Park**, which has coral to rival the Great Barrier Reef. **Gascoyne** is the centre of what is called the Mid-West and within striking distance are the blowholes of **Quobba Station** and **Mt Augustus**, which is more than double the size of Ayers Rock. The **Avon Valley** is a fertile farming area within an hour's drive of Perth, with the river, which it is named after, winding around the main town of **Northam**. Then comes the South-West, the garden of Western Australia, with some of Australia's greatest vineyards, the magnificent harbour of **Albany** and the three National Parks of **Esperance**. Finally there is **Kalgoorlie** and the gold towns, which are, yes, the Wild West, where 200,000 prospectors crowded in the 1890s in search of a fortune.

Agriculture is the main industry of the state and ranges from open-range grazing to orchards and vineyards. The seas off Western Australia also provide a large harvest and the state is one of the world's major suppliers of lobsters, prawns and pearls.

But the wealth of Western Australia lies in its mineral and energy resources, with extensive natural gas reserves and more than 270 operating mines. Western Australia is a leading supplier of alumina, diamonds, iron ore and mineral sands. It also produces 70% of Australia's gold. Kalgoorlie is reputedly the richest square mile on earth, while nearby **Coolgardie**, a mining town that had started to disappear, has been given a new lease of life to mine the new gold – tourism. This is the growing industry, with over half a million overseas visitors and about another 5 million Australians coming to the state; although the income it provides is perhaps only a fifth of that supplied by mining, it is growing rapidly in importance.

CLIMATE

Perth and the south-west corner of the state enjoy a truly Mediterranean climate. There is an average of 8 hours sunshine a day and around 120 clear days every year. The maximum temperatures range from 17°C in July to 30°C in February. The rain falls mainly in the winter months, which resemble a pleasant British spring, with minimum temperatures never below 5°C. The afternoon sea breeze, the 'Fremantle Doctor', offers relief to coastal towns during the warm summer months. The tropical north has hot, sticky, wet summers and warm dry winters. From May to November, the nights are mostly cool and crisp and the days are sunny with blue skies. Desert areas have hot, dry summers and mild, dry winters. The Mediterranean climate of the south has hot, dry summers and mild, wet winters. Once you start to get away from the coast, rainfall decreases (in some cases almost disappears) and the variations in temperature become more pronounced.

GETTING AROUND

There are good sealed highways linking regional centres to Perth and two national highways, north and south for interstate traffic. But, simply because of its size, Western Australia is not the place for a normal motoring holiday. The distances between places are much too great. The chapters that follow include some long routes for the more determined driver, but the easiest way to see the state is to fly to the major destinations and hire a car . To see the whole of Western Australia would be a lifetime's task. To see just the highlights requires time and travel. Time and travel well spent.

FLORA AND FAUNA

Western Australia calls itself the **wildflower state**. Isolated by the sea on three sides and with an inhospitable desert on the fourth, the region has developed a unique range of vegetation. There are about 10,000 varieties of flowering plant to be found in the state; the jarrah forests in the south-west alone have over 3000 species. The Australian spring, Aug–Nov, is the best time to see this amazing variety of wildflowers although the season starts in late winter in the north and is still going strong well into the summer months down on the south coast. There are tours to view the wildflowers but, in truth, they are almost everywhere and the display in **King's Park** in the heart of Perth is in itself of world class. Close to Perth they can be found in profusion in the **Nambung, John Forrest** and **Walyunga National Parks**. Then there are wildflower routes through the Midlands, **Geraldton**, along the Brand and the Great Southern Highways. In the outback there are years when the ranges are carpeted for kilometre after kilometre with wildflowers – and other years when they are very scarce on the ground. The tourist office will have the latest news and there is an Internet site solely devoted to showing where the flowers are in bloom.

When it comes to animals the state is home to a number of marsupials: kangaroos, quokkas, possums, dunnarts, numbats, wombats, koalas, platypuses and echidnas. The **black swan**, the West's most famous bird, is the state symbol.

Western Australia is an angler's idea of heaven. The 12,000 km of coastline runs right from the sub-tropics to the Great Southern Ocean and the range and profusion of fish is arguably among the greatest in the world. The coast has massive coral reefs, mangrove creeks, kilometres of beaches for surf casting and cliffs running out to deep water.

PERTH

Back in 1962 astronaut John Glenn referred to Perth, the capital of Western Australia, as the City of Lights, because that is how he saw it as he orbited the earth. All the lights had been turned on for his orbits. It was, perhaps, at the time, a little flattering. But since then Perth has developed into a modern, cosmopolitan city, much aided in its development by its involvement in the Americas' Cup.

The 1987 defence of the Cup brought a flood of visitors to the area and initiated a major building boom. While it is true that many people involved in the later growth of Perth – and especially WA Inc., which was the term used for a group of capitalists and developers working with the state government – have fallen dramatically from grace, the city has survived and retained the benefits of modern development.

TOURIST INFORMATION

Western Australian Tourism Commission; *tel: 220 1700.*

The main tourist office *(tel: 9483 1111)* is across the road from the East Perth Interstate Rail and Bus Terminal using a road bridge from the Transperth station – the centre for Perth's excellent suburban services of both bus and train – in the Forrest Chase precinct. It is unbelievably easy to get lost in this area and you will have to ask for directions. Once you get there you will find plenty of useful and free information.

There is also the **Pinnacles Tourist Centre**, *tel: 9221 5411,* which is on the corner of *Hay and Pier Sts.*

WEATHER

Perth enjoys the best climate in any Australian capital with a mean temperature of 23.5°C in the hottest month, Feb, and a mean of 13°C in the coldest month, July. A US vice consul once referred to it as the sort of climate that California thinks it has. The only minor problem is that the sun is stronger than you think and to avoid sunburn, and possibly skin cancer, you should wear a hat, shirt and sunglasses, and be liberal with a broad spectrum SPF 15+ sunscreen cream. Don't worry about standing out, because everyone else does the same.

ARRIVING AND DEPARTING

Airports

It is better by far to fly to Perth either internationally or domestically. If you are coming to Australia from Asia, Perth is an excellent gateway as it is only a short flight and you quickly become acclimatised. Domestically, there are daily direct flights to every other capital in Australia and connecting flights to pretty well everywhere else.

The domestic terminal at Perth is some 13 km to the east of the city and the international airport is about 3 km further out. There are shuttle buses meeting the main arrivals at both. The fare from the international terminal is $7 and from the domestic terminal $6. There are always taxis available and the cost of a trip to town is something just over $20.

By Car

You can get to Perth by road by driving over the **Nullarbor Plain** from, if you like, as far away as Sydney. This drive has little to recommend it – it is a long, boring journey, with stretches sometimes as long as 17 km without the slightest bend.

By Train

There is a third option which is to arrive by

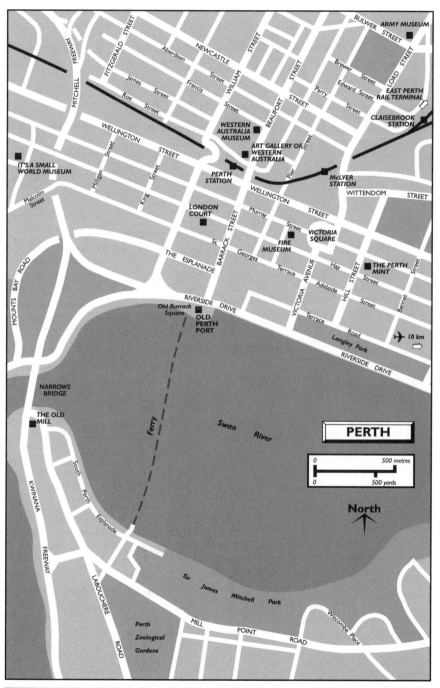

ARMY MUSEUM
BULWER STREET
LORD STREET
NEWCASTLE STREET
Aberdeen Street
FITZGERALD STREET
MITCHELL FREEWAY
James Street
Francis Street
Roe Street
WILLIAM STREET
BEAUFORT STREET
Brewer Street
Edward Street
Parry Street
EAST PERTH RAIL TERMINAL
CLAISEBROOK STATION
WESTERN AUSTRALIA MUSEUM
ART GALLERY OF WESTERN AUSTRALIA
WELLINGTON STREET
IT'S A SMALL WORLD MUSEUM
Milligan Street
King Street
Malcolm Street
PERTH STATION
Pier Street
McLVER STATION
WELLINGTON STREET
WITTENDOM STREET
LONDON COURT
Murray Street
VICTORIA SQUARE
BARRACK STREET
St. Georges Terrace
FIRE MUSEUM
Hay Street
HILL STREET
THE PERTH MINT
Bennet Street
THE ESPLANADE
VICTORIA AVENUE
Adelaide Street
RIVERSIDE DRIVE
Terrace
Road
Langley Park
10 km
291
RIVERSIDE DRIVE
Old Barrack Square
OLD PERTH PORT
NARROWS BRIDGE
THE OLD MILL
Ferry
Swan River
PERTH
0   500 metres
0   500 yards
North
South Perth Esplanade
KWINANA FREEWAY
LABOUCHERE ROAD
Sir James Mitchell Park
Wiccombe Place
Perth Zoological Gardens
MILL POINT ROAD

MOUNTS BAY ROAD

train on the **Indian-Pacific** (see p. 404). (*Railway Terminal, Summers St; tel 13 2232.*)

The **East Perth Rail and Interstate Bus Terminal** (not Perth Station on *Wellington St*) is where trains, buses and Westrail country buses arrive.

GETTING AROUND

Perth is now a large city covering 5369 sq km, but it is still attractive, still easy to explore and enjoy. The **Swan River** – named after the unique black birds discovered there more than 166 years ago – runs through the city. A park and recreation area on the foreshore, on the south side of the central business district, gives the city an open and spacious feeling. At the western end, the city slopes towards **Kings Park**, which is one of the jewels of this city and is arguably the finest city park in Australia. It was created as a public reserve in 1872 as Perth Park but was renamed in 1901. It covers about 4 sq km on the slopes and summit of **Mt Eliza** – more a prominent hill than a mountain – and overlooks the city and the river. Early in the morning the views are quite stunning and anyone who visits Perth and does not spend some time in Kings Park is making a serious error of judgment. It is beautiful all year round, but in the wildflower season the displays are spectacular.

To help you enjoy the pleasant climate there are 19 beaches in the city area. Although not to be compared with Sydney in this regard – Sydney has over 50 – they are all within easy reach using the suburban train and bus network and, because of the climate, are nearly always useable. **Leighton** is popular with windsurfers, **North Cottesloe** is known for topless sunbathers and the younger ravers head for **Swanbourne. Burns Beach** is small and safe, being protected by a reef. **Mullaloo Beach** is a very safe family swimming beach as are **Waterman's Bay, North Beach** and **Hamersley**, which all provide very safe reef-protected areas for families. **Scarborough Beach** is very good for surfing, but can be very dangerous for inexperienced swimmers when the surf is rough.

There is truly a beach for everyone. Most metropolitan beaches are patrolled at weekends and public holidays during the summer season, which runs from October to March.

Perth is a compact city so getting around is fairly easy. Indeed, walking is the preferred mode of transport as Perth is a city that takes its pedestrians seriously. Perth also has more cycling pathways than any other city in Australia and they extend as far as the port of **Fremantle** in the south and to **Marmion** in the north. There are cycling trails along the banks of the river and through Kings Park. This, and the climate, make Perth a cyclist's delight. (On **Rottnest Island**, only 22 km offshore, it is, indeed, the only way to go. See p. 296.)

Public Transport

Within the Free Transit Zone, basically the business district up to one station each side of the main Perth railway station, bus travel is free – an excellent price. For more information *tel: 13 2213.*

One of the better ways to explore Perth is on the **Perth Tram**. This is not really a tram, but a wooden replica built to resemble the first trams which operated in Perth from 1899. The full tour takes about 1½hrs but you can get off at any of the places that it visits and reboard later on. The driver gives a commentary, which is informed and not overly-intrusive.

There is another of the converted buses trams touring the city, which gives you a tour lasting much more than an hour and covers all the main tourists sites of the city for $12. You can get on and off the tram as often as you like. More information; *tel: 9367 9204.*

Taxis can be hailed in the street or called on the easily memorised numbers of *9333 3333* or *9444 4444.*

STAYING IN PERTH

Accommodation

Hyatt Regency Perth Hotel, *99 Adelaide Terrace; tel: 225 1234.* **Sheraton Perth Hotel**, *207 Adelaide Terrace; tel: 325 0501.* **Perth Parmelia Hilton**, *Mill St; tel: 322 3622.* **Perth Parkroyal** (*SPH*), *54 Terrace Rd; tel: 325 3811.* **Mercure Hotel – Perth**, *10 Irwin St; tel: 325 0481.* **Novotel Langley Hotel**,

Adelaide Terrace and Hill St; tel: 221 1200. **The Sebel of Perth Hotel**, 37 Pier St; tel: 325 7655. **Princes Hotel – Perth** (Accor), 334 Murray St; tel: 322 2844. **Orchard Hotel** (FL), corner Milligan and Wellington Sts; tel: 327 7000. **Kings Perth Hotel**, 517 Hay St; tel: 325 6555. **Perth Travelodge** (SPH), 778–788 Hay St; tel: 321 9141. **Criterion Hotel**, 560 Hay St; tel: 325 5155. **Chateau Commodore Perth Hotel**, 417 Hay St (corner Victoria Ave); tel: 325 0461. **Perth Ambassador Hotel**, 196 Adelaide Terrace; tel: 325 1455. **Miss Maud Swedish Hotel**, 97 Murray St; tel: 325 3900. **Sullivans Hotel**, 166 Mounts Bay Rd; tel: 321 8022. **Inntown Hotel**, corner Murray and Pier Sts; tel: 325 2133. **New Esplanade Hotel Perth**, 18 The Esplanade; tel: 325 2000.

Airways City Hotel, 195 Adelaide Terrace; tel: 323 7799. **City Waters Lodge Hotel**, 118 Terrace Rd; tel: 325 1566. **Baileys Parkside Motel-Hotel**, 150 Bennett St; tel: 325 3788. **Wentworth Hotel Plaza**, 300 Murray St; tel: 481 1000. **Carlton Hotel**, 248 Hay St; tel: 325 2092. **Court Hotel**, 50 Beaufort St; tel: 328 5292. **Pacific Motel**, corner Harold and Stirling Sts; tel: 328 5599. **Lone Saloon City Backpackers**, 167 Beaufort St; tel: 328 7566.

There are four youth hostels in the city: **HI: Newcastle St** (just E. of Pier St); tel: 328 1135; **HI: Northbridge**, 42–48 Francis St; tel: 328 7794; **HI: Britannia Backpackers**, 253 William St; tel: 328 6121; **HI: Scarborough Beach**, Mandarin Gardens Hostel, 20–28 Wheatcroft St; tel: 341 5431.

Eating and Drinking

Il Fiume Ristorante, South Shore Plaza, corner Mends St; tel: 474 300. **Tequila Sunrise**, 38 Roe St; tel: 328 3770. **Individual Thai Restaurant**, 101 Edward St; tel: 227 6122. **Chada Thai Restaurant**, 326a Wellington St; tel: 322 2829.

Sri Melak, 313 William St; tel: 328 6406. **Kung Thai Restaurant**, 75 Aberdeen St; tel: 228 0878. **Moorings Restaurant**, Barrack St Jetty; tel: 325 4575. **Romany Restaurant**, 188 William St; tel: 328 8042. **Tien Court Restaurant**, 19 Lake St; tel: 228 2188. **Thai**

House Restaurant, 63 Aberdeen St; tel: 328 6074. **Fraser's Restaurant**, King's Park; tel: 9481 7100. Licensed. Serves breakfast as well as lunch and dinner daily, and has wonderful views over Perth.

Money

There are **Thomas Cook Foreign Exchange** branches at the following locations: Shops 22–23 Wesley Centre, 760 Hay St, tel: 321 2896; API/Bankwest, 15 William St, tel: 322 7111; and Shop 13, Perth Plaza Arcade, 650 Hay St, tel: 325 4655.

SHOPPING

The main shopping area is around the parallel streets of Hay and Murray with shopping arcades joining the two. It is a shopping area of international standards. To the north of the city is **Northbridge**, which could be thought of as the restaurant and night life area of the town.

Off the **Hay Street Mall** is **London Court**, which you may have mixed feelings about. It was built in 1937 in a pastiche of English Elizabethan architecture and is an arcade full of shops catering mainly to tourists. At each end of the court is a clock, and at the strike of the hour St George comes out and slays the dragon. Some visitors find it an unhappy anachronism, others find it cute and appealing.

SIGHTSEEING

Museums and Galleries

Perth seems to have more museums and well-preserved historic houses than any other comparable sized Australian city, although that may be because the city goes out of its way to publicise them.

Perhaps the most important is the **Western Australian Museum**, Francis St; tel: 328 4411, which is the largest in the state. It contains among its many displays Aboriginal artefacts, vintage and veteran cars and motor cycles, and the 11-tonne **Mundrabilla** meteorite. All this plus a dinosaur gallery. It may sound an odd and eclectic collection, but it seems to hang together and some of the displays are riveting. Open Mon–Fri, Sat 1300–1700, Sun

293

1030–1700. The complex in which it resides is also home to some of Perth's oldest buildings, including the old gaol and an early settler's cottage.

The **Fire Museum**, *corner Murray and Irwin Sts; tel: 323 9468*, was originally the head-quarters of the city fire brigade and has many displays of relatively modern fire fighting equipment. Open weekdays 1000–1500.

The **Old Mill**, *Southern end of the Narrows Bridge; tel: 367 5788*, was built in 1835 and was originally the only flour mill in the colony. This is a genuine windmill in the traditional style and, unlike other early windmills in Australia, it actually works. It was very important to the young colony, so important that the foundation stone was laid by the Governor, James Stirling. It worked as a mill until 1858, after which it was used for a series of different purposes ending up, along with the miller's cottage and surrounding grounds, as a museum of pioneer life in early Perth. Open Thur–Mon 1000–1600.

Tranby House, *Johnson Rd, Maylands; tel: 272 2630*, is one of the oldest houses in the state, built in 1839 by yeoman farmer Joseph Hardy. In 1975 it was taken over by the National Trust and restored as a colonial farmer's home. Open Wed–Sat 1400–1700, Sun 1100–1700 in winter; rest of the year Mon–Sat same hours. Closed in June.

Another colonial home houses the **Army Museum of Western Australia**, *2 Bulwer St; tel: 227 9269*, which boasts a major collection of military memorabilia. Open Sun 1300–1630.

Woodbridge, another colonial home, was built between 1883 and 1885 by Charles Harper. This two-storey historic home, which overlooks the Swan River in *Ford St, West Midland*, was at the time it was built considered to be one of the finest homes in Australia. It has now been restored by the National Trust and furnished in the appropriate style. Open Mon–Sat 1300–1600, Sun 1100–1700.

Stirk Cottage was the first home built in the Kalamunda district in 1881. Around it, on the site of the old **Kalamunda Railway station**, a history village has been built and this is now the largest folk museum in Western Australia. Open weekdays 1000–1500. Sun 1330–1630. Closed Thur.

At the **Motor Museum**, *Lord St, Whiteman Park; tel: 249 9457*, there are normally about 85 historic cars and 25 motor bikes on show. These are privately owned and the display seems to be totally changed about four times a year. Open Wed–Sat 1000–1600, Sun 1000–1700.

The **Museum of Childhood**, *Edith Cowan University, Claremont Campus, Bay Rd, Claremont, tel: 442 1373*, has a superb collection of dolls, toys and games along with a bush classroom plus several interactive displays. Open Mon–Fri 1000–1600, Sun 1400–1700. $2.

Art Gallery of Western Australia, *Perth Cultural Centre, Northbridge; tel: 328 7233*, has one of the better collections of aboriginal art in Australia. Open daily 1000–1700. Guided tours Tues–Fri at 1215 and Sat–Sun 1500.

The **Perth Mint**, *310 Hay St, E. Perth, tel: 421 7277*, is thought to be the world's oldest mint operating from the original premises. Among other delights, it produces the world's largest gold coin weighing in at 1 kg. It was established on the current site in 1899 and is now a specialist coin maker to the rest of Australia. Open weekdays 0900–1600, Sat 1000–1300; $3. From the viewing gallery you can see coins and medallions being minted and, from time to time, gold being poured into moulds. There is a museum of coins and prospecting and a shop which sells souvenirs, including gold coins.

Modern Attractions

There are also a lot of more modern attractions in the city. **Perth Institute of Contemporary Arts (PICA)**, *Perth Cultural Centre, 51 James St, Northbridge; tel: 227 6144*, promotes the creation, presentation and discussion of new and experimental arts. It covers all areas of art, including painting, sculpture, photography, performance art, film, video, computer art and writing. Open Tues–Sun 1100–1800. Admission free.

The **Scitech Discovery Centre**, *corner Railway Parade and Sutherland St, W. Perth; tel: 481 6295*, has well over 160 exhibits, which all promote the learning of scientific principles – and can keep you as happily employed as any fun-fair arcade. Open daily 1000–1700.

History

Captain James Sterling and a group of colonists first arrived in Perth on the *Parmelia* in 1829. On Aug 12 of that year, the **Swan River** was proclaimed Australia's third colony and the first of free settlers. For some years the Swan River served as the main means of communication.

The colony quickly progressed. In 1832 there were only 360 people but four years on there was a court house – the oldest surviving building – and Perth was proclaimed a city only 20 years later. There were no convicts in the Perth area until 1859, when the first convict ship *Scindian* arrived, and transportation continued until 1868.

The city had its first major push towards sizeable growth with the gold rushes to **Kalgoorlie** and **Coolgardie** in 1890. Presaging the future massive boom in modern office buildings within the city, the first steel and concrete building in Australia – **Her Majesty's Theatre** – was erected between 1901 and 1904.

The city was originally a group of interconnecting wards rather than a true city, but the **Greater Perth Movement** that ran from 1906 to 1912 saw them amalgamated into one city.

It's a Small World, *12 Parliament Pl., W. Perth; tel: 322 2020*, boasts that it has the finest collection in the world of miniature models in Australia, including animated displays of fairy tales, a miniature car museum, a model train display and dolls houses. Open Sun–Fri 1000–1700, Sat 1400–1700.

Ten minutes walk from the city centre is what was called the Barrack Street Jetty but which is now **Barrack Square**. This is a relatively new complex of cafés, shops and attractions known as **Old Perth Port**. This is where the **South Perth** ferry departs, which will take you across the river and to the zoo. There are also cruise boats, which go down river to Fremantle or on to Rottnest Island.

Wildlife

Lovers of wildlife are well catered for in Perth. The claim is that the **Perth Zoological Gardens** is the most popular zoo per capita of population in Australia, which is an odd sort of claim to make. It is only 15 mins from the city centre by bus or ferry from the Barrack St Jetty, and is set amid splendid gardens with walkways and picnic areas. The zoo, *Labouchere Rd, S. Perth; tel: 367 7988*, has a wide range of Australian fauna in the Australian Wildlife Park within the zoo, including numbats, quokkas, emus, kangaroos, wombats, wallabies and koala. There is also an African Savannah and a Nocturnal House. You will find plenty of pelicans at the zoo, but then you will find them on pretty much all of the waterways in the area, where they have bred prolifically. Open daily 1000–1700.

Caversham Wildlife, *Park Arthur St, West Swan; tel: 274 2202*, is in the Swan Valley, near **Guildford** and its main focus is Australian fauna. Open daily 0900–1700.

Armadale Reptile Centre, *South West Hwy 3 km south of the Albany Hwy; tel: 399 6927*, has what is claimed to be Western Australia's largest collection of reptiles – over 200 of them. There is also a walk-through enclosure with quokkas and Australian parrots.

Cohuna Koala Park, *Mills Rd E., Gosnells*, is in bushland in the **Darling Range** and has a koala show every day. There now seems to be evidence that koalas suffer from stress when held and cuddled by visitors, and this is now going out of favour. There are also walks through aviaries with Australian birds and the park has a wide selection of Australian animals. Open 1000–1700 daily.

Hillary's Boat Harbour in **Sorrento** is well worth a visit if only for the **Underwater World**, the Perth seaside oceanarium, which is right next to **Sorrento Quay**. Like most modern aquariums it has a submerged acrylic tunnel so that you can have a fish-eye view of the world and can inspect some of the 2000-odd marine animals on display. There is also an audiovisual presentation in the 100-seat marine theatre. Aquarium open daily 0900–1700.

Adventure World, *179 Progress Dr.; tel: 417 9666*, is at **Bibra Lake** and is billed as

295

A Literary City

Perth has ever been a literary sort of city. In recent times Elspeth Huxley wrote in *Their Shining Eldorado* (1967): 'Most cities use the rivers on which they lie primarily as highways and sewers. Perth is the only modern city I can recall that puts first the uses of embellishment, as Venice must once have done.' In writing that she followed in a great tradition of people commentating, nearly always favourably, about what has been claimed to be the remotest city on earth.

Indeed, the only unfavourable comments come from the earliest discoverers and settlers. In 1697 Willem de Vlamingh sighted what he called 'Swaene rivier' and described the land as 'arid, barren and wild.' Lieutenant Henry Bunbury was posted there in the British army from 1836 and wrote in his reminiscences, *Early Days in Western Australia*: 'Perth itself is a most dismal place, duller than anything you imagine, but as I came here of my own accord I have no right to grumble.'

After that it was praises all the way. In 1901 May Vivienne in *Travels in Western Australia* wrote: 'I can never ride or drive through that Park (Mount Eliza) and gaze in the beautiful scene below without feeling that God has indeed given us a lovely world to live in.'

Earlier, the much travelled Anthony Trollope wrote in 1872 that Perth was 'a very pretty town built on a lake of brackish water formed by the Swan River.'

The water is no longer brackish but Perth still is, indeed, 'very pretty.'

Western Australia's biggest water-based fun park, with some thirty different rides to entertain the bold and scare the timid. Open daily 1000–1700, Oct–Apr.

You can get a taste of the countryside only 40 mins from Perth at the **Tumbulgum Farm**, *South West Hwy, Mundijong; tel: 525 5888,* which is a working farm that has a farm show, including sheep mustering and shearing, whip cracking and an Aboriginal corroboree. Open Wed–Sun 0930–1700.

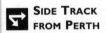

SIDE TRACK
FROM PERTH

ROTTNEST ISLAND

Tourist Information: Rottnest Island Authority; *tel: 372 9729.*

One of the most popular holiday resorts for the people of Perth is the island of Rottnest, which is only 21km north-north-west of Fremantle, opposite the mouth of the Swan River. The island is low lying and mainly sand. Rottnest covers 1900 hectares and is about 11 km long by 4½ km wide.

The island has five salt, shallow lakes of over 200 hectares. The beaches and bays of the island are mainly protected by offshore reefs, which makes swimming very safe. No cars are allowed on Rottnest and the favourite way of getting around is by bicycle. You can hire a bike or take a tour of the old convict buildings, Aboriginal prison and the gun emplacements from World War II. The island has nearly 40 km of coastline and offers excellent skin diving because of the multiplicity of wrecks in the area. There are over 150 species of fish in the surrounding waters.

In 1696, the Dutch captain, William Vlamingh, landed on the island and named it Rottnest, which is Dutch for rat's nest. This is because he mistook the local marsupials – quokkas – for large rats. They are, in fact, wallabies that are only found in their wild state on Rottnest, and are protected. Many of them have become quite tame.

There is a ferry to the island from *Barrack St Jetty*, Perth, Fremantle or Hillarys Boat Harbour. There are also regular flights from Perth Airport. ⬟

PERTH–ALBANY

In driving from Perth to Albany you are travelling along one of the most favoured parts of the country. It attracts English people like a magnet and, as you get to the sheltered bays and rugged headlands of the Rainbow Coast, it seems as if you are, indeed, in a British colony. Perhaps it is the temperate climate, perhaps the scenery, perhaps the number of like-minded people in the area, but the number of relatively wealthy Poms who settle in this area is quite remarkable.

There is only 410 km, between Albany and Perth but the country around Albany is very different with bays, karri forests and the Porongurup and Stirling Range National Parks.

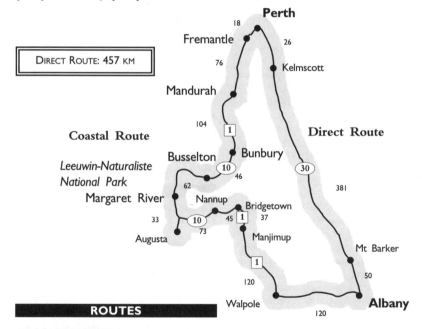

DIRECT ROUTE: 457 KM

Perth
18
Fremantle   26
76
Kelmscott
Mandurah
104
Coastal Route
1
Direct Route
Busselton   Bunbury
Leeuwin-Naturaliste   10   46   30
National Park   62   381
Margaret River   Nannup
33   10   45   1   37   Bridgetown
73   Manjimup
Augusta
1
50
120   Mt Barker
Walpole   Albany
120

297

ROUTES

DIRECT ROUTE

The easiest way to drive to **Albany** is to follow Rte 30, the Albany Hwy, south-east from the centre of Perth. At Kelmscott, 26 km out of the city centre, Rte 20 branches off south, but stay on the left and on Rte 30, which cuts across the south-west corner of the state all the way to Albany via Kojonup and **Mt Barker**, a journey of about 6 hrs.

COASTAL ROUTE

A more interesting route, with plenty of worthwhile overnight and longer stops, is to follow the coast right around, keeping first the **Indian Ocean** and then the **Southern Ocean** on your right. Take Rte 1 from central Perth. The road crosses the **Swan River** as the Kwinana Freeway. Once safely across the river, it turns smartly to the right towards the sea, changing its name to Leach Hwy. It heads towards the port of **Fremantle**, a suburb of Perth, with a style and atmosphere of its own.

On the outskirts of Fremantle Rte 1 takes a 90-degree turn to the right, now under the name of *Stock Rd*, which shortly becomes *Rockingham Rd* as it wends its way down the coast. Rte 1 changes its road name – but keeps its route numbering – several times in the next 20 or so kilometres. It changes to *Patterson Rd* before it gets to **Rockingham**, 47 km from Perth, and changes again to *Ennis Ave* as it leaves. Then, for the run down to **Mandurah**, 75 km from Perth, it becomes the *Fremantle Rd*.

The road runs directly through Mandurah, hugging close to the coast as the *Old Coast Rd*, with the waters of the Harvey Estuary on its left and Lake Clifton on the right, and beyond that the Indian Ocean. The road runs almost as straight as an arrow, with lakes almost always between the road and the sea, until it reaches first **Australind** (there is a major bypass), and then the outskirts of **Bunbury**, which is 180 km south of Perth – a relaxing morning or afternoon drive in Australian terms.

Leave Rte 1 at Bunbury to head right, and south-west, down Rte 10, the Bussel Hwy, and follow the coast down to **Busselton**. Rte 10 turns sharply inland here, to run as the Russell Hwy through Cowaramup to **Margaret River**. Leave Rte 10 as it turns inland and continue along the coast road to **Dunsborough** and then 13 km to **Cape Naturaliste**, where you have entered the **Leeuwin-Naturaliste National Park** that stretches for 120 km along the coast to **Augusta**. If you visit Cape Naturaliste you will need to track back the short distance to Dunsborough and then you can follow the *Caves Rd* for 102 km to Augusta and then to **Cape Leeuwin**. The route runs through the 15,500-hectare coastal park which contains scenic coastline, coastal heathlands and a wide range of woodlands. This is one of the clearly marked tourist drives which, following international convention, are marked with brown signs, in this case Tourist Drive 250.

Halfway along this drive you come to the Margaret River. To visit or overnight at the town of **Margaret River**, you will have to drive some 9 km inland from the *Caves Rd*.

Having visited Cape Leeuwin back-track the 5 km to Augusta, and continue to Karridale to pick up Rte 10 again – now called the Brockman Hwy. This takes you to **Nannup** and from there it is 45 km east to **Bridgetown** to rejoin the South West Hwy, Rte 1, turning south (right) onto this road and proceeding through **Manjimup** to the coast again at **Walpole**, on the Nornalup Inlet of the Southern Ocean. Now calling itself the South Coast Hwy, Rte 1 continues eastwards out of Walpole, through Denmark to **Albany**.

Although the Coastal Route may sound slightly complex, it manages to take in some of Western Australia's most charming scenery in a distance of only about 734 km, which is comfortable over several days.

TRAINS AND BUSES

Two trains a day make the 2-hr journey from Perth to Bunbury, OTT table 9036. There are also buses (2½ hrs to Bunbury) which also call at Mandurah (just over 1 hr). OTT table 9134 details these services and bus connections from Bunbury to Busselton (another 1 hr) and Albany (6 hrs from Bunbury). Alternatively there are bus connections from Perth to Albany which do not travel the route of this chapter, taking 5¾ hrs – OTT table 9139.

FREMANTLE

Tourist Information: Information Centre, *Fremantle Town Hall; tel: 430 2346.*

ACCOMMODATION AND FOOD

Esplanade Hotel Fremantle, *corner Marine Terrace and Essex St; tel: 432 4000.* **Tradewinds Hotel**, *59 Canning Hwy, E. Fremantle; tel: 339 8188.* **Pier 21 Resort**, *7–9 John St; tel: 336 2555.* **Fremantle Hotel**, *corner High and Cliff Sts; tel: 430 4300.* **Sunny's Shining On The Swan Hotel**, *6 Canning Hwy; tel: 339 1888.* **Norfolk Hotel**, *47 South Terrace; tel: 335 5405.*

Sukho Thai Restaurant, *6 Bannister St; tel: 335.* **Wesley Way Lunch Bar**, *12 Wesley Way Arcade, Fremantle; tel: 430 4147.* **Bengal Curry House**, *18 Philimore St; tel: 335 2400.* **Regal Diamond Seafood Restaurant**, *2 Market St; tel: 430 8845.* **Oreinthyia**

Restaurant, *corner South Terrace and Parry St;* *tel: 430 7797.*

When the main way of getting to Australia was by passenger ship, Fremantle rejoiced in the title of 'Gateway to Australia'. In time the liner was replaced by the jet aircraft and Fremantle slipped back into small-town somnolence. Then Australia won the Americas' Cup and the defence was set to be held in Fremantle in 1987. As it happened, Australia lost the cup but Fremantle won the prize. In preparation for the Cup defence it was renovated, painted and generally remodelled, and a slew of new buildings appeared. After those heady Cup days the city did not return to somnolence. Rather it has become the vibrant port city of Perth. Yes, there are people who regard Fremantle as merely a suburb of Perth, but Fremantle is a destination in its own right – one of the best preserved 19th-century seaports in the world, with over 150 buildings classified by the National Trust. It is a visual delight.

The name comes from Captain Charles Howe Fremantle of the *Challenger,* which was one of the three ships that brought the first European settlers to Western Australia in 1829. Indeed, it was Captain Fremantle who, at the age of 28, formally took possession of Western Australia for Britain that same year. The town started in 1829 and by 1832 a well-designed plan was in place to construct a suitable port for the new colony. The first town trust was established in 1848, although industry, in the form of whaling and boat building, had already been established a dozen years or more.

The first convicts, brought there because of a shortage of servants, arrived in 1850 and the last were some Irish Fenian rebels who arrived in 1868. (They were to escape in 1875 on the American whaler *Catalpa.*)

The port boomed. First with the gold rush at the end of the century, and further when the liners started to arrive; as late as 1960 a new passenger terminal was built to welcome the arrivals. Then came the lull with the decline of liner traffic, followed by The Americas' Cup defence. Alan Bond's *Australia 2* syndicate had taken the Americas Cup from the New York

Yacht Club in 1983, thus breaking an unbeaten run of 132 years. The defence brought spectators from all over the world. Now Fremantle is once again a busy port – but this time for container ships and a largish fishing fleet.

To get to Fremantle, you can either cross over the Swan River from the northern suburbs, drive in from the east past **Cantonment Hill**, or arrive by ferry down the Swan River.

Fremantle's distinctive style can perhaps best be flavoured along the **South Terrace**, sometimes called the **Cappuccino Strip** because of its outdoor cafés. Although Fremantle is small in area, it is very rich in attractions. The buildings are classified by the National Trust because of their gold rush-era architecture and the **markets** are lively, even strident. Perhaps the one that best gives the true flavour of the port is the market held at *84 South Terrace* from about 1000 until late every Fri, Sat and Sun.

Among the sights worth seeing is the **Western Australia Maritime Museum**, *Cliff St; tel: 355 8211* (open Mon–Thur 1030–1700, Sat–Sun 1300–1700). This has displays of maritime history connected with the port, as well as a reconstruction of timbers from the 1629 wreck of the *Batavia,* which was wrecked off the west coast. **The Fremantle Museum and Arts Centre**, *1 Finnerty St; tel: 430 7966,* was built by convicts and was once an asylum for women. It is considered one of the most distinguished buildings in a port full of distinguished buildings. It has an excellent history of the port and the adjoining coast. Open Thur–Sun 1300–1700.

The first gaol in the Swan River colony was the **Round House**, *10 Arthur Head,* which was completed in 1831 and is thus the state's oldest public building. There is a tunnel that runs from the grounds, which is where the whalers carried their supplies down to **Bathers Beach**. Open daily 1000–1700. A more up-to-date prison – the Round House was only in use as such for a comparatively short period of time – is **Fremantle Prison**, *1 The Terrace; tel: 430 7177,* which was finished in 1855 and was in use as a prison until relatively recently. Open daily 1000–1800. And for those with a sense of the macabre there are candlelight tours Wed and Fri at 1930.

299

Boats are part of the way of life of Fremantle and the **Historic Boats Museum**, *B shed Victoria Quay; tel: 335 8211*, has nearly twenty craft on display. Open daily 1300–1700.

MANDURAH

Tourist Information: Mandurah Tourist Bureau, *5 Pinjarra Rd; tel: 535 1155*.

ACCOMMODATION

Silver Sands Resort, *Mandurah Terrace; tel: 535 7722*. **Atrium Resort Hotel**, *Ormsby Terrace; tel: 535 6633*. **Mandurah Gates Resort**, *110 Mandurah Terrace; tel: 581 1222*. **Crabshell Motel**, *corner Gibson and Sholl Sts; tel: 535 5577*. **Blue Bay Motel**, *11 Oversby Rd; tel: 535 2743*. **Brighton Hotel**, *Mandurah Terrace; tel: 535 1242*.

EATING AND DRINKING

Mandurah Internet Café, *Shop 2/49 Pinjarra Rd at the Sutton St lights; tel: 9586 1414*. 7 days 1000–2100. Coffee and snacks whilst trawling the Internet. **Chasers Restaurant**, *Greyhounds, Gordon Rd; tel: 9581 7244*. Mon, Fri dinner. **Dancing Dolphin**, *3 Rees Pl.; tel: 9534 4106*. Tues–Sun lunch/dinner. **Edwards Waterfront**, *5a Mandurah Terrace; tel: 9581 1248*. Sun–Fri lunch, 7 days dinner. **Hog's Breath Cafe**, *115 Mandurah Terrace; tel: 9581 1122*. 7 days, 1130–late.

Jolly Frog, *Captains Court, Florida; tel: 9534 4144*. Daily lunch/dinner. **Outlaws Mexican**, *149 Mandurah Terrace; tel: 9535 5525*. 7 days lunch/dinner. **Chinese Smorgasbord**, *98 Mandurah Terrace; tel: 9581 3992*. Dinner. **Sunbreakers**, *Upstairs 84 Mandurah Terrace; tel: 9581 5556*. Tues–Fri 1200–1400, 7 days from 1800. **Princess Palace Randell's Restaurant**, *corner Pinjarra Rd and Randell St; tel: 9535 2187*. Wed–Sun dinner, Wed–Fri lunch.

SIGHTSEEING

Mandurah has a population of just under 50,000 and is rapidly expanding. The name comes from an Aboriginal word *mandjar*, which means either 'trading place', 'watering place' or 'meeting place of tribes'. This popular resort, only 60 km south of Perth and an easy 1 hr drive by road, is on the **Peel Inlet**, where the

waters of the Murray, Serpentine and Harvey rivers all enter the sea. The result is a very large inland expanse of water that includes the Peel Inlet and the **Harvey Estuary**. These are connected to the Indian Ocean by the artificial Dawesville Cut and the natural estuary that runs past Mandurah downtown. Running parallel with it and separating it from the Indian Ocean is the long skinny shape of **Lake Clifton**.

This profusion of waterways plus the range of beaches facing on to the Indian Ocean means that Mandurah is a major centre for boating and fishing, as well as birdwatching around Lake Clifton. But the major effect is that it attracts possibly more bottle-nosed dolphins than anywhere else in Australia and, indeed, has frequently been referred to as the **Dolphin Capital**. The pods travel along the coastline and then swim into the estuary and the rivers. These dolphins have become very used to human companionship and will, for example, race kayaks up the river. One of them, distinguishable by a fin with part chopped off, is well known to the locals as 'U-boat' and literally seems to want to play with humans.

The Peel Inlet is named after Thomas Peel (the town was originally called Peeltown), who was a pioneer settler, arriving in 1830. He was a great eccentric who intended to reintroduce the old English feudal system and planned extensive town and estates. It failed when the labourers refused to be serfs. Peel died in Mandurah in disillusionment and squalor 30 years after he arrived. The town was not founded until sixty years later and even today is still a sleepy seaside town, depending mainly on resort spending for its income, although it has its share of commuters to Perth. However, this sleepiness can be something of an illusion as no small town in Australia uses the Internet as aggressively and as intelligently as Mandurah. It even has most of its shops listed in a cybermall.

The **Peel Region** covers nearly 5700 sq km in total, comprising of the City of Mandurah and the Shires of **Murray**, **Waroona**, **Boddington** and **Serpentine-Jarrahdale**. In addition to the 75 km of attractive coastline, this region has some of Western Australia's finest Jarrah forests. The Peel Inlet covers an area of 155 sq km and is so protected that it is perfect for small boat sailing and cruising. Boats, canoes, surfcats and houseboats can be hired. Fishing is also a major attraction, as is crabbing. At the **Western Rosella Bird Park** on the *Old Pinjarra Rd*, 5 km from Mandurah, there is a large selection of Australian birds – this area is famous for the variety of its avian life – in a natural bush setting.

Currently being built, and moving through a staggered opening schedule, is **The Boardwalk**. A 500m boardwalk, already built, leads visitors past al fresco-style restaurants and cafés, tourism-related shops, boat and ferry moorings and into **Mandjar Square**. The facilities at The Boardwalk include a Performing Arts Centre, the Peel Discovery Centre, a new War Memorial and gardens, and a cinema complex.

A much older establishment is **Hall's Cottage** (*Leighton Rd;* open Sun 1400–1700), which was built in 1835 and is maintained by the local historical society. The house was originally built by early settler Henry Edward Hall and now contains a record of the history of the town. The same theme can be found in the **Mandurah Community Museum**, also on *Pinjarra Rd*. It was originally a brick school built in 1898. Open Tues and Sun.

BUNBURY

Tourist Information: Bunbury Tourist Bureau, *Old Railway Station, Carmody Pl.; tel: (097) 217922.*

ACCOMMODATION

Lord Forrest Hotel, *Symmons St; tel: 21 9966.* **Admiral Motor Inn,** *56 Spencer St; tel: 21 7322.* **Welcome Inn** *(FL), Ocean Dr.; tel: 21 3100.* **Clifton Beach Motel** *(BW), 2 Molloy St; tel: 21 4300.* **Lighthouse Inn Beach Resort,** *Carey St; tel: 21 1311.* **Fawlty Towers Lodge Motel,** *Ocean Dr.; tel: 21 2427.* **Bunbury Motel** *(BU), Forrest Ave; tel: 21 7333.* **Bussell Motor Hotel,** *Bussell Hwy; tel: 21 1022.* **Prince of Wales Hotel,** *41 Stephen St; tel: 21 2016.* **Rose Hotel,** *Victoria St; tel: 21 4533.* **Ocean Drive Motel,** *121–135 Ocean Dr.; tel: 21 2033.* **Parade on the Water,** *100 Stirling St; tel: 21 2093.* **Burlington Hotel,** *Victoria St; tel: 21 2075.* **Captain Bunbury Hotel,** *8 Victoria St; tel: 21*

2021. **Highway Motor Hotel,** *Forrest Ave; tel: 21 4966.*

EATING AND DRINKING

Memories of Bond Store, *next to the Entertainment Centre, Victoria St; tel: 9791 2922.* **Eagle Towers,** *192 Spencer St; tel: 9721 2762.* Open Tues–Sun. Seafood. Licensed. **Top of the Town Garden Restaurant,** *4th Floor, 91 Victoria St; tel: 9721 6979.* Wed–Sun 1830–2200. **Garden Palace Chinese Restaurant,** *8 Old Coast Rd, Australind; tel: 9725 1333.* 7 days 1700–late. **Bussell Bistro,** *Bussell Hwy; tel: 9721 1022.* Mon–Sat 1200–1400, 1800–2100. **A Lump of Rump,** *119 Beach Rd; tel: 9721 8691.* Tues–Sun 1800–2030. Steak, chicken, fish. **Uncle Vinnies,** *113 Spencer St; tel: 9721 7247.* Tues–Fri 1200–1400, Tues–Sun 1730–2030. Italian.

SIGHTSEEING

Some 180 km south of Perth and facing the Indian Ocean, Bunbury is the second largest town in Western Australia. It lies on the junction of the **Collie** and **Preston Rivers** and covers 61.2 sq km. The name comes from Lt Bunbury, who explored the district in 1836. The town was originally called Port Leschenault and this name is remembered in the Leschenault Estuary, which points like a long finger to the town. The name comes from a French expedition to the area in 1803, led by Captain Louis de Freycinet. The early farmers in the area had a ready market with American whalers who sheltered in **Koombana Bay**. The township was laid out in 1836 and convict labour was imported in the 1850s to assist in the construction of roads and buildings and the development of farms. **St Marks Anglican church** in the nearby hamlet of **Picton** was built in 1842. This is the oldest church in Western Australia.

Bunbury is the centre of an area that the CSIRO – the Australian government scientific research body – has identified as the most comfortable climatic environment for human existence.

Just north of Bunbury is **Australind**, which is on the edge of an estuary system that provides sheltered waters for sailing.

301

Bunbury grew in importance as a port for the timber industry in the nearby hardwood forests and then switched to agriculture and, of late, has been involved in the export of minerals. The Greater Bunbury Area includes, **Australind, Eaton** and **Gelorup**, which have become commuter territory for Bunbury.

The Leschenault Inlet abounds with bird life, with pelicans, ducks, black swans, magpies, wagtails, parrots and many others. In the area are also kangaroos, wallabies and possums but its true wealth lies in the abundance of flora – the wildflowers which have made Western Australia famous.

Koombana Bay has a **Dolphin Education Centre**, and most days, if you arrive early, you will be greeted by dolphins. They apparently enjoy swimming with humans, but you are advised not to touch them.

Fishing in Bunbury is very popular. In the crabbing season Blue Manna crabs are caught by the thousand in the harbour and the estuary. **Big Swamp Wildlife and Bird Park**, *Prince Phillip Dr.,* (look for signs off *Ocean Dr.*), 3 km from the city centre, has most Australian mammals in abundance. It also has a large walk-in aviary where you are invited to feed the lorikeets. Open daily except Tues 1000–1700.

The City itself has several attractive heritage buildings dating from around the 18th century. Many have been totally rehabilitated. The tourist office has *Walk About* and *Browse Around* brochures, offering self-guided tours.

The Bunbury Art Gallery, *Wittenoom St,* is in what was the **Old Convent of Mercy** building. This was opened and blessed in December 1897 and stands on the site of the original Catholic Chapel, which was built in the late 1860s. In 1981 the Convent was purchased by the Bunbury City Council and the building developed as the **Bunbury and Western Australia Art Gallery and Community Arts Complex**. Open daily.

The Bunbury Entertainment Centre, on the shores of the Leschenault Inlet, was opened in 1990 and contains the largest entertainment venue in regional Western Australia. A state of the art, multifunctional complex, it can cater for straight theatre, concerts, films, conferences and exhibitions.

BUSSELTON

Tourist Information: Busselton Tourist Bureau, *Civic Centre Complex, Southern Dr.; tel: (097) 521 268.*

ACCOMMODATION AND FOOD

Geographe Bayview Resort, *Bussell Hwy; tel: 55 4166.* **Abbey Beach Resort**, *595 Bussell Hwy; tel: 01 800 017 097.* **Amaroo Motor Lodge**, *25 Bussell Hwy; tel: 52 1544.* **Vasse River Resort**, *70 Causeway Rd; tel: 018 81 222.*

Beaches Café, *51 Bussell Hwy; tel: 52 2558.* **Lump Of Rump Steakhouse**, *Queen St; tel: 52 1872.* **The Fig Bistro**, *42 Fig Tree Lane; tel: 52 3561.* **Tiffins Indian Restaurant**, *48 Queen St; tel: 52 2549.* **Tails Of The Bay**, *42 Adelaide St; tel: 52 4032.* BYO. Seafood. **Ching's Dynasty Chinese Restaurant**, *20 Queen St; tel: 52 2668.*

SIGHTSEEING

Busselton, 229 km south of Perth, can truly be regarded as the gateway to the Cape as it is the northernmost town in the south-west **Cape Region**. It is a seaside town on the shores of **Geographe Bay** and has several broad beaches and sheltered coves. This was one of the first areas settled in the state, and takes its name from the early settler family headed by John Bussell. One of the main features of the town is the wooden jetty, which is about 2 km long. It was initially erected in 1865 with further extension being made over the years. It was abandoned as a commercial proposition in 1972 and the weather and fires have taken their toll. The jetty, off *Queen St*, has now been given a new lease of life by the local **Jetty Preservation Society** and is a most attractive place to stroll or ride the train – not on rails – which travels slowly up and down the jetty.

In the town near the **Vasse River** is **St Mary's Church** which is built of limestone with a shingled roof of oak. This is the oldest stone church in the state having been consecrated in 1848. It was built with help from the congregation of St Mary's church in Portsea, England where John Bussell's father served.

The **Ballarat Loco** is in *Victoria Sq.*, on the corner of Queen and Albert Sts, and is reputedly the first steam locomotive in Western Australia. It was built in 1871 for the price of 800 Australian pounds and its job was to haul hard wood logs from the local forests.

The **Busselton Historical Society** has taken over and restored the **Old Butter Factory** in *Peel Terrace* and now runs it as a local museum concentrating particularly on the early days of the butter industry. **Wonnerup House**, which dates from 1834 when it was owned by George Layman, is a historic home site which has been restored by the National Trust, as has the school opposite. It is a short drive along *Layman Rd*, north of the town.

Old Courthouse Arts Centre, *Queen St*, is now the home of the **Busselton Arts Council**. It contains an art gallery and a series of studios for artists working on a variety of crafts.

LEEUWIN-NATURALISTE NATIONAL PARK

The Leeuwin-Naturaliste National Park is a spectacular stretch of coast between Cape Naturaliste – named after a French survey vessel and not another example of Australian misplaced gentility – and Cape Leeuwin. This is perhaps the most important of Western Australia's national parks and is the result of an amalgamation in the 1970s, which ended in a park of 15,439 hectares, covering most of the coastline with a break in the middle where the **Margaret River** comes down to the sea.

The scenery of the park is varied, ranging from some very wild seashores to some beautiful sheltered beaches, which offer excellent surfing, and rugged granite ridges running down to rocky headlands. There are also heathlands and forests which are mainly karri. Inland the water eating its way through the limestone has created a wide range of caves, including the **Yallingup Cave**, renowned for its crystalline formations, which runs for 40m underground

Within the park there are several camping and caravan sites and, as it is only 260 km south of Perth, this is a very popular weekend attraction. Car access to the park is easy, as *Caves Rd*, a major tourist highway, skirts its edges. When walking on this coast take great care to avoid the dangers presented by crumbling cliff edges.

MARGARET RIVER

Tourist Information: Margaret River Tourist Bureau, *corner Tunbridge Rd and Bussell Hwy; tel: (097) 57 2911*.

ACCOMMODATION AND FOOD

Captain Freycinet Inn – Margaret River *(FL)*, *corner Bussell Hwy and Tunbridge St; tel: 57 2033*. **Margaret River Hotel**, *Bussell Hwy; tel: 57 2655*. **Colonial Motel**, *Wallcliffe Rd; tel: 57 2633*. **Edge of the Forest Accommodation**, *25 Bussell Hwy; tel: 57 2351*. **1885 Inn Motel**, *Farrelly St; tel: 57 2302*.

Leeuwin Estate, *Stevens Rd; tel: 57 6253*. **Mama's Oriental**, *Bussell Hwy; tel: 57 2622*. **Margaret River Chinese Restaurant**, *135 Bussell Hwy; tel: 57 2788*. **Harry's Mexican Wave**, *157 Bussell Hwy; tel: 57 2703*. **Country Kitchen Delights**, *99 Bussell Hwy; tel: 57 2611*. **The 1885 Inn and Restaurant**, *Farrelly St; tel: 57 3177*. Licensed. **Café Forte**, *101 Bussell Hwy; tel: 57 3101*.

SIGHTSEEING

There is Margaret River the town and Margaret River the area which, at a stretch, could be thought of as occupying a substantial part of the territory defined by Cape Naturaliste in the north and Cape Leeuwin in the south. It is to the landward side of the Leeuwin-Cape Naturaliste National Park which intermittently defends the coast. The Margaret River area is famous in Australia for two reasons – surf and wine. It could be argued, it is certainly argued by West Australians, that the best wine in Australia comes from the Margaret River vineyards. And it could also be argued that the best surfing is off the coast of the Margaret River area. To surfing and wine you could add caves, because this is one of the finest areas in Australia for pot holing and caving, and the caves contain many important fossils.

The area is defined by the *Caves Rd*, which meanders gently down the coast from **Dunsborough** to **Augusta**. Much of the land west of the road is part of the Leeuwin-Naturaliste National Park, which protects and displays its caves, forests and coastline. It contains the **Boranup Forest** with massive stands of western karri, some of the world's tallest trees.

303

The town, which is 277 km south of Perth and 10 km inland from where the river flows into the Indian Ocean, was named after Margaret Wicher, a friend of the Bussell family, a local family of settlers who settled along the **Vasse valley** in 1834 and gave their name to Busselton. It was at Margaret River that Alfred Bussell, in 1865, tried to emulate a grand English country house by building **Wallcliffe**. The town developed slowly between 1910 and 1920. The railway arrived in 1927 and closed thirty years later. Then, in the early 1970s, wine growing was successfully attempted and since then the district has boomed.

There is an amazing cave structure running throughout the area. The best known are **Lake**, **Jewel**, **Mammoth** and **Moondyne**, which are open for guided tours. At the Lake Cave a winding staircase leads down to a gigantic crater. There is an underground lake, stalactites and stalagmites that reflect the lighting of the cave. Just 8 km north of Augusta, on *Caves Rd*, is **Jewel Cave**, which was only discovered in 1957. The 27,000 year old Tasmanian Tiger (Thyiacine) fossil was found here and other fossils are still being discovered. The cave was so named because the stalactites reflect like sparkling gems. **Mammoth** is 21 km south of Margaret River and contains fossils, some of which are over 35,000 years old. The cave was first noted in 1850, explored some 45 years ago and was opened to the public in 1904. **Lake Cave** is 3.2 km further south and has limestone formations. It was first noted in 1867 by Fanny Bussell. **Moondyne** is also on *Caves Rd*, some 8 km north of Augusta. For this cave you don full caving gear before you explore the interior.

The surfing on the 130 km long Indian Ocean coast is considered some of the best in Australia with rocky bays, pretty much deserted white sand beaches and powerful waves rolling in. Ideal for children are the sheltered waters of **Geographe Bay** in the north with 30 km of beaches, and the **Augusta river** mouth in the south.

Margaret River, though a relatively late starter on the scene has, in little more than twenty years, come to be regarded as one of the world's great winemaking regions. Margaret River supplies 10% of Australia's premium market, which is extraordinary remarkable for a region that supplies overall only about 1% of the total.

There are some 50 vineyards and 30 vineries with most of them in the **Willyabrup Valley**, although you will find them throughout the whole area. Most wineries offer cellar tastings and sales, and many offer light meals using Margaret River produce.

It would be wrong to list all of the vineyards in Margaret River. There are so many and they all have their special attractions. Those that follow are but a random selection:

Vasse Felix, *Harman's Rd South, Cowaramup; tel: 55 5242*, is a pioneer vineyard of the area, established in 1967 by Dr Tom Cullity, thus following the great tradition of doctors producing Australian wine. Open daily 1000–1630. **Rivendell Vineyard**, *Wildwood Rd, Yallingup; tel. 55 2090*. Gallery of local art. Home-made jams, pickles. Pick-your-own strawberries and other seasonal flowers and fruit. Cellar door tastings and sales. Open daily 1000–1700. **Leeuwin Estate**, *Stevens Rd, Margaret River; tel: 57 6253*. Founded in 1978, this is one of the top wineries in Australia and is noted as the site for splendid bushland performances by some of the major orchestras of the world each year. Great if pricey wines. Open daily 1000–1630. **Cape Mentelle**, *Wallcliffe Rd, Margaret River, tel: (097) 57 3266*. This is one of the Australian wine houses in which the French Champagne house Veuve Clicquot, has made a major investment. Open by appointment only. **Ashbrook Estate** *Harman's Rd South, Willyabrup; tel: 55 6262*, is a colonial-style winery built from mud bricks. Open daily 1100–1700.

ALBANY

Tourist Information: Albany Tourist Bureau, *Old Railway Station, Proudlove Parade; tel: (098) 411 088.*

ACCOMMODATION AND FOOD

The Esplanade Hotel, *corner Adelaide Terrace and Flinders Parade; tel: 42 1711*. **Travel Inn** *(FL), 191 Albany Hwy; tel: 41 4144*. **Quality Inn – Albany**, *369 Albany Hwy; tel: 41 1177*. **Albany Dog Rock Motel**, *303 Middleton Rd;*

tel: 41 4422. **Albany Frederickstown Motel**, *corner Frederick and Spencer Sts; tel: 41 1600.* **Albany International Motel** *(BW), 270 Albany Hwy; tel: 41 7399.* **Amity Motor Inn**, *234 Albany Hwy; tel: 41 2200.* **Albany Hotel**, *244 York St; tel: 42 3337.* **Ace Motor Inn** *(BU), 314 Albany Hwy; tel: 41 2911.* **White Star Hotel**, *Stirling Terrace; tel: 41 1733.* **Royal George Hotel Motel**, *Stirling Terrace; tel: 41 1013.* **Ryans Premier Hotel**, *York St; tel: 41 1544.*

Albany Hotel, *244 York St; tel: 0998 423 337.* Licensed. Open lunch and dinner daily. **Genevieves**, *Albany Hotel, Middleton Beach; tel: 098 421 711.* Licensed. **The Penny post**, *33 Stirling St; tel: 098 411 045.* Open dinner daily. Licensed. **Cravings**, *1 Mermaid Ave, Emu Point; tel: 098 441 111.* BYO. Open daily lunch and dinner. **Adelaides**, *Forts Rd; Mt Adelaide; tel: 098 421 90.* Open daily lunch and dinner. BYO. Set in the historic forts precinct.

Albany is 409 km south-east of Perth and an easy 4½ hr drive down the Albany highway. If you are flying from Perth there are daily air services and the flight takes about 1½ hrs. Albany is a coastal town which could perhaps be considered the capital for the **Great Southern Region** – that section of Western Australia that basks in a Mediterranean climate. The climate, by Australian standards, is truly temperate with a summer average of 22.4°C and a winter average not much below that at 17.9°C. The rain tends to be concentrated in the winter months but there is not a truly dry season. The most popular time to visit Albany is from Aug–Oct when the wildflowers are in bloom and the whales pass in their annual migration. But, in truth, this is a year round tourist destination with the weather always welcoming.

King George Sound is a remarkable maritime paradise. Throughout the year it has sea lions, dolphins and seals, but, between Aug–Oct, it is temporary home to schools of whales on their annual migration. There are several whale watching tours offered. **Southern Ocean Charters** *(tel: 41 7176)* has 3 hr tours starting at $30. On the coast near Albany are the blowholes, where in rough weather the force of

the water sends spurts of air and water through cracks in the rocks.

Whaleworld, *Frenchman's Bay Rd; tel: 9844 4021,* is claimed to be the world's largest whale museum and Australia's last whaling station. It has hundreds of artefacts and a continuous historical video. Tours lasting 40 mins start every hour. Open daily 0900–1700. Admission $5.

There are two museums in Albany. The **Old Gaol** was built in 1852 as a convict hiring depot, a centre of cheap labour. It has been transformed by the **Albany Historical Society**, although it is still a sombre place to visit. There is an audio-visual display recounting the history of the place. **Patrick Taylor cottage** was built in 1832 of wattle and daub. The cottage has been restored as much as possible to its former state and is now a museum containing clothes of the period, household goods, old clocks and silverware. *(Corner Stirling Terrace and Parade St; entry fee for both $3.50.)*

The strangely named **Deer-o-Dome and Nature Park**, *Link Rd, off Albany Hwy; tel: 41 7436,* is a deer breeding farm and a tourist attraction. There is a wide range of deer, as well as kangaroos and other animals. Open Thur–Mon 1000–1600; daily in school holidays.

Multimedia has become very much a buzz word for the tourist industry and the **Extravaganza Gallery**, *Adelaide Crescent, Middleton Beach; tel: 421 551,* takes it to its logical conclusion by having over 2000 pieces of multimedia artworks plus a showcase of a collectors' cars. Open 0900–1700 daily. $5.

There are miniature train rides through bushland and a shady picnic area at **Locomotion Miniature Railways** *(Nannup Rd, Lower Kalgan Bridge; tel: 447 756)* which also has a tearoom in a historic tram.

CONNECTION TO ESPERANCE

From Albany you can reach **Esperance** on the Perth–Kalgoorlie route (pp.306–313), a distance of 482 km through **Jerramungup** and **Ravensthorpe** to Esperance, which is on the coast. It is then a 206 km run inland on what is now the Esperance Hwy – still Rte 1 – to **Norseman** and so to Kalgoorlie.

PERTH–KALGOORLIE

Kalgoorlie is 595 km east of Perth which is, in Australian terms, not an overly long distance and although this leads to the start of the long and boring run over the Nullarbor Plain, the road as far as Kalgoorlie has much of interest.

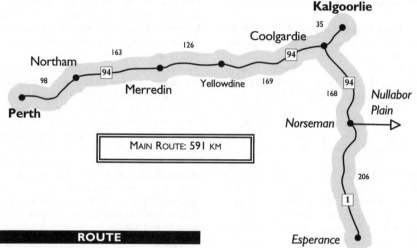

MAIN ROUTE: 591 KM

ROUTE

The route lies along the Great Eastern Hwy, Rte 94, for most of the way. Out of Perth you follow Rte 51 on the north side of the Swan River until, after 12 km, you come to the suburb of **Midland**. From Midland you take the Great Eastern Hwy 23 km to **Mundaring**, which is the site of a weir built in 1904 to provide water for the goldfields 500 km to the east (see p.313). The road now goes through Sawyers Valley to Manaring Lake, 17 km away.

The road then divides and, somewhat misleadingly, the Great Southern Hwy heads west and over the Great and the Little Ebenezer Flats, while the Great Eastern Hwy – our road, still Rte 94 – starts off as if going north and then turns north-east towards **Clackline**, a 30 km distant. From there the road runs to **Northam**, in the heart of the Avon Valley. You are now 98 km, just over an hour's drive, east of Perth.

From Northam the Great Eastern Hwy heads through a series of small wheat belt towns – Meckering, Cunderdin, Tammin and Kellerberrin, which is 203 km east of Perth and is one of towns along the way that benefited from the Goldfields Water Scheme. Now there is a run of 53 km to **Merredin** and then the Great Eastern Hwy heads for 126 km through Burracoppin and Moorine Rock to **Yellowdine**. From here there are few towns for the next 169 km until you arrive at the ghost town of **Coolgardie**, which is 550 km east of Perth.

From Coolgardie you can begin a long side track south to **Norseman** and the start of the Eyre Hwy across the Nullarbor Plain or on to **Esperance** on the coast; or you can continue for 39 km to **Kalgoorlie-Boulder**. (The side track can be picked up from here as well.)

This is by no means a difficult drive, with a good-to-excellent sealed road on the way. You need to be wary of other traffic, especially the very fast and large trucks hammering their way to the eastern states, but apart from that it is quite a relaxing run. As you drive it is also fascinating to see the scenery change from the green pleasantness of Perth to the dry, sere and brown outback country around Kalgoorlie.

TRAINS

The route is paralleled by the **Trans-continental Railway** running from Perth to Sydney by way of Kalgoorlie; this is the line which carries the **Indian Pacific** (see p. 403). There is at least one train a day between Perth and Kalgoorlie, not all calling at intermediate stops, as well as the Indian Pacific on Mondays and Fridays. Northam is 1¾ hrs from Perth East, Merredin 3¾ hrs, and Kalgoorlie 6–7½ hrs, depending on the train caught. OTT table 9033.

BUSES

Gold Rush Tours buses run three times a week from Perth to Leinster calling at Merredin (4 hrs), Coolgardie (8 hrs) and Kalgoorlie (8½ hrs). A daily Greyhound Pioneer Perth–Adelaide coach follows the whole of this chapter's route including the side-track as far as Norseman; Kalgoorlie is just under 8 hrs, Norseman 10¾ hrs. OTT tables 9127, 9132, 9138.

NORTHAM

Tourist Information: Northam Tourist Information Bureau, *138 Fitzgerald St; tel: (096) 222 100.*

ACCOMMODATION

Northam Motel, *13 John St; tel: 22 1755.* **Shamrock Hotel**, *112 Fitzgerald St.* **Commercial Hotel Motel**, *190 Fitzgerald St; tel: 22 1049.* **Grand Hotel**, *426 Fitzgerald St; tel: 22 1024.*

SIGHTSEEING

This is a favourite spot for Perth residents because it is only an hour or so drive away – 98 km on a very good road, the Great Eastern Hwy – and it is the heart of the **Avon Valley**, set on the river itself. The river, as it flows through the town, has a series of grassy banks which are ideal for picnics and strolling. The

river has a large selection of bird life including a colony of white swans, which are descendants of swans introduced early this century. The local swan is, of course, black. At the tourist centre they will not only give you a map of the town and a town walk guide but also bread to feed the swans.

There are many attractions within Northam itself. The oldest building is **Morby Cottage**, (open Sun 1030–1400), which was built in 1836 for the first settlers on this spot, the Morrell family. The town was named after a village in Devon by the then governor. The area was first settled in 1831 and was gazetted and officially recognised four years later.

Like so many other towns in Australia it was the gold rush that brought the town prosperity and expansion at the end of the last century. A dam was built across the Avon in 1900 but was almost immediately destroyed by floods. The current dam was built in 1907. On *Katrine Rd*, which here is listed as part of the Tourist Drive, is **Katrine Barn**, which was built of stone in 1858 and has now been restored as an arts and crafts centre with a small museum. Open Sundays; *tel: 223 790.*

It is possible to take a camel ride through the bush starting at the **Blue Gum Camel Farm**, near *Spencer Brook Rd* in the nearby town of **Clackline**. If you wish you can go on a full day tour – bookings *tel: (096) 574 1480* or try a test run of a few minutes.

The **old railway station** has been listed by the National Trust and converted into a museum. Open Sun 1000–1600.

MERREDIN

Tourist Information: Merredin Tourist Centre, *Barrack St; tel: (090) 411 666.*

ACCOMMODATION

Potts Motor Inn, *Great Eastern Hwy; tel: 41 1755.* **Northside Tavern**, *58 Bates St; tel: 41 1635.* **Merredin Motel & Gumtree Restaurant**, *10 Gamenya Ave; tel: 41 1886.* **Merredin Oasis Hotel-Motel**, *8 Great Eastern Hwy; tel: 41 1133.* **Commercial Hotel**, *62 Barrack St; tel: 41 1052.* **Merredin Olympic Motel**, *Great Eastern Hwy; tel: 41 1588.*

307

SIGHTSEEING

This town on the road to the goldfields is 260 km east of Perth. It was seen as a halfway stopping point by the diggers as they made their way east from one waterhole to the next. At the time the resting spot was **Merredin Peak**, which is 3 km away from the present town. The railway to the goldfields reached here in 1893 and was significant to the town's development as Merredin became an important railway junction between 1910 and 1925. Marking its importance, the station has now become a **Railway Museum** with rolling stock and the old complex signal box on display.

The name Merredin probably comes from an Aboriginal phrase meaning 'tree used for making spears.' Although a station was established there in 1864, there was no serious move to create a town until 1890 and it was gazetted in 1891.

Merredin has the first heritage trail established in Western Australia. This retraces the early history of Merredin and its links with the goldfields and the railway. The trail has two sections, the first a half-hour walk through the town and the second a 6 km walk around Merredin Peak and the original town site.

COOLGARDIE

Tourist Information: Coolgardie Tourist Bureau, *Bayley St; tel: (090) 266 090.*

ACCOMMODATION

Coolgardie Motel, *Bayley St; tel: 26 6080.* **Coolgardie Motor Inn**, *Great Eastern Hwy; tel: 26 6002.* **Caltex Coolgardie Motel**, *110 Bayley St; tel: 26 6049.* **Denver City Hotel**, *73 Bayley St; tel: 26 6031.*

SIGHTSEEING

This is the best known ghost town in Australia. It began life in 1892 when Arthur Bayley and William Ford discovered alluvial gold on **Fly Flat**. They called it **Bayley's Reward**.

The following year the prospectors Patrick Hannan, Tom Flanagan and Daniel Shea went on a prospecting trip to the west of the town (see opposite). One of the horses cast a shoe near **Mt Charlotte** and the group had to camp for the night, 20 km short of their intended destination. They had camped on a fortune. Over the next few days they collected 100 ounces of nuggets and Hannan registered his claim in Coolgardie on 17 June 1893. All hell broke loose at the news. It was a gold rush that surpassed those of earlier years.

An instant town was formed and by 1898 the town had 15,000 inhabitants with another 10,000 in the immediate district. To service them there were 23 hotels, seven newspapers and two stock exchanges set up to service the 700 companies floated in London to mine the field. The boom was, as is inevitable, followed by the bust and by 1902 the gold had started running out, even though the state had set up a gold crushing battery.

There was another mini-boom in the 1930s but it was basically all over, although Bayley's Reward only finally closed as an operating mine in1963. There are still attempts to repeat the trick and there are constant stories about prospectors being on the verge of a great discovery. And, who knows, it may well happen. In the **Golden West**, as the area is called, anything is possible.

The name Coolgardie comes from the Aboriginal language and possibly means 'mulga tree in hollow.' In its time it has also been known as Bayley's Find, Fly Flat, Old Camp and Old Diggings. The town began mainly as a tent city. The first building was probably the post office, which was erected in 1895. The following year the railway arrived and a year later the town had electricity and a swimming pool. But the town gradually went downhill until in 1985 there were only 700 people left, many of the old buildings were disappearing and when you drove past you hardly noticed the city that was. It had, indeed, become a ghost town.

In recent years there has been a strong movement to preserve and restore the old buildings and today their size and opulence shows the town that once was. The main street is wide and imposing as it was laid out on the principle that it had to be wide enough for a camel train to turn. The streets are lined with grand stone and brick buildings mixed with corrugated iron and timber homes, reflecting both the wealth and impermanence of the gold rush.

Gold Mining

The key to understanding the growth of Australia is not convicts or agriculture – it is gold. Starting in 1851 Australia experienced a series of gold rushes which changed the character of the country forever. Until that time it was a convict settlement 'gone decent' with nearly all of the emphasis on agriculture. With the discovery of gold two things happened. First there was a massive surge of migrants in search of a fortune – and when that didn't materialise they hung around anyway. The gold rush doubled the population of the country in five years. Secondly the metal brought a flood of money into the country and many towns in the bush achieved unbelievable prosperity.

The towns then went one of two ways. If gold was the only reason for their existence they became ghost towns almost overnight. The houses decayed until frequently there was nothing left to show but a few piles of bricks, a few gravestones and a large number of bottles.

In New South Wales gold was first seriously discovered in 1851 (there had been some small claims as early as 1823) near Ophir, about 250 km from Sydney, by Edward Hargreaves, who had taken part in the California gold rush two years previously. From there gold fever spread across the country and many major discoveries were made.

In Kalgoorlie the first major gold strike was made by three Irishmen – Patrick Hannan, Tom Flanagan and Dan Shea. They all claimed they were the first to make the strike although it is Hannan who has the statue in the main street of Kalgoorlie, *Hannan St.* Their find did not make them rich – Hannan needed a government pension to retire – but they started a major gold rush that eventually found the Golden Mile between Kalgoorlie and Boulder, which is one of the richest strikes the world has ever known.

But none excites the Australian imagination so much as Lasseter's mountain of gold – the legendary Lost Reef. Lewis Hubert Lasseter was an explorer, who in 1930 set out on an expedition into the bush. Although the expedition was well funded things started to go wrong, the spotting aircraft crashed and Lasseter decided to go on alone. He died of starvation in Jan 1931 near Shaw's Creek but left his diaries behind. He had discovered a reef of solid gold bringing riches beyond the dreams of avarice. And he had staked out the claim. Sadly, he failed to give precise details of where the reef was to be found and although there have been several expeditions no one has found a trace of it.

Was Lasseter as mad as a barking dog when he wrote those diaries and invented the reef? Or is there, somewhere out there in the outback, an immense reef of gold awaiting discovery? Most Australians will bet on the latter being the case.

309

The most imposing building is the **Warden's Court**, which was built in 1898 using local stone and is solid Victorian architecture at its best. It houses, among other things, the tourist office, the **Goldfields Exhibition**, the **Mining Registrar's Office** and the **Courthouse**. The exhibition within the building tells the story of the gold prospector by way of contemporary photographs and models. Comparing the photographs, which are less than a century old, with today's reality, shows how far Coolgardie has moved from its former glory. Open daily 0900–1700. Americans should note that President Herbert Hoover spent time on the West Australian goldfields.

Around the town are a series of historical markers, which also help you to get an idea of the original size of the town. The **railway station** in *Woodward St,* which played such a major part in the life of the town, has now been converted into a museum.

In *Hunt St,* on the other side of the old railway bridge, is **Warden Finnerty's residence**, built in 1894 for John Michael Finnerty, Warden and Resident Magistrate of Coolgardie Goldfields. An imposing residence for a man with an imposing title. It has been restored by the National Trust and is open Mon 1300–1600 and Sun 1000–1200. $2. Almost next door is the **gaol tree**, where prisoners awaiting trial were chained.

You can imitate early explorers and ride a camel at the **Camel Farm**, which is 3 km to the west. Open daily 0900–1700, it offers walks around the yard, which might be the safest bet, as well as 1 hr and 1 day treks.

↱ SIDE TRACK
FROM COOLGARDIE

At Coolgardie turn right on Rte 94 (you can go through to Kalgoorlie and join this road by way of a bypass that runs through the mining town of **Menzies**). Then pass through **Widgemooltha** to **Norseman**, which is 187 km south of Coolgardie, 742 km from Perth and 724 km from the state border. Three weekly **Westrail buses** run from Kalgoorlie (one of them via Coolgardie) to Norseman (nearly 3 hrs) and Esperance (just over 5 hrs).

NORSEMAN

Tourist Information: Norseman Tourist Bureau, *Roberts St; tel: (090) 391 071.*

ACCOMMODATION

Great Western Motel *(FL), Kalgoorlie Esperance Hwy; tel: 39 1633.* **Norseman Eyre Motel**, *Robert St; tel: 39 1130.* **Railway Hotel-Motel**, *106 Roberts St; tel: 39 1115.* **Norseman Hotel**, *Robert St; tel: 39 1023.*

SIGHTSEEING

This is yet another town that owes its existence to the discovery of gold. The story is that a horse called Norseman pawed the ground and found a gold nugget, starting the Norseman gold rush. It is very difficult to find any historical substantiation of this story. What is known is that a main mine was established in 1894 and named after an early settler's horse. There is now a statue to the alleged gold-finding horse in the main

street because the mine still operates and the whole economy of Norseman has revolved around gold.

The tourist office can supply you with a map showing you the **Dundas Coach Road Heritage Trail**, which runs for 33 km and follows the turn of the century Cobb & Co. Coach route. Along the way, 6 km from Norseman, there is a site where you can try your hand at gold panning.

Norseman lies at the western end of the Eyre Hwy, Rte 1, which passes the Nullarbor Plain on its way to the border with South Australia and on to Adelaide (see opposite).

ESPERANCE

Tourist Information: Esperance Tourist Bureau, *Museum Village, Dempster St; tel: (090) 71 2330.*

ACCOMMODATION AND FOOD

Bay of Isles Motel, *32 The Esplanade; tel: 71 3800.* **Bayview Hotel**, *31 Dempster St; tel: 71 1533.* **Captain Huon Hotel**, *5 The Esplanade; tel: 71 2383.* **Esperance Motor Hotel**, *14 Andrew St; tel: 71 1495.* **Jetty Motel**, *1 The Esplanade; tel: 71 5978.* **HI: Blue Waters Lodge**, *Goldfields Rd,; tel: 71 1040.*

Beachfront Café, *19 The Esplanade; tel: 71 7107.* Open daily 0700–2000. **Carusoe's**, *Centrepoint Arcade, Dempster St; tel: 71 7771.* Open daily 0730–2300. **Seasons**, *Hospitality Inn; The Esplanade; tel: 71 1999.*

SIGHTSEEING

This south-east destination, 721 km from Perth and 476 km from Albany, is beginning to be recognised as a serious holiday destination. The beaches and waters around Esperance have been described as some of the clearest and best in Australia and, indeed, the world. The Esperance archipelago has over 100 islands and a wealth of sea life including seals, sea lions and dolphins.

The waters of the area are also regular visiting grounds for the Southern Right Whales, who visit from July–Nov to calve

The Eyre Highway

The Eyre Highway, which takes you from Western Australia to the eastern states across the Nullarbor Plain, is not a road to be taken lightly. The drive is long and tedious and passes through desert country. Nowadays the road is sealed all the way through – this was not so until comparatively recently – and any ordinary car can make the trip without any special precautions. If you break down you will be given assistance although it will make a serious dent in your budget. It is generally accepted that to try and make the run without good air-conditioning is an exercise in masochism and it is advisable to carry fresh water both to drink and to wash your windscreens because the petrol stations, of which there are more than enough, only offer bore water for washing windscreens, which is something less than totally effective.

The Western Australian part of the journey runs for 1474 km from Perth to just the far side of **Eucla** on the coast of the Great Australian Bight. Between Norseman and Eucla there is nothing – 712 km of it. Twelve kilometres after Eucla you arrive at the border with South Australia and ahead of you stretches the great wasteland of the **Nullarbor National Park** and 300 km later on, **Ceduna** in South Australia (see p. 369), which is the start of civilisation again, with **Adelaide** only a further 793 km to go.

The civilised way to make this journey is by air, or by the Transcontinenal **Indian Pacific** train (see p. 403), although this runs a lot further north, parallel to the Eyre Highway. Or you can take the **Greyhound Pioneer** bus – 29 hrs from Norseman to Adelaide (see OTT table 9132 for full timings).

in the warm and sheltered waters. The area is of particular appeal to scuba divers and anglers because of the clarity of the waters and the wealth and variety of fish life.

Divers are catered for by the **Esperance Diving Academy**, *56 The Esplanade; tel: 71 5111*, which has a charter vessel working in the clear waters of the **Recerche Archipelago**. For anglers there is **Esperance Fishing and Charter**, *33 Mitchell St; tel: 71 2178*.

The history of Esperance is recorded in the **Esperance Municipal Museum**, *corner James and Dempster Sts; tel: 71 1579*. Open daily 1330–1630.

There are six national parks around Esperance. Moving down the coast to the east you come first to **Cape Le Grand National Park** and then just past Duke of Orleans Bay is **Cape Arid National Park**. To the west on the coast is **Stokes National Park** and further along the park is the Fitzgerald River. All of these national Parks have amazing beaches and blue waters and all are accessible by sealed road.

 Connection to Albany

To join up with the Perth-Albany route (p. 297), you can drive the 480 km west along the South Coastal Hwy (Rte 1) to **Albany**.

KALGOORLIE-BOULDER

Tourist Information: Kalgoorlie-Boulder Tourist Centre, *Hannan St; tel: (090) 211 966*.

ACCOMMODATION

Mercure Plaza Hotel – Kalgoorlie, *45 Egan St; tel: 21 4544*. **Tower Motel**, *corner Bourke and Maritana Sts; tel: 21 3211*. **Midas Motel**, *409 Hannan St; tel: 21 3088*. **Federal Hotel**, *1 Hannan St; tel: 21 2426*. **Hannans View Motel** *(BU), 430 Hannan St; tel: 91 3333*. **Quality Inn – Kalgoorlie**, *Hannan St; tel: 21 1433*. **Hospitality Inn Kalgoorlie Motel**, *Hannan St; tel: 21 2888*

Albion Shamrock Motor Hotel *(GC), corner Lane and Plesse Sts; tel: 93 1399*. **Star and Garter Motel Hotel**, *497 Hannan St*. **Hannans Hotel**, *Hannan St; tel: 21 2576*. **Mount Lyell Hotel**, *Boulder Rd; tel: 21 2263*.

Sandalwood Motor Inn *(FL)*, *Lower Hannan St; tel: 21 4455.* **Exchange Hotel**, *Hannan St; tel: 21 2833.* **Palace Hotel**, *corner Maritana and Hannan Sts; tel: 21 2788.* **York Hotel**, *259 Hannan St; tel: 21 2337.* **Union Club Hotel**, *1–3 MacDonald St; tel: 21 1749.* **Golden Mile Village Motel**, *240–262 Forrest St; tel: 91 2803.* **Piccadilly Hotel**, *164 Piccadilly St; tel: 21 2109.* **Inland City Hotel**, *93 Forrest St; tel: 21 2401.* **Criterion Hotel**, *117 Hannan St; tel: 21 2271.*

EATING AND DRINKING

Albion Shamrock, *60 Bart St; tel: 93 1399.* Open 0530–0830, 1200–1400, 1730–2030, á la carte and steaks. **Amalfi at the Midas**, *409 Hannan St; tel: 21 3088.* Mon–Sat 1800–late, Sun 1800–2000, Mediterranean. **Amy's at Flanagans**, *1 McDonald St; tel: 21 1749.* Tues–Sat 1800–late. Continental and Australian. **Basil's on Hannan**, *268 Hannan St; tel: 21 7832.* Mon–Tues 0800–1700, Wed–Sat 0800–late, Sun 0900–1630; pasta, Italian and Continental. **Best West Hospitality**, *Lower Hannan St; tel: 21 2888.* Prospector Room; Mon–Sat 1800–2100, Sun 1800–2000, seafood specials, à la carte. **Bullion Bistro**, *240 Forrest St; tel: 91 2803.* Open 0445–0800, 1645–2000; hearty. **Crock Pot**, *Graeme St; tel: 21 2907.* Open Wed–Fri 1100–1500, Wed–Fri 1700–late; hearty. **Cornwall Hotel**, *25 Hopkins St; tel: 91 2510.* Sun–Fri 1100–1500, Mon–Sat 1830–2330; counter meals. **de Barrales**, *193 Hannan St; tel: 21 4534.* Open Mon–Sun 1200–1500, Sat 1800–2100, Sun 1800–2000; seafood, pasta, steaks, game.

Hannans Hotel, *400 Hannan St; tel: 21 2576.* Mon–Fri 1800–2030, counter meals, seafood. **Inland City Garden**, *93 Forrest St; tel: 21 2401.* Mon–Sat 1800–late, Sun 1800–2100, steaks, buffet servery. **Kadees Bistro**, *6 Maritana St; tel: 21 7235.* Tues–Sun 1830–late. Continental, Italian. **Kalgoorlie Café**, *277 Hannan St; tel: 21 3002.* Mon–Fri 1000–1500, Mon–Sat 1730–2300, Sun 1730–2130, homestyle German sweets. **Kalgoorlie Food Court**, *84–90 Brookman St; tel: 91 6118.* Open 1130–1430, 1700–2100. BYO. Variety of Australian and international

stalls. **Kalgoorlie Hotel**, *319 Hannan St; tel: 21 3046.* 1200–1430, 1800–2100; blackboard and grills. **Loaded Cactus**, *90 Egan St; tel: 21 7347.* Tues–Sun 1800–late. BYO, Mexican. **Main Reef Tavern**, *32 Dwyer St; tel: 93 1132.* 1800–2100, bistro. **Mangia Bene**, *46 Maritana St; 21 3553.* Mon–Tues 1630–2100, Wed, Sun 1130–2230. Italian.

Daniel O'Shea's – Mercure Hotel, *45 Egan St; tel: 21 4544.* Mon–Fri 0600–0900, Sat–Sun 0630–0900, 7 days 1830–2100. **Mercure Inn Overland**, *Lower Hannan St; tel: 21 1433.* 0600–0900, 1800–2100. Buffet breakfast, á la carte. **New Hong Kong**, *248 Hannan St; tel: 21 1336.* 7 days 1130–1400, Mon–Wed and Sun 1700–2100, Thur 1800–2130, Fri–Sat 1700–2200. Chinese. **Varischettis and Hoovers at the Palace Hotel**, *corner Hannan and Maritana Sts; tel: 21 2788.* Mon–Fri 1200–1400, Mon–Sun 1830–late, Mediterranean. **Top End Thai**, *71 Hannan St; tel: 91 4027.* Mon–Sat 1800–2100. BYO; Thai – spicy.

SIGHTSEEING

It was gold that made Kalgoorlie-Boulder – Kal to the locals – the town that it is. A British magazine described it as the 'mad bastard capital of Australia,' which is somewhat vicious but not totally inaccurate. Kalgoorlie, 595 km from Perth and another country when it comes to climate, has always had an image of being a hard living, hard drinking town, which had legalised prostitution and gambling while the rest of Australia had the pubs closed at tea time. It is the last of the towns of the gold-rush – mining gold is still by far the largest industry – and it has retained, for its many and nefarious sins, the reputation of being the wildest town in a wild west.

This was probably true some years ago and there are still pubs where you wouldn't take your maiden aunt but these days you sometimes get the impression that Kalgoorlie is trying to live up to the reputation of its wild and disreputable youth.

In truth, nowadays it is a fairly typical prosperous and industrious Australian community with some stunning public buildings, reflecting the fact that it sits on the **Golden Mile**, the

Golden Water

There is a story attached to the growth of Kalgoorlie that shows how tough it was to be a pioneer. When the goldfields first opened, hundreds died of typhoid – mainly because of the lack of water. It was selling at the then staggering price of 2s 6d a gallon. Progress on the fields was seriously held up.

The problem was solved by the engineering genius of Charles Yelverton O'Connor, the State engineer-in-chief. He overcame the problem in 1903 by damming the Helena River at Mundaring and devising a scheme to pump the water to Kalgoorlie.

He designed a system to do that apparent impossible – pump 22,700 cubic metres of water from the plentiful supplies of Mundaring Weir, lift it 355m with only eight pumping stations, and deliver it to the dry goldfield towns 560 km away.

There were, as always, many instant experts who mocked his scheme and said it could never work. They were wrong and he was right.

However, because of the unjustified criticism – mainly from the press and politicians – C.Y.O'Connor shot himself only months before the system came into full operation.

It was discovered early on in the century that the way to get at the gold was through reef, open cut and deep shaft mining, which is the way it has been mined to this day. The super pit in the Golden Mile is the premier mine of the region and in 1995, 720,000 ounces were recovered from this mine alone. Kalgoorlie is currently the largest open cut mining operation in the world.

To see how gold is mined in Kalgoorlie, an early visit should be made to **Hannans North**, *Broadarrow Rd; tel: 914 074*. This has a gold pour demonstration, a locomotive ride to take visitors right around the 7 hectare site and a trip underground. Open daily 0900–1700. Another view can be had at **School of Mines Museum**, *Cassidy St; tel: 805 000*. Open Mon–Fri, 1000–1600 except Dec–Jan vacation.

In *Sutherland St* is the **Mt Charlotte Reservoir and Lookout**. Here you can see the remarkable design of C.Y.O'Connor (see box) and marvel at the fact that the water takes ten days to make the journey.

If you want to try and emulate the early diggers there is a 'prospecting for gold' self-tour package which has been put together by the Tourist Centre in *Hannan St*. **The Boorara Fossicking Area** lease is 18 km from Kalgoorlie and you can hire a metal detector from the Centre to increase your chances – which are very slim – of stumbling onto a fortune.

In *Outridge Terrace* you will find **Paddy Hannan's Tree**, which marks the site where Hannan, Flanagan and Shea struck lucky in 1893 (see p.309).

The Historical Society has a display at the **railway station**, *Burt St; tel: 931 157*, which recounts the history of the area through displays of early goldfield life. Open daily 0900–1200. Also at the railway station is the terminus for the **Loopline Railway**, which was once the busiest in Western Australia. There is an hour-long tour on the 'Rattler' with commentary. Train departs daily at 1000 with an extra tour at 1045 weekends and holidays (*Burt St; tel: 933 055*.)

In the bush around Kalgoorlie there are over sixty species of eucalyptus to be found, including many flowering varieties. In the season the displays of wildflowers are outstanding.

313

richest square mile of gold bearing earth in the world. Having said that, the echoes of Kalgoorlie-Boulder's boisterous past are still to be found. *Hannan St, Kalgoorlie, and Burt St, Boulder*, offer a glimpse of the way things were in the roaring 1890s.

There is much to see in Kalgoorlie but it is best to give the high summer months of Dec and Jan a miss as the heat becomes oppressive for those not used to it. This is also the holiday season for the residents of Kalgoorlie and much of the town is closed down. In September the combined attractions of wildflowers and local horse races can make accommodation difficult to come by.

PERTH–CARNARVON

The run from Perth to Carnarvon along the North West Coastal Highway, our old friend Rte 1, is something just less than a 1000 km journey, which can nearly be split into two at Geraldton.

Almost the whole of the way you will be driving along what used to be called the Batavia Coast by the early Dutch mariners, who were the first Europeans in the area. And it has a colourful history of mutiny, stranded sailors, massacres, shipwrecks and even sunken treasure. This area is a magic place of sun – and surf and miles of beach. But, as the wrecks show, it has its harsh side.

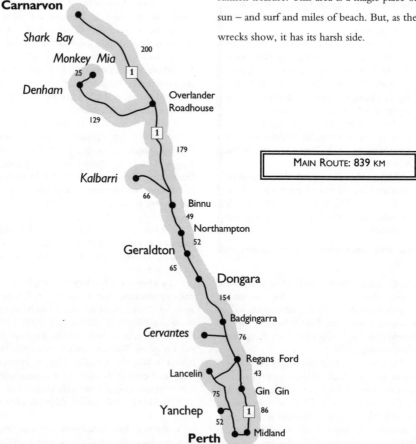

MAIN ROUTE: 839 KM

ROUTE

The route from Perth to Carnarvon follows Rte 1 north, part of which is known as the North West Coastal Hwy, as it runs alongside the coast, for 902 km in all. From Perth, the easiest way is to head west out of town on *Guildford Rd* – Rte 51 – for 12 km to **Midland** and then take Rte 1 (here called the Great Northern Hwy) northwards, heading out through **Bullsbrook**. Rte 1 then becomes the Brand Hwy to run 30 km to the **Gin Gin** by-pass. From there it runs for 43 km, still as the Brand Hwy, to the minor road point which is **Regans Ford**, only of note because it has a filling station.

Alternatively, start out from Perth on Rte 60 and head towards the suburb of **Wanneroo**, which is 54 km from the city centre. From there the road runs past **Lake Joondalup** on the right and continues on past **Quinns Rocks** to the turn-off towards the sea to **Yanchep** and **Two Rocks**, which is another 54 km along the road.

From Yanchep backtrack to Rte 60 and head north along it again past Guilderton and Seabird, which is on Cape Leschenault. From there Rte 60 heads towards the seaside town of **Lancelin**, which is 35 km distant. Just 10 km before Lancelin there is a minor turn-off that runs first 10 km to *Sappers Rd* and then turns right for 14 km to *Orange Springs Rd,* a right turning at a clearly marked crossroads. This brings you, after 17 km, back to Regans Ford and Rte 1, the main route. The last part of that diversion before Lancelin is, admittedly, somewhat complex, but it does allow you many small diversions to the beach as you go along.

From Regans Ford Rte 1 runs 54 km to **Badgingarra**. From there it is 73 km to Eneabba, where the road turns north-west and after 50 km reaches the sea. If you want to reach the coast earlier, there is a minor road, which is a left turning from Eneabba. This reaches the sea and joins the *Coast Rd* after 28 km, at Coolimba. The *Coast Rd* then runs north along the seafront, until 37 km later it rejoins Rte 1.

Dongara comes 24 km later, with **Port Denison** within easy reach. The highway then runs up the coast to **Geraldton**, 424 km from Perth. This is a solid day's drive and many would prefer to break the journey at Dongara.

From Geraldton the road runs 44 km north and inland to **Northampton**. It then goes 442 km to Carnarvon, the only major breaks being the turn offs at **Binnu** to **Kalbarri** and at the **Overlander Roadhouse** to **Shark Bay** and **Monkey Mia**, which comes 280 km after Geraldton.

Tour buses make it in one day to Monkey Mia from Perth – but the drivers know the road well. Driving such a distance in that time is not for the tourist. Many visitors might find it less demanding to fly to Carnarvon from Perth and pick up a hire car there to explore Shark Bay and the Gascoyne Valley. On the other hand locals think of this as an easy drive and cannot see what all the fuss is about.

BUSES

Greyhound Pioneer and Westrail run coaches from Perth to Monkey Mia (13 hrs). There is a choice of several daily along this route: all run as far as Geraldton (6 hrs or longer). Most terminate there but some go on to Kalbarri (8 hrs). OTT table 9133.

YANCHEP

Tourist Information: Information office Yanchep National Park; *tel: (095) 61 1004.*

ACCOMMODATION

Club Capricorn, *Two Rocks Rd; tel: 561 1106.* **Yanchep Inn and Units**, *Yanchep National Park; tel: 561 1001.*

SIGHTSEEING

Yanchep is on the *Yanchep Beach Rd* turning, off the *Wanneroo Rd* – Rte 80. This is an odd sort of a place, in that it was initially a commercial development that was taken over by the National Parks. Much of it has been landscaped, and what were the swamps of **Yanchep Lake** have been drained, trimmed and returned to life as the lawns of **Loch McNess** – sometimes misleadingly spelled Loch Ness. The koalas you will see have been imported and the wildflowers are grown in beds.

There are more natural areas within the 2800 hectares of the park, with woods of marri

315

and jarrah, and flowering heaths underneath. Getting around the park is fairly easy as there is an extensive range of fire trails, which makes for relaxed bushwalking.

The east end of the park has limestone caves and there are guided tours within the **Crystal Cave**. Visitors are asked to wear rubber soled shoes.

Yanchep is popular with Perth residents, especially for golfing weekends.

The road from Yanchep runs for 5 km along the coast to **Two Rocks**, a very small town on the sea.

◤ SIDE TRACK FROM THE BRAND HIGHWAY

Most people driving along the Brand Hwy from Perth to Carnarvon take the time to make a detour to **Cervantes** to see the miracle which is the **Pinnacles Desert**, within the **Nambung National Park**. The turn off is 250 km north of Perth, 12 km before **Badgingarra**, to the left on the *Bibby Rd*, which runs 25 km to *Munbinea Rd* and then into *Cervantes Rd* for the 29 km run down the township and the sea.

Note that the road into the park from Cervantes is not sealed and you need to check that it is passable before proceeding.

CERVANTES

Accommodation is available at the **Cervantes Pinnacle Hotel**; *tel: (096) 527 145*.

The town is a major windsurfing centre and the **Windsurfing Carnival** held every December brings contestants from interstate. It has one motel, a caravan park and a small shopping centre, which has a supermarket, take-away pizza and a newsagent. But its true importance is as the gateway to the Pinnacles. The entrance to the Nambung National Park is only 2 km east of town, while the Pinnacles are a further 15 km away.

NAMBUNG NATIONAL PARK

Tourist Information: **Nambung National Park**, *tel: (096) 52 7145*.

The park gives easy access to the sea at two points on its 26 km coastline – **Kangaroo Point** and **Hangover Bay** – but the main point of the exercise is the Pinnacles Desert. This is a true desert with a flat, sandy terrain, but it is punctuated as in a science fiction lunarscape with many limestone pillars, some up to 5 m tall. There is a 3 km drive which will take you around the pinnacles, but it is a magic place to explore, especially at sunrise and sunset, when the angled light throws the pillars into strong relief.

The Pinnacles were created centuries ago when sand, rich in lime, was blown inland to form high dunes, which were unstable and moved from spot to spot. Then rain came and took the lime from the upper layers, combining it with the sand at the base to make a soft limestone cement. A hard topping of calcrete formed over this limestone – still to be seen as a cap on many of the pinnacles – while water seeped down plant roots to start sub-surface erosion of some of the limestone.

The Pinnacles that you see today are what is left of that limestone layer, which was exposed when the pretty-well perennial, strong south-westerly winds blew away the surrounding quartz sand. The process is still going on, and in a strong wind the Pinnacles appear to be wreathed in a mist – which is the sand being blown away, as it has been for centuries. ◣

DONGARA

Tourist Information: Tourist Information Centre, *5 Waldeck St; tel: (099) 27 1404*.

ACCOMMODATION

Dongara Motor Hotel, *Moreton Terrace; tel: 27 1023*. **Old Mill Motel**, *Brand Hwy; tel: 27 1200*. **The Priory Lodge**, *St Dominics Rd; tel: 27 1090*. **HI: Dongara Backpackers**, *32 Waldeck St; tel: 27 1581*.

SIGHTSEEING

This is a small, pleasant fishing village specialising in crayfish, 65 km south of **Geraldton** and, on the Brand Hwy, 359 km north of Perth. It has an even smaller next door neighbour in **Port Denison**. The two towns face each other across the **Irwin River**, which is a great place for bird watchers.

The area was first settled by Europeans sometime around 1859, when the town was known as Port Irwin. By 1868, a permanent policeman had arrived – in those times a sure and certain sign of civilisation. The police station now houses the tourist information centre. In the same year the jetty was built and the town was gazetted as Port Denison which was, in fact, next door. *Waldeck St* contains the police station, the Anglican rectory, which was built in 1882, and the church which followed two years later. The tourist office has a brochure describing a Heritage Trail around the two towns.

The main street of the town, *Moreton St*, boasts a Moreton Bay Fig tree, which is at least 85 years old.

The name of Dongara, which eventually came to be used, probably comes from an Aboriginal word *thungarra*, meaning 'mouth of the river'.

GERALDTON

Tourist Information: Geraldton Tourist Office, *Bill Sewell Complex; tel: (099) 21 3999.*

ACCOMMODATION

Hospitality Inn Geraldton, *Cathedral Ave; tel: 21 1422.* **Ocean Centre Hotel**, *Foreshore Dr.; tel: 21 7777.* **Batavia Motor Inn**, *Fitzgerald St; tel: 21 3500.* **Tarcoola Tavern Motel**, *107 Brand Hwy; tel: 64 4777.* **Wintersun Hotel**, *441 Chapman Rd; tel: 23 1211.* **Abrolhos Reef Lodge** *(BU), 126 Brand Hwy; tel: 21 3811.* **Club Sun City Resort Motel**, *137 Cathedral Ave; tel: 21 6111.* **Queens Motor Hotel**, *97 Durlacher St; tel: 21 1064.*

Hacienda Motel, *Durlacher St; tel: 21 2155.* **Sunseeker Hotel-Motel**, *21 Marine Terrace; tel: 21 3422.* **Freemasons Hotel**, *Marine Terrace; tel: 64 3457.* **Mariner Motel**, *298 Chapman Rd; tel: 21 2544.* **Colonial Hotel**, *Fitzgerald St; tel: 21 4444.* **Geraldton Hotel**, *19 Gregory St; tel: 21 3700.* **Victoria Hotel**, *Marine Terrace; tel: 21 1133.*

EATING AND DRINKING

Fiddlers, *103 Marine Terrace; tel: 21 6644.* Daily lunch and dinner. Crayfish, but of course, a speciality. **Ocean Centre**, *Foreshore Dr.; tel: 21 7777.* Seafood. **Skeetas**, *George Rd; tel: 64 1619.*

SIGHTSEEING

Geraldton calls itself the lobster capital of the world and the travel publicists would have you call it Sun City. Allowing for some hyperbole, there is truth in both those titles.

Sun City, because it averages 8 hrs of sunshine – every day of the year. Few cities in the world can make that claim. And the fishing grounds around the **Houtman Abrolhos Islands**, where the Dutch merchant vessel *Batavia* went aground, support a major lobster catching industry.

The name Geraldton comes from the governor-general of the time, Charles Fitzgerald. **Champion Bay**, on which the town stands, is named after the first British ship which arrived there in 1840, although a shipwrecked naval officer had made a favourable report on the area the previous year. The town was surveyed in 1849 and the **Geraldton Hotel** was built the following year.

Copper was discovered nearby in 1852 and this led to a jetty being built in 1874, which was extended and improved, until it eventually became the current dock. The crayfish – rock lobster – industry started in the 1960s and is now an important part of the economy of the area.

In 1852 a convict depot was established to provide cheap labour and they went on to build the residency, which was completed in 1861 and later converted into a hospital. The first Australian woman member of parliament, Edith Cowan, who was elected in 1921, was born here in 1861.

The nearby group of Houtman Abrolhos Islands – there are a hundred of them just 60 km off the coast – has a mystery surrounding their name. The second part may come from the Portuguese *abre alhos* meaning 'look out' because of the danger of the reef, although no one knows for certain.

Houtman is the man, who in the *Dordrecht*,

317

reached and named the islands in 1619. The reefs are, indeed, dangerous, as the captain of the *Batavia* found out in 1629 when his ship was wrecked on the reef. Divers have brought up many of the timbers and some artefacts from the wreck, and these are now on display in the **Fremantle Maritime Museum**.

Nevertheless the **Geraldton Maritime Museum**, *Marine Terrace*, has a fascinating display on the shipwreck and other wrecks off this treacherous coast. Open Mon–Sat 1000–1700, Sun 1300–1700.

Geraldton is the third largest city in Western Australia and a port. It is also the administrative centre of the Mid West region of gold production, mining, agriculture and fishing, as well as a popular resort destination famous for its windsurfing and skin diving.

The **St Francis Xavier Cathedral** in *Cathedral Dr.* was completed in 1938, having taken 25 years to build. It is a wonderful example of the work of the architect turned priest, Monsignor John Hawes. There is a John Hawes Heritage Trail, where you can trace his other works. The tourist office will provide you with a map.

Geraldton is in the shire of Greenough, which is named after the river. It is well known for its 'leaning trees' – eucalypts that contort into strange shapes as if ducking the wind. It is, in fact, the salt content of the wind that causes the trees to lean.

The Houtman Abrolhos Islands are famous for the range of skin diving sites. These are created by the warm water of the **Leeuwin Current**, and the range of fish life and coral rivals that of the Great Barrier Reef.

Best diving months are Feb–May but the **Batavia Coast Dive Academy** (*tel: 214 229*) runs charters to the area all year round.

> ### ◤ SIDE TRACK
> ### ◤ FROM BINNU
>
> **Kalbarri** is a popular holiday town, 661 km north of Perth, situated between Geraldton – 166 km away – and Carnarvon on the Murchison River estuary.
>
> It is 66 km from the turn-off, a few kilometres after Binnu on Rte 1.

Tourist Information: Allen Community Centre, *Grey St; tel: (099) 37 1104.*

ACCOMMODATION

Kalbarri Beach Resort, *Clotworthy St; tel: 37 1061.* **Kalbarri Palm Resort**, *Porter St; tel: 37 2333.* **Kalbarri Motor Hotel**, *Grey St; tel: 37 1000.*

EATING AND DRINKING

Finlay's Fresh Fish BBQ, *Magee Crescent; tel: (099) 37 1260.* Open daily 1730–2030. Mentioned in every guidebook that covers Kalbarri as the definitive place for a meal. Open air. Great atmosphere.

SIGHTSEEING

When the *Batavia* was wrecked on the Houtman Abrolhos Islands, it suffered a mutiny among the crew. Two of the mutineers, who were both Dutch, were marooned at Kalbarri as punishment. These two miscreants are believed to be the first two permanent European settlers in Australia.

In 1697, William de Vlamingh landed here seeking fresh water, but the first serious European settler in the region was C. von Bibra, who established **Murchison House** at the mouth of the river in 1858. The town was very slow in developing and, in fact, was not gazetted until 1951, with the adjacent National Park being established some 12 years later.

Kalbarri is known for its excellent fishing, the amazing wildflower displays in the season and the spectacular gorges of the **Kalbarri National Park**. The park covers 186,000 hectares and through it comes the 100 km long Murchison River, which has cut gorges with names like **The Loop, Z Bend, Ross Graham Lookout** and **Hawks Head**. All of these gorges are well-signposted and accessed by way of well-maintained gravel roads, followed by hikes down well marked trails.

During the season the park is a paradise of wildflowers and more than 850 varieties have been discovered.

To the south of the town there are a string of cliff faces with evocative names like **Red Bluff**, **Rainbow Valley**, **Pot Alley** and, last of all, **Natural Bridge**. The road is fine to **Wittecarra Gully** – there is a cairn there to mark the site of the first permanent landing of Europeans – but after that it is unsealed and uneven and great care should be taken.

From Nov–June, the crayfish fleet is normally somewhere in the area, and it is common to see as many as 60 crayfishing boats moored in the river at one time.

Every morning at 0845 the pelicans are fed on the river bank along *Grey St.* Local volunteers give a brief account of these birds as they feed them fish.

Another species of bird is to be found at the **Rainbow Jungle**, *Red Bluff Rd; tel: (099) 371 248,* which is a parrot breeding centre and has a successful programme for breeding Australia's endangered species. Open Tues–Sat 0900–1700, Sun 1000–1530. $5.

Cruises are available up the Murchison River on the **Kalbarri River Queen**, *tel: (099) 37 1104,* or go self propelled in a hired canoe from **Kalbarri Canoe Safaris**, *tel: (099) 37 1245.*

SIDE TRACK
FROM OVERLANDER

To reach **Shark Bay** you turn off left opposite the **Overlander Roadhouse** on the Northwest Coastal Hwy. At 30 km along the turn-off, you will come to the **Hamelin Pool Telegraph Station**, which was originally built in 1884 and is now a visitor's centre full of information about the area.

The road will lead you to two peninsulas that run parallel to the coast, into Shark Bay. The first runs out past the **Hamelin Pool** and **Shell Beach** to the town of **Denham**. The road from Rte 1 as far as Denham is 129 km long. From Denham it is a short distance to **Peron**, the **Monkey Mia Dolphin Resort**, and finally, the lighthouse. The second eventually ends up as

Dirk Hartog Island and is somewhat longer than the first.

SHARK BAY

Tourist Information: Shark Bay Tourist Centre, *53 Knight Terrace, Denham 6537; tel: (099) 48 1253.*

ACCOMMODATION

Tradewinds Holiday Village, *Knights Terrace; tel: 48 1222.* **Shark Bay Hotel Motel**, *43 Knight Terrace, Denham; tel: 48 1203;* **Heritage Resort Hotel**, *Knight Terrace; tel: 48 1133.* **Monkey Mia Dolphin Resort**, *Dolphin Beach; tel: 48 1320.*

EATING AND DRINKING

Bough Shed Restaurant, *Money Mia Dolphin Resort; tel: 48 1320.* Open daily, breakfast, lunch and dinner. **Old Pearler Restaurant**, *1 Knight Terrace, Denham; tel: 48 1373.* Open seven days lunch and dinner. Licensed.

SIGHTSEEING

Tourist authorities around the world cannot resist in trying to rename areas and so Shark Bay is now part of what we are told is the **Outback Coast**, which is more generally called the **Gascoyne** area, and includes Shark Bay, **Monkey Mia**, and then past **Carnarvon** to the **Ningaloo Reef**.

The first Europeans came here in October 1616, when Captain Dirk Hartog landed at Cape Inscription and left behind an inscribed pewter plate to record the fact. This was the first European landing in Australia.

Dirk Hartog was followed 81 years later by another Dutch explorer, Captain William de Vlamingh, who replaced the original pewter plate with one of his own. The Hartog pewter plate is now on display at the **Rikjsmuseum** in Amsterdam, while that of de Vlamingh is on show at the **Fremantle Maritime Museum**.

After the Dutch, the English and French came in quick succession, and it was William Dampier who named the area

Shark's Bay in 1699, while 73 years later Francois St Allouam laid claim to the territory for the French. It is worth noting that Hartog predated Cook by 152 years.

Predating all of these humans are the **stromatolites** in Hamelin Pool, which are rather like coral growths covered in blue-green algae, and are claimed to be the oldest and largest living fossils in the world. They are formed by micro-organisms, which are closely related to those that existed on earth 2000–3000 million years ago. They can easily be seen from the end of the *Hamelin Pool Rd.*

While the naming of Shark Bay is clear, that of Monkey Mia is shrouded in mystery. The most likely suggestion is that it is a combination of the name of the colonial survey ship *The Monkey,* which visited in 1830, and an Aboriginal word *mia,* meaning 'place' or 'home.'

Shark Bay has several claims to fame. The first is that it is a **World Heritage Marine Park** within a very long day's drive from Perth – 750 km, which makes flying there and hiring a car locally the better proposition.

The park boasts ten species of mammals, 98 species of reptiles and over 100 species of land based, wading and migratory birds, living along the shore and in the coastal desert of the bay. About 10% of the world's population of **dugong** – about 10,000 of them – live in Shark Bay in the seagrass meadows, which grow in the warm, shallow and sheltered waters of the bay. A dugong, a Malay name, is a warm blooded water mammal with a typical mermaid's tale. It is possible that it is the origin of the mermaid myth to be found in so many cultures. Like humans they live for 70 years, measure about 2.7 m and weigh in at around 250 kg.

There are also manta rays, turtles and other aquatic life; all easy to view because of the clarity of the waters.

Monkey Mia is unique in that it has bottlenose dolphins – *Tursiops truncatus* –which although remain wild, interact with humans and come in to the shallow waters every day to be fed. Understandably, everyone is concerned that this felicitous relationship should continue.

There is a small charge for entering the reserve and you should visit the **Dolphin Information Centre** on the beach (run by the National Park and Wildlife Service), and get the leaflet that outlines the way in which you should approach and feed these most attractive of animals. In truth, the situation has almost got out of hand with the visitors growing in numbers each year and it is only a matter of time before very strict controls are imposed.

The practice started back in the 1960s, when a visitor who was there fishing began feeding one of the dolphins from a boat. The others soon joined in and over the course of three generations, they have become so adapted that they now swim right into the beach to be fed. These dolphins are about 4 m in length and truly appear to enjoy and understand this relationship with humans.

Between Denham and Monkey Mia is the **François Peron National Park**, which is only truly accessible by four-wheel-drive. There are several tours from Denham to the park so you can leave the worry of driving to someone else.

The park is named after the French zoologist who accompanied the Nicolas Baudin scientific expedition to Southern and Western Australia in 1801. The park covers an area of 52,500 hectares and is true wilderness with salt lakes and arid scenery, at the northern extreme of the **Peron Peninsula**.

As Shark Bay is neatly positioned at the northern extreme of the southern wildflower varieties and at the southern extreme of the northern varieties, it has the longest wildflower season of any part of Western Australia, with over 700 species of flowering plants, many of which are exclusive to the Shark Bay World Heritage Region.

Shell Beach, which is easily accessible from the *Denham-Hamelin Rd,* has been formed by countless tiny white shells of the burrowing bivalve (*Fragum erugafum*). Some of the deposits of shells are buried as deep as

10m and the beach, depending how you measure it, runs for nearly 100 km.

Bilanden Birds, *Monkey Mia Rd, Denham*, is a new complex with a wide range of Australian birds on display, with over 100 aviaries. Open daily; $5. 🏃

CARNARVON

Tourist Information: Carnarvon Tourist Bureau, *90 Robinson St; tel: (099) 41 1446.*

ACCOMMODATION

Fascine Lodge Hotel-Motel, *1002 David Brand Dr.; tel: 41 2411.* **Gateway Motel**, *309 Robinson St; tel: 41 1532.* **Hospitality Inn Carnarvon**, *West St; tel: 41 1600.* **Mount Augustus Tourist Resort**, *Mt Augustus via Carnarvon; tel: 43 0527.* **Carnarvon Motel-Hotel**, *Olivia Terrace; tel: 41 1181.* **Gascoyne Hotel-Motel**, *Olivia Terrace; tel: 41 1412.* **Port Hotel-Motel Carnarvon**, *Robinson St; tel: 41 1704.* **HI: Backpackers Paradise**, *10 Robinson St; tel: 41 2966.*

EATING AND DRINKING

Gypsy's Restaurant, *26 Robinson St; tel: 9941 1445* **Dragon Pearl Chinese Restaurant**, *17 Francis St; tel: 9941 1941.*

SIGHTSEEING

This town is some 201 km to the north of Shark Bay and 905 km from Perth along the North West Coastal Hwy. It is the commercial centre of the Gascoyne area and is situated on the mouth of the Gascoyne River, overlooking a picturesque inlet called the **Fascine**.

Carnarvon was once a centre for the whaling industry and although those times are thankfully well past, it is still well placed for whale-watching as the humpback whales make their annual slow migration to and from their breeding grounds.

Dominating the skyline is a huge satellite tracking station, which is no longer used but is becoming something of a historical monument, because it was here that Australia received its first satellite broadcast and played its part in the space race.

The local jetty is a favourite place for fishing here, being 1 km in length. The blowholes along this stretch of coastline are quite spectacular with water spouts of 20m or more. The best blowholes are along *Blowholes Rd*, which runs 49 km to the north to **Point Quobba**.

Carnarvon is an excellent base for visiting the outback, in particular **Mt Augustus National Park**, 460 km to the east. The park contains the world's largest monocline – like Ayers Rock but twice as big, yet hardly known to tourists. To get there, you drive 173 km parallel to the Gascoyne River to **Gascoyne Junction**, a typical West Australian outback town with a pub, general store and petrol station, serving the pastoral stations in the region. Many of these stations welcome visitors and you can get details from the tourist information centre.

To the north of Carnarvon is the **North West Cape**, which is a peninsula extending into the Indian Ocean. You get there from Carnarvon by following the North West Coastal Hwy north for 118 km until you reach the **Minilya Road House** where the road forks, and you take the left hand turn along *Learmonth Minilya Rd*, which runs first to the small resort of **Coral Bay** – 78 km – and then about the same distance to **Exmouth**.

Both of these towns are places to access the **Ningaloo Reef**, which runs for 260 km along the western side of the peninsula.

The **Ningaloo Marine Park** is a totally protected area and you could think of it as a miniature version of the **Great Barrier Reef**. Inland the same protection is offered for much of the way by the **Cape Range National Park**. This is a marine life wonderland with dugongs, whale sharks, greenback turtles and, in June, July, Oct and Nov, humpback whales, as they cruise along the coast.

Exmouth is one of the newest towns in Australia, having been built in 1967 as a service town for the US Navy base, which has since been closed.

Both of these towns offer some tourist facilities, but they are both very small and cater, in the main, for skin divers.

321

CARNARVON–WYNDHAM

This is a *very* long route, mainly along the coast of the Indian Ocean. Carnarvon to Broome is 1463 km and Wyndham is another 1064 km from Broome, and the drive is not practical for the average tourist. But it can be done, and among its attractions are access to the Kimberley region and some other less-visited areas of Australia, such as the new National Park of the Bungle Bungles. And, if you persevere with a drive to Katherine, you can reach the Northern Territory routes to Darwin (see p. 265) or Alice Springs (p.279).

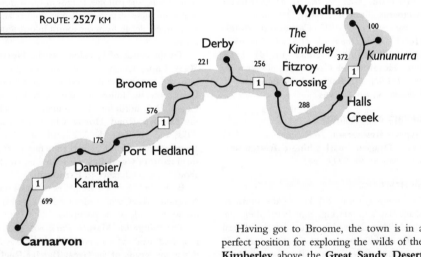

ROUTE: 2527 KM

322

Carnarvon to Broome is a continuation of the road from Perth to Carnarvon. The North West Coastal Road – Rte 1 – cuts inland from Carnarvon and heads north-west across country until it gets to **Karratha** and **Dampier**.

From there the road runs 226 km to **Port Hedland**. From Port Hedland there is a 475 km run to **Broome** with no towns along the way, although you can get petrol at the **Pardoo Roadhouse** (133 km from Port Hedland) and the **Sandfire Roadhouse** (291 km). Broome is a 25 km turn-off left from Rte 1.

Having got to Broome, the town is in a perfect position for exploring the wilds of the **Kimberley** above the **Great Sandy Desert** right up to Wyndham, which is as far north as you can easily get in Western Australia.

From Broome, rejoin Rte 1 – now the Great Northern Hwy – which runs for 146 km up to the **Willare Bridge Roadhouse**, where there is, turning left towards the sea, a 36 km road to **Derby**.

From Derby return to Willare Bridge, from where Rte 1 heads inland 217 km to the town of **Fitzroy Crossing**, entrance to **Geikie Gorge**. Two-thirds of the way along the road there is a turn off to the left to **Windjana Gorge**.

From Fitzroy Crossing it is 289 km along the lower slopes of the **Mueller Ranges** to

Halls Creek, which is above the Tanami Desert and the notorious Canning Stock Route. The road runs for 314 km over the Bungle Bungle range, through the small town of Warmun, until you come to a fork in the road. The left fork goes 56 km to Wyndham, while the right fork, which follows Rte 1, provides a side track to Kununurra and a possible continuation to the Northern Territory, ending at Katherine, on the Darwin–Alice Springs route (see p. 275).

BUSES

Greyhound Pioneer buses cover this whole route. One bus a day runs from Carnarvon as far as Port Hedland (11¾ hrs). From South Hedland (on Rte 1, 20 km by bus from Port Hedland) a separate service stops at Broome (7¾ hrs), Derby (10½ hrs), Halls Creek (16½ hrs), Wyndham (19 hrs) and Kununurra (20½ hrs), before continuing to Katherine and Darwin. OTT table 9133.

DAMPIER AND KARRATHA

Tourist Information: *Dampier Community Association, High St; tel: 9183 1243.*

ACCOMMODATION

Mercure Inn Dampier, *The Esplanade; tel: 9183 1222.* Peninsula Palms, *The Esplanade; tel: 9183 1888.* King Bay Holiday Village Resort, *The Esplanade; tel: 9183 1440.* Mermaid Hotel Motel, *The Esplanade; tel: 9183 1222.*

EATING AND DRINKING

Dampier Chinese Restaurant, *Dampier Shopping Centre; tel: 9183 1555.* Barnacle Bob's Restaurant, *The Esplanade; tel: 9183 1053.*

SIGHTSEEING

You need to think of these two towns as one. Dampier and Karratha are practically the same, two parts of the same largish town. Dampier itself is the commercial port for Hamersley Iron's mines. These are at Tom Price, Paraburdoo and Marandoo, and are linked to the port by a railway that runs 350 km.

These are not tourist destinations, although there is plenty of accommodation, modern shops and a very few restaurants.

You can go for a cruise among the islands of the Dampier Archipelago (named after the reformed buccaneer who charted this coast) with Coral Coast Tours *(tel: 9183 1269)* and it is possible to explore the nearby Burrup Peninsula, which has a large amount of Aboriginal engraving.

Karratha is 1535 km north of Perth on the Pilbara Coast. The town grew because of the development of the Hamersley Iron Project, the start of the Dampier Salt Project and the discovery of immense off-shore gas reserves by Woodside's North West Shelf Gas Project. The town is opposite the Dampier Archipelago and is a prime spot for fishing.

PORT HEDLAND

Tourist Information: *13 Wedge St; tel: 9173 1650.*

The post office is opposite the tourist office, where most banks are also situated.

ACCOMMODATION

Esplanade Hotel Motel, *Anderson St; tel: 9173 1798.* Hospitality Inn Port Hedland Motel, *Webster St; tel: 9173 1004.* Pier Hotel, *Esplanade; tel: 9173 1488.* Sandfire Roadhouse & Tavern Motel, *Great Northern Hwy, Sandfire; tel: 9176 5944.* South Hedland Motel, *Court Pl.; tel: 9172 2222.* Mercure Inn, *corner Lukis and McGregor Sts; tel: 9173 1511.* Mercure Inn Airport, *N.W. Coastal Hwy; tel: 9172 1222.*

EATING AND DRINKING

Malay Curry House, *Edgar St; tel: 9173 3435.* Mon–Fri 0900–1400, from 1700, Sat 1000–1400, from 1700. Oriental Galley Chinese Restaurant, *Edgar St.* Mon, Wed, Fri 1130–1330, Mon–Sun from 1700. Bangkok Rose, *Edgar St; tel: 9173 2629.* Tues–Sun from 1800, Thai. Dynasty Gardens Chinese Restaurant, *Tonkin St, S. Hedland; tel: 9172 3266.* Tues–Sun from 1800. Saltys Bistro, *Mercure Inn, corner Lukin and McGregor Sts; tel: 9173 1511.* Mon–Sun lunch and from 1800. Mangrove Room, *Mercure Inn Airport, N.W. Coastal Hwy; tel: 9172 1222.* Mon–Fri lunch and from 1900. **Arabella's**, *Last Chance Tavern, corner Throssel and Tonkin Sts, S. Hedland; tel: 9171 1222.* Tues–Sun 1130–1400, from 1800. **Kath's Kitchen Cafe**, *Wedge St; tel: 9173 2885.* Mon–Sun 0500–2100. **Natalie's Cafe**, *Richardson St; tel: 9173 2635.* **Shares Cafe**, *Boulevard Shopping Centre; tel: 9173 2630.* Mon–Sat 0830–1800.

SIGHTSEEING

The town is 1637 km north of Perth by way of the Great Northern Hwy. This is not an over-populated area – the whole of the shire of Port Hedland has a population of something under 4000 people. This area was one of the first dis-covered in Australia when the Dutch ships sailed by in the 1600. However, it was not until 1829 that Captain Peter Hedland discovered the entrance to the mangrove inlet which leads to the port.

More than thirty years were to pass before there was any further activity, which started with a sheep station and picked up momentum when pearls were found off-shore in the 1870s. Soon Port Hedland had become the home port for a fleet which consisted of around 150 pearling luggers.

In the 1950s, metal exploration was fol-lowed by tin, gold and manganese mining with iron following shortly afterwards. Nowadays the town is the main centre of iron ore in Western Australia, although the economy is moving slowly away from one industry reliance.

This is a commercial town where BHP, the biggest mining company in Australia, has sprawling works which are, in a sense, so ugly they become industrial art. Everything in the town eventually gets coated in pale-red iron dust. It has been reported that there are no automatic teller machines in Port Hedland because of the all-pervasive dust that gums up the works, but this has now been shown to be an urban myth. It can still be a very dusty town.

The town lives on its industry and is, indeed, very proud of its connections with commerce, calling itself The Port of Big Ships. Massive ore carriers – the largest in the world – operate from the port almost every day of the year. There is a tour available of the **BHP**

324

loading facility which runs for 90 mins Mon–Fri and costs $8.

The other export is salt, which can be seen as salt dunes alongside the North West Coastal Hwy, ready for shipment overseas. This salt is not mined. It is produced by solar evaporation in ponds close to the town.

The few attractions include a section of the old **Port Hedland to Marble Bar railway line**, complete with crane and tender, in the Lions Park. It is possible to visit the **Royal Flying Doctor** base on *Richardson St* Mon–Fri at 1115. No charge, but a donation is requested.

The **Town Observation Tower**, behind the tourist information offices, is 26 m tall and allows you to watch the big ships easing their way in and out of harbour. There are also whale- and turtle-watching tours Nov–Mar.

BROOME

Tourist Information: Broome Tourist Bureau, *corner Bagot St and Broome Rd; tel: 92 2222.*

ACCOMMODATION AND FOOD

Cable Beach Club, *Cable Beach Rd; tel: 92 0400.* **Continental Hotel**, *Weld St; tel: 92 1002.* **The Mangrove Hotel**, *Carnarvon St; tel: 92 1303.* **Roebuck Bay Hotel Motel**, *Carnarvon St; tel: 92 1221.* **Tropicana Inn Broome Motel**, *corner Saville and Robinson Sts; tel: 92 1204.* **Ocean Lodge**, *Cable Beach Rd; tel: 93 7700.* **Mercure Hotel**, *Carnarvon St; tel: 92 1212.* **HI: The Last Resort**, *2 Bagot St; tel: 93 5000.*

Dampiers on the Terrace, Continental Hotel, *Weld St; tel: 92 1002.* Licensed. **Charters, The Mangrove Hotel**, *Carnarvon St; tel: 92 1303.* Licensed. **Asian Affair**, *Cable Beach Club, Cable Beach Rd; tel: 92 0400.* **The Portlight, Mercure Hotel**, *tel: 92 1212.*

SIGHTSEEING

Broome is 2230 km north of Perth and 1885 km south of Darwin, and was once the pearl capital of the world. Up until, and just after, the turn of the century, there were often more than 400 pearling luggers working out of Broome, with many of the employees Asians, imported for the task. You can see reminders of Broome's pearling past all over the town in the houses that were built for the pearlers. Worth visiting are **China town**, which was once home to 3000 Asians and is now the small commercial centre of the town, and the **Japanese cemetery**, for pearling was always a dangerous task.

The first inhabitants of the Broome area was a tribe of Aborigines called the **Djugan**, and it is also very probable that the area was visited by Asian seafarers.

William Dampier, a buccaneer turned explorer, was probably the first European to visit the area, arriving in 1688. There was then a hiatus of more than a century until the arrival of Charles Darwin in the *Beagle*, which made a survey of the coast. There was another gap until 1880, when a settlement was started to support the eighty small boats in the pearling fleet that had moved north from Shark Bay. The town was named in 1883 after the then governor of the state, Sir Frederick Napier Broome.

Pearling was at its height in the 1920s when the town was, indeed, the pearl capital of the world – although most of the profits were made from the mother-of-pearl used for buttons – but after that the crop declined.

During the war there was a Japanese air raid on Broome and the wrecks of some allied aircraft can still be seen at low tide in **Roebuck Bay**. When hostilities ceased and much had been forgiven, the Japanese, great experts in this area, established pearl culture farms at **Kuri Bay** in 1956 and later at **Cygnet Bay**. If you want to see how pearls are harvested, the **Willie Creek Pearl Farm** in *Lullfitz Dr. (tel: 93 6000)*, has demonstrations and tours.

What brought the town out of the doldrums was the opening of a sealed road to Perth in 1982 and the fact that, only a year or so later, the rich and philanthropic Lord McAlpine fell in love with the place. He was directly or indirectly responsible for much of the refurbishment of the town and for the erection of the up-market **Cable Beach Resort**. After a few years he slowly started to withdraw from Australia, back to London, but the work he carried out is still there and Broome has become an almost perfect laid-back tropical resort.

There are some odd aspects to Broome. For example, there is a beach in front of the resort,

---

The Kimberley

Broome is the gateway to the **Kimberley Region**, which is vast, almost unknown to tourists and contains some of the best cattle country and the largest cattle stations in the world. The Kimberley region has diamonds near **Lake Argyle**, gold at **Hall's Creek** and pearls, even to this day, at Broome.

---

where the sea recedes as far as ½ km at low tide. And then there is the cinema. The **Sun Pictures**, in Chinatown, is not a picture theatre – it is a 'picture garden', as it is run in the open air. It is claimed that this is the world's oldest theatre of its type, as it opened in 1916. As it was the only entertainment in the area, it was immensely popular and often enjoyed Saturday night crowds of over 600. You can still see movies under the stars and even bring a picnic dinner with you.

Cable Beach, 6 km out of town and running for 22 km with sand like talcum powder, is so called because it was the terminus of the cable across the **Timor Sea** from **Java**. It is one of the few beaches in the world that can offer exploration on camel back. You are also allowed to drive a car on to the beach at a maximum speed of 15 kph. But be warned, the sea comes in like a racehorse after the tide turns, and in a bad year a dozen cars can be caught and ruined by the tide.

The **court house** in *Hamersley St* was originally a cable station, which was shipped there by mistake in 1888. It was sent from England and should have gone to Kimberley, South Africa. Not the Kimberley in Australia.

Broome is a multi-cultural town because of the Japanese, Filipino and Malay pearl divers, who form an essential part of its history. The town does not forget its cultural heritage and Chinatown, with its unique mixture of occidental and oriental buildings, has been restored and even the street signs are in five languages. The tourist office has a guide to a **Heritage Trail** through the town. There is an annual festival called **Shinju Matsuri** every

325

August, which manages to combine elements of several Asian celebrations.

Five kilometres past Cable Beach is **Gantheaume Point**, which has a cast of dinosaurs' tracks embedded in the sandstone at the base of the cliffs – the originals can only be seen at very low tide.

Broome is also popular with bird-watchers, with the **Broome Bird Observatory**, on Roebuck Bay, rated as one of Australia's top non-breeding grounds for migrant Arctic waders, which come to visit from Siberia. Nearly 250 different types of birds are to be found in the area.

The Broome Historical Society Museum is housed in the old customs house in *Saville St*. Open Mon–Fri 1000–1600 Apr–Nov and sporadically Nov–Apr. It is very small but extremely well done, without the over-ordered structure which is so off putting in some museums.

To the south of Broome is **Eighty Mile Beach**. This is unique among features named in this way as it is indeed 80 miles long. To be precise it is 85 miles – 137 km – in length and is the result of the **Great Sandy Desert** meeting the Indian ocean.

DERBY

Tourist Information: Derby Tourist Bureau, *1 Clarendon St*; tel: *(091) 91 1426.*

ACCOMMODATION

King Sound Resort Hotel, *Loch St; tel: 93 1044*. **Derby Boab Inn**, *Loch St; tel: 91 1044*. **Spinifex Hotel**, *Clarendon St; tel: 91 1233*.

SIGHTSEEING

Derby is more than 2300 km by road from Perth, 220 km from Broome and 36 km from the Great Northern Hwy. It is on **King Sound** at the mouth of the Fitzroy River. The town is the administrative centre for several aboriginal communities and the commercial centre of the central portion of the Kimberley. The port was originally established in 1880 and is surrounded by mudflats and tidal marsh. The tide has a rise and fall of 12 m, which made mooring for ships difficult. This is perhaps why it has not been used as a port for over a dozen years.

Although there had been cattle runs in the area from 1855 onwards, the town was not gazetted until 1882, when it was named after Lord Derby, the then Secretary of State for the Colonies. The cattle runs were stocked through one of the epic journeys of Australian pioneers. The MacDonald brothers drove stock from Goulburn in New South Wales to Derby to stock the early properties, over a distance of 6440 km, which makes it the longest cattle drive in the world. There were only 30 cattle left alive when they arrived at Derby. Why did they take them overland? There simply was no other way. And, believe it or not, thirty cattle were enough to start a major cattle empire.

This is the nearest town to some of the most spectacular gorge country in the world. It is possible to get to some of the gorges in a two-wheel-drive vehicle during dry weather, especially if the grader has just been through levelling the road. The Gibb River Rd will take you to **Windjana National Park**, before looping back towards the Great Northern Hwy. This section of the road is acceptable for two-wheel-drive conventional vehicles if you drive slowly and with great care. The rest of the Gibb River Rd goes right through the Kimberley, all the way to Wyndham and it is not recommended for anything except a four-wheel-drive, with an experienced driver. Even after grading, the surface is very rough with corrugations that test even a four-wheel-drive. This is truly rugged country and all proper precautions regarding carrying water and the suitability of the vehicle must be taken.

The best way to explore all of the gorges is with a four-wheel-drive tour, which you can arrange in Derby. Two tour operators are **Hot Land Safaris**, *Stanley St; tel: 9193 1312*; and **Boab Tours**; *tel: 91 1237*.

Windjana Gorge, which is 145 km away in Windjana National Park, features well-preserved fossil reefs and the water streaked-walls of the gorge, through which the **Lennard River** flows and, in the wet season, can rise as high as 100 m. This best way to view the gorge is by following a 3.5 km trail that winds through the gorge. Note that the 21,000 hectare park is inaccessible during the wet season, as is much of the Kimberley.

Tunnel Creek is a natural tunnel gouged through limestone above Western Australia's oldest cave system. In the last century Kimberley Aborigines, led by **Jundumurra**, rebelled against the invading Europeans and used these caves as hide-outs. Jundumurra was tracked down and killed by the police in 1897. These caves are within the National Park off *Gibb Rd* and you can wade 750m through the tunnel – sometimes the water can be chest high in some of the permanent pools. You need a powerful torch, which will allow you to see the colonies of bats. At the end you come out on the other side of the **Napier range**. This is most certainly not recommended for anyone who has the slightest touch of claustrophobia.

Just outside Derby, 7 km away, you will find a huge boab tree, which is 14m in diameter. It was once used to hold Aboriginal prisoners overnight.

FITZROY CROSSING

Tourist Information: Fitzroy Cross Tourist Office, *Flynn Dr.; tel: (091) 91 5355.*

ACCOMMODATION

Crossing Motor Inn, *Skuthorp Rd; tel: 91 5080.* **Fitzroy River Lodge Motel**, *Great Northern Hwy; tel: 91 5141.*

SIGHTSEEING

This very small outback town is 243 km from Derby along the Great Northern Hwy, just under 400 km from Broome and 2524 km from Perth. Fitzroy Crossing is 114m above sea level and is in the middle of the floodplains of the Fitzroy River. The name is literally correct as the town is on a crossing of the Fitzroy River.

This was always an area of Aboriginal unrest against the European intruders. The telegraph office was attacked and burned down in 1894. The following year there was a pitched battle between a police patrol and a group of Aboriginals who had hidden out in **Geikie Gorge**. In 1967, in more peaceful times, Geikie Gorge – the name is pronounced Geekie with a hard 'g' – was established as a National Park.

The park, 17 km from the town and accessible by car from the highway, is the major attraction for visitors as the small town has little

to offer. During the dry season – Apr–Nov, but more safely May–Oct – there are boat tours along the Fitzroy River through the gorge, which is 14 km long and has walls that are up to 30m high. The walls are a stunning mixture of colours – yellow, ochre and grey. You can see how high the floodwaters rise in the wet because they leave the lower part of the walls a creamy white. Where the gorge narrows the line goes much higher, showing how the flood waters are blasted through. The water comes from a catchment area the size of Victoria, so although the actual rainfall is low – say 500mm a year – the flow in full spate is tremendous; technically about 29,000 cubic metres a second.

The gorge is full of wildlife, including harmless crocodiles and, amazingly, stingray and sawfish, who over the centuries have adapted to a freshwater environment. **Fitzroy Crossing Tours** – *tel: (091) 91 5155* – have twice daily tours to the gorge, including a boat trip up the river through the gorge. You can check on current conditions with the park ranger; *tel: (091) 91 5121.*

HALLS CREEK

Tourist Information: Halls Creek Tourist Centre, *Memorial Park, Great Northern Hwy; tel: (091) 68 6262.*

ACCOMMODATION

Halls Creek Kimberley Hotel/Motel, *Roberta Ave; tel: 68 6101.* **Halls Creek Motel**, *Great Northern Hwy; tel: 68 6001.*

SIGHTSEEING

There are two towns of this name – the original site, which is now a ghost town, and the present day town. The original town was named after Charles Hall, who reported finding gold here in 1885, 6 years after the district was first explored by a European, Alexander Forrest. That gold find of 1879 led to other finds in the area and the gold rush to the Kimberley in 1886, which was the first gold rush in Western Australia. This involved some 10,000 diggers, although this is often disputed and 2000 is suggested as being a more likely figure. The gold soon petered out though, and Halls Creek started to become the ghost town that it is today. Indeed, the phrase ghost town flatters it, as it is basically a pile of empty bottles with the occasional glimpse of a mud brick foundation. The new Halls Creek was established in 1948, 15 km from the old town and 2832 km from Perth.

Basically this is a Kimberley cattle town, right on the edge of the **Great Sandy Desert**. Despite its small size, this is the largest town in the Kimberley even though it is most definitely the outback. The town has two attractions nearby. The first is **China Wall**, which looks as though it was constructed like the Great Wall of China but is, in fact, a freak of nature, with the weathered white quartz set back from the stone as if it were mortar and the resulting apparent wall running for many kilometres across country. The wall is 5 km east of the town, about 1.5 km off the road.

The second is fossicking for gold around the old town site and, yes, it is quite possible that you will strike moderately lucky. If you get nothing you can visit the **Arts Centre** in *Duncan Rd,* which sells jewellery made from Halls Creek gold.

SIDE TRACK FROM HALLS CREEK

BUNGLE BUNGLE

The newest national park in Western Australia – gazetted in 1987 – is **Bungle Bungle**, which is 175 km south of **Kununurra** with access off the Great Northern Hwy. Vehicle access is only by four-wheel-drive as this is very rugged country. Every precaution should be taken, including registering with the park ranger on *(091) 68 0200,* before setting off.

It is best to take a conducted tour and, indeed, perhaps the best way to appreciate the Bungle Bungle is from the air. There are flights from Kununurra and from **Halls Creek.**

WYNDHAM

Tourist Information: Wyndham Tourist Bureau, *Old Post Office Building, O'Donnell St; tel: (091) 61 1054.*

ACCOMMODATION

Wyndham Town Hotel, *O'Donnell St; tel: 61 1003.* **Wyndham Community Club Inc,** *Great Northern Hwy; tel: 61 1130.*

SIGHTSEEING

Wyndham is the most northerly proper town in Western Australia although the little hamlet of **Kalumburu** might make a challenge for that title. Originally Wyndham was known as Anton's Landing, but this was changed in honour of the son of Lady Barker, the wife of the governor.

The town started as a port on the **Cambridge Gulf** to service the gold fields of the Kimberley in 1886. It was also the point through which the telegraph line from Perth passed, although there were problems in the early days from Aboriginals, who made the insulators into spearheads. Wyndham was one of the few Australian towns attacked by the Japanese in the war and experienced air raids in 1942, although no one was killed. The port now serves some large mango and banana plantations, which were the end result of the ill-fated **Ord River Irrigation Scheme**. In the initial stages, the damming of the Ord resulted in crops ruined by disease and birds. Now the scheme has changed direction and different crops are being planted with better results.

A new town has grown up some 3 km east of the original site on the Great Northern Hwy, and this is now the main residential area.

There is a Heritage Walk around the buildings in the old port area and the tourist office can provide a printed guide. The historic buildings include the old **Shire Hall**, the **Post Office**, which now houses the tourist information centre, and the court house, which is now a museum.

There are a number of charter flight operators working out of Wyndham and one of these flights will give you a quick oversight of the area. **Ord Air Charter** *(tel: 61 1335)* offers the **Atlantis Experience**, which takes you over King George's Falls and some of the rugged outback country on a 2 hr 20 min flight that costs around $140 a person. Another flight goes across the Kimberley cattle country and gives you a tour of a working station.

SIDE TRACK FROM WYNDHAM

Rejoin Rte 1 from Wyndham, and turn left (eastwards), until you reach Kununurra, about 100 km from Wyndham.

KUNUNURRA

Tourist Information: Kununurra Tourist Bureau; *Coolibah Dr.; tel: (091) 68 1177.*

ACCOMMODATION

Quality Inn – Kununurra, *Duncan Hwy; tel: 68 1455.* **Kimberley Court Private Hotel**, *corner River Fig Ave and Erythrina St; tel: 68 1411.* **Hotel Kununurra**, *Messmate Way; tel: 68 1344.*

SIGHTSEEING

This is a new town that was created in the 1960s as the centre of the Ord River Irrigation Scheme. The name comes from the local Aboriginal for the area, which is *gananoorong*.

It is situated on **Lake Kununurra** – sometimes more prosaically called the **Diversion Dam** (which is the structure that is responsible for its creation) on the **Ord River**. This is the ideal base for exploring the wonders of **Lake Argyle**, created by the **Argyle Dam** in 1971, which is 50 km to the south. It also has many tour operators offering trips into the hinterland, especially to the **Bungle Bungle**, which is a very recently explored part of outback Australia.

Because of Kununurra's position on the lake, it has become a centre for water sports. Below the dam there is good fishing, but swimming is not recommended because of crocodiles.

Mirima National Park is 2 km from the centre of town and contains the **Hidden Valley**, which is a steep gorge with wonderful colours and striations and is a sort of miniature version of the Bungle Bungle (see p.328).

Two hundred and fifty kilometres to the south are the **Argyle Diamond Mines**, which you can only visit on a conducted tour. Although this mine produces some 35% of the world's diamonds, most of them are destined to be used on the end of cutting tools. However, the mine also produces the rare pink diamonds, which in recent years have soared in value and are now more valuable, carat for carat, then ordinary diamonds.

Lake Argyle contains nine times the water of Sydney Harbour and covers an area of 700 sq km. It was created by damming the River Ord and flooding a valley – the islands in the lake were originally peaks within the valley. There is now commercial fishing on the lake.

Argyle Downs Homestead, from which you can explore the lake, was founded in the late 1880s by Patsy Durack and his two brothers, who arrived there after a two-year trek from Queensland, bringing with them 2000 head of cattle. This herd formed the start of the current Kimberley beef industry. Their homestead would have been flooded by the lake, so it was dismantled and reconstructed at the head of the dam. This reconstructed homestead is now a museum; open daily 0830–1630 May–Oct, $2.

The homestead was the subject of a famous book about Australian outback life in the Kimberley, *Kings in Grass Castles,* by Mary Durack, essential reading if you are visiting this region.

The homestead is now in the centre of **Lake Argyle Tourist Village**, *tel: (091) 68 7360,* which is the old dam construction workers' camp, revitalised, redesigned and much rebuilt. From the village you can take cruises across the lake to see the wildlife and **Zebra Rock Island**.

Connection to the Northern Territory

By continuing on Rte 1, the Victoria Hwy, past Kununurra, you reach the Northern Territory border after 100 km. Another 454 very empty kilometres brings you to Katherine, from where you can drive north to Darwin or south to Alice Springs (see Darwin–Alice Springs route, p. 274).

WESTERN AUSTRALIA NATIONAL PARKS

INFORMATION AND OVERVIEW

Western Australia Dept of Conservation and Land Management, *tel: (07) 9334 0333.*

The size of the state means that the many national parks are, in some cases, considerable distances from each other and this needs to be borne in mind when planning a tour of the state.

Perth, luckily has many national parks within relatively easy reach. Perhaps the most important is **Leeuwin-Naturaliste National Park,** which is the result of an amalgamation in the 1970s which ended in a park of 15,500 hectares which covers most of the coast line with a break in the middle where the **Margaret River** comes down to the sea. In fact the town **Margaret River,** 11 km inland, is a perfect base for exploring this park, which covers the coastline of the Indian Ocean between the two caps at the south-west corner of Australia.

The scenery of the park is very varied, ranging from some very wild seashores to beautiful sheltered beaches. Inland the water eating its way through the limestone has created a wide range of caves, including the **Yallingup cave** which runs for 40 m underground and is renowned for its crystalline formations.

There are no problem with car access to this park as the Caves Road, a major tourist highway, skirts its edges. The only problem in this park is that crumbling cliff edges can lead to tragedy and great care should be taken.

Kalbarri National Park to the north of Perth beyond **Geraldton** covers 186,000 hectares and has dramatic river gorge scenery with the **Murchison River** meandering 80 km through the park. It is possible to drive on unsealed roads – entrance by way of the Ajana Road – to the edges of the gorge, which range in height up to 150 m above the river itself. The park not only has the magnificent gorge

but also a coastline with soaring cliffs and some amazing rock formations, best seen just to the south of the town of Kalbarri off the road to Port Gregory (unsealed but normally quite passable for two-wheeldrive vehicles). The park is safe enough for short walks but canoeing and serious hiking require permission in writing from the park ranger – *tel: (099) 37 1140.*

The **John Forrest National Park** is very close to Perth – 25 km to the east –and was the first national park in Western Australia having been listed at the turn of the century. The park covers some 1600 hectares and the original intention appears to have been to try and turn it into as much like a large English country garden as possible. This was unfortunate, and the park still has a scraped disciplined look about it which plainly has little to do with its original state. In the wildflower season, Aug–Oct, it can have magnificent displays. Access is easy from the Great Eastern Highway.

The **Walyunga National Park** is just 45 km from Perth and covers 1800 hectares of wooded slopes on the **Darling Scarp** and drops from 280 m to 30 m above sea level. In the park is the **Swan River,** which has cut a large channel down to granite beds and these connect as a series of large pools which are ideal for swimming and canoeing. These pools can turn to rapids in the wet season. Car access is off the Great Northern Highway 8 km past **Upper Swan.**

Right up north near **Derby** and **Fitzroy Crossing** is the **Windjana Gorge National Park,** which covers 21,000 hectares and is only accessible during the dry season. Nearby are the National Parks of **Geikie Gorge** and **Tunnel Creek.** The newest national park in Western Australia – gazetted in 1987 – is **Bungle Bungle,** which is 175 km south of Kununurra, with access off the Great Northern Highway. Vehicle access is only by four-wheel-drive, as this is very rugged country and every precaution should be taken – including registering with the park ranger on *(091) 68 0200* before setting off. It is best to take a conducted tour and, indeed, perhaps the best way to appreciate the Bungle Bungle is from the air. There are flights from Kununurra and from Halls Creek.

Even more wild and even more inaccessible is **Drysdale River National Park** which is 350 km north west of Kununurra; the 440,000 hectares remained basically unexplored by Europeans until a major expedition was mounted as recently as 1975. Note that vehicular access of any sort is still virtually impossible and perhaps the only way to see this rough and rugged terrain is by helicopter. The park ranger is contactable on *(091) 68 0200*.

REGION BY REGION

This listing for the most part ignores the national parks and nature reserves that are a long way from the recommended routes in this book.

In and around Perth
Avon Valley
John Forrest *No campsite.*
Kalamunda *No campsite or picnic area.*
Moore River *No facilities.*
Neerabup *No facilities.*
Serpentine Falls
Waylunga *No campsite.*
Yalgorup *No campsite, picnic area or walking trail.*
Yanchep *No campsite or picnic area. See p. 315.*

The South Western Highway
The Perth–Albany route, pp. 297–305, is designed to take in the most important of these parks.
Beedelup *No facilities*
D'Entrecasteaux *No picnic area or walking trail.*
Hassell *No facilities.*
Leeuwin-Naturaliste *See p. 303.*
Mount Frankland
Porongurup *No campsite.*
Scott *No facilities.*
Shannon
Stirling Range
Trent Forest

Torndirrup *No facilities*
Walpole-Nornalup
West Cape Howe

The Brand Highway
The route from which to visit the majority of these parks, all on the coast to the north of Perth, is Perth to Carnarvon, pp. 314–321.

Alexander Morrison *No facilities.*
Badgingarra *Walking trail but no other facilities.*
Kalbarri *No campsite.*
Mt Lesueur *No facilities.*
Nambung *No campsite.*
Stockyard Gully *Picnic area only.*
Tathra *No facilities.*
Watheroo *No campsite.*

The Pilbara and North-west
Some of these parks can easily be visited from towns along the Carnarvon to Wyndham route, pp. 322–329, in particular from Dampier and Karratha. Others are a long, long way from any route in this book.

Barrow Island Nature Reserve *From Dampier or Karratha.*
Collier Range No facilities
Dolphin Island Nature Reserve. *From Dampier or Karratha.*
Karijini *From Dampier or Karratha.* .
Kennedy Range. *About 100 km east of Carnarvon.*
Millstream Chichester *Accessible from Dampier and Karratha.*

The Kimberley
Bungle Bungle *See p. 328.*
Drysdale River *No facilities.*
Geikie Gorge
Purnululu
Tunnel Creek *No campsite.*
Windjana Gorge

The South Coast
These two coastal parks lie between Albany and Esperance – see p. 305.

Fitzgerald River *No picnic sites.*
Stokes *No walking trails.*

331

SOUTH AUSTRALIA

You will rarely hear an Australian speak badly about South Australia. It is, to many Australians, almost another country. And an admirable country at that. It produces large amounts of wine – some of it Australia's best. It has a biennial arts festival, which is the envy of every other state. And it has the only gambling casino in the country with any pretensions to style. As a final bonus, its capital city is one of the only two cities in Australia that has been built to a plan.

GEOGRAPHY

South Australia has always very firmly followed its own course and not fallen into line behind its neighbours. Its geographical position might have something to do with it. To the south it is bounded by the Southern Ocean, to the east by New South Wales, Queensland and Victoria, to the west by Western Australia and the northern boundary – wild, rugged country – abuts the

Northern Territory. It is contiguous to all the mainland states. South Australia, half as big again as Texas, covers 984,377 sq km, about an eighth of the whole of Australia. Although half the state is pastoral land, the northern part of the state is some of the toughest desert country in Australia, which is why most of the population lives in the southern coastal zones beneath the 32nd Parallel. Think of the state as two separate parts – the green and verdant south and the harsh and inhospitable north. The southern third is all accessible from Adelaide by road, with no journey needing to be longer than three hours. According to the last census, the population of the state is about 1½ million, of whom a million live in and around Adelaide. After Adelaide the two largest towns are Whyalla at 25,527 and Mt Gambier at 21,155.

The coastline of South Australia has two major indentations: Spencer Gulf, between the **Eyre** and **Yorke Peninsulas**, and Gulf of St Vincent, between the Yorke and **Fleurieu Peninsulas**.

The gulfs create a sort of trident shape of land coming into the Southern Ocean. Off Gulf St Vincent is **Kangaroo Island**, the largest of

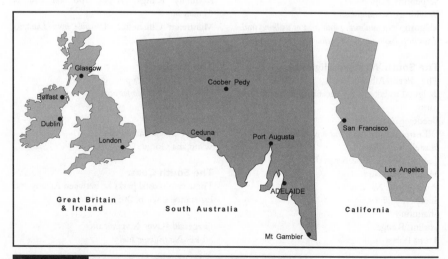

the islands off the coast of South Australia, some 480 km in circumference.

East from Adelaide, towards the border with New South Wales, is the **Barossa Valley**, one of Australia's prime wine growing areas. Once you travel north as far as **Hawker**, past **Port Augusta**, you start running into the arid lands until you come to the **Lake Eyre National Park**, through which runs the Birdsville Track, while to the west the **Simpson Desert** eventually comes to the boundary of the Northern Territory.

By and large the state is not mountainous and the inland area is mainly plains and deserts. The **Mt Lofty-Flinders Ranges** run for about 800 km from Lake Torrens to Cape Jervis and in the south never reach more than 727 m. In the north the highest point is **St Mary's Peak**, which rises to 1166 m. Much of the interior is taken up by National Parks. The only major river of the state is the mighty **Murray**, which meanders through the state and enters the sea in the **Coorong** through a heavily silted estuary 80 km south of Adelaide.

The northern Flinders Ranges is surrounded by a series of episodic lakes, which only ever become filled after heavy rain and most years look like shallow depressions with encrusted surfaces. The largest of these lakes is **Lake Eyre**, which is 15 m below sea level.

Wine forms a major part of the South Australian economy. The state holds about 42% of Australia's vineyards: over 25,000 hectares are being used for growing grapes, to make wines which are now widely recognised as being of world standard. Agriculture is mainly sheep – merinos – and cattle. But South Australia also has a solid mineral industry and **Roxby Downs**, in the mid north, holds what is potentially the world's largest copper and uranium mine. **Whyalla** is an iron and steel town and **Coober Pedy**, **Andamooka** and similar towns produce about two-thirds of Australia's opals.

CLIMATE

The climate of South Australia in its southern half is close to ideal. There are hot dry summers offset by relatively mild nights and cool – by Australian standards – winters, and most of the rainfall comes between May and August. It does not amount to much: the average is 528 mm making it the driest of the states – 80% of the state gets an average of less than 250 mm a year. South Australia is often described as the driest state in the driest continent on Earth and must be unique in having a government that sponsored advertisements saying 'Save water; shower with a friend'. The capital Adelaide and most of the coastal belt has a Mediterranean climate - Adelaide has roughly the equivalent latitude to Malta and the Greek islands

HISTORY

South Australia was the first of the Australian states, and one of the first places in the world, to give voting rights to women, in April 1896.

The state owes much to Colonel William Light, who in 1836 carefully designed and placed the capital 10 km in from the sea. The strip, of which it was the centre, was ideal for wheat and within twenty years the land between the St Vincent Gulf and the ranges had been taken up by wheat farmers. South Australia became the granary of Australia because of the climate and the easy access to a port. In the 1840s and 1850s a wave of German migrants fleeing religious oppression arrived and moved into Adelaide Hill and the Barossa Valley and started growing vines. From the beginning there were German influences. There were some thirty satellite villages to Adelaide by the 1840s and some of them, such as **Hahndorf, Klemzig** and **Lobethal**, were German settlements, whose wine festivals are still celebrated with oom-pah-pah bands.

The decision was made in the early days to have a different gauge railway to Victoria and the bulk of produce either had to be shipped from the Port of Adelaide or along the Murray by paddle steamers. One of the problems was that the river sometimes dried up and in trade South Australia was always at a disadvantage compared to Victoria and New South Wales. The gauges of the railway were not brought into uniformity until 1950. Incidentally, when Douglas MacArthur, made his famous 'I shall return' speech, after being forced out of the Philippines by the Japanese in 1942, he was at a railway station in South Australia.

333

ADELAIDE

Adelaide, named after William IV's queen, was planned by William Light and built in stone by a solid society enjoying new-found prosperity. The early, and still impressive buildings, have been challenged in recent times by office buildings of, perhaps, less apparent solid worth. Yet the feeling of an elegant city of Victorian solidity prevails. And the architecture truly reflects the society, which is stable, entrenched and based on old values and old money, and is far removed from what are regarded as the flash trivialities of Sydney.

TOURIST INFORMATION

The South Australian Travel Centre, *corner North Terrace and King William St; tel: 8212 1505.*

ARRIVING AND DEPARTING

Getting to and from Adelaide is basically by air. You can drive from Sydney by way of **Broken Hill** along the Barrier Hwy, but it is a long drive. The distance of 1401 km is roughly the same as London to Rome. You could also drive from **Darwin** through **Alice Springs** and **Coober Pedy** to Adelaide, and that way you would have traversed the whole of Australia from north to south, and driven 3045 km into the bargain. Finally you could drive across the **Nullarbor Plain** from **Perth**, which would be 2709 km of fairly boring scenery. Having driven all of these routes, I believe that flying is the answer. There are daily international and interstate flights and the airport is only about a quarter of an hour from the city centre.

GETTNG AROUND

For the visitor the easiest way to think of Adelaide is as six areas – the city, North

Adelaide, **Glenelg**, **Port Adelaide**, the outer suburbs and the beaches. The city is a long strip set on a flat, fertile corridor of land, which runs between **Gulf St Vincent** and the **Mt Lofty Ranges**.

Getting around Adelaide is easy. This is a city where the weather and the layout – most of the city is flat – were made for walking. The public transport system is unusually efficient and the tickets are the same whether you travel by bus, tram or train. For buses the TransAdelaide office, on the corner of *King William and Currie Sts* has timetables and transport maps. Trains run from the Railway Terminal on *North Terrace*. The only remaining electric tram is the one which runs to the seaside resort of Glenelg from Adelaide's **Victoria Square**. There is a rapid transit system of buses called the **O-Bahn**, which run along a special track from the city to the north-eastern foothills. This is said to be the world's longest guided bus way. The bus services also include the free central city **Bee Line. The Adelaide Explorer tram** – *tel: 8364 1933* – tours the main attractions of the city on a loop that takes 2½ hrs, and you can get on and off as you wish. It is not a true tram, but does look like one.

STAYING IN ADELAIDE

Expensive – $250 plus
Hyatt Regency Adelaide Hotel, *North Terrace; tel: 8231 1234.* **Hindley Parkroyal**, *65 Hindley St; tel: 8231 5552.*

Fairly expensive – $150–$250
Stamford Plaza Adelaide, *150 North Terrace; tel: 8461 1111.* **Holiday Inn Park Suites** *(FL), 255 Hindley St; tel: 8231 8333.* **Hilton Hotel Adelaide**, *233 Victoria Sq; tel: 8217 0711.*

Moderate – $70–$150
Country Comfort Inn Adelaide, *226 South Terrace; tel: 8223 4355.* **Adelaide Meridien**

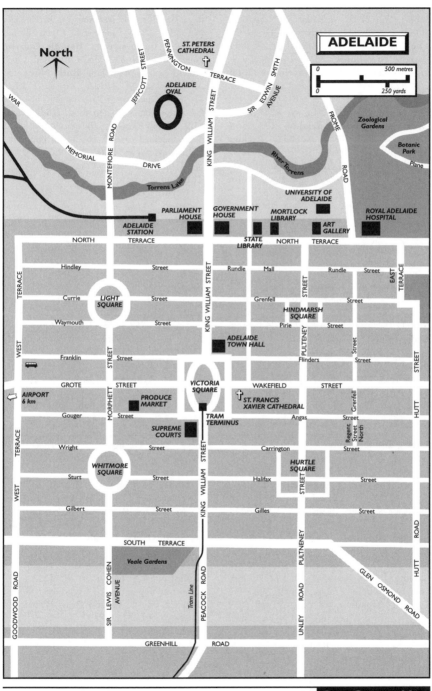

ADELAIDE

| 0 | | 500 metres |
| 0 | | 250 yards |

North

Motel *(FL), 21–37 Melbourne St, N. Adelaide 5006; tel: 8267 3033.* **Richmond Hotel On The Mall,** *128 Rundle Mall; tel: 8223 4044.* **Barron Townhouse Hotel,** *164 Hindley St; tel: 8211 8255.* **Adelaide Travelodge Hotel,** *208–223 South Terrace; tel: 8223 2744.* **O'Connell Inn Motel** *(BW), 197–199 O'Connell St, N. Adelaide; tel: 8239 0766.* **Grosvenor Hotel Adelaide,** *125 North Terrace; tel: 8231 2961.* **Adelaide Paringa Motel** *(GC), 15 Hindley St; tel: 8231 1000.* **Quality Hotel Adelaide,** *62 Brougham Pl., N. Adelaide; tel: 8239 0189.* **Regal Park Motor Inn** *(FL), 44 Barton Terrace; tel: 8267 3222.* **Strathmore Hotel,** *129 North Terrace; tel: 8212 6911.* **The Directors Studio Hotel,** *259 Gouger St; tel: 8231 3572.* **Festival Lodge Motel,** *140 North Terrace; tel: 8212 7877.*

Cheap – under $70

Motel Adjacent Casino, *25 Bank St; tel: 8231 8881.* **Ambassadors Hotel,** *107 King William St; tel: 8231 4331.* **City Central Motel,** *23 Hindley St; tel: 8231 4049.* **Princes Lodge Motel,** *73 Lefevre Terrace, N. Adelaide; tel: 8267 5566.* **Adelaide City Parklands Motel** *(BU), 471 Pulteney St; tel: 8223 1444.* **Brecknock Hotel,** *401 King William St; tel: 8231 5467.* **Clarice Motel,** *220 Hutt St; tel: 8223 3560.* **Plaza Hotel,** *85 Hindley St; tel: 8231 6371.*

Eating and Drinking

Jarmers, *297 Kensington Rd, Kensington Park; tel: 8332 280.* Licensed. Open Mon–Sat. Dinner. **The Earl of Aberdeen,** *316 Pulteney St; tel: 8223 6433.* Licensed. **Magic Flute,** *109 Melbourne St, North Adelaide; tel: 8239 0804.* Open lunch Tues–Fri, dinner Mon–Sat. Licensed. **Alphutte,** *242–244 Pulteney St; tel: 8223 4717.* Licensed. Open lunch, dinner Mon–Fri. Swiss. **Adelaide South Park Skyline,** *1 South Terrace; tel: 8212 1277.* Open breakfast, dinner 7 days, lunch Wed–Fri. Licensed. **Amadora,** *18 Leigh St; tel: 8231 7611.* Licensed. Open lunch Mon–Fri, dinner Mon–Sat. **Astor,** *437 Pulteney St; tel: 8223 2442.* Licensed. Open lunch, dinner Mon–Sat. **Original Barbecue Inn,** *196 Hindley St; tel: 8231 3033.* Licensed. Open lunch, dinner 7

days. **Bacall's,** *149 Melbourne St, N. Adelaide; tel: 8267 2035.* Licensed. Open dinner Mon–Sat. Cajun cooking. **Botanic Garden,** *North Terrace; tel: 8223 3526.* Licensed. Open lunch 7 days. Non smoking. **Bossa Nova,** *153 Melbourne St, N. Adelaide; tel: 8267 3018.* Licensed. Open lunch Sun, dinner Tues–Sun, late supper Fri–Sat. Latin food. **Bridgewater Mill,** *Mount Barker Rd, Bridgewater; tel: 8339 3422.* Licensed. Open 7 days, lunch Thur–Sun. **Cactus Mexican Café,** *236 Rundle St; tel: 8224 0631.* Licensed. Open lunch, dinner Tues–Sun.

Ceylon Hut, *27 Bank St; tel: 8231 2034.* Licensed. Open lunch Mon–Fri, dinner Mon–Sat. **The Chesser Cellar,** *29 Chesser St: tel: 8223 3791.* BYO. Open lunch Mon–Fri. **d'Arry's Verandah,** *Osborn Rd, McLaren Vale; tel: 8323 8710.* Licensed. Open lunch Wed–Sun, dinner Fri–Sat. **De Saru,** *330 Unley Rd, Hyde Park; tel: 8373 1133.* Licensed. Open lunch Thur, Fri, Sun, dinner 7 days. Malay/Indonesian. **Durham's,** *2 Durham St, Glenelg; tel: 8294 8224.* Licensed. Open lunch Thur, Fri, Sun, dinner Wed–Mon. **Duthy Thai,** *19–21 Duthy St, Malvern; tel: 8272 0465.* Licensed. Open lunch Tues–Fri, dinner Tues–Sun. **Empress of India,** *30 Nelson St, Stepney; tel: 8362 9156.* Licensed. Open lunch Wed–Fri, dinner Wed–Sun. **Eros Ouzeri,** *275–277 Rundle St: tel: 8223 4022.* Licensed. Open lunch Sun–Fri, dinner 7 days. Greek meze. **The Grange,** *Adelaide Hilton, 233 Victoria Sq; tel: 8217 2000.* Licensed. Open dinner Tues–Sat.

House of Chow, *82 Hutt St; tel: 8223 6181.* Licensed. Open lunch Mon–Sat, dinner 7 days. **Jolleys Boathouse,** *Jolleys Lane; tel: 8223 2891.* Licensed. Open lunch 7 days, dinner Mon–Sat. **La Casalinga,** *77 Unley Rd, Parkside; tel: 8271 7991.* Licensed. Open lunch Tues–Fri, dinner Tues–Sat. Italian. **La Guillotine,** *125 Gouger St; tel: 8212 2536.* Licensed. Open lunch Wed–Fri, dinner Mon–Sat. French. **Lemon Grass Bistro,** *289 Rundle St; tel: 8223 6627.* Licensed. Open lunch Tues–Fri, dinner 7 days. Thai. **Lenzerheide,** *146 Belair Road, Hawthorn; tel: 8373 3711.* Licensed. Open lunch Tues–Fri, dinner Tues–Sat. **The Manse,** *142 Tynte St,*

N. Adelaide; tel: 8239 2048. Licensed. Open lunch Tues–Fri, dinner Mon–Sat. **Matsuri,** *167 Gouger St; tel: 8231 3494.* Licensed. Open lunch Fri, dinner Wed–Mon. **Mount Lofty House,** *Mercure Grand Hotel, 74 Summit Rd, Crafers; tel: 8339 6777.* Licensed. Open breakfast, dinner 7 days, lunch Fri. **Mona Lisa's,** *160 Hutt St; tel: 8223 3733.* Licensed. Open lunch Mon–Fri, dinner Mon–Sat. Mediterranean. **Oli's Brasserie,** *Hindley Parkroyal, 65 Hindley St; tel: 8231 5552.* Licensed. Open dinner Mon–Sun. **Pavilion on the Park,** *Veale Gardens, South Terrace; tel: 8212 1991.* Licensed. Open lunch Tues–Fri, dinner Thur–Sat.

The Post Office, *192 Chandlers Hill Rd, Happy Valley; tel: 8322 7766.* Licensed. Open lunch Fri–Sun, dinner Tues–Sat. **Red Ochre Grill,** *129 Gouger St; tel: 8212 7266.* Licensed. Open café 7 days, lunch Mon–Fri, dinner 7 days. **Rising Sun Inn,** *60 Bridge St, Kensington; tel 8333 0721.* Licensed. Open lunch, dinner Mon–Sat. **Shiki,** *Hyatt Regency, North Terrace; tel: 8238 2382.* Licensed. Open dinner Tues–Sat. Japanese. **Sweet Water,** *187 Rundle St; tel: 8223 7748.* Licensed. Open lunch Tues–Fri, dinner 7 days. Thai. **Universal Wine Bar,** *285 Rundle St; tel: 8232 5000.* Licensed. Open lunch, dinner Mon–Sat. **The Chargrill at The Unley on Clyde Hotel,** *27 Unley Rd, Parkside; tel: 8271 5544.* Licensed. Open lunch Mon–Fri, dinner Mon–Sat.

Money

There are **Thomas Cook Foreign Exchange** branches at *45 Grenfell St; tel: (08) 212 3354* and *49 Jetty Rd, Glenelg; tel: (08) 294 3533.*

EVENTS

Apart from the bi-annual festival (see p. 338), there is a lot of entertaining nightlife in Adelaide, although popular repute is that the city is dead after 2000. But this simply is not so. Your start should be *The Guide,* which runs in the Thursday edition of the *Adelaide Advertiser,* although in almost any tourist centre you will be assailed by a series of free guides and magazines, with *Rip It Up* giving, as you would expect, the gig listings, and the *Adelaide Review*

adding tone to what would be otherwise a vulgar brawl by covering the arts in detail.

As in every Australian city, most of the band action takes place in the pub, but in the area of Hindley St there are several clubs and music joints, which might not be quite as antiseptic as you would wish. Listing all of the pubs that have live music would be excessive, but very well spoken of are **The Austral** at *205 Rundle St,* which normally has music Thur–Sun, no entrance charge; and **The Exeter Hotel,** a little further along the road at *246 Rundle St.* It is not exactly spit and sawdust, but it has not been made over in the dreaded yuppie style. Music Tues–Sun and, again, it is free.

The **Old Lion Hotel** at *165 Melbourne St, North Adelaide,* was once a brewery and now serves a wide assortment of real ales and has cabaret acts of international standards.

SHOPPING

The centre of shopping in Adelaide is **Rundle Mall,** which for much of its length is a pedestrian precinct, containing many of the major stores as well outdoor cafés, fruit and flower stalls and buskers. There are other streets which cater to a blend of enjoyable shop browsing with antique shops, speciality shops and cafés all mixed together – places where shopping becomes more of a social exercise. In Adelaide the places to look for are *Melbourne St* in **North Adelaide,** *The Parade* in **Norwood,** *Unley Rd* south of the parklands, *King William Rd,* **Hyde Park,** *Jetty Rd, Magill Rd* and *Stepney Rd* in **Glenelg** and *Glen Osmond Rd* in **Glen Osmond.** A most unusual way to go shopping is to take a **Market Adventure Tour** (**Adelaide Central Market;** *tel: 018 842 242),* which lasts about 90 mins and finishes with tastings at some of the stalls in the Adelaide Central Market. There are also several other markets in Adelaide, including one off *Rundle St* in the city. As is common with most Australian cities there is late night shopping on Thursday.

SIGHTSEEING

Light laid out Adelaide in 1836 on a square mile grid pattern of wide streets and squares, with the ever-important green buffer zone. This is all pretty much still in place and as a result,

337

Adelaide has a clearly defined style. One of the best places it can be seen is the *North Terrace* boulevard, which is lined with museums, galleries, the university campus, **Government House**, **Parliament House** and a casino.

Settlers, led by John Hindmarsh, followed Light in 1837, and only 2 years later the foundation stone for the Holy Trinity Anglican Church was laid. Government House followed the year after and was expanded throughout the remainder of the century as the colony expanded. In its early days, South Australia was far from being a financial success and had to be shored up with government loans, but by 1850 the tide had turned. The **Murray River** became the connecting link with the eastern states and prosperity surged forward.

Adelaide was to become known as a city of churches – built in fast succession were: **Christ Church** in North Adelaide, begun in 1848; **St Francis Xavier's Roman Catholic Cathedral**, 1856; **St Peter's Anglican Cathedral**, 1869. The **Quakers' Meeting House** was built in 1840, as was the Queens Theatre, which was later to become the supreme court for 4 years before being rebuilt as the **Royal Victoria Theatre**.

The attractions of Adelaide are many. Like every other Australian city it has clambered on the casino bandwagon, but with great style. The **casino**, *North Terrace; tel: 8212 2811,* is housed in the railway station, built in the 1920s in the solid stone, Victorian style. The result is totally stylish and worth visiting, even if you do not intend to gamble one brass razoo (an Australian slang phrase indicating a coin of the lowest possible denomination). It has all the usual games plus the uniquely Australian 'two up.' Open Mon–Fri 1000–0400, weekends 24 hours.

Parliament House, *corner North Terrace and King William St; tel: 8237 9100.* Open on non-sitting days 1000–1400; to see Parliament sitting from 1400 onwards. It was built in two stages and is a solid pile of Kapunda marble on granite with Corinthian columns giving it presence. This is the parliament that was shocked to its conservative core when in the 1960s, the then premier Don Dunstan, turned up wearing a pair of pink shorts.

Perhaps even more important to the style and the reputation of the city than parliament is the **Adelaide Festival**, which occurs every even year. The Festival has been held since 1960 and is an Australian institution. For those three weeks in March everything possible in the way of the arts is on show at the city's theatres, galleries, nightclubs, halls and open spaces. Although the festival is spread out right across the city, with performances taking place beyond the fringe, the **Adelaide Festival Centre**, *(King William Rd; tel: 8216 8600),* is the epicentre. Lying in the heart of the city on the banks of the **River Torrens**, its stages cover an area of 1.2 hectares.

The complex includes a concert hall and three theatres, as well as an open air amphitheatre. There is a theatre museum in the basement, which has more than 40,000 items on display showing the history of the performing arts, using that term in its widest sense. Open Mon–Fri 0900–1700; *tel: 8216 8767.*

The centre perhaps suffers, as it is placed in direct comparison with the solid stone and marble architecture behind it, but if not an artistic triumph it is at least non-offensive. It is home to the **State Theatre Company** as well as the biennial Arts Festival, and has regular exhibitions and events. The park in front is an especially pleasant place, and is a favourite with city workers at lunch time.

The number of art galleries and museums in Adelaide reflect the fact that this is a cultured city – possibly the most cultured city in Australia. **The Art Gallery of South Australia**, *North Terrace; tel: 8207 7000,* was originally opened in 1841 and has four main areas; prints and drawings, Australian decorative arts; European and Asian decorative arts and painting and sculpture. The collection of Australian art is particularly strong. It has what is claimed to be the world's largest and most comprehensive collection of Australian Aboriginal artefacts. **Ngurunderi** is a superb audiovisual presentation, bringing the Aboriginal Dreaming (see p.226) and the culture of the Ngarrindjeri people of the Coorong and lower Murray River to life. Open daily 1000–1700.

The first art in Australia was, of course, Aboriginal and this has been a continuing

The City of Light

Adelaide is indeed the City of Light, in that it was surveyed by the surveyor-general Colonel William Light in 1836, and laid out by him the following year along the banks of the **Torrens River**, with large areas reserved as parkland. This far-seeing use of parkland exists to this day, forming clear separation between Adelaide and the suburb of **North Adelaide**.

The city has inevitably spread, and is now a long, thin developed area with the sea as one boundary and the **Mt Lofty Ranges** as the other. But luckily there are strong town planning regulations so that the towns surrounding Adelaide remain separate and distinct. And Col Light's master plan still commands the city.

It is not often that a father and son design and develop two disparate cities. In Penang, in 1786, Captain Francis Light, William Light's father, developed **Georgetown** on Penang, which had been sold by the Sultan of Kedah to the East India Company for the then British Empire. It is said, on dubious authority, that he cleared the site by firing a cannon loaded with silver coins into the jungle and told the locals there was a fortune waiting for them there if they could find it. They hacked down the jungle and Georgetown was born. Adelaide is now its twin city.

tradition. One place to see it is **Tandanya**, *253 Grenfell St; tel: 8223 2467*, which is an Aboriginal multi-arts complex including galleries, a workshop and performing areas. Tandanya is the local Aboriginal name for the Adelaide area. If you make an appointment, Aboriginal guides will give introductory talks on various aspects of Aboriginal heritage and culture. There are several exhibitions as well as work for sale. Open daily 1000–1700.

A sort of extension of the fringe of the Adelaide Festival is the **Lion Arts Centre**, *corner North Terrace and Morphett St; tel: 8231 7760*, which is an old food factory that has been transformed into a mixed arts centre with several exhibition and performance areas.

Yet another food factory which has found a new life in the service of the arts is **The Jam Factory Craft and Design Centre**, *19 Morphett St; tel 8410 0727*. Open Mon–Fri 0900–1700, Sat–Sun 1000–1700. There is a viewing platform so you can watch crafts people at work and there are free guided tours.

Adelaide is particularly well endowed with museums. **The Old Treasury Museum**, *corner King William and Flinders Sts; tel: 8226 45133*, is one of the imposing buildings which Adelaide is blessed with. It dates back to 1839 and is primarily focussed on the history and techniques of surveying. It is worth mentioning, in passing, that Adelaide exported its

method of dealing with real estate transactions to the rest of Australia and to the world, and a Torrens title is internationally recognised.

The original Destitute Asylum has been transformed into the **Migration Museum**, *82 Kintore Avenue; tel: 8207 7570*. Open Mon–Fri 1000–1700, Sat–Sun 1300–1700. You can take a chronological walk through the history of immigration to settlement in South Australia since 1836. It includes the impact of white settlement on Aborigines and graphically tells the story of the waves of migration that came to South Australia. **The South Australian Museum**, *North Terrace; tel: 8207 7500*, has an international reputation for its collection of Aboriginal artefacts.

The original mounted police barracks, built in 1851, have now been converted into the **South Australian Police Museum**, *Kintore Ave; tel: 8274 8597*, and by recounting the history of the state's police, it also tells the story of the state. Open Sat–Sun 1300–1700.

Aviation has always played a major part in the history of Australia and this is reflected in the **Historical Aviation Museum**, *11 Mundy St, Port Adelaide; tel: 8278 5328*, which has everything from early prop planes to over 50 rockets and missiles. Open Sat–Sun 1000–1700.

For train spotters **Port Dock Station**, *Lipson St, Port Adelaide; tel: 8341 1690*, is a small heaven for there are 26 locomotives on

339

various track gauges – Australia for years had different gauges for each state – and there are two steam trains, which you can ride on, if only a short distance. Open daily 1000–1700.

The **South Australian Maritime Museum**, *126 Lipson St, Port Adelaide; tel: 8240 0200*, is more a collection of buildings than a traditional monolith of a museum. It spreads over several sites, including an 1850s bond store, the 1869 lighthouse and a wharf with vessels alongside.

For a more direct feeling of the history of the recent past, the **Old Adelaide Gaol**, *18 Gaol Rd, Thebarton; tel: 88231 4062*, allows sleepovers in the dormitories for a minimum group of 15 people, who have booked ahead. It was first opened in 1841 and closed in 1988. Open Sun 1100–1530.

Following Colonel Light's original design, Adelaide is a green city with plenty of air and space. It also has the **Adelaide Botanic Gardens and Bicentennial Conservatory**, *North Terrace, tel: 8228 2311*, which were begun, almost with the founding of the city, in 1855. It boasts the oldest greenhouse in a botanic garden in Australia and the Bicentennial Conservatory next door, built in a giant arc, holds a tropical rain forest. Open Mon–Fri 0800–sunset, Sat–Sun 0900–sunset.

Nearly as impressive are the **Zoological Gardens**, *Frome Rd; tel: 8267 3255*, which are one of the oldest in Australia. There are moated enclosures, walk-through aviaries and an excellent reptile house. Open daily 0930–1700.

It is easy to forget that Adelaide is almost a seaside town. Only 15 mins from the city is the suburb of Glenelg, with golden beaches extending to Port Adelaide in the north and Marino to in the south. The water is safe for both swimming and sailing. If you want to swim in a heated pool the **Adelaide Aquatic Centre**, *Jeffcott Rd, North Adelaide; tel: 8344 4411*, is Australia's largest indoor heated pool complex. Open daily 0700–1000.

There is a launch called **Popeye** that leaves from Elder Park (*off King William Rd; tel: 8203 7777*) for a 35 min cruise upstream to the **Zoo** and down to the weir, where the lake again becomes a river.

From the zoo you can take a **Venetian**

gondola (operates 1200–1600 and 1800–2400 Tues–Sat; *tel: 8415 7611*), which carries two to six persons to a boat and provides a romantic cruise along the Torrens. Bookings are essential.

SIDE TRACK FROM ADELAIDE

It is 30 mins by scheduled daily air services from Adelaide to Kangaroo Island and there are daily passenger and vehicle ferry services from Adelaide and **Cape Jervis**. There is little public transport on the island itself but there are bicycles, scooters and cars for hire.

KANGAROO ISLAND

Tourist Information: Department of Environment and Natural Resources, *37 Dauncey St, Kingscote; tel:(0848) 22381.*

ACCOMMODATION

Wisteria Lodge Motel *(FL), 7 Cygnet Rd, Kingscote; tel: 8553 2707.* **Ellson's Seaview Motel**, *Chapman Terrace, Kingscote; tel: 8553 2030.* **The Island Resort Motel**, *4 Telegraph Rd, Kingscote; tel: 8553 2100.* **Ozone Seafront Hotel**, *Foreshore, Kingscote; tel: 8553 2011.* **Queenscliffe Family Hotel**, *Dauncey St, Kingscote; tel: 482 2254.* **Wanderers Rest Of Kangaroo Island Inn**, *Bayview Rd, American River; tel: 8553 7140.* **Matthew Flinders Terraces – Boutique Motel**, *American River; tel: 8553 7100.* **Linnetts Island Club**, *American River; tel: 8553 7053.*

SIGHTSEEING

Kangaroo Island has been little developed and although it is Australia's third biggest island, 147 km long by 60 km wide, it is still a nature reserve with an abundance of wildlife. The scenery is spectacular, with cliffs and caves standing guard against the great rollers coming in from the Southern Ocean, originating in Antarctica. The interior of the island includes untamed wilderness, huge blackboys, farmland and forest.

The island is a lozenge running roughly east and west, with the **Investigator Strait** separating it from the mainland. The eastern end of the island – about a quarter of the land area – is taken up by the **Flinders Chase National Park**, and the south of the island has the **Cape Gantheaume Conservation Park** jutting out into the Southern Ocean. To the east of the island there is a head sticking out, which is the **Dudley Peninsula**. Here are two smaller national parks – there are 18 national parks on the island in all – as well as the town of **Penneshaw**, which is where the ferries come in.

The island was first sighted by a European in 1802 and Matthew Flinders gave it its name. The French explorer Nicholas Baudin sailed around the island and landed the following year. The same year American sealers stayed at what is now **American River** and constructed the first ship to be built in South Australia.

The first European settlement in South Australia was founded at what is now the main island town of **Kingscote** in 1836, although it closed four years later.

In 1852, the **Cape Willoughby lighthouse** was built – the island was notorious for wrecks and there are still over forty in the seas off the island – and this was followed by the **Cape Borda lighthouse** some six years later. As far as is known, tourism on the island started just after the turn of the century.

Flinders Chase National Park covers 73,662 hectares and is the largest national park in South Australia, covering the western end of the island from **Sanderson Bay** in the south to **Cape Borda** in the north. The coast of the park has some of the most amazing proliferation of animal and plant life in Australia. There are sea lions, sea eagles, osprey and Cape Barren geese on the coast. Inland are kangaroos, wallabies, koalas, bush-tailed possums, the rarely-seen platypus and an amazing range of bird life. There are well-marked trails throughout the park.

Within the park, at **Cape du Couedic**, is the natural formation **Admiral's Arch**, which is a haven for New Zealand fur seals,

who bask on the rocks around the arch. Also in the park is Cape Borda lighthouse, perched on a 155 m high cliff.

In the centre of the park is a substantial clearing, which is home to a large number of kangaroos and Cape Barren geese. This is the site of the park headquarters – *tel: (0848) 37235.*

The other major park on the island is **Cape Gantheaume Conservation Park**, which covers 21,254 hectares. This is on the southern coast and extends as far inland as **Murray Lagoon**. The park has a rugged coastline of cliffs and caves and the vegetation near the coast is mainly heath. No vehicles are allowed, but the park has a lot of wildlife especially around Murray Lagoon, which when full after rain, can cover 2000 hectares and is home to more than 200 species of birds. The park headquarters is at the *Seagers Rd* entrance – *tel: (0848) 28233.*

Although **Seal Bay Conservation Park**, at 750 hectares, is relatively small, it is home to about 500 Australian sea lions, which is probably about 10% of the world's population. These sea lions seem pretty tame and accept visitors, but every now and again they get irritable and charge at humans. Therefore the number of visitors is restricted.

At the **Interpretative Centre** – *tel: (0848) 94207* – there is a series of displays explaining the life cycle of the sea lion. Note that the bay is an aquatic reserve and swimming and fishing are prohibited.

The capital of Kangaroo Island is **Kingscote** on Nepean Bay, which has a population of around 1400. The other town is Penneshaw with a population of 300. It is only 16 km from the mainland.

One odd note. In Aug 1881, Freibig brought 12 hives of bees from the province of **Liguria** in Italy, and established an apiary near Penneshaw. Since then no other breeds of bees have been introduced to Kangaroo Island and so all present-day honey bees on the Island are descendants of those 12 hives. The bees on the Island are therefore pure Ligurian and are unique. ↵

341

THE FLEURIEU PENINSULA

This is a gentle drive from Adelaide that will take you on to the furthest point in the Cape of St Vincent, the Backstairs Passage and to the Southern Ocean. The full circular tour begins in the wine country of McLaren Vale and continues to Victor Harbor and Granite Island before reaching Cape Jervis at the end of the Peninsula, from where an easy coastal run takes you back to Adelaide. A side track to Kangaroo Island is also possible. Alternatively, you can decide to make it a straight there-and-back trip along the coast.

> FULL ROUTE: 389 KM

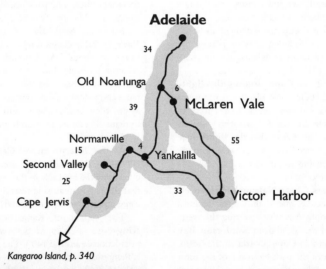

Adelaide
34
Old Noarlunga
6
39
McLaren Vale
Normanville
15
4
55
Second Valley
Yankalilla
25
33
Cape Jervis
Victor Harbor

Kangaroo Island, p. 340

ROUTE

There are several ways to drive to this lovely part of the country but an easy to follow route is to drive out to the **Airport** and from there run along the shore to **Marion**, which is right on the edge of the **Sturt Gorge Recreation Park** – a journey of about 18 km. From there through **Morphett Vale** 16 km to **Old Noarlunga**. Turn left just after Noarlunga to the wineries of **McLaren Vale** some 6 km

distant. From there a right turn onto a minor road takes you through **Willunga**. Just past Willunga turn right onto the main road, which travels up and over the **South Mount Lofty Ranges** and, 31 km further on, to **Victor Harbor**, which faces the Southern Ocean.

From Victor Harbor you cut back inland and westwards over the Peninsula for 33 km to **Yankalilla**. Turn left for a short run of 4 km to **Normanville** which is on the sea again, but this time the Gulf of St Vincent. Continue along the coast; from here the Peninsula gets narrower as it passes, after 15 km, the tiny hamlet of **Second Valley**. This is 92 km south of Adelaide and it was here that Colonel William Light came in 1837. He climbed a steep hill and looked down at the wide valley and said, 'I have hardly seen a place I like better.' The present population (of 40 souls, all told) agree with this early judgement. The road then runs 18 km through **Delamere** to **Cape Jervis**, the very tip of the Fleurieu Peninsula.

To return to Adelaide, retrace your route as far as Yankalilla, but there keep to the left to take the road north through **Aldinga** back to Old Noarlunga and so back to Adelaide.

TRAINS

The **Steamranger** train from Adelaide to Victor Harbor follows a different itinerary from the driving route above, stopping at Mt Barker and Goolwa, on the coast east of Victor Harbor. This train departs on Sun only and takes 2¼ hrs. OTT table 9022.

MCLAREN VALE

Tourist Information: There is a kiosk at *The Cottage, BRL Hardy, Main Rd*. For more information contact **Barossa Tourist Information & Wine Centre**, *66 Murray St, Tanunda; tel: 8563 0600.*

ACCOMMODATION AND FOOD

McLarens on the Lake Motel, *Kangarilla Rd; tel: 8323 8911*. **McLaren Vale Motel**, *corner Main Rd and Caffrey St; tel: 8323 8265.*

The Barn, *Main Rd; tel: 8323 8618*. Open 7 days lunch and dinner. **McLaren's on the Lake**, *Kangarilla Rd; tel: 8323 8911*. Lunch Fri–Sun. Dinner Fri–Sat. **Salopian Inn**, *corner McMurtie and Willunga Rd; tel: 8323 8769*. Lunch daily, dinner Fri–Sat.

SIGHTSEEING

There are about 50 wineries in the McLaren Vale area and they cover a fairly wide range of wines, from ones of international importance to boutique wines which are just finding their way in the world. The town has a population of 4000 and is 39 km south of Adelaide but the

wine area extends from **Reynella** in the north to just the other side of **Blewitt Springs** in the west and 4 km or so to the south of the town of McLaren Vale.

The vineyards of McLaren Vale started, as did so many other vineyards in Australia, because of the belief of a doctor in the Biblical injunction, 'Use a little wine for thy stomach's sake and thine often infirmities,' *Timothy 1: 23*. The medical man was Dr A.C.Kelly and he and Thomas Hardy (like his famous namesake, a Dorset man) started in the 1860s. The wine was an instant success and by the turn of the century the area was selling 3 million litre vintages. Then came two World Wars and the disruption of trade and by the 1970s McLaren Vale was in parlous straits because white wine was in vogue. This meant extensive replanting but in the end this worked in the Vale's favour because the wide variety of grapes now grown gives it a strength in diversity.

Almost without exception, the vineyards offer cellar door tastings and sales and most of them can offer some sort of a snack meal; some of them have high quality restaurants associated with the vineyard. The majority are open daily 1000–1700. The Tourist Association has a free publication, *South Australian Wine and Food Guide*, comprehensive and intelligently written.

One vineyard worth a special mention. **Luong Rice Winery** (open daily 1000–1700; *220 Main South Road, McLaren Vale; tel: 8323 8156*) produces rice wine, mainly for cooking, although it does have a drinkable liqueur port fortified with rice brandy.

VICTOR HARBOR

Tourist Information: Victor Harbor Tourist Information, *10 Railway Terrace; tel: (085) 52 4255.*

ACCOMMODATION AND FOOD

Colonial Motor Inn *(FL), 2 Victoria St; tel: 8552 1822*. **Apollon Motor Inn & Restaurant & Convention Centres** *(FL), Hindmarsh Rd; tel: 8552 2777*. **City Motel**, *51 Ocean St; tel: 8552 2455*. **Hotel Victor**, *Victor Harbor; tel: 8552 1288*. **Whalers Inn Resort**, *The Bluff, 121 Franklin Parade; tel: 8552 4400*. **Kerjancia Motor Lodge Motel** *(BU), 141*

343

Hindmarsh Rd; tel: 8552 2900. **Wintersun Motel**, Hindmarsh Rd; tel: 8552 3533. **Bayview Victor Motel & Bowley's Restaurant**, 17–19 Hindmarsh; tel: 8552 1755. **Family Inn Motel** (BU), 300 Pt Elliot Rd; tel: 8552 1941. **Ocean Crest Motel & Restaurant**, 117 Mentone Rd; tel: 8552 3233. **Grosvenor Hotel**, Ocean St; tel: 8552 1011.

Apart from some of the hotels, Victor Harbor offers only milk bars and cheap take-away food to hungry visitors.

SIGHTSEEING

Victor Harbor is 83 km south of Adelaide and was named by Captain Richard Crozier, anchoring in the lee of Granite Island in 1837, after his ship HMS *Victor*. It was proclaimed a port in the following year. The American-style spelling of Harbor has always been used.

At one time serious consideration was given to making the town the capital of South Australia. Instead it first became a whaling station and then the unofficial capital of the Fleurieu Peninsula. By the early years of this century Victor Harbor had ceased to be an important port and had started to become the holiday resort that it is to this day.

It has many natural attractions. **The Bluff** is a few kilometres west of Victor Harbor and is a 100m high outcrop of granite which was used in the early days as a lookout for whales to alert the whaling fleet. It is still used for spotting whales to this day but the whaling fleet is no more.

Victor Harbor has the delightful **Cockle Train**, which departs from the railway station – tel: 8231 1707 – 16 km for **Goolwa**, running along the front near the beaches and sandhills. It was originally built in 1854 for horse-drawn trams but now has a steam engine and carriages dating from the beginning of this century. The ride takes half an hour.

It is claimed that the town is unique in the southern hemisphere in that it has a horse-drawn tram which travels across a causeway to **Granite Island**. The causeway was begun in 1864 and extended to Granite Island in 1875. The tram began service in 1894. The island is famous for its fairy penguins, which come out

at sunset to feed. There is a chairlift to the summit of the island and this gives stupendous views.

The Old Customs House and Station Master's House, 2 Flinders Parade; tel: (085) 524 081, was built in 1886 and is now a museum. Open Sat public and school holidays.

Victor Harbor was once the centre for the whaling fleet. You can learn more about this at the **South Australian Whale Centre**, Railway Terrace; tel: (085) 52 5644, which has three floors of displays about the southern right whales. Open 7 days 0900–1700.

About 5 km down the road to Adelaide is the **Urimbirra Wildlife Park**, Adelaide Rd; tel: (085) 54 6554, which is a 16 hectare nature farm for more than 70 species of Australian animals and birds. The name is Aboriginal, meaning 'to preserve'. The park has a nocturnal house. Open daily 1000–1700.

CAPE JERVIS

This is the tip of the Fleurieu Peninsula, with **Deep Creek Conservation Park** just to the east. The world's longest footpath, the **Heysen Trail**, begins near Cape Jervis and ends 1500 km north in the Flinders Ranges. From Cape Jervis it follows the coast to turn inland to **Myponga Conservation Park** then north east to **Mt Compass** (between McLaren Vale and Victor Harbor) and north through the **Mount Lofty Ranges**. The trail is marked with orange triangles but parts of it require bushwalking skills. Information on this trail is available from **Recreation SA**; tel: 8226 7301.

⤴ SIDE TRACK FROM CAPE JERVIS

You can travel, with or without your vehicle, from Cape Jervis to **Penneshaw** on **Kangaroo Island**. The crossing, by **Kangaroo Island Sealink**, takes one hour. If you are not driving, you can catch a courtesy bus from Adelaide to Cape Jervis to connect with the ferry. The bus travels down the west side of the Peninsula and takes approx 2 hrs. OTT table 9054. For Kangaroo Island, see p. 340. ⤴

ADELAIDE–WARRNAMBOOL

The first part of the trip involves getting around the large and amorphous estuary of the mighty Murray, Australia's biggest river, before continuing down the coast to

Mt Gambier. The town of Mt Gambier is about as south as you can get in South Australia. It is but 16 km from the Victoria border and 38 km from Carpenter Rocks. Yet it is only 460 km south east of Adelaide and driving there takes you through some singularly interesting country. The route continues into Victoria to Warrnambool, from where the route on p. 134 takes you to Melbourne.

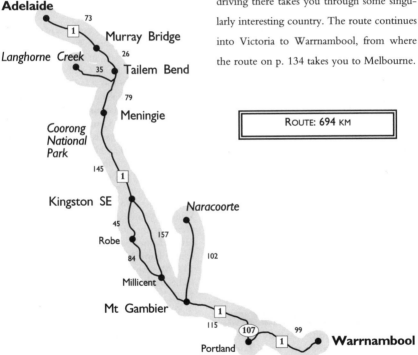

Adelaide

73

1

Murray Bridge

Langhorne Creek 26

35 **Tailem Bend**

79

Meningie

Coorong National Park

145

1

Kingston SE

45

Naracoorte

Robe 157

84 102

Millicent

Mt Gambier

115

1

107 99

1 **Warrnambool**

Portland

ROUTE: **694** KM

345

From Adelaide take the **South East Freeway**, Rte 1, through the inner suburb of **Ashton**, the wine capital of **Hahndorf** and then to **Murray Bridge**. This is 80 km from Adelaide and is South Australia's largest river town. It is an ideal place to arrange cruises on the river,

which is an ideal way of seeing important and interesting parts of South Australia. From Murray Bridge it is 27 km, still along Rte 1, to the railway workshop town of **Tailem Bend**, which is on the junction of the Duke, Mallee and Princes Hwys, as well as being on the

Murray River. Now called the Princes Hwy, Rte 1 turns towards the coast and runs alongside **Lake Alexandrina** to **Meningie**, which is on **Lake Albert**. This is the start of that amazing phenomenon **The Coorong**, an immensely elongated waterway, protected by the **Younghusband Peninsula** from the Southern Ocean; Princes Hwy runs on its landward side. From Meningie to **Kingston SE** is 197 km, and there is not a metre of the road when you are not in sight of water.

At Kingston SE it is possible to take a diversion and follow the coast road 42 km to **Robe** and then past **Lake Ellis** and **Lake George** to **Millicent**, where you rejoin the Princes Hwy, which then runs 49 km to **Mt Gambier**, from where you can side-track to **Narracoorte**. From Mt Gambier the route continues 115 km to **Portland** and another 99 km on to **Warrnambool**.

TRAINS

The daily Adelaide–Melbourne 'The Overland' train stops at Murray Bridge (just over 2 hrs) and Tailem Bend (2½ hrs) but then leaves the course of this route, arriving in Melbourne in 13 hrs from Adelaide. OTT table 9035.

BUSES

Several buses a day leave Adelaide along this route, not all stopping at every place listed in the chapter. Murray Bridge is 1¼ hrs from Adelaide, Tailem Bend 1–1½ hrs depending on the bus taken, Mt Gambier 5¾ hrs. Some buses also run via Narracoorte, 5 hrs.

Several daily services connect Mt Gambier with Warrnambool, taking about 3¼ hrs. OTT tables 9121, 9123.

MURRAY BRIDGE

Tourist Information: Murray Bridge Community Information and Tourist Centre, *3 South Terrace; tel: 8532 6660.*

ACCOMMODATION

Murray Bridge Motor Inn, *212 Adelaide Rd; tel: 8532 1144.* **Murray Bridge Oval Motel & Caravan Park**, *4 Lemessurier St; tel: 8532 2388.* **Olympic Pool Motel**, *34 Standen St; tel: 8532 2359.* **Motel Greenacres** *(BU),*

Princes Hwy, (East Side); tel: 8532 1090. **Bridgport Hotel**, *2 Bridge St; tel: 8532 2002.* **Murray Bridge Hotel**, *corner Fifth and Sixth Sts; tel: 8532 2024.*

SIGHTSEEING

Murray Bridge is 78 km east of Adelaide and is the state's largest town on the Murray River. The town started off in 1850 as Edward's Crossing, named after the first settler, and this transmuted to Mobilong. But the road bridge was laid across the river in 1879 and then the rail bridge in 1925 and the name made a logical change. Now there are three bridges over the river – the original road bridge, the rail bridge and the new **Swanport Bridge**, which opened in 1979.

Cruising the river is a great way to see a vital part of South Australia. There are several ways you can do it, one of the options being a paddle steamer from **Goolwa** at the river mouth. **PS Mundoo**, *Goolwa Wharf; tel: 8555 2203,* is a replica of a paddle steamer of the last century. From **Mannum**, 39 km away, are **Lady Mannum Cruises** *(tel: 8269 1438).* From Murray Bridge is the **Murray Princess** *(tel: 8269 2511),* which is Australia's largest inland paddle steamer. The paddle steamer **Proud Mary** sails out of Murray Bridge on 2 day cruises – *tel: 8231 9472.*

You can also hire a houseboat at Murray Bridge – you need no more nautical skills than a current car driving licence – from **Jubilee Line Houseboats**, *tel: 8378 3122;* the oddly named **Lady Muk Houseboats**, *tel (018) 813 536;* **Mystique Houseboats**, *tel: 8344 7303;* and **Shore to Please Houseboats**, *tel: 8295 7798.*

Apart from the river, Murray Bridge has several land-based attractions. It boasts the smallest **Anglican Cathedral** in Australia, which was built in 1887. The walk-through **Butterfly House**, *off South-Eastern Freeway; tel: 8532 3666,* has hundreds of tropical butterflies as well as a nocturnal animal sanctuary. Open daily; $7.

A cottage built by a Captain Johnson in 1890 has been carefully restored as a museum of pioneering days in South Australia. The **Captain Cottage Museum**, *Thomas St; tel:*

8531 0049, is modest but charming and even has a doll collection. Open weekends 1000–1600.

Ten minutes by car from Murray Bridge – 11 km west on Princes Hwy – is **Monarto Zoological Park**, a 1000 hectare park of grassland and mallee forest with herds of blackbuck, deer, bison, giraffe, antelope, ostrich, zebra and other animals, including such endangered species as the Przewalski's and Mongolian wild horses. The only way to see the park is by safari bus. Open Sun 1000–1700. Admission $10.

TAILEM BEND

Tourist Information: Tailem Bend Tourist Information, *87–89 Railway Terrace; tel: 8572 3537.*

Accommodation is available at **Tailem Bend River's Edge**; *tel: 8572 3307.*

SIGHTSEEING

Tailem Bend is a very small town at the junction of the Dukes and Princes Hwys, 99 km from Adelaide. The town is built on a cliff overlooking the Murray. The town was once an important railway town on a junction where lines left to service the Murray and the **Mallee** areas. Now the train traffic has all but died away and these days the town services the local farming community.

Old Tailem Bend Pioneer Village, *South Eastern Freeway; tel: 8572 3838*, is a true village about 5 km north-west of the town and has more than 70 restored buildings – most of them moved here from other places – including a school, a church, a railway station, a general store, a wine shop, a police station and at the other end of the scale, a cow dung hut and a fisherman's hut, which seems to have been constructed from oil drums that have been beaten flat. It has become a museum of the pioneering days on the Murray. Open daily 1000–1700. Admission $8.

Nearby **Poltalloch Station**, *Narrung Rd; tel: 8574 0043*, runs sheep and cattle. It was developed in 1876 by John Bowman and is now operated by his fifth generation descendants. The homestead is in an exquisite setting overlooking Lake Alexandrina. It is open for tours and overnight guests. Phone for bookings.

From Tailem Bend you can take the ferry across the river to **Jervois**.

SIDE TRACK
FROM TAILEM BEND

Ten kilometres south of Tailem Bend turn right to cross the Murray and drive 35 km, through Wellington, to the vineyard area of Langhorne Creek.

LANGHORNE CREEK

This small town – population 1900 – is 67 km from Adelaide and is one of the oldest wine growing areas in Australia. It was originally settled in 1850 by Frank Potts. It is on the banks of the Bremer River, close to the shores of Lake Alexandrina, and in 1994 became the fastest growing vineyard area in South Australia. One of the many wineries in the area is **The Bleasdale Winery**, *Wellington Rd; tel: (085) 37 3001.* It was first established in 1850 and has been classified by the National Trust. It still has a huge wine press of red gum wood, which was made in 1892 and used until 1962, on display. Open daily, Mon–Sat 0900–1700, Sun 1100–1700.

The Wine Vat Restaurant, *Wellington Rd; tel: (085) 373 242*, is open daily for lunch and dinner by arrangement.

MENINGIE

Tourist Information: Melaleuca Centre, *76 Princes Hwy; tel: 8575 1259.*

ACCOMMODATION

Lake Albert Motel, *Princes Hwy; tel: 8575 1077.* **Meningies Waterfront Motel**, *Princes Hwy; tel: 8575 1152.* **Coorong Hotel-Motel**, *Princes Hwy, Policemans Point via Meningie; tel: 8575 7064.* **Mill Park**, *Yumali Rd; tel: 8575 6033.*

SIGHTSEEING

This small town, on the eastern shores of the fresh-water Lake Albert, is 152 km south-east of Adelaide. The town is on the Princes Hwy and also at the northern tip of the **Coorong National Park**. It started life as a proclaimed

347

town in 1886, as a terminus for paddle steamers crossing the lake from **Milang**. Travellers from Adelaide to Melbourne in those days crossed the lakes by steamer before taking a coach south. Meningie is now very much a fishing town and there are 40 professional anglers working from this town mainly in the Coorong, to which the town is the gateway.

This 100 km stretch of water is only 2 km wide and has a narrow range of sand dunes separating it from the Southern Ocean. Coorong is an Aboriginal word possibly meaning 'long neck of water', which is an apt description.

The Coorong, along with the associated lakes **Albert** and **Alexandrina** – at 50,000 hectares the largest permanent fresh-water lake in Australia – have some of the most prolific bird life in Australia and they are protected by the Coorong National Park.

Just 12 km to the south of the town is **Camp Coorong**, an Aboriginal museum and cultural centre run by the **Ngarrindjeri Lands and Progress Association** – *tel: 8574 5557.* Aboriginal guides are available to take visitors on day walks to ancient Aboriginal fish traps and introduce them to plants and shrubs the Ngarrindjeri used as medicine.

On the road from Meningie to Kingston SE you pass **Chinamans Well**, which is a well on the route taken by the Chinese diggers as they travelled from South Australia to Victoria in search of gold. The well has been restored by the National Parks Service and is clearly signposted from the Highway.

THE COORONG NATIONAL PARK

Tourist Information: Salt Creek Visitor Centre; *tel: 8575 1200.*

This National Park covers 46,745 hectares and is one of the finest nature preserves in Australia. It is one of Australia's greatest surviving tracts of wetlands. The name is said to come from a Ngarrindjeri Aboriginal word *karangk,* which has been translated as meaning 'narrow neck' or 'long finger of water.'

The Coorong is a series of lagoons created initially by the estuary of the Murray River. The river appears to lose all of its power as it approaches the coast and the flow is so depleted

that bulldozers have to be used to effect an exit to the sea. Its silted and salted waters spread slowly to Lakes Alexandrina and Albert, and along the Coorong. The resulting shallow lagoons stretch for 145 km and are bordered on one side by the **Younghusband Peninsula**, which is mainly sandhills occasionally bound by coastal mallee, wattle and boobialla. This peninsula totally protects the Coorong from the waves of the Southern Ocean.

The Coorong runs from the mouth of the Murray to Kingston SE and includes a 9000 hectare game reserve. At any given time it has as many as 240 species of native birds, which are based there but may migrate annually to Siberia, Japan and China. The bird life is profuse, with literally millions of them feeding from the lagoon and also fishing in the Southern Ocean.

Long before the Europeans arrived this was the traditional home of the **Ngarrindjeri** people and archaeological sites suggest that they have been here for as long as 40,000 years.

Among the birds that breed in the Coorong are giant pelicans, wild duck, shags, ibis, cormorants, spoonbills, black swans, gannets and plovers and tern. There was an Australian children's film called *Storm Boy,* which was filmed here and was about the friendship between a boy and a pelican.

Fishing is allowed in the park and anglers enjoy considerable success from beach casting and from small boats on the lagoon. The upper Coorong is normally accessible from **Goolwa** by boat.

There is car access to the park off Princes Hwy and there are two crossings, which span the Coorong to the ocean. **42 mile Crossing** is available throughout the year while **Tea Tree Crossing** is a summer crossing as at other times it can be flooded up to ½m in depth. The park headquarters is south of **Salt Creek**, about 64 km from **Meningie** along the Princes Hwy, and just opposite the **Messent Conservation Area**, which covers 12,250 hectares. At Salt Creek there is a nature trail, which explains the formation of the sand dunes and the assorted vegetation within the park. A tour company specialising in the Coorong is **Coorong Nature Tours**, *tel: 8574 0037,* which uses four-wheel-drive vehicles to access the park.

KINGSTON SE

Tourist Information: The Big Lobster, *Princes Hwy; tel: 8767 2555.*

ACCOMMODATION

Kingston Lobster Motel *(FL), Princes Hwy; tel: 8767 2322.* **Beehive Motor Inn,** *corner Hanson St and Marine Parade; tel: 8767 2444.* **Mobil 190 Mile Roadhouse & Motel,** *Princes Hwy; tel: 8767 2419.*

SIGHTSEEING

Why the initials for this town? To distinguish it from Kingston OM, where those initials stand for on the Murray. SE denotes that this Kingston stands in the south-east of the state, on **Lacepede Bay.** (It is 296 km south-east of Adelaide on Princes Hwy.)

The name comes from the surveyor Sir George Strickland Kingston, who arrived in 1836 and built a house on the site of the town four years later. Before it was formally named by Governor McDonnell, it was informally known as Maria Creek and then Port Caroline. In 1840, 26 pioneers survived the wreck of the brig *Maria* and came ashore here, only to be later killed by Aborigines.

Now the town is a the rural centre for a farming area. It also has a major crayfishing fleet and this is marked by a **Big Lobster** – another example of a peculiar Australian affliction, the love of outsize models – which stands at the entrance to the town on Princes Hwy. The Big Lobster is known tolerantly by the locals as Larry and is 17m high and weighs 4 tonnes. Behind Larry is a café and a tourist information centre.

The town marks the beginning of a coastal playground with many fine beaches and scenic drives in and around Lacepede Bay.

Cape Jaffa lighthouse was built on **Margaret Broch Reef,** 8 km offshore, in 1871 but was dismantled in 1975. It has now been re-erected in the town next to the **Len Lampit Reserve** and is open during the school holidays. There is an excellent view from the top. There is a **National Trust Pioneer Museum** in *Holland St.*

In **Apex Park,** within the town, is an **Analemmatic Sundial,** which is one of only two in Australia. The clock is made up of a series of carved fish. You are instructed to tell the time by standing on the analemma when your shadow is cast on the time. The use of the word analemma is dubious, as the Oxford Dictionary gives its primary meaning as 'sundial'. Whether the name is correct or not, this method of computing the time does not lead to great accuracy.

Kingston is within easy reach of the Coorong National Park and three other parks – **Mt Scott, Jip Jip** and **Butchers Gap.**

Jip Jip Conservation Park covers 142 hectares and is about 50 km north-east of Kingston. It is characterised by large granite boulders and a wide variety of wildlife. **Mt Scott Conservation Park** is 1238 hectares in extent and 20 km east of Kingston. It is part of a former coastal dune system and has brown stringy bark forest while its wildlife includes sugar gliders, wombats and the uncommon mallee fowl. **Butchers Gap** is 6 km south-west of Kingston, covers 178 hectares and is a seasonally flooded wetland, which has a wide variety of bird life.

The Granites is a unique rock formation on the beach 18 km to the north of Kingston. There is a vineyard in the area. **Cape Jaffa Wines,** *Cape Jaffa Rd; tel: 8768 5053,* is open daily with a sign on the road advising the times of visiting. The cellar door is at the top of a hill overlooking vineyards with a view of the countryside and the Southern Ocean. The cellar is in fact a cave that has been dug into the side of a limestone hill.

MT GAMBIER

Tourist Information: Lady Nelson Information and Interpretive Centre, *Jubilee Highway E.; tel: 8724 1730.*

ACCOMMODATION

Terrace Motor Inn & Apartments *(GC), 203 Commercial St E.; tel: 8725 5433.* **Presidential Motor Inn** *(FL), Jubilee Hwy W.; tel: 8724 9966.* **Southgate Motel** *(BW), 175 Commercial St E.; tel: 8723 1175.* **Mt Gambier International Motel** *(FL), Millicent Rd; tel: 8725 9699.* **Commodore Motel,** *corner Jubilee Hwy and Penola Rd; tel: 8724 9666.* **Mt**

349

Gambier Hotel, *2 Commercial St W.; tel: 8725 0611*. **Arkana Motor Inn and Terrace Apartments** *(GC), 201 Commercial St E.; tel: 8725 5433*. **Motel Mt Gambier** *(BU), 115 Penola Rd; tel: 8725 5800*. **Grand Central Motel** *(BU), 6 Helen St; tel: 8725 8844*. **Mid City Motel**, *15 Helen St; tel: 87 257277*. **Avalon Motel**, *93 Gray St; tel: 8725 7200*. **Tower Motor Inn**, *140 Jubilee Hwy W.; tel: 8724 9411*. **Le Cavalier Court Motel**, *37 Bay Rd; tel: 8725 9077*. **Blue Lake Motel** *(BW), Kennedy Ave; tel: 8725 5211*. **Gambier Lodge-In Motel**, *92 Penola Rd; tel: 8725 1579*. **Mount View Motel**, *14 Davison St; tel: 8725 8478*. **Jens Hotel**, *40 E. Commercial St; tel: 8725 0188*. **Federal Hotel-Motel**, *112 Commercial St E.; tel: 8723 1099*.

EATING AND DRINKING

Artists Restaurant, *6 Commercial St (East); tel: 8725 9782*. **Fasta Pasta**, *102 Commercial St; tel: 8723 0011*. **Golden Chopsticks Restaurant**, *95 Commercial St; tel: 8725 3935*. **Jacksons Café Bistro**, *76 Commercial St (West); tel: 8725 3006*. **Le Cavalier Restaurant**, *37 Bay Rd tel: 8725 9077*. **Mt Gambier Mandarin Restaurant**, *68 Commercial St (West); tel: 8723 2100*.

SIGHTSEEING

The name applies to both a town and a mountain. The mountain is a long-extinct volcano, which was sighted by Lt James Grant in 1800, and named after the commander of the fleet at the Battle of Copenhagen in the Napoleonic wars.

The town is built on the slopes of the volcano in the middle of some of the largest softwood plantations in Australia. It has a population of 23,000 and is 460 km south-east of Adelaide and half way between Adelaide and Melbourne. The sea is 38 km to the south at **Carpenter Rocks**, which is on the edge of the **Canunda National Park, Bucks Lake Game Reserve** and **Lake Bonney**.

The first dwelling in the district was built in 1841 and the town was started in 1854 as a private venture. One of the distinguishing features of the town is the use of local white stone for the buildings. This, along with an abun-

dance of parks and green spaces, makes Mt Gambier a pleasant place to visit. There is a heritage walk which takes in all of the buildings of significance and a leaflet is available from the tourist centre.

The town's main attraction, however, is **Blue Lake**, which is something of a mystery. Every November, in time for the summer, the colour of the waters change from grey to an intense turquoise blue and when the summer ends it goes back to being grey.

The lake is in one of the volcano's craters and is very deep – it is claimed to be 197m at its deepest point. There is a 5 km scenic drive around the lake and a 3 km walking track closer in, running below cliffs that rise as high as 76m. The lake is used for Mt Gambier's water supplies but when the water comes out of the tap it is colourless.

On a cliff opposite the Blue Lake there is a placard at a point from where poet-horseman-politician, Adam Lindsay, made a daredevil leap on horseback to a ledge below the crater rim. This was a most amazing feat of horsemanship, which has never been repeated.

This area is full of caves and beneath the streets of the city is the **Engelbrecht Cave**, which was used in the last century as a dump by a whisky distiller. The cave sometimes partially floods with underground water but most of the time it is open to visitors. *Tel: 8723 2893*.

The Mt Gambier Courthouse, *Bay Rd; tel: 8723 2041*, was opened in 1865 and operated for the next 110 years. The jury box, judge's chamber and cells are open to the public along with an exhibition showing Mt Gambier history. Open daily 1200–1600.

In the **Lady Nelson Tourist Interpretative Centre**, *Jubilee Hwy E.; tel: 8724 1730*, there is a full size replica of the *Lady Nelson*, which was the brig used by Lt Grant when he first sighted Mt Gambier and, at the same time, made the first eastward passage along southern Australia. Also in the centre is a time walk, a cave walk and geology and wetlands exhibitions. Open daily 0900–0500; $5.

There is a wide range of Australian animal life at the **Mt Gambier Animal and Reptile Park**, *Wandilo Forest Rd; tel: 8723 0619*, as well as an animal nursery for children. Open daily.

SIDE TRACK FROM MT GAMBIER

From Mt Gambier you head north to Tarpeena which is 24 km away. The road is, incidentally, almost exactly parallel with the state border, which is about 10 km to the east. From Tarpeena the road runs a further 20 km to Penola and then 50km through Coonawarra to Naracoorte.

It is also possible to side-track from Kingston SE, 91 km via Reedy Creek and Lucindale, although the journey is more circuitous.

NARACOORTE

Tourist Information: Tourist Information Centre, *The Sheep's Back Museum, MacDonnell St; tel: 8762 1518.*

ACCOMMODATION

William MacIntosh Motor Lodge *(FL), Bordertown Rd; tel: 8762 1644.* **Country Roads Motor Inn**, *28 Smith St; tel: 8762 3900.* **Belvedere Motel**, *17 Fourth Ave; tel: 8762 3655.* **Greenline Motel** *(BU), Bordertown Rd; tel: 8762 2599.* **Naracoorte Hotel-Motel**, *73 Ormerod St; tel: 8762 2400.* **Commercial Hotel**, *20 Robertson St; tel: 8762 2100.* **Kincraig Hotel**, *144 Smith St; tel: 8762 2200.*

SIGHTSEEING

The area was once known as the **Mosquito Plains** but, thankfully, the problem no longer exists to justify that name. Naracoorte comes from an Aboriginal phrase meaning 'the place of running water'. The first station – the **Naracoorte Run** – was established here in 1842 and the town, run as a private enterprise and then named Kincraig, started in 1847 but two years later became a government town. Naracoorte is 337 km south east of Adelaide, and among the major attractions of the town are the limestone **Naracoorte Caves** – there 60 in all – which are listed by the World Heritage and contain fossils of giant kangaroos, monster wombats and marsupial lions. The caves are 13 km from the town centre in the 410 hectare **Naracoorte Caves Conservation Park**, *tel: 8762 2340.* These caves were one of the first organised tourist attractions in Australia – as early as 1869 a local publican was organising tours. Nowadays, guided tours take visitors to the four main caves – **Victoria**, **Alexandra**, **Blanche** and **Wet**. There are guided tours to the first three ($4) but Wet is freely open to the public.

There is also the **Bat Cave**, which is not open to visitors and has a collection of about quarter of a million bats which come out in waves in the evening. But you can view the inside through infra-red cameras. $6.

In the town is the privately owned **Naracoorte Museum and Snake Pit**, *Jenkins Terrace*, which is sometimes more accurately listed as the **House of 100 Collections**; it actually has more than that number, ranging from local fossils to butterflies. The venomous snakes are behind glass for safe viewing. Open Mon–Thur 1000–1700, Sat–Sun 1400–1700. Closed mid July–end Aug. $5.

Based in what was originally an 1870 flour mill, **The Sheep's Back**, *Macdonnell St; tel: 8762 1518,* is a National Trust operated museum which has three levels showing how the sheep industry developed in Australia. Open daily 1000–1600.

One of the states finest areas of wetlands is 24 km south of the town at the **Bool Lagoon** – *tel: 8764 7541* – which covers 3600 hectares, and the adjoining **Hacks Lagoon Conservation Park**, covering 2000 hectares. Combined they contain a stretch of over 14 km of shallow freshwater lagoons. This has been designated by UNESCO as a wetland of international significance.

These wetlands are a drought refuge and breeding ground for over 150 species of birds, and are full of freshwater fish and other wildlife. Each September some 200,000 straw-necked ibis invade the area to breed. There are guided tours and self-guided tours along a boardwalk raised out of the water.

WARRNAMBOOL

See p. 142.

ADELAIDE–MILDURA

From Adelaide one of the easiest and pleasant runs is to the Barossa Valley, possibly Australia's best-known wine country, and then up to Renmark and the Riverland.

There are no big distances involved here but in 80 km or so you come across great changes in style and at almost every turning there is something of interest.

ROUTE: 390 KM

Danggali
Conservation
Park

Calperum   Mildura

Waikerie   45   Renmark   59

Nuriootpa   20   20

33   Barmera   15   Berri   79   Cullulleraine

102   16

Tanunda

Gawler   Lyndoch

41

Adelaide

352

ROUTE

From the centre of Adelaide, leave by way of *King William Rd* and *O'Connell St* until you come to the *Main North Rd* which is, in the first stretch, Rte 1. Then in 5 km it branches off as Rte 20, still the *Main North Rd,* through Parafield on the road to Gawler. The road – still Rte 20 – becomes the Sturt Hwy and heads directly to **Gawler**. From Gawler, which is 40 km north-east of Adelaide, you head out on the Barossa Valley Hwy for 32 km through the towns and villages of the **Barossa Valley** – including **Lyndoch**, **Tanunda** and **Nuriootpa**. From Nuriootpa head out on the Sturt Hwy, still Rte 20. You pass the **Brookfield Conservation Park** along the 99 km to **Waikerie** and continue another 34 km to Kingston OM – Kingston on Murray. Heading on from there you encounter a series of small river towns – Cobdogla, **Barmera** on Lake

Bonney, Glossop and then the appropriately named **Berri**, famous for its dried fruits. From there it is only a 20 km run to **Renmark**, in the heart of the Riverland and one of the oldest irrigation areas in Australia. You are still only 260 km from Adelaide. From Renmark follow Rte 20 across the Victoria border, through Culleraine to **Mildura**, to connect with the Melbourne–Mildura route, p.156, and the Mildura-Wodonga route, p.168.

BUSES

A variety of companies, including Greyhound Pioneer and McCafferty's, provide a choice of daily buses between Adelaide and Mildura, stopping at, among other places, Gawler (1¼ hrs), Berri (some services only, nearly 4 hrs) and

Colour section (i): The Sun Pictures, Broome (p. 323); Bungle Bungle in the Kimberley (p. 327).
(ii) Tanunda and Chateau Yaldara, in the Barossa Valley (p. 353); Mine workings, Coober Pedy (p. 378).
(iii) Port Arthur (p. 389).
(iv) Cradle Mountain and Dove Lake (p. 396).

Renmark (just over 4 hrs). The full journey to Mildura takes about 6¾ hrs. OTT table 9110.

GAWLER

Tourist Information: Gawler Tourist Information Centre, *2 Lyndoch Rd; tel: 8522 6814.* **Accommodation: Prasads Gawler Motel**, *1 Main North Rd; tel: 8522 5900.*

The town is the gateway to the Barossa and 44 km from Adelaide. Gawler is one of South Australia's oldest and most historic country towns, displaying many beautiful colonial buildings. It is also the oldest country town in South Australia – it was planned by Colonel Light (see below) and settled in 1839. It is named after the resident South Australia commissioner George Gawler and was originally known as Gawler Town. The site, at the junction of the North and South Para Rivers, was selected by William Light in 1837 and by 1840 the town was well under way. The railway station opened in 1857, providing a direct link to Adelaide. An agricultural college was established at nearby **Roseworthy** in 1883, and in 1936 this became an oenological – vine growing and wine making – college, which now has true international fame.

The town's prosperity over the years can be seen in the Heritage listed **Church Hill** district, which starts next to *Murray St,* and there is a Heritage walking tour with brochures available at the Information Centre. The oldest public building in Gawler is the **Old Telegraph Station**, *Murray St; tel: 8522 2548,* built in 1859 and now the **Gawler Heritage Museum**. This National Trust property has displays depicting early life in the area with a pioneer kitchen, laundry, sitting room and bedroom. Open daily 1300–1600. The same applies to **Para Para Mansion** *(Penrith Ave),* a 15-room house built in 1862, which has, in the main, been restored to its original condition.

Within the boundaries of the town is **Dead Mans Pass** at the end of *Murray St,* which is a scenic reserve with walking trails beside the river and **Clonlea Recreation Park**, the site of the first farm settlement in the area.

THE BAROSSA VALLEY

The history of the Barossa Valley is fascinating.

The man who you might call the father of the area is Colonel Light, who has never quite been paid his historic due. He came from a quite remarkable family – his father was responsible for the design of Georgetown in Penang, Malaysia. Col. Light was, of course, responsible for the liberal and intelligent design of Adelaide (see p. 334). In 1837, as surveyor-general, he came to the Barossa in search of a north-east route from Adelaide to the eastern states. Instead he found this area of great fertility – a valley between 3–11 km wide and about 30 km long. In naming the area there was some misspelling. Light had served in the Peninsular Wars of the Napoleonic era and Barossa is named after the Battle of Barrosa in Spain. **Lyndoch** is also misspelled: Col. Light named it in memory of his friend Lord Lynedoch, who fought alongside him in that same battle.

Three years later the potential of the valley was brought to the attention of George Fife Angas, an investor and merchant banker, by Johann Menge, a German geologist and mineralogist, who had found minerals in the hills around. George Angas was on the committee of the South Australian Land Company, which had been created to help colonise South Australia with free settlers as opposed to convicts sentenced to transportation. Angas extended this idea to encouraging settlement by religious dissenters. At the time the German Lutherans were under extreme pressure in their homeland and a group of 25 families came to South Australia in 1838. They, and the ones that followed over the next 20 years, brought with them their language, their customs and their religion. Even the way the villages were built followed the German pattern of *strassendorf* or *hufendorf* villages. Although there is a residual cultural effect it is difficult to see obvious traces of this wave of settlers except perhaps in the villages of **Krondorf** and **Bethany** and in the cemeteries and churches of **Gomersal**, **Seppeltsfield**, **Ebenezer** and **Gruenberg**.

These were not large settlements but they were self-contained owing to language difficulties, and the benefits of this have been passed on to this day. Households produced almost all their own food including smoked meats, cheese and wine. The houses and outbuildings in the

353

villages – cellars, smoking rooms – reflect this diversity.

The first wines made were by Johann Gramp in 1850 and were table wines for immediate use although after a few years fortified wines such as port and tokay were produced. In the period 1858–1876, 21 distillation licences were issued in the Barossa. Export of the wines started in the 1890s and this led to the opening of new wineries, some of which are still in production to this day. These days the Barossa Valley is almost certainly the most visited and probably the best-known wine-producing area in Australia. The main flood of visitors comes with the **Barossa Vintage Festival**, which is held every 2 years on the odd numbered years.

The Barossa Valley wineries produce a very wide range of wines. It could be argued that its strength is in the dry whites and the dry reds, leaving the seriously heavy reds to the **Hunter Valley** in New South Wales (see p.76) although there are many exceptions to this rule.

There are two sub-regions in the Barossa Valley itself, which includes **Nuriootpa, Tanunda** and **Lyndoch**, and the **Barossa Hills** with the towns of **Eden Valley, Springton** and **Angaston**. Many of the grape growers are descendants of the original German settlers.

There are many ways of seeing the Barossa and walking is one of them. There are marked trails all over the valley and the low ranges and the tourist information offices all have brochures giving detailed instructions. In the Barossa region there are about fifty wineries and almost all of them welcome visitors for cellar door tastings, guided tours and cellar sales. Most of them offer light refreshments as well. The Barossa crushes, but does not necessarily grow, about a quarter of the Australian vintage. (A substantial percentage of the grapes processed in the Barossa are in fact grown elsewhere.)

LYNDOCH

Tourist Information: Kies Estate Cellars, *Barossa Valley Way; tel: 8524 4110.*

ACCOMMODATION AND FOOD

Chateau Yaldara Estate Motor Inn *(FL), Barossa Valley Hwy; tel: 8524 4268*
Errigo's Cellar Restaurant, *23 Barossa*

Valley Way; tel: 8524 4015. Licensed. Open lunch seven days a week.

SIGHTSEEING

This village of 700 inhabitants is at the southern end of the Barossa Valley. Dating from 1838, it is one of the oldest towns in South Australia. However, there were no wineries in the early days when the water mill, built in 1853 and driven by the **Para River**, was used for grinding corn. The first winery did not arrive until 1896.

Fine examples of early dwellings survive. A nearby château style winery has a remarkable collection of antiques and European porcelain. **Rosedale**, a short distance from Lyndoch, has a quaint cemetery and an interesting herb farm.

The Mechanical Music Museum, *Barossa Valley Hwy; tel: 8524 4014,* has a collection of 19th-century mechanical music machines including the cylinder and music boxes that preceded the gramophone, the Edison wax cylinder machines that followed and the Berliner phonographs, which brought in the record player. Open daily 0900–1700.

TANUNDA

Tourist Information: Barossa Wine and Visitor Centre, *66-68 Murray St; tel: 8563 0600.* Caters not just for Tanunda but the whole of the Barossa wine industry.

ACCOMMODATION AND FOOD

Barossa Weintal Hotel *(FL), Murray St; tel: 8563 2303.* **Barossa Junction Resort,** *Barossa Valley Way; tel: 8563 3400.* **Barossa Motor Lodge** *(FL), Murray St; tel: 8563 2988.* **Tanunda Hotel,** *51 Murray St; tel: 8563 2030.*
1918 Bistro and Grill, *94 Murray St; tel: 8563 3408.* Open daily lunch and dinner. Licensed. Garden setting. **La Buona Vita,** *89a Murray St; tel: 8563 2527.* Licensed. Lunch and dinner daily. **The Park Restaurant,** *2a Murray St; tel: 8563 3500.* **Zinfandel Tea Rooms,** *58 Murray St; tel: 8563 1822.* Lunch and tea daily.

SIGHTSEEING

Widely regarded as the most German of the towns in the Barossa, Tanunda is 70 km north-east of Adelaide. The name of the town

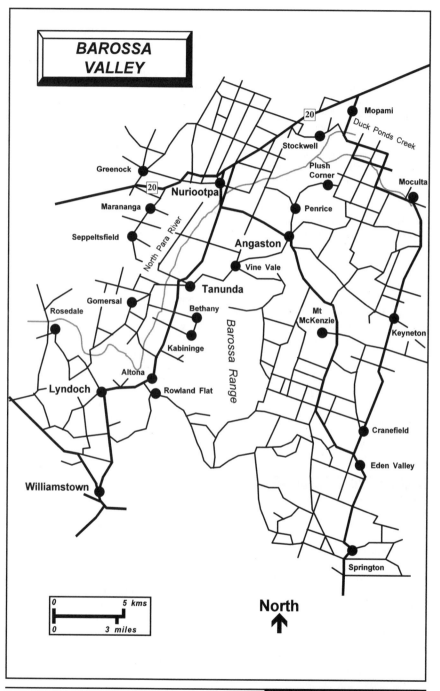

BAROSSA VALLEY

Mopami

20

Duck Ponds Creek

Stockwell

Greenock

Plush Corner

Moculta

20

Nuriootpa

Marananga

Penrice

Seppeltsfield

Angaston

North Para River

Vine Vale

Tanunda

Rosedale

Gomersal

Bethany

Mt McKenzie

Keyneton

Barossa Range

Kabininge

Altona

Lyndoch

Rowland Flat

Cranefield

Eden Valley

Williamstown

Springton

0	5 kms
0	3 miles

North

355

originates from an Aboriginal rather than a German word, meaning 'watering hole'. Originally it was a small village called Langmeil and was the second of the German settlements in the Barossa, with **Bethany** being the first. It is still possible to see the outlines of the old village around **Langmeil's Goat Square**, **Rose Bridge** and **Kegel Alley**. The four Lutheran churches of the town bear testament to the religious belief that took settlers far from their native land. The culture is reflected in the cuisine of some of the restaurants, which offer bratwurst and a variety of German breads and pastries.

A little way out of town at **Dorien** is the **Kev Rohrlach Technology and Heritage Centre**, *Barossa Valley Way; tel: 8563 3407.* This is an esoteric and eclectic private collection including everything from space rockets and a 1902 electric car to horse-drawn carriages and old clothes and curios.

Despite its off-putting name the 7-hectare **Barossa Kiddypark**, *corner Magnolia St and Menge Rd,* has everything to keep young children happy including an electric train, dodgem cars and an American western fort. There is also a wildlife section with kangaroos, wallabies, emus and wombats.

The Keg Factory, *St Hallett Rd; tel: 8563 3012,* makes kegs and then, by extension, wine racks and barrel furniture – almost any application of the craft of coopering. Open daily.

Mengler's Hill Lookout, *Mengler's Hill Rd* to the east of Tanunda, has views of the valley.

NURIOOTPA

Tourist Information: Barossa Wine and Visitor Centre, *66-68 Murray St; tel: 8563 0600.*

ACCOMMODATION AND FOOD

Nuriootpa Vine Inn Hotel-Motel *(BW), Murray St; tel: 8562 2133.* **Top of the Valley Tourist Motel**, *49 Murray St; tel: 8562 2111.* **Barossa Gateway Motel**, *Kalimna Rd; tel: 8562 1033.*

Kaesler Restaurant, *Barossa Valley Way; tel 8562 2711.* Open daily lunch and dinner. Licensed. Part of the Kaesler Estate. **Nuriootpa Vine Inn**, *14 Murray St; tel: 8562 2133.*

Licensed. Open daily lunch and dinner. **The Wild Olive Restaurant**, *Pheasant Farm Rd; tel 8562 1286.* Open lunch Wed–Sun. Dinner Thur–Sat. Licensed. **Saltram Winery and Bistro**, *Nuriootpa Rd, Angaston;* tel: 8564 3355. **Barossa Brauhaus**, *42 Murray St, Angaston; tel: 8564 2014.* Open lunch daily, dinner Tues–Sun. First licensed in 1849.

SIGHTSEEING

Non-residents tend to pronounce the name of the town incorrectly. There is a story of a severely wounded digger being carried on a stretcher from an aid station and abusing the orderly: 'It's not Nuriopta, it's Nuriootpa, you dummy.' Or words to that effect. It's best to get the pronunciation correct, as the locals are very touchy on the subject. The town is 76 km from Adelaide on the Barossa Valley Hwy.

Nuriootpa is the commercial centre of the Barossa Valley. The name that causes such pronunciation problems comes from an Aboriginal word, translated as 'meeting place' or 'rock of the giant'. The town was originally called Greenock Green, when William Coulthard and Mathias Lange built a red gum slab pub – hotel is too grand a word – called the **Red Lion** to serve travellers and bullock trains on their way from Adelaide to Kapunda. Coulthard's house is now a National Trust museum, *corner Murray and Penrice Sts.* The **North Para River** meanders through the town which, with the open spaces and interesting old buildings, make it a pleasant town to visit.

Near Nuriootpa is the small village of **Light Pass**. There are two Lutheran churches and cairn that mark the place where Colonel Light and Captain Sturt met. Nearby is **Luhr's Cottage**, which was built in 1848 by the Barossa's first German schoolteacher, J.H. Luhrs. The house has been restored in the authentic German style and is heritage listed. Three kilometres from Nuriootpa in the opposite direction is **Marananga**. It was originally named Gnadenfrei by Silesian settlers, meaning 'freed by the Grace of God.' During the anti-German feeling, approaching hysteria, which marked World War I, the name was changed to Marananga, an Aboriginal word, translated as 'my hands'.

Marananga may be small – population a nominal 200 – but it has a wonderful church, restored barns and cottages and its own brass band. Nearby, is the **Seppeltsfield Winery**, established by Joseph Seppelt in 1852. Seppeltsfield was established as a château complete with a mini-family village. On top of the hill they built the family mausoleum. Now the beautifully maintained gardens add to the impressive buildings, making it one of the show places of the Barossa.

Just 7 km out of Nuriootpa, at the eastern end of the Barossa Valley is **Angaston**. This is a small town of parks and open spaces set in the highest reaches of the Barossa (which is not that high, at 361 m above sea level). The town is named after George Fife Angas. There is a 2½ km Heritage Walk laid out to take you around the town. Worth seeing in the area is the **Collingrove Homestead**, *Eden Valley Rd; tel: 8564 2061*, which was built in 1856 as a home for John Howard Angas, second son of George Fife Angas. The grand homestead remained in possession of the Angas family until 1976, when it was given to the National Trust. It still contains many of the original furnishings. Open 1300–1630 weekdays, Sat–Sun 1100–1630.

BARMERA

Tourist Information: **Barmera Travel Centre**, *Barwell Ave; tel: 8588 2289.*

ACCOMMODATION

The Lake Resort Motel, *Lakeside Dr.; tel: 344 6477*. **Barmera Hotel Motel**, *Barwell Ave; tel: 8588 2111.*

SIGHTSEEING

The town is situated on the edge of **Lake Bonney** – named after the explorer Charles Bonney, who came here in 1838, when droving cattle along the Murray River to the market in Adelaide. The name of the town comes from a local Aboriginal word which could be interpreted as 'water place' or 'lake dwellers.'

By 1848 this was cattle country with several major properties in the area. After World War I, the area was opened up to soldier settlers and the village was established. The blocks along the southern and western shores of the lake produce grapes, citrus, stone fruits and vegetables, which, with tourism, is the major industry.

Lake Bonney has several attractive beaches, of which the nudist beach at **Pelican Point** is the most widely known. The **Donald Campbell Obelisk** on *Queen Elizabeth Dr.* marks Campbell's 1964 attempt on the world water speed record.

To the north of town along the lake shore are the ruins of **Nappers Accommodation House**, one of the earliest buildings in the area, which was built on the stock route in 1850. About 15 km away on *Morgan Rd* is the **Overland Corner Hotel**, which functions both as a hotel and a museum. Only 5 km west of Barmera is **Cobdogla**, a small irrigation settlement that was first developed by Europeans in 1851. The early settlers cleared the land and dug the irrigation channels, which are still used today. You can see how the system worked at the **Cobdogla Irrigation Museum**, *Main Rd; tel: 8588 2289*, originally a pumping station dating from the turn of the century. It has the world's only working Humphrey pump, which acts like a giant water cannon by driving water upwards by a series of explosions. Other exhibits include a fully restored 1906 steam locomotive and a 1920 traction engine, both operate as rides. Ring to check opening hours but usually 1100–1630 most holiday weekends.

357

BERRI

Tourist Information: **Berri Tourist Information Centre**, *24 Vaughan Terrace; tel: 8582 1655.*

ACCOMMODATION

Big River Motor Inn, *Sturt Hwy 20; tel: 8582 2688*. **Berri Lodge Motel** *(BU), 11 Zante Rd (Sturt Hwy); tel: 85 82 1011*. **Berri Resort Hotel**, *Riverview Dr.; tel: 8582 1411*. **Glossop Motel**, *Sturt Hwy, Glossop via Berri; tel: 8583 2379.*

SIGHTSEEING

Berri is very much the commercial centre of the Riverland. It is the home of one of the largest wineries/distilleries in the southern hemisphere, **Berri Estates**. The name is said to come from an Aboriginal phrase *berri berri*, which means 'wide bend in the river', which is pretty accurate. It is also the name for a species of bush. The first explorer in the area was Charles Sturt in 1830, but the town dates from the proclamation of the **Berri Immigration Area** in 1910. The town was formally founded in 1911. Until that time the site had been part of the Cobdogla sheep station and was a mooring point for boats working the river. Berri Estates started as a distillery in 1918 to make spirits from waste dried fruit. The town has several pretty picnic areas and **Martin's Bend** 2 km east of Berri is a good water skiing spot. Two vehicular ferries cross the river at Berri.

On *Riverview Dr.* is a sculptural and environmental installation on the river bank, commissioned by the **Riverview Cultural Trust**, which honours the famous Aboriginal tracker Jimmy James, who worked with the police for more than 30 years. To get an idea of how the district developed the **Berrivale Orchards Showroom and Theatrette**, *Sturt Hwy; tel: 8582 3321,* has a 10 min video to give you the background and a showroom displaying all the produce of the town. Open Mon–Fri 0830–1630, Sat 0900–1200.

Berri is another town that cannot resist proclaiming it presence with a Big something. This time it's **The Big Orange**, 3 km from town on the Sturt Hwy and sadly you cannot miss it. However from the top of the Orange there is an excellent view over the district and the River Murray. An even better view is from **The Lookout Tower**, *corner of Fielder St and Vaughan Terrace.* Originally this was a 15.8m water tower.

Katarapko National Park (information from **Riverland National Parks**, *Vaughan Terrace; tel: 8585 2111*), is 17 km south-west of the town. **Katarapko Creek**, one of the many minor tributaries of the Murray, runs through the centre of the park, which is famous for its bird life. The **Kia Kia Nature Trail**, also runs through the park and takes about 20 mins. Canoe hire is available for exploring the park.

Glossop, between Berri and Barmera is a very small town (population 250) and is named after Captain Glossop of HMAS *Sydney*, the warship which sank the German battleship *Emden* in World War I.

RENMARK

Tourist Information: Renmark Tourist and Heritage Centre, *Murray Ave; tel: 8586 6704.*

ACCOMMODATION

Renmark Country Club, *Sturt Hwy; tel: 8595 1401.* **Renmark Hotel-Motel**, *Murray Ave; tel: 8586 6755.* **Citrus Valley Motel**, *210 Renmark Ave; tel: 8586 6717.* **Ventura Motel**, *234 Renmark Ave; tel: 8586 6841.* **Fountain Gardens Motel**, *Renmark Ave; tel: 8586 6899.* **HI: Renmark Holiday Hostel**, *16th St; tel: 8586 6937.*

SIGHTSEEING

Renmark, Australia's first irrigation town, is 257 km north-east of Adelaide on the Sturt Hwy. The town was founded in 1887, when the Canadian Chaffey brothers started an irrigation scheme, using water from the Murray. They went bankrupt in 1892 and the government took over the scheme, which is still in operation today. The town was named by George Chaffey. Suggestions are that the name comes from the Aboriginal word meaning 'red mud' or that it was named after William Renny, an early settler. Renmark has another first to its name – the **Renmark Hotel** was the first community-owned hotel in Australia. These days Renmark is a provincial centre on a beautiful bend of the Murray. Tourism is a source of income for the area along with wheat, wool, fruit, wine and brandy production.

Renmark has many attractions for the visitor. **Olivewood**, *21st St; tel: 8586 6175,* was built of pine logs in 1887 for George Chaffey. It is now a museum telling the story of Renmark's pioneering days and is set in attractive grounds with palms, olive trees and citrus groves. Open Thur–Mon 1000–1600, Tues 1400–1600. $3.50. Next door to the tourist information office is an **Interpretive Centre** (open Mon–Fri 0900–1700, Sat 0900–1600, Sun 1200–1600; $3), which tells the full story of the River Murray – its history from ancient times, its geology, the story of the local Aboriginal inhabitants, the irrigation scheme and the boats that plied the Murray.

Moored close to the centre is a reminder of

the importance of the Murray as a major highway. **The PS Industry**, *Murray Ave; tel: 8586 6704*, is a working river boat (PS stands for Paddle Steamer). Open Mon–Fri 0900–1630, Sat 0900–1530, Sun 1200–1530. The *Industry* was built in Goolwa in 1911 for the Engineering and Water Supply Department to go up and down the river removing snags that were a danger to navigation. It has been fully restored to working order and turned into a museum. But it is a museum that can, and still does, regularly steam up and down the river. It is an impressive sight as it churns up the river with its tall single funnel, its massive white boom over the bow and the two massive paddle wheels at the stern. The tourist office has information about cruise times and prices.

Bredl's Wonder World of Wildlife, *corner Sturt Hwy and 28th St; tel: 8585 1431*, is one of the largest private zoos in Australia and reportedly has the biggest collection of reptiles with over 200 species on display as well as crocodiles and other animals and birds. Open 7 days 0900–1800. The 74 sq m mural at **Harding's Folklore Gallery**, *Murtho St; tel: 8586 6972*, is a matter of personal taste. It depicts the bushrangers of Australia and is said to have taken more than 3000 hours to create. Open 1000–1100 Sat–Sun.

↗ SIDE TRACKS
FROM RENMARK

Renmark is also the gateway to the **Murray Riverland**, which extends down the river from Renmark through Berri, Glossop, Barmera, Cobdogla, Kingston on Murray and finally Blanchetown.

Renmark is surrounded by National Parks and reserves. **Calperum Station** is 17 km north of Renmark and covers 24,000 hectares. It was originally established as a property in 1865 by Richard Holland and the original lease included the current site of Renmark. In the flood season this is one of the major centres for breeding water birds in the state and these wetlands form part of the total **Riverland Wetland**, which has been declared of international importance.

Further to the north, 90 km from Renmark, is **Dangalli Conservation Park**, which touches the border of New South Wales, formed by putting together four major sheep stations with a total area of 253,000 hectares. Just below Dangalli and 50 km east of Renmark is **Chowilla Game Reserve**, which is 18,400 hectares of floodplains and wetlands. It is accessible from either *Wentworth Rd* or *Murtho Rd*. All of these form part of the **Bookmark Biosphere Reserve** (park information; *tel: 8595 8010*). This is rugged country with no facilities whatsoever and should only be approached in serious expedition mode.

The **Murray River National Park** is much softer and more accessible. It has four separate areas – **Katarapko Creek, Lyrup Flats, Bulyong Island** and Eckert Creek. The nearest to Renmark is Bulyong Island, which covers 2380 hectares and which you get to by way of Renmark North. Then down river towards Berri and to the southwest of Renmark is Lyrup Flats at 2000 hectares, which is accessible by road from the Sturt Hwy. And beyond Berri, again hanging down in a great loop towards Loxton, is Katarapko, which is the biggest section at 8905 hectares and, again, is accessible by car from the Sturt Hwy. Lyrup Flats and Eckert Creek is where you can best see the potential problems of irrigation with most of the trees killed either by salt or high flood levels. As it stands it is a bleak landscape but it is an amazing breeding and feeding ground for wild birds. In fact, nearly 150 different species have been recorded within the park, which is full of quiet backwaters and horseshoe lagoons.

All of these waters, as indeed all of the waters of the Murray, are excellent for canoeing and fishing. The Murray is home to six main species of fish: catfish, silver perch, European perch or redfin, golden perch or callop, European carp and Murray cod. There are also shrimps and yabbies. Murray cod can grow up to 2m in length and are protected.

359

MILDURA

See p.166.

THE YORKE PENINSULA

The Yorke Peninsula, which is never more than 50 km across but is 187 km long – hangs like a defensive arm forming the Gulf of St Vincent to protect Adelaide and has on its other side Spencer Gulf.

Some of the towns on this peninsula have a surprising Cornish influence, thanks to the thousands of miners who made their way here from the west of England in the last century, and the area even stages a Cornish festival.

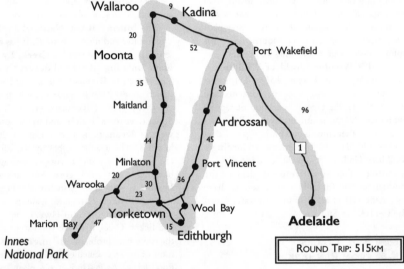

360

ROUND TRIP: 515KM

Follow Rte 1 north from the city centre and then along the west coast of the Gulf of St Vincent through **Salisbury, Two Wells, Lowler Light, Dublin, Windsor, Wild Horse Plains, Inkerman** and then **Port Wakefield**, which is 97 km from the city centre and is the gateway to the Yorke Peninsula.

Just after Port Wakefield the road splits and you turn left off Rte 1 towards Kadina. After 8 km comes another junction: turn left again, sharply to the south, on the road to **Ardrossan**, 49 km from Wakefield, which runs along the west side of the peninsula. From Ardrossan the road runs along the coast through **Pine Point** and the turn off for Port Vincent (44 km away)

and continues through **Stansbury, Wool Bay** and then jigs around **Salt Creek Bay** to arrive at **Edithburgh**. From there **Yorketown** is 15 km inland. Alternatively turn right before Wool Bay to reach Yorketown more directly.

From there to the tip of the Peninsula there is a mainly unsealed road that runs 16 km to the coast and then circumnavigates **Sturt Bay** and **Foul Bay** until after 47 km it comes to **Marion Bay**, which could be thought of as the gateway to **Innes National Park**, which is the very tip of the Eyre Peninsula.

To get there using only sealed roads you drive the 23 km from Yorketown to **Warooka** and then from there to **Marion Bay**, 2 km from the Innes National Park.

To make the return trip to Adelaide you can go up the other side of the peninsula. From Yorketown north to **Minlaton** is 30 km. Going from Marion Bay, drive to **Corny Point** by unsealed road, passing the **Warrenben Conservation Park** on the way – 33 km. Then from **Warooka** back on sealed roads to Minlaton, a 20 km distance.

From Minlaton the road runs in a straight line 44 km to **Maitland** and then another 35 km to **Moonta** on **Moonta Bay**. From there it is 18 km to **Wallaroo** and another 9 km to **Kadina**. From Kadina drive 41 km through **Kulpara** until rejoining Rte 1 back at Port Wakefield. Turn south on Rte 1 to retrace the route to Adelaide.

BUSES

There are 2 buses Mon–Fri and 1 service Sat–Sun operated by Premier Roadlines, connecting Adelaide with Kadina, Wallaroo and Moonta, but not going south into the peninsula. The same services run in the opposite direction. Journey time to Moonta is 3 hrs. OTT table 9128.

TOURIST INFORMATION

Yorke Peninsula Visitor Information Office, *Town Hall, 51 Taylor St, Kadina; tel: 8821 2093.*

ARDROSSAN

Tourist Information: *BP Road House, Main Coast Rd; tel: 8837 3048.*

ACCOMMODATION

Ardrossan Motel-Hotel, *36 First St; tel: 8837 3008.* **Royal House Hotel-Motel**, *1 Fifth St; tel: 8837 3007.*

SIGHTSEEING

This town with a Scottish name was originally known by the first Europeans to visit the area as Clay Gully or Parrara. In 1873 Governor Fergusson proclaimed the town Ardrossan after its namesake in Ayrshire. The town is situated 149 km from Adelaide on 25 m clay cliffs overlooking Gulf St Vincent, and is the largest eastern seaport, being constructed to handle the shipping of the locally mined dolomite and of

grain, for which it is the third largest port in the state. Besides all this industrial activity it is a very popular holiday and fishing resort.

Among the attractions are the **Ardrossan and District Historical Museum**, *Fifth St; tel: 8837 3048,* in the old power house, which was run by the brothers Clarence and Richard Smith, who invented the stumpjump plough. This plough can go across a field of mallee roots – the worst kind – and jump over the obstacles instead of snagging and breaking. There is a collection of original implements, drawings and other archival material. Open Sundays 1430–1630.

EDITHBURGH

This is an immensely popular destination for skin divers. It still retains many of its original buildings and has the feel of a 19th century coastal port. There is a Heritage Walk brochure available from the **Boathouse Tearooms** in *Edith St (tel: 8852 6109),* which lets you take a self-guided tour of the port. The town was named after Governor Fergusson's wife, Edith.

Offshore from Edithburgh is **Troubridge Island Conservation Park** with a lighthouse and a large sea bird population including penguins and cormorants.

The **Edithburgh District Museum**, *Edith St; tel: 8852 6214,* has an excellent account of the local marine and salt mining industries, which grew up together. Open Sun 1400–1630. In town is the **Edithburgh Flora Reserve**, *corner Robert Ave and Anstey Terrace,* which covers 17½ hectares of bushland and is full of a wide range of wildflowers and bird life.

YORKETOWN

Tourist Information: *EJ Braunds, 2 Standbury Rd; tel: 8852 1005.*

ACCOMMODATION

Yorke Hotel, *Yorketown; tel: 8852 1221.* **Melville Hotel-Motel**, *1 Minlaton Rd; tel: 8852 1019.* **Anchorage Motel**, *25 O'Halloran Parade.*

SIGHTSEEING

The first industry in this area, and still carried out to some extent, was the harvesting of some

361

of the 300 salt lakes scattered in the vicinity, some of which are pink. Later came agriculture and later still tourism.

The town is 230 km west of Adelaide and 15 km from the sea.

SIDE TRACK FROM YORKETOWN

From Yorketown it is 53 km by sealed road to **Innes National Park**. For **park information**: *tel: 8854 4040*.

INNES NATIONAL PARK

Right on the toe of the Yorke Peninsula, the Innes National Park covers some 9100 hectares and has spectacular coastal scenery. There are large, and frequently windswept beaches backed inland by large sand dunes. Tall and heavily weathered cliffs divide the beaches. Moving inland there are salt lakes and low lying scrub land, which make a fairly deserted and almost desolate scene. This is a good place to see kangaroos and emus, especially at dawn and dusk.

There is a good camping area with all facilities at **Pondalowie Bay**; *tel: 8854 404.*

Within the park there is a ghost town, **Inneston**, which is well signposted to show its history.

MOONTA

Tourist Information: Town Hall, *George St; tel: 8825 2622.*

ACCOMMODATION

Cornwall Hotel, *20 Ryan St; tel: 8825 2304.* **Moonta Bay Patio Motel**, *196 Bay Rd; tel: 8825 2473.*

SIGHTSEEING

This Cornish town is 18 km south-west of Kadina and 165 km north-west of Adelaide. Although the name is an Aboriginal word, possibly meaning 'impenetrable scrub', it should mean large fortune. **The Moonta Mining Company** was formed in 1861 by a Scot, not a Cornishman; Captain Walter Hughes.

He enticed Cornishmen – 'Cousin Jacks' – from the **Burra Mines**, which are 154 km north of Adelaide. Many of them trekked overland with their belongings in wheelbarrows. This was the first mine in Australia to pay £1 million in dividends.

In the area the **Moonta Mines State Heritage** is a must. It has Cornish cottages, the church, **Hughes Pump House** and other ruins. **The Miner's Cottage and Garden**, *Vercoe St; tel: 8825 3422,* has a typical Cornish cottage, built around 1870 from wattle and daub, mud bricks, clay and limestone and furnished in period style. The garden has also been re-created in the style of the period. Open Wed, Sat–Sun 1330–1600. Cornish miners were religious and their religion was Methodism. **The Moonta Mines Methodist Church**, *tel: 8825 3422,* built in 1865, seats 1250 worshippers and has a magnificent organ with over 600 pipes. Open Wed, Sat–Sun

---

The Cornish Connection

In the last century the Yorke Peninsula switched from being a place of agriculture when rich copper ore deposits were found. This was followed by an influx of Cornish miners; first from other parts of Australia and then from Cornwall itself. At one time there were so many there that the area around Wallaroo, Moonta and Kadina became known as Little Cornwall. In every town on the peninsula there are small museums – at least 16 altogether – run by the local historical societies which commemorate this influence. Perhaps the most recent is **Moonta Mines Museum** *(tel: 8825 3422)*, a large, old school building dating from 1878 which, in its prime, had more than 1000 pupils. Now its classrooms are dedicated to the Cornish miners and their homes. The displays include photographs, lamps, clocks, needle and lace-work, kitchen and laundry utensils, household items and furniture.

On the peninsula you can still get a Cornish pasty in many of the pubs, although one would not like to vouch for the authenticity of the recipe. Especially when served with tomato sauce.

1130–1630. **The History Resource Centre** is in the old **Moonta Mines School House**, *Verran Terrace; tel: 8825 3422*, (see box opposite) and is part of a mining museum. It has a comprehensive collection of rare documents and newspapers, many of them stored on microfilm. Open Wed, Sun 1330–1600.

One of the delights of Moonta is that there is a **narrow gauge railway** with hourly departures from the station next to the museum (*tel: 8825 3422*). The train takes you around the old mining area showing you how it was worked.

WALLAROO

Tourist Information: Wallaroo Tourist Information Centre, *Town Hall, Irwin St; tel: 8823 2023.*

ACCOMMODATION

Esquire Motor Inn, *27 Lydia Terrace; tel: 8823 2303.* **Sonborn Lodge Motel**, *18 John Terrace; tel: 8823 2291.* **Peninsula Hotel-Motel**, *9-11 Bagot St; tel: 8823 2545.*

SIGHTSEEING

Wallaroo's copper mines had started production when a shepherd discovered a new and major deposit around a wombat burrow 20 km away. The name is alleged to have come from an Aboriginal phrase *wadlu waru* meaning 'wallaby's urine'. Originally it was Wall Warroo, which was corrupted to its current name. The shepherd discovered copper in 1859 and Wallaroo Mine was soon followed by Moonta. In the 1880s the ore yielded 30% copper, at the time a world record.

There is a **Heritage and Nautical Museum**, *Jetty Rd; tel: 8823 2366*, which was built in 1865 as the town's first post office. It is now a National Trust property and depicts Wallaroo's history. The maritime complex covers the history of one of the state's busiest ports. Open Wed, Sat, Sun 1400–1600.

There is yet another railway at Wallaroo and this runs to Kadina only on the second Sun of every month at 1300 from the **Wallaroo Railway Yards** (*tel: 8821 1356*).

KADINA

Tourist Information: Yorke Peninsula

Visitor Information Centre, *51 Taylor St; tel: 8821 2093.*

ACCOMMODATION

Kadina Gateway Motor Inn, *Adelaide Rd; tel: 8821 2777.* **Kadina Village Motel**, *28 Port Rd; tel: 8821 1920.* **Kadina Hotel**, *29 Taylor St; tel: 8821 1008.* **Wombat Hotel**, *19 Taylor St; tel: 8821 1108.*

EVENTS

In the north of the Yorke Peninsula are a trio of Cornish towns: **Kadina, Moonta** and **Wallaroo**. They hold the only Cornish festival in the world outside Cornwall – the biennial **Kernewek Lowender**, held in May in odd numbered years.

SIGHTSEEING

Kadina, 150 km north-west of Adelaide, is the largest town on the Yorke Peninsula. Its fortune was built on copper, discovered at nearby Wallaroo – 10 km west of the town – in 1861 and thousands of Cornish miners flocked to the area. In a period of 63 years, 1861–1923, 3.4 million tonnes of ore were sent to the smelter. So although the town has a name which may be derived from an Aboriginal word meaning 'lizard plain', it is a town with a Cornish history and, indeed, many of the houses were built in the Cornish style. There are several examples throughout the town with the oldest cottage at *63 Taylor St,* which has a parapet to prevent non-existent snow building up on the scullion roof. There is a heritage trail through the town and the tourist information office has copies.

The **Banking and Currency Museum**, *Graves St; tel: 8821 2906,* is Kadina's oldest surviving bank building, having been built in 1873. No longer a bank it now has collections of used and proof coins, gold coins and the old ledgers, cash books and promissory notes. Open Sat–Wed 1000–1700.

The **Kadina Heritage Museum**, *Matta Rd, off Moonta Rd; tel: 8821 1083,* is part of the complex dealing with the history of the area, part mining, part agricultural. It also includes **Matta House**, a mine manager's residence built in 1863. Open Wed 1400–1630, Sat–Sun 1400–1630.

363

THE EYRE PENINSULA

The Eyre Peninsula is a triangle of land bigger than Tasmania – 1000 km east–west and 400 km north–south. It produces a tenth of Australia's wheat crop and still half of it is kept as parks, reserves and bushland. It is also the start of the Nullarbor, under which runs the world's longest cave system. The coast which abuts the Spencer Gulf is sheltered, calm and full of excellent and safe beaches. The west coast, which faces the fury of the Southern Ocean, is rugged with spectacular scenery and yet has resort towns which prosper where shelter can be found from the precipitous cliffs and pounding surf.

The coastline was first seen by Dutch explorer Peter Nuyts in 1627, then Matthew Flinders in 1802, followed by Edward Eyre in 1839, who made a 1000 km trek to Western Australia.

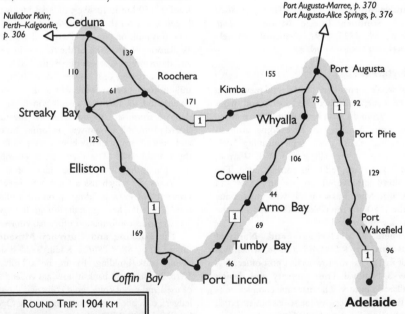

Port Augusta-Marree, p. 370
Port Augusta-Alice Springs, p. 376

Nullabor Plain;
Perth–Kalgoorlie, p. 306

Ceduna

139

110

Roochera

155

Port Augusta

61

Kimba

171

75

1

92

Streaky Bay

1

Whyalla

Port Pirie

125

106

Elliston

Cowell

129

44

1

Arno Bay

1

Port Wakefield

169

69

Tumby Bay

1

96

Coffin Bay

46

Port Lincoln

Adelaide

ROUND TRIP: 1904 KM

ROUTE

From Adelaide it is a 96 km run on Rte 1 to **Port Wakefield**. From there the road runs through a series of small towns – **Beaufort, Lochiel, Snowtown, Meriton, Warnertown** – until 129 km further on you come to **Port Pirie**. From Port Pirie the road now does a major hook by way of **Port Augusta** around Fitzgerald Bay.

Just 26 km from Port Augusta Rte 1 divides in two. Take the left-hand road, the Lincoln Hwy (Alternate Rte 1), which heads 48 km south-west to **Whyalla** and the sea. The road from Whyalla cuts between the Munyaroo Conservation Park and Mt Olinthus on its way to **Cowell**, 107 km from Whyalla, in the **Franklin Harbor Conservation Park**. From Cowell the road follows the coast through **Arno Bay** and **Tumby Bay** 170 km to **Port Lincoln**.

Now the road becomes the Flinders Hwy and goes up the west side of the Eyre Peninsula, along the coast of the Great Australian Bight, through the small towns of Coulta, Warrow, Mt Hope, Sheringa and **Elliston**, 169 km from Port Lincoln. After this the Flinders Hwy passes Lake Newland National Park and then Venus Bay and Port Kenny until it get to **Streaky Bay** and the town of the same name. From Streaky Bay to **Ceduna** is a run of 109 km; at Ceduna, turn back east along the main Rte 1, Eyre Hwy to **Roochera**. (Alternatively you can cut out Ceduna and 250 km of driving by taking a minor road from Streaky Bay to Roochera. Return to Port Augusta by Rte 1, via Wudinna and **Kimba**. From Port Augusta you can either retrace the road to Adelaide or head off on one of the routes to Marree (p. 370) or Alice Springs (p. 376).

BUSES

There is a good Stateliner bus service from Adelaide to Port Lincoln (9½ hrs). Intermediate stops include Port Pirie (3 hrs) and Cowell (5¼ hrs). Greyhound Pioneer buses take only 2 hrs to reach Port Pirie, en route for Ceduna (11½ hrs) but not entering the Peninsula itself. OTT tables 9130 and 9132.

PORT AUGUSTA

See p. 371.

WHYALLA

Tourist Information: Whyalla Tourist Centre, *Whyalla Maritime Museum, Lincoln Highway; tel: 8645 7900.*

ACCOMMODATION AND FOOD

Derhams Foreshore Motor Inn *(FL), corner Foreshore and Watson Terrace; tel: 8645 8877.* **Alexander Motor Inn** *(FL), 99 Playford Ave; tel: 8645 9488.* **Westland Hotel-Motel**, *corner*

McDouall Stuart Ave and Ian St; tel: 8645 0066. **Airport Whyalla Motel** *(BU), Lincoln Hwy; tel: 8645 2122.* **Country Inn Motel**, *95 Playford Ave; tel: 8645 0588.* **Sundowner Hotel-Motel**, *Lincoln Hwy; tel: 8645 7688.* **Bay View Hotel**, *13 Forsyth St; tel: 8645 8544.* **Hotel Eyre**, *Playford Ave; tel: 8645 7188.* **Spencer Hotel**, *1 Forsyth St; tel: 8645 8411.*

Spags, *83 Essington Lewis Ave; tel: 8645 2088.*

SIGHTSEEING

This is South Australia's largest regional city. Until the 1920s it was known as Hummock or Hummock Hill – the name Matthew Flinders gave it when he was here in 1802. This despite the fact that it had officially been named Whyalla – from an Aboriginal word thought to have meant 'deep water place' – in 1914.

The town arose through the discovery of iron ore at **Iron Knob**, 53 km away, in the 1880s. Whyalla is essentially a mining town and port. In 1901 a tramway was built to bring the iron ore from Iron Knob to Whyalla and in the following year a jetty was built to handle the shipping. Originally the ore went the short distance – less than 50 km – by sea across the Spencer Gulf to **Port Pirie** but a blast furnace was built in 1939. This was followed by a deep water port and a shipyard that ran until 1978.

The history of the town is well recorded in the **Whyalla Maritime Museum**, *Lincoln Way; tel: 8675 7900* (open daily 1000–1600, admission $5), which has on display the 650 tonne HMAS *Whyalla*. This was the first ship launched from the shipyard and is now based 2 km from the sea. Also included in the museum are relics recovered from ships wrecked in the Spencer Gulf. The museum includes what is possibly Australia's largest 00 gauge model railway, with 670m of track.

To orient oneself at Whyalla the best bet is to drive up **Hummock Hill**, where there is a magnificent look-out, which has views across Whyalla and out to sea as well as back to the **Flinders Ranges**. At the lookout there is an anti-aircraft gun that has been restored as a reminder of the gun battery that was positioned here in World War II.

365

The **Whyalla Fauna and Reptile Park**, *Lincoln Hwy; tel: 8645 7044* (open daily, 1000–dusk, admission $5) is in a bushland setting near the airport and has wallabies, koalas, dingoes, free-ranging kangaroos and emus and a walk-through aviary with more than 200 birds. **Mt Laura Homestead Museum** *Ekblom St,* behind the Westland Shopping Centre; *tel: 8645 3565* (open Sun, Mon, Wed 1400–1600, Fri 1000–1200; admission $2), is a National Trust Museum of local history in a former sheep station homestead. It also contains the first local lock-up, more than 60 fully restored and operation stationary engines and an 80-year-old locomotive.

The **Whyalla Conservation Park**, which is off the Lincoln Hwy near the turn-off to **Port Bonython** and **Point Lowly**, covers 1011 hectares and is typical of the bush and woodlands of the northern Eyre Peninsula. In the north-west corner of the park is **Wild Dog Hill**, accessed by a path from the picnic area. More than 70 species of birds have been counted in the park.

COWELL

Tourist Information: District Council of Lincoln Harbour, *6 Main St; tel: 8629 2019.*

ACCOMMODATION

Cowell Jade Motel, *Lincoln Hwy; tel: 8629 2002.* **Cowell Commercial Hotel**, *24 Main St; tel: 8629 2181.*

SIGHTSEEING

This town was named after Sir John Cowell, an engineer in the British army. The area where Cowell now stands was first sighted by a European, when Matthew Flinders sailed past in 1802 in the *Investigator*. Originally the town was known as Franklin Harbour, which then became Lake Flinders, settling on the current name in 1880.

Cowell is considered one of the finest and safest fishing areas in Australia. **Franklin Harbour**, on which it stands, is a land-locked bay covering 48 sq km, with only a narrow entrance to the sea. The range of fish is remarkable, including snapper, silver and spotted whiting, flathead, mullet, garfish, squid, razorfish,

snook and tommy ruff with the addition of crabs in the shallows.

Cowell is the only place in Australia which has a commercial **jade processing** operation. The jade, in one of the largest deposits known in the world at an estimated 80,000 tonnes, was discovered in the nearby **Marbie Ranges** in 1965. Jade boulders, which can weigh up to several tonnes, are brought to the town, where they are cut into shape using diamond-tipped saws. Samples of the jade are on display and for sale at the **Cowell Jade Motel** (see Accommodation).

The history of the district is on display at the **Franklin Harbour Historical Museum** sited in the Old Post Office, which was built around 1888. Opening times are uncertain and should be checked on the notice board outside the museum.

Just 16 km to the north is **Lucky Bay**, a small resort with a very safe beach for children. **The Knob**, 13 km to the north of Cowell, is also a very sheltered beach but has few facilities.

ARNO BAY

Accommodation: Hotel Arno, *tel: 8628 0001.*

Arno Bay is a very small town, so small that it does not have a tourist information office. It was originally a small port servicing the local farming district. The jetty and an old beacon remain as reminders of its original use. Now it is basically a holiday town. It is well known for the quality of its angling – from boats, the jetty and casting from the beaches. **Redbanks** is 6 km away and the rocks and cliff provide platforms for anglers mainly going for snapper. The Redbanks area has been declared a geological monument by the Geological Society of Australia.

TUMBY BAY

Tourist Information: Hales Mini art, *1 Bratten Way; tel: 8688 2584.*

ACCOMMODATION

Tumby Bay Hotel, *North Terrace; tel: 8688 2005.* **Sea Breeze Hotel**, *Tumby Terrace; tel: 8688 2362.* **Tumby Bay Motel**, *4 Berryman St; tel: 8688 2311.*

SIGHTSEEING

This again was originally a grain loading port and the first jetty was built in 1874. The town remains an important service centre for the area but is also a quiet and peaceful holiday resort with access to the national parks at the tip of the Eyre Peninsula, which are only 50 km away.

Some 20 km off the coast from Tumby is the **Sir Joseph Banks Group of Islands**, a marine conservation park with sea lions, dolphins and a very wide range of bird life, including the Cape Barren Goose, for which these islands are the main breeding ground. There are several cruises to the island, arranged by **Lower Eyre Peninsula Boat Charters**, *tel: 8682 2311*.

The history of Tumby Bay is on display in the **CL Alexander National Trust Museum** (open Fri, Sun 1430–1630; *tel: 8688 2198*), which was once a three roomed wooden schoolhouse.

PORT LINCOLN

Tourist Information: Port Lincoln Tourist Information Centre, *Eyre Travel, Tasman Terrace; tel: 8682 4577.*

ACCOMMODATION AND FOOD

Limani Motel, *50 Lincoln Hwy; tel: 8682 2200*. **Hilton Motel**, *11–13 King St; tel: 8682 1144*. **Navigator Restaurant & Motel**, *corner Lincoln Hwy and Normandy Pl.; tel: 8682 4313*. **First Landing Motel** *(BU), 11 Shaen St; tel: 8682 2344*. **Kingscourt Motel**, *Tasman Terrace; tel: 8682 2033*. **Blue Seas Motel**, *7 Gloucester Terrace; tel: 8682 3510*. **Grand Tasman Hotel**, *94 Tasman Terrace; tel: 8682 2133*. **Pier Hotel**, *33 Tasman Terrace; tel: 8682 1322*. **Boston Hotel**, *King St; tel: 8682 1311*. **Boston House Motel**, *Lincoln Hwy; tel: 8682 1872*.

Dockside Tavern, *on the Waterfront; tel: 8682 6141*. Daily lunch and dinner. **Grand Tasman**, *94 Tasman Terrace; tel: 8682 2936*. Licensed bistro. Daily lunch and dinner.

SIGHTSEEING

The town was named by the explorer Matthew Flinders after his home county of Lincolnshire. It is 664 km by road west of Adelaide – 250 km

as the crow flies – and is the town on the tip of the Eyre Peninsula. It stands on **Boston Bay**, which is protected by **Boston Island** and the encircling arms, which stretch from the tip of **Port Lincoln National Park** to **Point Boston**. This provides an area of protected water that is between three and seven times – both claims are widely made – the size of Sydney Harbour. Strangely, the town was considered as a site for the capital of South Australia by Colonel Light (see Adelaide p.334) but rejected because, as one report has it, he thought the harbour was unsafe. An alternative suggestion is that he was worried about the lack of fresh water. Nowadays, the harbour is the a base for a large commercial tuna fishing fleet.

The town was settled in 1839 and in the following year the **Lincoln Hotel** opened, which is the oldest on the Eyre Peninsula. In the same year a windmill was started but never completed because the grain harvest at the time did not justify the expense.

The town has many historic buildings, including **St Thomas Anglican Church**, which was started in 1849, the **Courthouse**, which was built in 1862 and the **Mill Cottage**, attached to the uncompleted mill, now the National Trust museum, in 1866. The first homestead in the area was **Mikkira** to the south of the town, which was built in 1840. It is open to the public except in summer but a permit is needed, which can be obtained from the tourist information centre. And **Mill Cottage** (open Tues–Sun 1400–1630) has a collection of artefacts covering pioneering life in the area.

But the main attractions of Port Lincoln are the national parks in the area. The 29,000 hectare **Lincoln National Park (park information** *tel: 8688 3177)* is to the south on the headland jutting into **Spencer Gulf**. It has both high cliffs and secluded beaches with rocky, undulating hills with a covering of tall mallee woodland. Among the birds in the park is the distinctive Port Lincoln parrot, as well as emus and a wide range of other birds. Kangaroos are common in the northern section of the park.

Much of the park is accessible to conventional drive vehicles although some of the areas

368

to the south require four-wheel-drive and a few require special permits from the **National Parks Office** in Port Lincoln – *Liverpool St; tel: 8688 3111.*

Coffin Bay National Park covers 30,380 hectares (**park information;** *tel: 8685 4047)* and covers the whole of the **Coffin Bay Peninsula** at the southern end of Eyre Peninsula. This is a true coastal wilderness of dunes and salt marshes but conventional vehicles can use the **Yangie Trail** from **Coffin** to **Yangie** and **Avoid Bays.** There is a wide variety of wild life in the park, including the Coffin Bay brumbies, and white-bellied sea eagles, ospreys, albatrosses and petrels are quite common.

↗ **SIDE TRACK FROM PORT LINCOLN**

COFFIN BAY

Tourist Information: Beachcomber Agencies, *Esplanade; tel: 8685 4057.*

Accommodation: Coffin Bay Hotel/Motel; *The Esplanade, tel: 8685 4111.*

The town is 51 km to the north-west of Port Lincoln at the head of the Eyre Peninsula on what is one of the most beautiful estuaries in Australia. The slightly funereal name comes form Matthew Flinders' friend Sir Isaac Coffin. This is very much a sailing town, with plenty of safe anchorages and sheltered waters. The town is literally surrounded by National and Conservation Parks with **Kellidie Bay Conservation Park** on one side and **Coffin Bay National Park** on the other.

The oysters of Coffin Bay have a statewide reputation and the **Oyster Farm** (open Mon–Fri 0800–1700; *The Esplanade)* is a specialist shop. There is also a 6 km **Oyster Walk** along the foreshore, which takes you to beyond **Crinolin Point.** The tourist office has a leaflet. Much of the outdoor sequences of the movie *Gallipoli* were shot on the nearby Farm Beach. There is a 10 km drive south by way of **Yangie Bay** lookout, which has stunning views over the

surrounding country as far as Point Avoid. ↗

ELLISTON

Tourist Information: District Council of Elliston, *Beach Terrace; tel: 8687 1977.*

ACCOMMODATION

Elliston Hotel/Motel, *Fifth St; tel: 8687 9009.* **Ellen Liston Motel,** *Beach Terrace; tel: 8687 9028.*

SIGHTSEEING

The town is 168 km from Port Lincoln and is on the shore of **Waterloo Bay,** surrounded by pleasantly undulating hills. The name is an elision of the name Ellen Liston, a governess to one of the pioneering families. On each side there are cliff walks and a very scenic coastline but in the immediate area there are several sheltered bays and Waterloo Bay itself is protected by **Point Wellington** and **Point Wellesley.** The harbour is full of fish, which can be caught from the jetty or boat. There is also good surfing at **Blackfellows Beach** and this surf is often enjoyed by schools of dolphins. **Flinders Island** is about 35 km off the coast and the **Waldegrave Islands** are about 4 km offshore to the north of the town.

Lake Newland Conservation Park is 15 km north of the town and is an elongated lake system with a wide variety of bird life, including Cape Barren geese.

STREAKY BAY

Tourist Information: Streaky Bay Tourist Centre and Auto Mart, *15 Alfred Terrace; tel: 8626 1126.*

ACCOMMODATION

Streaky Bay Community Hotel, *33 Alfred Terrace; tel: 8626 1008.* **Streaky Bay Motel,** *13–15 Alfred Terrace; tel: 8626 1126.*

SIGHTSEEING

The name was given by Matthew Flinders because of the streaking effects of seaweed in the area. The town was proclaimed in 1839 and in the following year Edward Eyre used it as a base for his epic trek to Albany in Western

Australia. The site of the depot is known as **Eyre's Waterhole** and can still be seen 3 km out of town, just off the road to **Port Kenny**.

The **Old Schoolhouse Museum**, *Montgomery Terrace, tel: 8626 1142*, contains artefacts recording the history of the area. Open 1400–1600 Tues and Fri.

Murphy's Haystacks are 40 km south-east of Streaky Bay and 2 km off the Flinders Hwy on the road into **Calca** and **Point Labatt**. These are wind-worn granite inselbergs, which look like giant toadstools and are thought to be over 1500 million years old. They are on the **Murphy property** (*tel: 8626 5054*), which is run by the grandson of the original Murphy. A donation at the gate is expected.

CEDUNA

Tourist Information: Ceduna Gateway Tourist Information Centre, *58 Poynton St; tel: 8625 2780*.

ACCOMMODATION

Nullarbor Hotel Motel *(FL), 300 km west of Ceduna on the Eyre Hwy; tel: 8625 6271*. **Ceduna Community Hotel-Motel** *(BW), corner O'Loughlin and South Terrace; tel: 8625 2008*. **East West Motel** *(FL), Eyre Hwy; tel: 8625 2101*. **Highway 1 Motel** *(BU), Eyre Hwy; tel: 8625 2208*. **Pine Grove Motel**, *49 McKenzie St; tel: 8625 2201*.

SIGHTSEEING

Ceduna, which is South Australia's largest far west coast town, lies on the shores of **Murat Bay**, which faces out to the Great Australian Bight. The name is said to have come from an Aboriginal word meaning 'to sit down and rest' and was originally used for a waterhole, which is 2 km outside the town. A settlement called Denial Bay was established here in the 1840s about 12 km from where the town now stands and the ruins can still be seen on the road to **Davenport Creek**. The present town was proclaimed in 1901 and it is the business centre for the surrounding farming area. It is also the last major stop before you cross the **Nullarbor** to Perth.

The seaport of Ceduna is called **Thevenard** and it is 2 km to the south-west of the town.

The Treeless Plain

Ceduna is the gateway to the **Nullarbor Plain**, which comes from the Latin for 'no trees' and not, as most people imagine, from an Aboriginal word. The Nullarbor stretches for 1000 km across the base of Australia and is 250 km wide. Driving across you could be forgiven for think it is dull and boring but it is, perhaps, worth knowing that underneath the desert is one of the longest cave formations in the world complete with subterranean rivers and streams. Some of the caves are so large they have sand dunes and beaches.

As a drive, however, it truly has little to commend it although these days the road is sealed throughout and the filling stations are close enough together – some with motels attached – so that the journey has become monotonous rather than somewhat perilous.

369

This is the home port for the fishing fleet and is also equipped for the bulk handling of grain, gypsum and salt.

There are two small islands, **St Peter** and **St Francis**, visible from Thevenard, which were first recorded and named by Peter Nuyts and Francis Thyssen, who sailed past in the *Gulden Zeepard* in 1627. These islands have precisely the same latitude and longitude as the islands where Gulliver met the miniature people of Lilliput. Swift wrote his satire in 1714 and one wonders whether he had read Nuyts' account of his voyage. No trace has been found of a race of miniature people on either of the islands despite extensive searches.

The Old School House Museum, *Park Terrace; tel: 8625 2210*, is a National Trust site which tells the story of the district. There is a room dedicated to the history of the Church Bush Aid Society. More ominously, the museum also displays items from **Maralinga**, the site of the British atomic weapons programme. Open Mon, Tues Thur–Sat 1000–1200; Wed 1400–1600.

PORT AUGUSTA–MARREE

Going from Port Augusta to Marree you are heading from an industrial town right into the outback of Australia. Although Maree is only 645 km north of Adelaide it is on the junction of the Birdsville Track and the Oodnadatta track. The area is surrounded with desolate saltbush country and you are, as the saying goes, well beyond the Black Stump. It is difficult to put across how much these two tracks mean to Australians. They are, indeed, at the core of the Australian experience. If you drive to Marree and go but a short way up the Birdsville Track it is something to boast about afterwards.

Birdsville Track

Oodnadatta Track ◁

Marree

83

113

Leigh Creek   123   *Arkaroola*

North Flinders Ranges

159   83   209

Wilpena

Hawker   52

100

47

Port Augusta   40   Quorn

◁ *Eyre Peninsula Route, p. 364*

370

ROUTE: 412 KM

later, Wilson Ruins, followed by Yourambulla Caves. At 100 km from Quorn comes **Hawker**, an outback town in the centre of the Northern Flinders Ranges.

From Hawker you can take a 53 km side track on sealed roads to **Wilpena Pound** and **Wilpena** in the middle of the **Flinders Ranges National Park**.

At Hawker switch to Rte 83, which runs 156 km through Parachilna to **Leigh Creek**. For most of this part of the journey **Lake Torrens National Park** lies 20 km to the right. The name 'lake' is misleading. There has been no water there for many years: it is a salt-soaked desert. From Leigh Creek the sealed road goes 34 km north until it gets to the very small hamlet of **Lyndhurst** and then it stops. From now on it is unsealed road.

ROUTE

From Port Augusta you head south on the Princes Hwy – Rte 1 – for just 6 km, until you come to the turning on the left, which is Rte 47 heading towards **Quorn**, 47 km away near the Dutchmans Stern Conservation Park.

From there the road runs 66 km to Death Rock and Kathyaka Ruins and then, 12 km

The road from Lyndhurst goes 79 km through the ghost town of **Farina** to **Marree**, which is the start of the **Oodnadatta and Birdsville Tracks** and serious expedition country.

Also from Lyndhurst runs the **Strzlecki Track** which is, again, only suited for well-equipped four wheel drive expeditions with an experienced driver. To the right, the south-east, of this Track is a most amazing anomaly. This is the **Gammon Ranges National Park**, within which is the privately owned **Arakoola-Mt Painter Sanctuary**, an example of how the land can be reclaimed from over-grazing. This is reachable by road from Leigh Creek or by an extension of the previous side track to Wilpena. The best way to visit, however, is to fly there.

DRIVING SAFETY

The Flinders Ranges, especially the Northern Flinders, can be seriously tough country and should not be tackled lightly. Certainly, you need to think most carefully if you are going to travel much north of Leigh Creek, which involves unsealed roads. If the grader has been recently smoothing out the bumps then many unsealed roads are perfectly acceptable to a conventional vehicle. If they have not been well maintained they can try the toughest four-wheel-drive.

This can be a harsh and unforgiving land – unlike the verdant greenery in the south of the state – and the rule is always, but always, listen to local advice before proceeding, especially that supplied by the **National Parks and Wildlife Service**. If a ranger tells you that you should not attempt to go over part of a route or crossing then take that advice or you could experience difficulties.

BUSES

Stateliner buses from Adelaide run twice weekly (Wed and Fri) through Port Augusta on their way to Quorn (45 mins from Port Augusta), Wilpena Pound (3 hrs, not served by all buses) and Leigh Creek (5½–6 hrs).

One bus on Sundays makes the same trip but starts from Port Augusta not Adelaide. OTT table 9130.

PORT AUGUSTA

Tourist information: Port Augusta Tourist Information Centre, *41 Flinders Terrace; tel: 8641 0793.*

ACCOMMODATION

Standpipe Golf Motor Inn, *corner Hwys 1 and 87; tel: 8642 4033.* **Port Augusta Hiway One Motel** *(FL), National Hwy One; tel: 8642 2755.* **Augusta Westside Motel** *(FL), 3 Loudon Rd; tel: 8642 2488.* **Myoora Motor Inn** *(BW), 10 Eyre Hwy; tel: 8642 3622.* **Port Augusta East Motel** *(BU), National Hwy One; tel: 8642 2555.* **Pampas Motel,** *76 Stirling Rd; tel: 8642 3795.* **Flinders Hotel-Motel,** *39 Commercial Rd; tel: 8642 2544.* **Acacia Ridge Motor Inn,** *33 Stokes Terrace; tel: 8642 3377.* **Motel Poinsettia,** *24 Burgoyne St (Hwy 1); tel: 8642 2856.*

EATING AND DRINKING

Barnacle Bill Family Seafood Restaurant, *60 Victoria Parade; tel: 8641 0000.* **Crossroads Restaurant,** *33 Stokes Terrace; tel: 8642 3191.* **Fernleigh Restaurant,** *4 Tassie St; tel: 8642 3906.* **Great Northern Hotel,** *4 Tassie St; tel: 8642 3906.* **King Po Chinese Restaurant,** *39 Flinders Terrace; tel: 8642 5851.* **Tucker Box Bistro,** *41 Flinders Terrace; tel: 8641 0755.*

SIGHTSEEING

Port Augusta is frequently called the crossroads of Australia, as from here you can either head out across the Nullarbor to, eventually, Perth, or go in the other direction to Broken Hill and then Sydney. Or head north to Alice Springs and, eventually again, Darwin. Or amble gently down 332 km south to Adelaide. To best see why it is called Australia's crossroads you can climb the **Water Tower Lookout** in *Mitchell Terrace*. This tower, built in 1882, has been converted to a viewing station.

The town was named in 1852 after Lady Augusta Young, the wife of the governor of the day. Stock drives were made from the district to Port Lincoln in the 1840s but the town did not start to grow until the following decade. By the 1860s it was developing into an important port at the top of the **Spencer Gulf.**

It is only a short drive from the start of the

Flinders Ranges and it has been neatly described in tourist brochures as a garden on the rim of a desert.

You can learn about the history of the town at the **Homestead Park Pioneer Museum** *Elsie St; tel: 8642 2035,* which is a railway and pastoral museum, centred around the 130-year-old **Yudnapinna Homestead**. The homestead, the only log homestead in the state, was transported here from its original site 100 km away. It is furnished and decorated in the style of its times. Open Mon–Sat 1000–1600.

An excellent introduction to Aboriginal culture is the **Wadlata Outback Centre**, *Flinders Terrace; tel: 8642 4511* (open Mon–Fri 0900–1730, Sat–Sun 1000–1600, which has a three screen theatre and other audio-visual presentations to make it both entertaining and instructive.

The north part of the state is as arid as the south is green. **The Australian Arid Lands Botanic Garden**, *tel: 8641 1049,* is 2 km north of the town on the Stuart Hwy and is a first for Australia. The site covers 200 hectares and has panoramic views of the Flinders Ranges to the east. This is an important new kind of botanic garden, showing how an arid region still manages to display an impressive array of plants.

QUORN

Tourist Information: Quorn Tourist Information Centre, *Council Office, Seventh St; tel: 8648 6419.*

ACCOMMODATION AND FOOD

The Mill Motel, *Railway Terrace; tel: 8648 6016.* **Transcontinental Hotel**, *Railway Terrace; tel: 8648 6076.*

Quorn Mill Restaurant, *Railway Terrace; tel: 8648 6016.* Licensed. Daily lunch and dinner. In a National Trust and Heritage listed building. **Old Willows Brewery Restaurant**, *Pichi Richi Pass; tel: 8646 6391.* Licensed. Dinner daily.

SIGHTSEEING

This town is in a valley in the Flinders Ranges and is 330 km to the north of Adelaide. It started as a railway town in 1879 and was, for a

while, an important junction in the days of narrow gauge railways. When the gauges of Australia were standardised in 1956 the new gauge went through **Marree**, by-passing Quorn, and the town then became something of a backwater.

The **railway station** *(tel: 8276 6232)* is not defunct. Every second and fourth Sunday in the month, Mar–Nov, the train is fired up and runs on the narrow gauge railway through the **Pichi Richi Pass** to **Woolshed** – a 33 km run, which is a 3 hr return journey. The line is an amazing feat of engineering, cutting its way through the rugged terrain to open up the outback to the rest of South Australia. The station, designed in modified Spanish baroque, is now a museum with steam trains and carriages from the original Ghan railway.

Near the town is **Dutchmans Stern Conservation Park**, which overlooks the valley.

HAWKER

Tourist Information: Hawker Tourist Information Centre, *Hawker Motors, corner Wilpena and Cradock Rds; tel: 8648 4014*

ACCOMMODATION

Hawker Hotel–Motel *(BW), 80 Older Terrace; tel: 8648 4102.* **Outback Motel**, *1 Wilpena Rd; tel: 8648 4100.*

SIGHTSEEING

Hawker was a railway town 429 km from Adelaide until the line was moved away in 1956. After that it went into a quiet period, out of which it is emerging as a tourist centre. Its current population is 300.

Jarvis Hill Lookout is on top of a hill some 6½ km to the south-west of Hawker and gives excellent views over the central Flinders.

The Kanyaka Ruins – pronounced locally Kanika – was a homestead that started in the 1850s and at one time supported up to 70 families. Substantial over-grazing, a series of poor seasons and a bad drought in the 1860s forced the station to close.

Another aspect of the area is shown at **Teague's Museum**, *corner Cradock and Wilpena Rds; tel: 8648 4014,* which has on display a collection of gemstones, minerals, Aboriginal artefacts, fossils, antique bottles and Flinders memorabilia. Open Mon–Sun 0730–1800.

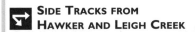

SIDE TRACKS FROM HAWKER AND LEIGH CREEK

WILPENA

There is no tourist information centre as such. **Accommodation: Wilpena Motel,** *tel: 8648 0004.*

At the last census the official population of this town, 481 km north of Adelaide, was 15 people altogether. Not counting tourists passing through.

The main reason for its existence as far as the traveller is concerned is **Wilpena Pound**, which is arguably the greatest single feature of the Flinders Ranges National Park and, indeed, of the Flinders Ranges altogether. The Pound, a vast natural basin, is surrounded by the **Wilpena Wall**, which rises to as high as 500m. There is a single entrance above **Sliding Rock** through a narrow gorge when you can see the multi-coloured cliffs – purple shale blending into red stone with white topped peaks – that surround and contain the basin. The Wilpena Pound is easily reached by a sealed road from Wilpena.

It is possible to drive on from there 2 km to the **Stokes Hill Lookout**, which gives spectacular views over the park, including the eastern escarpment of Wilpena Pound. From Stokes Hill Lookout, after travelling north 29 km, the road divides. One branch heads north to **Blinman, Glass Gorge** and rejoins the main road at **Parachilna**. The left branch, travelling due west, passes the **Branchina Gorge**. This gorge meanders through sharp saw-tooth ridges of quartzite and limestone. Branchina Gorge was once used as a pass, with bullock teams pulling the loads through. It is alleged, on slim authority, that the name comes from an Aboriginal word signifying a mythical argument between two birds over a grindstone. There is a **Corridors Through Time Geological Trail** through the gorge with

interpretive signs. The wildlife in the area includes wedge-tailed eagles, yellow-footed rock wallabies, western grey kangaroos and over 70 different varieties of birds.

On the Hawker to Wilpena road, some 20 km south of Wilpena is **Rawnsley Park**, which is located at the foot of the southern rampart of Wilpena Pound. The park provides cabin accommodation and there are a series of marked walking tracks in the area. ⛺

ARKAROOLA

You can reach Arkaroola by road from Leigh Creek via **Copley** or, more lengthily, from Wilpena, but these are unsealed roads (although they are generally well maintained). However, there is an airstrip and it is possible to fly in. Contact **Arkaroola Travel Centre**, *50 Pirie St, Adelaide; tel: 8212 1366.*

Accommodation: **Arkaroola-Mt Painter Sanctuary Resort**, *Northern Flinders Ranges; tel: 8648 4848.* **Mawson Lodge**, *Northern Flinders Ranges; tel: 212 1366.*

This is perhaps how outback tourism should be conducted. This is a 61,000 hectare, privately owned sanctuary with more than 160 species of native birds and a range of marsupials.

The story of this remarkable resort dates back to 1968, when the owners took over a sheep station that was over-grazed and the haven of thousands of feral goats that ate anything that grew. Conservation methods were introduced and 80,000 feral goats have been shot or trapped. The property is now starting to recover.

It is almost mandatory if you stay there to take the award-winning four-wheel-drive **Ridgetop Tour**. It has been described as Australia's most spectacular scenic drive. It takes you along a heart-stopping track, which was used for mineral exploration with immense, apparently vertical drops and climbs and eventually goes up to **Sillers Lookout**. The terrain is truly rugged – towering granite peaks, razorback quartzite ridges, slashed by precipitous gorges.

373

Also at Arakoola is an **Astronomical Observatory**, which has computerised telescopes for scanning the universe under the extremely favourable conditions that exist in the area.

Nearby are the euphoniously named **Nooldoonooldoona, Barranna** and **Bolla Bollana** waterholes. Also in the area are a series of old mining sites, which have mainly been abandoned because the terrain is so difficult, even though the area is rich in mineral deposits. Copper and zinc were mined in the last century and you can see the ruins of the 1861 round smelters at Bolla Bollana, 12 km north of Arkaroola.

There are also scenic flights over the area: **Arkaroola Air Services** is run by the resort – *tel: 8648 4848.*

MARREE

Accommodation: Marree Hotel, *Main St; tel: 8675 8344.*

The town was originally known as Hergott Springs but its current name comes from an Aboriginal word meaning 'possum'. Marree started life in the latter half of the last century as a staging post for the camel trains, which were the main way of moving supplies and heavy loads in the outback. Until 1980 it was also what was known as a railway break station on the Ghan journey to **Alice Springs**. That was where the gauge of the railway changed and everything had to be switched from one train to another. This all changed in 1980 with the final rationalising of the gauges to a single standard all over Australia and the new track now runs some 190 km to the west of the town. This is saltbush flat country and Marree has become a service centre for the vast properties to the north of the state.

Marree has many symbols to remind you of its adventurous past. In the town there are remnants of the date palms planted by the Afghan camel herders, who in the 1880s drove their camel trains through an outback terrain hardly less hospitable than Afghanistan. There is a memorial in the main street that commemorates the crossing of the **Simpson Desert** on camel back by a party led by Cecil T. Madigan in 1939.

374

SIDE TRACKS FROM MARREE

In Australia the two legendary outback tracks are the **Oodnadatta** and the **Birdsville**. They both start in Marree.

THE OODNADATTA TRACK

The Oodnadatta Track provides an alternative, a very tough alternative, to the sealed Stuart Hwy that now runs between Adelaide and Darwin in the Northern Territory by way of **Alice Springs**. The surface is earth with sandy patches; it tends to be impassable after rain and there are some large creek crossings. It is vital that anyone attempting this run should first check with the **Northern Roads Condition Hotline** *(tel: (08) 11633)* before starting the journey.

The route the road takes is determined by mound springs, which were found around the rim of the **Great Artesian Basin** and allowed the pastoral settlement of the outback but also determined the path of the Overland Telegraph, the Ghan railway and the Oodnadatta Track. They include **Bubbler, Blanchecup** and **Coward Springs**.

The Oodnadatta between Marree and **Marla** (see p. 376) follows the route of the explorer John McDouall Stuart – and the Overland Telegraph Line and the original Ghan narrow gauge – passing as it does through **William Creek** and **Oodnadatta**. Both these towns have petrol and accommodation. The track from Marree to Marla is 619 km long and these two towns almost precisely split it into thirds. There are no other supplies whatsoever between Marree and Marla and sufficient water and petrol must be carried.

On the road from Marree to William Creek – 3 km west of Marree – is a turn-off to **Lake Eyre North**. It passes **Muloorina Homestead** and then on to **Level Post Bay**, which is 90 km north of Marree. This route to the lake is only one of two. The other is 7 km on the Marree side of William Creek and runs 53 km to the east to **Halligan Bay** to the south-west corner of

Lake Eyre. The lake is a dry salt bed and it was here that in 1964 the late Sir Donald Campbell set a world land speed record of 645 kph in the jet-powered car, *Bluebird*.

The **Lake Eyre National Park** covers 1,288,000 hectares of remote, arid desert and it includes all of Lake Eyre North and the **Tirari Desert**. Lake Eyre is a salina, that is, a dry salt lake. But it is also episodic and a playa, in that it does flood occasionally. Vegetation within the park is sparse: samphire, saltbush and bluebush.

Lake Eyre North covers 8430 sq km, is 144 km long and 77 km wide and is 15.2m below sea level at its lowest point. Note that it is both daft and illegal to drive on the lake surface as it is only a crust, which can crack under the weight of a vehicle.

Back on the Oodnadatta Track, which now heads towards William Creek but first runs past the mound springs, which are 6 km south of the track and have been fenced off to preserve them. **Coward Springs** and the ruin of the old railway siding are a true oasis in the desert, with palms, an extensive pond and warm water bubbling to the surface. Next is **William Creek**, a very small town in one of the world's largest cattle stations – **Anna Creek** – which is 30,028 sq km, about half the size of Tasmania.

Then on to **Oodnadatta**, which was an important railhead between 1891 and 1929 and is just over 1000 km from Adelaide. Oodnadatta is an Aboriginal word that could be translated as 'blossom of the mulga'. The railway station is now a museum and there are nearby water-holes for swimming.

The Birdsville Track runs from Marree to **Birdsville** in Queensland and was developed originally as a stock route in the 1880s to bring cattle from the rich grazing country of south-west **Queensland** to the rail head at Marree.

The track runs through some of the driest places in Australia between the **Simpson Desert** and **Sturt's Stony Desert**. In recent times the track has been upgraded for beef cattle transports, which are monster trucks, which take up all of the track; great care must be taken if you have to pass one while driving.

The track is 514 km long and is split pretty close to the middle, 203 km from Marree by **Mungerannie**, which has petrol, basic supplies and a place to rest. Apart from that there are no supplies whatsoever on the Birdsville Track. After leaving Marree the track comes, after 30 km, to **Lake Harry**, which was once a busy camel trading post and a date palm plantation. Lake Harry is, of course, a dry saltpan.

A few kilometres north of Lake Harry you come to the biggest fence in the world. The **Dog Fence** is part of the 9600 km fence across the outback from the Great Australian Bight to the NSW border, which was built to keep the dingo from southern sheep country. It is now falling into disrepair.

Along the track you come to the **Cannuwaukaninna Bore**, where the water comes out of the ground so hot it has to run 800m or so before it is cold enough for cattle to drink.

Then comes **Cooper Crossing**, with a ferry. When the Cooper is in flood the ferry operates in daylight hours. Under normal circumstances not a drop of water will be seen. On display at the crossing is the old barge *Tom Brennan*, which was used from 1949 to 1956.

From there the track passes through the **Natteranie Sandhills**, which run through to the Simpson Desert and average about 9m in height. Then come the ruins of two abandoned homesteads and **Mungerannie**; the **Mungerannie Roadhouse** has most things you will need, including emergency repairs.

You cross the normally dry **Derwent Creek** and then proceed to the **Mugerannie Gap**, which is the highest point of the track at 150m. From here you pass two hot water bores and then continue across the border with Queensland to the town of Birdsville itself. ◼

375

PORT AUGUSTA–
ALICE SPRINGS

Nowadays it is a sealed road all the way but for early explorers the trip into the Red Centre was one fraught with privations, danger and, in many cases, death. The Stuart

Hwy, which runs from Port Augusta to the Alice and then, from there right up to Darwin, was the last great road construction of Australia. The Highway has been sealed all of the way for just over ten years and it is now just a question of cruising along in air-conditioned comfort. And if you do, try to remember the early explorers who came slogging this way with camels and horses and, normally, a desperate thirst.

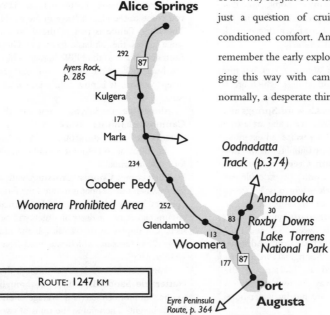

Alice Springs

292

Ayers Rock, p. 285

87

Kulgera

179

Marla

234

Coober Pedy

Woomera Prohibited Area   252

Glendambo

Woomera

Oodnadatta Track (p.374)

Andamooka
30
83   Roxby Downs
113   Lake Torrens
177   National Park

ROUTE: 1247 KM

Eyre Peninsula Route, p. 364

Port Augusta

87

ROUTE

Head north out of Port Augusta on the Stuart Hwy, Rte 87, towards **Woomera**, which is 173 km away with very little in between except for some hills – nothing spectacular – and some lakes, which are only true lakes after a series of heavy rainstorms (and those may be years apart).

At Woomera there is a possible side track that runs 92 km on a sealed road to **Roxby**

Downs and then still on a sealed road over the end of the **Ardrossan Ranges** to the northern end of the **Lake Torrens National Park** and to **Andamooka**, with its opal fields.

On the main route, from Woomera and heading north-west on the Stuart Hwy you will first skirt around and then pass through the **Woomera Prohibited Area**. The road and a small strip on either side of it are exempt from the prohibition but otherwise you must keep out of this area unless you have a permit. Camping is totally forbidden. The road runs on 113 km to **Glendambo** passing the **Lake Gardner National Park** as it does so until, 365 km from Woomera, it arrives at **Coober Pedy**, just outside the Woomera Prohibited Zone, with the **Tallaringa Conservation Park** to the east.

Rte 87, still the Stuart Hwy, carries on for 152 km to the **Cadney Homestead** and halfway there starts to run parallel with the railway. From the homestead the road goes 83 km to **Marla**, which is one end of the **Oodnadatta Track** (see p. 374). From Marla the road continues north until after a 100 km or so it passes over the border into the Northern Territory just before **Kulgera**, on its way to **Alice Springs** (and eventually to Darwin). There is a road junction 74 km north of Kulgera, which leads west to Ayers Rock (Uluru), another 244 km – see p. 285.

TRAINS

The Ghan railway line runs from Adelaide to Alice Springs through Port Augusta, Woomera and the prohibited area, by-passing Coober Pedy, but stopping at Kulgera (but the station is along way east of the town). For more details see pp. 403–404 and OTT table 9034.

BUSES

Greyhound Pioneer, McCafferty's and Stateliner run services along this route, giving a choice of at least one bus a day. From Port Augusta, Woomera is 2 hrs, Coober Pedy 7½ hrs, and Alice Springs 14¼ hrs. OTT table 9125.

WOOMERA

Tourist Information: Wadlata Outback Centre, *Flinders Terrace, Port Augusta; tel: 8641 0793.*

Accommodation is available at the **Eldo Hotel**, *Kotara Cres., Woomera; tel: 8673 7867.*

The town, 502 km north of Adelaide, was established in 1947 to test experimental rockets for, in the first instance, Britain and later Europe and the United States. The result was that Australia was the third country, after the United States and what was then the USSR, to

launch a satellite. Woomera, appropriately, is an Aboriginal term for a spear throwing tool.

Altogether – nobody is publishing full and frank figures – there have been in excess of 3000 test firings. The most famous of the rocket test series was ELDO, which stands for the European Launcher Development Organisation, which operated from 1964 until 1970. From 1960 until 1972 the United States operated a NASA deep space tracking station at nearby **Island Lagoon**.

It should not be thought that all this has gone without comment or, indeed, protest from the Australian public but Woomera is so far from anywhere that effective protest has been muted and the government of the day has always seen it as a 'nice little earner'. At the moment it is pretty quiet but there are rumours that the Japanese and even the Chinese governments are interested in using the facilities.

The village of Woomera has a population of just 800 people, although in its heyday there were more than 7000 residents. Until 1982 it was a restricted area and to this day it is administered by the Defence Department. The range and the communications station **Nurungar** are still restricted.

In Woomera there is a **Missile Park**, displaying examples of rockets, aircraft and weapons associated with the testing range. Next door the **Missile Park Woomera Heritage Centre**, *tel: 8673 7042*, ironic though the name may appear to be, has been established to keep together all of the artefacts and publishable information connected with the range since its inception. Open daily 0900–1700 Mar–Nov; admission $2.50. It is possible to go on a tour of the rocket range. **Woomera Rocket Range Tours**, *tel: 8671 0788*, does a tour of the local attractions, which takes 3 hrs.

⌖ SIDE TRACK FROM WOOMERA

There is a sealed road leading 83 km to **Roxby Downs** from Woomera on the Stuart Hwy. An unsealed road runs 125 km from Roxby Downs to join the **Oodnadatta Track** (see p. 374) just south of **Lake Eyre South**. The 25 km road from Roxby

377

Downs to **Andamooka** is also now sealed, which makes access to the town extremely easy. It is possible to take a thrice-weekly Stateliner bus from Woomera to Andamooka, journey time 1½ hrs.

ROXBY DOWNS

Tourist Information: *Olympic Dam Visitors Centre; tel: 8671 0788.*

Accommodation: Roxby Downs Motor Inn, *Richardson Pl; tel: 8671 0311.*

This new town, 580 km north-west of Adelaide, was created in 1986 to service the giant copper, gold, uranium and silver mining operation at **Olympic Dam**, 15 km north of the town. It is named after the pastoral lease on which it is established. Roxby Downs is a purpose-built modern town in a wilderness of red dunes. The centrepiece is a motel with a bedouin-like tent structure above the main complex, which is reminiscent of the architecture employed at Yulara (see p. 285).

The huge mine extracts 2½ million tonnes of copper, uranium, gold and silver ore a year and is open to conducted tours Mar–Nov. Contact the visitors' centre. The actual dam, built at the time of the Melbourne Olympic Games in 1956, is near the discovery drill site.

ANDAMOOKA

Tourist Information: Opal Creek Showroom, *Main St; tel: 8672 7193.*

ACCOMMODATION AND FOOD

Andamooka Motel, *Main Rd; tel: 8672 7078.* **Andamooka Opal Hotel-Motel & Restaurant**, *Andamooka Opal Fields; tel: 8672 7078.*

SIGHTSEEING

The name comes from an Aboriginal word, which may mean 'comet' or 'meteorite'. The first step in the creation of the town was when the explorer John McDouall Stuart discovered a large waterhole near Andamooka in 1858. The discovery of opal came in 1930, when two drovers from **Andamooka Station** saw flashes of brilliant colour on a hillside after a thunderstorm.

Opal is mined close to the town in shafts 3–10m below the surface. There are 24 mine fields in the area, all of them close to the town. This is a very different mining system to Coober Pedy (see below). Bulldozers carve down to the opal level, which was formed during the Tertiary Period. Occasionally the opalised bones of ancient creatures like the giant plesiosaurus are brought to the surface. The first semi dug-out permanent homes of the early miners and buyers are now given Heritage listing. Noodling – searching the waste tips by hand – is tolerated, but ask for permission first.

A local landmark is **Dukes Bottle Home** (*tel: 8672 7021* or *8672 7062*), which is made entirely from discarded beer bottles. Nearby is **Andamooka Station** (*tel: 8671 0754*), a 2950 sq km station on **Lake Torrens**, which welcomes visitors and even has a small museum built inside the blacksmith's workshop. ▣

COOBER PEDY

Coober Pedy Tourist Information Centre, *Council office, Hutchison St; tel: 8672 5298.*

ACCOMMODATION

Desert Cave, *Hutchison St; tel: 8672 5688.* **Underground Motel**, *PO Box 375; tel: 8672 5324.* **Radeka Dugout Motel**, *Oliver St; tel: 8672 5223.* **The Opal Inn Motel**, *Hutchison St; tel: 8672 5054.* **Budget Motel & Backpackers**, *corner Oliver and Brewster St; tel: 8672 5163.* **Umoona Opal Mine Museum & Motel**, *Main St; tel: 8672 5288.*

SIGHTSEEING

Coober Pedy is one of Australia's strangest towns, sited in the middle of the most inhospitable waterless outback 863 km north-west of Adelaide and 270 km from Woomera. It exists for one reason only – opal. The name is said to come from the Aboriginal *kupa piti*, which means 'white man's hole in the ground', and that is an exact description of the way that opal is extracted here. The first opal mined here, in 1911, was of very poor quality. The first serious strike came in 1915, which led to a town of sorts being established that year. Possibly the largest opal ever mined in the world, **Olympic Australia**, was mined here in 1956 and Coober Pedy officially made it as a town in 1960.

The town is like a set from the film *Mad Max III*, with a strange lunar landscape of dumps and mines scattered around the town. Indeed, this is where much of the film was shot. The scenery is flat with pink mounds of waste showing where the mines were or are. There are reputedly over 25,000 mines in the area.

Although visitors are welcome to the town it is not possible to explore the mines on a solo expedition. There are two reasons for this. The official reason is that the holes in the ground could cause an accident – which is true. The mine areas are, indeed, dangerous to wander around unescorted, especially for children, and you should be very careful in your exploration. The second reason is that the diggers are desperately defensive about their individual claims and do not want potential competition digging around. There are fines for trespassing on registered claims, although diggers tend to take more immediate and direct action.

If you want to dig for opal using a shovel and a pick or any other instrument you need a prospecting permit from the Department of Mines and Energy. However, if you do not use digging tools – this is called noodling – no permit is required, but ask permission first.

Coober Pedy suffers from very high extremes of heat and cold and many of the 4000 or so inhabitants – there is no exact count – choose to live underground in dug-out homes (called dugouts), which maintain a fairly constant temperature of 24°C.

The Coober Pedy workings are made up of over 70 different fields, some producing, many dormant, covering a substantial area of ground. The newest is **Mt Penrhyn**, 50 km to the south; the **Shell Patch** is 34 km to the north west and **Russo's Folly** is 15 km to the west. This area produces most of the opal in the world. The town is full of shops, some of which are also display mines. A typical example is **Old Timers Mine**, *Crowders Gully Rd; tel: 8672 5555* (open daily 0900–1700, admission $3), which is an historic opal mine dating from 1918

Opals

Opals are a form of hydrated silica. Over 95% of the world's opals come from Australia – certainly most of the attractive ones – and the lion's share comes from Coober Pedy. Probably the most beautiful is the black opal, which is normally only found at Lightning Ridge (see p. 112). Years ago the *Saturday Evening Post* said of it, 'It is more beautiful than diamonds or rubies. Australian black opal is, without doubt, the finest gem in the world.' There are several other kinds, including a light, milky opal. To make the stone go further it is often sold in layered form – doublets and triplets. When you visit Australia at some point, some time, someone will offer you opals. It may be in a jeweller's shop; it may be in an opal mine; it may be in a pub in the outback. Only one thing is certain – you will not make a fortune from the investment. Buy opals if you like them, if they appeal to you, if you will enjoy wearing them. Do not buy them as an investment. You will be lucky to get your investment back. I once did buy a major bargain in Lightning Ridge black opal – but in Amsterdam, not Australia.

379

with a walk-through tour and a shop selling the gems. Another is **The Big Winch**, *tel: 8672 5264* (open daily 0700–2000), which is a lookout and a landmark on top of the town centre and is also Coober Pedy's largest opal and art gallery. The display includes the largest opalised sea shell fossil in the world.

There are two underground churches – the **Church of St Peter and St Paul** and **Catacomb Church**. The **Desert Cave Motel** is also partially underground, with glowing pink walls.

The **Breakaways Reserve** is 32 km north of the town; it covers 40,000 hectares and includes some of the most colourful landscapes in the area. The colours in the rocks change continually as the sun moves across the sky. This area is ecologically very fragile and you are asked to stay on the defined roads and tracks.

SOUTH AUSTRALIA NATIONAL PARKS

INFORMATION AND OVERVIEW

National Parks and Wildlife, *tel: (08) 8204 9000.*

The state is blessed with an abundance of national parks, conservation parks, game reserves and wilderness protection areas. There are over 300 of them: 17 national parks, 211 conservation parks, 13 recreation parks, 10 game reserves and 7 regional reserves. Over 20 per cent of the area of the state, in total something over 200,000 sq km, is under some kind of conservation order or another.

Several major parks are within striking distance of Adelaide in the south east of South Australia. Perhaps the most important is **The Coorong**, which protects the lakes and estuary where the Murray River slowly and reluctantly comes to the sea. This is one of the bird havens of the state and more than 280 species of birds have been spotted in the park.

Another park in this part of the state, with a prolific bird life, is **Bool Lagoon,** which cover 3,600 hectares and is 24 km south of Naracoorte. It has formally designated by UNESCO as a wetland of international significance. The lagoon is a drought refuge and breeding ground for thousands of birds, freshwater fish and other wildlife. There are 79 bird species to be seen in the park.

Close in to Adelaide is **Cleland Conservation Park**, which only covers 725 hectares but contains an amazing series of king ferns in a few peat bogs on the side of Mt Lofty (which belies its name by only climbing to 725 m). The **Black Hill** and **Morialta Conservation Parks** are also close to Adelaide and together 1,300 ha mostly covered in eucalypts but with the gorge of Morialta Creek adding variety and rock climbing opportunities.

Mt Remarkable is a park of the same name in the southern Flinders Ranges and is a foretaste of the rugged country to the north.

The park covers 8649 hectares and most of that is the mountain, which rises to 995 m.

The north of the state has the Flinders Ranges, containing three national parks. The **Flinders Ranges National Park** itself covers 94,908 hectares and includes the famous **Wilpena Pound**. The **Gammon Ranges National Park** has the private park **Arkaroola** nearby. Then there is **Lake Eyre National Park**, with its immense salt lake, covering 13,492 sq km, which makes it as big as a small country.

Witjira National Park is 120 km to the north of Oodnadatta and covers 776,900 hectares. It is basically desert with gibber plains, salt pans, sand dunes, flat-topped hills and numerous mound springs that are part of the **Great Artesian Basin**, bringing life to the desert. In the park **Dalhousie Mound Springs** is one of the best known and the largest in Australia.

The **Innamincka Regional Reserve** covers an amazing 1,382,765 hectares at the end of the **Strzelecki Track** and includes extensive wetlands associated with the Cooper Creek drainage system, particularly Coongie Lakes. In contrast the **Simpson Desert Conservation Park and Regional Reserve** is nearly as dry as the Sahara. It covers 3,656,200 hectares and is a endless series of red sand dunes and salt lakes. No one know the exact limits of the dunes but they cover something around 140,000 sq km. The parts of the desert not listed as national park have been declared a regional reserve under control of the National Parks and Wildlife Service.

On **Kangaroo Island** in the south of the state there are several national parks. The largest is the **Flinders Chase National Park**, which covers 73, 662 hectares and occupies the entire western end of the island. Most of the park is in its natural state and the animal and plant life have been little affected by the incursions of civilisation. The coasts in the park are a haven for sea lions, sea eagles, osprey and Cape Barren geese, while inland there is a wide range of marsupials.

Then, at the tip of the Eyre Peninsula there are the **Lincoln National Park** and the **Coffin Bay National Park**, which between them cover most of that end of the peninsula.

In the west the major park is the **Nullarbor** which is 230,000 hectares of arid desert and coastline above a complex structure of caves and caverns.

REGION BY REGION

In this listing, all parks are national parks except where otherwise stated, and have campsites, picnic areas and walking trails, again unless it says otherwise.

In and around Adelaide and the Fleurieu Peninsula

See the Fleurieu Peninsula route, pp. 342–344.

Belair *No campsite*
Black Hill Conservation Park
Cleland Conservation Park
Deep Creek Conservation Park
Newland Head Conservation Park

Kangaroo Island

See Adelaide chapter, pp. 334–341.
Cape Gantheame Conservation Park
Cape Hart Conservation Park
Dudley Conservation Park
Flinders Chase
Kelly Hill Caves Conservation Park
Lathami Conservation Park
Western River Conservation Park
Vivonne Bay Conservation Park

Barossa Valley Region

These parks lie along the Adelaide to Mildura route, pp. 352–359.

Brookfield Conservation Park
Chowilla Regional Reserve *North of Renmark.*
Danggali Conservation Park *North of Renmark.*

Moorundie Wildlife Park
Swan Reach Conservation Park
Murray River *This national park is further east, near Renmark.*

Eyre Peninsula

These parks can be accessed from the Eyre Peninsula route, pp. 364–369.

Coffin Bay *No campsite or picnic area but bush camping possible.*
Franklin Harbour Conservation Park *Near Cowell.*
Lincoln *No campsite or picnic area but bush camping possible.*
Middlecamp Hills Conservation Park. *Near Cowell.*
Mt Remarkable *Bush camping possible.*
Venus Bay Conservation Park
Waldegrave Island Conservation Park *Near Elliston.*
Whidbey Isles Conservation Park
Yeldulnie Conservation Park *Near Cowell.*

Coastal Parks South of Adelaide

See the Adelaide to Warrnambool route, pp. 345–351, for more details of these parks.
Beachport Conservation Park
Coorong *Bush camping possible.*
Canunda *Bush camping possible.*
Little Dip Conservation Park

North of the State

See Port Augusta to Marree route, pp. 370–375.

Arkaroola *Private park on the edge of Gammon Ranges.*
Gammon Ranges *Bush camping possible.*
Flinders Ranges *Bush camping possible.*
Lake Eyre *No campsite, picnic area or walking trail but bush camping possible.*
Simpson Desert Regional Reserve *No entry without a Desert Parks Pass.*
Strzelecki Regional Reserve
Witjira *No entry without a Desert Parks Pass. No walking trail. Bush camping possible.*

381

TASMANIA

Tasmania is a state of Australia, whereas New Zealand is a sovereign country in its own right. Visitors get this wrong more frequently than you would imagine, and Australians get it wrong all the time, as you can tell by those maps of Australia which leave off Tasmania. Tasmania is Australia's most southerly and smallest state, only 0.9% of the total Australian land mass with an area of 68,331 sq km, including at least 20 offshore islands. It has a population of less than 500,000.

HISTORY

Tasmania was given its first European name – Van Diemens Land – by **Abel Janszoon Tasman**. He was the commander of the ships *Heemskirk* and *Zeehan,* who had been sent to discover the mysterious Southern Land by Antony Van Diemen, Governor General of the Dutch East Indies Company. In Nov 1642, Tasman sighted the west coast of Tasmania. He landed on the **Forestier Peninsula**, near **Blackmans Bay**, on the western bank of the Derwent River. And 150 years later the British came to make this a convict settlement and one of the furthest reaches of the British empire.

It would be wrong to write about Tasmania without mentioning its tragic history. At the time of the establishment of the first white settlement there were thought to be about 5000 Aboriginal people in Tasmania. The first flocks of sheep were grazed at **Woolnorth** on **Cape Grim**, which was prime Aboriginal hunting land. When hunting parties began to take sheep, whites indiscriminately killed Aborigines in retaliation. Around 1826, a group of Aboriginal men seeking revenge for the rape of their women speared a shepherd and killed 100 sheep. In retaliation a group of 30 unarmed Aborigines were killed by shepherds, and their bodies thrown over a cliff which is now misleadingly called **Suicide Cove**. In 1828, Governor Arthur declared martial law, expelling all Aboriginal people from the settled districts and, in practice, giving settlers a licence to shoot on sight. The British Government, alarmed by these events, planned to round up the remaining Aborigines and confine them to **Bruny Island**. In 1830, a mass militia of 3000 settlers formed an armed human barrier, the Black Line, which was to sweep across the island, clearing Aborigines before them, in preparation for 'resettlement'.

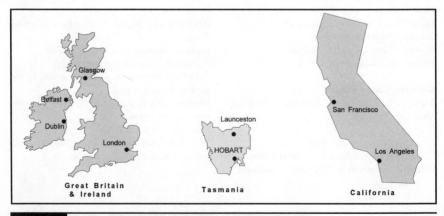

Great Britain & Ireland

Tasmania

California

Tigers and Devils

Tasmanian tigers were common toward the start of the century, but were hunted extensively because they threatened sheep. The tiger was about 1.5 m long, had light brown fur with dark stripes across its lower back.

The tiger has been extinct since 1933, when the last one died in the Hobart zoo. That is the official story. The number of sightings since has rivalled those of flying saucers. In Jan 1995, a Parks and Wildlife Service officer observed a tiger in the **Pyengana** region of eastern Tasmania. The government has launched an investigation to confirm the existence of the tiger. Tiger skins and a preserved tiger can be seen at the **Tasmanian Museum and Art Gallery** in Hobart.

The Tasmanian devil has been described, with some accuracy, as 'an unprepossessing, mostly-black animal, something like a badly proportioned dog, with ferocious looking teeth.' The colouring is basically black with some brown tints. It has large jaws and strong teeth and an evil disposition. You do not want to pick it up for a cuddle. Ever.

The line failed, and in the end only 135 Aboriginals were found alive, to be moved to a makeshift settlement on **Flinders Island**. Within four years most of these people had died. In 1837, the 47 survivors were transferred to their final settlement at **Oyster Cove**.

GEOGRAPHY

Tasmania lies 240 km south of the Australian mainland, separated from it by the Bass Strait. It is closer to the Equator than Rome and is warmer, on average, than Madrid. Nowhere on Tasmania is more that 115 km from the sea.

Tasmania has four major towns. **Hobart**, the capital, in the south, and **Launceston**, in the north, are rated as cities, although Hobart has a population of 190,000 and Launceston 90,000. The port towns of **Burnie** and **Devonport** are on the north-west coast. Despite claims by Tasmanians – called Taswegians by most other Australians – traffic jams do not exist in Tasmania.

Of the 20 or so islands scattered around its shores, some are inhabited, many are not. In the **Bass Strait** are **King Island** and the **Furneaux Group**. Until something like 12,000 years ago, these were part of a land bridge that connected mainland Australia and Tasmania.

At the other end of the state, and halfway between Tasmania and the Antarctic continent, is **Macquarie Island**, home to, among other things, elephant seals and 4 million penguins. There are other islands, which are much easier to reach, such as **Maria** and **Bruny Island** on the east coast.

Tasmania is also a state of mountains. Its highest is **Mt Ossa**, reaching 1617 m on the central plateau, which has an alpine environment, averages over 1000 m in the south and has over 3000 lakes of assorted sizes. In general the mountains are not overly tall, but the proportion of mountainous country within the state is very high, by far and away the highest in Australia. The central plateau slopes south-east and on the western edge ends in a range of mountains running parallel to the west coast. This region is sparsely populated.

383

FLORA AND FAUNA

As it has been separated from the mainland for many centuries, Tasmania has a unique wildlife and flora. It is not generally realised that the most impenetrable jungle in the world is in Tasmania. Parts of the state are still unexplored – it is too difficult to hack your way in. More than 20% of the island consists of national parks or reserved areas. It is extremely easy to explore the island by car.

CLIMATE

Tasmania is the most southerly of the Australian states, and so it escapes the excesses of the summer heat, although it is still warm. The average summer temperature is 21.5°C and the winter average is 12.5°C. Even in the summer the evenings can be cold and warmer clothes are useful no matter what the season.

HOBART

Hobart is the elegant city on the Derwent River, which provides one of the world's best deep-water harbours. For the visitor, this city, the capital of the Tasmania, is lively all year round. But it explodes when the Sydney to Hobart yacht race – one of the world's great sailing events – ends at Constitution Dock, between Christmas and the New Year, as it has since 1949. The end is celebrated by The 'Little Drink', when the quantity of beer drunk per head of crew defies all belief. That is the city's once-a-year party, but throughout the full twelve months Hobart operates with an immense amount of style.

TOURIST INFORMATION

Tasmanian Travel and Information Centre, *20 Davey St; tel: 6230 8233.*

ARRIVING AND DEPARTING

Airport

The airport is at Cambridge, which at 26 km, is probably the furthest sited of the domestic airports. A central shuttle bus to the city, run by **Redline**, costs $6, while a taxi – a rank is at the airport – will cost something over $20.

By Ferry

The ferry from the mainland to Tasmania does not go to Hobart. Instead, it sails between Melbourne and **Devonport**. The **Spirit of Tasmania** *(tel: Devonport 13 2010)* sails from Melbourne three times a week on Mon, Wed and Fri, leaving at 1800 and arriving at 0830. It then heads back to Melbourne that evening.

The 14 hr trip over the Tasman Straits can be quite rough. But there is a bed in both the hostel sections and in private cabins. To pass the time, there are restaurants, bars and entertainment. The ferry tends to be fully booked in the summer months and, especially if you are taking a car, you need to book well in advance. The trip starts at around $85 in the winter, with a cabin costing about $140–160 per person. Add to that the fee for the car, which ranges between $125–175. If you are in Sydney it is normally much less expensive to fly direct and hire a car when you get there.

By Car

An extensive road system connects Hobart with other cities and towns in Tasmania.

GETTING AROUND

Hobart stands on the banks of the Derwent River, which flows from Lake St Clair (see p. 396) to the estuary, before joining the waters of Storm Bay and out to the Tasman Sea. The city is positioned on a 20 km strip between Mt Wellington and the river. Most of it is on the flat, although some of the suburbs are on the steep side of the mountain. Although Hobart is the most southerly city of Australia, and therefore the one nearest the South Pole, it is totally protected by two arms of land and the barriers of the two Bruny Islands, which are separated from the main island by the D'Entrecasteaux Channel.

Walking around Hobart – the best way to see the city, although there is an excellent bus system – you realise that this is a city that has made a serious effort to preserve its past. The streets are arranged in a logical grid pattern and are mainly on flat ground. The civic centre is **Franklin Square**, which is bordered by *Macquarie* and *Davey Sts,* and in this area there is a concentration of restored and listed historic buildings. In the centre of the business district is **Elizabeth Street Mall.** The street itself starts in North Hobart and comes to an end at the **Elizabeth Street Pier** on **Franklin Wharf.** The eastern shores of the Derwent are linked to

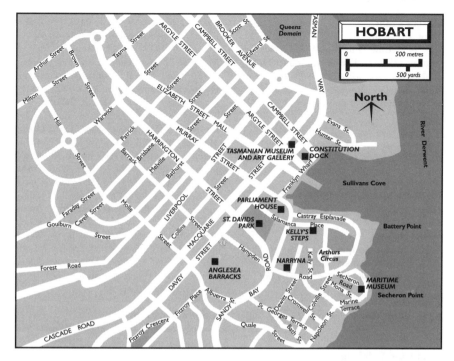

the rest of the city by the five-lane concrete-arch **Tasman Bridge**, and the four-lane **Bowen Bridge**.

Public Transport

There is an excellent public transport system called the **Hobart Metro**. The best buy is a pack of ten tickets (slightly discounted), which you can get at the **Metroshop**, *18 Elizabeth St,* opposite the GPO. You can also catch the bus to most destinations from here – **information hotline**; *tel: 13 2201.* There is also a peak-hour ferry service from **Brooke St Pier**, which goes to **Bellerive** on the other shore, but this only operates on weekdays.

Taxis can be hailed in the street and there is a big taxi rank near the town hall on *Elizabeth St.* For radio cabs: **City Cabs Co-op**; *tel: 34 3633;* **Combined Services**; *tel: 13 2227.*

STAYING IN HOBART

Central Hobart

Hotel Grand Chancellor Hobart, *1 Davey St; tel: 6235 4535.* **Salamanca Inn**, *10 Gladstone St; tel: 6223 3300.* **Islington Private Hotel**, *321 Davey St; tel: 6223 3900.* **Westside Hotel**, *156 Bathurst St; tel: 6232 6255.* **The Elms of Hobart Hotel**, *452 Elizabeth St; tel: 6231 3277.* **Hobart Mid City Motor Inn**, *96 Bathurst St; tel: 6234 6333.* **Hobart Macquarie Motor Inn**, *167 Macquarie St; tel: 6234 4422.* **Country Comfort Hadleys Hotel** *(CC), 34 Murray St; tel: 6223 4355.* **Valley Lodge Motel** *(BW), 11 Augusta Rd; tel: 6228 0125.* **Hobart Pacific Hotel** *(FL), Kirby Court; tel: 6234 6733.* **Astor Private Hotel**, *157 Macquarie St; tel: 6234 6611.* **Fountainside Motor Inn** *(BW), corner Brooker Ave and Liverpool St; tel: 6234 2911.* **Black Buffalo Hotel–Motel**, *14 Federal St; tel: 6234 7711.* **Brisbane Hotel**, *3 Brisbane St; tel: 6234 4920.* **Brunswick Hotel**, *67 Liverpool St; tel: 6234 4981.* **Coupe De Ville**, *145 Elizabeth St; tel: 6234 3501.* **Black Prince Hotel**, *145 Elizabeth St; tel: 6234 3501.* **Brooker Hotel**, *405 Brooker Ave; tel: 6272 4722.* **Freemasons Hotel**, *58 Harrington St; tel: 6224 1093.*

Battery Point

Ascot of Battery Point, *6 Colville St; tel: 6224 2434.* **Blue Hills Motel**, *96A Sandy Bay Rd; tel: 6223 1777.* **Lenna of Hobart Hotel**, *20 Runnymede St; tel: 6232 3900.* **Prince of Wales Hotel**, *55 Hampden Rd; tel: 6223 6355.* **St Ives Motel**, *67 St Georges Terrace; tel: 6224 1044.*

Bellerive

HI: *52 King St; tel: 6244 2552.*

New Town

HI: Adelphi Court, *17 Stoke St; tel: 6228 4829.*

North Hobart

Argyle Motor Lodge, *2 Lewis St; tel: 6234 2488.* **Rydges Hobart Hotel**, *corner Argyle and Lewis Sts, North Hobart; tel: 6231 1588.*

Sandy Bay

Wrest Point Hotel Casino *(FL), 410 Sandy Bay Rd; tel: 6224 0112.*

Eating and Drinking

Astor Grill, *157 Macquarie St; tel: 6234 3809.* Traditional English grill. Lunches Mon–Fri. Dinner 7 nights. **Bertie's Pasta Restaurant**, *115 Collins St; tel: 6223 3595.* Mon–Fri 0900–2300; Sat 1800–2300. Fresh pasta. **Bistro Pinot**, *corner Little Arthur St and Burnett Pl., North Hobart; tel: 6231 5566.* Lunch Tues–Sun. Dinner Tues–Sat. Licensed. French cuisine. **Caesar's Restaurant**, *160 Sandy Bay Rd, Sandy Bay; tel: 6223 4533.* Lunch Tues–Sat. Dinner Tues–Sun. A short walk from Battery Point, Salamanca and the Casino. BYO. **Dragon Palace Restaurant**, *63 Liverpool St; tel: 6234 5885.* Lunch Mon–Fri. Dinner 7 nights. BYO. **Drunken Admiral**, *17-19 Hunter St, Old Wharf; tel: 6234 1903.* In one of Hobart's oldest waterfront warehouses. **Mures Upper and Lower Deck**, *Victoria Dock; tel: 6231 2121.* Seafood caught by Mure's own fishing boats. Two-level food centre set among yachts and fishing boats. Licensed. Open Mon–Sat lunch, dinner. One of the few with an Internet address – *mures@trump.net.au.* **Panache Café**, *89 Salamanca Pl.; tel: 6224*

2929. Licensed. Outdoor dining. Open 7 days till late. **Roches Restaurant**, *9-11 Murray St; tel: 6223 7983.* Lunch Mon–Fri, dinner Mon–Sat. Licensed. Historic sandstone building circa 1846. **Royal Botanical Gardens Restaurant**, *Lower Domain Rd; tel: 6234 4849.* Open 7 days a week for lunch. **Salama**, *305 Elizabeth St, North Hobart; tel: 6236 9833.* Open 7 nights. BYO. **The Last Drop**, *Westside Hotel, 156 Bathurst St; tel: 6232 6255.* Dinner 7 days a week, lunch Mon–Sat. Colonial décor. **The Pier Waterfront Restaurant**, *opposite Parliament House, Sullivans Cove; tel: 6224 8636.* Open 7 days lunch, dinner. Licensed. Port views. **Vanidol's Asian Cuisine**, *365 Elizabeth St, North Hobart. tel: 6234 9307.* Dinner Tues–Sun. BYO. **Wrest Point Hotel Casino**, *410 Sandy Bay Rd; tel: 62250112 Ext. 8.* Asian restaurant open dinner Tues–Sat. Revolving restaurant. Open seven days lunch and dinner.

Communications

The post office is at the corner of *Elizabeth* and *Macquarie Sts* and is open Mon–Fri 0800–1800.

Money

All the major banks are represented and most of their offices are in *Elizabeth St.*

Thomas Cook change money and traveller's cheques at *40 Murray St, PO Box 306, Hobart 7000; tel: (02) 34 2699; fax: (02) 24 0573.* Open Mon–Fri 0845-1715.

SHOPPING

The Department of Tourism, Recreation and Sport Outdoors runs the **Sport and Rec Shop** in *Macquarie St,* which is a bookshop on Tasmania's sporting and outdoor life as well as an information centre: *tel: 33 8011.* A shop with a strong reputation for renting camping gear is the **Jolly Swagman**, *107 Elizabeth St; tel: 34 3999.* **Paddy Pallin**, *76 Elizabeth St; tel: 31 0777,* is part of an Australia-wide chain of sports and outdoor equipment shops that both sell and rent. Paddy Pallin himself is one of the great men of Australian bushwalking.

SIGHTSEEING

Start with **Salamanca Place**, which is logical,

Origins

Hobart was carefully selected as the first town of Tasmania. Lt Col David Collins was sent from England to establish a colony and had found an earlier site 'wholly unfit for the settlement.' In 1803, Lt John Bowen led a party of 24 convicts from Sydney to settle on the eastern shores of the Derwent River at **Risdon Cove**, but the site lacked drinking water. On 20 Feb 1804, David Collins transferred his settlement from Risdon Cove to **Sullivans Cove** on the western banks of the Derwent, and that is the site of present day Hobart. This was the first permanent European settlement of Tasmania, with 262 colonists, of whom 31 were free settlers.

The settlement rapidly developed into a city. **Pitt's Farm** at Glenorchy was built in 1806, making it the second oldest building in Australia. A warehouse, built in 1808, now containing the museum, is probably the oldest building in central Hobart. It was named after the British statesman, Lord Robert Hobart (1760–1816) and was originally known as Hobart Town. It became the capital of Tasmania in 1825 and was chartered as a city in 1857.

for this is the heart of the city. Salamanca Place, in a sense, typifies Hobart, in that it is on the fringe of the waterfront and has elegant, lovingly preserved Georgian warehouses. These sandstone buildings date from the early 1800s, when whales ventured into the Derwent Estuary and Hobart was a thriving whaling port. The weekly **Saturday market** is almost an alternative lifestyle market, charming, stylish and throbbing with an inner life. As you shop you are serenaded by a harpist, who is a classical musician of considerable repute.

At the north end of Salamanca Place are the **Houses of Parliament** and the **Supreme Law Courts**, and beside them, **St David's Park**. This park is on the site of the first cemetery and has some of the tombstones of the very early settlers, moved and set into two sandstone walls at the bottom of the park.

When it was built by convicts in 1835, Parliament House was the original customs house, but in 1856 self-government changed its role. The lower ground level is now a historical archive museum and is open to the public. On the approach to the building there is an oak plantation, which was planted at the time the building was constructed.

Just up Kelly's steps from Salamanca Place is **Battery Point**, arguably the most historic precinct of the city, and named after the battery of guns which protected the city from a possible invasion. It still has the **Anglesea Barracks**, which were started in 1814, making

it the oldest military establishment in Australia. Many of the buildings in this area are listed by the National Trust. Battery Point is covered with a maze of winding lanes and buildings, which include **Arthur Circus**, a group of 16 Georgian cottages built in 1847, which positively reek charm.

Hampden Rd is the main road through the area, with antique shops, coffee houses and colonial cottages. **Narryna** is one of the mansions dating from the last century, located at *103 Hampden Rd*. It operates as a museum and is furnished with period antiques. Inside is the **Van Diemen's Land Folk Museum**, which is the oldest of its kind in Australia; in the grounds is a blacksmith and a collection of horse-drawn vehicles. Open Mon–Fri 1000–1700, Sat–Sun 1400–1700. $5.

The **Maritime Museum**, *21 Secheron Rd, Battery Point; tel: 6223 5082,* was established in 1974 and is a community museum conducted by volunteers. It has an extensive collection of models, artefacts, artworks and photographs showing Tasmania's shipping history since 1804. The museum is in a former colonial mansion, **Secheron House**, which was built in 1831 for the Surveyor General of the colony, George Frankland. It is considered one of the best examples of Georgian architecture in Hobart. A wide verandah, added in the 1840s, overlooks the Derwent River. Open daily 1000–1630; $3. Close by is one of Hobart's landmarks, **St. George's Anglican Church**,

387

The Sydney to Hobart Yacht Race

Not long after the World War II, a group of sailing enthusiasts in Sydney formed the Cruising Yacht Club. One of the members, Peter Luke, suggested a cruise to Hobart. A guest of the club, Captain John Illingworth RN, was extremely enthusiastic about the event and took the idea a step further – a race from Sydney to Hobart.

The first Sydney to Hobart race was held in 1945 with nine starters. Only one yacht completed the course – *Rani* skippered by Illingworth. Rough weather forced the others to withdraw. This set the scene for the annual race, when rough weather is almost always encountered. In 1977, for example, winds reached about 50 knots, and of the 131 competitors 59 withdrew. And in 1984, 104 of the 150 yachts withdrew. Similar figures were seen yet again in 1993 when only 38 of the 104 yachts finished.

The race finish at Hobart is always celebrated by the 'Little Drink', which is famous throughout Australia. The quantity of beer drunk is well in excess of 40 cans per drinker in less than 24 hours. Altogether a truly remarkable race.

at the top of the hill. The other, which is somewhat less felicitous, is the **Hobart Casino**.

One of the best ways of seeing this delightful area is the **Battery Point Walking Tour**, which is run by National Trust volunteers. Tours Sat 0930–1230, departing from the *Wishing Well, Franklin Sq; tel: 237 570.* The $5 charge includes morning tea.

Around from Battery Point, following the banks of the River Derwent, you come to **Sandy Bay**, which boasts the casino and the **Royal Yacht Club**.

The **Tasmanian Museum and Art Gallery**, *40 Macquarie St; tel: 6235 0777,* was established by The Royal Society of Tasmania, which is the oldest Royal Society outside England and was established by Sir John Franklin, the explorer. It includes the commissariat store (1808), which issued the supplies for the people and the new colony; the Bond Store (1824); and the Cottage, built originally as a private store or stable before 1810 and converted into a residence for the Governor's Secretary in 1828. It contains some splendid photographs of the allegedly extinct Tasmanian tiger, and an Aboriginal room which has a full account of their near-extermination. There is also a section devoted to the convicts, who were among the first residents of Tasmania and were brutally used. Open daily 1000–1700.

The **Theatre Royal**, close to the city centre, *corner Sackville St; tel: 34 6266,* is the oldest theatre still operating in Australia – it was built

in 1837. It has a most elegant interior with Regency décor.

The **Allport Library and Museum of Fine Arts**, *State Library, 91 Murray St; tel: 6233 7484,* is one of the four collections of the State Library Service. The Allport family settled in Van Diemen's Land in 1831. Henry Allport, a Hobart solicitor, died in 1965 and gave his collection of 18th- and 19th- century furniture, colonial paintings, silver and objets d'art, fine china and rare and antique books to the people of Tasmania. It is housed on the ground floor of the **State Library**. **Penitentiary Chapel and Criminal Courts**, *28 Campbell St; tel: 6231 0911,* is a reminder of grim times past. Open 1000–1400. Tours are $4.

In Sandy Bay is the **Wrest Point Casino**, the first legal casino in Australia, completed in 1973. It is a prominent, if unlovely, landmark. Its revolving restaurant has panoramic views of the city. **The Queens Domain** is to the north of the city centre and is, basically, a hill on the banks of the Derwent.

At the base of the hill are the **Royal Botanical Gardens**, which have some superb formal gardens. One interesting piece of early scientific endeavour is the wall built in the Botanical Gardens in 1829 by convicts. It is connected to Government House and could be heated by means of internal fireplaces, allowing exotic plants to grow in the appropriate atmosphere.

Mt Wellington provides a wonderful backdrop for the city, rising 1271m, and it is only a 22 km drive away, with an observation and information centre on the summit. In the winter the strength of the wind up there could 'blow a dog off its chain' and you need to take care when getting out of the car. On a clear day you can see about 100 km inland. The road to the summit is somewhat tortuous and is sometimes closed due to snow in the winter.

Chocoholics should take the trip out to **Claremont** to visit the **Cadbury's Factory**. The factory is in a garden setting and a tour includes as much chocolate as you can eat as you go around. These tours, which, as one might expect, are called Death by Chocolate, last 2 hrs and take place Mon–Fri at 0900, 0930, 1030, 1115 and 1300. The $10 ticket must be paid for in advance at the time of booking at the **Tasmanian Travel Centre**.

 SIDE TRACKS FROM HOBART

A short and pleasant tour from Hobart is down and around the **Huon Peninsula**. Drive out of Hobart through Sandy Bay on the A6, which takes you 12 km to **Kingston**. Just out of town is the **Australian Antarctic headquarters**. From Kingston the Channel Hwy, now the B68, runs to **Margate** on the coast of **North West Bay** and then through **Electrona** and **Snug** to **Kettering**, which is 36 km from Hobart. This is where the vehicle and passenger ferries leave for **South Bruny Island**. The Channel Hwy now runs on a big coastal loop along the **D'Entrecasteaux Channel** for 48 km, through **Middleton**, **Gordon** and **Garden Island Creek**, fetching up at **Cygnet**. There is then a gentle 17 km run along the Huon River estuary to **Huonville**, where the road rejoins the A6. An easy 37 km along that road, with the last half hugging the edge of **Wellington Park**, and skirting **Mt Wellington**, brings you to Hobart.

KINGSTON

Tourist Information: *Council Offices, Channel Hwy; tel: 6229 5555.*

In recent years this small town has

effectively become a suburb of Hobart. The **Australian Antarctic Headquarters** – *tel: 6229 0209* – is on the outskirts of town, 2 km to the south. An exhibition showing what it does is open weekdays 0900–1700.

Pierson Point on the **Tinderbox Peninsula**, which is a pleasant, short drive from the town, has tremendous views of **Bruny Island**. Then there is the small blowhole at **Blackmans Bay**, 7 km south of *Blowhole Rd*, which has spectacular displays in stormy weather.

On the road to **Taroona**, about 3 km from the town, is the old **Shot Tower**, which has wonderful views of the **Derwent Estuary** from the top.

KETTERING

Tourist Information: Bruny D'Entrecasteaux Visitor Centre, *Ferry Rd; tel: 6267 4494.*

Accommodation: Oyster Cove Inn, *1 Ferry Rd; tel: 6267 4446.*

The centre of a major fruit growing area at the head of Little Oyster Cove, its principal interest lies in the fact that it is the terminal for the Bruny car ferry.

CYGNET

Tourist Information: Talune Wildlife Park, *Gardners Bay; tel: 6295 1775.*

Accommodation: Cygnet Hotel, *119–123 Mary St; tel: 6295 1267.*

The town was originally named Port de Cygne Noir – black swan port – by the French explorer Admiral D'Entrecasteaux. It has good beaches on both sides – notably **Randalls Bay** and **Verona Sands** – and 6 km south east at **Gardners Bay** (misleadingly 6 km inland) is **Talune Wildlife Park**. This has a wide range of marsupials, water fowl, owls, emu, parrots and farm animals. The park itself has a large koala exhibit and over 1000 sq metres of exhibit space for the Tasmanian devils, of which there are over a dozen. Entrance is $5.

In driving around this area you pass many of the **Huon Valley Wineries**, which are noted for the quality of their wine. Two near Cygnet, at Gardners Bay,

389

are **D'Entrecasteaux**, *Woodbridge Hill Rd;* *tel: 6295 1864,* which is normally not open to the public, and **Hartzview Wine Centre**, *Gardners Bay; tel: 6295 1623,* open 1000–1700 daily in the summer and at weekends in the winter.

PORT ARTHUR

Tourist Information: Visitor Information Office, *Historic Site, Arthur Hwy; tel: 6250 2363.*

ACCOMMODATION

Port Arthur Motor Inn *(FL), Arthur Hwy; tel: 6250 2101.* **Fox & Hounds Holiday Resort**, *Arthur Hwy; tel: 6250 2217.*

SIGHTSEEING

A sad, sad place. Sad because of the recent massacre in April 1996, where 35 innocent lives were lost. Sad because, from 1830 to 1877, it was the most infamous convict settlement of them all, Australia's **Devil's Island**. In all, about 12,500 convicts served sentences there. Even though, on a sunny day, Port Arthur can be beautiful and charming, there is still a chill in the air to remind visitors of the disasters of the recent past and the last century.

Despite this Port Arthur is officially Tasmania's number one tourist attraction. Getting there from Hobart is very easy and this is the most popular day trip for visitors to Tasmania. You drive from the city centre across the bridge to the other bank and drive along the A3, the Arthur Hwy, 36 km to **Sorrell**. It is then 74 km through **Dunalley** and down the **Forestier Peninsula**, across the narrow restraints of **Eaglehawk Neck** to Port Arthur. Many of the buildings are well preserved and some have been restored. There is a $13 admittance charge but this includes free tours, which leave hourly 0930–1530 from the information office. **The Granary** was built in 1843 and was the largest building in Port Arthur. It was later changed from a Granary into a prison, which housed 678 men after the closure of the Norfolk Island Penal settlement in 1857.

The Model Prison was in a separate building and had a terrible punishment, which had also been used in London at Pentonville. The prisoner was placed in solitary confinement and not allowed to speak. When the prisoners took exercise they had to wear masks. In church the pews had separate compartments for each prisoner, only offering a view of the pulpit. This church was built in 1836, but gutted by fire in 1884. Most of the other buildings do not have such sinister overtones. They were built to house the military detachment, which at one time was 300 men and their families.

The prison was closed in 1877 and the place was deserted to be damaged time and time again by the bush fires that regularly sweep the area. The National Parks and Wildlife Service made funds available in 1973 to preserve and restore what is possibly the most important historic site in Australia.

The **Tasman Peninsula** on which Port Arthur was built, was connected to the mainland by Eaglehawk Neck, which is, at one point, only 100m wide. And it was said that the surrounding waters contained many sharks that would attack prisoners who tried to escape but that, even then, was probably a myth propagated by the warders. Even if they escaped the sharks, the coastline was stark and forbidding. Certainly some managed to get around the obstacle, even though it was manned by guards, who ran a chain from one side of the neck to the other, and tethered between 9 and 18 savage dogs to it.

Four spectacular natural formations are a short drive from the Neck. **Tasman Arch** is a natural arch between two cliffs cut by wave action. At **Devil's Kitchen** the waves roar onto the rocks hundreds of feet below. The sea rushes in under the rock and shoots into the air at the **Blowhole**. The **Tesselated Pavement** is a natural formation of rocks, which to visitors looks as though it was laid by a maritime bricklayer. On a lighter note, nearby is the **Bush Mill** – *tel: 6250 2221* – which has a 4 km railway with a steam engine and many recreations of pioneering time. Entry is $12. ▲

HOBART–
CRADLE MOUNTAIN

This route takes you along Tasmania's east and north coasts before heading inland, in the shape of a giant question mark, to finish in a national park of world-class scenery.

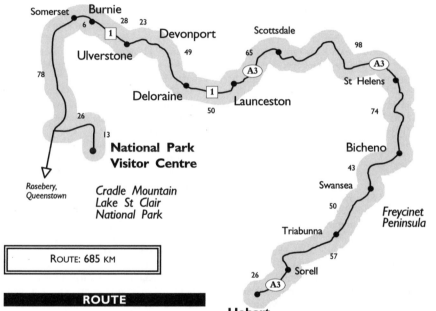

ROUTE: 685 KM

391

ROUTE

In Hobart you cross the bridge over the Derwent and follow the A3 road north-east. After 26 km you come to Sorrell. From there the highway runs along the coast past Maria Island though **Triabunna** until, after 113 km, it comes to **Swansea**, which is opposite the **Freycinet Peninsula**. The road swings 32 km across the head of the peninsula to **Bicheno**, at the very south end of the **Douglas–Apsley National Park**. From there it hugs **MacLean Bay** and runs through **Seymour** until, after 30 km, it comes to **Chain of Lagoons**. The A3 stays with the coast past Four Mile Creek to **Falmouth**, when it swings inland and meets the junction with the A4, the Esk Main Road. Stay on the A3, the Tasman Hwy, which continues back to the sea, 37 km to **St Helens**, on Georges Bay.

From St Helens the A3 starts to swing inland across the broad top of Tasmania, running for 99 km to **Scottsdale**. The road heads 70 km from Scottsdale to Tasmania's second city and capital of the north, **Launceston**. From Launceston take Rte 1 – the Bass Hwy – 51 km west to **Deloraine** and then 49 km north to **Devonport** – on the coast again, but now facing the Bass Strait, which separates Tasmania from the rest of Australia. Now Rte 1 hugs the coast through **Ulverstone** until, after 51 km it comes to the coastal industrial town of **Burnie**.

After Burnie continue west on the Bass Hwy, now the A2, for about 6 km until you reach **Somerset**. There take the A10, the Murchison Hwy, to the left and then head south towards the interior of the island. The Murchison Hwy runs for 78 km, passing several villages and the **Hellyer Gorge State Reserve**, until it reaches the turn-off left towards the **Cradle Mountain Lake St Clair National Park**, which comes about 16 km south of the junction for Guildford. Continue along this minor road for about 26 km and then take the right turn to the Park Visitor Centre.

If you continue down the Murchison Hwy instead of turning towards the Park, another 38 km will bring you to **Rosebery**, which is a possible base from which to visit the Park. A further 50 km along the A10 (by now called the Zeehan Hwy) is Queenstown, which is one end of the Hobart–Queenstown route (p.398), enabling you to complete a full circular tour of Tasmania.

BUSES

At least one bus a day connects Hobart with Swansea and Bicheno and along the line of this route up the east coast as far as Launceston. Alternatively, you can catch a Hobart Coaches or Tasmanian Redline bus following the more direct way to Launceston along the Midland Hwy, ignoring the coast; approx. 2½ hrs. The same buses continue to Devonport, Ulverstone and Burnie; the latter is 5½ hrs from Hobart.

From Launceston (Tasmanian Wilderness Transport), Burnie (Tasmanian Redline) and Devonport (both companies) there are buses to Cradle Mountain itself, taking respectively 4 hrs, 3 hrs and 2 hrs.

OTT tables 9150, 9160 and 9161.

BICHENO

Tourist Information: Bicheno Penguin Adventure Tours, *Tasman Hwy; tel: 6375 1333.*

ACCOMMODATION AND FOOD

Beachfront Motel, *Tasman Hwy; tel: (003) 75 1111.* **Waubs Bay House**, *16 Tasman Hwy.* **Freycinet Lodge Resort**, *Coles Bay, Freycinet National Park; tel: 6257 0101.*

Cyrano French Restaurant, *77 Burgess St; tel: 6375 1137.* Brasserie style, dinner 7 days a week. Licensed.

SIGHTSEEING

Bicheno, 195 km from Hobart, is the gateway to the **Freycinet National Park**, which occupies most of the Freycinet Peninsula and all of the seaward side and the head. And just to the north and inland of Bicheno is the relatively new **Douglas-Apsley National Park** which is basically forest.

The name of the town is pronounced 'Bisheeno'. It was renamed by Lt-Governor Denison after James Ebenezer Bicheno, the Colonial Secretary of the time. The town is also a holiday destination in its own right. It started life about 1803 as a sealing and whaling town, but those wild and wicked days were over by about 1840 and today crayfishing and tourism are the two largest industries.

The town was originally known as **Waubs' Harbour** from the Aboriginal woman Waubedebar. She had been kidnapped by the sealers, had married one and is said to have rescued two sealers – one of whom may have been her husband – during a storm. There is a reconstructed grave for Waubedebar near *Burgess St.* Bicheno has a famous little penguin colony 6 km to the north on **Diamond Island**. To protect them visits are on an organised basis from **Bicheno Penguin Tours** (see Tourist Information) and only small groups can walk near the birds at any one time. The price for the tour is $12. Tasmania has only one glass-bottom boat expedition and that is out to the sheltered waters of **Bicheno's marine park**; price also $12.

This is one of the better dive sites in Tasmania with a Marine Reserve on the eastern side of **Governor Island**, which has spectacular large drop-offs and vertical rock faces. **The Bicheno Dive Centre** (*4 Tasman Hwy; tel: 6375 1138*) has rental gear and diving courses.

Just beyond the harbour is the famous **Blowhole**. Blowholes occur when part of the roof of a tunnel eroded by waves close to sea level along a weak zone in the rock collapses. The waves compress the air at the rear of the tunnel and the high pressure causes a hole to be blown out through the rock. Water is forced up through the hole in the roof to form a water spout. This is also the location of the **Rocking Rock** – 81.3 tonnes of solid granite which has been rocking slightly with each wave for thousands of years.

Back down 11 km on the Tasman Hwy as if you are returning to Hobart is **Llandaff**. From there the road runs 31 km to **Coles Bay** – named after Silas Coles who used to burn shells of the beach to make lime – which is the entrance to the **Freycinet National Park**. This has its information centre (*tel: 6257 0107*) about 1 km from Coles Bay. Tracks into the park begin at the Walking Track Car Park, 4 km from the information centre. There is a range of walks which are well signposted and the most common walk is to **Wineglass Bay** and that is a leisurely 1 hr each way.

LAUNCESTON

Tourist Information: Tasmanian Travel Centre, *corner St John and Paterson Sts; tel: 6336 3133.*

ACCOMMODATION

Abel Tasman Airport Motor Inn *(BW), 303 Hobart Rd; tel: 6344 5244.* **Aberdeen Court Motel,** *35 Punchbowl Rd; tel: 6344 5811.* **Balmoral Motor Inn Motel–Launceston** *(FL), 19 York St; tel: 6331 8000.* **Batman Fawkner Inn Hotel,** *35–39 Cameron St; tel: 6331 7222.* **Coach House Motor Inn Motel** *(BW), 10 York St; tel: 6331 5311.* **Colonial Motor Inn Hotel,** *31 Elizabeth St; tel: 6331 6588.* **Commodore Regent Motor Inn Motel** *(FL), 13 Brisbane St; tel: 6331 4666.* **Great Northern Hotel** *(FL), 3 Earl St; tel: 6331 9999.* **The Maldon Motel,** *32 Brisbane St; tel: 63 31 3211.* **Mews Motel,** *89 Margaret St; tel: 6331 2861.* **Novotel Launceston Hotel,** *29 Cameron St; tel: 6334 3434.* **Olde Tudor Motor Inn,** *Bass Hwy; tel: 6344 5044.* **Parklane Motel,** *9 Brisbane St; tel: 6331 4233.* **Penny Royal Watermill,** *147 Paterson St; tel: 6331 6699.* **Prince Albert Inn,** *corner Tamar and William Sts; tel: 6331 7633.* **Sandors On The Park Hotel-Motel,** *3 Brisbane St; tel: 6331 2055.* **St George Hotel,** *119 St John St; tel: 6331 7277.*

St James Hotel, *122 York St; tel: 6331 6122.* **Tamar River Motor Inn** *(FL), 23–27 Elouera St; tel: 6327 1022.* **Windmill Tourist Lodge Motel,** *22 High St; tel: 6334 3292.*

EATING AND DRINKING

Arpar's Thai Restaurant, *Charles and Paterson Sts; 6331 2786.* Licensed. Daily for dinner. **Calabrisella,** *56 Wellington St; tel: 6331 1958.* Open dinner except Tues. BYO. **Cucina Simpatica,** *Margaret and Frederick Sts; tel: 6334 3177.* Daily lunch and dinner. BYO. **Montezuma's,** *63 Brisbane St; tel: 6331 8999.* Dinner 7 nights, lunch Wed–Fri. Licensed. Mexican. **Shrimps,** *George and Patterson Sts; tel: 6334 0584.* Lunch Mon–Fri. Dinner Mon–Sat. Licensed. Seafood. **Tairyo Japanese Restaurant,** *25 Yorketown Sq; tel: 6334 2620.* Lunch Tues–Fri. Dinner Mon–Sat. BYO.

SIGHTSEEING

Launceston is the second city of Tasmania and there is a certain rivalry with Hobart, although it is nowhere near as intense as that between Sydney and Melbourne. This city has it own range of splendid restored Georgian and solid Victorian buildings. It also uniquely has **Cataract Gorge** as its green heart, only 10 mins walk from the city centre and containing the world's longest single span chair-lift.

The city was named in 1824 after Governor King's birthplace in Cornwall in England, after it had a brief period when it was known as Pattersonia. One of the major rivers of Cornwall is the **Tamar** and the river that runs through Launceston was also given that name. The city is on the junction of the Tamar and the **North and South Esk** rivers, which join here before flowing 64 km to the Bass Strait.

The first settlement was in 1805 and it became the headquarters for northern Tasmania in the following year. A major step forward came when the road to Hobart was opened in 1818.

The **Brisbane Street Mall** marks the centre of the city, which is arranged in a grid pattern.

There are several places of interest in the city. **The Queen Victoria Museum and Art Gallery,** *Wellington St,* has a good collection

393

and a planetarium. It also has a **Chinese joss house** built in the 1870s by Chinese workers who were brought to work the tin mines. Open Mon–Sat 1000–1700, Sun 1400–1700.

The Old Umbrella Shop, *60 George St; tel: 6331 9248*, is listed by the National Trust as an example of a mid-Victorian shop. It was built in the 1860s and is beautifully lined with Tasmanian Blackwood. Open Mon–Fri 0900–1700, Sat 0900–1200.

The Community History Museum, *corner Cimitiere St; tel: 6337 1391*, is in the old **Johnston and Wilmot Store**, built in 1842 and still in its original condition. Open Mon–Sat 1000–1600, Sun 1400–1600; $2.

But what defines Launceston for most people is the **Gorge** and its amazing chair lift (daily 0900–1630; 6 mins; $3) which swings you across 457m. While it is true the views from the chair lift are spectacular, it is not for the timid or those who suffer from vertigo. There are some who find the alternative just as worrying. This is **Alexandra Suspension Bridge**, which is called the 'swinging bridge' locally, for it feels something less than totally solid and you, like me, might find that slightly disturbing.

Both the chair lifts and the bridge take you to the **Cliff Grounds**, which have gardens with a Victorian feel leading to a rotunda containing a display of early photographs of the area.

Close to the Gorge is the **Penny Royal World** (daily 0900–1630; admission $19.50) which is a remarkable complex containing a water mill with a working cornmill and a tramline connecting to a gunpowder mill. This area was originally a deserted quarry and the current presentation started being developed over twenty years ago. The entrance fee includes a cruise on the paddle steamer *Lady Stelfox* and a ride on a Launceston tram.

DELORAINE

Tourist Information: Visitor Information Centre, *29 West Church St; tel: 6362 2046*.

ACCOMMODATION AND FOOD

Bonney's Inn, *17 West Parade; tel: 6362 2974*.
   Arcoona, *East Barrack St; tel: 6362 3443*. Daily lunches and dinner. Licensed and BYO.

SIGHTSEEING

Deloraine is on the Meander River in a valley of rich farmland, with **Quamby Bluff** at 1256m overlooking the town. To the south are the **Western Tiers**, where the Central Plateau drops abruptly to the plains. The tiers are right on the edge of the Central Plateau Protected Area – a form of national park – and the **Great Lake**. Deloraine is exactly at the mid-point between **Devonport** and **Launceston** on the Bass Hwy. No one is quite certain where the name of the town comes from although it is suggested that it is from a character in Sir Walter Scott's *Lay of the Last Minstrel*, since one of Scott's relatives, James Scott, surveyed the district in the 1820s. The Meander River bisects the town and the first bridge across was built by convict labour but destroyed in a flood in 1844.

The river often sees Deloraine shrouded in morning mist, which suits its historic buildings. **Bonney's Inn**, *17 West Parade*, which was built in 1830, is the town's oldest remaining building and is now used as a restaurant.

Deloraine is important as a base for walkers, walking tracks throughout the area range from easy strolls to three-day serious expeditions. The information office has brochures on many of these. Several organisations in the area offer guided walks; **Cadman and Norwood Environmental Consultancy** – *tel: 6369 5150* – in the nearby town of Meander has bush walks guided by qualified field naturalists.

Deloraine is also at the centre of a serious caving area. **Mole Creek**, 24 km to the southwest, has **Marakoopa** and **King Solomons Caves** for which there are guided tours starting at 1000, with a charge of $12 for the two. Both are lit with electricity but Marakoopa, the bigger of the two, also has glow-worms and is the only glow-worm cave in Tasmania open to the public.

DEVONPORT

Tourist Information: Tasmanian Travel and Information, Devonport Showcase, *5 Best St; tel: 6424 4466*.

ACCOMMODATION AND FOOD

Gateway Inn, *16 Fenton St; tel: 6424 4922*.

Barclay Lodge Motel, *112 North Fenton St; tel: 6424 4722.* Trelawney By The Sea Resort, *6 Chalmers Lane; tel: 6424 3263.* Sunrise Motor Inn *(FL), 140 North Fenton St; tel: 6424 8411.* Argosy Motor Inn, *Tarleton St; tel: 6427 8872.* Hotel Formby, *82 Formby Rd; tel: 6424 1601.* Elimatta Motor Inn, *15 Victoria Parade; tel: 6424 6555.* Edgewater Motor Inn, *2 Thomas St; tel: 6427 8441.*

Alexander Hotel, *78 Formby Rd; tel: 6424 2252.* Bistro. The Greendoor, *10 Oldaker St; tel: 6424 6000.* Licensed. Tues–Sat. Rialto Gallery, *159 Rooke St; tel: 6424 6793.* Lunch Mon–Fri. Dinner Sat, Sun.

SIGHTSEEING

Devonport was once two towns: **Formby** on the west bank and **Torquay** opposite. They merged in 1890. This is an industrial port and the terminal of the Bass Strait Ferry. The town is about an hour's drive from Launceston and is an excellent starting place for Cradle Mountain and the other national parks and now has several companies catering for travellers.

Worth seeing is the **Tiagarra Tasmanian Aboriginal Cultural and Arts Centre**, *tel: 6424 8250,* which is on a bluff north of the town centre. It has dioramas showing the lifestyle of the Aboriginal people from the region, and is close to the Aboriginal rock carvings. Open daily 0900–1630; closed July; admission $2.50.

Home Hill, *77 Middle Rd,* is the former home of Sir Joseph Lyons, the only person ever to be Premier of Tasmania and Prime Minister of Australia – up to the start of World War II – is a National Trust property. Open Tues, Thur, Sat, Sun 1400–1600; $5.

The Don River Railway is run by enthusiasts who have restored 3½ km of the original railway that closed in 1950. It starts at **Don Recreation Ground** 4 km out of town on the Bass Hwy and runs along the Don River to **Coles Beach** from 1100–1600 hourly; *tel: 6424 6335.* $6 return. On Sundays and public holidays steam locomotives are used, the rest of the time it is diesel. The museum associated with the railway has the largest collection of locomotive carriages and traction engines in Australia.

ULVERSTONE

Tourist Information: *Car Park Lane; tel: 6425 2839.*

ACCOMMODATION AND FOOD

Furners Hotel, *42 Reibey St; tel: 6425 1488.* Lighthouse Hotel, *corner Victoria and Reibey Sts; tel: 6425 1197.* Beachway Motel, *Heathcote St; tel 6425 2342.*

Bass and Flinders Restaurant, *49 Eastlands Dr.* Mrs Simpsons, *31 King Edward St.*

SIGHTSEEING

Ulverstone is the central town of the north-west coast and stands on the Leven River, 21 km from Devonport and 122 km from Launceston. It has an undeserved reputation of being a dull and conservative town even though it has much to offer the visitor. Along the banks of the river there is a series of parks and recreation spots.

The Ulverstone History Museum *50 Main St,* is run by the local historical society and concentrates on the lives of the European pioneers. Open Sat, Sun 1330–1600, $2. **Ulverstone Lookout** in *Upper Maud St* has an excellent view of the town.

Out of town **Leven Canyon**, 41 km from Ulverston, has spectacular scenery and bushwalking tracks.

The Gunns Plains Caves, *tel: 6429 1388,* is a limestone cave system which has an underground river. The caves, which show some truly remarkable formations, are home to both platypuses and possums. Open daily 1000–1600, $6.

There are several waterfalls in the immediate area. The **Castra Falls** is in the local rain forest. **Preston Falls** are between **Preston** and **Gunns Plains**. **Winterbrook Falls** is a dense rain forest with 2000-year-old King Billy Pines.

BURNIE

Tourist Information: Tasmanian Travel Centre, *Civic Square, off Little Alexander St; tel: 6434 6111.*

ACCOMMODATION AND FOOD

Ocean View Park-A-Tel, *253 Bass Hwy; tel:*

395

6431 1925. **Voyager Motor Inn**, *Wilson St; tel: 6431 4866.* **Wellers Inn**, *36 Queen St; tel: 6431 1088.*
  Rialto Gallery, *46 Wilmot St; tel: 6431 7718.* Italian. **Moods Restaurant and Glopots**, *139 Wilson St; tel: 6431 4455.* **Partners Restaurant**, *104 Wilson St; tel: 6431 9393.*

SIGHTSEEING

Originally called Emu Bay, the site was chosen by Henry Hellyer for the Van Diemen's Land Co in 1827. In 1843 it was renamed after a director of the company, William Burnie. Many of the streets in the town are named after other company notables. Burnie was proclaimed a municipality in 1907 and granted city status in 1988. Burnie is very much a commercial centre, home to one of the state's largest enterprises, a pulp and paper factory. The town is 49 km from Devonport and 150 km from Launceston.

  The Pioneer Village Museum, *Little Alexander St; tel: 6430 5746,* is in the Civic Centre and is a reconstruction of a street in the last century. About 30,000 articles are housed in units built of authentic 19th-century materials. The colours used and the architectural variations are those which were fashionable along the North-West Coast from 1880 to 1910. Open Mon–Fri 0900–1700, Sat, Sun 1330–1630; $4.

  The Burnie Regional Art Gallery, *Wilmot St; tel: 6431 5918,* is a gallery serving north-western and western Tasmania. It holds touring and local exhibitions and is also building a permanent collection. Open Tues–Fri 1030–1700, Sat, Sun 1330–1630.

CRADLE MOUNTAIN LAKE ST CLAIR NATIONAL PARK

Tourist Information Centre: at the entrance to the park near **Cradle Mountain Lodge**; *tel: 6492 1133.* Open all year.

ACCOMMODATION AND FOOD

Right on the boundary of the park is the **Cradle Mountain Lodge** (*tel: 6492 1303*) which has a wide range of accommodation, an excellent restaurant, a provision store and even a petrol pump.

SIGHTSEEING

The Cradle Mountain Lake St Clair National Park is one of the great treasures of Tasmania, covering as it does some 126,000 hectares of wilderness. Within the park Cradle Mountain itself, which rises to 1545 m, is one of the most popular destinations for tourists coming to the state. The odd name for it was given by Joseph Fossey in 1827, who thought it looked like a cradle. It was also known for a time as **Rock Rib Crest** but the easier to remember name is the one that has survived. The great man of this mountain was **Gustav Weindorfer**, who explored and pioneered the area. He emigrated to Australia in 1900 and six years later married a Tasmanian woman, a naturalist called Kate Julia Cowle, and moved to Tasmania, where they farmed.

  Cradle Mountain had been climbed by Europeans – explorer Henry Hellyer was the first person known to do so in 1831 – but it was difficult of access. Although climbing the mountain was no great achievement, getting into the area made it a rare event. Gustav Weindorfer decided to change this and bought land, cleared walking trails, named many of the features of the mountain – **Mt Kate** and **Crater**, **Dove** and **Hanson Lakes** – and prepared the way for tourists. He built **Waldheim Chalet** and opened it for tourism in 1912. Cradle Mountain has never looked back. The chalet is still there, with eight extra bushwalker huts built around it.

  The terrain was created by ancient glaciers – this is one of the most glaciated areas in Australia. It is full of lakes and mountain tarns and is the highest in Australia. **Mt Ossa** is the highest spot in the state and, at the other end of the park, **Lake St Clair** is Australia's deepest clear water lake, with a maximum depth of over 200 m. The lake is in a massive basin that glaciers scooped out of the earth.

  The distance between Cradle Mountain and Lake St Clair is 85 km and this is traversed by the **Overland Track**, which can lay claim to being the best-known walk in Australia and, indeed, has a worldwide reputation. The route

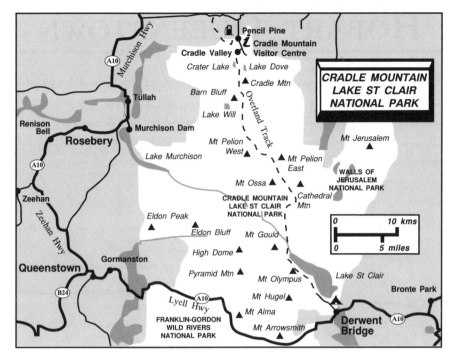

CRADLE MOUNTAIN LAKE ST CLAIR NATIONAL PARK

397

takes you along the slopes of Cradle Mountain and then past **Lake Windermere** and over **Pine Forest**. From there the track passes between **Mt Pelion East** and **Mt Pelion West** with Mt Ossa in the distance. The track then goes past **Kia Ora Falls** and over the **Duncan Range** and then comes down the west side of the **Narcissus River** to Lake St Clair and goes along the lakeside under the shadow of **Mt Olympus** until it reaches **Cynthia Bay** and the end of the track.

The National Parks and Wildlife Service has done its best to see that no one actually perishes on the track by erecting huts, which are normally full in summer. It has also tried to lessen the impact of the army of walkers – up to 100 a day – by laying boardwalks on several stretches. But the fact remains that this is a serious walk that will take six days and will task the toughest. For the whole of the distance there are no roads. The track crosses forests of beech, Tasmanian myrtle and King Billy pine and plains covered with buttongrass. And every now and again in the summer – the only time

to walk – a sweep of wildflowers to lift the spirit.

Before walking you must register at the extremely well-equipped information centre at the entrance to the park (see Tourist Information above). You must also attend an obligatory briefing and have your gear checked.

There are guided tours on offer, of which **Cradle Mountain Huts** (*22 Brisbane St, Launceston; tel: 6331 2006*) is the most inviting, as you stay in private lodges with beds and hot showers. But you still have to walk every step of the way.

Not that you need to walk the Overland Track to enjoy the park. At the impressive modern **Cradle Mountain Visitor Centre** there is an abundance of information on the many **day walks** available in this area of the park. As a starting point next to the centre is the **Rainforest-Pencil Pine Falls Walking Track** which is less impressive in length than its name, covering only 500m of boardwalk. But it is an easy and enthralling introduction to the local scenery.

HOBART–QUEENSTOWN

It is possible to get from Hobart to Queenstown by following the route in the preceding chapter and then hooking down to Queenstown. The much quicker and more direct route goes on the Lyell Highway straight through the Franklin-Gordon Wild Rivers National Park. Queenstown provides another base from which to visit Cradle Mountain–Lake St Clair, and you can side-track to the historic towns of Strahan and Zeehan.

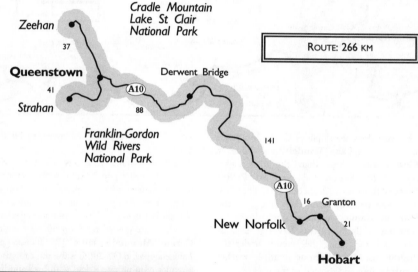

ROUTE: 266 KM

Zeehan
37
Queenstown
41
Strahan
88
Cradle Mountain Lake St Clair National Park
Derwent Bridge
A10
Franklin-Gordon Wild Rivers National Park
141
A10
16   Granton
New Norfolk   21
Hobart

ROUTE

Leave Hobart northwards on the A10 road, which runs up the east side of the Derwent River. After 21 km you come to the very small town of **Granton**. Take the left-hand road, still the A10, the Lyell Hwy. (The right-hand road, Rte 1, does provide a detour which will eventually bring you back onto the main route, but involves a stretch of road which is currently unsealed.)

The Lyell Hwy turns sharply towards the west above the expanse of Wellington Park until it gets to **New Norfolk**. From there it starts easing its way cross–country through some small villages until after 90 km it comes to the B11 turn-off (which is where the detour mentioned above rejoins the Highway). This is pretty much the exact centre of Tasmania. To the south and west of the road is nothing but wilderness and national parks stretching to the coast.

From the B11 junction, the Lyell Hwy goes 26 km to the minute village of **Derwent Bridge**, which is on the edge of **Cradle Mountain Lake St Clair National Park**.

From here the A10 goes 86 km straight through the park until it reaches **Queenstown** on the other side.

BUSES

Tasmanian Redline and Tasmanian Wilderness Transport provide a bus service from Hobart to Queenstown along this route. There is one bus a day (none on Mon or Thur), taking between 6 and 7¾ hrs depending on the day of the week and the operator. OTT table 9165. There are also local services from Hobart to New Norfolk.

NEW NORFOLK

Tourist Information: Council Offices, *Circle St; tel: 6261 2777.*

ACCOMMODATION

Amaroo Motel, *Lyell Hwy and Pioneer Ave; tel: 6261 2000.* **Bush Inn,** *Montagu St; tel: 6261 2011.*

SIGHTSEEING

Although New Norfolk is only 53 km from Hobart it is by no means a suburb and has a very distinct character of its own. The town started and got its name through the resettlement of settlers from Norfolk Island after it was closed down in 1807. In fact, from 1811 to 1825 it was known as Elizabeth Town after Governor Macquarie's wife. There is a charming story that an Irish convict, Denis McCarty, was appointed the first police constable in 1808 and built the first house in 1812 on the site now occupied by the Boyer Mill.

This is one of the oldest towns in Tasmania because land was granted to the settlers as they arrived. **The Bush Inn** *(49 Montagu St; tel: 6261 2011)* was built in 1815 and was licensed from 1825, starting with Anne Bridger as the licensee. It claims to be the oldest licence on a single site in Australia. It has hardly changed since it was first licensed and still has plain stained floorboards.

Another ancient hostelry is the **Old Colony Inn** *(21 Montagu St; tel: 6261 2731)* which now displays antiques and artefacts and has a restaurant attached. The town was associated with hops and hop fields almost from its inception and the district was dominated by the hop-growing industry until very recently. Indeed, it is often said that the immediate countryside is reminiscent of Kent in England.

Reflecting that involvement with hops, the **Oast House** (open daily 1000–1700, *tel: 6261 1030,* $3.50) which is off the Lyell Hwy is a museum recounting the history of hops. The Oast House was built in the 1820s and converted by Ralph Terry into a kiln for drying hops in 1867.

St Matthews Church of England facing **Arthur Square** on *Bathurst St* was built in 1823 and is Tasmania's oldest surviving church. It has been much modified since it was first built. It is unusual in that it is set in a garden full of flower beds instead of the traditional bushes and lawns which surround most churches.

New Norfolk is one of the oldest towns in Australia and has some of the oldest buildings. But this is balanced by the river which is an important part of the town. The **Derwent** at New Norfolk is much narrower than it is at Hobart, is perfectly clean and safe for swimming and is tree-lined.

Hop growing was pretty much over by 1970 and new industries arose to fill its place. One of these was trout farming. The first rainbow and brown trout in the southern hemisphere were bred in **Salmon Ponds** at **Plenty** 9 km away. That was in 1864. This is still going on although this site is under the management of the Inland Fisheries Commission as a historic site. The farm is open for inspection, *Lower Bushy Park Rd; tel: 6261 1076.* Open daily; $3.50. How did the trout travel so far, back in 1864? The eggs were carried in an ice chest on the clipper *Norfolk* to Melbourne, from there to Hobart on a steam ship called HMS *Colonial.* Then by river steamer, horses and finally messengers to the Salmon Ponds. Some of the fish to be seen today are over half a metre in length.

Only an hour's drive away is **Mt Field National Park** and close to the park entrance are **Russell Falls**, a wildlife park and a fish farm. Mt Field was one of Tasmania's first national parks and the area within the park around Russell Falls, near the entrance, was made into a reserve in 1885.

The park itself is one of the major refuges

399

for the Tasmanian Devil. Some of the eucalypt trees in the park are over 400 years old, 90m high and 20m around the base.

QUEENSTOWN

Tourist Information: Royal Automobile Club of Tasmania, *Orr St; tel: 6471 1974.*

ACCOMMODATION

Westcoaster Motor Inn *(BW), Batchelor St; tel: 6471 1033.* **Silver Hills Motel** *(BW), Penghana Rd; tel: 6471 1755.* **Gold Rush Motor Inn,** *Batchelor St; tel: 6471 1005.* **Queenstown Motor Lodge Motel,** *54–58 Orr St; tel: 6471 1866.* **Mt Lyell Motor Inn,** *1 Orr St; tel: 6471 1888.*

SIGHTSEEING

For many years Tasmanian Tourism pushed Queenstown as a destination of great historic interest. That is debatable. What is certain is that it shows the effect of years of uncontrolled mining on an area. Queenstown and its surrounds look like the time that time forgot. It is surrounded by a series of hills, which form a bleak moonscape and although there is talk of reforestation it seems unlikely the area can ever recover in less than a century or so.

Having said that and understanding that this is a mining town where no environmental controls were ever applied you can go on to explore its interesting aspects. Queenstown is 180 km from Burnie and 256 km from Hobart. It exists first because gold was found to the south of **Mt Lyell** in 1881 and the **Iron Blow** area was pegged two years later. Mining has been continuous ever since.

The first mining town was **Penghana** but this was destroyed by fire in 1896 and Queenstown was established further down the valley.

In 1892 copper was discovered and the hills in the area were stripped of all trees to provide timber for the smelters and the mines. Then rain eroded the soil and exposed the underlying rock. No trees grew back because of the sulphur fumes although now the fumes have stopped and mining activity is cut back to an almost zero level it is possible to hope. In its time it produced over 900,000 tonnes of copper, 547 tonnes of gold, 26,400 kg of gold and a landscape to rival the moon.

One way of getting an overall view of the area is to ride the chairlift which rises to 150m and takes about 15 mins to make the return journey. It is off *Penghana Rd* and is run by **Queenstown Ropeways** – *tel: 6471 2338* – and the ride costs $4.

Eric Thomas Galley Museum, *corner Driffield and Stitch Sts; tel: 6471 1483,* is a photographic collection of the life of mining in the area. Twenty one rooms are now open to the public with a variety of collections. Open daily Mon–Fri 1000–1630, Sat–Sun 1300–1630.

Queenstown has the only gravel sports oval in Australia – and both football and cricket are played on it regularly.

There are daily tours of the **Mt Lyell Mine** with bookings and departures from the **Western Arts and Crafts Centre** at *1 Driffield St; tel: 6471 2388.*

Next door to the mine is the National Parks and Wildlife Service office *(tel: 6471 2511),* which is the base for the **Franklin Lower Gordon Wild Rivers National Park**.

☑ SIDE TRACKS FROM QUEENSTOWN

There are two interesting destinations which are within easy reach of Queenstown. **Strahan** is 41 km out of town along the B24 road (a continuation of the Lyell Hwy). There is also a twice-daily bus service, taking 45 mins (OTT table 9162). **Zeehan** is 37 km north of Queenstown, along the A10.

STRAHAN

Tourist Information: Wharf Centre, *The Esplanade; tel: 6471 7488.*

ACCOMMODATION AND FOOD

Strahan Motor Inn Motel *(FL), Jolly St; tel: 6471 7160.* **Hamer's Hotel,** *The Esplanade; tel: 6471 7191.*

Franklin Manor, *The Esplanade; tel: 6471 7311.* Open daily for dinner. Seafood. **Hamers Craypot Inn,** *The Esplanade; tel: 6471 7191.* Open for dinner daily. Seafood.

This is the only town and port on the whole of the west side of Tasmania. It is on the natural and massive **Macquarie Harbour**. This is the second largest harbour in the southern hemisphere after Sydney and has an 80m wide entrance. This was known as **Hells Gate** by arriving convicts heading for Sarah Island, a convict settlement in use between 1822 and 1830. This penal settlement was a brutal punishment camp, where unruly convicts were transported and used to fell Huon pine and float it down river. The settlement was closed after the theoretically, escape-proof **Port Arthur** was opened 1834.

Strahan is the only safe anchorage on Tasmania's west coast. Strahan's glory years were at the turn of the century when, during the west coast's boom mining days, it became the third largest port in Tasmania but the weather, which could close the entrance, made it unreliable.

The trade went elsewhere and Strahan started to take on the appearance of a ghost town. Now it is a small fishing village with a population of under 600 but a strong and growing tourist trade. The declaration of a World Heritage Area has meant that tourists now come in sizeable numbers to see the river.

To cope with the tourists the wooden and iron **Strahan Visitor Centre** has been opened with stunning views over the harbour and there is a serious redevelopment plan for the foreshore. This centre has a planned and coherent display with an ecological slant, which is superior to that of any other tourist centre in Australia.

Next to the tourist centre is **Morrison's Saw Mill** (open daily 0800–1700), which is open to visitors and has some excellent pieces on sale.

The Strahan Historic Foreshore Walkway is a gravel track following the harbour around to **Regatta Point**.

Strahan sits on the edge of the southwest wilderness, the wettest part of Australia after the tropical lowlands of north Queensland, with rugged coastlines, wild rivers, open plains, thick rain forest and spectacular peaks. This is tough and unforgiving country and is pretty much inaccessible to all but very experienced and well equipped bushwalkers. The easiest way to see at least some of this wilderness is by cruising up the river.

The main reason for Strahan's new lease of life is the **Gordon River**. This deep, dark brown river – the brown comes from the tannin from the buttongrass plains and does not affect the drinking qualities of the water – has been bitterly and successfully defended from any encroachments. You can take a cruise boat 14 km up the river to **Heritage Landing**, where there is a boardwalk above the rain forest floor.

The wet and swampy conditions are ideal for **Huon pines**, found only in Tasmania, and the second-oldest living things on earth after the bristlecone pines of North America.

Just outside the town, the 30 km long **Ocean Beach** is the longest in Tasmania.

Tourist Information: West Coast Pioneers Memorial Museum, *Main St; tel: 6471 6225.*

Heemskirk Motor Hotel, *Main St; tel: 6472 3451.* **Zeehan Motor Inn and Lodge**, *Main St; tel: 6471 6107.*

Zeehan is a 30 min drive from Queenstown. Mining brought it a boom period at the end of the last century when it had 26 hotels and a population of 10,000 and was Tasmania's third largest town.

Today it has a tin mine still operating as a reminder of its glory days. But many of the historic buildings from the boom period have survived, including the **Gaiety Theatre**, at one time the largest theatre in Australia. **The West Coast Pioneers' Memorial Museum** (open daily 0830–1700) has mining and railway displays.

TASMANIA NATIONAL PARKS

INFORMATION AND BACKGROUND

Parks and Wildlife Commission, *tel: (03) 6233 8011.*

The National Parks have been in Tasmania in one form or another for well over a century. In 1863, land in Tasmania was first set aside as 'reserves for scenic purposes'. These reservations were made under the Waste Lands Act of 1863 and subsequently under the Crown Lands Act. By 1899 Tasmania had 12 reserves. The government passed more comprehensive scenery preservation legislation in 1915 and established the Scenery Preservation Board. In 1916, **Mt Field** – known until 1937 simply as **National Park** – and **Freycinet** became Tasmania's first national parks. Six years later, following a long campaign led by Gustav Weindorfer, a scenic reserve and wildlife sanctuary covering an area of 63,900 hectares was established between **Cradle Mountain** and **Lake St Clair.**

The government of Tasmania has not always been conservation-conscious. In 1972 it flooded Lake Pedder for a hydro-electric scheme; the **Wilderness Society** was formed and procedded to start a war – campaign is too soft a term – against the Hydro Electricity Commission's next plan, the damming of the Franklin. This was Tasmania's last wild river. The protests ran for nearly ten years. In 1981 the whole south-west area was proposed for the World Heritage list. The government ignored this and continued with its plans. The Franklin Blockade, organised by the Wilderness Society, began on 14 Dec 1982 and continued for two months, with protesters lying down in front of the bulldozers. In all 1,200 protesters made the journey up-river from Strahan.

Then the Labor government of Bob Hawke as voted in and in March 1983 the federal government forbade further work on the hydro-electric scheme. This created immense bitterness among the Tasmanians that supported the dam, who believed that they were being denied employment by mainlanders who rarely visited the state. The Wilderness Society still exists, still campaigns but some of the tensions are starting to ease as Tasmanians find that the wealth of national parks is attracting more and more tourists with tourism now a substantial industry.

The **Franklin Lower Gordon Wild Rivers National Park** is the result of those protests. It was declared in June 1980 and in 1982 was included with the adjoining parks on the World Heritage List. Note that access to this park is almost non-existent. You can fly over it, or explore the edges by cruising the Gordon River or, if you are adventurous you can go on a raft down the Franklin – but only between Dec and Mar and not always then, for this is by far the most dangerous rafting river in Australia. The full trip takes 8–14 days.

THE NATIONAL PARKS

All of these parks have at least one campsite, picnic site and walking trail unless otherwise noted.

Ben Lomond *No picnic area.*
Cradle Mountain Lake St Clair *Bush camping possible. See p. 396.*
Douglas Apsley
Franklin-Gordon Wild Rivers *No campsite but bush camping possible.*
Freycinet *Bush camping possible. See p. 392.*
Maria Island *Bush camping possible.*
Mt Field *See p. 399.*
Mt William *Bush camping possible.*
Rocky Cape *No campsite.*
Southwest *Bush camping possible.*
Strelzcki (Flinders Island) *Bush camping possible.*
Walls of Jerusalem *No campsite but bush camping possible.*

CLASSIC TRAIN JOURNEYS

Australia offers the opportunity to enjoy some of the world's most fascinating train journeys. Named trains run regularly on long- and short-distance routes, often taking the traveller through scenery and to places which would be impractical or wearisome to visit by car. This chapter looks at some of these classic rail journeys, which range from the adventurous and characterful to the luxurious. Sleeping accommodation is available on overnight services, often to a high standard of comfort. All the trains are non-smoking in Queensland.

INFORMATION AND BOOKING

All of the trains described here can be booked through Thomas Cook in Australia itself (see p. 37 for further details). Alternatively, you can obtain information and brochures, and make bookings, through the following agents in your own country:

UK and Republic of Ireland: Leisurail, PO Box 113, Peterborough, PE3 8HY; tel: (01733) 335599; fax: (01733) 505451.

USA and Canada: Forsyth Travel Library, 1750 E. 131st St, PO Box 480800, Kansas City, MO 64148-0800, USA; tel: 800 367 7984 (toll free). ATS Tours, 2381 Rosecrans Ave, Suite 325, El Segundo, CA 90245, USA: 800 423 2880 (toll free). Goway Travel, 3284 Yonge St, Suite 300, Toronto, Ontario M4N 3M7, Canada, tel: (416) 322 1034.

France: Australie Tours, 129 rue Lauriston, Paris 75116; tel: (331) 4553 5893.

Germany: Brits: Australia, Plinganser Str. 12, 81369 München; tel: (89) 725 79550.

Japan: Japan Travel Bureau, Overseas Travel Department, JTB Building, 3rd Floor, 1-6-4 Maraunouchi, Chiyouda-ku, Tokyo 100; tel: (3)

3824 7303. Toyo World Co Ltd, Adyama Ten-X Building, 7th Floor, 5-50-6 Jingu-Mae Shibuya-Ku, Tokyo 150; tel: (3) 3489 7636.

Netherlands: Incenta BV, PO Box 1067, 1400 BB Bussum; tel: (35) 69 55 111.

New Zealand: Intercity Management Ltd, PO Box 3625 Beach Road, Auckland; tel 0800 801 060 (toll free). Tranz Rail Ltd, Private Bag, Christchurch; tel 0800 808 900 (toll free).

South Africa: Go Australia, Holiday House, 158–160 Hendrik Verwoerd Dr., Randburg 2125; tel: (11) 289 8112.

South-east Asia: Westminster Travel Ltd, 16/F1 Oriental Centre, 67 Chatham Road, Tsimshatsui, Kowloon, Hong Kong; tel: 2369 5051. Seoul Travel Service Ltd, 7F Keumjung Building, 1-KA, Ulchi-Ro, Chung-Ku, Seoul, Korea; tel: (2) 755 9696. Linbert Travel Exchange, 35 Selegie Road, # 09-28 Parklane Shopping Mall, Singapore 188307; tel: 337 9227.

These agents can also supply rail passes (see p. 37), and information. Bookings on fully escorted tours by rail and bus such as 'Queensland's Sunshine Rail Experience' are also available in the UK through Leisurail.

Those interested in railway heritage should contact the **Australian Railway Historical Society**, tel: (02) 9699 1714. Their publications include the Guide to Australian Heritage Railways & Museums, which gives details of museums, sites and special railways. Colin Taylor's Australia and New Zealand by Rail (Bradt/Globe Pequot) has useful information for those touring the country mainly by rail. It is available from bookshops or in the UK direct from Thomas Cook Publishing at £12.45 inc. P&P.

THE GHAN

Possibly Australia's most famous train, named after the Afghan camel drivers who once trekked this route into the Red Centre of Australia. In 20 hrs The Ghan transports you 1559 km from Adelaide to Alice Springs. From the train you'll see the world's biggest sheep

403

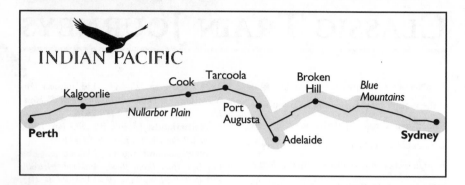

INDIAN PACIFIC

stations, the red-baked earth of the Simpson Desert, oceans of sandhills, the brilliant Outback sunset and the best view you'll ever have of the Milky Way in the night sky.

The train leaves Adelaide at 1400 every Thur and returns every Fri at 1400. First class sleeping accommodation is twin or single cabins with en-suite facilities (no showers in single cabins) and dedicated conductors. Holiday Class provides private cabins with showers and toilets at the end of each carriage. Coach Class gives budget passengers comfortable reserved seating. Catering ranges from the fine dining of Stuart Restaurant in First Class and Matilda's Restaurant in Holiday Class to the Ghan's buffet car for Coach Class passengers.

THE INDIAN PACIFIC

On the Indian Pacific you cross the entire continent in style, from the Pacific Ocean in Sydney to the Indian Ocean at Perth, a distance of 4532 km. En route you travel through an amazing variety of terrains: the Blue Mountains, the mining country of Broken Hill (see p.107), the red Outback and the journey across the Nullarbor Plain includes 478 km – the world's longest stretch – of straight track.

Towns connected en route include Port Augusta (see p.321) and Kalgoorlie (see p.311). Accommodation and catering is provided for First, Holiday and Coach Classes, First Class including the facility of the lounge cars for cocktails and afternoon tea.

THE SPIRIT OF THE OUTBACK

Travelling from Brisbane past the sugar town of Bundaberg, of rum fame, to Rockhampton and then west across the Great Dividing range to Longreach, home of the Australian Stockman's Hall of Fame, 'The Spirit' enables passengers to see the stark, hot wilderness of Australia's 'last frontier' from cool and comfortable lounge, bar and dining cars. Sleeping accommodation is provided in First and Economy Classes and there are also seat-only arrangements in Economy.

Making the round trip twice weekly, The

404

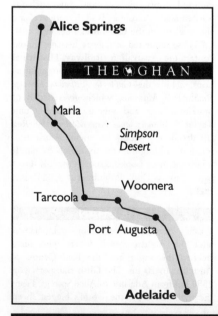

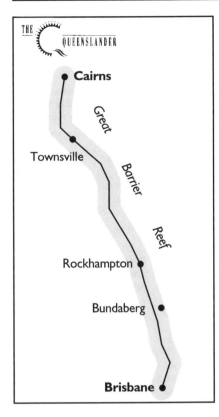

THE QUEENSLANDER

- Cairns
- Townsville
- Rockhampton
- Bundaberg
- Brisbane

Great Barrier Reef

Spirit of the Outback takes around 24 hrs to cover the 1325 km.

THE QUEENSLANDER

This is the way to see the best of coastal Queensland in stylish and luxurious surroundings. Making a leisurely 32 hr journey between Brisbane and Cairns in both directions, the Queenslander epitomises land cruising by rail. The train takes passengers past misty rain forests and the million-year-old Glasshouse Mountains and through oceans of sugar cane to the Great Barrier Reef.

THE SAVANNAHLANDER

Running from Mt Surprise to Forsayth and back, this 121 km, 5½ hr rail trip takes a fascinating look at the country in northern Queensland west of Cairns (see p.249), retracing the steps of the pioneers who mined for

gold, copper and gemstones. The driver is also your guide and host, pointing out places of interest and telling tales of the past. Trains depart Mt Surprise Mon and Thur, returning Tues and Fri. Buses connect with Cairns.

THE INLANDER

Running inland twice weekly from Townsville in northern Queensland to the mining capital of Mt Isa in the Gulf country, the train provides sleeping accommodation in First and Economy Classes and seat-only in Economy. From Mt Isa there are bus connections to the Gulflander route.

THE GULFLANDER

A chance to see the Gulf country and an adventure not to be missed, the twice-weekly Gulflander runs the 94 km between Normanton (p.255) and Croydon in approx. 4 hrs. Bus services connect the route with Cairns and Mt Isa. A 'jack of all trains', this small railmotor (referred to by locals as the 'Tin Hare') carries passengers, freight and just about anything else to remote stations in 'the land that time forgot'. Schedules are also forgotten when the driver stops to point out places of interest along the way!

405

KURANDA SCENIC RAILWAY

Taking 1½ hrs to travel the 34 km north from Cairns to Kuranda, trains pass high over deep gorges surrounded by rain forest and past spectacular waterfalls. Kuranda station itself is almost a botanical garden in its own right.

THE SPIRIT OF THE TROPICS

A favourite with budget travellers and the young at heart, this 32-hr trip between Brisbane and Cairns rocks and rolls through Queensland's tropical scenery, providing nonstop fun in the fully licensed Club Loco, complete with dance floor.

THE SUNLANDER

The same route as the Spirit of the Tropics, but here the emphasis is on luxury and relaxation. On-board facilities include the Waterways Restaurant, Macrossan's Lounge, with colonialstyle furnishings and the Tropics Club Car.

INTERNAL FLIGHT TIMES

The following sample domestic flight times are meant as a guide only; actual journey durations can vary widely between services on the same route. Note that many flights make more than one stop and this affects the overall journey time significantly. For each route the fastest non-stop service (where one exists) has been used as the sample time in this table. There are of course many more domestic airports and routes than we have space to show here.

	Hours
Adelaide to . . .	
Alice Springs	2
Ayers Rock	3¼
Brisbane	2¾
Canberra	2
Darwin	3¾
Hobart	3
Melbourne	1¼
Mildura	2¾
Mt Gambier	1
Perth	3½
Sydney	2

	Hours
Alice Springs to . . .	
Adelaide	2
Ayers Rock	1
Brisbane	5½
Canberra	4
Darwin	2
Hobart	5
Melbourne	2¾
Perth	4¼
Sydney	3

	Hours
Brisbane to . . .	
Adelaide	2¾
Alice Springs	5½
Ayers Rock	3¾
Cairns	2¼
Canberra	2
Darwin	4
Melbourne	2¼
Mt Isa	2½
Perth	5½
Rockhampton	1¼
Sydney	1½
Townsville	2

	Hours
Canberra to . . .	
Adelaide	1¾
Alice Springs	5
Ayers Rock	6½
Brisbane	1¾
Darwin	6
Hobart	2¾
Melbourne	1
Perth	5¼
Sydney	¾

	Hours
Darwin to . . .	
Adelaide	3½
Alice Springs	1¾
Ayers Rock	4½
Brisbane	3¾
Broome	2¾
Canberra	7
Melbourne	6½
Perth	4
Port Hedland	4¼
Sydney	4¾

	Hours
Hobart to . . .	
Adelaide	3
Alice Springs	6
Ayers Rock	9
Canberra	2½
Melbourne	1¼
Sydney	2

	Hours
Melbourne to . . .	
Adelaide	1¼
Albury	¾
Alice Springs	2¾
Ayers Rock	5¾
Brisbane	2

Canberra	1
Darwin	6
Hobart	1¼
Mildura	1¼
Perth	4
Sydney	1¼

	Hours
Perth to . . .	
Adelaide	2¾
Albany	1
Alice Springs	5¼
Ayers Rock	2½
Broome	2½
Canberra	5½
Carnarvon	2¼
Darwin	3½
Esperance	1½
Hobart	7
Kalgoorlie	1
Kununurra	4
Melbourne	3¼
Port Hedland	2
Sydney	4

	Hours
Sydney to . . .	
Adelaide	2
Alice Springs	3½
Ayers Rock	3½
Brisbane	1½
Broken Hill	2½
Cairns	3
Canberra	¾
Darwin	4½
Dubbo	1
Griffith	1¼
Hobart	2
Melbourne	1¼
Perth	5

HOTEL AND MOTEL CODES
AND CENTRAL BOOKING NUMBERS

The following abbreviations have been used throughout the book to show which hotel and motel chains are represented in a particular town. Central booking numbers of these, or the numbers to call for information, are shown in bold – use these numbers whilst in the Australia to make reservations at any hotel in the chain. Where available, numbers that can be called in your own country are also noted. (Can=Canada, Ire=Ireland, NZ=New Zealand, SA =South Africa, UK=United Kingdom, US = United States of America, WW=Worldwide number).

AIM **Australian Independent Motels**
1 800 066 835

BU **Budget Motel Chain**
(051) 43 1077
for a free directory (no bookings)

BW **Best Western**
13 1779 or
Ire 800 709 101
NZ (09) 520 5418
SA (011) 339 4865
UK 800 393130
US 800 528 1234

CC **Country Comfort**
1800 065 064

Fl **Flag**
13 2400

GC **Golden Chain**
1 800 023 966
no bookings but provide toll-free numbers for each motel, or a booklet.

Hn **Hilton**
(02) 9209 5209
NZ 800 448 002
SA (011) 880 3108
UK (0345) 581595
US 800 445 8667

Hy **Hyatt**
13 1234
Ire 800 535 500
NZ 800 441 234
SA (011) 773 9888
UK (0345) 581666
US 800 233 1234

HI **Hostelling International**
(612) 9565 1699
(information only)
Can/US 800 444 6111
UK (0171) 248 6547

SP **Southern Pacific**
1300 363 300

B4 **Big 4 Holiday Parks**
1 800 632 444
no bookings, but will provide information

The following international hotel chains have a small number of properties in Australia:

Holiday Inn
800 221 066
Can/US 800 465 4329
Ire 800 553 155
NZ 800 442 222
SA (011) 482 3500
UK 800 897 121

Hyatt
13 1234
Can/Us 800 233 1234
UK (0345) 581 666

Ibis
(2) 563 0888
NZ 800 444 422
Can/US 800 221 4542

InterContinental
800 221 335
Can/US 800 327 0200
NZ 800 654 343
SA (011) 331 7422
UK (0345) 581 444

Marriott
800 251 259
NZ 800 441 035
UK 800 221222
US 800 228 9290

Mercure
800 642 244
Can/US 800 MERCURE
NZ 800 444 442
UK 0181 741 3100

Novotel
800 642 244
Can/US 800 221 4542
NZ 800 444 422
UK 0171 748 3433

Radisson
800 333 333
Can/US 800 333 333
Ire 800 557 474
NZ 800 443 333
UK 800 191991

Ramada
800 222 431
Can/US 800 854 7854
Ire 800 252 627
NZ 800 441 111
UK 800 181737

Renaissance
as Ramada and
US 1 800 HOTELS

Sheraton
800 073 535
Ire 800 535 353
NZ 800 443 535
UK 800 353 535
US 800 325 3535 or
800 325 1717
(hearing impaired)

407

CONVERSION TABLES

DISTANCES (approx. conversions)
1 kilometre (km) = 1000 metres (m) 1 metre = 100 centimetres (cm)

Metric	Imperial/US	Metric	Imperial/US	Metric	Imperial/US
1 cm	3/8ths in.	10 m	33 ft (11 yd)	3 km	2 miles
50 cm	20 in.	20 m	66 ft (22 yd)	4 km	2½ miles
1 m	3 ft 3 in.	50 m	164 ft (54 yd)	5 km	3 miles
2 m	6 ft 6 in.	100 m	330 ft (110 yd)	10 km	6 miles
3 m	10 ft	200 m	660 ft (220 yd)	20 km	12½ miles
4 m	13 ft	250 m	820 ft (275 yd)	25 km	15½ miles
5 m	16 ft 6 in.	300 m	984 ft (330 yd)	30 km	18½ miles
6 m	19 ft 6 in.	500 m	1640 ft (550 yd)	40 km	25 miles
7 m	23 ft	750 m	½ mile	50 km	31 miles
8 m	26 ft	1 km	5/8ths mile	75 km	46 miles
9 m	29 ft (10 yd)	2 km	1½ miles	100 km	62 miles

24-HOUR CLOCK
(examples)

0000 = Midnight	1200 = Noon	1800 = 6 p.m.
0600 = 6 a.m.	1300 = 1 p.m.	2000 = 8 p.m.
0715 = 7.15 a.m.	1415 = 2.15 p.m.	2110 = 9.10 p.m.
0930 = 9.30 a.m.	1645 = 4.45 p.m.	2345 = 11.45 p.m.

TEMPERATURE
Conversion Formula: $°C × 9 ÷ 5 + 32 = °F$

°C	°F	°C	°F	°C	°F	°C	°F
-20	-4	-5	23	10	50	25	77
-15	5	0	32	15	59	30	86
-10	14	5	41	20	68	35	95

WEIGHT
1 kg = 1000 g 100 g = 3½ oz

Kg	Pounds	Kg	Pounds	Kg	Pounds
1	2¼	5	11	25	55
2	4½	10	22	50	110
3	6½	15	33	75	165
4	9	20	45	100	220

FLUID MEASURES
1 litre(l) = 0.88 Imperial quarts = 1.06 US quarts

Litres	Imp.gal.	US gal.	Litres	Imp.gal.	US gal.
5	1.1	1.3	30	6.6	7.8
10	2.2	2.6	35	7.7	9.1
15	3.3	3.9	40	8.8	10.4
20	4.4	5.2	45	9.9	11.7
25	5.5	6.5	50	11.0	13.0

MEN'S CLOTHES

Aus/UK	Europe	US
36	46	36
38	48	38
40	50	40
42	52	42
44	54	44
46	56	46

MENS' SHOES

Aus/UK	Europe	US
6	40	7
7	41	8
8	42	9
9	43	10
10	44	11
11	45	12

LADIES' CLOTHES

Aus/UK	France	Italy	Rest of Europe	US
10	36	38	34	8
12	38	40	36	10
14	40	42	38	12
16	42	44	40	14
18	44	46	42	16
20	46	48	44	18

MEN'S SHIRTS

Aus/UK	Europe	US
14	36	14
15	38	15
15½	39	15½
16	41	16
16½	42	16½
17	43	17

LADIES' SHOES

Aus/UK	Europe	US
3	36	4½
4	37	5½
5	38	6½
6	39	7½
7	40	8½
8	41	9½

AREAS
1 hectare = 2.471 acres

1 hectare = 10,000 sq meters

1 acre = 0.4 hectares

INDEX

READER SURVEY

If you enjoyed using this book, or even if you didn't, please help us improve future editions by taking part in our reader survey. Every returned form will be acknowledged, and to show our appreciation we will give you £1 off your next purchase of a Thomas Cook guidebook. Just take a few minutes to complete and return this form to us.

When did you buy this book? _____

Where did you buy it? (Please give town/city and if possible name of retailer)

When did you/do you intend to travel around Australia?

For how long (approx.)? _____
How many people in your party? _____

Which cities, national parks and other locations did you/do you intend mainly to visit?

Did you/will you:
- ☐ Make all your travel arrangements independently?
- ☐ Travel on a fly-drive package?
Please give brief details: _____

Did you/do you intend to use this book:
- ☐ For planning your trip?
- ☐ During the trip itself?
- ☐ Both?

Did you/do you intend also to purchase any of the following travel publications for your trip?
Thomas Cook Travellers: *Sydney & New South Wales*
A road map/atlas (please specify) _____
Other guidebooks (please specify) _____

Have you used any other Thomas Cook guidebooks in the past? If so, which?

Please rate the following features of Touring Australia for their value to you (Circle VU for 'very useful', U for 'useful', NU for 'little or no use'):

The 'Travel Essentials' section on pages 16–39	VU	U	NU
The 'Driving in Australia' section on pages 40–43	VU	U	NU
The 'Touring Itineraries' on pages 50–54	VU	U	NU
The recommended driving routes throughout the book	VU	U	NU
Information on towns and cities, National Parks, etc	VU	U	NU
The maps of towns and cities, parks, etc	VU	U	NU
The removable colour road map	VU	U	NU

Please use this space to tell us about any features that in your opinion could be changed, improved, or added in future editions of the book, or any other comments you would like to make concerning the book:

_____
_____
_____
_____
_____
_____
_____

414

_____
_____

Your age category: ☐ 21-30 ☐ 31-40 ☐ 41–50 ☐ over 50

Your name: Mr/Mrs/Miss/Ms
(First name or initials) _____
(Last name) _____

Your full address: (Please include postal or zip code)

_____
_____
_____
_____

Your daytime telephone number: _____

Please detach this page and send it to: The Project Editor, Touring Australia, Thomas Cook Publishing, PO Box 227, Peterborough PE3 6PU, United Kingdom.

We will be pleased to send you details of how to claim your discount upon receipt of this questionnaire.

415

Australia via the World with Qantas & British Airways.

416